Library of
Davidson College

Religion and rural revolt

Religion

and rural revolt

Papers presented to the
Fourth Interdisciplinary workshop on Peasant Studies,
University of British Columbia, 1982

JÁNOS M. BAK and GERHARD BENECKE *editors*

MANCHESTER UNIVERSITY PRESS

Copyright © Manchester University Press 1984

While copyright in the volume as a whole
is vested in Manchester University Press
copyright in the individual papers belongs to their respective authors,
and no paper may be reproduced whole or in part
without the express permission in writing of author,
publisher and editors.

Published by
Manchester University Press
Oxford Road, Manchester M13 9PL
and
51 Washington Street, Dover,
New Hampshire 03820, USA

British Library cataloguing in publication data

Interdisciplinary workshop on Peasant Studies (*4th:
    1982; University of British Columbia*)
    Religion and rural revolt.
    1. Religion and politics – History – Congresses
    2. Revolutions – Congresses
    I. Title   II. Bak, János M.   III. Benecke, Gerhard.
    322.4'2 09   BL66.P7
    ISBN 0–7190–0990–1 (cased)   0–7190–0991–X (paperback*)

Library of Congress Cataloging in Publication Data

Interdisciplinary Workshop on Peasant Studies (*4th:
    1982: University of British Columbia*)
    Religion and rural revolt.

    1. Peasant uprisings – Religious aspects – Congresses.
I. Bak, János M.   II. Benecke, Gerhard.   III. Title.
D210.I57 1982   909.08   83–18698
    ISBN 0–7190–0990–1 (cased)   0–7190–0991–X (paperback*)

*The paperback will not be published simultaneously with the cased edition

Photoset in Garamond
by Northern Phototypesetting Co., Bolton
Printed in Great Britain
by Butler & Tanner Ltd., Frome

Contents

Editors' Preface	page ix
Introduction	1
Religion *and* revolt?	2
Religion as an ideology of domination *Herbert Frey*	14
Icon and ideology in religion and rebellion 1300–1600: *Bauernfreiheit* and *religion royale* *Lionel Rothkrug*	31
Western and Southern Europe	63
Preface *Harvey Mitchell*	64
Mediterranean Europe 1500–1800: notes and comparisons *Peter Burke*	75
From Lollards to Levellers *Christopher Hill*	86
Religion and peasant movements in Normandy during the French religious wars *David Nicholls*	104
Religion and rural revolt in the French Revolution: an overview *T. J. A. LeGoff* and *Donald M. G. Sutherland*	123
Central and Eastern Europe 1525–1848	147
Preface *Christopher R. Friedrichs*	148
Miners, pastors and the peasant war in Upper Austria 1524–26 *Karl-Heinz Ludwig*	154
Rural revolt and urban betrayal in Reformation Switzerland: the peasants of St Gallen and Zwinglian Zurich *Philip Broadhead*	161
Religion, confession and peasant resistance in the German territories in the sixteenth to eighteenth centuries *Günter Vogler*	173
Bureaucratic tenure, peasant leadership and *politiques* during the Austrian Counter-Reformation *Hermann Rebel*	188
Religious ideologies in Russian popular movements in the seventeenth and eighteenth centuries *Viktor I. Buganov*	206
'Irreligiosity' in seventeenth and eighteenth century peasant uprisings in Russia *Aleksandr I. Klibanov*	214
Religious patterns of interpretation and mobilisation in *Vormärz* Germany *Rainer Wirtz*	223

Middle East and Africa — 239

Preface *Hans G. Kippenberg* — 240

Limits of Islamic civilisation: Mahdist movements in Abbasid Iran *Hans G. Kippenberg* — 243

The Babi movement in Iran 1844–52: from merchant protest to peasant revolution *Kurt Greussing* — 256

The revolt of Eshaq Khan in Afghan-Turkestan in 1888: peasant mobilisation and re-formation of patron–client relationships *Jan-Heeren Grevemeyer* — 270

Popular Islam, Kurdish nationalism and rural revolt: the rebellion of Shaikh Said in Turkey (1925) *Martin van Bruinessen* — 281

Mahdism, Messianism and Marxism in the African setting *Thomas Hodgkin* — 296

Religions and rural protests in Makoni District, Zimbabwe, 1900–80 *Terence Ranger* — 315

Modern China — 337

Preface *Daniel L. Overmyer* — 338

Taipings and Triads: the rôle of religion in inter-rebel relations *Elizabeth J. Perry* — 342

God's country in the family of nations: the logic of modernism in the Taiping doctrine of international relations *Rudolf G. Wagner* — 354

The fate of the Heavenly Gates: rebellion, religion and repression in Republican China *Ralph Thaxton* — 373

Ideology, organisation and rebellion in Chinese sectarian religion *Robert Weller* — 390

Latin America — 407

Preface *Catherine LeGrand* — 408

Evangelisation, protest and ethnic identity: sixteenth century missionaries and Indians in Northern Amazonian Ecuador *Blanca Muratorio* — 414

Religion and clergy in the Atusparia uprising, Peru, 1885 *William W. Stein* — 424

The *Cristiada*: peasant war and religious war in revolutionary Mexico, 1926–9 *Jean A. Meyer* — 441

Religion, rebellion, and working class consciousness in Bolivian tin-mining communities *June Nash* — 453

	Contents	vii
	Epilogue	469
	The politicisation of the transcendent: a quasi-sociological postscript *Ivan Varga*	470
	Authors	482
	Index	485

MAPS

1. Normandy in the Religious Wars — 106
2. Peasant movements during the French Revolution — 127
3. Some mining communities in sixteenth century Upper Austria — 155
4. Areas of the Shaikh Said rebellion in Turkey — 284
5. The *Cristiada* in Mexico — 445

Editors' preface

This volume of studies grew out of our interest in the problems raised by the German Peasant War of 1525 and the literature about it. While working independently on collections of articles for its 450th anniversary, we felt the need to look at some of its salient features in a wider than national or even wider than early modern European context. Such a need was also mentioned by authors in our volumes, and by reviewers. We are grateful for these suggestions, and hope that the present volume will be another step towards a genuine interdisciplinary study of one of the major issues of peasant wars and uprisings.

We were pleased with the response received from colleagues whom we asked to contribute, and from those who provided suggestions and further advice. Our gratitude belongs first to the authors, many of whom participated in the Fourth Interdisciplinary Workshop on Peasant Studies, University of British Columbia, Vancouver, Canada, April, 1982, which enabled us to improve the collection. We owe thanks to our colleagues, and especially to those who took time at the UBC to prepare critical comments on the papers for the workshop: Hermann Rebel, Tim LeGoff, Rodolphe De Koninck, Don Sutherland and Lyman Legters. We also appreciate the assistance received in the translation of French and Russian texts from Gamma H. Bak and György Szöke, and from Kurt Greussing, Jan-Heeren Grevemeyer and Jack McIntosh in the transliteration of arabic and slavic words. We have chosen simplified transliterations, comprehensible to the general reader, and we apologise to the specialists for neglecting linguistic nuances and diacritical marks.

Preparation of the manuscript was greatly assisted by the staff of our universities. Ruth Mirza and Joyce Tiplady (UBC) helped János Bak get some texts through the mires of a word-processor, while Doreen Revitt, Sue Macdonald and their colleagues in the Secretarial Office at Darwin College (UKC) took the trouble of re-typing manuscripts with Gerhard Benecke's hieroglyphic corrections.

The workshop at UBC, of which the present volume is an expanded record, was supported by grants from the Social Science and Humanities Research Council of Canada, the Dean of Arts, and the Institute of Asian Research at the University of British Columbia. Additional financial help was received for the final stages of preparation from Social Sciences and Humanities Grants, from the Faculty of Arts at the University of British Columbia, and from the University of Kent at Canterbury, for which the editors are very grateful.

Editors' preface

The kind permissions of Christopher Hill, Thomas Hodgkin, the Commissie tot uitgave van Documenta Anabaptistica Neerlandica, and the University of Khartoum Press respectively to reprint copyright materials are gratefully acknowledged.

Finally, we thank Terence Ranger and above all Béla Király for invaluable support.

Vancouver and Canterbury, Summer, 1983

J.M.B.
G.B.

Introduction

Religion and *revolt?*

At first sight the project of this volume and of the workshop that preceded it would seem to be paradoxical. There has been hardly any religion in the history of mankind that would have advocated open resistance or rebellion. However, students of social upheavals and particularly of rural revolts have noted in a great number of cases that religion was a significant force in the rebellion. Few of them would seem entirely to lack any religious implication, although its intensity varies from case to case. In many movements religion served as the major ideological underpinning supplying the language of resistance and the frame of a programme. In others, the religious community played a paramount rôle in uniting peasants and other rural folk, or their leadership was religiously legitimated. For what reasons do the two apparently antithetical notions of religion and revolt so often come into close proximity with one another? What are the conditions that bridge a seemingly unbridgeable gap between preaching acceptance of the state which the Lord prescribed us and violent attempts at changing such a status quo? The essays in this volume address themselves to these questions, hence it may be useful to outline some of the possible answers as a frame of reference.

Great historical religions contain two elements which can lead to their inclusion into the set of ideas that justify or mobilise revolt, namely, their eschatological promise and their mandatory system of moral values. To them may be added a third ingredient, which occasionally played a rôle of supplying an ideology for rural revolt, namely the idea of holy war against enemies of the faith. Once enemies of the people are identified as enemies of the faithful, the oppressed and disenfranchised were able to call upon the tradition of *jihad* or crusade, and fight a 'just and holy war' against their oppressors. Elements of such thinking can be detected in the programme of Styrian and Carinthian peasants who in the late fifteenth century attacked their lords, because, so they argued, the *Herren* were in cohouts with the enemy, the Ottoman Turks. In neighbouring Hungary in 1514 the peasants who had flocked under the flag of an anti-Turkish crusade turned against their lords who failed to join them or even hindered them in their crusading zeal. They declared themselves a *sancta turba cruciatorum*, and fought a regular peasant war against the landowners [*Szűcs, 1976; Bak, 1983*]. Somewhat differently, under seigneurial leadership, the rebellion of Eshaq Khan in 1888 against the modernising and anti-clerical king of Afghanistan, also claimed to be a Holy War, as it did, by extension, with the revolt of the Cristeros in twentieth century Mexico. But Crusades in Europe, when they were not called against outside enemies, were mostly against rebellious subjects, heretics and against peasants refusing to pay the tithe. So religion played here its more usual rôle of justifying domination.

The appearance of an eschatological element in rural and occasionally also in urban revolt is a much more widespread phenomenon. The promise of equality and justice on the *dies illa* inherent in the great monotheistic religions, seems to have been one of the major factors that allowed religious ideas to serve the aims of the poor and disenfranchised. Messianistic, millenarian or Mahdist prophecies were part of orthodox teaching in Judaism, Christianity and Sh'ite Islam. Their function was to juxtapose future eternal bliss with secular patience, and to sway the faithful towards repentance and obedience. The transfer of these promises from the *eschaton* into the here and now was a significant mode of religious motivation in a number of important oppositional movements and uprisings. The millenarian elements in the different Mahdist movements, in the Babism of mid nineteenth century Iran, in the Taiping vision of a Heavenly Kingdom, and in the many variants of Brasilian cultic protest movement are unequivocal. In Europe many a medieval heresy [Hilton, 1973: 107–9] and the famous Anabaptist commune of Münster in 1534 are major examples, to which one may add the virtuous republic of early seventeenth century Astrakhan, and related movements in Russia.

The second major aspect inherent in the great religions that often lent itself to a justification of resistance is the duty of the orthodox to refuse communion with those transgressing the commands of their religion. In the western medieval context the Pataria of Milan comes to mind. Here, laymen and lower clergy attacked, with papal approval, those churchmen who did not conform to the standards set by the Gregorian reformers. It cannot be disproved that social motives played a rôle in this religious rebellion, neither that they did in other 'reforming' heresies that raised the flag against unworthy priests and their lay patrons [Werner, 1953, 71–79]. Such reforming fervour may, under certain circumstances, go far beyond the 'disciplining' of those members – or leaders – who do not conform to the preached core values. The conflict between the élite that does not live up to those standards which it demands from the other members of society and those other members can frequently change from mere 'spiritual' purification to demands for a tangible social reform. Under special conditions it led to revolt, as evinced in the German Peasant War or in the Babi movement in Iran. The step from religious reform as proposed by a Luther or a Sayed Ali Mohammad (the 'Bab') to the demand for social transformation was often made under the leadership of a radical theologian, such as a Thomas Münzer or a Mohammad Ali Barforushi. By attempting to obtain support for the reform, they tended to mobilise masses, whose complaints may not have been inherently centered on religious issues but which were ready to rise, once an articulation of their demands had been formulated in terms more broad and general than local grievances. Without wanting to overplay the significance of religion in the many sided conflicts of societies, or to overstress the importance of social and economic causes in religious reform, the two do come together at certain times of crisis as a kind of theological radicalism with strong social-revolutionary overtones. The 'astonishment' of religious reformers when they realised that their critique had been translated into secular confrontation, was surely quite sincere, even though few of them went as far as Luther in openly denouncing the radical followers, and hardening his attitudes once conflict had broken out.

Less spectacular are those peasant revolts in which religious sets of ethical commands constituted the backbone of the grievances and of the emerging programme. As far as the historian is able to ascertain, the religion of the participants in such uprisings was mostly a simplified extract of the official faith, containing only such elements that coincided with something that can be seen to have been a popular perception of justice [*cf. Obelkevitch, 1979*]. Most of the moral principles sanctified by the universal religions appear to peasants in the societies studied here as being so 'natural' that their origin in religious teaching is hardly ever made overtly conscious. Knowledge of Christian theology even among European peasants of, say, the eighteenth century was probably limited to a few tenets about the sacraments (more or less as protective magic) and a number of ethical commands that might be labelled 'natural' for simplicity's sake. How far ethical norms are in fact eternal and natural to human society we do not feel able here to go into. It may suffice to record the contradiction between popular religiosity and peasant notions of 'Christian conduct' on the one hand and the dominant social and political system sanctified by clergy and church on the other.

Whether millenarian, reforming or 'moralist', the frame of resistance in these cases was at least *pro forma* defined by the same religion that also justified the status quo. In historical reality, however, the religious ideas that played a part in peasant struggles were never identical with the prevailing established religion of the given society. Even less were they to be equated with its institutional manifestations, namely the official church and its clergy, who were incorporated into the system of domination. In the more 'typical' cases the religion of the social élite and that of the rebellious low strata differed more or less explicitly. That may be argued to hold true also where the opponents of the 'establishment' saw their religion as the true church in contrast with the corrupted church of the rich prelates or secular-minded believers. There exist many other variations on this theme. Popular religion and religiosity may be synchretist, containing elements of both the ecclesiastical religion and beliefs of different origin, be they survivals of an earlier culture, as with pre-colonial beliefs still detectable among Bolivian miners, Ecuadorian Indians and Peruvian peasants, or parts of religious tenets transplanted from elsewhere as in the sects of Taiwan or Africa. The social status and ideological solidarity of parish priests and mendicant friars is also not as simple as implied by the dichotomy clergy *versus* laity. Some of the complexities in this field are being mapped out by students of popular heterodoxy [*Ginzburg, 1979; Henningsen, 1980*].

A logical example of religious motivation for a revolt is probably the case where religion that has tended to justify and mobilise resistance is expressly different from the approved church of the state. This was the case with Protestantism in Catholic regions of early modern Europe, with Old Belief in Orthodox Russia, and with fundamentalist Christianity coloured by popular beliefs in Confucian China. In these conflicts, which perhaps can be termed confessional rather than religious in general, the alternative religion acquired oppositional character by the mere fact that it was suppressed by the same authority that imposed social and economic order on the lower classes. These seem to be the main types of movements in which the inherent possibility of religious ideas is transformed into resistance to existing social structures. The most contentious issue seems to be to decide how 'extraneous' these religious justifications were – a matter to which we will return.

Thus, religion and revolt are by no means as divorced from each other as the more conventional analysis of the 'classical' legitimatory role of religion might suggest. What is the rôle of such different types of religion in resistance movements? Two major groups can be discerned, and they are not mutually exclusive. In the first one, religious ideas and types of discourse supply programme and legitimation, in the other religious communities serve as the organisational nuclei of resistance. These two types coincide with what may be called religion-as-aim and religion-as-reason, or rather, – frame, of revolt.

The two rôles of religion in revolt need closer definition as regards their position in pre-industrial religiosity as a whole, and it is within this wider framework that most of our contributors have written. The basic recent study to attempt to deal with this is probably Guenter Lewy's *Religion and Revolution* [*1974*], in which the author considers the unique characteristic of religion to have been belief in superhuman powers that assist or harm man. In order ostensibly to perform consistently as rural cultivators, peasants have always had their activities institutionalized and regularized in terms of ritual and calendar [*O'Neil, 1976*]. The result has been at least animistic, magical and naturalistic worship [*Freud, 1960: 77; Granet, 1975*], and after a while, a set of answers to speculations eschatological and anthropomorphic have followed. The problem arises when reconciling in a cultivator's and his community's mind what he, as a peasant, has to do (and therefore, can expect as just to be done unto him) and what landlords or priests have to do, and what their God is expected to stand for as a guarantee of morality, its sanction and justification. Because he produces the material basis of life, year-in and year-out, the peasant has a view of nature, time and justice which is linked to a set of contracts with family and landlord, tied by custom and inheritance. Policy can make it go right, and policy can make it go wrong. Either way, religion stays, snake-like and Janus-headed. The conditions under which religion becomes a force for revolt rather than social integration, which interested Lewy [1974] in general, interests us here in the particular case of rural society.

The study of pre-industrial, feudal and early modern Europe has recently been focussed especially on religion in an urban context. The mass of work on the German and central European Reformations in the sixteenth century, as well as studies of mentality in France and western Europe in the transition from scholasticism to humanism, early science and rationalism often have been centred on the urban bourgeoisie and landed aristocracy. In the great central European conflicts of the 1470s which lasted to the peasant wars of the 1510s and 1520s essential links between town and country, farm, village, and walled market were explored as long ago as 1850 by Engels [1977], recently developed in contributions edited by Bak [1975] and Scribner and Benecke [1979]. But more has to be said about peasant ideology and belief. A start has been made by George Rudé, who argues for the interplay between inherent (i.e. backward looking) and derived (i.e. from the upper-class culture and therefore forward looking because hegemonically false class-conscious) culture as 'the political, philosophical or religious ideas that, at varying stages of sophistication, became absorbed in the more specifically *popular* culture' [1980: 33].

It is appropriate to ask whether it is indeed true that rural, agrarian populations (part-societies, classes) are more likely to fight their social struggles under religious flags than others of a more secular, material kind. The argument has often been advanced that peasants (or cultivators in general) are by their way of life and productive processes so closely bound to the natural, annual cycle and so dependent on natural forces beyond their control that they tend to be 'religious' by definition. It is assumed that they are prone to believe in superhuman, supernatural powers that regulate the all-important forces to which they are subject – rain, drought, flood, hail, plague and pestilence. This also holds true of another nature-bound group of pre-industrial society, the miners whose lives depend on natural conditions in the bosom of the earth, just as those of peasants do on weather and soil. We might compare here the carnivalesque belief systems of the Bolivian tin-miners with the crypto-Protestant Christian biblicism of the Inner Austrian miners. As an ancient activity, mining is often more close to a rural, marketing and township scene than to a modern, urban and big-city way of life [*Mitterauer, 1979*].

The literature on religiosity in terms of nature-magic among cultivators is ample and need not be rehearsed further here; but is it really as relevant to peasant revolts as is usually somewhat too readily assumed? We might perhaps do better by not prejudging rural protest movements and rural rebels in terms of some kind of natural determinism of our own making. However, church, clergy, and religious rituals are beyond doubt central to most villages of the world, both topographically and mentally. A basic reason for this may partially be due to the need for supernatural mediation between cultivators and the forces they are unable to control. These, of course, include not only natural phenomena but also such interconnected social forces as lordship, markets, and the state and so on. But it is doubtful whether in most of the more established and mature rural cultivator societies, which our authors have reviewed here, this original connection was still immediately relevant. It was probably no longer consciously explicit. It seems rather that other aspects of religion that accrued to it in the course of centuries played a much more important rôle.

First, without implying its being more important, one might argue that religious justification of certain revolts did not in essence originate with peasants or rural rebels but was rather imposed on them, as it were, from outside. At least since Marx and Engels it probably counts as more or less established that in ages in which religion was the dominant or hegemonial ideology, opposition and rebellion had inevitably to be expressed in religious terms. Pre-capitalist societies are essentially legitimated by religious tenets – hence, one may regard it as logical necessity that these systems be attacked in religious terms, that is, first by challenging or denying their divine and eternal legitimation. The problem is that this interpretation rather presupposes an unbroken chain from royal appointing through to the pulpit of the village church and down to the peasants without any perceivable gap in the ecclesiastical domination of thought and belief. But since we know that the transmission of lofty political theology from the coronation ceremonies to the sermons urging the tenants to pay the tithe was by no means linear, the more lateral and more capricious mechanisms and ways of domination need also to be explored.

In the age of mass peasant movements of the later Middle Ages the crisis of ecclesiastical legitimation was manifest, and the uprisings could build on this fact. The challenge did not originate among the oppressed masses but rather among critical clerics and scholars questioning the authority of one or both of two or even more popes and anti-popes, as well as among literate urban folk spreading disbelief about the efficacy of sacraments. The Roman church itself gave away some of its powerful tools of domination by granting individual indulgences, whereby laymen acquired what may be called infinitesimal fractions of the Power of the Keys to be used of their own free choice for saving the dead who were condemned to eternal suffering, or in order to free themselves from future punishment in Purgatory. In capitalist-imperialist societies the ecclesiastical legitimation plays a less central part, and here the critique of social injustice and the alternative programme can be expressed in vocabularies other than religious, beginning with folk wisdom (the language of tale and proverb) and ending with social science.

The main problem with this 'ideological' interpretation appears to most of us to be in its functionalist approach to religion. In whatever way this explanatory model is formulated, it does not convincingly bridge the gap between the peasants (or other rebels) and religious concepts; the question remains open, what is really meant when grievances are couched in religious language. What we are in fact able to register is the cohesion offered by shared ideals, which are both religious and secular; or the language of scriptural rhetoric (Biblical, Q'uranic or otherwise) articulating secular demands perceived as claims to restoring a divinely blessed just order. It is in this context that the problem of belief – at least in the efficacy of sacraments and rites – becomes a historical question. Although few historians feel themselves qualified to discuss matters of social psychology, the religious dimension of pre-industrial popular movements has important mental, spiritual aspects. It is by no means obvious what peasants who fought for social justice with the battle-cry, *Viva Maria*! meant by this slogan.

The general argument about rural folk being religious because of their closeness to nature and apparently super-human forces is too vaguely connected to these historical events to be convincing. While in most of the studies printed below the functional, external aspect of religion will necessarily be an object of inquiry, it should be born in mind that recourse to religion as a guide and solace in critical situations is an important part of human reality. That this also applies to social crises which end in armed struggle is one of the possible links between religion and revolt in the critical interplay between internalised and externalised motives, actions and their self-generated justifications. The immediate relevance to active rural movements of peasant religiosity, either in terms of protective magic or in those of individual belief, remains an open issue.

Many of our authors demonstrate that another function of religion may have been most significant in coupling religious solidarities with rural resistance movements: its community-building character. It may be fair to say that, while the almost exclusive ready availability of a religiously formulated ideology is a characteristic of pre-modern societies, in which domination is legitimated mainly by clerical blessing, in secularised societies the function of religion is more precisely described by its offering the most inclusive bond of solidarity and cohesion in rural society. The issue is complex in colonial societies, as for example the Spanish-American, where clerical support for foreign domination had always been centrally organised, but where popular Christianity has always been very diffuse, some versions of which have been oppositional. This is not to propose that the ideological-legitimising aspect is absent entirely from more modern uprisings, nor that the organising function of religious community would not play a significant part in the earlier uprisings against hallowed hierarchies. The two aspects probably merge in all movements where religion and church community are important factors, but the relative significance of the two would seem to shift from the former to the latter.

Our studies of seventeenth and eighteenth century Europe, nineteenth century Afghanistan, and twentieth century Mexico and Taiwan point forcefully to the cohesive social character of various religious solidarities as vital aspects in rebellions. The resistance of Muslims against Spanish Catholicism, of Protestants against the Counter-Reformation, and of Catholic peasants against a reforming or revolutionary state opposing 'their parish' and 'their priest', can not be reduced to a monocausal factor. It is variously a defence of traditional culture against outside interference; a cluster of social relations connected with church rituals that are being challenged by the secular state; a response to the Counter-Reformation threat to an accepted system of tenure and office-holding.

In these and other similar instances religion appears much less as a set of ethical ideas or as a vocabulary for the formulation of egalitarian expectation, but rather as the common denominator uniting rural folk, often across economic and social barriers. Put another way, religion may be seen less as a supplier of scriptural legitimation and justification, but rather as the unifying force of a village and regional community. In some cases the latter predominates, as when, for example, peasants in Normandy resist the banditry of Catholic League nobles in the name of Protestantism, or alternatively use Catholicism against Huguenot incursions. More complex is its manifestation in the Cristero movement of modern Mexico, where state closure of churches mobilised thousands of peasants against the government, its clients in the countryside and against all officers of state. The opposition of French villagers to the Revolution's interference with their parishes might not have been as vehement as it was in the Vendée and elsewhere, had the Parisian attack been aimed at a rural institution less emotionally deep-rooted than was the church, even though the uprisings were essentially motivated by the rural communities' resistance to outside interference.

It thus appears that the specifically natural way of life of rural folk was hardly the immediate cause of the religious influence on their resistance movements. The need to counter religious legitimation with religious delegitimation, and also to justify revolt by use of sacred texts and doctrines accounted for much of the religiosity apparent in rural uprisings, especially in feudal or similar societies. In most of the movements against the increasingly secularised state rural solidarity as expressed in terms of a community of believers played the central rôle. In uprisings against the secular state, the organising-bonding aspect was perhaps the most significant contribution of what surfaced as religious colouration. Yet the strength of this bond cannot be separated from religious belief, at any rate not from religious ritual and life-ordering sacraments and festivities, for it appears that these lie at the roots of communal cohesion, its form and its wide appeal, although the elements of solidarity are themselves more basic than their theological formulation.

Considering all these possible explanations for the rôle of religion in rural revolts and allied popular movements, we are still faced with another traditional query of modern scholars, which is especially puzzling for those whose sympathies lie with the working people and the poor, and who regard themselves as 'progressive' historians and social scientists in really wishing to understand people as they were. The question, roughly put, is that of the often so called reactionary, counter-revolutionary or restorative character of rural revolts in general, and of movements informed by religious ideologies in particular. It is an old quandry for democrats, populists and socialists of different observance; namely, how to explain the alliance of poor peasants, rural labourers and even miners with religion and with clergy, without being, therefore, forced to label men and women fighting against oppression and unfreedom as reactionaries. This issue is of course much wider than the topic of this volume and cannot be handled without a full discussion of the place of rural revolts in the over-all scheme – if indeed there is such a one – of class conflicts and their outcome. Surely, under the conditions of colonialism and imperialism, the orthodox socialist and heavily Eurocentric assessment that regards peasant revolts as immature anticipations of the only genuine liberation struggle, the one led and organised by the proletariat and leading to the socialist revolution, cannot be upheld. It does not stand up to historical scrutiny even within Europe. But in the present project we merely set out to explore the religious dimension of rural resistance, regardless of the issue whether peasant risings are 'revolutionary' or not.

An aspect of this question has already been discussed when we noted that the religiosity of rural producers and their solidarity with the local church and its clergy may not be at all identical with the kind of religion which justifies hierarchies and that kind of ecclesiastical institution which legitimises inequality. One other aspect may be raised here, particularly because its characterises very much the religiously motivated (or formulated) programmes of rural resistance, namely, the defensive and apparently restorative, or more succinctly, recuperative aims. We tend to regard the defence of religious freedom from an oppressive absolutism, or in general the fight for liberty of conscience against an all-intrusive state power, as legitimate and progressive. This is partially motivated by our democratic-libertarian convictions, partially based on the fact that in many cases the dissenting religious groups were in fact proponents of social progress against a conservative or reactionary state. Hence the rebellious Protestant Camisards pose little problem, and even the Russian Old Believers, although defenders of the unreformed traditional faith against the absolutist Petrine state, can be accommodated. The same holds true for the entrepreneurial tenants of Protestant upper Austria resisting the reimposition of intolerant Catholic bureaucratic seigneuries under the Habsburgs. When missionaries subject Indians of the tropical forest to slave labour, then the shaman-led revolt inspired by a mixture of tribal religion and demonisation of the Catholics is surely a legitimate defence of inborn liberty, however 'backward-looking' its ideology may be. And in an extreme case, when the ritual calendar of pre-colonial religion *cum* popular Catholicism inspires the militant labour organisation of Bolivian miners, even the orthodox socialist observer will have to admit that the strike hits home, whatever the loose ends may be.

Yet the issue becomes much more problematic when ritual Catholicism is defended against the enlightened anti-clericalism of the Convent, and when Mexican peasants seem to be manipulated by clergy and great landowners against the 'revolutionary' agrarian reform of the secular state. Careful analysis is able to show that these conflicts – just as similar ones – are much more complex. The correlations between land-holding patterns and resistance to revolutionary clergy or the place of the *agraristas* in Mexico offer certain clues that place the discussion on an entirely different plane. There, however, the issue of 'progress' and 'conservatism' or even 'reaction', can be much more meaningfully debated. Naturally, all this is in one way or another connected with that other Janus-faced term: 'modernisation', and we may surely be pardoned for not wishing to embark on its discussion in a paragraph or two, when others are writing volumes about it. Still, without, so we hope, becoming Romantic defenders of allegedly idyllic peasant communes, as were the Russian populists or the Latin American *indigenistas*, there are especially in our times many peasant movements that oppose imperialism and exploitation precisely by fighting for the restoration of an earlier stage, in which land and labour of independent rural producers were not alienated to the extent that they are now. One may ask oneself, whether it was true only in twentieth century China that rural poor and uprooted peasants had to fight 'backward towards revolution' [*Friedman, 1974*] for rights, land and territory taken away from them by landlords and other agents of colonial and domestic oppression.

Finally, we should offer some thoughts about the question of *cui prodest*: what did religion add to or deduct from a rural movement? What can be said about the value of religious elements in programme, legitimation and organisation of rural resistance? It has been noted by most of our authors, and this was in a sense our sixteenth century point of departure, that a programme formulated in terms of divine justice and scriptural justification can to a very great extent widen the appeal of a resistance movement. The change from local grievances in the name of traditional custom ('old law') to general indictment of the ungodly oppressors in the name of Biblical justice ('godly law') was crucial to the spread of those peasant revolts that added up to the German Peasant War. Similar mechanisms can be observed in the revolt of Eshaq Khan, the *Cristiada* and the Taiping uprising. On the other hand, religious appeal may cut down and limit the possible alliances of the rebels, as it seems to have done in Taiping–Triad relations, where the puritan morality of crypto-Christians repelled the heterodox and Buddhist secret society members whose military aid was thus ultimately denied to the rebel, anti-Manchu cause as an effective, cohesive tool for transferring the mandate of heaven. Or an example in reverse: the 'official' irreligiosity of Russian movements of the seventeenth-eighteenth centuries had assured their appeal to people of many religions and ethnic traditions. Regarding the programmatic aspect of religious rural revolt, one notes that religiously influenced aims, especially millenarian ones, tend to open up maximalist vistas of a new, just society. They create a Heavenly Kingdom of one sort or another, mobilising imagination and enthusiasm far beyond the power of a 'realistic' programme of social change. But again, exactly these eschatological aspects make for poor strategies. The millenarian expectation is an immediate end of the old world, an enormous historical discontinuity which virtually precludes any thought regarding retrenchment, regrouping and advance planning. This shortcoming was fatal for the Babi in Iran no less than for the Taiping after the capture of Nanjing. The scenario defined by the vision of Hong Xiuquan gave guidance only up to the moment of apparent victory, after which the new world was to begin. Thereafter the Taiping host had no guidelines for further fighting and final defeat of their enemies. In turn, if religious vision was a factor in the defeat of many uprisings, it was at least a useful ideology for accepting such a fate, as its essential teachings on suffering and martyrdom enabled the crushed and decimated peasant troops to face the victor's revenge, and often permitted the survivors and subsequent generations to rise again in the memory of the martyrs.

The wide ranging collections of examples about religion's rôle in rural resistance, revolt and uprising which form this volume are presented as preliminary findings for cross-cultural discussion. The editors invite comment in order to set up a further dialogue across the social sciences and humanities.

References

Bak, J., 1975, ed., *The German Peasant War of 1525*, London.
Bak, J., 1983, 'Delinquent Lords and Forsaken Serfs', in: *Society in Change: Studies in Honour of Béla K. Király*, S. B. & A. H. Vardy, eds., Boulder, 291–304.
Engels, F., 1977, *The peasant war in Germany*, Moscow.
Freud, S., 1960, *Totem and Taboo*, London.
Friedman, E., 1974, *Backwards toward Revolution*, Berkeley.
Ginzburg, C., 1979, *The Cheese and the Worms*, London.
Granet, M., 1975, *The Religion of the Chinese People*, New York.
Henningsen, G., 1980, *The Witches Advocate*, Lincoln, Nevada.
Hilton, R., 1973, *Bond Men Made Free: Mediaeval Peasant Movements and the English Rising of 1381*, London.

Lewy, G., 1974, *Religion and Revolution*, New York.
Mitterauer, M., 1979, *Grundtypen alteuropäischer Sozialformen. Haus und Gemeinde in vorindustriellen Gesellschaften*, Stuttgart.
Obelkevitch, J. ed., 1979, *Religion and the people*, Chapel Hill.
O'Neill, W. M., 1976, *Time and the calendars*, Manchester.
Rudé, G., 1980, *Ideology and popular protest*, London.
Scribner, Bob, and G. Benecke, eds., 1979, *The German Peasant War of 1525. New Viewpoints*, London.
Szücs, J., 1976, 'Die Ideologie des Bauernkrieges', in: G. Heckenast, ed. *Aus der Geschichte der Ostmitteleuropäischen Bauernbewegungen im 16.–17. Jahrhundert*, Budapest, 157–88 [repr. in J. Szücs, *Nation und Geschichte: Studien*, Budapest, 1981, 329–69].
Werner, E., 1953, *Die gesellschaftlichen Grundlagen der Klosterreform im 11. Jahrhundert*, Berlin/GDR.

Religion as an ideology of domination

HERBERT FREY

The title of this volume implies, *prima facie*, a direct relationship between religion and rural revolt. The authors have posed themselves the question, what kind of rôle did religion play in different rural resistance movements, and most of them established a positive correlation between the two notions. However, if one considers the traditional functions of religion, it is more appropriate to start out by positing an inverted relationship between religion and revolt. The cases in which religion stimulated rebellion will appear to be the exceptions. Because, surely, the essential function of religion in all developed class societies has always been to assure, in the sphere of ideas, the social reproduction of the existing society by legitimating the prevailing relations of exploitation and the forms of expropriation of surplus, and thus establishing that basic consent that is essential for their survival.

A religious interpretation of the world has always had to explain two major spheres, nature and society, and in its explanation has sought to control the impact of natural forces on human existence. No religion can ever evade the task of interpreting natural phenomena, be it a 'primitive', and 'archaic' or a 'historical' religion [*Bellah, 1973*], be it 'mythology', 'polytheism' or 'monotheism' [*Dobert, 1973*]. It was exactly this naming of the unknown, or, as Hans Blumenberg phrased it, the intrusion of names into the chaos of the nameless world, that constituted the specific achievement of Greek myth. This also applies to all the preceding stages of religious development.

> Myth is an expression for the fact that the world and the powers acting in it are not arbitrary. Whatever it may be called, be it division of powers, codification of responsibilities, or legalisation of relationships, in essence it amounts to a limitation of arbitrariness [*Blumenberg, 1979: 50*].

The chaos that had surrounded man was changed by myth into a cosmos. Nature, now filled with divine beings, lost its alien and frightening character. Fears of the unfamiliar world were turned into stories through the mythological personification of nature. The realm of gods with human passions made men familiar with the world and nature, and eliminated his fear of the unknown. On this level of development, where kinship relations and not class distinctions defined the distribution of the fruits of labour, the aim of religious theory and practice was naming and explaining. In the pre-scientific age, analogy dominated human thinking. Hence nature was perceived in analogous terms. Natural forces and invisible realities were imagined anthropocentrically, that is, as subjects, as individuals with consciousness and ability to communicate among themselves, and with humans. These man-made fictions appeared as a consistent, organised world to dominate both the consciousness and the *praxis* of men and women [*Godelier, 1974: 333*]. In other words, it was the intention of primitive as well as higher forms of religion to arrive at a total understanding of the universe [*Levi-Strauss, 1980: 29f*].

The attempted personalisation of natural forces implied that nature could be tamed. This gave rise to the illusion of communication with phenomena that were in fact not controllable. The actual inability of men in the pre-capitalist age to control natural forces made these appear as belonging to an extra-human sphere. Concepts of gods as acting persons, accessible to human prayer, sacrifice and veneration, led to the expectation that they could be forced to respond in definite ways to human activities. The early phases of religious development, such as animism, were characterised by identifying certain kinds of natural events with a divine being. As social development became more complex, this identification was replaced by gods who were seen as distinct persons in charge of a certain part of nature. Increased personalisation meant that although natural phenomena were seen as manifestations of divine will, yet they were thereby no longer identified with the divine being itself. Thus nature lost much of its sacrality and, in consequence, it became possible to interfere with natural processes without coming into conflict with divine beings.

We can only touch briefly on the unfolding of early religions and their relations to society, since our main task here is the function of religion in the developed class society. Yet we do have to outline the process whereby religion became the most important form of legitimising. Social differentiation was continually reflected in religious ideas. Social institutions emerged from their hitherto less problematic existence to become the object of mythological constructs. Kingship and state ceased to be self-evident. Instead, they had to be re-sacralised continuously by state rituals and protected by distinct gods. The hierarchies that developed in actual society supplied the model for a stratification of gods. It produced a religious explanation of subordination which sanctified the existing social structure. At this point mythical interpretations of nature passed from merely relieving fear of the unknown towards acceptance of a definite form of society, which was based on class domination.

In the stage preceding the emergence of social classes, social division of labour was defined by sex and age. The relations of production by which society controlled natural resources and organised its confrontation with nature as well as its distribution of the fruits of labour, were essentially kinship relations [*Godelier, 1979: 7f; 1980: 16*]. In such a society the prestige of most individuals was defined by their rôle in the productive process. Yet the prestige of elders, for example, was not based on their immediate participation in the actual process of production, but rather on the knowledge of the forces of nature, which they acquired through lifelong confrontation with nature. They constituted a collective memory, enabling society to confront nature on an increasingly effective level. It was a historical development which encouraged the accumulation of an ever-increasing surplus. However, the prestige of the elders was not based on any real insight that they had into a more materially effective process of survival, but rather on the assumption that they were able to communicate with the ancestors, and through them with the gods, by which process they were thought to bring prosperity and fortune to the community. A monopoly of communication with personalised natural forces held by distinct social groups was to make them develop into a class as soon as higher social prestige included the appropriation of surplus product. *Godelier* formulated this as follows:

> In order to develop a lasting form within a pre-class society, the relations of production and domination have to present themselves as relations in the form of exchange of mutual services. Only thereby can these relations be made acceptable by obtaining the active and passive consent of the dominated. The internal differentiation of social positions and the gradual development of new hierarchies based on divisions into estates, castes or classes seems to be given further momentum by the fact that the services which the rulers rendered, relate to the invisible realities and forces. These are the forces perceived by society to control the reproduction of the world and of life [*1979: 18*].

Acquisition of a monopoly in securing communication with extrahuman powers thus became the means for legitimising the appropriation of production. In other words the ruling class obtained their rents and services by exercising tight control over all avenues of communication with so-called extra-human belief systems of their own manufacture. Class division appeared as a differentiation of mental from physical work. While the former by use of religion gave the right to supervising the process of production, the latter enforced the inexorable, routine performance of labouring tasks. This type of structure is characteristic for all societies under a so-called Asiatic mode of production in which the priests and bureaucrats are the masters of production.

> The real appropriation through the labour process happens under these presuppositions, which are not themselves the product of labour, but appear as its natural or divine presuppositions. . . . The surplus product – which is, incidentally,

determined by law in consequence of the real appropriation through labour — thereby automatically belongs to this highest unity [*Marx 1973: 472f*].

The identification of an Asiatic mode of production with geographical areas where natural phenomena such as temperature, rainfall or flood are exactly predictable, was not mere coincidence, since labour had to be mobilised there at precisely, predictably fixed times.

Two societies illustrate the point here, namely Ancient Egypt and the Maya Empire. Even though they precede by many centuries the period covered by the articles in this volume, a brief discussion of the function of religion in these earlier societies is warranted for purposes of contrast and comparison with societies based on later forms of class domination. While Egypt's civilisation was based on the cultivation of the alluvial valley made fertile by the annual floods of the Nile, the economic basis of the Maya Empire was its cultivation of corn. In both societies harvest depended on the precise knowledge of the dates of Nile's high waters or the arrival of the rainy season respectively. A correct forecast appeared easily as the creator of the harvested surplus. As corn needs a definite amount of humidity in its early growth but may suffer from too much water, it was essential to find methods for deciding the optimal date for sowing. The need for exact dating triggered the development of astronomy in both societies [*Broda 1981a, 1981b*].

A combination of favourable geographical conditions with expert construction of irrigation secured in the Nile valley and on the Yucatan Peninsula such an enormous agrarian surplus that not only a priestly and bureaucratic caste could develop, but also a secondary industry to supply it with luxury items. Ruler and priests appropriated surplus produce automatically as a seemingly just equivalent for services rendered to their self-manufactured invisible super-human powers seen as regulating the source of all bounty. In his sacral relationship with natural forces, the king or pharao as supreme proprietor of all land guaranteed the stability of the forms, and hence the production and survival of all cultivators [*Sohn-Rethel, 1970: 100*]. Thus in the so-called Asiatic mode of production, religious relationships decided the distribution of production: religion assumed the function of relationships of production. Acceptance of religion implied acknowledgement of a distinct class relationship, and thus an intrinsic connection was established between interpretation of nature and legitimation of social order. Religious beliefs made expropriation of the social product by priests and officials appear as a legitimate appropriation. In turn, any opposition to the social order was seen as an attack on divine ordination. These close connections contributed much to the stability — and, we may add, to the stagnating character — of these societies.

The division of mental from physical work increased with the development of class society, especially with the emergence of such auxiliary tasks in the expropriation of surplus as writing, accounting and the like [*ibid., 101*]. In fact, mental labour, more or less closely linked with religion, developed not primarily as an aid to material production but rather as an aid in the further appropriation of the surplus by non-producers. Even though the impressive intellectual achievements of Egyptian and Maya priests did include elements of considerable use to production, their legitimation was based on mystical knowledge of natural processes. It was their apparent confidence in handling natural phenomena, regardless of its religious interpretation, that had the really significant impact on social structure, and it legitimated class positions.

With apologies for flying over centuries of history, something should be said about how classical Greek society and religion was underpinned by a slave-holding economy. When the exploiting class originates in a social system which is different from that of the exploited, the necessity of a religious explanation of class differences becomes superfluous. That is why antique religion and philosophy was not confronted with the problem of domination. As *instrumenta vocalia*, slaves were essentially deprived of human quality, and their exploitation needed little further thought as regards ideological justification. Early Greek myth had of course interpreted nature in the service of an agricultural society dependent on natural forces. 'By contrast with urban craftsmen, who are almighty in their own small sphere, what agriculture and war have in common is that men engaged in them feel that their success depends on the help of divine powers' [*Vernant, 1973: 254*]. With increased use of slave labour inserted between free men and nature, the rôle of religion in mastering natural forces became secondary. Greek polytheism could thus concentrate on interpreting its own society without differentiating between religious commands and social norms. The integration of Greek society was achieved not on a religious but on a political plane. Hence Greek society had a relatively great tolerance in matters of religion. The notion that the cosmos was full of gods expressed a certain openness of myth, so much so that there could even be a temple dedicated to an 'unknown god'. In spite of its imagery, Greek mythology was flexible and was not confined to petrified idols.

> This myth could eschew ancient fears as defeated monsters because it did not need them for the protection of *one* truth and *one* law. The institution supporting it was not aimed at frightening and scaring its public. Instead it presented the fear that had been overcome to bring assurance and security to increasingly beautiful things [*Blumenberg, 1979: 266*].

This liberation was achieved by the creation of a Pantheon consisting of gods that were neither less subject to fate nor more ethical than the mortals. One could therefore live with them, without being goaded into rebellion by the impeccable sanctity represented by the god of monotheistic religions.

Before turning to the main thrust of my argument about the specific rôle of Christianity in feudal society, it is worth outlining some of the major features of monotheism. Limitation of space forces us to forego detailed examination of Judaism and the primitive Christianity closely linked to it, but a few issues can be outlined.

Unlike earlier religions, Christianity as one of the universal monotheistic religions is transcendental in character. In these universal religions the old cosmological monism is being dissolved, and a sphere entirely distinct from the empirical world is postulated. This sphere claims to represent men's highest values [*Weber, 1966; Weber, 1968; Wach, 1962; Bellah, 1973*]. By the discovery of this new sphere of religious reality the existing, tangible cosmos is implicitly devalued, hence a denial of the world (*contemptus mundi*) becomes a general feature of these religions. This other-worldliness ascribes to the actual world a merely transitory character, making it a mere vale of tears which must lead to the only valuable life which is in the hereafter. Hierarchical orders which were present in earlier stages of religious development now receive a greatly increased significance. This world is subject to control of a higher valued 'otherworld'. Both are structured in hallowed hierarchies, which reflect the actual increase of class differentiation in society.

> The appearance of universal monotheistic religions is part of a general transition from the archaic system of two classes into that of four, typical for all historical civilisations up to our own time. These contain two upper strata, the political-military and the cultural-religious elite; and two lower, the rural peasant, and urban trader and craftsmen producers [*Bellah, 1973: 287*].

For the masses, this dualism is reflected in distinctions drawn between this life and that of the hereafter. Religious thought from earlier such as classical Greek times, which was primarily orientated towards this world, turned towards that other sphere which was thought to be either much more exalted, such as heaven, or infinitely more debased, such as hell. Salvation became the central issue of religion.

Monotheistic religions differed from earlier religions also insofar as they were universal. That is, they were not limited by tribal particularism. It became irrelevant to what tribe or clan the faithful belonged or what particular god originally had been worshipped. Decisive was merely their faculty for salvation. This made it possible for the first time to postulate man as such. The carriers of the new religious systems were its individual members who made up the universal community of the faithful. Their decision to lead a life pleasing to god was no longer predetermined by the immutable tribal and ethnic identity into which they were born.

Universalism, however, implies not merely granting to everyone his or her own faculty for salvation, but also insisting on a monopoly of one religion as the only truth. Universal religions tend to contain this core of totalitarianism. They sanctify violence as holy war, and grant to it a legitimation and justification which is above mere political expediency [*Weber, 1968: 474f*].

> As a rule, prophetic religion is naturally compatible with the status feeling of the nobility when it directs its promises to the warrior in the cause of religion. This conception assumes the exclusiveness of the universal god and the moral depravity of unbelievers who are his adversaries and whose untroubled existence arouses his righteous indignation [*ibid., 473*].

The image of god in monotheistic world religions is essentially different from that of the older ones. The irrational, spontaneous actions of the ancient gods are gradually transformed by ethics and rationality, adding the qualities of love, goodness and justice to the old attributes of power and omniscience of god. The concept of the lonely, womenless god emerges, bereft of his own myth, sole creator and ruler of the universe. Not tolerating other gods besides himself, all the powers of the many earlier ones are concentrated and multiplied in him. Neither the Olympic Zeus, nor the Greek philosopher-god would have been permitted to claim such total lordship over world and man. The new god has absolute claims on human conduct, which leads to a new kind of human responsibility perpetually confronted with divine commands. No longer is it sufficient to conform to social norms. Correct conviction is also demanded, whereby the invisible god is an omniscient judge who reads the minds of all men and women. External ritual and sacrifice are replaced by the internal views of godly thought and unwavering faith. This god cannot be magically coerced by properly conducted rites. Men can pray and supplicate to him but the result is uncertain, since the omnipotent addressee alone will decide whether he is to grant a mortal's wishes.

This transformation of the concept of god is accompanied by autochthonous religious institutions and social structures reflecting the essential dualism. As noted above, the undifferentiated elite of archaic societies is being split into two roughly autonomous hierarchies: a political and a religious one. Consequently, legitimation of domination and exploitation become a problem as they depend on a balance of power between the two ruling strata. They generally support each other, but specific conflicts between the political and ideological leadership do cause serious crises in society. The outcome can be subordination of the one to the other, and establishment of a new concept of legitimation. If that fails, the social order may collapse and be replaced by a new one.

These characteristics describe monotheistic systems in general, without defining the specifics of the one that interests us most, namely Christianity. As all religions carry the mortgage of their origins, so in Christianity the heritage of monotheism, is still seen as first elaborated in its immediate precursor, namely Judaism. The intellectual independence expressed in that Jewish god of universal salvation was surely a response to the continuous threat posed to the Israelites by the existence of mighty neighbours. 'The anxious bewilderment by the political events of the world provoked ever new mental constructs in the sphere of religion' [*Weber, 1966: III, 220*]. The Judaic god was essentially a heavenly king, similar to the gods of the sky among other peoples of the desert, where they were in charge of rain and hence of survival [*ibid., I, 298*]. But Jahwe received his characteristics due to the specific political-military conditions of ancient Israel. A small kingdom at the crossroads of menacing world empires, it had to construe a supermundane 'god of the hosts' who had a personal relationship with his chosen people. In an earlier stage Jahwe, too, was a nature god, master of tempests and catastrophes with strongly anthropomorphic traits. The particular achievement of ancient Judaism was that the Jahwe of the storms, residing on the top of high mountains as a strange and distinct god, was transformed into one that had been chosen by Israel (and Israel by him) in a covenant established between them [*Schluchter, 1981: 33*]. The world view could now be built around the idea of obedience to the positive divine law expressed in this covenant. If Israel acted accordingly, divine reward was granted. If Israel trespassed, negative sanctions could be expected. Thereby the political ups and downs of the Jews could be interpreted as punishments meted out by an almighty god.

> This made possible the assumption that when enemies conquered, or when other calamities befell one's group, the cause was not the weakness of the god but rather his anger against his followers, caused by his displeasure at their transgressions against the laws under his guardianship. Hence, the sins of the group were to blame if some unfavourable development overtook it. The god might well be using the misfortune to express his desire to chastise and educate his favorite people [*Weber, 1968: 437*].

In this sense Jahwe appeared as a superhuman but still 'understandable personal lord, demanding obedience' [*Weber, 1966: III, 239*]. The categories of the perception of god grew out of historical reality, and hence Max Weber could state, in a surprisingly Marxist manner, that 'the god of the Near East was formed on the model of the earthly king' [*ibid., I, 298*].

The establishment of the Ten Commandments meant both the theologising of law and the rationalisation of religious ethics. A systematic catalogue of sins was set up for the first time by which traditional commands were unified, and ethical norms divorced from ritual and social norms. A unified religious ethic corresponded to the demand for an exclusive relationship with god, since fulfillment of these norms became the paramount test for salvation. These structural elements of Judaism became constitutive parts of a Christian concept of the divine. The historical deed of Paul was to turn the sacred book of the Jews into the holy writ of Christianity by clarifying its position when faced with attacks of gnostic intellectualism. Furthermore, the passion of Jesus was declared to have eradicated the persecuted and abject state of the Jews, hence opening the road to Christian universalism with its mission to 'Jews and Gentiles'.

It took many centuries for Christianity to change from being a religion of the oppressed into being the religion of the oppressors. The precondition of this was a socio-economic change in the Roman Empire: the transition from a slave economy to one based on peasants holding plots from a landlord in course of the feudalisation of society. Christianity, as interpreted by St Augustine, increasingly satisfied the needs of this emerging feudal society. It was based on the truce that the late Roman Emperors had made with Christianity since the fourth century. State power and ideological domination were synchronised as emperors assumed the rôle of defenders of the church in return for ecclesiastical legitimation. At the same time Christianity was protected by the officers of the State against the pagan Gods of Ancient Rome that were suppressed, if necessary, even with violence. Christian monotheism brooked no rivals in religion, just as emperors tolerated no rivals in politics. A totalitarian inner coherence emerged in which there was no room for heterodoxy. The church developed rationally with centralised piety under a monarchic head whereby a supra-worldly God was represented by an earthly ruler of mighty power and ability to regulate all forms of life. The church assumed a monopoly of interpretation over nature, society and the extrasensory world, as expressed in dogma, a set of beliefs enforced by extreme sanctions. Myth did not need a constant defence against variant interpretations. Dogmatic theology is a particularly rigid form satisfying the need for knowing the exact truth about the invisible from vortex to God's grace or gravity to the Holy Trinity, and laying down the law on what was to be believed once and for all. It is based on the assumption that everything depends on the very exclusive finality of the one definite truth which is the cause of an infinite variety of consequences. 'Whoever won the monopoly of defining the truth was to be the church, and acquired the right, in cooperation with the state to declare others to be sects' [*Blumenberg, 1979: 265*]. That gave rise to a new and quite peculiar set of distinctions between *ecclesia* and *secta* between the singular orthodoxy of ought and must versus multiple heterodoxy, with a splintering, regrouping and resplintering of belief systems. Thus all divergent understandings of belief and social order became heresies in medieval and early modern times, when the Catholic Church held the ideological monopoly.

The question emerges as to why Christianity should prove to be the most adequate expression of ideological domination in feudal systems. The feudal system was a specific type of exploitation related to the generalised forms of dependence, to serfdom, although the development of servitude was tied to geographical and regional peculiarities. Whereas in the western Mediterranean region, the transformation from slave to serf status brought with it a certain amount of freedom, in central and northern Europe the move to serfdom from Germanic or Slav commoner worsened the position of the lower social strata. The consequence was a standardisation of unfreedom across the whole European peasantry which in the end was only to a very limited extent variegated by regional peculiarities.

Since the exploited now came from the same society it was hardly possible to hold them down by the mere exercise of violence. Hence it became necessary to legitimate the feudal system by obtaining the widest possible consent for the exercise of power within it. This was achieved by the Christian religion when it interpreted nature and society in the way demanded from it, especially since Christian legitimation was flexible, offering a certain amount of room for modest and therefore more harmless heterodoxy. The low economic development of the productive force only allowed for an irrational explanation of natural phenomena, which meant that any objective explanation of reality had to be cloaked in religion [*c.f. Marx, 1971: 93–4; Kofler, 1966: 56*].

According to the Christians, God's will manifested itself in nature and in history, whereby phenomena were understood as an expression of God's intervention in the running of the world. Bad harvests and plagues were regarded as God's reaction to man's behaviour whereby only the church could beg for mercy and seek to deflect His wrath.

> The medieval church thus acted as a repository of supernatural power which could be dispensed to the faithful to help them in their daily problems. It was inevitable that the priests, set apart from the rest of the community by their celibacy and ritual consecration, should have derived an extra cachet from their positions as mediators between man and god. It was also inevitable that around the church, the clergy and their holy apparatus there clustered a horde of popular superstitions, which endowed religious objects with a magical power to which theologians themselves had never laid claim [*Thomas, 1973; 35*].

Between magician and Christian priest the difference in attitude towards the powers of nature lies in that magic seeks to be coercive whereas the priest's prayer is solely dependent on the grace of God. This performance has social implications. Whereas the magician loses prestige or even his own life when the powers of nature fail to do his bidding, the Christian priest avoids any such immediate consequences if his prayer fails. For it was the inscrutable will of God to test man through His punishment, for in that case man had sinned too much to be allowed God's grace. It sets up a dialectic between the higher power and the subjective guilt of the faithful, which always exonerates the Christian priesthood of the West from blame. Whereas the priests of Asia and pre-Columbian America are directly dependent on success in their dealings with nature if they are to retain their influence in society, by contrast, the Western Church seems to increase its power over the faithful in catastrophic situations. In such a way the medieval Catholic Church secured a monopoly over interpretations of nature without once ever having to put itself to the test. Thereby the religious world-view severely limited a more scientific approach to nature, and the modern European revolution in natural science had to fight its way against theology all along [*Blumenberg, 1973: 125*]. But for medieval man a division between theology and natural observation was impossible. The consequence of having an all-powerful, all-seeing yet inscrutable God precluded any notion of such a split [*ibid., 125–6*].

In medieval agrarian society Christian interpretation of nature functioned rather like myth in ancient Greece. Both gave protection against fear of the unknown, with the added bonus that the Christian religion also thereby stabilised the social system. Medieval agrarian society was dependent on the goodwill of nature, which was regarded as the expression of an even stronger subjective force in the face of which man could only remain a gratefully passive receiver. It resulted in the view that man's daily production was achieved not merely as a result of his own labour, but at least just as much because of the mercy of God. Here was a case for the view that man's work was part of God's nature rather than that man by his toil was making his own exclusive use of nature [*cf. Lefevre, 1978: 60*].

The church now appeared in the guise of arbiter between God and man in that its prayers seemed to involve it directly in obtaining surplus production from the natural world. Tithe was thus its legitimate reward for services rendered. However, this argument for the confiscation of surplus production was probably only really valid in Asian societies with their more direct religious attitude towards influencing nature, whereas in the Christian West it was merely another argument to justify the levying of tithe.

Up to now we have concentrated on the question of how the monopoly of interpreting nature strengthened the power of the church. We go on to examine how the Christian religion dealt with social relations. It is perhaps best to go back to the transition from slave to feudal society, and to add to it the thesis that it is necessary to establish one area within it which represents the inner coherence of society. In Ancient Greek society the polity was a community of freemen constituted in public affairs. In feudal society it was the equality of all souls in the eyes of God, which would however only be carried out after death. Hereby the church monopolised the hopes of serf-peasants by contrasting their poor existence on earth with the Utopia of a free, equal and self-sufficient society in heaven. In this belief-system self-sufficiency was raised to the status of Utopia at the day of Last Judgement which was always spiritually imminent. Thereby other-worldliness was imported into actual every-day living consciousness as a spiritual element which began to look forward to a life after death even long before death was likely to take place [*Tomberg, 1973: 162*].

In the feudal system serfs were assigned a politically passive place. They had to accept their subordinate rôle and hand over their surplus production. Yet in the religious sphere they were provided with a view of the future Kingdom of God with its freedom and equality which was an opiate for the toils of everyday life. It allowed for the development of an inner freedom among the exploited classes, which was indifferent to the social world outside it for that was only a kingdom of the earth which would soon moulder away.

Without doubt there was for the peasants a lasting contradiction between a Godly inner life and the real, earthly world of power-relations outside. Yet this contradiction was usually tolerated as long as exploitation was kept under control by customary laws which partly favoured the peasants and which were honoured by the ruling classes. But each delivery of rents and tithes made it clear to the peasants that they were unfree; that perpetually they were thereby negating their own independence [*Marx, 1973: 299*]. By showing their dependence in this way feudal peasants tacitly accepted social relations as being just as unchanging and static as they thought nature itself to be. Very little mobility in the social system instilled in the peasants a view that for them to be suppressed was just an eternal fact, whereby they just became a specifically suffering object over and against the ruling class. Feudal hierarchy was underpinned by ideological dependencies in such a way as thereby to express the inner strength of such relationships since one was morally bound to uphold loyalty to the system wherever direct supervision was not possible. Feudalism therefore needed its own organisation to instill such moral principles which allowed all its members to feel that they were always in direct, spiritual contact with God. Such a service was supplied by the feudal church.

The church is a member both of the secular and the spiritual world [*Tomberg, 1978: 196*]. She must preserve the identity of each world whilst at the same time uniting hierarchy with community. Feudal lords delegated their younger sons into running the church where they fused with the serfs as their leaders in a single community. Faith became identical with loyalty and obedience which integrated the community into the church and bound it to ruling-class society. Yet some elements in medieval Catholic faith strove ultimately towards participation in the freedom of the kingdom of heaven. The authorities of the church on earth could not in the last resort be anything other than mere arbitrators between the masses and heaven. It applied also to loyalty. Any obedience towards worldly and spiritual authority was merely based on the belief in God. By treating the faithful as equal members of the church solely in the eyes of God, Catholic social theory was thereby capable of ignoring totally their social inequality here on earth. The village community came together as God's children during church service in a symbolic gesture to produce an imaginary sense of local unity. A collection of unequal people practised a common ritual in the church whereby each person went through the inner gates into the other world where they all met again as a community of saints undivided by class or status. Once the church service was over this spiritual act of unity remained as a vague and hopeful memory [*Tomberg, 1973: 166–7*]. In this manner the church created a bond of unity within feudal society. The peasant was bound to the village on Sundays generally, and during the sermon from the pulpit especially, whereby the status quo was perpetuated. Yet beyond the church with its rituals and symbols the real bonds holding the village together were its communally held lands. Tenancy and ownership were carefully distinguished from each other. The more land-holding was the basis of feudal society, so the less did it serve to provide the inner ideology of that society. Land ownership increasingly masqueraded in the restricted sense of private property [*Lefevre, 1978: 57*].

It was the church that had to hold the two ends of society, the serfs and their feudal lords, together as a unified whole, as each found their different places in the hierarchy of land-holding and land-ownership. The rise of private property, whether from the side of the peasantry or that of the nobility, broke through this delicate feudal compromise by destroying the older system of land-holding whilst at the same time overturning the hold of the church over its tithe system. Tithes were carved up among peasants or nobles according to the rules of each particular political practice. The church had to retain an overall interest in the feudal system since only that guaranteed it the most substantial rents and incomes. In the ensuing battle between peasants and nobles over the last remnants of common lands, the church tended to support the nobles when it came to upholding property rights, but when the nobles tried to drive the peasants off the land the church changed sides. The church was thus incredibly powerful because of its unique rôle in justifying social relations; and uniting social differences. That the church was perhaps unconscious of what it was doing on the ideological plane is a question which we can not go into here since we have only been concerned with the self-interpretation of the church in so far as it clarifies our understanding of the whole system of feudal exploitation.

Since the medieval Catholic Church regarded life on earth merely as a preparation for the after-life the historical process of the every-day was debased in advance and also belittled. Human existence was only a testing-ground for the coming life after death which was especially directed at the subjected mass of peasants, for thereby the most piteous type of existence was given inner strength and value. The division between the real world on earth and the ideal city of God was well characterised in the early feudal era by St Augustine when he expostulated that God only grants eternal happiness to the pious in His Kingdom of Heaven, and He leaves the kingdom of the earth to the faithless and unclean. The world was thus tarred with the brush of sin and it became merely a place which was worth leaving as fast as possible. Yet St Augustine still had the task of interpreting serfdom and unfreedom in his theology. According to St Ambrose, it ran along the lines of 'he who sins, is in bondage to his sin': Serfdom was derived from the Fall in the Bible [*Puiggros, 1969: 112*].

But to St Augustine there were problems with this. The sinner could not be a slave to sin, since his soul was free. He had the freedom to sin, to repent and to do penance. By creating this notion of freedom, St Augustine placed the responsibilities of the world on man who now had the task of letting the good overcome the bad within him. There was thus no escaping from the view that the way of the world lay totally in the freedom of man who was a sinner right from the start [*Blumenberg, 1979: 469–70*]. Serfdom was thus a degeneration from an original law of nature in which all men were equal before God but because of the Fall, they had lost their equality. The ten commandments now had to help sinful Adam along. He was far removed from the Golden Age of the Garden of Eden when freedom and peace had been a common property to all. After the Fall, only a weak and relative law of nature remained which was now available to justify the church. It took over the ordering of the world from the original biblical communism. Medieval natural law was a very pale reflection of Ancient Stoicism. It even sanctioned slavery. It certainly sanctioned violent rule with power of the sword. The Fall of Adam gave natural law the rôle of chastiser against human sinfulness [*Bloch, 1972: 38–9*]. It allowed for a clear distinction between the freedom of the soul and the bondage of the body. In having the teachings of St Augustine applied to him the serf only attained his freedom through passive toleration of his bondage here on earth which would cease after death when he had reached the world of God. The soul could only be freed when all earthly resistance was avoided. Nothing was to interfere with God's plans of salvation for man on earth. The earthly kingdom was not worth fighting for since it was sinful and temporary and God had his own plans for it [*Kojève, 1947: 345f*]. Everything had its Godly place and the serf had to accept his status as a test of God, which if quietly accepted would be his passport into heaven after death.

Let us finally ask, why medieval society regarded the social structure as something static, unchangeable and God-given which had at all costs to be obeyed. People regarded nature as subjective and the man who worked in its fields and forests was its mere object. Since economic and technological progress was relatively modest in the feudal era, the relationship between man and nature remained static and dependent on the caprice of the weather. The peasant saw himself as passive in the hands of nature. He saw no way of taking production and society into his own hands. From here everyone was given his place in society [*Ullmann, 1966: 42f; Hauser, 1951: 187–8*]. Status and *ordo* were unequal constellations, fixed by God with a parallel in the angelic hierarchy around the heavenly throne [*Huizinga, 1924: 46ff*]. Everyone had his own particular God-given job to do. Each had his calling which was the end-product of Christianity according to which each individual had been delegated his own particular task in life [*Duby, 1978: 11–35; Ullmann, 1966: 43*].

Given all this passivity, then what social and economic changes strengthened the element of resistance within the Christian religion? What destroyed the cosy legitimation of the feudal-catholic world view? What led Catholicism into reorganising itself internally? Since Catholicism claimed a monopoly in interpreting the world, any differences of opinion were branded as heresy and this applied also to social movements that tried to change the outdated social structure. The feudal view of reality did not allow a rational explanation of nature and society, which meant that all conflicts had to take on a religious language. Heresy and sectarianism were as natural to medieval society as were strikes in industrial society. Most heretical movements took the Catholic teaching of poverty, equality, celibacy and fraternity seriously over and against the mere cynicism of ecclesiastical pragmatism. The Church authorities were forced time and again into reforms only as an unwilling, necessary response to sectarian idealism [*Kofler, 1966*].

We have sought to outline the comparative origins, structure and development of official monotheistic religious ideology as eventually also institutionalised in medieval feudal Europe, and to show how priests and rulers held their agrarian populations in a spiritual vice. How did the common people break out of this stranglehold? It happened when priest and noble fell out with each other, however indirectly, over sharing the spoils of their exploitative power and jurisdiction; when urbanisation and commercialisation created new classes and avenues of communication for rural producers to find new marketing outlets and take on financially oppressive obligations, when peasants and small townsmen made their own apocalyptic biblical interpretations, sometimes using violent, secretive, heterodox religion to break down institutional orthodoxies with their interpretations of exploitative loyalty and obedience. The ideology has moved from animism and naturalism to monotheism. From there it has gone towards objective, rationally secular science after the eighteenth century, corresponding *economically* with stages of human development from the pre-historic to ancient, to feudal, and from there to capitalist and socialist forms of production.

We have sought to provide a very brief overview. For it is surely a task of *Religion and Rural Revolt* to examine the global implications of the agrarian and feudal, pre-industrial stage of human existence, and how it survives in an irregular geographical spread across, and bordering on, more advanced social formations. With all their scientific technologies, industrial societies still carry with them moral codes and fears of change, called traditions, from earlier times of feudal-agrarian production and marketing, gathered together by monotheistic religions. These religions make rural revolts both necessary and socially unsuccessful –

rebellious rather than revolutionary – precisely because rural life has had such terrible difficulty in shaking off and replacing positively, the psychological and political assumptions which religion and tradition impose.

References

Anderson, Perry, 1974, *Passages from Antiquity to Feudalism*, London.
Aston, M. E., 1960, 'Lollardy and Sedition, 1381–1431', *Past and Present*, No. 17.
Bloch, Ernst, 1972, *Naturrecht und menschliche Würde*, Frankfurt.
Bloch, Ernst, 1977, *Thomas Münzer als Theologe der Revolution*, Frankfurt.
Bellah, Robert, 1973, 'Religiöse Evolution', C. Seyfahrt and W. Spondel, eds., *Seminar: Religion und gesellschaftliche Entwicklung*, Frankfurt.
Blumenberg, Hans, 1973, *Der Prozeß der theoretischen Neugierde*, Frankfurt.
Blumenberg, Hans, 1979, *Arbeit am Mythos*, Frankfurt.
Broda, Johanna, 1981a, *Astronomy, Cosmovision and Ideology, in praehispanic Mesoamerica*, New York.
Broda, Johanna, 1981b, 'Ideologia y represion en al estado mexica', *VI Reunion de historiadores mexicanos y norteamericanos*, 8–12 de Septiembre, Chicago.
Dobert, Rainer, 1973, 'Zur Logik des Übergangs von archaischen zu hochkulturellen Religionssystemen', K. Eder, ed., *Seminar: Die Entstehung von Klassengesellschaften*, Frankfurt.
Duby, George, 1978, *Les trois ordres ou l'imaginaire du féodalisme*, Paris.
Ginzburg, Carlo, 1980, 'Volksbrauch, Magie und Religion', R. Romano, ed., *Die Gleichzeitigkeit des Ungleichzeitigen*, Frankfurt.
Godelier, Maurice, 1974, *Economia, fetichismo y religion en las sociedades primitivas*, Madrid.
Godelier, Maurice, 1979, 'Infrastructura, sociedades, historia' *En Teoria*, 2.
Godelier, Maurice, 1980, 'Las relaciones hombre-mujer: el problema de la dominacion masculina', *En Teoria*, 5.
Hauser, Arnold, 1951, *The Social history of art*, I, London.
Hilton, Rodney, 1977, *Bond men made free*, London.
Huizinga, Johan, 1924, *The Waning of the Middle Ages*, London.
Kofler, Leo, 1966, *Zur Geschichte der bürgerlichen Gesellschaft*, Neuwied.
Kojève, Alexandre, 1947, *Introduction à lecture de Hegel*, Paris.
Kuchenbuch, Ludolf, 1977, 'Zur Struktur und Dynamik der feudalen Produktionsweise im vorindustriellen Europa', *Feudalismus-Materialien zur Theorie und Geschichte*, Frankfurt.
Lefevre, Wolfgang, 1978, *Naturtheorie und Produktionsweise*, Neuwied.
Levi-Strauss, Claude, 1980, *Mythos und Bedeutung*, Frankfurt.
Marx, Karl, 1971, *Das Kapital*, vol. 1 MEW 23, Berlin.
Marx, Karl, 1973, *Grundrisse*, (trans. M. Nicolaus) Harmondsworth.
Mollat M., & P. Wolf, 1973, *Popular Revolutions of the Late Middle Ages*, London.
Negt, O., & A. Kluge, 1981, *Geschichte und Eigensinn*, Frankfurt.
Puiggros, Rodolfo, 1969, *Genesis y Desarollo del feudalismo*, Buenos Aires.
Schluchter, Wolfgang, 1981, 'Altisraelische religiöse Ethik und okzidentaler Rationalismus', *Max Webers Studie über das antike Judentum*, Frankfurt.
Sohn-Rethel, Alfred, 1970, *Geistige und körperliche Arbeit*, Frankfurt.
Sohn-Rethel, Alfred, 1971, *Warenform und Denkform*, Frankfurt.
Thomas, Keith, 1973, *Religion and the Decline of Magic*, Harmondsworth.
Tomberg, Friedrich, 1973, *Polis und Nationalstaat*, Neuwied.
Tomberg, Friedrich, 1978, 'Thesen zur geschichtlichen Konstitution der sozialistischen Persönlichkeit aus der Folge der Gesellschaftsformationen', *Argument-Sonderband AS-32*.
Ullmann, Walter, 1966, *The Individual and Society in the Middle Ages*, Baltimore.

Vernant, Jean-Pierre, 1973, 'Arbeit und Natur in der griechischen Antike', K. Eder, ed., *Seminar: Die Entstehung von Klassengesellschaften*, Frankfurt.
Wach, J., 1962, *Vergleichende Religionsforschung*, Stuttgart.
Weber, Max, 1968, *Economy and Society*, G. Roth and C. Wittich, eds., New York.
Weber, Max, 1966, *Gesammelte Aufsätze zur Religionssoziologie*, 3 vols., Tubingen.
Wittfogel, Karl, 1977, *Geschichte der bürgerlichen Gesellschaft*, Hannover.

Icon and ideology in religion and rebellion 1300–1600: Bauernfreiheit *and* religion royale*

LIONEL ROTHKRUG

Ever since Marc Bloch compared rural rebellions in seigneurial regimes to industrial strikes in contemporary capitalist enterprises and asserted that rural insurgents were a normal feature of the French countryside even on the eve of the Great Revolution [*1960: 174–5*], social historians have emphasized the routine character of popular insurrection in medieval and early modern Europe. A considerable amount of new evidence for the frequency of uprisings and riots has been presented since, which also reveals wide variations in the character of insurrection. Insurgent bands behaved differently from one another, and they expressed dissimilar points of view. This paper argues that rebels everywhere developed fundamental notions of personal rights, but diverse patterns of religious practices influenced people to understand these rights differently from one region to another. Finally, the geographical pluralism in viewpoint both corresponded and contributed toward cultural differentiation among European populations.

In 1549 at Mousehold heath outside Norwich, Robert Kett, at the head of a small army of followers, presented to government officials twenty-nine demands, a list of grievances about rents, enclosures, weights and measures and the like. However, one article, number 16, carries a clear ideological message:

> We pray thatt all bonde men may be made ffre for God made all ffre wt his precious blood sheddyng [*Fletcher, 1968: 143*].

Since bondmen had virtually disappeared from Norwich in Kett's day the insurrectionary appeal to the Grand Manumission at Calvary, dissociated as it was from any institutional specificity, must have had a wider signification. It was

---

* Werner O. Packull (University of Waterloo) has been most generous in sharing his knowledge with me. I owe to him almost all the references to the 'common man' in late medieval Germany.

Also I thank my colleagues, Charles Bertrand, John Hill and Jim Moore for reading the manuscript and for their helpful suggestions.

a generalized, biblically inspired protest against any conditions thought to resemble those of bondage.

This slogan had already appeared in *The Twelve Articles of the Peasants* drawn up in February 1525 in Memmingen, in the name of insurrectionary peasants from Upper Swabia, Baltringen, Allgäu and Lake Constance, called the Christian Peasant Union. No other single document was more widely publicized in the great Peasant War. The third article explains that:

> it has until now been the custom for the lords to own us as their property. This is deplorable, for Christ redeemed and bought us all with his precious blood, the lowliest shepherd as well as the greatest lord, with no exceptions. Thus the Bible proves that we are free and want to be free [*Blickle, 1981: 197*].

These words or one of their several versions promulgated in Germany in 1525 [*ibid.: 58–64*] may have inspired Kett's invocation on Mousehold heath. In any event Rodney Hilton [*1977*] insists that Kett's appeal to the Grand Manumission 'epitomizes the chief desire of rebellious serfs throughout medieval Europe'. Certainly German bondmen demanded emancipation from servile status, but in declaring their intention many said nothing about the Grand Manumission. For example, Peter Blickle explains that historians have overlooked how defiant peasants, especially serfs, sought persistently to express 'notions of *personal, individual rights*' (Blickle's italics). Without mention of the Grand Manumission, peasants formulated the most forceful references to 'rights' in their complaints against serflike (*leibherrlich*) duties, even when the duties had not been recently enforced. According to Blickle, the clearest notions of personal rights came from bondmen who had the least to fear from their hard-pressed lords [*Blickle, 1980: 302*].

Blickle thinks bondmen may have assimilated their own growing horizontal mobility with the freedoms enjoyed by urban artisans to sell their labor, to marry whom they chose and to go where they pleased. When he transferred urban freedoms to the countryside, argues Blickle, the peasant may have universalized and imparted to these liberties the character of a natural law [*ibid.: 302*]. The point to be made, however, is that when other peasants – probably some of whom were not serfs – invoked the Grand Manumission they consciously appealed to a *divine* principle, indeed to the central mystery of the faith – *not* to a natural law – to justify their insurrection.

It is clear, therefore, that German peasants advanced dissimilar notions of personal rights to justify armed rebellion. Did Protestant teachings influence those insurgents, rural and urban, who appealed to the Grand Manumission? The answer is yes, but in very different ways. Henry J. Cohn [*1979*] recently reminded us that monasteries, chapters, and, to a lesser extent bishops had been a chief object of rebel fury throughout the fifteenth century, especially after 1450, when uprisings grew progressively in size and intensity. Although the waxing discontent is attributable largely to demographic, fiscal and political factors that intensified constraints – here in one way, there in another – on the entire population, Cohn also shows that a fierce anti-clericalism often animated recurrent uprisings against seigneurial policies of restriction and coercion. Clerical landlords, sometimes hard pressed, regularly resorted to weapons unavailable to lay lords. Their routine recourse to papal privileges, ecclesiastical courts, excommunication, denial of sacraments, refusal of marriage, refusal of last rites or denial of burial in sacred ground, onerous penances and the like encouraged many south Germans to be attentive to Lutheran, Zwinglian and Bucerian strictures against a parasitic, money gouging and tyrannical clergy and to call upon divine law and holy scripture to justify a general assault against, in their eyes, the material and spiritual oppression of the Church. In this way, argues Cohn, anti-clericalism provided 'the essential link between the economic grievances of peasants and townsmen and the appeal of the Reformation' [*ibid.: 25*].

Cohn explicitly accepts Gunther Franz's classic thesis that when rural insurgents invoked the 'old law' or custom they appealed only to local sentiments and their goals remained conservative. Only if they sought justification in divine law and in scripture could they universalize their appeal and radicalize their demands. Certainly the authors of *The Twelve Articles* called upon divine law – a principle superior to terrestial codes – in order to effect changes in areas outside religion. They also 'found in Holy Scripture' evidence to prove they were freemen. Perhaps they also understood the principle of 'the priesthood of all believers' to be a corollary to the view that Christ had shed His blood 'for the lowliest shepherd as well as the greatest lord'.

Be that as it may, Cohn's powerful description of a pervasive anti-clericalism makes Franz's thesis possible only for rebels who espoused the Reformation. What about those who remained Catholic? For example, in May 1525, the city of Freiburg capitulated to rural insurrectionaries. The victorious peasants told the citizens that they could keep their customs and rights 'so far as Holy Gospel permits and until the awaited reformation of these usages shall have taken place'. At the same time, however, the peasants still kept their Catholic beliefs ... the treaty with Freiburg was in fact concluded with an oath to *God and the saints* [*Bergsten, 1978: 220*]. In short to apostrophize divine law and scripture in the midst of a rebellion was one thing; but it was clearly quite another to abandon deeply rooted religious practices. That is why historical maps show little correspondence between the theatres of insurrection and Protestant jurisdictions in South Germany. Only a map indicating areas of strong and weak relic worship, to be determined, as I have shown [*Rothkrug, 1980, passim*], from the distribution of pre-Reformation pilgrimage sites dedicated to saints, will reveal whether local practices made it easy or difficult for people to accept Reformation teachings.

In other words Henry J. Cohn and Gunther Franz certainly help us to understand why and how Reformation doctrine provided an immediate and powerful ideological stimulus for revolution, especially among populations suffering from landlords who used their priestly offices to exploit more effectively the people to whom they owed pastoral care. But armed assaults against monasteries, chapters and other ecclesiastical institutions do not *ipso facto* testify to acceptance of Reformation piety. To attack landowning monks and churchmen who wielded priestly powers as instruments of oppression required a religious justification which Reformation teachings did provide. To transform this God-given right to rebel into an institutionalized expression of personal piety, however, was a further step, one especially difficult for people accustomed to make relics a central feature of their religious life.

This distinction between rebels who used scripture to justify insurrection and those who went on to join congregations organized to hear a systematic exposition of the Bible does not, by itself, tell much about the several types of appeals to personal rights made in the German Peasant War. Further information comes from the unusual meaning that insurgents gave to the plenary indulgence. Many thought it legitimated both spiritual and territorial authority; therefore they interpreted 'salvation by faith alone' to mean a repudiation of these two dimensions of clerical competence. To explain this development requires, however, a very brief digression into the earlier history of indulgences, especially in France.

Beginning in the early Middle Ages people advanced from simple to more complex levels of devotion according to the expansion in space and in time of interpersonal loyalties, a phenomenon largely revealed by shifting patterns of peregrination. Slow, successive increments in the geographical and temporal range of social bonds caused the faithful to enhance the dignity of the supernatural personages to whose powers of protection they accorded continuous territorial extensions. A persistent expansion in the geography of social, political and religious obligation, contributing to a progressive differentiation of people's concept of the sacred, had by the fifteenth century effected an upward displacement in both supernatural ascription and in the compass of political authority so vast as to expand people's notions about the Church and society beyond the limits of mere personifiable representation.

By repeatedly projecting outward their bonds of fidelity and, at the same time, by progressively enhancing the dignity of the celestial patrons who protected the inhabitants of newly integrated space, people regularly imputed a religious value to their expanding webs of distant affiliation; and in the course of time they ultimately confounded divine will with their sense of solidarity with others far away. Thus by a series of ascriptive displacements people not only advanced from primitive to more sophisticated perceptions of the sacred, but the means whereby they proceeded piecemeal from local to transregional loyalties also caused them to confuse celestial volition with the common purposes of a society whose members were unknown to one another.

In the course of this protracted conquest of space the faithful registered their early advances by supplanting the relics of local saints with those of ancient martyrs. There followed a period of further hierarchization among Europe's vast collection of relics until the twelfth century when, outside of Germany, west of the Rhine, they all yielded first to Mary and then to Jesus, celestial personages who, having left no bones, that is, living in no location, were therefore conceived to reside in a realm situated outside spatial and temporal processes. The passage from relics of neighborhood thaumaturges to the cult of the Virgin and, finally, in 1215, to the doctrine of transubstantiation diminished the efficacy of relics, and, at the same time, also took the faithful further and further away from their dead. In the course of this progressive desacralization of relics – manifested above all by an indifference to being in their physical proximity – people sought less protection from the dead; and the dead, in turn, increasingly assumed the role of grateful supplicants for the prayers of the living [*Rothkrug, 1980: passim*].

Ultimately, after the Great Year of Jubilee in 1300, when perhaps two million pilgrims received plenary indulgences [*Southern, 1970: 141; Sumption, 1975: 235*], the cult of purgatory gradually transferred responsibility for spiritual care of the dead from corporate bodies to the penitential initiative of individual Christians. By the later fifteenth century private access to general and limited remissions for penalties for sin had become well nigh universal. In principle, therefore, every Christian could acquire for his own or for specified, indeed even for unspecified souls in purgatory qualified powers of redemption that had been previously a prerogative of monasteries and of other primarily penitential institutions. Probably all, certainly most penitents knew that these remissionary powers came from the infinite merits purchased by the Lord's blood – one drop would suffice 'to redeem the entire human race', declared Clement VI, in 1343 [*Paulus, 1922, II: 202*]. Since every penitent should be able to procure indulgences it followed, as German peasants later explained in *The Twelve Articles*, that 'Christ shed His precious blood to redeem and to purchase all of us without exception, the shephered as well as the highest born'. The peasants formulated this statement as a fact, making no appeal to authority; only the subsequent inference that 'we are freemen' required a reference to Scripture.

Early notions of personal rights, therefore, proceeded directly out of a long established practice, peculiar to the cult of purgatory, to make the instruments of salvation available to everyone. In insurrectionary Germany, however, as Cohn has so persuasively explained, anti-clericalism prevailed among all categories of rebels. Also we saw that those least conditioned by relic devotion probably found it easier to rebel and to convert than others who may have invoked divine law and the Bible to justify insurrection without joining Protestant congregations. But insurgents who appealed to the Grand Manumission at Calvary propounded a slogan conceived to be the direct antithesis of the plenary indulgence. Protestants and Catholics alike all believed that redemption came from the Lord's sacrificial blood. But in the early years of the Reformation only the educated understood Luther's theological invalidation of indulgences. What could rebellious rustics who repudiated penance have understood from the Reformer's clarion call to salvation 'by faith alone?' Knowing nothing of theology and having always understood the plenary indulgence to be the chief instrument of salvation through Christ's blood, the insurgents who insisted that Jesus shed His blood for *everyone* – no hint of predestination here – must have conceived *sola fides* to mean a plenary indulgence *without* penitential obligations.

After all a controversy about indulgences thrust Luther – as it had Hus a century earlier [*Spinka, 1966: 113*] – on to the public scene. The Reformer's widely publicized contempt for 'good works' had a special resonance in regions where penitential authority permitted priestly landlords to exercise oppressive, sometimes even terrifying powers. Luther's protest that his attack on Rome's theology of indulgences had provided no warrant for peasant uprisings did not, even in Luther's own eyes, diminish the Reformation's scorn for the penitential system. Both Luther and the insurgents who appealed to the Grand Manumission agreed that routine recourse to the infinite merits earned by the Savior's blood distorted the central Christian mystery. The issue Luther failed to consider is that peasants who labored for priestly potentates could not *peacefully* repudiate the penitential authority of governors whose right to rule proceeded from their ecclesiastical status. Under these conditions Luther's public demand for wholesale abrogation of indulgences *was nothing less* than a full blooded call to revolution – a fact of course unknown to the great Reformer and ignored by most people who lived far away from warrior prelates. That is probably why the ideological content of insurrectionary calls to the Grand Manumission have remained hidden from scholarly attention. Revolutionary rustics simply assumed that freedom from penitential obligations also released them from seigneurial tyranny. Probably few if any of them understood the contradiction between the predestinarian content of Luther's *sola fides* and their own claim that Jesus' blood redeemed everyone – a notion that they may have also projected into Luther's early announcement of the 'priesthood of all believers'. Thus their appeal to the Grand Manumission as a universal redemption transformed *sola fides* into a doctrine of indulgence removed or abstracted from its penitential context.

Before the common access to plenary indulgences monks had assumed much of the penitential responsibility for a layman's sins. The corporate character of expiation had assured the unity of mankind in that the 'communion of saints' –

the faithful on earth, the souls in purgatory and the saints in heaven – all worked for the entry of mankind as a whole into the Kingdom of Heaven at the Last Judgment. Subsequently, after 1300, when Everyman sought increasingly to enter paradise without monastic assistance, he also took up the penitential burdens previously expiated by the regular clergy. As responsibility for spiritual care of the dead shifted gradually from the monastery to the private penitent people everywhere sought to help each other enter paradise *before* the Last Judgment.

The faithful enrolled their *own* dead into sodalities and confraternities that, by offering a maximum of penitential assistance, minimized the purgatorial ordeals reserved for each living and departed member. These lay penitential cooperatives proliferated throughout the fourteenth and fifteenth centuries, vastly diversifying practices associated with penance. Previously corporate and cenobitic forms of expiation united all souls throughout time – the Feast of All Souls (998), following that of All Saints, embraced *all* souls from the beginning to the end of time. People sought the proximity of the dead and the presence of their saints. For the routine asceticism of monks and the exceptional mortifications performed by saints sanctified the dead and invested relics – perceived to be the living persons of the saints – with thaumaturgical powers; and because God held the dead in special esteem cemeteries – virtually the sole sites of miracles until about 1100 – were holy places frequented by all sections of the population. But after 1300 the growing ubiquity of full pardons and a parallel multiplication of societies for penitential self-help reversed earlier relationships. For to make departed souls depend more and more on *lay* forms of expiation was to deprive the dead of the sanctifying powers of institutionalized asceticism, on the one hand, and to deny that ascetic accomplishments communicated a divine potency to saintly relics, on the other.

In sum from 1300 to 1500 European religious life showed (i) progressive intensification of regional differences in penitential practices; (ii) a decline of confidence in the monastic vocation; (iii) a diminished holiness of the dead and a corresponding desacralization of relics. Also since laymen increasingly took over penitential responsibilities from the regular clergy one can speak of a secularization and a democratization of these responsibilities as well as an intensified religious activity among laymen. All of these developments, associated as they were with progressively easier access to full pardons, especially in the fifteenth century, prompted ordinary people to claim that their equal right of entry into paradise entitled them to more esteem and to better treatment from their social superiors.

Moreover popular claims to greater personal respect received support from the extraordinary record of military success by low born soldiers and archers in the fourteenth and, more spectacularly, in the fifteenth centuries. Even today school children are familiar with the myth of William Tell, the battle of Agincourt and tales of Hussite valor. But the common man's new importance, occasionally his real prominence, contributed to social radicalism only when, as Rodney Hilton points out [*1977: 124, 207–213*], the lower clergy helped to lead their flock into rebellion, as in the English uprising of 1381 and in the Taborite insurrection of the 1420s. These clerical revolutionaries gave a new urgency to the problem of the 'common man'. That is probably why *Piers the Plowman* (1363–1386) and the *Plowman from Bohemia* (1400), masterpieces of world literature, emanate from the only two societies in the late Middle Ages where Christian social radicalism had assumed revolutionary or at least major insurrectionary proportions. Both texts, each in its own way, insist that the religious destiny of Everyman is inseparable from profound social transformations that, in the one view, will precede and, in the other, will follow man's entry into the Kingdom of God. The two works make Everyman's enjoyment of social justice a condition essential to his participation in the unfolding of God's plan in the world.

Throughout the late Middle Ages, therefore, insurgents who were led by priests seem to have been most able to formulate demands that, going beyond simple statements of grievance, invokes some general principle of justification. To be sure those German rebels who, from about 1430, appealed episodically to a higher or divine 'law' in order to radicalize and to universalize their revendications may have had few or no priests to assist them. But these insurgents remained a minority among their fellows until, in 1525, *religious* reformers drafted *The Twelve Articles* to justify insurrection throughout the Empire.

Most insurgents failed to find higher justification for insurrection because the intensely local character of penitential practices in fifteenth-century Germany conflicted directly with federative or transregional associations among rebel bands. In a study based upon analyses of 1,036 places of pilgrimage founded in Germany *before* the Reformation I show that relic cults never took firm root where people had been converted by the sword, chiefly in non-Romanized Germany. Charlemagne's repeated campaigns against the Saxons began a long history of forcible conversions, *Heidenmissionen*, that, down to the eve of the Reformation, divorced pagan peoples from their past and separated them from their dead. Subjugation and conversion rendered them incapable of perceiving saints either among their conquerors or among their own communities of unwilling proselytes [*Rothkrug, 1980*].

Saint veneration flourished most in Upper and Lower Bavaria, the Innviertel, the Upper Palatinate, in Franconia, in the farrago of fragmented Habsburg possessions called *Vorderösterreich* ('nearer Austria' situated largely in lands lying immediately west, south and east of the Duchy of Wurttemberg) and in parts of Baden as well as in all ecclesiastical territories. But the multitude of saints who worked their miracles in these regions were so to speak imported from abroad.

The notorious scarcity of native German holy men prompted clerics elsewhere in Europe to regard the idea of a German saint as anomalous; to discover any at all would be a miracle, they argued [*Delooz, 1969: 201, note 1*].

Never having had indigenous reserves of sanctity to transfer to overarching structures, Germans could sustain the emotional force of religious life at only the very local level. This severance of the emotionally bonding aspects of religion from its public or constitutional dimensions, therefore, had to some extent always marked German patterns of worship. But first the Interregnum (1254–1273) and then, much more decisively, the Great Year of Jubilee began two centuries of descent into progressively more intense forms of cultic regionalization. For the inflation of indulgences and the corresponding decline in monastic supervision of spiritual care for the dead encouraged, in Germany, a proliferation of authorized and unauthorized sodalities and sworn associations that, unlike France and England, did not find legitimation within a wider framework of transregional institutions. That is why accounts of commotions, demonstrations, conflicts over unlawful forms of expiation such as flagellant processions, mass pilgrimages of children and those of adults, as well as reports of open rebellion fill the pages of local religious histories of the fourteenth and fifteenth centuries. Ultimately Luther's appearance on the public scene polarized the sundry forces that contended here and there for control of local penitential practices. Each region responded to his message largely on its own, according to patterns of authority and piety established long before the great Reformer's birth.

These considerations explain a great deal about the ideological statements of German rebels in the many insurrections leading to the Revolution of 1525. Most scholars accept Gunther Franz's distinction between an insurgent call to the 'old law' or custom and one to 'godly law' or 'godly justice'. Franz counts thirteen appeals, all in the fifteenth century, to 'godly law' [*1977, app., map 1*]. More recent studies show that some uprisings fall in neither category [*Bierbrauer, 1980: 41–42*]. But all scholars agree that the great majority of rebels continued to invoke the 'old law' or custom, even as late as the autumn of 1524 [*Blickle, 1981: 87–91*]. Only in 1525 did *The Twelve Articles* establish 'godly law' as a generally accepted principle of legitimation.

When insurgents invoked the 'old law' or custom they confirmed the very arrangements against which they rebelled. From at least the 1430s a minority of rebels did appeal to divine law. According to Franz, these efforts to justify their demands in terms of a general principle helped to prepare a majority of insurgents, in time, to take the same step [*1977: 41–42*]. Why did an idea comprehensible to some at one date require almost an additional century for others to learn? Does sheer psychological inertia explain why for generations people rose up in the name of a self-defeating principle when they knew that other fellow insurgents appealed all the while to a superior formula of justification?

Franz observes that to invoke 'godly law' required rebels to join others from elsewhere in sworn associations. He goes on to explain that these confederated conspirators were plagued repeatedly by premature betrayal of their plans; whereas he knows of no single such betrayal among scores of rebellions made in the name of the 'old law' or custom [*ibid., 43*]. Late medieval brotherhoods routinely required their members to perform penance and prayer for *all* the association's dead. Since cultic regionalization attained its apogee only on the eve of the Reformation, it follows that people accustomed to dissimilar penitential practices found it more difficult to accept one another's dead as their 'own' at the end of the fifteenth century than at the beginning. This would explain the specificity of betrayals among sworn associations of rebels – the first one occurring in 1493. Also local custom derived much of its sanctity from the dead. To recognize a plurality of penitential practices, to renounce thereby a loyalty to one's 'own' dead – an act tantamount to burying relatives and friends among strangers [*Rothkrug, 1980: 73–75*] – was to withdraw from the dead their power to sanctify custom and, by extension, to suggest that this incapacity also made meaningless the notion of consecrated ground. That is why, I think, most insurgents could not bring themselves to invoke God's name in order to reject 'old law' or custom.

Indirect support for this view comes from a bitter pre-Reformation controversy. In 1507 the theological faculty at Cologne, including most of the 'Obscure Men' later satirized by Ulrich von Hutten, condemned a distinguished Italian scholar, Peter of Ravenna, then visiting Cologne, for his complaints expressed in writing and in teaching about the improper burial of executed criminals in Germany [*Nauert, 1970*]. The issue aroused intense emotions, and public controversy about the subject continued until 1511! At one point the doctors of Cologne even threatened to have Peter burned at the stake. Why? According to Peter, German princes routinely left executed criminals exposed on the gallows even though they had previously repented of their crimes, shown true contrition and had become reconciled to the Church. The doctors acknowledged this to be the practice. But they were enraged when Peter declared the princes to be guilty, therefore, of mortal sin. To leave repentent criminals exposed on the gallows, argued Peter, was to deny them the spiritual benefits of Christian burial, unjustly prolonging their ordeals in purgatory. Peter especially insisted that since a right to burial in consecrated ground originates exclusively in the sacrament of penance the burial itself has a virtually sacramental character.

Thus the controversy divided those who affirmed from those who denied that burial in consecrated ground is an extension of the sacrament of penance. In south Germany we distinguished between insurgents who refused and those who accepted the dead from communities with different penitential practices. We are confronted by parallel divergences that proceeded out of contrary perceptions about the intimacy or the distance of penance from burial. Those who appealed to 'old law' or custom and others who invoked the 'godly law' may, therefore, have acted according to principles identical with those expounded by the protagonists in Cologne. On both the learned and popular plane people differed in that some associated and others distinguished between true piety and our loyalty to the dead.

Luther's message swept away the hitherto insurmountable barriers that progressive cultic regionalization had raised among scattered groups of insurgents. For by attacking the very notion of penance, by his call for salvation 'by faith alone', Luther dissociated rebellion from penance and unwittingly authorized insurgents to rise up with or without reference to the expiation of sin. But a license to appeal to 'godly law' in rebellion encouraged no agreement among widely dispersed insurgents either to accept as their 'own' the dead from elsewhere or to reject entirely the practice of penance. Most regions remained remarkable for the homogeneity of their practices and their piety. That is why the confessional geography of early Reformation Germany conforms so closely to the distribution of medieval pilgrimage sites.

Among Germans, therefore, people who tended to impute a sacramental value to interpersonal ties and to communal sympathy, the faithful who remained enmeshed in self-contained penitential communities, being rarely inclined to project the affinities they formed in common worship beyond the bounds of social affiliation, could not, like many among Joan of Arc's countrymen, make loyalty to the Crown a feature of their personal piety. The increasing habit of imparting the force of religious precept to neighborhood allegiances and to parochial stratifications aroused more and more popular resentment during the course of the century. Open protest exploded first in the famous 'commotion' at Niklashausen in 1476 – events associated also with several remarkable victories won by Swiss peasant soldiers against the flower of Burgundian chivalry. Fear of fury from below prompted south German authorities to begin a literary campaign to villify, occasionally even to demonize the 'common man'. The degree of hatred unleashed against him finds no parallel, so far as I know, in French and English literature of the period. We shall see that this incredibly bad press for the 'common man' goes a long way toward explaining the subsequent prominence of the 'evangelical peasant' in Lutheran broadsheets during the first years of the Reformation. Also since Luther rebelled against the ecclesiastical hierarchy that had long tyrannized and maligned the 'common man' perhaps figures like those of Karsthans, who peopled Lutheran *Flugschriften* from 1520 to 1525, helped to make respectable a previously despised anti-clerical billingsgate. They may have thereby intensified the social hostility long inherent to German anti-clericalism even though throughout the *Flugschriften* the 'evangelical peasant' remained always entirely free of social animus [*Scribner, 1975*].

In 1476 Hans Boheim an adolescent shepherd and drummer (or piper) preached at a Marian pilgrimage shrine at Niklashausen. Despite his extreme youth, despite his illiteracy – even basic elements of the creed may have been unknown to him – the boy attracted common people from all over south Germany. Specialists in the history of the Revolution of 1525 point to Boheim's violently anti-clerical preaching, to his immense popularity, to his arrest and execution by the Bishop of Würzburg, to the popular indignation that followed and to its possible influence in subsequent rebellions. They all agree that the events at Niklashausen form part of the prelude to the great Peasant War. The piper preached his millenarian, anti-clerical message when Swiss infantry and Swiss peasant archers, simple rustics, had defeated Charles the Bold's splendid cavalry at Hericourt (Nov. 1474), at Grandson (Feb. 1476), at Murton (June 1476); in their final victory at Nancy (Jan. 1477) they also slew Charles and destroyed the Burgundian state. Ten years later, in 1486 members of the *Bundschuh* explained that they hoped 'at least to be as free as the Swiss and, like the Hussites, to participate in the direction of religious affairs' [*Buszello 1969: 85*].

This association of the Swiss with heresy will reappear in another context. Meanwhile especially noteworthy are Boheim's personal attributes: a poor illiterate adolescent who preached at a Marian shrine. Why did *common* people flock from all points of the compass to hear an illiterate shepherd boy? We shall see that at Niklashausen people wanted their pilgrimage, one undertaken by the common man, to supplant recent mass peregrination by children to alleviate widespread distress. They sought to transform processions of puerile supplicants into an adult journey to call on God to witness a public protest. They wanted to abolish once and for all practices wherein attributes from juvenile and adult forms of dependency were amalgamated so as to portray collective holiness to be a condition of shared or common minority. In 1475 several thousand children from the Rhineland and Bavaria, travelling in groups of about eight hundred, arrived at irregular intervals at Mont-St-Michel, in France, among other things, to implore for help to drive the Turk out of Germany [*Gäbler, 1969*]. Perhaps they also reminded the Archangel that he had recently assisted Joan of Arc to rid France of her hereditary foe.

One year later new juvenile armies departed from northern Germany to visit St Michael at Monte Gargano. Contemporaries were struck by the children's poverty, and in the towns along their route enthusiastic spectators often fed and lodged them. Indeed sources suggest that a restlessness to escape from poverty at home may have motivated some of the youngsters to peregrinate abroad [*Sumption, 1975: 282–288*]. This certainly seems to have been the case in 1475, just one year before the 'commotion' at Niklashausen, when several thousand children from Franconia, Hesse and Meissen – many of them bereft of funds –

travelled to the shrine of the Bleeding Host at Wilsnack, near Wittenberg in Saxony. The Turk and other symbols of great public causes had vanished from their attention. In this mass peregrination undertaken for no ostensible purpose more than one thousand poverty-stricken children perished or disappeared [*ibid.: 283*].

The Wilsnack journey in 1475 finds striking parallels in the pilgrimage to Niklashausen a year later. All south Germany seems to have suffered from poor harvests in 1475 and 1476. But distress was more acute in the Prince-Bishopric of Würzburg, a principality remarkable for an unrelieved record of corrupt and incompetent government [*Franz, 1977: 47*]. Several weeks before Boheim's public appearance Rome had launched a campaign to preach the Jubilee indulgence throughout south Germany. In this time of unusual religious excitement and widespread deprivation the Virgin visited Boheim; and she entrusted him with a mission to preach to the world – perhaps in the style of a Jubilee preacher – from her own residence at Niklashausen. The Virgin also promised Boheim that the faithful who followed his instructions would receive a plenary indulgence.

The thousands who peregrinated to Niklashausen – leaving records of prodigious offerings – indicated no more ostensible purpose for their collective quest than did the children who visited Wilsnack. Both journeys originated amidst deprivation and poverty. Boheim's extreme youth, his illiteracy and his poverty made him a representative figure capable of giving voice to the distress of his audience and he was also ready to express their common hatred of the clergy. In sum, thousands of pilgrims converged on a Marian shrine where, secure in the Virgin's promise of a plenary indulgence, they mounted a massive demonstration against the entire ecclesiastical establishment. This extraordinary pilgrimage to listen to a shepherd boy needed no direct sequel. For unable to ignore or to forget the elemental fury it revealed, the rich and well-born, prelates and lay lords, associated the events at Niklashausen with insurrection, with heresy and with satanic forces.

Their state of mind explains the bestial traits German literature ascribed to the 'common man' in the generation before Luther. We saw that in 1486 members of the *Bundschuh* wanted to be as 'free' as the Swiss and wished to direct their religious life in the manner of the Hussites. The very same year also saw the first printing of the well-known *Malleus Maleficarum* wherein William Tell exemplifies the archetypical male witch – described as the leader of 'archer-wizards' who spill Christ's blood by shooting arrows at His images on Good Friday [*Kramer, 1971: 323*]. At this time William Tell enthusiasm was at its height in the Swiss cantons. South German insurgents who extolled Swiss republicanism [*Bak, 1975: 44–45*] and who admired alleged Swiss religious practices probably participated in the festive mood. Perhaps some of them were among the rural and urban populations who sang the William Tell *Lied*. They may also have visited William Tell shrines dedicated to Sankt Kümmernis, a legendary figure native to a region, Friesland, known for its popular archery contests as well as for its violent anti-clerical Chambers of Rhetoric [*Rothkrug, 1981*: addendum to Chapter 8].

In the myth William Tell leads a rebellion against the Empire; no mention is made of hostility toward priests. Why then did the prelates who wrote the *Malleus* portray Tell and his archers as enemies of God? Because they could not dissociate the fury expressed at Niklashausen from the victories of the Swiss peasant soldiers, low-born warriors every bit as fierce as their earlier Hussite counterparts. In fact the 'pilgrims' at Niklashausen probably did celebrate the Swiss triumphs as a sign from heaven or a portent from the apocalyptic Virgin who had visited Boheim, who had promised redemption to all his followers, and whose cryptic message some scholars see in contemporary woodcuts representing the events at the Marian shrine [*Chadraba, 1964: 55ff*]. For this would explain the extraordinary measures taken by the authorities to obliterate popular memories of the piper, on the one hand, and the tenacity of these memories, on the other.

After his execution bishops, princes and town councils located in the shrine's vast catchment area coordinated their efforts to stop further pilgrimages to Niklashausen. Meanwhile the authorities confiscated all offerings left at the shrine; they razed the church to the ground, and they laid Niklashausen under interdict. Even Boheim's ashes had been strewed in the Tauber. Leaving no relics, destroying all monuments and other artifacts associated with the piper, the authorities manifestly feared people would perceive Boheim to be a martyr. Had he become a popular saint – possibly among the very first Germans to be viewed as a martyr by his countrymen – Boheim would have been the first saint in history to be venerated for having advocated the removal of the Pope and the Emperor – an ambition imputed to William Tell in the *Malleus*!

Despite these efforts popular respect for Boheim's memory proved sufficiently strong to prompt the Bishop of Würzburg, the prelate responsible for the piper's execution, to commission for publication diffamatory verses about Boheim [*Jöst, 1976: 274*]. Were the authors of the *Malleus* inspired by similar motives when they wrote the chapter about male witches? In the absence of an alternative explanation these passages become intelligible only as an attempt to demonize south German insurgents who were portrayed as archers to symbolize their admiration for the Swiss. Their alleged hatred for Christ points of course to the anti-clerical passions that continued to nourish popular memories of Boheim and the Swiss.

Fourteen printings of the *Malleus* appeared in Germany between 1486 and 1520. During these decades south Germany developed into virtually the sole center for publication of a unique literary genre, called *Neithartschwänke*. Accompanied by an impressive series of woodcuts, these writings depict the peasant to be a species of *Untermensch*. His animal physiognomy arouses revulsion among more gentle folk and the rustic's moral viciousness permit his social superiors to delight in applying physical torture to his person [*ibid.*]. I know of no parallel literary genre in the West at this time. Paying no particular regard to *Neithartschwänke*, K. Uhrig [*1936*] presents a detailed account of peasant portraits throughout the other literature of the period, most of it south German. The picture is vastly more composite, but features expressive of turpitude and depravity remain massive.

Prior to figures like Karsthans, Fryhans, Flegelhans and others who people the immensely popular Reformation *Flugschriften*, therefore, champions of the 'common man' – who was often represented by the peasant or by his son, as Till Eulenspiegel – could do little to alter a pervasive propaganda of hate. Nevertheless consider for a moment an apparently trivial item: the time and places where people translated the couplet associated with John Ball and the peasant revolution in 1381:

When Adam delved and Eve span
Who was then the gentleman?

Englishmen had read a minor variant almost a century earlier [*Hilton, 1977: 211*]. According to Peter Burke, the verse was 'virtually confined to the Germanic languages'; in the late fifteenth century it was recorded in Swedish, German and Dutch [*1981: 53*]. Perhaps the couplet's 'Germanic' diffusion and the time of its translations are attributable less to language affinity and more to its reception in areas of powerful peasant militancy. For example, Swedes took a fancy to the verse on the eve of the battle of Hemmingsted (1500), when Dithmarscher peasants successfully defended their *Bauernrepublik* against seasoned troops. In Germany the lines, known long before they were published [*Schubert, 1975: 895–896*], first appear in print in 1493, in Bamberg [*Epperlein, 1975: 141*], the year when Joss Fritz raised the standard of the *Bundschuh* near Sélestat. Of course the Dutch, especially in Friesland, had always expressed moral support for peasant struggles against their seigneurs.

Nowhere and at no time do the couplet's lines suggest anti-clerical sentiment. Yet in Germany a Bamberg printer, Hans Sporer, first published the proverb as part of a poem that gave voice to both anti-clerical and social animosity [*ibid.*]. Insertion of the lines in an anti-clerical context provides an antithetic parallel to the portrayal of William Tell as an enemy of God. The analogy goes several steps further. For not only did Sporer publish the couplet in the year that Joss Fritz led an insurrection in Alsace, but Fritz also raised the standard of the *Bundschuh* at the very moment when a papal legate preached a plenary indulgence.

A Jubilee indulgence preached throughout south Germany had also played a role in the events at Niklashausen. Perhaps the immediacy of the full pardon had encouraged Boheim and his audience to appeal to 'godly justice'. At any rate the 'pilgrims' at Niklashausen – coming as they did from the four points of the compass – could scarcely have appealed to an 'old law' or custom. Their voyage to the Marian shrine permitted them, therefore, to break through the constraints imposed by self-contained penitential communities. Would they have travelled so far to hear the piper without the atmosphere of portent created by the Jubilee indulgence – especially when it was preached amid widespread economic distress? To pose the question is to raise again a fascinating query made recently by François Rapp [*1974: 472*]. He suggests that Joss Fritz may have planned his insurrection to coincide with the preaching of a plenary indulgence in order to give dramatic effect to an invidious contrast between competing appeals to heaven: one to abolish a servitude endured by the common man on earth; the other to remit future suffering in a promised purgatory. If so, Fritz may have reflected on the meaning of the events at Niklashausen.

If German insurgents were powerfully influenced by religious emotions throughout the late middle ages and during the Peasant War, the contrary was true in France where, before the Wars of Religion, rebels showed little interest in holy symbols or in credal pronouncements [*Le Roy Ladurie, 1977, I/2: 828*]. A comparison of insurrectionary patterns in the two countries reveals a feature peculiar to the French countryside: prior to 1548–1549, when the *Pétaults* in Guyenne rose up against the Gabelle, *all* major rural rebellions occurred in a period of population *decline* – precisely the reverse of the German example. Demographic growth appears to set in everywhere from about 1450–1470. In Germany rebellions multiplied precipitately after 1450; after 1475 the insurrections, while remaining stable in number, grew greater in size and seriousness down to the great Peasant War [*Bierbrauer, 1980: 26–28*].

In contrast most French *émeutes*, several legendary for their size and fury, flared up in the fourteenth century. The more memorable among them are related to the Hundred Years War: the great *Jacques* in Beauvaisis and to a lesser extent in Picardie and Champagne, the *Tuchins* in Languedoc and Auvergne and the *Chaperons Blanc* in Normandy. Although major uprisings continued into the fifteenth century they disappeared rapidly from the countryside. An especially violent outbreak in Lyon, the *rebeyne* of 1436 [*Fédou, 1972: 242*], marks the approximate date when serious rebellions became an exclusively urban, and a less frequent phenomenon.

Thus from the end of the Hundred Years War to the beginning of the Wars of Religion in 1560 only one important revolt, the *Pétaults*, disturbed French rural life. This century of relative pastoral peace coincided exactly with the hundred years when *la religion royale* flourished as it never had before. Today undergraduates learn that in 1431 Joan of Arc's martyrdom contributed powerfully to the recovery and the reconciliation of France. At that time many people thought Joan, not the *roi de Bourges*, Charles VII, had protected the Crown. They explained that *la pucelle* – a peasant virgin, a folk personification of *Notre Dame* clad as a knight, a rustic Queen of Heaven in chivalric attire – restored to the Crown the sanctity from which royal power flowed. The rise of *la religion royale* after Joan is a story often recounted, [*Giesey, 1960*]. Remarkable here is the chronological parallel. For peasants accorded the greatest degree of sanctity to the Crown precisely when they enjoyed the highest level and the longest period of social peace in their entire history! That is why the *Bauernfeindlichkeit* so pervasive in German literature after the 1470s is largely absent from French writing in the same period.

To be sure, the generally reduced tensions between landlord and tenant that followed from a previous century of demographic decline contributed to social peace, encouraging agrarian populations to identify domestic tranquility with victory abroad and the King's ascendancy at home. Widespread reverence for the monarchy also intensified long established practices whereby, as I show elsewhere, people transferred to the Crown the sanctity they had earlier ascribed to relics and to the dead [*Rothkrug, 1980*]. The immemorial character of the practices contributing to the triumph of *la religion royale* points both to the past and the future. For their persistence in time illuminates the behaviour of rebels in the long periods of civil war that immediately precede and follow the age of the Crown's resplendency. In each of these widely separated struggles one of the protagonists made common cause with a foreign power – the Burgundians with the English, the League with the Spanish.

In both conflicts rioters and rebels expressed in symbolic acts, sometimes in rites and ceremonies, loyalty and hostility, allegiance and defiance to *la religion royale*. Its history, therefore, throws light on features peculiar to French uprisings. Its antecedents are ancient. In the present context the First Crusade, above all its profound association, indeed in some respects its identity with the plenary indulgence, provides a decisive turning point in the history of the Crown's sanctity. The Pope who preached the Crusade in 1095, Urban II, was also the first pontiff to issue plenary indulgences, a general remission of penalties for sin that assured martyrdom – the first rank of sainthood – and paradise to every crusader who died on his mission. Everyone from prelate to shepherd conceived the Crusade to be a pilgrimage, and ordinary people rapidly assimilated into their peregrinational practices the symbols and usages of crusaders. Clergy and laymen together offered special prayers to the Virgin, celestial patron of the Crusade. Indeed when Urban II announced this remarkable enterprise at Clermont-Ferrand he did so from the site of perhaps the first and certainly the most famous

French Madonna in Majesty. Only after this date did people visit local shrines dedicated to Mary, and the statues are direct successors of Majesties like the one at Clermont-Ferrand [Forsyth, 1972: 25, 42, 95–99].

Everyone knew about Mary's mission to the Holy Land. Some hastened to join the People's Crusade. Other Frenchmen, however, remained content to visit Mary at local shrines. But before departing they insisted that their staffs, sacks and insignias be blessed in the manner of a crusader's weapons [Garrison, 1965: II, 1172]. Also at this time, about 1100, Frenchmen started to baptize children with Christian names, especially those of famous crusaders [Yonge, 1884: 457]. Subsequently, for two centuries after 1095, virtually all unauthorized mass religious demonstrations were either crusades intended for the Holy Land or intimately connected with them. The list is a familiar one: 'King Tafur's' paupers' crusade in 1198; the Children's crusade in 1212; a 'commotion' in Flanders and Northern France in 1224–1225, the Pseudo-Baldwin, was a sequel to the Fourth Crusade; the *Pastoureaux* in 1251 pillaged, plundered and murdered for provisions on their way to help God and to rescue their King, Louis IX, then prisoner of the Moslems.

The last insurrectionary 'crusade', the Second *Pastoureaux*, wended its violent way in 1320. Its tattered participants continued to invoke the Virgin and to display her picture on their banners in the manner of those before them. They and all their predecessors were millenarians, people persuaded that their loyalty to the Virgin and their own salvation was related somehow to the recovery of Palestine, an accomplishment thought to be preparatory to the Last Judgment [Norman Cohn, 1970]. Similarly, since the twelfth century, most other Frenchmen were also convinced that Mary's special interest in recovering the Holy Land was connected in some way to the place she reserved in paradise for all those who entered into the circle of her allegiance. This redemptive preoccupation with Palestine is attributable to the inability of most Frenchmen — except crusaders and people able to finance an overseas pilgrimage — to procure a plenary indulgence. For, prior to 1300, full pardons had *never* been widely accessible. The faithful, therefore, sought redemption directly from Mary, celestial patron of the Crusade. Accordingly, the Virgin worked her wonders so as to admit into paradise countless souls from among the humble and the outcast — presumably few of whom had been able to procure a full pardon [Herolt, 1928].

Mary's efforts were prodigious. Nevertheless the *fleurs de lis* supplanted her picture on the pennants carried in the great *Jacques* of 1358 [Mollat and Wolff, 1973: 125–126]. And the metamorphosis from rebellious 'crusaders' to loyal rebels proved during the next four centuries to be singularly shock-resistant. For down to 1789 insurgent rustics continued, even in the most desperate circumstances, to assert their loyalty to the monarch. The irreversibility of the change is no doubt striking, but to substitute the *fleurs de lis* for a picture of the

Virgin signified, for Frenchmen in 1358, neither a diminished devotion to Mary nor an indifference to her great mission in the Holy Land. Prior to 1300 Mary had redeemed multitudes who, although denied access to full indulgences, remained convinced nevertheless that their salvation had something to do with the recovery of Palestine. When in 1300, the Great Year of Jubilee, countless pilgrims sought full pardons in Rome, not in Jerusalem, the papacy did much more than legitimize a hitherto plebian effort to democratize redemption. The Church also dissociated the full indulgence from crusade and pilgrimage to the Holy Land, thereby undermining for the now plebian recipient the belief that events in Palestine could influence the course of his own salvation.

Meanwhile other developments had also influenced people's thoughts about paradise and Palestine. For in the mid-thirteenth century Saint Louis had done much to territorialize the prevailing notions of redemptive crusade. And, as we shall see, Saint Louis' campaign to recover the Holy Land prompted most Frenchmen to perceive the *fleurs de lis*, not the then unattainable indulgence, to be the symbol of *France's* divine mission – therefore a primarily royal rather than a papal enterprise. Urban II had powerfully encouraged a militarization of European (and especially French) sanctity when he promised paradise to every warrior who took the Cross. Hitherto monks differed from warriors in that the former frequently attained sainthood, the latter almost never. For the patron saint of France, Martin of Tours, was especially notable for having *abandoned* the career of arms in order to enter a monastery. Under his surveillance military prowess provided no entry into the ranks of sainthood. That is why few, perhaps even no kings of France chose to be buried near Saint Martin in his residence at Tours [*Erlande-Brandenburg, 1975: 65*].

One generation after Urban II called warriors to the Cross, however, Saint Bernard, in 1128, drafted a Rule adapted from the Cistercians for the knights Templar – called by him a *religio militaris*, by them *une religion de chevalerie* [*Taylor, 1951 : I, 546–549*]. In this new world where monastic orders crossed with those of knights and knightly virtues assumed distinctly monkish traits Saint Martin found few champions. The Kings of France, therefore, replaced him with Saint Denis – thought to be Dionysius the Areopagite who – in a further confusion of legends – supposedly suffered martyrdom while converting the Gauls, a death crusaders found especially congenial [*Graus, 1975: 148–158*]. Four years prior to the Templars, in 1124, according to one account, Louis VI, deciding to become a vassal to Saint Denis, took the Saint's banner, the Oriflame, in the sight of his exposed relics and before a great assembly of dignitaries. In any event the Monarch's son Louis VII (1137–1180) and Abbot Suger presented a new abbey church to Saint Denis. Indeed in 1143 Louis personally transported the Saint's relics to his new residence constructed over the graves of many previous kings and later, after Saint Louis, was to become France's *necropole dynastique*. Four years later, in 1147, when Louis VIII departed at the head of the Second Crusade, he was, so far as I know, the first king of France to emblazon *fleurs de lis* on his standard [*Chéruel, 1855: I, 441–2*].

Subsequently, when Saint Louis took the Cross at the head of his warriors, they all displayed *fleurs de lis* on their shields. Also recent research, revealing fact previously unknown to Marc Bloch, shows that the French monarch's miraculous power to cure scrofula with his touch, perhaps a faculty occasionally exercised in an earlier age, first developed as a *regular custom* 'in the French royal court probably in Louis IX's reign. And the most likely time for its consolidation was *after* [italics added] the King's return from his six years' Crusade in 1254' [*Barlow, 1980:24*]. In sum, Saint Louis departed on a Crusade under the aegis of the *fleurs de lis*, and he returned from the Holy Land possessed of a divine power henceforth to be regularly exercised in solemn ceremonies held for ordinary Frenchmen throughout the realm.

The healing character of the king's touch like the healing properties of relics emanated from a sanctifying, a divine source. It was fitting, therefore, that a saint – Louis IX was canonized in 1297 – should have established the royal healing taction as a *regal* power, a potency originating in the office of kingship, not in the person of its occupant. To be sure the sanctity lodged in the monarch's touch had its origins also in the bodies of saints – their relics – resident on French soil. For the miracles they performed transmitted holiness to the Crown. To protect their travail in France was, therefore, among the king's first duties. That is why, for example, Saint Louis attended numerous translations of relics [*Jordan, 1979: 191*]. Also, in 1239, the King received, for a fabulous sum, relics from the Passion. The occasion prompted Gregory IX to declare France to be a holy kingdom; seventy years later Clement V proclaimed Frenchmen to be 'a peculiar people chosen by the Lord to carry out the orders of heaven' [*Strayer, 1971: 312–3 and n. 51*]. Under Saint Louis it was even widely believed that an English saint, Archbishop Edmund Rich of Canterbury, who died in France in 1240, could not bear to be buried outside France's sacred soil; his corpse performed repeated miracles while in transit so as to make known his wish to be interred in the Cistercian abbey at Pontigny [*Jordan, 1979: 191*].

Finally we know that in January, 1322 the empty litter destined to transport Philip V's remains to Paris 'was draped with a great gold cloth adorned with *fleurs de lys* . . . while another gold cloth of *fleurs de lys* covered Philip's body' [*Brown, 1980: 278*]. Taken together this evidence would strongly suggest that the participants in the great *Jacques* of 1358 – a time when even the papacy was located in Avignon – thought the *fleurs de lis* symbolized the crusading mission that their forbears in a previous age had ascribed to the Virgin. But other considerations disclose wider religious, political and social dimensions to the actions of the rebels, particularly with respect to how a subsequent decline in aristocratic prestige hastened the sanctification of the Crown. And all these issues also go back to the development of *la religion royale* in the two centuries separating the First Crusade from the Great Year of Jubilee.

From about 1150 to about 1235 at least nineteen major medieval romances, including correlated works, were composed and form what today is called the Arthurian cycle. A library of devoted scholarship suggests that the fascination of the Grail and its quest fosters a state of mind by no means peculiar to the knights of romance. That the Arthurian cycle is a literature crusaders found congenial is evident even to a cursory reader. Recruitment of warriors into the first ranks of sainthood encouraged knights to think their relationship to God to be unusually intimate. Of special interest is the date — sometime between 1220–1230 — when readers of Arthurian romances first learned, in the prose *Lancelot*, that the Grail was a dish from the Last Supper confided by our Lord to Joseph of Arimathea, and Joseph poured the blood of the crucified Christ into the sacred vessel.

This text may have been composed in the very year, 1230, when canon lawyers first drew Christendom's attention to the existence of a *Treasury* wherein were deposited the infinite merits from Christ's blood. Only the pope had access to the Treasury, insisted the lawyers, because merits from Christ's sacrificial blood communicate a supreme power or pardon, the source of the papal plenitude of power. Since pontiffs must promulgate plenary indulgences to promote crusades for defense of the Holy Land and for protection of the Christians resident there, argued the lawyers, it follows that the sole right to confer full pardons for penalties for sin also provide Rome with an exclusive authority to preach a crusade [*Russell, 1977: 204*]. Thus knights portrayed divine forgiveness to be a reward reserved for those able to fulfill an heroic quest or pilgrimage about the time that Rome located this forgiveness in the plenitude of its power, conceived to originate in the same source as the Grail. This parallel appropriation of holiness marks the later limits of an era when, beginning with the establishment of the Cistercians and the Knights Templar, both clergy and crusaders could, each in their own way, find martyrdom and therefore enter into the first ranks of sainthood. To identify this century as the single period when military saints flourished is perhaps sufficient to explain an enigma first formulated in 1940 by Sidney Painter:

> From the middle of the twelfth century to the middle of the thirteenth the lives of noblemen appear to have been sacred. . . . Assassination and execution for political or criminal offenses was so rare as to be practically unknown. I can advance no explanation for this interesting phenomenon . . . [*1957: 93*].

But Rome discovered its Treasury of Merits early in Saint Louis' reign when, as we saw, a movement developed that would assimilate the knight's quest with a national mission symbolized in the *fleurs de lis*. Subsequently the Great Year of

Jubilee and the Monarchy's portentous conflict with Boniface VIII — events closely associated in time — combined to divorce the nationalized quest or French mission from Rome's plenitude of power in a way so as to change radically prevailing notions about the agencies of salvation. Plebian access to full pardons not only prompted Frenchmen to separate paradise from Palestine, but it also made available to the faithful a way to salvation free from monastic assistance.

Similarly, at a higher level, the altercation with Rome severed not only France's mission to Palestine — an undertaking not immediately feasible after the fall of Acre in 1291 anyway — but *all* French missions from the only authority hitherto recognized, the plenitude of power and the Treasury of Merits from whence it proceeded. When the Knights Templar were founded as a new *religio* Frenchmen first associated their own redemption with recovery of the Holy Land. Correspondingly people ceased to think events in the Holy Land related to their personal salvation when, two centuries later, the Templars were disgraced and suppressed. For when the Crown took over from the warrior-monk France's missionary responsibility Frenchmen imputed a new meaning to the *fleurs de lis*. They assimilated the emblem and its signification, *la religion royale*, with the past and the expected or future advent of Christ. People imagined that the *fleurs de lis* had appeared on the Lord's banner at His first coming. At His second coming He would carry the blood-red Oriflamme — the banner of St Denis — to wage war on sinners [*Strayer, 1971: 307*]. Thus when Frenchmen made sinners rather than heathens the enemies of God and, therefore, of France, they retained the *fleurs de lis* as the symbol of France's mission, but by shifting its locus from Palestine to Europe the faithful reenacted as it were Boniface VIII's transfer of Christendom's peregrinational capitol from Jerusalem to Rome.

It may be more than coincidence that the trial of the Knights Templar (1307–1314) — perhaps the most sensational proceedings and possibly also the most lurid in European history to that time — began only a few years after ordinary Frenchmen started to enter heaven on an equal footing with the rich and well born. As early as 1275 Jean de Meun tells the reader of *Le Roman de la Rose* [*lines 18,589–18,605*] that 'the body of a prince is worth not one apple beyond that of a plowman, a clerk, a squire. . . . As far as the condition of humanity is concerned [they are] all on an equal footing.' Perhaps similar sentiments inspired townsmen at Bruges first to rise up and massacre the French garrison, and then to lead a union of urban and peasant militias to slaughter the French army at Courtrai in 1302. The action was memorable, for it seemed extraordinary that a force of townsmen and peasants could crush an army of French knights.

But Courtrai proved to be only the harbinger of greater humiliations. The impotence of French chivalry before common archers and low-born infantry at Crécy (1346) and at Poitiers (1356) — defeats considered the more disgraceful because of the knights' numerical superiority in both encounters — utterly discredited French chivalry in the eyes of peasants compelled to pay money for ransoms to free seigneurs who time and again failed even to protect them from bands of roving soldiers. Two years after the disaster at Poitiers rebels in the great *Jacques* directed their fury at nobles, destroying their places of residence. Throughout the fourteenth and early fifteenth centuries French rustics continued to show a strong animus toward the nobility. To be sure at this time English, German and Italian insurgents, albeit to a lesser extent, also directed their anger against the aristocracy. 'When Adam delved and Eve span who was then the gentleman' was a slogan that – although not yet well-known on the continent – expressed a defiance that was most deeply rooted in France – a country where an equal right of entry into paradise encouraged rural populations to resist seigneurial abuse while the nobility undermined its own moral authority in repeated failures to defend either themselves or their peasants, even from lowborn soldiery. Also the more democratic character of redemption and a growing contempt for aristocracy was intimately connected with radical changes in the dress of commoners. Inventories of personal effects left by deceased bourgeois reveal that until 1300 even the most wealthy commoners dressed more modestly than nobles. After that date, however, records testify to the disappearance of vestamentary deference. Rich townsmen possessed wardrobes that rivaled in magnificence the most sumptuous aristocratic attire [*Vincent-Cassy, 1980: 263*].

Aristocratic prestige continued to decline during the first third of the fifteenth century, among the very darkest periods in French history. Indeed only the nobility's widespread disrepute permitted a peasant girl to assume the role of a knight in arms so as to become the symbol of French resistance to an invader. Aristocratic decadence was most manifest, therefore, in the period when *la religion royale* began to show its greatest strength. And this fact will help to explain striking contrasts between rural uprisings in France before and after the extended, relatively peaceful century separating Joan's martyrdom from the massacre at Amboise.

When Etienne Marcel, in 1356, encouraged peasants in the Ile-de-France to rise in the Jacques so as to further the goals of his own insurrection in Paris – to subject the monarchy to the control of Estates representing the communes of France – he intensified urban-rural animosities and thereby complicated the subsequent task of reconciliation. The future Charles VI (1364–1380) rose to the challenge, however, and his success presaged the new standard of kingship he would later establish in a program to restore order among a troubled, vexed and distracted people. Called Charles the Wise and loved for his efforts to pacify France, also admired for his appointment of the renowned constable, Du Guesclin, it was fitting for this Monarch to establish as a regular practice that the royal coat of arms carry three *fleurs de lis*, arranged in a triangle. One generation later, in 1415, when France entered her time of deepest crisis, the *fleurs de lis* banner replaced the Oriflamme – the red ensign of Saint Denis – as the standard French armies would henceforth carry into battle [*Chéruel, 1855: I, 441–2*].

Historians frequently quote Joan of Arc's dramatic exclamation: 'all those who war against the sacred kingdom of France do battle against King Jesus' [*Strayer, 1971: 313, n. 52*]. Perhaps Joan uttered in the form of a battle cry as it were the century-old belief that the *fleurs de lis* had appeared on the Lord's banner at His first coming. But in the earlier formulation the *fleurs de lis* had pointed among other things to the nobility's readiness to carry out France's providential assignment. Joan's statement is remarkable, therefore, not for her insistence on France's sacrality, but for her *silence* about a French mission. Joan's exclusion of the aristocracy from France's ultimate destiny corresponds to a process, beginning in Joan's day but completed only in the course of several generations, whereby Frenchmen transformed the office of kingship into a sacramental institution that incorporated in itself the powers of sanctity that had been invested here and there throughout the realm since the monarchy's inception.

In the course of the fifteenth century, especially in the later period, Frenchmen organized royal funerals around a ceremonial separation of the king's two bodies – his effigy, the symbol of the Crown, and his corpse [*Giesey, 1960*]. Juxtaposed as it was to his cadaver, the king's effigy was the Crown made flesh. In this way a funeral ceremony joined Frenchmen to the immortal, transfigured body of the king – just as the Mass joined the faithful to the body of Christ – to form what contemporaries called '*un corps mystique*' [*Rothkrug, 1980: 32–3*]. Since French kingship assumed a sacramental character only in the mid to late fifteenth century, it follows that after this date kings *had* to be innocent. For the Crown's sacramental power necessarily confers innocence upon the official acts of its occupant just as God communicates religious efficacy to the Mass celebrated even by a sinful priest.

That is why only after the end of the Hundred Years War, largely beginning in the mid-sixteenth century, did rural insurrectionaries regularly invoke the king's innocence as they rose in rebellion. The force and the tenacity of this practice resides in the religious belief that justice was a sanctifying power originating in the office of kingship and communicated through the monarch's person to subalterns who, occupying no God-given position and therefore usually self-serving, often perverted the necessarily pure intentions of royal authority. Beyond its strictly sacramental qualities, additional properties accrued to the Crown from the special protection it had always accorded to the saints and their relics resident on French soil. And we shall see that the monarchy's intimate relations with its saints powerfully influenced French collective behaviour – both authorized and rebellious – in the Wars of Religion.

Just as saints became members of the living body of Christ so did they also reside in the *corps mystique*, the mystical union of the Crown – embodied by the king – and its subjects. In Saint Louis' Court the royal healing taction had been conceived to be a *regal* power emanating from the anointing of the King. In 1485, however, Frenchmen transmuted this hitherto regal faculty into a force communicated to the king by relics, in this case the relics of Saint Marcoul [*Bloch, 1961: 281–93*]. Indeed since *no* documentation shows that French kings had *ever* exercised a miraculous touch between 1308–1485 [*Barlow, 1980: 14*] it is possible that a long lapse in the practice – perhaps related to the factors explained above – made it easier for Charles VIII (1483–1498) and his officials to project the reliquary, indeed the peregrinational qualities emphasized by Marc Bloch [*1961: 261–83*] into a ceremony that, in a previous age, had always divorced the king's healing taction from the relics of any particular saint.

Mere absence of documentation of course – even for almost two centuries – may testify to the disappearance of sources rather than to a medieval desinence and a renaissance revival of the practice. Hopefully someone will someday throw light on the issue. Meanwhile, for whatever reasons, relics do not enter the picture until after Charles VIII's coronation, also the first king to be buried with all the ceremonies indicative of the Crown's sacramental attributes [*Giesey, 1960: 105–12*]. Nowhere is the central place relics will occupy after 1485 more evident than in the events following the affair of the *placards* in 1534.

During the night of 17 October 1534 members of the 'so-called reformed religion' posted broadsheets – printed by Antoine Marcourt [*Berthoud, 1973*] in Neuchâtel and recently smuggled into France – that on the next morning outraged many citizens in Paris, Orleans, Blois, Rouen, Tours and Amboise. The headline alone summarized both the content and the tone of the message:

THE TRUE ARTICLES AGAINST THE HORRIBLE, GROSS, AND INSUPPORTABLE ABUSE OF THE POPISH MASS, invented directly contrary to the holy supper of Jesus Christ [*Kelley, 1981: 13*].

All scholars agree that the incident marks a major turning point in the events leading up to the Wars of Religion. Two days later the King, Francis I, set in motion all available forces of repression, and French Protestantism went underground – Calvin being among the many who fled into exile. Early in January a 'perpetual and irrevocable' edict enlisted the faithful to help hunt down the 'imitators of Lutherans', promising informers a quarter of the property confiscated from convicted heretics about whom they had provided information.

At the same time officials also announced that on 21 January the King would lead a propitiatory procession to make manifest his 'hatred' of heresy. The spectacle was among the most grandiose in France's history. But before describing the extraordinary place of relics in this historic ceremony, it might be helpful to pause to ask why a few score heretical posters galvanized the government into full scale mobilization to combat Protestant influence at home. The answer, I think, is that in 1534 royal officials – not enjoying the advantage of hindsight – had every reason to perceive Protestantism as a revolutionary movement that appealed primarily to artisans and peasants. The great Peasant War was a memory less than a decade old. The multiplication of Anabaptist sects and the propagation of radical Zwinglian doctrines could hardly be seen as anything other than a ground swell of rebellion. More immediately alarming, however, was the occupation by radical Anabaptists of Münster (Westphalia) in February 1543. Indeed even in October, when Marcourt's heretical placards had appeared simultaneously in six major French cities, Münster *still* remained under revolutionary rule! The language of the broadsheets seemed formulated to appeal to the great unwashed; and the synchronous timing of their appearance suggested a well organized network of subversion. And if the Peasant War and Münster were any indication of the dimensions that possible French insurrections might assume, then royal reaction – however mistaken in fact – seemed both timely and commensurate with the perceived danger.

Fearful that repression alone might prove inadequate, the King and his councillors had recourse to all the supernatural powers of the Crown. On 21 January 'The entire Church, nay, the whole kingdom ... progressed with its monarch to manifest its hatred of heresy and its devotion to the Blessed Sacrament.' Even during the preparations regiments of archers made way among spectators massed so thickly that 'entire streets appeared to be paved with human heads'. The excitement grew, however, as processions from the monasteries and churches began to appear:

> Les paroisses avec leurs bannières, leurs reliquaires ... se rendent à Notre-Dame où des religieux viennent d'apporter les châsses [reliquaries] précieuses de Sainte Geneviève et de Saint Marcel. De la cathédrale, tous se dirigent, chantant et portant châsses et reliques vers Saint-Germain-l'Auxerrois d'où partira le cortège ... [Les] Cordeliers et Jacobins, chacun avec un chapelet de Notre-Dame, Augustins et Carmes tous ... portant les saintes reliques de leurs églises. Un véritable cortège de châsses leur faisait suit. . . .

Almost an entire page follows, enumerating 'les chasses' carried by every major corporation in Paris. Finally toward the end of the procession:

> passaient les plus précieuses reliques de la Sainte Chapelle, aux mains de divers prélats: 'la saincte couronne d'espines . . ., reliquaire inestimable, lequel, de mémoire d'homme n'avoit esté porté en quelque procession que ce fust, et . . . faisoit dresser les cheveulx de la teste à ceux qui le voyoient et rendoit tous ravis en Dieu' [*Berthoud, 1973: 190–194*].

These relics, together with those of the True Cross, the staff of Aron, the milk of the Virgin and many, many more formed a multitude called upon to defeat the forces of heresy. Conversely, French Protestant mobs directed their fury not only against relics and other sacred objects, but Huguenot iconoclasm sought above all to attack *la religion royal*. Protestant mobs destroyed Louis XI's tomb, elsewhere rioters cut off the nose and arms of his statues, burned the heart of Francis II, pillaged the sepulchres and scattered the bones of William the Conqueror and Queen Mathilda, pulled down the statues of Joan of Arc, exhumed the bones of Jeanne de France and desecrated the tombs of the Bourbons [*Mariejol, 1911: 63–5; Crew, 1978: 116; LeGoff, 1980*]. Meanwhile Catholics looked to their cemeteries. After all, if the faithful were forbidden to associate with a heretic in life, all the more reason for them to avoid him after death. To inter him alongside Catholics, insisted one pious spokesman, would nullify the Church's witness to penances performed by the faithful in life. Cemeteries are holy. They are places of habitation set aside for God to hear testimony about the penance, contrition and tribulations endured in the life of each resident. To wipe away the traditional 'disjuncture and distinction in places of burial, [a practice] always observed according to the virtues and vices and the qualities of persons in sole respect to religion' would forever contaminate the travail of the saints and the sufferings of the faithful [*Henri de Sponde, 1597: fols. 32–37*]. This dreadful confusion in the graveyard also sweeps away the Crown's protection of the saints resident on its soil. A pollution so pervasive is bound to incur God's wrath. News of sacreligious burials, therefore, set Catholic mobs into action: they stormed the cemeteries and dragged offending corpses to the nearest offal heap [*Benedict, 1981: 64*].

Huguenots who desecrated and destroyed the objects and symbols identified with the Crown's sanctity were manifest rebels. Could they have behaved otherwise or were they in a position similar to that of the south German peasants who denied the penitential powers of their clerical landlords? Clearly the Crown was a sacramental institution. Also the cult of relics and its attendant train of religious epiphenomena appeared in the procession of 21 January as major, perhaps even the chief components of *la religion royale*. In Germany warrior prelates had politicized their penitential powers in the course of the fifteenth century. During the same period the French Crown – in a development already apparent in 1415 and especially prominent after 1485 – progressively sanctified its political authority. That is why relic cults proved to be essential to the divinization of territorial governments in both countries, however dissimilar may have been the processes permitting prelates and kings to acquire their celestial mandates. In sum, very different streams of events combined so as to produce a substantial overlap, a hidden homology in the causal patterns of two sixteenth-century revolutions.

The two revolutions reveal also profound differences. Everyone agrees that the German Peasant War was a revolution from below; whereas French uprisings assumed proportions of a full scale civil war only because more than half the aristocracy joined and led Huguenot forces in combat. In Germany imperial cities could support the Protestant cause for the most part without serious changes in the structure or social composition of urban government. The countryside, however, saw different types of confrontation that, in general, may be subsumed under two categories: conflicts between people who were and those who were not conditioned by powerful relic cults may be distinguished from rebellions against the clerico-seigneurial tyranny of ecclesiastical landlords and, secondarily, against many of their secular neighbors.

In France cultic regionalization proved less intense. For the Crown had gradually assimilated into its own rites and ceremonies traits common to local practices, leading villagers to imagine that in neighborhood cults people throughout the realm participated with their king in a common piety. Prominent features of *la religion royale* went back to the First Crusade, others even earlier; their meanings evolved over time, and intense conflict developed ultimately around changes in signification, especially about the concept of martyrdom. In the early Church, for example, a martyr was a saint. Subsequently monks extended the meaning of martyrdom to include systematic denial of the flesh as well as self immolation. Later crusaders earned martyrdom if they died in their mission to the Holy Land. In time stories of the Grail point to knights other than crusaders who entered the ranks of martyrs. After 1500, when more and more Frenchmen imagined they were united with their monarch in a mystical body, the nobility claimed martyrdom for those who died in defense of *la couronne de France* [*Rothkrug, 1980: 33–4*].

But a universal access to full pardons – releasing both noble and commoner from dependence on penitential aid from monks – dissociated the notion of a military martyr from the cenobitic and religious context in which it it had always been embedded. At this juncture when most of the nobility associated neither martyrdom nor sacrifice with monastic traditions the Crown, first in 1485 then more spectacularly in 1534, took a precisely opposite tack, and reestablished at the center of *la religion royale* the monastery with its relic veneration and its entire train of associated religious epiphenomena. By appropriating a sanctity unique to the monastic ethos the Crown declared seditious forms of worship – and therefore notions of martyrdom – conflicting with relic veneration and the cult of saints. So fundamental a contradiction about the meaning of sacrifice made uncertain the warrior's very *raison d'être*. This crisis of identity explains, I think, the massive defection of France's aristocracy in the Wars of Religion.

Against this background on the Continent consider the host of people who stood outside one of the prevailing official religions in later Tudor and Stuart England. Many argued that their convictions signified no diminution of their loyalty to the monarch – a point of view possible only where the government made no claim to sacramental power. Perhaps that is why, in England, relics never legitimated the royal healing taction [Bloch, 1961: 318–9].

Here one might think that France furnishes a distant parallel during the Wars of Religion. For the Politiques are renowned for their pleas to remove the Crown from the arena of religious contention. That their message remained in the deepest sense unintelligible may be seen by comparing for a moment the writings of rebels on both sides of the Channel during the English Civil War and the *Fronde*. Between 1647–1650 a number of English small tradesmen, artisans and farmers formed a group called the Levellers; they propounded with remarkable clarity arguments that later characterized revolutionary liberalism in the eighteenth and nineteenth centuries. In contrast, thousands of French *Mazarinades* reveal mostly a multitude of complaints; only the rare pamphlet rises above denunciation and mere statements of grievance. When popular discontent in the one country contributed significantly to political theory, why did public protest in the other remain intellectually barren? Because to argue, as did the Levellers, that natural rights of individuals limit the legitimate powers of government was to assert, in Counter-Reformation France, that powers emanating from reliquaries and other repositories of sanctity, sources of the Crown's sanctifying potency, are defeasible or subject to human regulation. The message of English radical democracy, like the ideas of earlier *Politiques*, were rendered unintelligible, therefore, not by written works, but by the widespread reverence paid to Saint Frances of Sales, Saint Vincent of Paul and to entire contingents of saints active in seventeenth-century France. This reverence was manifest in the multitude of shrines dedicated to other saints while its royal dimension was strikingly demonstrated by the 1,700 'sick' who gathered at Versailles on 8 June 1715 to be touched by Louis XIV, a public act he performed while standing visibly at death's door [Bloch, 1961: 363].

References

Bak, J., 1975, ed., *The German Peasant War of 1525*, London.
Barlow, F., 1980, 'The King's Evil', *English Historical Review*: 95, 1–27.
Benedict, P., 1981, *Rouen during the Wars of Religion*, Cambridge.
Bergsten, T., 1978, *Anabaptist Theologian and Martyr*, Valley Forge.
Berthoud, G., 1973, *Antoine Marcourt*, Geneva.
Bierbrauer, P., 1980, 'Bäuerliche Revolten im Alten Reich', in P. Blickle, ed., *Aufruhr und Empörung?*, Munich: 1–68.
Blickle, P., 1980, 'Bäuerliche Rebellionen im Fürststift St Gallen', in Blickle, *Aufruhr*.
Blickle, P., 1981, *The Revolution of 1525*, Tr. T. A. Brady and H. C. E. Midelfort, Baltimore.
Bloch, M., 1960, *Les caractères originaux de l'histoire rurale française*, Paris.
Bloch, M., 1961, *Les rois thaumaturges*, Paris.
Brown, E. A. R., 1980, 'The Ceremonial of Royal Succession in Capetian France', *Speculum*, 55: 2.
Burke, P., 1981, *Popular Culture in Early Modern Europe*, New York.
Buszello, H., 1969, *Der deutsche Bauernkrieg als politische Bewegung*, Berlin.
Chadraba, R., 1964, *Dürers Apokalypse*, Prague.

Chéruel, A., 1855, *Dictionnaire historique*, Paris.
Cohn, H. J., 1979, 'Anticlericalism in the German Peasants' War 1525', *Past and Present*, 83: 3–31.
Cohn, N., 1970, *The Pursuit of the Millennium*, New York.
Crew, P. M., 1978, *Calvinist Preaching and Iconoclasm in the Netherlands, 1554–69*, Cambridge.
Delooz, P., 1969, *Sociologie et canonizations*, The Hague.
Du Bruck, E., 1978, 'The Emergence of the Common Man in Fifteenth Century Europe', *Fifteenth Century Studies*, 1: 83–109.
Epperlein, S., 1975, *Der Bauer im Bild des Mittelalters*, Leipzig.
Erlande-Brandenburg, A., 1975, *Le roi est mort*, Paris.
Fédou, R., 1972, 'A popular revolt in Lyons in the fifteenth century: the Rebeyne of 1436', in P. S. Lewis, ed., *The Recovery of France in the Fifteenth Century*, New York: 242–64.
Fletcher, A., 1968, *Tudor Rebellions*, London.
Forsyth, I. H. 1972, *The Throne of Wisdom*, Princeton.
Franz, G., 1977, *Der deutsche Bauernkrieg*, Darmstadt.
Gäbler, U., 1969, 'Die Kinderwallfahrten aus Deutschland und der Schweiz zum Mont-Saint-Michel, 1456–9', *Schweizerische Kirchengeschichte*, 63: 221–323.
Garrison, F., 1965, 'A propos des pèlerins et de leur condition juridique', *Etudes d'histoire du droit canonique dediées à Gabriel Le Bras*, 2 vols., Paris.
Giesey, R. E., 1960, *The Royal Funeral Ceremony in Renaissance France*, Geneva.
Graus, F., 1975, *Lebendige Vergangenheit*, Cologne.
Herolt, J., 1928, *Miracles of the Blessed Virgin Mary*, Tr. C.C. Swinton Bland, London.
Hilton, R., 1977, *Bond Men Made Free*, London.
Jöst, E., 1976, *Bauernfeindlichkeit. Die Historien des Ritters Neithard Fuchs*, Göppingen.
Jordan, W. C., 1979, *Louis IX and the Challenge of the Crusade*, Princeton.
Kelley, D. R., 1981, *The Beginning of Ideology*, Cambridge.
Kramer, H. and J. Sprenger, 1971, *Malleus maleficarum*, Tr. M. Summers, London.
LeGoff, J., 1980, 'Jeanne d'Arc', *Encyclopedie universalis*, 9: 416–8.
Le Roy Ladurie, E., 1977, 'Les masses profondes: la paysannerie', in F. Braudel and E. Labrousse, ed., *Histoire économique et sociale de la France*, I/2, *Paysannerie et croissance*, Paris: 483–865.
Lorris, F. de and J. de Meum, 1971, *The Romance of the Rose*, Tr. C. Dahlberg, Princeton.
Mariejol, J.-H., 1911, 'La Réforme et la Ligue, 1559–98', *Histoire de France*, 6, ed. E. Lavisse, Paris.
Mollat, M. and P. Wolff, 1973, *The Popular Revolutions of the late middle ages*, London.
Nauert, C. G., 1970, 'Peter of Ravenna and the 'Obscure Men' of Cologne', in A. Molho and J. A. Tedeschi, eds., *Renaissance studies in honour of Hans Baron*, Florence: 609–40.
Packull, W. O., 1982, 'The Image of the 'Common Man' in the Early Pamphlets of the Reformation, 1520–5', unpublished address, University of Waterloo.
Painter, S., 1957, *French Chivalry*, Ithaca.
Paulus, N., 1922, *Geschichte des Ablasses im Mittelalter*, Paderborn.
Rapp, F., 1974, *Réformes et réformation à Strasbourg*, Paris.
Rothkrug, L., 1980, 'Religious practices and collective perceptions', *Historical Reflections*, 7.
Rothkrug, L., 1981, 'The "Odour of Sanctity" and the Hebrew Origins of Christian Relic Veneration', *Historical Reflections*, 8: 95–142.
Russell, F. M. 1977, *The Just War in the middle ages*, Cambridge.
Schubert, E., 1975, 'Bauerngeschrey', *Jahrbuch für fränkische Landesforschung*, 34–5: 883–907.
Scribner, R. W. 1975, 'Images of the peasant, 1514–25', in Bak, ed., *Peasant War of 1525*.
Southern, R. W., 1970, *Western Society and the Church in the middle ages*, London.
Spinka, M., 1966, *John Hus' Concept of the Church*, Princeton.
Sponde, H. de, 1597, *Les cimtières sacrés*, Bordeaux.
Strayer, J. R., 1971, 'France: the Holy Land, the Chosen People, and the Most Christian King', in *Medieval Statecraft and the Perspectives of History*, Princeton: 300–14.

Sumption, J., 1975, *Pilgrimage*, London.
Taylor, H. O., 1951, *The Medieval Mind*, 2 vols., Cambridge, Mass.
Uhrig, K., 1936, 'Der Bauer in der Publizistik der Reformation bis zum Ausgang des Bauernkrieges', *Archiv für Reformationsgeschichte*, 33: 71–125.
Vincent-Cassy, M., 1980, 'L'envie au moyen âge', *Annales*, 35: 253–71.
Yonge, C. M., 1884, *History of Christian Names*, London.

Western and Southern Europe 1500–1800

Preface

HARVEY MITCHELL

The tenacity of popular religious rituals, beliefs and practices, both within the institutional structures of the major confessions, as well as, existing uneasily alongside but outside them, evoked, as we well know, a mixture of incredulity, impatience, and little sympathy in the more rarefied atmosphere of the educated, the sensitive, and the sensible, the people for whom Schiller's disenchanted world was welcome and a certain sign of civilizations' advance. It is not amiss, I think to stop for a moment and consider the cool, but not cold, responses of a figure who, while revealing instances of all the emotions listed above, did not express them fully, for he could not but hold himself in reserve before the awesome power of religion. What struck Adam Smith was the innovative strength of the people to find effective ways to protect themselves against the terrors of urban life which they encountered on leaving behind the comparative safety of rural closeness and solidarity. Stifling as the latter were, they were a source of identity. The abundance of sects in the city functioned to give the displaced the identity they had foresaken or lost. Smith was as sure of the 'role' religion played in the different milieux of town and country, as he was uncertain of the effects the sects produced in the city. If, as he claimed, they ensured orderliness and regularity, why did Smith [*1937: 748*] in the next breath speak about 'the poison of enthusiasm and superstition' in the inferior ranks?

The answer is not clear, but he may have been thinking of the sects' radical past. In any case, he advised the filtering down of science and philosophy to the people and public displays of all the arts to serve as an antidote to religious enthusiasm. The ambiguities are dissolved in the remedies. None at all were present in his forthright assertions that in societies with an established church, it was incumbent upon the sovereign to determine its teachings and activities, while never disturbing its clergy by force or violence, lest such persecution increase their popularity and pose a danger to society and to the state [*ibid., 750–51*]. Smith possessed a fair understanding of what was at stake, and he showed the need for prudence as well. The major point is that, for all his obvious distaste for the phenomena he was describing, he gave them their due and did not underestimate their power.

To shift from the eighteenth to the twentieth century is to expand the problem, as I shall do, by making use of Jürgen Habermas's understanding of the identify-endowing functions of religion. Although it forms part of his understanding of the legitimation of authority, the focus on the need for individual and group identity is almost the same as Smith's [*Habermas, 1975 [1973]: 118–19*]. Habermas's citation of Peter Berger's [*1967: 22ff, cited ibid.*] belief that men are instinctually drawn to impose order upon reality attests to Smith's insight as well. But Habermas's further discussion of the 'meaning' promised by religion moves in a direction which Smith did not follow. Smith was almost too ready to conflate 'meaning' with the passions of enthusiasm and superstition of which he disapproved so prudishly. He was not willing to entertain the idea that 'truth' might have been the goal of religious enthusiasts, though he was prepared to recognize that their beliefs acted as a consolation for those unlettered ranks who had the misfortune to lack other philosophical and psychological supports. Long before the troublesome concept of ideology was invented, Smith anticipated that the real truth could be established, or at least that falsehood could be minimized. Habermas is no stranger to the opacity of truth. He is certainly no opponent of modernity [*Habermas, 1981*], but he is intensely alive to the force of religion in human existence.

With Smith at one end of this two hundred year period, which is about the present age of the modern study of the human sciences, and Habermas at the other, we have proof of how the mysteries of religion have commanded the efforts of major intellectuals. They continue to pose extraordinarily difficult problems. Religion lurks on the edges of and rarely becomes an integral part of the central concerns of the authors of the papers in this section. The reader will not fail to note that the most apparent intellectual current in these studies is to avoid the dangers of releasing the coiled spring of the subjective aspects of the past, the very essence of religious experience, especially as they are expressed at the popular level. This feat is achieved by approaching them with a discrete wariness and locking them up in a sort of addendum or appendix after the 'real' work of historians, that is, the social and economic analysis, has been completed. My remarks, needless to say, are not intended to restore religion to some separate and hallowed space, for that would only provide a reverse but equally distorted image. Since each of these images is predicated on notions of primacy and reductionism which is its corollary, they might preferably have been avoided.

It is odd to be making these remarks forty years after Lucien Febvre who, in reviewing Gabriel Le Bras's *Introduction á l'histoire de la pratique religieuse en France* in 1943, complained that he was being compelled to repeat the dismay and disappointment he had first uttered in 1932, occasioned, he said, by the sectarian blindness of French university scholars (he was alluding to the thorough and suffocating laicization of the republican tradition) to the importance of popular religion, as if it were, one might add, a microbial survival of a shameful past. Could it be, he asked as he reflected on this intellectual resistance, because,

'Once you start taking the temperature of yokels, you might run into danger. You never know with the people' [Febvre, 1973: 269]. It is as if Febvre were challenging his generation to test their ability to survive the temptations of élitism, thereby revealing the extent of their debt to the Enlightenment, and enter into a pact of sympathetic understanding with subjects of their future studies without succumbing to folkloristic exuberance. The brilliant attempts to expose the richness of popular cosmologies and consciousness are now available to us in the works of Ginzburg [1980], Thomas, [1971], and Le Roy Ladurie [1978]. Too few of their skills and imagination are to be found in the studies presented here.

Their strengths lie in the more positivistic aspects of the historian's craft, and they are not to be belittled. Nevertheless this preface takes its cue from the theme of the volume and will relentlessly stick to it. My major observations will be devoted to the paper by Le Goff and Sutherland, for I have some expertise in French revolutionary and religious studies, but I shall begin with some briefer remarks on the papers contributed by Burke, Hill, and Nicholls.

Peter Burke's description of religion 'as end and as means', leads him, to use his own words against him, to make 'a simple distinction' [*Burke, below*]. Its simplicity, moreover, seems to have beguiled not only him but others, so that rather than groping with the extremely tortuous relationships that were fashioned between religion and revolt, the older explanations of the struggle for or against religion, or the accounts of manipulative exploitation of religion, are revived. In this kind of explanatory scheme, religion must either appear in 'pure' garb, or in a form or forms contaminated by dirty power. Since the content of its 'purity' is difficult to articulate, it is customarily glossed over. In brief, the dualism Burke posits is nothing more than a return to one of the oldest versions we have of religion and revolt: 'purity' leading the legions or conspirators leading the legions in the name of the 'pure' cause. He glides over the implications of some of his own examples, because he seems to think that there is no problem in his allusion to the legitimizing effects of having priests on your side, and he is content to say, in the instances he cites, that 'religious ideas were instruments in the struggle, and religion an ideology' [*ibid.*]. This is an unconscious parody of Marxism, or if I may borrow François Furet's phrases, it is an 'extremely simplified and simplistic Marxism', an 'elementary textbook Marxism' [*Furet, 1981, [1978]: 87, 96*]. So far has the term ideology crept into the literature without any appreciation of Marx's own difficulties with the concept, or acknowledgment of the many recent attempts to give is some real meaning. For all that, the scale of Burke's survey is daunting, and it is salutary to be reminded of how many revolts were not strictly speaking rural, but urban, even though peasants were involved in them.

Though not directly concerned with a systematic study of revolt and religion,

Christopher Hill makes two points which at this stage of research require more work. I will deal with his second first, since it bears more directly on the theme of this volume. Hill has rarely, if ever, been such an insularist in his insistence on the original character of English religious dissent and radicalism, seeking example after example in the earliest manifestations of Lollardism and relating them to their seventeenth-century variants and extensions. As part of this major contention, Hill puts great weight on his other thesis: the peculiar geography of Lollardism. Geography, sociology, and religious dissent constitute a trinity which kept alive a tradition of religious and communitarian beliefs. For centuries these survived an underground existence. They reemerged with startling vitality during the conflicts of the seventeenth century. After 1660, but more so after 1685, the radicals went underground again, only to surface at crucial periods in the eighteenth century and with greater force in the more tempestuous period of the early industrial revolution. Whatever the merits of Hill's proposals to create a continuous chain of religious and political dissent from the Lollards to the Levellers and to the Chartists, one can see why Hill's concerns are of pertinence in this volume. They conjure up a state of chronic revolt which are inconceivable without their religious elements, and which were never wholly expunged from popular consciousness.

The fit between arable areas and the 'stable docile communities subordinated to parson and squire, on the one hand', and the fit between 'pastoral, forest, moorland and fen areas' and large parishes 'where ecclesiastical control was less tight', may be compared with attempts to find similar fits in France [*Hill, below*]. Paul Bois, for example, found that in the *bocage*, an area of counter-revolutionary activity, the moral scrutiny of the priest was not so crushing, if only because it was an area of scattered settlement, while in the plains area anti-clericalism grew in defiance of the close surveillance of the priest [*Bois, 1960, 614*]. Observers at the time of the Revolution referred to the exalted religious sentiments of the *bocage* inhabitants. One could almost infer that the power of popular religiosity was inversely proportional to the omnipresence of the church, were it not for the fact that the *bocage* was also an area of active missionary work from the mid-eighteenth century [*Pérouas, 1964*]. The evidence is, however, confusing. Missionaries and resident priests appeared to evoke different reactions from the local populations. The comparison with English counties unfortunately cannot be complete, but what it does demonstrate is that the gulf between élite and popular expressions of religion was to be found in both countries and that the restricted impact of the first on the second allowed the latter to assume an aggressive response to authority.

David Nicholls is also struck by the need to establish a religious geography in his study of revolt in Normandy during the religious wars. Before they broke out, the defence of forest rights united seigneurs, peasants and forest officials against the crown's incursions. Once the wars began, it became more and more obvious, according to Nicholls, that the fundamental causes of unrest were not religious, that the incessant pillage and bloodshed were not 'outbursts of "primitive" religiosity or millenarianism', and that 'clergy were enlisted as mediators between village communities and the outside world' [*Nicholls, below*]. Once again, the question appears to be wrongly posed, for how is one to distinguish so confidently what root causes are, unless one is committed to an unreflective monism? When Nicholls writes that, 'Peasant religion was a support to a system of law and moral economy, based firmly on the rationality of a precarious economic system,' and then adverts to the defence of the community, he comes closer to the realities of rural revolt, just as Burke does in his brief allusion to the facts of urban protest in Tuscany in the late eighteenth century, which he views as a 'moral economy' protest, and in his concluding assessment that the rebels he had looked at were fighting to resist attempts to intervene in their lives and change them [*Nicholls, below; Burke, below*]. At least this openness to what really happens in communities frees historians from the narrower obsession with causality and brings them within hailing distance of the emotive powers associated with small and large-scale examples of popular defiance.

Le Goff and Sutherland claim to possess a theory at once less ambitious and more realistic than those they reject. We can only express our gratitude for an analysis that has a discernible point of view and takes no pride from the mistaken assumption that the facts speak for themselves. What have they rejected as unifying themes and what have they substituted for them? They have set aside the modernization thesis which served Charles Tilly [*1964*] and Gwynne Lewis [*1978*], who followed Tilly's model in his study of the Gard, though with modifications and qualifications. They have refused to accept Marcel Faucheux's [*1964*] theory of immiserisation; and they are not receptive to the correlations between counter-revolution and militant dechristianisation. What they give us is a restated version of Georges Lefebvre's major historical achievement. It is within Lefebvre's life-long attachment to the idea of an autonomous peasant revolution that Le Goff and Sutherland place their modest proposal, namely, that by depicting why and how 'dominant groups in rural society and the way in which they held their land ... stood up for the revolution in their communities [*Le Goff and Sutherland, below*], we will be enabled to ascertain the reason for the political positions assumed by antagonists on either side of the Revolution. The tenant farmers constitute for Le Goff and Sutherland the crucial core within the dominant groups in the west and in the north, while the peasant proprietors served the same function, although not consistently and under very particular circumstances, in areas of the south.

There are a number of obvious attractions to this singling out of the dominant groups in rural society and finding within them, in the three main areas of conflict, the catalyzing element that set things in motion for or against the Revolution. It helps to focus our attention on the groups that presumably can articulate support for or arouse resentment of the Revolution. It allows us to attribute to them a leadership role, since one of the difficulties in assessing how support or opposition is mobilized, is to find criteria for determining how social structures and the exercise of power can be seen and appreciated as a continuous whole. And it explicitly opens up the possibilities of exploiting this explanatory model in assessing its ultility in those areas of France in which the dominant groups were recipients of benefits which justified their intervention within the larger frame of the Revolution in its various phases, confirmed them as its friends, or minimally as its compliant collaborators. In such a construct, Lefebvre's major thesis is preserved, and is indeed expanded. For the key role Lefebvre gave to the tenant farmers in the North is extended to the west, and while it is too risky to do the same for them in the south, small peasant proprietors fulfil almost the same function there. Have Le Goff and Sutherland at last found the elusive invariable in French rural history?

It is tempting to answer in the affirmative, but besides surprising Le Goff and Sutherland, it would confound all historians, apart from the most extreme positivists among us. Most of us, I believe, are more in tune with d'Alembert's conviction that history is a highly speculative, conjectural kind of knowledge, reminding us of our limitations and teaching us tolerance and forebearance. But it is not only because certainty cannot be the goal of any sane historian that we must deny Le Goff and Sutherland what would turn out to be a meaningless accolade. My aim in this brief critique is, like theirs, just as modest.

The first major point is that modernization remains a useful tool of analysis, for even if it cannot be applied universally, it does, when more explicitly used in conjunction with the host of institutions, practices, and ideas associated with the transitions and transmission points from the moral to the market economies, provide great insight into the ways in which communities were structured and responded to the problems of a commercially revived seigneurial system or an intrusive capitalization of agriculture. Le Goff and Sutherland implicitly recognize the dual, though spatially differentiated, processes at work when they assess the varying expectations and responses to the alterations in the rural-social-economic system beginning on a large scale in 1789. Admittedly, modernization makes much more sense as a concept if it is seen as a phenomenon more closely or exclusively associated with the nodal points of a market economy which will rely on the mobilization of surpluses moving from local to regional and even national markets. Its power is negated, however, if it is seen exclusively as a technological process, rather than as a system of social relations, with contesting notions of property. If dominant groups in rural society become part of and contribute to the changes, then the rapidity with which they are effected and which they effect will have an impact on the rural economy as a whole, creating opportunities and revealing disadvantages at the same time, while spreading stress unevenly. The tenant farmers, if they are the pivotal group, as Le Goff and Sutherland make out, will then be ready to welcome, indeed, help to initiate the chain of events that will release them from former rural servitudes and simultaneously make them more effective participants in a newly-freed market. If, however, as in the west, they lack the resources or perceive that they do, following a series of anticipated benefits, they are thereby removed from the full advantages that a market economy can bestow upon them. It is not clear from Le Goff and Sutherland's account how the western tenant farmers differ substantially from those in the Nord, for the categories used by Le Goff and Sutherland in the two instances differ. In the west, they are classified economically; and we are thus enabled to see how close they are in income to those below them. In the north, they are also assigned an economic classification, but the other members of the rural society they tried to dominate are described in political terms. This confusion in categories clouds the sources of counter-revolutionary activity.

My reluctance to deal harshly with the concept of modernization does not, on the other hand, transform me, as I have already declared, into its partisan. I am anxious to stress that what still needs explanation, after all the ink that has been spilt on the subject, is how we got from one world to another, and how we should understand it. If those of us, who are studying what Barrington Moore Jr calls, 'economic growth, or more generally modernization, a term that emphasizes the social, political, and psychological aspects of this process', we need not, as he reminds us, believe it to be an irreversible or universal phenomenon [*1973 [1970]: 42*]. There are too many instances, we are beginning to see, of cultures resiting in ways, fathomable and unfathomable, the paths of modernity [*Godelier, 1974*]. If, moreover, modernization is not quite another name for Weberian rationality, it is hard to conceive of either without thinking of how they affected communities. 'The Revolution ... brought national politics to the village level, gave the force of the law to attempts by the minority of better-off people in the rural community to impose their way of life on the mass, ... and generally tried to enforce the writ of undoubtedly more enlightened but nonetheless unwelcome bourgeois morality on a countryside where it had hitherto been unknown' [*Le Goff, 1981: 359*]. I am quoting from a passage in Le Goff's book on Vannes, which, in its firmness of tone, bears a close kinship with my judgement that the Revolution was but a high point in a continuous effort to 'justify proposals for intervention in a rural society [which was] generally hostile...' [*Mitchell, 1979A: 82*].

This brings me to my second observation. No proper evaluation of the events after 1789 can be expected if the revolutionary period is treated in isolation from the developments of pre-revolutionary France. Le Goff and Sutherland know this. Indeed, in their other works, some of which are now in book form, they take the longer view. It should not be ignored in any synthesis, for without it we cannot possibly gain an appreciation of what was constitutive of communities. If we suppose the accuracy of Le Goff's and Sutherland's designation of the tenant farmers and peasant proprietors in the economic life of their communities, we cannot ignore how this was translated in the complex layers of relationships which tied them to others in the community, both above and below them, before the Revolution produced its great and prolonged strains. What we know, from the work done over the past few years, is that whole communities, or that, at least important sections of communities, turned against the revolution, and did so violently and for the purpose of selfpreservation against hostile external authorities intent on continuing the changes originally introduced by the reforming ministries of the old regime. If Le Goff and Sutherland are going to assign the central role to the tenant farmers and peasant proprietors, who, although part of the dominant groups in rural society, were yet somewhat removed from their economic superiors, and in a somewhat ambiguous relationship with their economic inferiors, it is important to consider whether they occupied their pivotal positions before the Revolution, or whether the Revolution stifled a more promising future rather than an existing reality.

More is at stake in my reflections on community. As it stands, Le Goff's and Sutherland's study does not, in my view, deal with the religious fact. The religious fact, of course, is not to be conceived of as a reification or a hypostatization. Nor should it be written off as an epiphenomenon or as the simple fulfillment of a tributary functional role. Because they do not confront the religious fact frontally, indeed, it is thrust away from what Le Goff and Sutherland see as fundamental, that is, from forms of landholding, they are sparing themselves the difficult task of seeking how forms of social solidarity may be expressed at both the mundane and sacred levels, without subsuming one to the other. In other words, it seems that Le Goff and Sutherland are adopting a variant of the second approach. I take no issue with their statement that 'peasants who supported the Church did not necessarily give up other aims which can be classed as revolutionary' [*Le Goff and Sutherland, below*]. Others and I have made the same or similar points elsewhere. But they stress much more their conviction that the 'continuing struggle in the name of a religious cause, firmly and sincerely upheld, [was] also a way of continuing other social conflicts' [*ibid.*]. Though put in the form of a question, it is most certainly a rhetorical one. We are clearly being induced to conclude that, while there was no question of the authenticity of peasant religious beliefs and practices, they were a kind of appendage to matters more fundamental and came to the surface under stress, as the normal cultural expression of people who had no other means of identifying themselves, poor souls.

There is, I would suggest, more to the religious fact than this. Its richness is severely diluted by making it a weakened analogue of social discontent. In such a perspective, we are compelled to accept mechanical notions of social conflict; we are driven more and more to a strictly structural explanation of human activity; and we are deprived in the end of the chance of exploring how we may deal with the subjective nature of experience, or with the intentional acts of subjects. When Le Goff and Sutherland write that, 'Peasant communities ... withdrew into themselves, showing their disgust at the religious reforms, not so much by petitions, demonstrations, or violent outbursts, as by refusing to have anything to do with public authority' [*ibid*.], they reveal that their perspective is not entirely confined within the frontiers of economic calculations. But they do not inquire further into a cognitive system, a set of cultural values, the threads that bound layman and priest together, sometimes uneasily, at other times in mutual tolerance, so that when they were threatened 'communities moved even more closely in on themselves and sought out their priests, as the figures of moral authority, to protect them through a reaffirmation of the sacred nature of their deepest and most intimate personal and social commitments' [*Mitchell, 1976 [1974]:283*].

What is missing from Le Goff's and Sutherland's admirable synthesis, as well as from the other accounts in this section, is a deeper awareness of how religion serves not only as a means of expressing resistance or conformity — for that way of interpreting subjective intention is incomplete. If religion is seen merely as a 'socially cohesive force according to so-called rational standards of behaviour ... the religious and social springs of behaviour would be identical, locked together in an unchanging and perfect balance' [*Mitchell, 1979B:37–38*]. When I refer to the religious fact, I intend to stress the facticity of religious beliefs and practices, not the perfectly reflecting power of religion to mimic the social world. I think it would be useful at this point to allude to Paul Ricoeur's alternative way of understanding mimesis, for it provides an imaginative way of rendering the facticity of which I am speaking more transparent. With Aristotle, Ricoeur is thinking of a *creative* (my italics) imitation, which does not reduplicate reality, but 'seeks to represent men as better ... than they are in reality' [*Ricoeur, 1981:292, citing the* Poetics *of Aristotle, 1448a*]. The forms and symbols of religious resistance may, I suggest, be seen in a similar way. Its language must be deciphered and read not only as a description of action. It possesses the power to transform. In its distance from reality, in whatever appeals it makes to the past or to a utopian future, it is of course the Ur-ideology, but to insist that in time the symbolic forms of a distorted consciousness will be dissipated is to lose sight of the significance of the meanings, which individuals search out, and to subordinate them to a putative higher truth, explanation, or understanding.

Although the agenda for the latter is in much dispute, it is highly unlikely that it will dispense with the place of subjective meaning. This may not be palatable to all historians or human scientists, but it will appeal to scholars who are not terrorized into accepting the incessant commands of the empirical tradition, who are instead showing sympathy for the hermeneutical character of their inquiries, and who know that subjective meaning, if we are to have any history of the past at all, means intersubjective meaning. Such an approach cannot rest easy with what Charles Taylor calls the 'validity of descriptions of social reality in terms of . . . brute data,' which is the 'point of view of empiricist epistemology' [*Taylor, 1971: 22*] that conceives of the development of human consciousness in terms of the individualist model bequeathed by Locke. The religious fact is embedded in community action, it is an expression of intersubjectivity; it is produced within what Taylor calls a common 'social matrix in which individuals find themselves and act' [*ibid., 27*]. Hermeneutics recognizes the historical specificity of intersubjective meanings, but more important it perceives that the very act of social belongingness renders full reflection impossible, or to put it another way, makes a non-ideological knowledge of ideology a dream [*Thompson, in Ricoeur, 1981: 24*]. But this is far different from the attitudes of the points of view presented in nearly all of the papers here, with the exception of Hill's where there is an implicit, not a consciously elaborated theory of how nostalgic and utopian longings are created within a social matrix. The others do not all dismiss religion as mere ideology, but neither do they give it the attention it deserves.

The individuals and communities that appealed to religion, that declared they were ready to die for it, and even, as was so often the case, took coercive measures to press their priests into service, were looking to its power to fill in the gaps, make the adjustments, and supply the interpretations which the 'cultural, contractual, and technical imperatives' of the mundane world could not or failed to make provision for [*Falk-Moore, 1975: 220*]. How much more that power grew in a period of great troubles! If during untroubled times, the religious world inverts that of the mundane world, so that it is critical of it, yet reinforces it at the same time (it promises 'truth', identity, and consolation), in times of unexpected change transformed by violent struggle, the religious world expands its critical role markedly. Henceforth religious experience for those trying to fill in the gaps becomes a way of learning about themselves anew, of opening themselves to fresh thoughts and judgments, to the contemplation of unaccustomed deeds, and to the assumption of roles until then unimagined. The religious fact certainly heightens the intensity of social conflict, but it is not a bare function of the social world, nor its reflection. It is its otherness from, not its similarity to, the social world that gives it significance. During the Revolution, it permitted individuals and communities under stress to know themselves and nourished the belief that they could create a reality superior to that which had been imposed upon them.

References

Alembert, J. le Rond d', 1967, 'Réflexions sur l'histoire', in *Oeuvres complètes*, II, Geneva.
Berger, P., 1967, *The Sacred Canopy*, New York.
Bois, P., 1960, *Les Paysans de l'Ouest. Des structures économiques et sociales aux options politiques depuis l'époque révolutionnaire dans la Sarthe*, Paris.
Falk-Moore, S. 1975, 'Epilogue', in S. Falk-Moore and B. Meyerhoff, (eds.), *Symbols and Politics in Communal Ideology: Cases and Questions*, Ithaca.
Faucheux, M., 1964, *L'Insurrection vendéenne de 1792. Aspects économiques et sociaux*, Paris.
Febvre, L., 1973, *A New Kind of History and Other Essays*. Edited by P. Burke, New York.
Furet, F., 1981 [1978], *Interpreting the French Revolution*, Cambridge.
Ginzburg, C., 1980 [1976], *The Cheese and the Worms. The Cosmos of a Sixteenth-Century Miller*, London.
Godelier, M., 1974, 'Anthropology and Biology: Towards a New Form of Co-operation', *International Social Science Journal*, XXVI.
Habermas, J., 1975 [1973], *Legitimation Crisis*, Boston.
Habermas, J., 1981, 'Modernity versus Postmodernity', *New German Critique*, no. 22.
Le Goff, R. J. A. 1981, *Vannes and its Region: A Study of Town and Country in Eighteenth-Century France*, London.
Le Roy Ladurie, E., 1978 [1975], *Montaillou. The Promised Land of Error*, London.
Lewis, G., 1978, *The Second Vendée. The Continuity of Counter-Revolution in the Department of the Gard, 1789–1815*, London.
Mitchell, H., 1974, 'Resistance to the Revolution in Western France', in D. Johnson (ed.), *French Society and the Revolution*, 1976, Cambridge.
Mitchell, H., 1979A, 'Rationality and Control in French Eighteenth-Century Medical Views of the Peasantry', *Comparative Studies in Society and History*, XXI.
Mitchell, H., 1979B, 'The World Between the Literate and Oral Traditions in Eighteenth-Century France: Ecclesiastical Instructions and Popular Mentalities', in R. Runte ed., *Studies in Eighteenth-Century Culture*, VIII, Wisconsin.
Moore Jr., B., 1973 [1970]. *Reflections on the Causes of Human Misery and Upon Certain Proposals to Eliminate Them*, Boston.
Pérouas, L., (ed.), 1964, *Mémoire des missions des Montfortains dans l'Ouest (1740–1779)*, par P.-F. Hacquet, Paris.
Ricoeur, P., 1981, *Hermeneutics and the Human Sciences. Essays on Language, Action and Interpretation*. Edited, translated and introduced by J. B. Thompson, Cambridge.
Smith, A., 1937 [1776], *An Inquiry into the Nature and Causes of the Wealth of Nations*. Edited by E. Cannan, London.
Taylor, C., 1971, 'Interpretation and the Sciences of Man', *Review of Metaphysics*, XXVI.
Thomas, K., 1971, *Religion and the Decline of Magic*, London.
Tilly, C., 1964, *The Vendée*, London.

Mediterranean Europe 1500–1800:
notes and comparisons

PETER BURKE

At first sight this may seem to be a 'snakes in Iceland' paper. Not that there was any shortage of revolts in Mediterranean Europe in the early modern period. However, urban revolts predominate over rural ones, and when the peasants do rebel, they do not seem, in most cases, to have been decisively influenced by religion. Why was this the rule? In what circumstances were there exceptions? These will be the major themes of this paper, which will confine itself to Italy, France, and Spain, omitting the world of Islam (with the important exception of Granada), and even part of the Catholic Mediterranean world (notably Portugal and Dalmatia).

A brief, and naturally incomplete chronology of the revolts of the period is given in the appendix. From this chronology the importance of the larger towns will be clear. In Italy, there was revolt in Florence, Milan, Bologna, Rome, Naples, Palermo, Messina; in Spain, revolt in Madrid, Barcelona, Valencia, Saragossa, Córdoba, Granada, Seville; in France, where this urban pattern was least pronounced, in Paris, Lyons, Bordeaux, Toulouse, Aix, Rennes. This urban predominance is not altogether surprising, given the number and the size of the towns in these parts. In 1550, some thirty-two European towns had populations of 40,000 or more, and of these, twenty-four were in our region; thirteen in Italy, six in Spain, and five in France. In these parts of Europe, many peasants lived in towns rather than in villages or hamlets, despite the effort involved in 'commuting' to their fields.

The countryside often remained quiet for long periods. Historians have commented on the lack of peasant revolt in France between 1675 and 1775, in Valencia between 1525 and 1693, in Tuscany before the 1790s. This need not mean that the peasants had no injustices to complain of. It might be the case that the suppression of earlier revolts had taught them a lesson about the dangers involved; it might be that they were too divided, and one wonders whether the *mezzadria* system, common in Tuscany and other parts of the Mediterranean, was a divisive factor; it might be that emigration offered itself as an alternative, as in the case of the countryside around Naples, which grew so rapidly in this period; it might be, as Braudel [*1976: 734f*] has suggested, that the men whom the authorities in Catalonia, Calabria, and elsewhere, labelled 'bandits', were in fact continuing revolt by other means [cf. Hobsbawm, *1959, ch. 2*].

There remains an appreciable number of rural revolts to account for. Recent research has shown that two major urban revolts were not confined to cities after all. In the famous revolt of Naples in 1647, the peasants came into town, armed with pitchforks, in order to take part, and there were so many rural disturbances that the movement has been called a 'peasant war', the most serious of its kind in seventeenth-century Europe [*Villari, 1967: 241*]. Peasants also took part in the revolt of the Comuneros in Castille in 1520–1 [*Gutiérrez Nieto, 1973*]. In Normandy in 1639, and in Catalonia in 1640, the peasants rose with the towns or soon after [*Foisil, 1970; Elliott, 1963*]. In France in particular, there can also be found numerous rural revolts with little or no urban participation, as in the case of the Croquants of Périgord (who were hostile to such towns as there were in their province), or the Camisards of Languedoc.

It is of course the French revolts which have been studied in most detail, thanks to the pioneering work of the Soviet historian Boris Porshnev [*1963*], of his adversary Roland Mousnier [*1971, etc*], and of Mousnier's pupils, notably Yves Bercé [*1974*], and René Pillorget [*1975*]. Where Porshnev explained the popular revolts of the period 1623–48 in terms of class conflict, the 'Mousnier model' presents them as alliances of nobles, townsmen and peasants in resistance to the ever-increasing demands made by the state, especially demands for taxes, levied in order to pay for wars on a similarly increasing scale.

The Mousnier model has the advantage of accounting for the chronology and geography of the revolts more precisely than its competitor. 1623–48 was indeed a period of steep rises in direct taxation. If a map of seventeenth-century French revolt is drawn, it immediately becomes clear that it was the periphery which had risen against the centre; Normandy, Brittany, Aquitaine, Languedoc and Provence against Paris and Versailles. The peripheral provinces had been incorporated into the kingdom last and on the most favourable terms, including the right to vote their own taxes. Their revolts were a form of resistance, ultimately unsuccessful, to the erosion of this privileged position.

The historian has of course to be careful not to treat these revolts as more homogeneous than they really were. It is unlikely on the face of it that so many risings (130 in Provence alone between 1596 and 1635, according to Pillorget), should have taken place for exactly the same reasons. What is needed is a typology, and Pillorget does draw useful distinctions between (i) revolts which divide a community internally, (ii) revolts opposing the whole community to an enemy from outside, and (iii) revolts opposing more than one community to royal power. In the case of divisions within a town or village, he stresses the importance of conflicts between factions rather than conflicts between classes, vertical solidarity rather than horizontal.

It is worth emphasising the difficulty, in any particular case, of deciding whether the Porshnev model or the Mousnier model fits the evidence better. In most cases we have to infer the attitudes of participants from their behaviour (more exactly, from descriptions, by members of the ruling class, of the behaviour of others, usually members of subordinate classes), and the problems of interpretation are acute. Take the case, common enough in seventeenth-century France, of peasants attacking and burning a local château. For Porshnev this is an attack of 'feudalism', Mousnier, however, tends to argue that the château was owned by a tax-farmer, or that the attack was organised by a noble from an opposing faction. In any single instance it is virtually impossible to decide who is right. At a more general level, however, these revolts suggest the importance of different forms of social and political conflict which sometimes reinforce but more often cut across each other; periphery versus centre, faction versus faction, but also tenant against landlord and poor against rich. It seems fairly clear that these seventeenth-century revolts were generally movements of community self-defence against increasing demands from the landlord or the state. A similar point might be made about the rural riots in the Ile de France in 1775, with their emphasis on the just price or 'moral economy': self-defence in a society which was now more commercialised than that studied by Porshnev and Mousnier [*Rudé, 1964: ch. 1*].

Spanish and Italian revolts have not yet been studied as a whole or even region by region in the French style, but it is worth asking whether they seem to diverge from the French pattern, and if so, how. Movements opposing whole communities to the central government include the revolt of Aragon in 1591 and the revolt of Catalonia in 1640, both risings of the periphery against the centre. The Catalan peasant rising of 1688 was also a revolt against the centre, directed like that of 1640 against the billetting of troops, but in this case upper-class support was lacking [*Kamen, 1977*].

In Italy, by contrast, there was no centre, and it is hard to find clear-cut examples of this type of revolt, even in states under foreign rule such as Milan, Naples and Sicily. In Naples and Palermo in 1647, as in so many French communities in the 1630s, revolt was triggered by increases in taxation to pay for the Thirty Years' War, but the revolts of 1647 in South Italy were not purely anti-Spanish. In Naples, for example, there were conflicts between the bourgeoisie (led by the lawyer Genoino), and the nobility, and also between the poor (led by the fisherman Masaniello), and the rich. For an example which fits the 'whole community' model of revolt we may have to go as far afield as the Corsican war for independence from Genoese rule, a war which broke out in 1564; and even this movement was complicated by conflicts between factions.

For in Italy, faction was at least as important as in Pillorget's Provence. The troubles in Friuli in 1511, for example, seem to have been essentially a battle between the Zamberlani and the Strumieri, each faction including both nobles and peasants. In Genoa in 1575, when a conflict developed between the old and the new nobilities, the former armed the peasants on their estates and brought them into town. However, it is not difficult to find examples of antiseigneurial revolt in Italy in this period, especially in the South; in Calabria in 1512, in Basilicata in 1513, and over a wide area in 1647, when the peasants demanded the return of the common lands usurped by the barons, as well as an end to the imprisonment and torture of the 'poor vassals' [*Villari, 1961*]. They failed. The assassination of oppressive landlords, far from uncommon in the South in the sixteenth century, was probably the most successful form of rural revolt. In other words, there was a remarkable contrast between peaceful Tuscany and the turbulent South. Perhaps landlords were less oppressive in Tuscany; but structural differences between the two regions should also be taken into account. Tuscany was the classic land of *mezzadria*, which divided the peasantry; the South was the equally classic land of latifundia, which united them. The contrast is not unlike that which can still be seen in Portugal, between the conservative Catholic smallholders of the North and the radical anticlerical agricultural labourers of the South.

And that brings us, at last, to the question of religion. For the sake of clarity it may be useful to operate with a simple distinction between two functions of religion in revolts; as end and as means. Most of the revolts of Mediterranean Europe were movements of Catholics against Catholics. Their essential aims were usually what we would call secular; a reduction of the demands made on them by state or landlord. They were concerned with taxes, seigneurial dues, the billeting of troops, encroachments on the commons. These concerns might bring them into conflict with the Church as an institution, the Church as landowner or collector of tithes, but it would be odd to describe their aims as 'religious'.

Yet religion did enter into many of these revolts. It was a means rather than an end. Its most characteristic function may be summed up in one Weberian word; legitimation. The peasants often marched to revolt behind their priests, as in the Angoumois in 1548 or Normandy in 1639. The priest was the natural leader of the parish, and his leadership was likely to give the movement a more religious tone. The rebels would generally declare that God was on their side, and they might appeal to the Virgin and the saints (as was done in Naples in 1647), and carry their images on their banners. When the revolt was suppressed and their leaders executed, the peasants might tell stories of their martyrdom and even miracles, as in Aquitaine in the early seventeenth century, where they told of a corpse refusing to putrefy and of a man coming down alive from the gallows [*Bercé, 1974: 665*]. It is hard to isolate the religious element in these revolts, and even harder to discuss it without falling into one of two opposite traps; the Scylla of reductionism and the Charybdis of literal-mindedness. I do not want to argue that the peasants or their priests merely dressed up secular grievances in religious language. It was normal to appeal to the Virgin and the saints in time of crisis, and to expect their support in a just cause. But it is unlikely that all the rebels were unaware of the strategic value of shouting *Viva Maria!*, a cry which, like *Vive le Roi!*, made their cause respectable. In that limited sense, religious ideas were instruments in the struggle, and religion an ideology.

In a few cases, however, rebellious peasants in Mediterranean Europe did more than justify themselves in religious terms; they had religious goals, they were concerned to change the religious situation. Not very often. I do not think that this was the case in 1525, when the Peasant War spread to the Trentino, though the messages carried by the sources are confused and contradictory. A chronicler declares that the revolt in the Trentino was the result of infection from the 'Lutheran plague', and emphasises the attacks on priests, monks and friars. On the other hand, the impression given by the published trial records is that participants saw themselves as engaged in a war of *povereti* against *signori*; tenants against landlords, poor against rich [*Sardagna, 1889: 94f, 193, 222*]. In 1647, churches were attacked in South Italy, in the Cilento, but in this case too it seems that it was the Church as landowner that was the true target [*Di Leo, 1973*].

Leaving aside the cases of the French wars of religion and the 'counter revolution' in the Vendée (discussed below by David Nicholls, and Timothy Le Goff & Don Sutherland), I know of only three major examples of revolts with religious goals in the Mediterranean world in the early modern period. The first is Spanish, the second French, and the third Italian; the first Muslim, the second Protestant, and the third Catholic. They are the revolts of the Alpujarras in 1586, of the Camisards in 1702–4, and of Tuscany and Calabria in the 1790s. I shall discuss them in chronological order.

In 1492, the troops of the 'Catholic Kings', Ferdinand and Isabella, finally conquered the Muslim kingdom of Granada. In the last phase of the war of reconquest, agreements were made with the defeated 'Moors', allowing them to continue practising their religion. However, in some places Muslims were forcibly baptised, an action which provoked a rising in the Moorish quarter of Granada in 1499 and another in the mountains of the Alpujarra in 1500. In Valencia, another region with a substantial Muslim minority, the great revolt of 1519–23, the Germanía, was directed in part against them. There were forced baptisms and also attacks on individuals – in other words, Moor-bashing. In 1525 the government, following local opinion rather than leading it, ordered the Muslims of Valencia to embrace Christianity. In some areas there was armed resistance, which continued till late 1526. There followed thirty years of relative peace, during which time the clergy did all they could to convert and assimilate the Moors, whether Muslims or converts (Moriscos). [*Domínguez Ortiz and Vincent, 1978: chapters 1–2*].

By the accession of Philip II, in 1556, there were signs of increasing tension between Christians and Moriscos, especially in Granada, where there were about 150,000 of these willing or unwilling converts, still speaking Arabic, wearing their distinctive dress (the women in particular), and observing their traditional customs; their baths, their dances, their treatment of Friday as a holiday, their abstinence from pork, their distinctive manner of slaughtering animals, and so on. Some at least of these Moriscos remained Muslims at heart. In 1563, the mufti of Oran wrote to the Moriscos of Andalusia, presumably in response to a request, giving them permission to 'adore the idols of the christians', and even to drink wine if necessary, provided their intentions were pure; in other words, to practice exterior conformity [*Longás: 1915, appendix*].

Whether the majority of Moriscos regarded themselves as Muslim or Christian by this time it is impossible to say. Degrees of assimilation or 'acculturation' varied, and in any case Moors and 'old Christians', as the Spaniards called themselves, defined Christianity in different ways. The problem of distinguishing between essential Christianity and the western customs which had become associated with it was one which cropped up again and again in the mission field in the sixteenth and seventeenth centuries. Some missionaries, such as the Italian Jesuits Matteo Ricci, in China, and Roberto de'Nobili, in South India, argued the case for the 'accommodation' of Christianity to the local customs, for allowing the Chinese Christians to carry on with 'ancestor worship', and for christian Brahmins to continue to practice the ceremony of the sacred thread, on the grounds that these customs were social and not religious.

Ricci and de'Nobili were of course in a tiny minority in a vast non-Christian continent. The Moriscos, on the other hand, had the disadvantage of being outnumbered by their Christian neighbours. These neighbours regarded Moorish customs with hostility and expressed this hostility in religious terms. The Morisco way of slaughtering animals looked to Christians like a ritual of non-Christian sacrifice; their baths were sometimes interpreted as Muslim ritual ablutions; even their language and their clothes, badges of a distinctive identity, fell under suspicion. There was a good deal of tension between the two communities at a local level, especially in the countryside. Priests accused their morisco congregations of missing Mass, of deliberately coming late, and of insulting the Host. The Moriscos in turn accused their priests of calling them 'moorish dogs' and of overcharging them for funerals and other services. The Inquisition was increasingly investigating and condemning Moriscos in an attempt to purify popular Christianity of 'pagan' elements (an attempt characteristic of Catholic Europe in the years after the Council of Trent) [*Bennassar, 1979: 167f*]. For its part, the central government was coming to see the Moriscos more and more as a problem, partly in response to pressure from below and partly as a result of the international situation. The Ottoman advance westwards by land and sea was making the fear of a Morisco 'fifth column' more acute, and at a time when Philip II also had the revolt of the Netherlands on his hands [*Hess, 1968*].

This was the context of the royal decree of 1567 which forbade the Moriscos to speak their own language and practice their native customs. Unable to change this policy of enforced acculturation by peaceful means, they turned to violence in 1568. An attempt to call out the Moorish quarter of the city of Granada failed but in the countryside, more especially in the Alpujarras mountains (the scene of a rising 68 years earlier), the Moriscos reverted to Islam, elected a king, and began a holy war against their Christian oppressors. The dominant religion was ritually profaned: churches were destroyed, images and altars smashed, Catholic liturgy parodied, and priests humiliated before they were dispatched. The rituals of Islam were celebrated with great pomp and there were apparently millenarian expectations in the air. It was said that 'the age of innocence had arrived'. But it did not last. Although it was not easy for the regular army to deal with the Morisco guerrillas, with their hit and run tactics, and their mountain refuges, and although Morisco 'bandits' remained active in the area for the rest of the century, the revolt had effectively been suppressed by the end of 1570 [*Marmol Carvajal, c1600: book 4; Braudel, 1976: 1060f; Garrad, 1955; Caro Baroja, 1957: 159f; Domínguez Ortiz and Vincent, 1978: chapter 3*].

The revolt of the Camisards resembles that of the Alpujarras in a number of ways. It was another movement of mountaineers in resistance to forcible acculturation. In the 1560s, the inhabitants of the highlands of the Cévennes, in Languedoc, went over to Calvinism, as did some of the villages of Aquitaine Béarn and Normandy at about the same time, although Calvinism was much more an urban than a rural movement. When Henri IV turned Catholic and ended the religious wars, his Edict of Nantes allowed the French Protestants to continue practising their religion, like the Moors of Granada after the Reconquest. As in the case of Granada, so in Languedoc the local laity and clergy disapproved of this policy of toleration and did all they could to undermine it. In the later seventeenth century, some 90% of the population of the Cévennes was Protestant, but the Estates of Languedoc were putting them in a less and less tenable position by excluding them from civic office, harassing their ministers and so on. Like Philip II, Louis XIV took action relatively late in the day, action which culminated in the Revocation of the Edict of Nantes in 1685. Calvinist worship was forbidden, the 'temples' pulled down and the pastors dispersed.

Why Louis took the decision to persecute the Huguenots when he did is a controversial question. Historians no longer explain the decision by the increasing piety of the ageing king, or the increasing influence of his devout mistress Madame de Maintenon, but instead point out the strength of local pressure groups. The problem of timing remains. Perhaps the persecution of Huguenots in the 1680s was an attempt to divert attention from the unsuccessful war with the Dutch, 1672–9, and to win popularity with the Catholic majority. The Spanish analogy is enough to make one ask whether Louis saw the Huguenots as a 'fifth column' likely to support his enemies the Protestant Dutch and English. In any case he wanted to be an absolute monarch, and, as his representative in Languedoc remarked at about this time, 'if subjects have a different religion from that of their prince, his dominance and their subjection cannot be complete.'

The Huguenots in general did not react to the Revocation of the Edict of Nantes as the Moriscos reacted to the royal decree of 1567, by almost immediate rebellion. Some emigrated; most conformed. In the Cévennes, however, they began to meet in secret, in the open air, in remote places, to sing psalms and listen to lay preachers. The atmosphere was one of millenarian expectation. The Cévenols discussed the Apocalypse and expected the imminent end of the world. A number of them prophesied the destruction of Antichrist and Babylon, and in 1701 one of these prophets, a young man called Abraham Mazel, took the step from words to deeds by assassinating the archpriest of the Cévennes. This action set off a revolt, known as the revolt of the Camisards (1702–4), a holy war seen by the participants in biblical terms with the psalm-singing rebels in the role of the people of Israel, Louis in that of Pharaoh. Churches were attacked and priests killed. For about two years the Camisards conducted a successful guerrilla war in the *maquis*, growing in strength and on one occasion defeating a whole regiment of regular troops. Then their leader was persuaded to submit, and the movement dissolved. There seem to have been no demands for social reform [*Le Roy Ladurie, 1974: 269f; Joutard, 1976*].

The revolts of the Alpujarras were at once spontaneously rural and intensely religious. It is difficult to think of an Italian parallel to these movements in the early modern period. The case of the holy wars of the 1790s, in Calabria and Tuscany, is rather more complicated. They form part of a counter-revolution (a term which was coined to describe the events of the 1790s). In 1799, after French invaders had defeated the Bourbons, a Neapolitan Republic was proclaimed, standing for liberty, equality and the sovereignty of the people. French troops also marched into Tuscany and there was a movement in their support. Liberty trees were planted.

However, counter-revolution was not far behind. In the same year, cardinal Fabrizio Ruffo led his Christian Army from Calabria to Naples to wipe out the enemies of 'heaven's most precious gift, our holy religion', in other words, Jacobins, republicans, and freemasons. Liberty trees were torn up and replaced by crosses. When the news of these events reached Tuscany, there were riots and also the destruction of liberty trees in a mood of religious exaltation in which a number of miracles were said to have occurred. The slogan here was *Viva Maria!* [*Cingari, 1957; Turi, 1969*].

There is no doubt of peasant involvement in these attacks on the 'Jacobins'. It was they who formed the rank and file of the Christian Army, singing 'equality is finished, liberty is finished, long live God and His Majesty'. It was they who pulled down the liberty trees. They were against the French Revolution, but exactly what they thought the Revolution was about is difficult to say, just as it is difficult to decide how far they were manipulated by the clergy. It is likely enough that their dislike for foreigners was spontaneous, and they were certainly conscious enough of their own interests to take over a good deal of land in some places [*Villari, 1961*].

As for the slogan, *Viva Maria*, it is possible to say something about its context and meaning. In Tuscany, the slogan went back to the riots of 1790. These riots were both urban and rural and they were protests against both the economic and the religious policies of the government. The urban protest was essentially a 'moral economy' protest against the high prices of grain and oil. The rural protest, on the other hand, was against the closing of certain churches and the suppression of certain confraternities and processions. In other words, it was a rejection of the 'Jansenist' policies of the government and of the bishop of Pistoia and Prato, Scipione de'Ricci, who had criticised certain popular devotions as examples of exterior religion. The peasants were protesting against attempts to reform popular religious culture. However, unlike so many popular religious revolts, there was no messiah here and no millennium. The Italian peasants of the 1790s behaved more like the Mexican *Cristeros* than like the Brazilian followers of Antonio Conselheiro [*Meyer, below; Da Cunha, 1944*]. The closest Italian parallel to the Conselheiro movement occurred as late as the 1870s, in the 'backlands' of Tuscany, on Monte Amiata. The Messiah of Monte Amiata was Davide Lazzaretti, whose dream of the 'Republic of Christ' came to an end when he was shot by the carabinieri in 1878 [*Hobsbawm, 1959 : ch. 4*].

I have discussed three revolts in relative detail. To what extent were they rural, and to what extent religious? None of them were purely peasant movements in the strict sense. Some of the leaders of the Alpujarras revolt were artisans, dyers in particular. Silk-growing was crucial in the rural economy, so that villagers are likely to have been market-oriented and outward-looking (as in many of the communities which took part in the German Peasant War). In the Cévennes, Protestantism spread through a network of rural artisans, shoemakers in particular; and craftsmen were also important in the revolt of the Camisards, whose leaders included a woolcomber, a baker and a blacksmith. Rural revolts, yes; peasant revolts, not exactly.

Were the revolts religious? I have already tried to distinguish between the language in which the movements were justified and their essential aims; it is also necessary to say something about 'preconditions' and 'triggers'. It does not look like coincidence that the revolt of the Alpujarras was preceded by the bad harvest of 1567, and in the longer term, by a decline in the silk industry going back to about 1550. Again, the Cévennes of the end of the seventeenth century was a region hit by famine and economic depression. The Messiah of Monte Amiata followed the agricultural crisis of the 1870s. To say this is not to say that revolt is merely a reaction to hunger, that religion is merely a rationalisation for material discontent. But in those hard times, would-be rebels may have felt that they had nothing to lose by violent protest.

Can we say that the aims of the rebels were religious? Religion is of course hard to define, difficult to distinguish from the rest of a group's culture. What is clear in all three cases is that the rebels were protesting against attempts by outsiders to change their culture. They were defending their traditions against assault; old traditions in the case of the Catholics and the Muslims, relatively recent ones – but already rooted – in the case of the Camisards. In that sense all three movements were, like so many revolts in the Third World in this century, 'nativistic'. 'Conservative' is a difficult word to define. Historians of the Peasant War of 1525 have argued that demands for return to the good 'old law' may mask innovation, that traditions may be reconstructed. It may well be that future research will interpret our three movements more subtly in this way. But the first thing to say about them is that they were defending traditional values, not attacking them.

Appendix. Chronology of the principal revolts in France, Italy and Spain, 1500–1800

1500	Alpujarras	1629	Milan
1509	Padua	1630	Aix (*Cascaveoux*)
1511	Friuli	1636–7	Angoumois, Saintonge, Périgord (*Croquants*)
1512	Calabria		
1513	Abruzzi, Basilicata	1639	Normandy (*Va-Nu-Pieds*)
1519–23	Valencia, Mallorca (*Germanía*)	1640	Catalonia
1520–21	Castille (*Comuneros*)	1644	Brescia
1525	Trentino	1647–53	Southern Italy, southern Spain, southern France
1525–6	Valencia		
1529	Lyons (*Rebeine*)	1658	Sologne (*Sabotiers*)
1531–2	Lucca (*Straccioni*)	1662	Boulogne (*Lustucru*)
1547	Naples	1670	Vivarais
1548	Guyenne, Angoumois (*Pitauts*)	1671	Bologna
1558	Aragon	1674	Messina
1564–9	Corsica	1675	Brittany (*Bonnets rouges*)
1568–70	Alpujarras	1677	Bologna
1579	Dauphiné (*Ligue des Vilains*) and Provence (*Razas*)	1688	Catalonia (*Segadors*)
		1693	Valencia (*Segunda Germanía*)
1585	Naples	1702–04	Languedoc (*Camisards*)
1589	Normandy (*Gauthiers*)	1707	Quercy (*Tard-Avisés*)
1591	Aragon	1725	Ile de France
1594	Limousin and Périgord (*Croquants*)	1736	Rome
		1766	Madrid (*Esquilache*)

1773	Palermo		1793	Sardinia
1775	Ile de France		1795–6	Arezzo
1790	Florence		1799	Calabria (*Sanfedisti*)
1792–9	Brittany (*Chouans*)		1799	Tuscany (*Viva Maria*)
1793–6	Anjou (*Vendée*)			

References

Bennassar, B., 1979, *L'Inquisition espagnole*, Paris.
Bercé, Y. M. 1974, *Histoire des Croquants*, Geneva.
Braudel, F., 1976, *The Mediterranean in the age of Philip II*, London (first published in French in 1949).
Caro Baroja, J., 1957, *Los moriscos del reino de Granada*, Madrid.
Cingari, G., 1957, *Giacobini e Sanfedisti in Calabria*, Florence.
Da Cunha, E., 1944, *Rebellion in the Backlands*, Chicago.
Domínguez Ortiz, A., 1973, *Alteraciones andaluzas*, Madrid.
Domínguez Ortiz, A., and Vincent, B., 1978, *Historia de los moriscos*, Bilbao.
Elliott, J., 1963, *The Revolt of the Catalans*, Cambridge.
Foisil, M., 1970, *La révolte des nu-pieds*, Paris.
Garlan, Y., and Nières, C., 1975, *Les révoltes bretonnes de 1675*, Paris.
Garrad, K., 1955, *The Causes of the Second Rebellion of the Alpujarras*, unpublished, Cambridge Ph.D thesis.
Gutiérrez Nieto, J. I., 1973, *Las comunidades como movimiento antiseñorial*, Barcelona.
Hess, A. C., 1968, 'The Moriscos: an Ottoman Fifth Column in Sixteenth-Century Spain', *American Historical Review*, LXXIV: 1–26.
Hobsbawm, E. J., 1959, *Primitive Rebels*, Manchester.
Joutard, P., 1976, *Les camisards*, Paris.
Kamen, H., 1975, 'La segunda Germanía', *Homenaje al Juan Reglà Campistol*, Valencia: 647–56.
Kamen, H., 1977, 'The Catalan Peasant Rising of 1688', *Journal of Modern History* XLIX: 210–30.
Di Leo, 1973, 'Le ripercussioni del moto di Masaniello nel Cilento', F. Malgeri, *La società religiosa nell'età moderna*, Naples: 741–50.
Le Roy Ladurie, E., 1974, *The Peasants of Languedoc*, Illinois, U.P., (fuller French edition published in 1966).
Longás, P., 1915, *Vida religiosa de los moriscos*, Madrid.
Marmol Carvajal, L.de, c1600, *Historia del rebelión y castigo de los moriscos*, Malaga.
Mousnier, R., 1971, *Peasant Uprisings*, London (first published in French in 1967).
Pillorget, R., 1975, *Les mouvements insurrectionels de Provence*, Paris.
Porshnev, B., 1963, *Les soulèvements populaires en France de 1623 à 1648*, Paris (first published in Russian in 1948).
Rudé, G., 1964, *The Crowd in History*, New York.
Sardagna, G. B., 1889, *La Guerra rustica nel Trentino*, Venice.
Turi, G., 1969, *Viva Maria: la reazione alle riforme leopoldine*, Florence.
Villari, R., 1961, 'Movimenti antifeudali dal 1647 al 1799', R. Villari, *Mezzogiorno e contadini nell'età moderna*, Bari.
Villari, R., 1967, *La rivolta antispagnola a Napoli*, Bari.

From Lollards to Levellers

CHRISTOPHER HILL

> Abridged version with shortened references of an essay which appeared in *CUDAN Bulletin* 12–13 (1980–81) 9–28, by kind permission of the author and the editors of the *Bulletin*. See also an earlier version in M. Cornforth, ed., *Rebels and their causes: Essays in honour of A. L. Morton* (London, 1978) 49–67.

In the 1640s, when the censorship broke down in England and church courts ceased to function, a whole host of radical ideas popped up and were freely expressed. The question I want to ask is how far these ideas had had an underground existence before 1640, so that the novelty is only in the freedom to express them: or were they novel ideas, the product of novel circumstances? In the space at my disposal I cannot do more than throw out a few suggestions, and that is fortunate, for I have no completed thesis to put forward, only a few working hypotheses, a list of questions I am asking myself.

Now of course there are very special problems in attempting to trace continuities of underground ideas. By definition those who held them were anxious to leave no traces. Before the nineteenth century we can very rarely hear the lower orders speaking for themselves in a natural tone of voice. We hear instead what JPs in Quarter Sessions, judges in ecclesiastical courts, heresy-hunting pamphleteers, thought their inferiors were thinking, with all the dangers of distortion from such sources ('Who writ the history of the Anabaptists but their enemies?' asked the Leveller Richard Overton; and the Leveller William Walwyn spoke of 'that lying story of that injured people, . . . the Anabaptists of Münster' [*Hill, 1975: 120*].) Alternatively, we have to rely on inference, from the survival of particular doctrines in particular areas. In putting together scraps of evidence, which have survived by chance, we are unlikely to arrive at decisive conclusions. The problems are perennial whenever we try to reconstruct the history of the common man, still more of the common woman. Nearly all our history is upper-class and male. One of the delights of the English Revolution is the exceptional nature of the surviving evidence, thanks to the exceptional political liberty and the relative cheapness of printing.

Let us remind ourselves how very radical some of the ideas were which surfaced in the 1640s and 1650s. Levellers advocated political democracy, a republic with a widely extended franchise, abolition of the House of Lords, election of magistrates and judges, drastic legal and economic reforms. The

Diggers and others carried the Leveller emphasis on natural rights to advocacy of a communist society. Sectaries and Milton extended the Puritan attack on bishops to rejection of the whole idea of a state church – its courts, its tithes, its fees, its control of education and the censorship, the very distinction between clergy and laity. They carried anti-sacramentalism to the point of regarding worship as discussion. Spiritual equality and the doctrine of the inner light were extended to rejection of the idea of 'sin', to a belief in human perfectibility on earth. Many denied the divinity of Christ, the immortality of the soul. Some ceased to believe in a local heaven or hell; the gospel story was treated as an allegory. Winstanley found the word Reason preferable to God. The protestant ethic, the dignity of labour, monogamous marriage, all came under attack.

Many of the proponents of these ideas looked back to Lollards and Marian martyrs as their ancestors. Foxe had of course accustomed Englishmen to this pedigree, to this answer to the question 'Where was your church before Luther?' England differed from most continental countries in having a 'respectable' prereformation heresy to appeal to. But Foxe, we know, often played down the radicalism of his heretics [*Horst, 1972: 146–6*]. Many of the views of Lollards and Marian martyrs would have been punishable under Elizabeth – which did not stop her making political capital out of Foxe's book. In the seventeenth century Levellers like Lilburne, Overton, Walwyn, a reformer like William Dell, emphasized the more radical elements in the heretical heritage. The point was regularly made from the other side. John Cleveland spoke of 'Presbyter Wyclif' and 'Tyler's toleration'; the sneer was repeated by other poets, Abraham Cowley and John Collop. Charles I, in his answer of 18 June 1642 to the Parliament's 19 Propositions, warned that, if opposition to him continued, 'at last the common people . . . [will] set up for themselves, call parity and independence liberty, . . . destroy all rights and properties, all distinctions of families and merit, and by this means this splendid and excellently distinguished form of government end in a dark, equal chaos of confusion, . . . in a Jack Cade or a Wat Tyler'. This Answer of Charles's became the classic royal statement of 'mixed monarchy', the King's acceptance of a Parliamentary share in government. He repeated the points at his trial in 1649, and the doctrine played its part in preparing for the restoration of 1660 [*Cleveland, 1687: 506; Cowley, ed. 1973: 88, 103; Collop, ed. 1962: 48; Rushworth, 1659–1701, V: 732*].

Continuities certainly exist between 15th and 17th century radicals. Some are doctrinal, some geographical. I shall try to look at both. Joan Thirsk and Alan Everitt have distinguished between champion arable areas of the country, with stable docile communities subordinated to parson and squire, on the one hand, and pastoral, forest, moorland and fen areas on the other. In the latter, parishes were often very large, so that ecclesiastical control was less tight, there were fewer lords of manors, and vagrants could squat in relative security ('out of sight or out of slavery', as Gerrard Winstanley put it). In the 17th century these forest cottagers formed a pool of labour for the new industries that were developing. Both Lollardy and later heresy are found especially in clothing counties, and in pastoral, forest, moorland and fen areas.

The Weald of Kent and Sussex was a region of forests, with few gentlemen and few manors. Parishes were large, and many families rarely attended church. It was a heavily populated and industrialized area (clothing and iron); the population was mobile and wayfaring, with 'multitudes of rogues and beggars', since there were many opportunities for casual labour. Masterless men abounded who were fodder for conscription in time of war. The Lollard areas can be roughly correlated with those that produced the most Marian martyrs, and with later Baptist and Quaker regions. Heresy was widespread in Kent in the fifteen-thirties; Peter Clark speaks of protestant pressure coming from below in Kentish towns. There were anti-Trinitarians in the fifteen-thirties and among the many Marian martyrs. Rye was especially Puritan, or worse. Its poorer townsmen, their pastor said in 1537, 'reeked of Lollardy and ribaldry'. There were 'free-willers' under Edward VI, and what Patrick Collinson calls 'rustic Pelagianism' under Elizabeth [*Fletcher, 1975; Collinson, 1967: 37, cf. 96–7; Clark, 1977*].

Radical heresy continued later in the century. Robert Master of Woodchurch denied the resurrection. Another man 'maintains ... usury and says there is no hell'. In the sixteen-twenties there were Brownists. There were political rebels in Kent in 1381, 1450, 1549 and 1554. There were food riots in 1630, and the Weald produced the largest single contingent of emigrants to Massachusetts later in the decade. Both John Taylor the Water-Poet, a man of conservative sympathies, and the radical George Wither thought it necessary to distinguish between Christendom and Kent. This tribute to the county's heretical reputation goes back at least to Sir Thomas Wyatt's time [*Clark, 1976; Burrage, II, 1912: 202–3*].

In 1638 ten labourers from the old Lollard centre of Tenterden were up before the church court for refusing to pay tithe on wages. 'What care we for his Majesty's laws and statutes?' the churchwardens of Little Horsted in the Sussex Weald were asking. The Kent and Sussex Weald was firm in support of Parliament during the civil war, unlike the western area of Sussex. A host of sectaries appeared in the forties, at Tenterden among other centres. Kent was one of the earliest areas to have women preachers. The county looms large in Thomas Edward's *Gangraena* of 1646. Kentish radicalism produced a strong Leveller movement, culminating in a Digger colony and a near-Digger pamphlet. It was a Muggletonian centre of some significance. Samuel Fisher, who evolved from a Baptist into a Quaker, and who argued in a scholarly folio that the Bible was not the Word of God, operated around Ashford [*Fletcher, 1975: 22; Hill, 1975: 46–7, 124–7, 239*].

Essex, my next county, is another woodland region, especially in the north, the traditional radical area. Itinerants and squatters abounded. The cottage clothing industry of this region was described as a breeding ground for Lollardy. John Ball had preached in Colchester. Essex participated in the Lollard revolt of 1414, and heresy survived into the 16th century. There were major disturbances in the county in 1549, the year of Ket's rebellion. There were more Marian martyrs from Essex than from any other county except Kent (and London). In 1566 there was an abortive rising in the clothing towns of the north-east of the county. Under Edward VI there had been groups of 'free-willers', under Mary lower-class conventicles, and under Elizabeth Familists, in Essex just as in Kent. The Legate brothers, one of whom was burned in 1612, the other dying in prison, came from Essex: they denied the existence of any true church on earth. In 1581 there was an illegal preaching place in the woods at Ramsey, with straw and moss for seating, 'and the ground trodden bare with much treading' [*Collinson, 1967: 223; Horst, 1972: 122–3; Cross, 1976: 28–32; Gordon, 1895: 16–17*].

Essex was also a county in which there was an unusually large number of indictments for witchcraft in the 16th and 17th centuries. Here I can only hint at the possible connections which caused Lollards, Anabaptists and early Quakers to be denounced as witches. When the famous Puritan William Ames was expelled from Christ's College, Cambridge, in 1610, he was promptly offered a city lectureship at Colchester. But the bishop ensured that he was not allowed to accept it. Men spoke of 'Colchester the Zealous'. The Puritan Thomas Shepard thought Essex the best county in England, John Hampden agreed that it was the place of most religion in the land. The Familist John Everard held a living at Fairstead in Essex [*Macfarlane, 1970; Sprunger, 1972: 24–5; Shepard, ed. 1972: 47*].

Essex is a county in which economic developments to the disadvantage of the poor are particularly well documented. Parish vestries and élites are busy imposing social discipline. There was an enormous increase after 1600 both in poor rates and in presentation of cottagers and lodgers. In the fifteen-eighties and nineties revolt was being foretold there. 'What can rich men do against poor men if poor men rise and hold together?' artisans were asking in 1594. Next year there were threats to hang sellers of victuals – a simple popular remedy against inflationary price increases. In 1629 there were two riots in Maldon, led by Anne Carter, a butcher's wife. She was hanged, with two others. Charles I's enforcement of forest laws in the 1630s hit small and large cultivators in Essex particularly hard. The Venetian Ambassador said that the total composition fines to be levied on the county's forest lands would have amounted to at least £300,000 – more than ten times the total collected in Ship Money. So it did not need the Earl of Warwick's encouragement for Essex to be the earliest and most outstanding of the counties defaulting on Ship Money payments. When 'intelligencers' news' was read in Colchester streets on market days, 'zealants' flocked to hear 'as people use when ballads are sung'. In 1637 a parson at Maldon, where Anne Carter had been hanged eight years earlier, was said to have preached that the King's sins were being visited upon the kingdom. He prayed for Charles's conversion, and urged the people to arm themselves if all else failed. Next year he prayed that God would 'utterly destroy those that are enemies to the plantations', because these offered a refuge to the godly [*Thomas, 1971: 406, 422*].

After 1638 Essex was the scene of violent anti-clericalism. The common people pulled down altar rails and images. In 1640 Laudian clergy were rabbled. Much popular iconoclasm was *social*, directed against the coats of arms of noble families depicted in churches. At the county elections in 1640 'rude vulgar people', fellows without shirts' (the English equivalent of sans-culottes?) threatened to 'tear the gentlemen to pieces' if the popular candidate were not elected. 'Many thousands' turned out to sack the papist Countess of Rivers's house. When manorial documents and evidences were destroyed at Colchester in 1641 the jury gave an 'ignoramus' verdict against the plunderers. They were indicted again at the assizes, but the sheriff could not get a jury to convict. At Milford 'no man appeared like a gentleman but was made a prey to that ravenous crew'. 'The rude people are come to such a head', said a Colchester gentleman, 'that we know not how to quiet them'. There were enclosure and other riots in 1641–2. They 'must take advantage of these times', said an Essex enclosure rioter in 1642, 'lest they never have the like again'. 'There was no law settled at this time that he knew', declared a poacher in the same county in the same year [*Holmes, 1974: 33–6, 43–4*].

In January 1642 6,000 Essex freeholders signed a petition against bishops. Thousands from Essex marched on London after the arrest of the Five Members. Bruno Ryves's account of the principles held by the lower classes of Chelmsford around 1643 is prophetic of much that was to be developed later: but it also recalls much that had gone before. Kings are burdens. The relation of master and servant has no ground in the New Testament; in Christ there is neither bond nor free. Ranks such as those of the peerage and gentry are 'ethnical and heathenish distinctions'. There is no ground in nature or Scripture why one man should have £1000 *per annum*, another not £1. The common people have long been kept under blindness and ignorance, and have remained servants and slaves to the nobility and gentry. 'But God hath now opened their eyes and discovered them their Christian liberty'. Gentlemen should be made to work for their living, or else should not eat. Learning has always been an enemy to the Gospel; it would be better if there were no universities, and all books except the Bible were burned. Any gifted man may be chosen by the congregation as its minister. Essex plays almost as big a part in Edward's *Gangraena* as does Kent. Baptists, Ranters and

Muggletonians were all to be found there in the forties and fifties. The main Quaker strength was in North Essex, the new drapery region, an area of arable small holdings. After 1660 Essex was the third county in numbers of ejected ministers [Hill, 1975: 37, 263; Reay, 1980].

The Chiltern hills of Buckinghamshire formed another Lollard area, where there was a revolt in 1413–1414. Again heresy survived. In 1521 more were persecuted for heresy in Buckinghamshire than in all the rest of England. A century later Isaac Pennington, the Long Parliament's Lord Mayor of London, later a regicide, came of a family resident in Buckinghamshire since the 1550s. In 1640 the elections of High Wycombe and Great Marlow provided classic examples of class conflict. County freeholders elected John Hampden, and rode up to London in their thousands to defend the Five Members against Charles I's attempt to impeach them in January 1642. Buckinghamshire Levellers sponsored anti-enclosure riots, and produced two pamphlets – *Light shining in Buckinghamshire* and *More Light Shining in Buckinghamshire* – which are close to the Diggers in sentiment, though both were published before digging started at St George's Hill. Winstanley's colony was endorsed by a third pamphlet from the Chiltern Hundreds. *A Declaration of the Wel-Affected in the County of Buckinghamshire* (May 1649). Like Kent, Buckinghamshire had a Digger colony, at the old Lollard centre of Iver, with its own pamphlet (May 1650). There had been Baptists in Buckinghamshire in the sixteen-twenties, and Mr Watts sees general Baptist strength in the county (and in Kent) as a Lollard legacy [Hill, 1975: 21, 117, 126; Cross, 1976; Watts, 1978: 277]. Quakers found an early welcome in the county of Pennington and Penn: High Wycombe was one of the centres of the near-Ranter Story-Wilkinson separation.

Readers of Dickens' admirable *Lollards and Protestants in the Diocese of York* will remember that many of the most savoury Lollard remarks came from the moorland and clothing areas of the West Riding of Yorkshire, another remote region of huge and uncontrolled parishes. Christopher Shuter, vicar of Giggleswick, a nominee of Archbishop Grindal, opened up or revived a radical tradition in the area. In the sixteen-twenties the Pennine valleys produced Grindletonians, who put the spirit before the letter of the Bible, and thought that heaven was attainable in this life; in the sixteen-forties the lower classes in the West Riding forced the gentry to take up arms for Parliament. John Webster, religious radical and would-be reformer of the universities, came from the Grindleton region; George Fox found his first congregations there in 1651, including James Nayler and many other subsequent Quaker leaders. There were Familists in Bradford in the sixteen-thirties, Ranters later [Collinson, 1979: 205–12].

From another Lollard area, Gloucestershire, the reformers William Tyndale and Robert Crowley came in the 16th century, the anti-Trinitarians John Bidle and John Knowles a century later. John Rogers of Colesbourn in 1636 told an audience of young people that women had no souls and therefore could commit any sin without fear of damnation; men could live as wickedly as they wished, confident that they could repent at leisure. The Forest of Dean was an area in which 'people of very lewd lives and conversations' found greater freedom for 'their villanies' than elsewhere; and this too was a heretical region. 'Those tried notorious foresters of Dean' were 'constant friends of the Parliament', 'ever ready to rise against his Majesty's forces' [*Sharp, 1980*]. Levellers and Quakers found their greatest support in south-western England in Bristol. There were antinomians, Brownists and enclosure riots in Gloucestershire in the sixteen-thirties, forties and fifties. There was a Digger colony: later there were Ranters.

The clothing towns of Berkshire (Newbury, Reading) nourished heresy from the 15th to the 17th century. There had been Lollards in Salisbury in 1443, Brownists and Barrowists in Salisbury and elsewhere in Wiltshire in the late 16th century. Mr Watts believed he could trace continuity in Somerset between late 15th century Lollards and 17th century Baptists. Mr Evans saw similar continuity between Lollardy and nonconformity in Norwich. East Anglia generally was a Lollard area. There were Lollards in Ely in 1457, Familists under Elizabeth and Quakers in the mid-17th century. Ely was well known as a haunt of sectaries in the forties, and a recruiting ground for Oliver Cromwell. There were East Anglian anti-Trinitarians in the fifteen-seventies and eighties. There were Quakers in the sixteen-fifties in parts of Cambridgeshire where there had been Familists 80 years earlier [*Watts, 1978: 335; Evans, 1979: 84; Reay, 1980: chapter 2; Spufford, 1974: 351*].

In Lincolnshire, Leicestershire and Warwickshire Professor Jordan suggested continuities between Lollards and Baptists. The Midlands industrial region around Coventry produced Lollards in the 15th century, heretics in the early 16th and again in the early 17th centuries, Ranters in the sixteen-forties and fifties. Celia Fiennes at the end of the century noted Coventry as a dissenting town. In London the parish of St Stephens, Coleman St, harboured heretics from Lollards to Foxe's martyrs and beyond. It had close links with Buckinghamshire and Essex heretics in the fifteen-thirties; in 1628 it produced libels on the Duke of Buckingham; in the forties it was London's most notorious radical centre. Ayrshire, traditionally radical in religion in the 17th century, had been one of the few Lollard areas in Scotland. There were 'Lollards' in Kyle in 1494; there were anti-clerical demonstrations in the county in 1511; heretics were being hunted there in 1537 [*Hill, 1975; Manning, 1976: 210–6; Cross, 1976*].

I do not want to impose too much organizational coherence upon those who transmitted the ideas I have been discussing: that is one of the dangers of historical hindsight. In the fifteenth and early sixteenth centuries the orthodox spoke of 'Lollards'; under Elizabeth of 'Anabaptists' or 'Familists'. There were indeed Lollard and Anabaptist groups, and the Familiy of Love also had so[me] sort of organization. We do not know very much about any of them yet: m[ore] research is needed. But I suspect that clerical inquisitors imposed classificatio[ns,] 'isms', for their own convenience. They started with some idea of what 'Lollards', 'Anabaptists' or 'Familists' ought to believe, just as they started with assumptions about what 'witches' believed. Leading questions would then encourage suspects to conform to the expected type.

So though there were 'Lollard', 'Anabaptists' and 'Familist' trends in popular thought, we should not necessarily postulate the existence of an organized underground. But there are tantalizing hints. A heretical meeting in Colchester in 1555 was so widely advertised that a servant attended from Cambridgeshire. If there was underground organization, itinerants necessarily played a considerable part in it. The clothier Thomas White, involved in Dudley's conspiracy in 1556, carried on treasonable activities under cover of 'collecting the wool'. Humphrey Newman, a cobbler at one time attached to the household of Sir Richard Knightley, was the principal distributor of the Marprelate Tracts in the Midlands and London. A travelling clothier from Berkshire was alleged to be spreading sedition in Chicester in the late sixteen-thirties. Elizabethan Familists are said to have been linked by itinerant weavers, basket-makers, bottle-makers, musicians, joiners. In 1622 Thomas Shepard in Essex knew about the Grindletonian Familists, lurking in the obscurity of a Yorkshire Pennine valley. The clothing industry linked Essex and the West Riding. The Grindletonians were to be associated retrospectively with Coppinger (who had Kentish connections) and the Yorkshire gentleman Arthington, disciples of William Hacket who in the fifteen-nineties believed he was the Messiah [*Spufford, 1974: 247, 351; Hill, 1975: 26–7, 45, 83–4; Thomas, 1971: 134–6; Loades, 1965: 206–7*].

Familists – like Lollards before them – tended when challenged to recant, but to remain of the same opinion still. This unheroic attitude was related to their dislike of all established churches, whether protestant or catholic. Their refusal of martyrdom no doubt helped their beliefs to survive, but it increases the historian's difficulty in identifying heretical groups with confidence. Only after the excitement of the reign of Edward VI were lower-class heretics for a brief period prepared to court martyrdom: after 1660 one suspects that many former Ranters and Baptists reverted to the ways of their Familist predecessors and returned formally and unbelievingly to the national church. The Ranters 'would have said as we said and done as we commanded, and yet have kept their own principle still', said Durant Hotham, stressing this Lollard and Familist way of acting as the main difference between Ranters and Quakers [*Hill, 1975: 257*].

Before 1640 the traditions I have been describing circulated verbally. Historians, themselves the products of a literary culture, relying so much on written or printed evidence, are always in danger of underestimating verbal transmission of ideas. Men did not need to read books to become acquainted with heresy: indeed censored books were the last place in which they would expect to find it. Again and again the great heresiarchs deny being influenced by their predecessors. Luther was astonished to find that he was reproducing Hus's heresies: Milton was astonished and delighted to find that many protestant divines had anticipated his views on divorce.

With all these reservations, let me now suggest some continuing lower-class traditions which burst into the open in the 1640s. There is no need to produce further evidence of the point I have already stressed, class hatred, since this has recently been fully documented in Mr Brian Manning's magnificent *The English People and the English Revolution*. More generalized illustrations of hostility to social subordination are refusal to remove the hat in the presence of magistrates or social superiors, and addressing them as 'thou' in symbolic assertion of equality. The Quakers inherited a long-standing lower-class tradition here. The fifteenth century Lollard William Thorpe kept his hat on in the presence of authority. So did Essex heretics in 1584, William Hacket in 1591, an oatmeal-maker up before the High Commission in 1630, the future Leveller John Lilburne in 1638, John Saltmarsh in 1647, and very many others. John Lewis, burnt at Norwich in 1583 for anti-Trinitarianism, 'did thou each wight'; so did Essex heretics under Elizabeth. Refusal to take the oath is also a rejection of political authority: we find it among Norwich and Essex Lollards, some Anabaptists, Barrowists, Lilburne. Again this was inherited by the Quakers. The myth of the Norman Yoke enshrines a similar anti-authoritarian and anti-aristocratic attitude, rejection of the ruling class and its law. So does the 1381 question, 'When Adam delved and Eve span/Who was then the gentleman?' quoted in the reign of Edward VI, in 1593 and often after 1640 – 'this levelling lewd text', Cleveland called it. Sneers about Jack Straw, Wat Tyler and Jack Cade were frequent. Fuller said the rebels of 1381 were 'pure Levellers'. Sir Thomas Aston referred in 1641 to 'the old seditious argument, that we are all the sons of Adam, born free; some of them say, the Gospel hath made them free.... They will plead Scripture for it, that we should all live by the sweat of our brows [*Emmison, 1973: 126, 309–10; Hill, 1975: 29; Rollins, 1920: 56; Lutaud, 1976: 60; Hill, 1968: 58–125*].

The Digger community at St George's Hill, we now know, was only one of ten or more such experiments; communist ideas are to be found in many writers not directly associated with the Diggers, such as the Ranter Abiezer Coppe and the author of *Tyranipocrit Discovered*; they were attributed to the Leveller Walwyn. John Ball, and Essex, Norwich and Worcestershire Lollards were alleged to have said that property should be common. Similar charges were made against participants in Cade's rebellion in 1450. Such accusations may be the product of the alarmed imaginations of the rich; but since community of property is commended in the New Testament it is unlikely that no lower-class Bible-reader would take the point. An Essex man did, late in Henry VIII's reign: Chelmsford radicals a century later were said to have done so. Tyndale came dangerously near to justifying community of property, and such ideas occurred in the mid-sixteenth century often enough for one of the 42 Articles of 1552 and of the 39 Articles of 1562 to be directed against them. The Presbyterian John Field found it necessary in 1572 to denounce communist theories [*Hudson, 1973; Smith, 1973: 144, 149; Horst, 1972: 147; Tanner, 1977*].

Turning to more specifically religious matters, Essex Lollards said that priests should marry and work, and attacked non-preachers. Pluralism was as bad as bigamy, asserted an Essex Lollard burnt in 1440. Another in the same county 17 years later said that the best man was the best priest, and that confession should be made only to God – anticipating the lay initiative in Puritanism and the sects. John Ball taught that tithes should be paid only by men richer than the priest. Many Lollards opposed tithes. Ministers should not be paid, said Augustine Draper of Essex in 1587; he also denied the immortality of the soul. Opposition to tithes and church courts became standard among the radicals of the revolutionary decades. Wyclif had thought that the exercise of civil jurisdiction by ecclesiastics, and in particular the use of force, was antichristian. So did many 17th century radicals, including John Milton [*Emmison, 1973: 110; Hill, 1971A: 121, 133; Hudson, 1973: 153, 155*].

The 17th century view that a layman is as good as a parson, that the whole ecclesiastical hierarchy is antichristian, that tithes and a state church should be abolished, together with universities as training centres for the clergy; advocacy of 'mechanic preachers' who enjoy the spirit of God, so much more important than academic education: these ideas are so familiar from Wyclif and the Lollards through Anabaptists and Familists to Levellers and sectaries that documentation would be superfluous. Some Lollards seem to have accepted that all believers were priests. Familist ministers were itinerant craftsmen, and indeed the conditions of underground sectarianism forced the emergence of mechanic preachers. Anti-sacerdotalism was a necessity as well as an ideology. Some Lollards, and the reformer William Tyndale, even thought that women might preach [*Tanner, 1977; Hudson, 1973: 151*].

Secondly comes a strong emphasis on study of the Bible, and use of its texts – as interpreted by the individual conscience – to criticise the ceremonies and sacraments of the church. Worship of images, for instance, was denounced as idolatry. Sacredness was denied to church buildings: worship and prayer could take place anywhere. Lollards as well as Edwardian radicals anticipated the iconclasm of the mid-17th century. Essex and Norwich Lollards were accused of scorning infant baptism; so did Francis Kett and Edward Wightman. This looks forward to Samuel Oates, weaver and button-maker, dipping in Essex in 1645–1646 as well as begetting Titus. Millenarianism, familiar in lower-class underground movements, was found among the later Lollards. Around 1580 Familists were alleged to believe that the saints were to judge the world, doctrine repeated by Thomas Collier, Gerrard Winstanley, George Fox, Fifth Monarchists. Ludlow, like John Cook and John Milton, saw regicide as an anticipation by the saints of the Last Judgment [*Thomson, 1965: 240–1; Tanner, 1977; Cross, 1976: 76–8; Moss, 1976: 190*].

Arminianism, the doctrine that men may save themselves by their own efforts, does not seem a particularly dangerous heresy to us today. But it did to orthodox 16th and 17th century Puritans. (We must distinguish between radical Arminianism, rejecting the sacraments of the church as aids to salvation, and Laudian Arminianism). Many 16th century English heretics rejected predestination, attached greater value to works than to faith, emphasized human freedom and effort — a sort of pre-Arminianism, which can be found among Familists as well as among continental Anabaptists, from one or other of whom it was taken over by the English general Baptists. A Kentish heretic, Henry Hart, a 'forward free-will man', who wrote a treatise against predestination in 1554, anticipated Milton in saying that human freedom to choose between good and evil was essential if God was to be absolved of responsibility for evil. There were 'free-will men' in London in 1560. An Essex heretic in 1592 thought that 'all the world shall be saved'; Thomas Edwards in 1646 attributed the idea of universal salvation to Familists and other radicals. It was certainly held by Winstanley and under the 1648 Blasphemy Ordinance was made an offence carrying the penalty of life imprisonment. Thomas Shepard's interest in the Yorkshire Grindletonians led him in 1622 to ask 'whether that glorious state of perfection might not be the truth?' The belief that perfection could be attained in this life had been held by London tradesmen in 1549 and 1631, and by many Familists in between. In the sixteen-forties Saltmarsh, Everard and Winstanley believed that Christ would not appear in the flesh but in the saints. Mrs Attaway and William Jenny did not think it could stand with the goodness of God to damn his creatures eternally: Walwyn was to say that eternal punishment was too great for 'a little sinning' [*Martin, 1976; Hill, 1975; Cross, 1976*].

Another recurrent heresy is anti-Trinitarianism. Some Lollards denied the divinity of Christ and the Holy Spirit. The rapid spread of anti-Trinitarianism both in the liberty of Edward VI's reign and in prisons under Mary gave rise to great alarm among orthodox protestants — so much so that the godly John Philpot had to apologize for 'spitting upon an Arian'. In 1549 an Arian said Christ was a prophet, the Son of God, but only the first-begotten amongst many brothers. This gives rise to thoughts about the connection of anti-Trinitarianism with attacks on primogeniture, familiar later among the Levellers [*Tanner, 1977: 91*].

In 1555 denial of the divinity of Christ by an itinerant joiner, later a well-known Familist, was the subject of illegal discussions in a Colchester tavern, to which servants and husbandmen travelled long distances from outside the county. Some of the Marian martyrs were probably anti-Trinitarians, and between 1548 and 1612 at least eight persons were burnt in England for heresies concerning the Trinity. Among them was Marlowe's friend Francis Kett, grandson of the leader of the Norfolk rebels in 1549, who was also a mortalist, an opponent of infant baptism and of the death penalty for heresy; he rejected the authority of ministers to excommunicate. Marlow, himself from Kent, was said to have called Christ a bastard; in 1560 a Kentish man had said that those who believed Christ sat on the right hand of the Father were fools. The Legate brothers from Essex, one of whom was burnt in 1612, were anti-Trinitarians: so was Wightman, the last Englishman to be burnt for heresy, also in 1612. Their courage made the common people, Fuller tells us, 'ready to entertain good thoughts even of [their] opinions'. When Archbishop Neile in 1639 wished to revive the practice of burning heretics his chosen victim would have been John Trendall, anti-Trinitarian stone-mason of Dover [*Thomson, 1965*].

Anti-Trinitarianism was associated especially with Familists, who rejected the whole theology of the Atonement, Christ's vicarious sacrifice: some abandoned belief in the historical existence of Christ. For them the word Christ was a metaphor for the divine spark which exists in every man. William Pynchon of Essex carried anti-Trinitarianism to Massachusetts in the sixteen-thirties; John Bidle of Gloucestershire, John Milton and very many others proclaimed it in England in the forties and fifties. Quakers and Muggletonians were accused of the heresy. The humanity of Christ enhanced the dignity of man.

Another heresy which recurs among underground groups was mortalism, the doctrine that the soul either sleeps from death until the general resurrection or dies with the body. Professor N. T. Burns has so thoroughly demonstrated the continuous existence of *Christian Mortalism from Tyndale to Milton* that I refer to him for evidence, though with a caution that mortalism existed in England well before the Reformation – among Essex Lollards, e.g. Tyndale was a mortalist. The 42 Articles of 1552 condemned mortalism, though the condemnation was omitted in the 39 Articles of 1562. Elizabethan Familists were alleged to be mortalists, believing that the resurrection occurred in this life. In the 1560s in Surrey and in the 1580s in Wisbech and Wiltshire there were those who believed that the soul was annihilated at death, with no ultimate resurrection. Among mortalists was Augustine Draper of Essex, who also thought the clergy should not be paid, and the anti-Trinitarians Francis Kett and Edward Wightman. Christopher Marlowe was said to be a mortalist; Donne – like Sir Thomas Browne – appears to have toyed with the heresy in his younger days. Mortalism too travelled to New England, where Mrs Anne Hutchinson and Samuel Gorton were accused in the 1630s of being mortalists as well as Familists. In the forties and fifties Richard Overton, Clement Writer, Henry Marten, Lodowick Muggleton and John Milton were some of a large number of adherents to the belief. The Quakers and Henry Stubbe were also accused of the heresy [*Burns, 1972; Emmison, 1973, 110*].

Mortalism was often accompanied by, or led to, a species of materialism. Wyclif, like some troubadours, was said to believe in the eternity of matter. In 1428 the Lollard Margery Backster anticipated Milton in a crude reference to the ultimate physical fate of bread eaten in the eucharist, in order to show that it could hardly be the body of Christ. Dickens quotes many similar remarks. A man from north-west Kent in 1538 denied that God had created him, and many early heretics believed – like Ranters in the 1650s and the rebel angels in *Paradise Lost* – that 'all comes by nature'. Ranters, like Milton, held that matter is good in itself. Such doctrines can by a natural progression lead to anti-ascetism, glorification of the body, a belief that life is to be enjoyed here and now. This may be expressed as an antinomian libertinism: the elect are exempt from the moral law since God is in them; they partake of God's nature. A Lollard lay 'priest' in 1389 was said to believe himself free from the possibility of sin. Such doctrines in England were denounced by Thomas Rogers in 1607. They surfaced in the 1640s. Baxter said in 1649 and 1654 that all men were naturally antinomians, especially the vulgar. Arminianism on the other hand was a heresy of the learned [*Lamont, 1979: 128, 143*]. John Milton is an example of a learned antinomian.

If at death the body returns into its elements, as a drop of water taken out of the ocean returns to it again, mortalism can also lead to scepticism about heaven and hell, which become states of mind rather than geographical locations. Some Lollards denied their existence, and placed purgatory in this world. The devil too was internalized. This could combine with allegorical interpretations of the Bible to make the whole Christian myth describe conflicts which take place only within the believer. Familists were said to hold that Christ and Antichrist were not real persons, heaven and hell not real places. Francis Kett the mortalist thought there would be no hell before the Last Judgment. In Wiltshire and in Somerset in the early 17th century men were denying the existence of a local heaven or hell. A preacher in Lancashire appointed by the Bishop of Chester early in James I's reign thought hell a mere delusion, invented to oppress and torment the consciences of men. In 1619 a Wiltshire heretic was accused of doubting whether the writings of the apostles and prophets were true. Saltmarsh and Everard treated the Scriptures as an allegory, though Everard added 'I deny not the history'. For Winstanley 'it matters not much' whether the Bible was true or not; from his earliest pamphlets he concentrated on their allegorical meaning. James Nayler more cautiously said 'there is no knowledge of heaven or hell'. In the 1620s the Grindletonians, like Thomas Müntzer before them and Gerrard Winstanley after them, emphasized the spirit as against the letter of Scripture, a doctrine not unknown to Milton. A Norfolk anti-Trinitarian in 1579 anticipated the Ranters by saying that the New Testament was 'a mere fable' [*Hill, 1971B: 142–3; Clark, 1977; Quaife, 1979: 64; Hill, 1974: 15*].

The poet Gower in the 15th century described labourers who were not satisfied with the bread and water on which they had been brought up but demanded good food and drink – and did not believe in God. There were 'libertines' in Essex in 1551, and later men who denied the existence of 'sin' and criticised the Bible in a way that looks forward to Clement Writer and Samuel Fisher in the 1650s. One described himself as an atheist [*Hilton, 1975: 24; Horst, 1972: 134*]. Antinomianism led to sexual heresies. Whenever suspected Lollards were up before the Norwich church courts in 1428–1431 they were asked, in a standard formula, if they believed in church marriage. Clearly the answer expected was No. Miss Hudson confirms this from other regions. Some Norwich suspects were accused of advocating community of women – a recurrent charge. 'Marriage is superfluous', the Venetian Ambassador reported heretics as saying in 1499. 'A lewd fellow out of Essex' in 1457 thought marriage should be a civil ceremony; Buckinghamshire heretics taught this in the first decades of Henry VIII's reign, the Barebones Parliament enacted it in 1653. In 1548 it was thought necessary to issue a royal proclamation attacking seditious preachers who advocated divorce. Sixteenth century Familists married and divorced by simple declaration before the congregation. The Yorkshire custom of 'handfast marriages' was taken up by Ranters and Quakers. Some Lollards may have advocated polygamy, though the evidence is doubtful. It was defended in 1548, in Kent in 1572, and by Milton. In 1592 Nashe referred to 'adulterous Familists'. Drunken Barnabee repeated the slander against Bradford Familists in the 1630s. It was entirely in keeping that James Nayler should be accused of saying that 'he might lie with any woman that was of his judgment'. Similar accusations were more plausibly made against Abiezer Coppe and Laurence Clarkson, who in the 1640s advocated free love. Underlying these radical theories of marriage and divorce was the widely attested fact that lower-class attitudes toward matrimony were much more casual and fluid than the ethic which middle-class Puritans wished to impose. Evidence for *de facto* marriage and easy divorce is overwhelming, especially – but not exclusively – among vagrants [*Thomson, 1965; Tanner, 1977; Hudson, 1973; Wrightson and Levine, 1979: 133*].

We isolate heresies for the purpose of analysis, but they normally came in combination. Sir Thomas More linked anti-Trinitarianism with advocacy of common ownership of property. Edmund Leach has suggested that anti-Trinitarianism, millenarianism and social revolt go together, among the early Christians and in seventeenth-century England. Radical Arminianism, rejection of infant baptism, antinomianism, mortalism and materialism were frequently linked with Leach's heresies in England, as Thomas Edwards noted in *Gangraena* in 1646. In the same year the respectable inhabitants of Great Burstead, Essex, saw similar connections. They petitioned against 'a dangerous sect' which had arisen in their parish, admitting and rebaptizing all comers, 'setting up mechanics for their preachers, denouncing the order and ministry of the Church of England as antichristian'. They taught 'unsound opinions' like universal grace, the abrogation of the law, the sinfulness of repentance. Their name was legion, and they had a long pedigree. [*Hill, 1975: chapter 25; Leach, 1972: 5–14; Edwards, 1957: 77–8*].

Looking back to Lollards and Familists helps to emphasise that, if there was a continuing heretical underground, it was essentially composed of laymen. This fits in with what we are coming to know about the initiative in Puritanism of lay members of congregations in refusing to allow their minister to wear the surplice or to conform to other ceremonies. The Puritan clergy were moderate reformers, safely educated at Oxford or Cambridge. They naturally had not much use for lay mechanic preaching. There were initially some Lollard hedge priests, but they counted for less and less with time. Familist ministers seem normally to have been craftsmen.

The church was the official meeting place; and it belonged to the official clergy. The meeting place of the unorthodox was the tavern or ale-house, from Lollards to Familists and on to Baptists, Levellers and Ranters. The only other popular meeting place was the open air; the Quakers preached there. Lawrence Clarkson said that a tavern was the house of God. [*Smith, 1973: 150; Hill, 1975: 200; Clark, 1977*]. The popularity of the ale-house, apart from the obvious reason, was partly due to the evolution of a new itinerant clothing working-class, which sought social intercourse and information about jobs in taverns. JPs deeply resented any attempt to remove control of ale-houses from their hands, whether by Buckingham's protégés Mitchell and Mompesson or by Oliver Cromwell's Major-Generals.

So I suggest as a hypothesis for further investigations that there may have been a continuing underground tradition – not necessarily organization – in which we can identify certain heretical and seditious beliefs. Professor Elton's notorious statement that there was no connection between Lollardy and the Reformation is true only if we interpret the Reformation in the narrowest sense as Henry VIII's act of state. But if we ask why England became a protestant country we cannot leave Lollardy out of account, though it was the more radical protestants who looked back to the Lollards. Bruce McFarlane was right to call his book *John Wyclif and English Nonconformity*. I think we can trace direct links in ideas from Lollards through Familists and Anabaptists to the radical sectaries, the Levellers, Diggers, Ranters and Quakers of the mid-seventeenth century.

This leads on to a final question. What happened after 1660? It took some time to realise that defeat was final, that the above-ground decades had been a mere interlude. In 1678–1681 something surfaced again in London. But the defeat of the radicals in 1685 facilitated the coup of 1688, when Whigs and Tories united against the radicals no less than against James II. Some emigrated to the West Indies, New England and the continent. There were Ranters on Long Island in 1699. Some of those who remained in England no doubt lapsed into silent bloody-mindedness. Some became sectaries; the Quakers cast off their radical wing and became pacifists. All sects were purged by the fierce persecution of the three decades after 1660. They had to recognize that Christ's kingdom was not to be built on earth, but was to be expected in heaven at a date later to be announced.

But the Levellers were never wholly forgotten. Goldsmith praised them. Jefferson quoted William Rumbold, who had been paraphrased by Defoe and cited in an almanac of 1708. There had been men who called themselves Levellers in revolt in Worcestershire in 1670, in anti-enclosure riots in 1724, in Ledbury in 1735, in the Lowlands of Scotland in the 1720s, in the Hudson valley in 1760, other American rebels under William Prendergast in 1765. The Leveller sea-green colours reappeared in the streets of London in 1681, and the Whig Green Ribbon Club took its name from them. London weavers in 1675 had rioted in green aprons, and green aprons soon came to be 'almost regarded as a badge of Quakerism'. The fact that the Chartist flag was green is usually attributed to Irish influence; but why did Irish protestants adopt the colour in the first place? In 1690 William III's troops in Ireland wore green, and some are said to have chosen the Leveller sea-green, so there may be continuity from Levellers through Whigs to United Irishmen and Chartists. At all events the Levellers were still remembered in the Chartist movement. [*Wolfe, 1957: 19; Thompson, 1975: 256; Capp, 1979; Jackson, 1946: 63*]. Was it only because of Robespierre's complexion that Carlyle labelled him 'sea-green'?

Nor is it only a matter of politics. A. L. Morton showed that Blake was aware of the Ranter past, and Burns may have been. How the ideas were transmitted is more difficult to document. A lay clerk of Norwich cathedral about 1700 was alleged to think that 'there is no heaven but a quiet mind and no hell but the grave' – almost a literal quotation from many Ranters. There were people called Ranters in Cumberland, Nottingham, near Inverness and elsewhere at the turn of the century. Wesley in the 1740s met antinomian preachers in the Black Country – an old Lollard/Ranter area – who believed in community of property and did not believe in monogamy. The linked doctrines of mortalism, millenarianism and the perfectibility of man on earth were still being discussed in a Kentish general Baptist congregation in the middle of the eighteenth century. In 1756 the Robin Hood Society met every Monday night at a pub in Butcher's Row, London. Here Deists, Arians, Socinians, Papists and Jews aired their doubts about the resurrection, the incarnation, the Trinity ('their everlasting butt'), the authenticity of the Scriptures, of the Gospel miracles. They were a set of mechanics – tailors, barbers, butchers and shoemakers [*Morton, 1966: 85–121; Hill, 1975: 380–2; Kensley, 1968: 136; Lewis, 1756: v–vi, 19*]. Where did the millenarian revivalism come from which accompanied the American as it had accompanied the English Revolution? What about the New England antinomians of the 1820s and 1830s, whose belief that perfection was attainable on earth led to sexual eccentricities and experiments as it had done in old England nearly two centuries earlier? If we look for them, I think we can find other traces, before 1640 and after 1660. One of the objects of this paper is to encourage others to look.

References

Burns, N. T., 1972, *Christian mortalism from Tyndale to Milton*, Harvard.
Burrage, C., 1912, *Early English Dissenters*, Cambridge.
Capp, B. S., 1979, *Astrology and the popular press*, London.
Clark, P., 1976, 'Popular protest and disturbance in Kent, 1558–1640', *Economic History Review*, XXIX.
Clark, P., 1977, *English provincial society*, London.
Cleveland, J., 1687, 'The rustic rampant', in *Works*, London.
Collinson, P., 1967, *The Elizabethan Puritan movement*, London.
Collinson, P., 1979, *Archbishop Grindal*, London.
Collop, J. (ed. C. Hilberry), 1962, *Poems*, Madison, WI.
Cowley, A. (ed. A. Pritchard), 1973, *The Civil War*, Toronto.
Cross, C., 1976, *Church and people, 1450–1660*, London.
Edwards, A. C., 1957, *English history from Essex sources*, Chelmsford.
Emmison, F. G., 1973, *Elizabethan life: morals and the church courts*, Chelmsford.
Evans, J. T., 1979, *Seventeenth century Norwich*, London.
Fletcher, A., 1975, *A county community in peace and war: Sussex 1600–50*, London.
Gordon, A., 1895, *Heads of English Unitarian history*, London.
Hill, C., 1968, *Puritanism and revolution*, London.
Hill, C., 1971A, *Economic problems of the church*, London.
Hill, C., 1971B, *Antichrist in seventeenth century England*, London.
Hill, C., 1974, *Change and continuity in seventeenth century England*, London.
Hill, C., 1975, *The world turned upside down*, Harmondsworth.
Hilton, R. H., 1975, *The English peasantry in the later middle ages*, London.
Holmes, C., 1974, *The Eastern Association in the English Civil War*, Cambridge.
Horst, I. B., 1972, *The Radical Brethren*, Nieuwkoop.
Hudson, A., 1973, 'The examination of Lollards', *Bulletin of the Institute of Historical Research*, London, XLVI.
Jackson, T. A., 1946, *Ireland her own*, London.
Kensley, J., 1968, 'Burns and the peasantry, 1785', *Proceedings of the British Academy*, LII.
Lamont, W., 1979, *Richard Baxter and the Millennium*, London.
Leach, E., 1972, 'Melchisedech and the Emperor: icons of subversion and orthodoxy', *Proceedings of the Royal Anthropological Institute*.
Lewis, R., 1756, *The Robin Hood Society, A satire by Peter Pounce*, London.
Loades, D. M., 1965, *Two Tudor conspiracies*, Cambridge.

Lutaud, O., 1976, *Winstanley*, Paris.
Macfarlane, A., 1970, *Witchcraft in Tudor and Stuart England*, London.
Manning, B., 1976, *The English people and the English revolution*, London.
Martin, J. W., 1976, 'English Protestant separatism', *Sixteenth Century Journal*, VII.
Morton, A. L. 1966, 'The everlasting Gospel', *The matter of Britain*, London.
Moss, J., 1976, 'Variations on a theme: the Family of Love in Renaissance England', *Renaissance Quarterly*, XXXI.
Quaife, G. R., 1979, *Wanton wenches and wayward wives*, London.
Reay, B., 1980, 'Early Quaker activity and reactions to it, 1652–64', D.Phil. thesis, Oxford.
Rollins, H. E., 1920, *Old English Ballads, 1553–1625*, Cambridge.
Rushworth, J., 1659–1701, *Historical Collections*, V, London.
Sharp, B., 1980, *In contempt of all authority: rural artisans and riot in the west of England, 1586–1660*, Berkeley, CA.
Shepard, T. (ed. M. McGiffert), 1972, *God's Plot*, Massachusetts U.P.
Smith, L. B., 1973, *Henry VIII*, London.
Sprunger, K. L., 1972, *The Learned Doctor William Ames*, Urbana, ILL.
Spufford, M., 1974, *Contrasting communities: English villages in the sixteenth and seventeenth centuries*, Cambridge.
Tanner, N. P., 1977, 'Heresy trials in the Diocese of Norwich, 1428–31', *Camden 4th Series*, XX.
Thomas, K., 1971, *Religion and the Decline of Magic*, London.
Thomson, J. A. F., 1965, *The Later Lollards, 1414–1520*, London.
Thompson, E. P., 1975, *Whigs and hunters*, London.
Watts, M. R., 1978, *The Dissenters from the Reformation to the French Revolution*, London.
Wolfe, D. M., 1957, *The image of man in America*, Dallas.
Wrightson, K., and Levine, D., 1979, *Poverty and piety in an Essex village: Terling 1520–1700*, London.

Religion and peasant movements in Normandy during the French religious wars*

DAVID NICHOLLS

Of all classes in Normandy, the peasantry was least receptive to Protestantism. Between 1520 and 1562 the new religion did make inroads into the countryside in the Pays de Caux, the Seine valley, the Bessin, the Saint-Lô area, the plaine de Caen, and in the immediate vicinity of the larger towns. It reached a peak in the early 1560s and was soon entrenched in a struggle for survival [*Nicholls, 1980*]. The religious geography created before 1562 proved enduring and was strengthened by movements of refugees [*Galland, 1898: xxv-ii, xxxi-ii*]. The areas most affected by peasant movements during the wars and where the Catholic League gained mass popular support were precisely those regions which had ignored the Protestant message from the beginning.

Rural unrest and legal resistance

But localised peasant unrest is detectable in solidly Catholic areas even before the coming of war in 1562. 'Micro-revolts' could break out at any time, but, since there was no major revolt, such as that of Guyenne in 1548, their appearance in surviving local sources is largely a matter of chance. For example it is only through the existence of the *privilège Saint Romain*[1] that we know of the incident in 1559 at the village of Saint-Georges-sous-Mesnil in the Lieuvin. Guillaume Guibel, *laboureur* of that parish, gave a full account of how he had landed in the prisons of Rouen [*ADSM, G2164: fols. 43v.–44v.*]. The sieur de Radepont, accompanied by fifteen or sixteen armed hangers-on, arrived in the village in the spring of 1559 to impound some animals that the inhabitants were grazing on land which de Radepont claimed was part of his fief of Le Mesnil. Guibel, who held his land from another *seigneur*, tried to act as mediator and arranged a

---

* I would like to thank the British Academy for financial support for research for this essay. For comments on earlier versions I am grateful to the editors of this volume and the members of the Early Modern History seminar at the University of Sheffield.

meeting between the two lords and some of the villagers. But de Radepont took matters into his own hands and tried to seize about a dozen animals and the women looking after them. With this initial act of violence by the unpopular *seigneur*, the church bell was rung. When Guibel arrived on the scene he found his father, mother and sister all wounded and defending themselves. Grabbing a stick from his mother, Guibel laid into the attackers, wounding three, one of whom later died. De Radepont instigated a case against Guibel and the other villagers, but, although Guibel was taken and sentenced to death, the other 'accomplices' were nowhere to be found, and the village was still virtually abandoned a year later when Guibel was released under the *privilège*.

Five years earlier, it appears that areas of the forests around Alençon, nearer the epicentre of the later *Gautiers* revolt, were in a state of complete lawlessness. The inhabitants of eighteen villages had on several occasions rung the *tocsin*, attacked forest officials, and even killed the *procureur général* of the duchy of Alençon. *Arrêts* of the Parlement against the villagers were ineffective because no-one dared try to enforce them, and, to make matters worse, many forest officials were in cahoots with the outlaws, happily eating and drinking with those who had been sentenced to death for the murder of the *procureur* [*'Arrêt...'*, *1896–99*].

That these two incidents centred on common lands and forest rights makes them exemplary of many disputes throughout the sixteenth century. Inhabitants of villages in and around forests clung stubbornly to their customary rights against attacks from *seigneurs*, whether noblemen or religious houses, and from the crown. Conflicts were placed before the courts, where they sometimes dragged on for years and often ended in compromise [Procacci, 1955: 73–88]. But when the crown tried one of its periodic 'reformations' of the Normandy forests, with the aim of extracting greater revenue from them, it ran up against a wall of obstruction from peasants, *seigneurs* and forest officials. But the threat of violent resistance was in the air in 1523 when the inhabitants of the forest of Pont-de-l'Arche resisted the letting out of fiefs in the forest, and the commissioners claimed to have been in danger of death from the people of Louviers [AN, J781, pièce l: fols. 7v., 19v.–20r.]. The commission of 1540–41 similarly decided that discretion was the better part of valour when confronted with the villagers of the forest of Evreux [*ibid., pièce 10: fol. 54r.–v.*]. The peasants were here defending both traditional rights and the new encroachments they had made in response to the demographic pressures of the early sixteenth century. They were adept at making excuses, raising objections, playing the game of the law, and thereby fighting the commissioners on their own ground. Two features of these pre-war struggles were to remain constant during the wars: the persistent legalism of the Norman peasants, eager to present their case before the properly-constituted authorities in the belief that their rights rested on legal bases, and the double

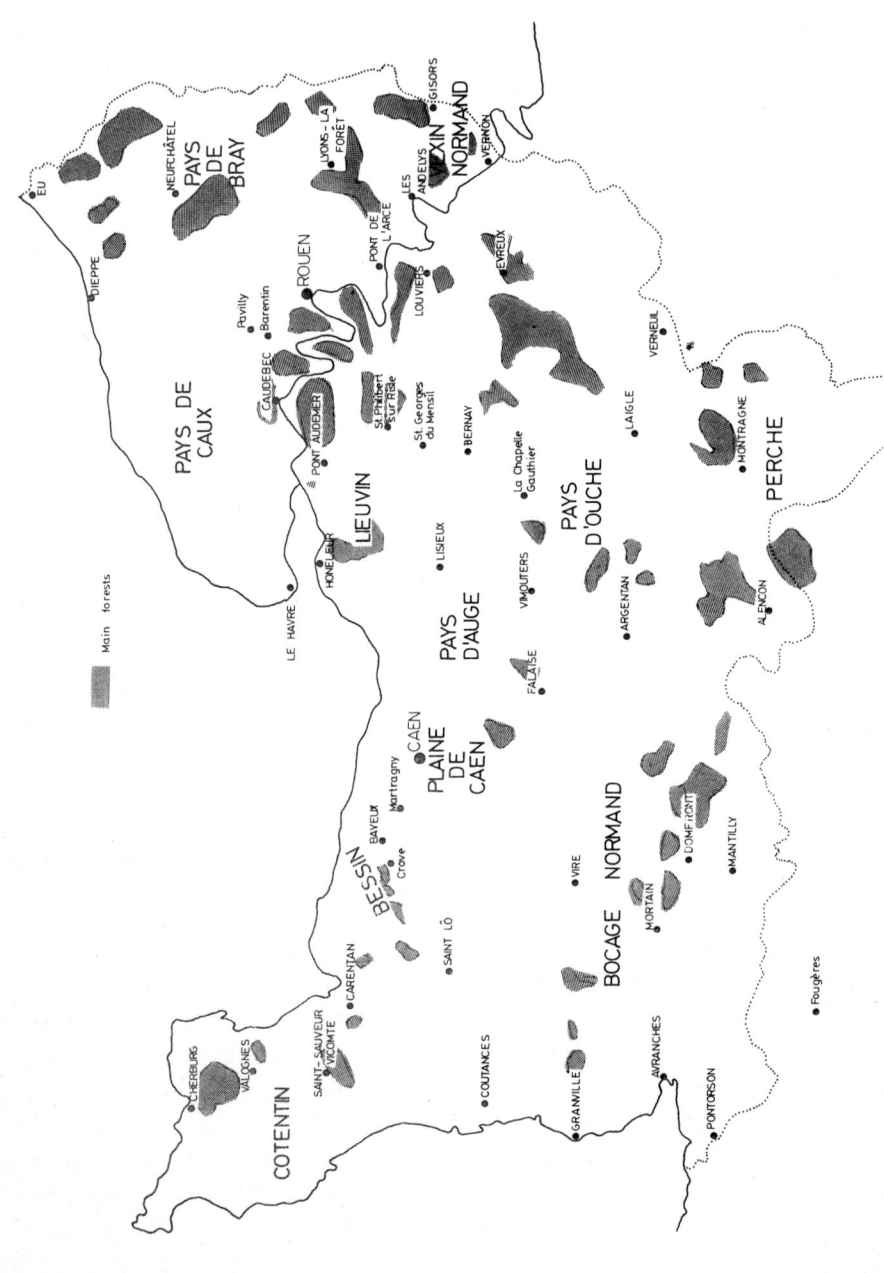

Map 1. Normandy in the religious wars

potential for conflict, on the one hand between peasants and *seigneurs*, and on the other hand local societies united against outsiders, whether agents of the crown or, in the forest of Alliermont, the Archbishop of Rouen.[2]

From self-defence to anti-Protestant violence

With the coming of religious war, however, legalism and obstruction were no longer sufficient means of defence, and the necessity for armed resistance took on a religious colouring. Defence of the village and defence of the church building and fabric against Protestant pillagers went together, and clergymen could often be found organizing it.

At the beginning of the wars in 1562 Protestantism was still an advancing, self-confident movement, and the association of militant Protestantism with the coming of disorder must have sealed the minds of the Catholic peasantry permanently against heresy. In July 1562 Protestant noblemen from Lower Normandy, with the comte de Montgommery to the fore, gathered together a large band of their co-religionists and proceeded eastwards leaving a trail of destruction behind them, throwing down images, pillaging churches and commandeering food from the peasantry [*BN, Ms. fr., 22470: p. 43*]. When they tried to take the priory of Saint-Philibert-sur-Risle, near Pont-Audemer, however, they found that the prior had foreseen events, gathered men, food and arms, and resisted them successfully [*'Discours abbrégé...', 1900: 225–27*]. At the same time, with Protestant-occupied Rouen besieged by a royal army, Protestants from Dieppe, prevented from reaching the city, pillaged the neighbouring villages of Pavilly and Barentin. The inhabitants of Pavilly, who had hitherto kept aloof from the fighting, now turned on all Rouennais and Protestants and killed a Protestant priest from Caudebec [*ibid., 238–39*]. South of the Seine, from Bernay to Laigle and Mortagne in the Perche, parishes chose 'captains', obtained arms and attacked Protestants, going so far, noted the shocked author of the *Histoire ecclésiastique* [*1883–89: ii, 334, 420–21*], as to pillage the houses of their own lords. We do not know whether such organization was used elsewhere, but in the area of greatest peasant resistance it was established from the beginning.

The dividing line between self-defence and hostility towards Protestants, then, became very thin or disappeared. The necessity for armed self-defence was imposed upon the peasantry by the nature of the wars, with bands of soldiery and local warlords loosely committed to one side or another, gangs of disbanded but unpaid soldiers, and more regular royal armies, all living off the land, that is to say the people, pillaging, requisitioning houses and goods, and being generally indistinguishable from the noble bandits and 'adventurers' who had long infested the countryside. The Estates of Normandy, meeting in November 1567, set the tone for the grievances of all classes, and the peasantry above all. In their *cahiers de doléance* they complained about the depredations of the soldiery and the 'infinite number of thieves, vagabonds and others, calling themselves soldiers, committing pillage and robbery on the people'; repeated the traditional but justified complaint that Normandy was overtaxed; demanded that many tax exemptions be abolished and no new taxes imposed; protested at farming of the *taille*; and demanded that Protestants be removed from all offices and their religion forbidden [*États de Normandie, Charles IX, 1891: 1–17*]. These complaints continued at every meeting of the Estates during the wars, with the tone becoming more desperate and the language more flowery as hardship became so unbearable that the Estates' relationship with the crown seriously deteriorated.

An attitude of sullen and watchful defensiveness prevailed through the late 1560s into the 1570s. Although the fourth civil war of 1572–73 was fought largely in the south, 1574, with the death of Charles IX and the fifth war, saw the invasion of Normandy by a Huguenot army under Montgommery. The barely-fortified towns of Lower Normandy were easily taken and just as easily lost, and townspeople fleeing from armies, especially Protestant armies, brought added problems for the countryside [*BN, Ms. fr., 23295: 541–42*]. In 1574 when Montgommery took Domfront only the handful of local Protestants stayed in the town [*Goulart, 1577: iii, 283–93*]. The subsequent slide towards anarchy turned sullenness into intermittent aggression tinged with desperation. In 1575 obscure incidents around Laigle led to surrounding villages being burnt to the ground by a royal army under François d'O [*BN, Ms. fr., 3389: fols. 11r., 12r.*]. Further south a 'popular sedition' was reported in 1577 against de Bouillé's royalist army, while in 1578 tax collectors were attacked in the Falaise area [*Dupont, 1870–85: iii, 519; BN, Ms. fr., 3389: fol. 88r.*]. But these remained localized events. Obscure attempts in 1578–79 to organize a 'League' in Lower Normandy and Brittany against taxation seems to have met with little response [*L'Estoile, 1875–96: i, 275–76, 310; Benedict, 1981: 154*].

The provincial Estates meeting in March 1575 stated categorically that the problems of religion were more worrying to them than those of the king and requested that, in view of the exactions of armed bands, 'we beg His Majesty to give permission to the nobility and the people to assemble at the sound of the *tocsin* and pursue all persons who wish to lodge with others than *hostelliers* and *cabaretiers* without the consent of the said hosts' [*États de Normandie, Henri III, 1887–88: i, 48–49*]. A similar request was made in 1585 when it was apparently intended to take legal action against parishes which had taken arms in this way, and the Estates wanted the proceedings quashed [*ibid., ii, 43*]. The villagers clearly wanted their actions recognized by the law and the crown. With no help coming from the crown and little from the nobility, many of whom were otherwise engaged, the peasants had to take the initiative in defending themselves. Once again, defence of the village and the church went together. The sounding of the *tocsin* — the ringing of church bells for the convocation of the *communauté d'habitants*, often after Mass — was now used to bring them together to defend their lives and belongings [Cf. *Doucet, 1948: i, 396–402; Babeau, 1915: ch. 2*]. Faced with marauders, peasants could either flee, attempt to buy them off (a foolish option), or defend themselves. When defence was organized between parishes it became a revolt, but some kind of ideological cement was needed to bind parishes together. As Antoine Séguier, the king's envoy in Lower Normandy in 1579–80, noted, the iniquities of taxation were not necessarily enough; each parish was concerned with lowering its own contribution, even at the expense of others [*BN, Ms. fr., 18941: fol. 27r.–v.*]. Similarly, in civil wars essentially fought between nobles, upper-class leadership could not provide the necessary cohesion. Those nobles not themselves leading pillaging gangs did support reducing the tax burden on the peasantry out of their own self-interest. The nobility at the 1583 Estates stated this clearly:

> Recognizing that without the Third Estate, which dispenses them from having to embrace the mechanical estate, they could not maintain themselves in their vocations, they very humbly beg His Majesty to reduce the great burden on the Third Estate, which weighs them down with intolerable *tailles* and subsidies which have so denuded them of means that even the said nobility feels the effects of their poverty, and cannot collect the seigneurial rents due to them or find anybody to work and occupy their lands [*États de Normandie, Henri III, 1887–88: ii, 43*].

But the nobility as a whole could not provide leadership. In this situation revolt could take on a hopeless, despairing quality. 'In two or three parishes', wrote Séguier in 1580, 'some badly-advised poor people have thrown themselves naked onto the soldiers' pikes' [*BN, Ms. fr., 18941: fol. 30v.*]. In retrospect it seems that peasants were almost begging for a religious movement to bind them together and give them hope. But the root causes of unrest were not religious.

It only took a certain degree of intelligence and sensitivity to see the real causes of the problem. When in 1579 the population of Martragny, near Caen, attacked a *sergent des tailles* and prevented the punishment of those responsible, the crown feared that nobles would try to profit from popular discontent, and Séguier was accordingly sent to Martragny where he arrested several villagers. But the problem, he said in his report, should be attacked at the root, and this was poverty, due to injustice in tax assessments to the benefit of the rich and the towns as against the poor and the countryside. This was a longstanding conflict in the Caen region, with better-off *laboureurs* setting themselves up as *bourgeois* of Caen to escape the *taille* and the crown making ineffective attempts to stop them [*Fontaine, 1953*]. The consequences of this impotence, Séguier saw, could be dangerous. The peasants were looking to the king for help, but were giving up hope and could join the nobility in disobedience: 'they are beginning to despise their prince, and this evil is trickling down from above. Poor subjects who are born only to obey want to throw off the yoke, a thing never before heard of'. Some nobles, he reported, had abandoned their houses and disappeared to 'places outside obedience to the king'. Some were of the opinion that 'all things were permitted them, going so far as to think that for them there was no law, no magistrate, no control'. The three main causes of misery, he concluded, were the passage of soldiers, injustices in taxation, and the actions of local officers who used any pretext to rob the people and pocketed up to one third of the taxes they collected [*BN, Ms. fr., 18941: fols. 46–54*].

A complete eradication of peasant unrest, then, would have required radical social change. Peasant self-defence had become normal, condoned and even actively supported by the local nobility, but by the mid-1580s it was clear that the more dangerous incidents could develop into widespread lower-class aggression with threatening consequences for the eternal social order. But the monarchy seemed powerless and unheeding of the danger signs, and those nobles who issued warnings to the crown were becoming increasingly frustrated.

When the League was revived in 1584 to exclude Henry of Navarre from the succession it did not gain an immediate response in Normandy. Indeed in 1585 a band of Leaguers in Lower Normandy were forced to retire to their hideout of the château of Neuilly-L'Évêque because of organized opposition to their exactions by the people of the villages between Saint-Lô and Carentan [*Dupont, 1870–85: iii, 536*]. But many nobles and others were sliding towards the League and would be susceptible to the themes of League propaganda. The Estates' *cahier* of 1585 called, for the first time since the early 1560s, for the prohibition and burning of heretical books, but also asked that Protestant sea-captains should be allowed to trade in Norman ports [*États de Normandie, Henri III, 1887–88: ii, 108–09, 126–27*]. Economic interest and religious frustration were here at odds, though by 1587 the future League leader Carrouges was informing the king that food could not be imported because of the activities of Protestant English ships in the Channel [*BN, Ms. fr., 3358: fol. 50r.*]. In 1586 the Estates' tone changed; it became bitter and sardonic. If the province does not get relief soon, they said, they will conceive a bad opinion of His Majesty's intentions. There were now taxes on everything, and the taxers 'have left out nothing, except for taxing air, so that people may not breathe without paying tribute'. They warned bluntly that new taxes and creation of offices would move the people to 'sedition' [*États de Normandie, Henri III, 1887–88: ii, 166–67*]. Both nobles and peasants were thoroughly disillusioned with normal channels of grievance, and it was becoming difficult to find noblemen willing to attend the Estates.

The Estates of 1587 ignored an important order: 'Being advised that M. de Guise... was carrying out his own *arrière-ban* of Caux, and that they were to ask for its revocation, declare that they wish to do nothing against the said sieur de Guise', with the significant clause, 'et principalement les prestres', hooked on at the end [*ibid., ii, 317*]. The threat of adherence to the Catholic League is clear: Henri de Guise was by now in open alliance with Spain, raising men in his county of Eu, on the northern borders of Normandy, and preparing to march against Navarre's German army in the three-cornered contest known as the War of the Three Henries, with a view to making himself master of Paris. The menace of revolt in Normandy was made plain to Henry III at Blois in October 1588: the province had been treated worse than any other; if its remonstrances were ignored even *gens de bien* would be pushed into rebellion; and the king's duty was to maintain the union of the Holy, Apostolic, Roman Catholic religion [*Harangue ..., 1588*]. Unfortunately, although we know of League preaching, we cannot be sure how far printed propaganda circulated in the Norman countryside. We may assume, however, that preachers took up its themes. The strength of this propaganda was in subsuming all the kingdom's and its peoples' problems, including taxation and the sale of offices, into the religious question. The Protestants were responsible for all the evils besetting France, which a return to true religion would put right, and the Catholic people were awakening to put an end to the heresy which had brought down calamity on their backs. This must have confirmed what the Catholic peasantry had always suspected. The point was summed up in a print in the *De tristibus galliae*, published in Lyons, showing a Huguenot monkey holding a sack full of tax money, sitting astride a hobbled and doleful lion of Gaul [*Goulart, 1602–04: ii, 453–54, 550–60; Pallier, 1975: 166–91; Baumgartner, 1976: 109, 114, 154; Blum, 1916: opp. p. 224*]. One pamphlet of 1587 called on the common people to take their revenge on Protestant soldiers, especially Germans, by assembling to pursue them [*Pallier, 1975: 179*]. The Normandy peasants needed no encouragement in this direction, and now some of them could see themselves as part of a broader movement acting in the interests of the whole kingdom.

The *Gautier* revolt and its aftermath

It is not surprising, then, that the League rebellion of 1588–89 encountered little resistance in rural Normandy, and that some peasants made, for a while, common cause with it. Villages cooperated with each other over a wide geographical area for the first and last time when for a short while it seemed that the League was sweeping all before it. The League may, paradoxically, have been seen by the peasants as a way of ending the fighting, replacing a discredited king, throwing out the Protestants, who were to blame for the whole mess, and creating a new authority in which the local clergy would play a prominent role. The clergy, who had made common cause with the Catholic peasantry in 1562–63, were almost entirely pro-League and whipped up enthusiasm with fiery preaching. Caen, Alençon and Dieppe held firm for the crown, as did Vire, Saint-Lô, Saint-Sauveur-le-Vicomte, Cherbourg, Granville, Carentan, Pontorson, Pont-Audemer, and Pont-de-l'Arche [*ibid., 19–20*]. But Protestants and moderate royalists were demoralised and scornful of the crown's inaction. Jacques-Auguste de Thou [*1866: 326*] reported from Dieppe in 1588 that 'he found the minds of the inhabitants, who were almost all Protestants, very strongly against the Guises, and well-disposed towards the king; but, like the people of Caen, they were hiding their feelings, realising that the king preferred to seek comfort, even at the expense of his dignity, than to recover his authority with vigour'.

Montpensier, the new governor of Normandy, arrived at Alençon in April 1589 and, gathering royalist noblemen en route, proceeded to Caen. Seeing the growing power of the League, he decided that decisive action against *ligueur* towns was necessary and accordingly moved off to lay siege to Falaise. But he quickly learned that a League army under the comte de Brissac had gathered around Laigle and Argentan and was marching to relieve besieged Falaise and that this army had with it companies of peasants called *Gautiers*. Thus was the union between the League and peasant unrest consummated, albeit for only a brief period and with ambiguous and treacherous attitudes on the part of the League nobles.

The *Gautier* army had its origins in by now traditional actions against soldiers of all sides and against taxes, but they had come to see Henry III, now in alliance with Henry of Navarre, as the source of their troubles. The name came from the village of La Chapelle Gauthier, said to have been where the revolt originated, and where the inhabitants had been organizing self-defence for the past two years. But rebellion spread rapidly around Bernay and Vimoutiers and became a true confederation, with clergymen joining the ranks and urging them on. They chose 'captains' from the nobility, including the baron d'Eschauffour, Longchamp, governor of Lisieux, and a professional soldier called Vaumartel, and were supposed to be organized under military discipline. Brissac evidently thought that Montpensier, faced with such an army, would give up the siege, but he was disappointed. The royalist commander, clearly believing that attack was the best form of defence, decided to break the *Gautiers* without further ado. The peasant army had grown to be thousands strong, but had no experience of organized offensive warfare. Encamped in villages around Falaise, they were no sooner installed than Montpensier and his *maréchal de camp* Villers attacked them and, at the second attempt, put them to flight. Brissac, who had turned his cavalry loose on the countryside in the usual fashion, stood by and did nothing. The *Gautiers* retreated but determined to defend themselves to the death in

Vimoutiers, Bernay and La Chapelle Gauthier, while Montpensier and Villers, anxious to press home their advantage and gain a first royalist victory in Normandy, pursued them. The *ligueur* warlords definitely abandoned their peasant allies: Longchamp scuttled back to his base in Lisieux, while the others went off looking for Brissac, hoping that he would know what to do. Vimoutiers was attacked first and fell easily; many *Gautiers* were killed, but prisoners were allowed to return to cultivate their land. Bernay, walled and better defended, was more difficult prey for the royalists, but artillery was brought up and in the successful bloody assault many more *Gautiers* killed by undisciplined troops with their tails up. The remaining *Gautiers*, seeing themselves abandoned and outgunned, nominated two priests to negotiate surrender. They thus abandoned their arms and returned to their usual occupations [*Davila, 1801: iv, 65–71; Palma Cayet, 1875: i, 133–34; Goulart, 1602–04: ii, 571–73; De Thou, 1734: x, 600–03; BN, Ms. fr., 23295: 542–43*].

The first royalist success in Normandy, followed shortly by the assassination of Henry III in July 1589, put an end to League hopes of rallying the province as a whole and turned it into the cockpit for the armies of Navarre and Mayenne and their allies. War damage got worse and worse. The officers of the *élection* of Alençon reported in 1590 that for every person not paying taxes through opposition to the crown there were two who could not pay through extreme poverty [*D'Estaintot, 1862: 110*]. This did not put an end to League agitation. Just after Henry III's murder the guardian of the Franciscan house at Bernay was preaching that 'we must kill the king of Navarre; we have started well, but the job must be finished; and all the king of Navarre's followers should get the same treatment as the late king' [*Floquet, 1840–42: iii, 482–83, 492*]. Leaguer monks travelling to Caen probably preached in the countryside, but without getting any response. The fate of the *Gautiers* must have had a considerable effect on the minds of the peasantry as a dreadful warning, and the coalition of Catholic peasantry, clergy and *ligueur* warlords broke down as quickly as it had appeared.

The balance of forces between royalists and the League and the resultant general chaos meant that the two sides and their hosts of loosely-connected bands were all competing to extract taxes and goods from the peasantry. After the collapse of the *Gautiers* Montpensier was extracting food and munitions in Lower Normandy, while the League was grabbing much of the tax revenue [*D'Estaintot, 1862: 24–25*].

On the other hand, there were limits to what could be extracted, and peasants could escape into the forests. After three years of chaos, in June 1592, the Leaguer Parlement sitting at Rouen authorized resistance by villagers against pillagers, and local chiefs on both sides did the same [*ibid., 259–61*]. Shadowy bands of refugees and deserting soldiers, glorified with names like *Lipans*,

Châteauverts and *Francs-Museaux* stalked the forests. The *Lipans* roamed in bands around Alençon in the spring and summer of 1590, while the woods around Cherbourg were also full of robbers [Lair, 1861: 110; D'Estaintot, 1862: 153]. Further east, the forest of Lyons was haunted by gangs of soldiers, brigands and refugees, who were making life perilous for travellers by robbing them and holding them to ransom [Bourgeois de Gisors, 1878: 39–40, 47, 83]. Bands of Leaguers operated from small châteaux, some of which had long been brigands' hideouts, and locals could be fleeced by them or could join with them. While both the royalist Parlement and Henry IV himself saw these as ruinous for the population, in 1593 in the *bailliages* of Alençon and Evreux villagers 'supporting the rebel party' were bringing 'much confusion' to the countryside, especially from the dwelling of a certain sieur de Pleuviers [Floquet, 1840–42: iii, 504–07; iv, 54–58; D'Estaintot, 1862: 119–20; États de Normandie Henri IV, 1880–82: i, 32–33].

In areas outside the influence of a local *ligueur* sheer exhaustion lay at the root of neutrality. The struggle for survival had taken precendence over all other considerations, and the psychological effects of devastation were not outbursts of 'primitive' religiosity or millenarianism, but war-weariness and a heartfelt desire for peace.

A concern about 'atheism' was discernable throughout France towards the end of the religious wars [Cf. Galpern, 1976: 187–88]. Partly this was due to reformist clerics discovering the limits of popular Christianity, but it grew when it did because of people being tired of the religious quarrels which had been tearing the country apart for so long. The Estates of Normandy duly recorded their apprehension in 1593, asking for proceedings of lèse-majesté against 'the blasphemers of the name of God, people given over to all vices, living without faith, law or religion, called atheists' [*États de Normandie, Henri IV, 1880–82: i, 3*]. We do not know if the Estates had any precise groups in mind here. It seems more likely that their fears merely reflected the general mood. The efforts of the League had resulted in nothing more holy than a desire for peace, so that, as far as peasant action was concerned, the religious wars in Normandy ended in a mixture of brigandage and exhaustion. A common proverb of the time – 'in civil war the great play while the common people fight' [BN, Ms. fr., 23296: p. 492] – echoed a worldly-wise cynicism which was no longer transmuted into social or religious radicalism.

The Lower-Norman countryside thus returned to a state of sullen resistance and sporadic unrest after the excitement of the *Gautiers* and was not to see another major revolt until 1639. A constant guerilla action was waged against taxes, but action through legal channels was still the most important means. A collector of the *taille* was murdered in 1617, but such violence was rare until the new demands of the 1630s engendered a rising crescendo of actions against taxmen and soldiers, paving the way for the *nu-pieds* rising of 1639 [*Caillard, 1963: 43–49*].

The historian of the *nu-pieds* notes the participation of lower clergy in the revolt, stating that 'confidence in them seems to be a characteristic and permanent trait of Lower-Norman mentality' [*Foisil, 1970: 203–06*]. This seems exaggerated, especially for the sixteenth century, when many parishes were without priests for long periods. [Cf. *Bourgueville, 1588: 162*]. Priests initially took part in peasant self-defence to preserve their own position and property, then reached their greatest influence during the League, but we have seen that this was temporary. Their literacy made them natural bearers of peasant demands or negotiators of surrender, but there is no evidence that they were necessarily followed, especially in the later stages of the League. Or perhaps the position varied from area to area. The *nu-pieds* rising had six epicentres – Avranches, Coutances, Vire, Mortain, Mantilly, and Domfront – all to the west of the *Gautier* area [*Foisil, 1970: 171*]. When the risings started in the Avranchin contemporaries remembered that Avranches had been 'l'allumette de la Ligue' [*Porchnev, 1963: 314*]. The League encountered virtually no opposition here in 1588–89, so there was no role for a separate peasant army, as the *Gautiers* had been necessary for resistance to Montpensier at Falaise, but once in command the League met with the passive resistance that was always encountered by the holders of power. A pro-League peasant movement in a particular area does not necessarily indicate that the area was unanimously *ligueur*, but is an indication that opposition to the League spurred the peasantry to action.

The original features of the sixteenth-century Normandy revolts are made clearer by comparisons with other regions. Le Roy Ladurie in his study of the carnival of Romans in 1579–80 [*1980: 290 and passim*] has proposed, or rather implied, a sort of grille in which particular episodes may be placed. At one extreme is pure faction fighting in which the lower orders are mobilized in support of quarrels which did not really concern them by leaders from urban élites; at the other extreme is pure class struggle, as occurred at Romans. Most popular insurrections are somewhere between the two, on a sort of sliding scale between one and the other. The Norman case is certainly 'impure'. Peasants initiated action; nobles supported it to defend their own interests; clergy were enlisted as mediators between village communities and the outside world when it seemed as if the League was going to clean out the Augean stables of France. But when it was clear that League overlordship was not significantly different from that of the rightful king and was prolonging the wars into a worse trough than ever, then self-defence, brigandage and non-cooperation were the order of the day. Hostility towards Protestants was ever-present, but not necessarily active.

Revolts in Brittany

A contrast has been drawn between the western revolts, in Normandy and Brittany, which were pro-League, and those of the south and east, straddling the country from the Limousin and Perigord across to Burgundy, which were anti-League [*Le Roy Ladurie, 1977: 835–47*]. Movements in Burgundy between 1592 and 1594, for example, were directed against League armies. They were similar to the Norman revolts in being essentially defensive, but were late and lacked upper-class support [*Drouot, 1937: ii, 288–93*]. But the two-way split should be modified, and Brittany considered as *sui generis*, going much further in both pro-League and anti-noble directions than did Normandy. Right through to 1595 confederations of Breton peasants actively opposed royalist nobles. True, the massacre at Roscanou in September 1590 was partly the result of misunderstanding, when a wedding party was mistaken for a gathering of royalist nobles preparing to wage war through the countryside, but the peasants had no compunction about murdering over ninety nobles at one fell swoop [*Moreau, 1960: 81–84*]. At the siege of the château of Kerouzéré in November 1590 the peasants killed some royalist nobles and wanted to kill the rest, but were restrained by League nobles [*ibid., 66–67*]. The levelling ideas of the Bretons showed themselves in the attempt, also in November 1590, to drive the royalists out of Carhaix. Peasants from over a dozen villages came together by ringing the *tocsin* and imposing their will on nobles, forcing them to lead their bands, but their attack was beaten off. The moralistic, pro-League canon, Jean Moreau, noted the effects of this defeat:

> [It] brought low their arrogance and pride, for they were prepared for a revolt against the nobility and town communities, boasting openly that they would be subject to no-one; and it is beyond doubt that, if they had returned victorious from Carhaix ... they would have attacked the houses of the nobility, sparing no-one of higher condition than themselves. And, by doing this, they said, all would be equal, no-one having power or jurisdiction over others. But God disposed otherwise, for they were so badly beaten at Carhaix, that they became docile and humble where they had been so arrogant [*ibid., 71–76*].

Even allowing for exaggerated upper-class fears, this testimony, coming from an observer on the same side of the political and religious divide, links these movements with the tradition of social radicalism and vestigial Breton nationalism stretching from the revolts of the late fifteenth century to the *bonnets rouges* of 1675. In the later stages of the League the peasants' main enemy was the royalist warlord, La Fontenelle. In June 1593 they besieged the royalist 'safe house' of the château of Le Granec for ten days before La Fontenelle arrived with reinforcements and, according to Moreau, slaughtered seven or eight thousand [*ibid., 117–18*]. Resistance to La Fontenelle did not end until June 1595 when he again massacred large numbers of peasants in a clash at Saint-Germain-Plougastel, near Douarnenez. Moreau was in no doubt as to the peasants' real motives:

> ... [they] wanted nothing other than a revolt against the nobility and all others not of their own estate, which they would have done had they found a leader ... Their intentions [were] to kill everyone except for peasants like themselves, and they did kill many in Cornouailles, even their captains who were leading them. But they were punished in several encounters ... and for every gentleman or soldier whom they killed they lost more than a hundred of their own men, which knocked down their courage to such an extent that they were rendered as docile as lambs [*ibid.*, 222, 281–82].

Such fears as Moreau's, and relief at peasant defeat, may have lain behind Brissac's abandoning the *Gautiers*, but the evidence suggests that the Bretons, now and later, were the nearest thing to 'revolutionaries' that the revolts of the *ancien régime* produced. Here was a genuine alliance of extreme Catholicism and social radicalism, unique in the French countryside [Cf. *Jacquart, 1975: 351–52*].

Comparisons and conclusions

There was less contrast between Normandy and the south than the royalist/League division suggests. The most developed movements were in the south-west, but unfortunately Bercé's massive study of this area [*1974a*] begins only in 1593, thereby abstracting the *Tard Avisés* of the Limousin and Périgord from earlier unrest, such as the localized revolts in 1582 and 1587, indicated elsewhere by Le Roy Ladurie [*1966: 400*]. Their assemblies grew out of earlier meetings for self-defence, but extensive sedition only started in the aftermath of Henry IV's abjuration of Protestantism in July 1593, with most *ligueur* towns and chiefs rallying to the crown. Hopes of peace were therefore associated with the crown, not with purified Catholicism. Nevertheless, there are striking similarities with unrest in Normandy. The *Tard Avisé* assemblies took place in *bocage*-like areas of Périgord in parishes already notorious for tax avoidance; their chiefs were elected peasants, village notables or minor nobles; the miseries of the times, they claimed, were caused by the exactions of the soldiery and the profiteering of upstart officials and the urban bourgeoisie; and they demanded the lowering of the *taille* to its pre-war level, the suppression of new offices, and recognition of the right to take arms against the enemies of the king and the people; they did not seek battle and had no overall plan beyond making their demands heard [*Bercé, 1974a: 257–93*]. Bercé automatically assumes that they had conventional Catholic religious feelings (later in his book he refers to seventeenth-century France as 'a wholly Christian society', without saying exactly what this could mean), but recognizes that the peasantry was weary with fighting over religion and could see that it was often merely a pretext for fighting among nobles [*ibid., ii, 666*].

Even in the southeast, where a much more complicated series of alliances between religious parties and peasants operated from 1575 onwards, similar basic features are recognizable. In the Vivarais between 1575 and 1580 the fundamental cause of unrest was the reign of terror inflicted by the warlords, but since the Catholic segment of the local Estates was levying taxes to pay for garrisons, Catholic peasants collaborated in resistance with Huguenot notables [*Salmon, 1979*]. While in Dauphiné, despite the social radicalism of the peasantry, fiscal problems were the focal point for numerous causes of rebellion, and the nobles' tax exemptions was 'the matrix of plebeian frustration' [*Le Roy Ladurie, 1980: 35–59*]. In Brittany and to a lesser extent in Normandy the League became another 'focal point', or rather two lenses, fiscal and religious, created a single focal point and briefly burned up the map of the western provinces.

It is possible, then, looking beneath the royalist/League division, to propose an alternative geography of peasant revolt, linking Normandy with the south-west and viewing Brittany and Daupiné as separate cases. Brittany was also exceptional in that League commitment persisted after 1590. Porchnev [*1963: 47*] placed the revolts of 1593–96 in a different cycle from those of 1570–90, seeing them as a progression beyond the influence of religion. But other writers have claimed that the sixteenth-century revolts show a greater element of class conflict than those of the seventeenth [e.g. *Davies, 1973: 123–24; Salmon, 1967: 41–42*]. Certainly, a 'long cycle' of revolt, essentially unchanging from the sixteenth century to the nineteenth can only be discerned (or artificially constructed) by virtually ignoring the revolts of the religious wars [*Bercé, 1974b: 49–50* and *passim*]. The religious content is evidently part of this difference, but a closer examination reveals several paradoxes.

Throughout the sixteenth century the Parlementaires of Rouen, many of whom were acquainted with peasants through their ownership of rural *seigneuries*, viewed the people of the countryside as fundamentally dangerous. The religious wars, they thought, showed that 'the peasants belong to no party' and that outside pressures, especially taxation, turned them away from their natural obedience. Urban people they saw as more intense in religious feelings and therefore more likely to join warring parties [*Dewald, 1980: 60–61*]. The experience of the League seems to bear out the magistrates' view. The main contrast is perhaps not between urban and rural as such, but rather between those large cities that experienced a popular League movement and the rest of the country. The small towns of Lower Normandy were too much the prey of opposed armies to develop autonomous religious characteristics. But in the

Parlementaires' own city of Rouen the League was accompanied by an extraordinary (if temporary) upsurge of penitential piety embodying an impulse towards communal purification based on religious feeling as a source of safety and solidarity in the city [*Benedict, 1981: ch. 8*]. There is no evidence of a similar religious fever at village level. This may be related to the different effects of war on a city asserting its civic liberties against the nascent absolutist state and an undefended village taking arms to save itself from undisciplined rabbles turned loose to live off the land; between a siege mentality and a survival mentality.

Norman opposition to the state during the religious wars was, as nearly always in early modern Europe, justified by appeals to the past: taxes should be reduced to the level of Louis XII's reign, new offices and 'innovations' of all kinds should be suppressed. The League in the cities, however, was able to combine the new elements of Counter-Reformation piety with 'medieval' appeals to communal identity in opposition to monarchical centralization [Cf. *Barnavi, 1978*]. Neither of these components existed in the countyside. The cadres of Counter-Reformation religiosity – oratories, the new orders, penitents – had not yet penetrated the villages, leaving a less fervent religion, in the words of one historian: 'less fuddled with theology' [*Kiernan, 1980: 95*]. Thus the religious justification for revolt was also an appeal to the past, not the expression of a new militant piety.

Le Roy Ladurie [*1980: 95*] notes that the Dauphiné movement was 'no brutal *jacquerie*, no peasant uprising in the usual and often pejorative sense of the word'. This raises the question of how many French peasant revolts ever conformed to the 'pejorative view'. Le Roy Ladurie himself also points out that popular revolt in the late sixteenth century 'drew on an ethical, religious value system implicitly understood by the people'. Justice and God were on their side against 'thieves' and 'robbers of the people' [*ibid., 69. Cf. Berce, 1974a: i, 272–77; Salmon, 1979: 26–28*]. The appeal to the past was in reality a demand for greater justice, which inevitably took on a class nature and radical appearance. The alliance with the League strengthened this appearance simply by opposing the monarchy, going beyond the normal peasant cry of '*Vive le roi – sans taille et sans gabelle!*'. But the League promised the removal of the hated Valois only to replace him with another king who, if experience of local *lingueurs* was anything to go by, would be just as bad or worse. The League thus provided a very limited alternative, temporarily overcoming the mood of resignation and legitimating resistance, but giving no realistic hope for a radical re-ordering of society. Peasant religion was a support to a system of law and moral economy, based firmly on the rationality of a precarious economic system. Revolts occurred in regions with what was still fundamentally a subsistence economy. Maintaining control over scarce resources was here of vital importance, hence the defence of communal rights. Rural economic transactions took on an ethical content, hence the demand that tithes should be used only for the support of conscientious priests, as part of a two-sided deal. *Curés* who took part in the defence of the community and presented its demands were perceived as fulfilling their part of the bargain, which must have helped the League until it became clear that the priests could not deliver lasting peace. Evidence from the Breton revolt of 1675 suggests that priests were judged by their actions: those supporting the rebellion were treated with respect, but those who were against it were attacked [*Garlan and Nières, 1975: 128–32*]. In sixteenth-century Normandy priests were not attacked: they were either followed or, possibly most of the time, ignored. Peasant 'conservatism' was thus not a backward-looking dreaming, but a moral-*cum*-religious rationality with its roots in the local economy. The Parlementaires thought peasants dangerous because they had a tendency to ignore legal pronouncements that went against their moral view of economic relations, a view which they were convinced was enshrined in just laws, hence the co-existence of legalism and turbulence.

The abiding impression left by the peasant movements in Normandy is indeed one of overriding reasonableness. Movements started in self-defence, for which official approval was sought, with no instances of unbridled peasant aggression against the innocent. The exact nature of religous feelings, apart from the early stages of the League, is difficult to determine, but it is clear that we can make no automatic assumptions based on ideas of a 'totally Christian society'. We can guess at an elementary Christianity or Deism based on a firm morality and resistance to a Protestantism associated with outsiders who first appeared as agents of destruction. Peasant action tended to strengthen the village community and thus to preserve existing religion. The desire for good priests, supported by just tithes and doing their duty to the community, was one aspect of a 'conservatism' which, if applied, would have led to enormous changes in society. But struggle for survival overrode all other concerns because it was based in the harsh reality of the local economy, and because the wars brought such destruction and chaos. Religious emotionalism was not allowed to interfere with this most basic of human concerns.

Notes

(1) This was a privilege belonging to the cathedral chapter of Rouen, which on the feast day of Saint Romain every year had the right to release a prisoner of their choice from the civil or ecclesiastical prisons, provided that he made a full confession of his crimes.
(2) For the reformation of 1550–56 see AN, Z1E 1131 and 1132, and the Archbishop's attempts at reformation of his forests in 1548 may be traced in AN, Z1E 1130.

References

ADSM = Archives Départementales de la Seine-Maritime (Rouen).
AN = Archives Nationales (Paris).
BN = Bibliothèque Nationale (Paris).

'Arrêt ...', 1896–99, 'Arrêt du Parlement de Normandie pour la rèpression de la révolte des usagers des forêts du duché d'Alençon, 1554', *Bulletin de la Société de l'Histoire de Normandie*, 10: 363–366.
Babeau, A., 1915, *Le village sous l'ancien régime*, Paris.
Barnavi, E., 1978, 'Centralisme ou fédéralisme? Les relations entre Paris et les villes à l'époque de la Ligue (1585–1594)', *Revue historique*, 256: 335–344.
Baumgartner, F. J., 1976, *Radical Reactionaries: the Political Thought of the French Catholic League*. Geneva.
Benedict, P., 1981, *Rouen during the Wars of Religion*, Cambridge.
Bercé, Y.-M., 1974a, *Histoire des croquants. Étude des soulèvements populaires au XVIIe, siècle dans le sud-ouest de la France*, 2 Vols. Paris and Geneva.
Bercé, Y.-M., 1974b, *Croquants et nu-pieds*, Paris.
Blum, A., 1916, *L'estampe satirique en France pendant les guerres de religion*, Paris.
Bourgeois de Gisors, 1878. *Journal d'un bourgeois de Gisors (1588–1617)*, ed. H. Le Charpentier and A. Fitan, Paris.
Bourgueville, C. de., 1588, *Les recherches et antiquitez de la province de Neustrie, à présent duché de Normandie, comme des villes remarquables d'icelle: Mais plus spécialement de la ville et université de Caen*, Caen.
Caillard, M., 1963, 'Recherches sur les soulèvements populaires en Basse-Normandie (1620–1640) et spécialement sur la revolte des nu-pieds', in *A travers la Normandie des XVIIe, et XVIIIe, siècles* (Cahiers des Annales de Normandie, No. 3), pp. 23–152.
Davies, C. S. L., 1973, 'Peasant Revolt in France and England: a Comparison', *Agricultural History Review*, 21: 122–134.
Davila, E. C., 1801, *Storia delle guerre civili di Francia*, 6 Vols. London.
D'Estaintot, R., 1862, *La Ligue en Normandie, 1588–1594*, Paris, Rouen and Caen.
De Thou, J.-A., 1734, *Histoire universelle*, 16 Vols, 'London' (Paris).
De Thou, J.-A., 1866, 'Mémoires de Jacques-Auguste de Thou depuis 1553 jusqu'en 1601', in Michaud and Poujoulat, *Nouvelle collection des mémoires relatifs à l'histoire de France*, XI, Paris.
Dewald, J., 1980, *The Formation of a Provincial Nobility: the Magistrates of the Parlement of Rouen, 1499–1610*, Princeton: Princeton University Press.
'Discours abbrégé...', 1900. 'Discours abbrégé et mémoires d'aulcunes choses advenues tant en Normandye que en France depuis le commencement de l'an 1559, et principalement en la ville de Rouen', in *Deux chroniques de Rouen*, ed. A. Heron, Rouen: Société de l'Histoire de Normandie.
Doucet, R., 1948, *Les institutions de la France au XVIe siècle*, 2 Vols, Paris.
Drouot, H., 1937, *Mayenne et la Bourgogne: Etude sur la Ligue (1587–1596)*, 2 Vols, Paris.
Dupont, G., 1870–85, *Histoire du Cotentin et de ses îles*, 4 Vols, Caen.
États de Normandie, Charles IX, 1891. *Cahiers des États de Normandie sous le règne de Charles IX*, ed. C. de Robillard de Beaurepaire, Rouen: Société de l'Histoire de Normandie.
États de Normandie, Henri III, 1887–88. *Cahiers des États de Normandie sous le règne de Henri III*, ed. C. de Robillard de Beaurepaire, 2 Vols, Rouen: Société de l'Histoire de Normandie.
États de Normandie, Henri IV, 1880–82. *Cahiers des États de Normandie sous le règne de Henri IV*, ed. C. de Robillard de Beaurepaire, 2 Vols, Rouen: Société de l'Histoire de Normandie.
Floquet, A., 1840–42, *Histoire du Parlement de Normandie*, 7 Vols, Rouen.
Foisil, M., 1970, *La révolte des nu-pieds et les révoltes normandes de 1639*, Paris.
Fontaine, A., 1953, 'Conflits à propos de la taille entre bougeois de Caen et habitants de la campagne aux XVIe. et XVIIe. siècles', *Annales de Normandie*, 3: 227–245.

Galland, J.-A., 1898, *Essai sur l'histoire du protestantisme à Basse-Normandie de l'edit de Nantes à la révolution (1598–1791)*, Paris.

Galpern, A. N., 1976, *The Religious of the People in Sixteenth-Century Champagne*, Cambridge, Mass.

Garlan, Y. and Nières, C., 1975, *Les révoltes bretonnes de 1675*, Paris.

Goulart, S., 1577, *Mémoires de l'estat de France sous Charles neufième*, 3 Vols, n.p.

Goulart, S., 1602–4, *Mémoires de la Ligue*, 3 Vols, n.p.

Harangue..., 1588. *Harangue faicte au roy par un députté de la ville de Rouen, dans son cabinet à Bloys, le 27 octobre 1588*, Paris.

Histoire ecclésiastique, 1883–89. *Histoire ecclésiastique des églises réformées au royaume de France*, ed. G. Baum and E. Cunitz, 3 Vols, Paris.

Jacquart, J., 1975, 'Immobilisme et catastrophes, 1560–1690', in E. Le Roy Ladurie (ed.), *Histoire de la France rurale, Tome 2, L'âge classique des paysans*, 175–353, Paris.

Kiernan, V. G., 1980, *State and Society in Europe, 1550–1650*, Oxford.

Lair, J., 1861, *Histoire du Parlement de Normandie depuis sa translation à Caen au mois de juin 1589 jusqu'à son retour en Rouen en avril 1594*, Caen.

Le Roy Ladurie, E., 1966, *Les paysans de Languedoc*, 2 Vols, Paris.

Le Roy Ladurie, E., 1977, 'Les masses profondes: la paysannerie', in F. Braudel and E. Labrousse (eds.), *Histoire économique et sociale de la France. Tome I: de 1450 à 1660, Vol 2, Paysannerie et croissance*, 483–865, Paris.

Le Roy Ladurie, E., 1980, *Carnival: a People's Uprising at Romans, 1579–80*, London.

L'Estoile, P. de., 1875–96, *Mémoires-journaux de Pierre de L'Estoile*, ed. Brunet et al., Paris.

Moreau, J., 1960, *Mémoires du chanoine Jean Moreau sur les guerres de la Ligue en Bretagne*, ed. H. Waquet, Quimper: Archives Départementales.

Nicholls, D., 1980, 'Social Change and Early Protestantism in France: Normandy, 1520–1562', *European Studies Review*, 10: 279–308.

Pallier, D., 1975, *Recherches sur l'imprimerie à Paris pendant la Ligue (1585–1594)*, Geneva.

Palma Cayet, 1875, *Chronologies novenaire et septenaire*, ed. J. A. C. Buchon, 2 Vols, Paris.

Porchnev, B., 1963, *Les soulèvements populaires en France de 1623 à 1648*, Paris.

Procacci, G., 1955, *Classi sociali e monarchia assoluta nella Francia della prima metà del secolo XVI*, Turin.

Salmon, J. H. M., 1967, 'Venality of Office and Popular Sedition in Seventeenth-Century France', *Past and Present*, 37: 21–43.

Salmon, J. H. M., 1979, 'Peasant Revolt in Vivarais, 1575–1580', *French Historical Studies*, 11: 1–28.

Religion and rural revolt

in the French Revolution: an overview

T. J. A. LeGOFF and D. M. G. SUTHERLAND

As in so many other aspects of French life, Lucien Febvre's injunction 'que la France se nomme diversité' is so evident to those who have spent even a little time studying the religious history of the French Revolution as to be a truism. Small wonder, then, that there seems little connection between the attitudes and behaviour of the Breton or Vendean peasant who took up arms, as his banners proclaimed, *'pro aris, rege et focis'* (with the accent on the first of the three) and the peasant of the South-East who assisted, more or less approvingly, in the Year II, at the local 'dechristianisation' ceremony, with the obligatory parade of the members of the local *société patriotique* decked out in ecclesiastical vestments, the profanation of the sacred species, the resignation of the parish priest, and the brave speech against fanatical prejudice, the whole brought to a triumphant conclusion by the *curé*'s marriage to a suitable patriotic spinster. Between such events, what possible common ground can there be? Nevertheless, if only for the sake of swimming against the tide, it is worth considering the relation between religion and the rural manifestations of the French Revolution in a common framework, one defined by Georges Lefebvre as 'a peasant revolution with its own autonomy in its origins, its action, its crises and its trends'. [*Lefebvre, 1933: 342–3*]. This peasant revolution, he made clear, was a movement of emancipation from the economic oppression of lay and ecclesiastical seigneurs, but it also included the struggles of tenants against their landlords and the tensions between rich and poor within the peasant community.

Lefebvre, however, thought of the autonomous peasant revolution as taking place within rather narrow limits. It provided part of the motive force for the political revolution in Paris because, down to the end of the radical phase of the political movement in 1794, marked by the fall of Robespierre and the onset of the Thermidorean reaction, there was always one more peasant discontent which could be satisfied at the expense of the *ci-devant* by the latest team of radical politicians in the National Assembly. The peasant revolution, like the Paris crowd, had its *grandes journées*: the anti-seigneurial revolts and the blind panic of the Great Fear which between them swept across most of provincial France in the summer of 1789, anarchic upheavals which so frightened the new Constituent

Assembly that it decided against its will to 'abolish entirely' the 'feudal regime' on August 4/5 1789, only to water down this achievement in the enabling legislation of the subsequent year; the peasants' disappointment and their violent reaction at this reneging; and the subsequent attempts by the radical rump of the Legislative Assembly once again to 'abolish feudalism' when the conservative politicians had fled Paris after the fall of the Monarchy on 10 August 1792; and the Jacobins' bid for rural support in eliminating the final vestiges of manorial tenure in July 1793.

Since Lefebvre's time, much research has focused upon a subject which he omitted from his general synthesis of peasant activity in the French Revolution: the origins of popular counter-revolution. These uprisings, once left to the fact-grubbers of royalist, clerical and jacobin historiography in search of further proof of the rightness of their particular causes and the wickedness of their opponents[1] and dismissed by mainstream historical writing on the Revolution as mere 'Church and King' riots [e.g. *Rudé, 1964: 135–7*] have aroused considerable interest since the early 1960s. Much of this interest is owing to the attempts to apply modernisation theory to them. This approach, which has been widely employed in the analysis of twentieth-century rural revolts, holds, in general terms, that peasant communities are ripe for revolt when they are dragged from a subsistence to a market-oriented economy. The disruption this causes to traditional ways of thought and habit, to the positions of established elites, to relations with the state and to time-honoured social relationships makes these communities highly vulnerable to social disorder. In various forms, the traumas of modernisation have been invoked by several historians as the ultimate explanation for the rebellion of the West in 1793, the White Terrors and their antecedents in the South in 1790–1801 and 1815, and the 'jacquerie' in the Midi in 1851.[2]

It seems appropriate, then, to examine the relation between religion and rural revolt in the French Revolution with these two complementary purposes in mind: to stretch Lefebvre's notion of a peasant revolution to include the popular counter-revolutionary movements of the 1790s and to test the usefulness of modernisation theory in explaining these rebellions.

By 1793, religion was in the camp of the counter-revolution, and those peasants who sympathized with the fate of the Church or stood up in its defence were out of the revolutionary movement as it has been traditionally described. The story has often been told of how the wish to help the parish clergy, extirpate abuses, and adapt the organisation of the Church to a changing country soured when the reforms were rushed through, without any consultation with the Gallican Church or the Pope, by an impatient Constituent Assembly eager to assert its absolute jurisdiction over all affairs within the French hexagon, and anxious to use Church lands to settle the unpaid bills of the old regime. A loyalty oath, to be taken in public, was foisted on the erstwhile parish clergy, now transformed into salaried and elected public servants as *ecclésistiques fonctionnaires publics*. In all, two fifths refused, rather more of the parish priests and rather less of their assistants; and of course in proportions which varied widely from one part of France to the other.³

It has often been pointed out, too, how this series of decisions by the National Assembly gave for the first time a mass following to the counter-revolutionaries, who up to then had mainly consisted of disgruntled nobles. A large body of Frenchmen — and, naturally, a large body of peasants — took sides with those clergymen who refused this and subsequent oaths. From here, it might seem, it was a short step to the mass risings of the Vendée and Brittany in March 1793, which were triggered by the Republic's demand for 300,000 men for the army, but in which discontent with the religious changes of the previous two years played a large part. Religion and rural revolt thus became religion and counter-revolutionary rural revolt.

Yet such a view is both narrow and superficial. Indeed, religion in the sense of a central cluster of beliefs and a traditional liturgy was rarely an issue during the Revolution, except perhaps during the ephemeral episode of 'dechristianisation' in 1793–4.⁴ Otherwise, whatever their private thoughts, the authorities seldom seriously attempted to impose new beliefs or practices on the countryside. Rather, the Civil Constitution of the Clergy and the legislation which flowed from it were attempts to reorganise the internal structure of the Gallican Church and its relation to civil society. The politicians and officials had a point when they claimed that abolishing the tithe, selling Church property, redrawing parish and diocesan boundaries, imposing lay election of priests and bishops and abolishing convents and monasteries challenged no fundamental religious beliefs or practices. In a wider sense, of course, apologists for the Church could claim that the revolutionaries were meddling in affairs that were no concern of theirs, that the Church had property rights too, that dissolving monastic vows or tampering with the hierarchy of authority was in a way just as corrosive of religion as an assault on dogma or liturgy.

These issues were the ones which revolutionaries and Catholic apologists debated in the Assembly, in pulpits, pamphlets, clubs and in the public place during the years 1790–1, and they occupy pride of place in religious histories of the Revolution down to this day. However, they do not precisely translate the questions in the way that laymen, particularly the mass of ordinary Frenchmen, saw them. A peasant who marched into battle with an image of the Sacred Heart stitched to his smock was not risking death merely for casuistical distinctions. For him, the Revolution was a series of changes which had altered for the worse his situation as a parishoner, as a citizen and as a taxpayer. It had also changed, often dramatically, his relationship with his neighbours, his former seigneur and his landlord, if he was a tenant farmer. In short, the laity's decision to support or reject the Civil Constitution of the Clergy and its attendant legislation depended a great deal upon the total effect of the Revolution, and particularly of its social legislation, on a given rural community. Peasants who supported the Church did not necessarily give up other aims which can be classed as revolutionary, ambitions which were often frustrated by the Revolutionary settlement of tenurial questions.

To attain a balanced assessment of the impact of that settlement throughout France on the basis of existing research is difficult, and only more or less informed estimates are possible. Lefebvre himself stressed that middling and poor peasants – the vast majority of Frenchmen in other words – got little or nothing from the sales of ecclesistical or émigré property, were completely frustrated in their attempts to stop the engrossing of land or leases and received less than they had hoped from the abolition of tax privilege, seigneurial dues and the tithe. It is possible to go even further and claim that rampant inflation, poor harvests, more or less indiscriminate requisitioning of victuals and animals and conscription of young men made their lives miserable for much of the time. Yet only certain regions were so outraged by the secular and religious reforms of the Revolution that they rejected it utterly. These regions are well known and can be identified in an approximate way on Donald Greer's map [*1935, frontispiece*] of the frequency of executions during the Terror: the Departments of the Pas-de-Calais and the Nord, the area west of an imaginary line running from Caen through Le Mans and ending around Poitiers, the zone lying along the Rhône valley south of Lyon to the Mediterranean coast and extending westwards through the departments of the South-West, which were to be the scene of a great rising against the Republic in 1799[5] (see map no. 2). In all these parts of the country, it can be argued, the material damage done by the Revolution so outweighed its benefits that defending the local priest against the revolutionary authorities became a way of manifesting discontent. For people in these regions, protests against the new regime's demands for a show of loyalty – such as the obligation imposed on parish priests to take an oath to the Civil Constitution of the Clergy – became the occasion for a kind of plebiscite against the regime. The results of plebiscites are rarely to be explained solely by reference to a single variable; they require an explanation in terms of patterns of political choice and social conflicts within given communities. In short, because religion had become counter-revolutionary, did this mean that peasants in revolt had ceased to be revolutionary? Or was their continuing struggle in the name of a religious cause, firmly and sincerely upheld, also a way of continuing other social conflicts?

The religious policies of the Revolution provoked widely varying reactions among country people. In many regions, the response seems to have been muted,

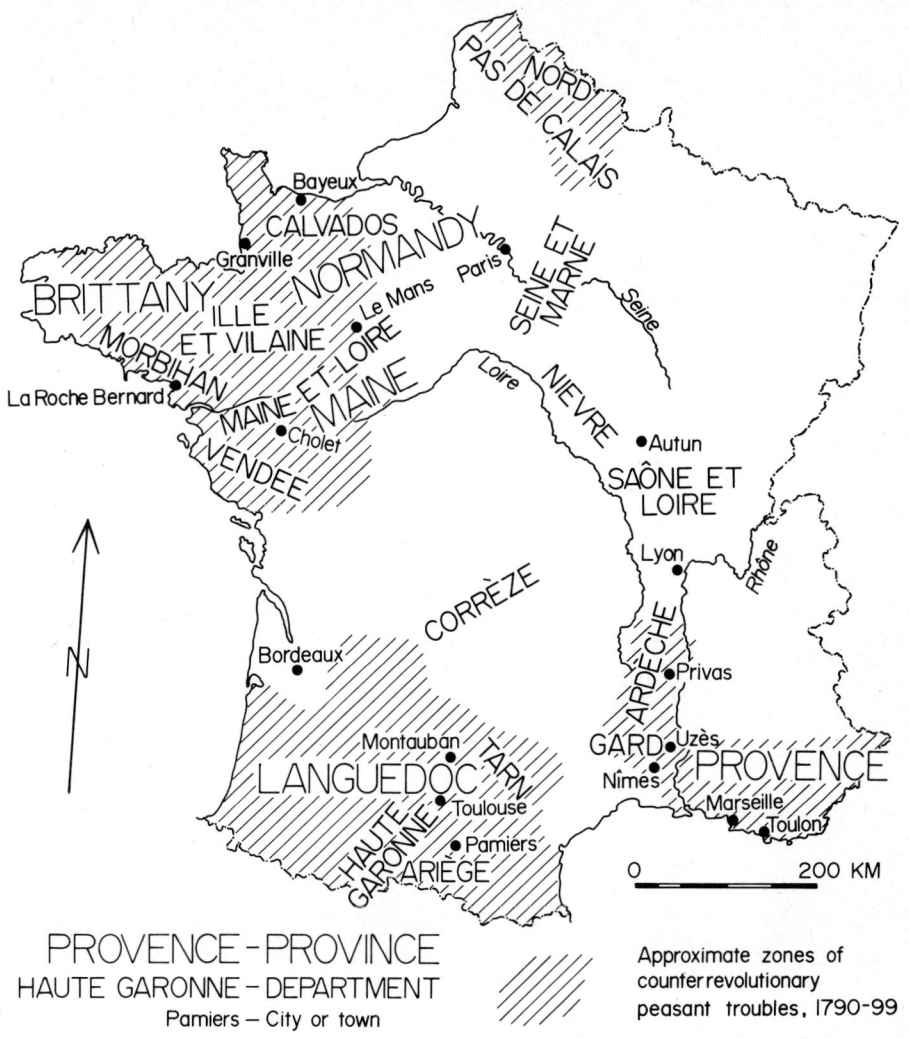

Map 2. Peasant movements during the French Revolution

ranging from nostalgia for better times to grumbling discontent which only sporadically became violent. For example, the inhabitants of Chartres-de-Bretagne, despite the local reputation of their parish as a republican outpost in a violently counter-revolutionary region, nevertheless petitioned the Convention in 1795 to have their old priest returned because, they said, 'nous en avons besoin pour nous consolé (sic) dans nos peines et nos malheurs. Nous ne voulons point vivre comme des bêtes, comme nous avons déjà fait pendant trois ans.'[6] In the Department of the Nièvre, where the dechristianisation campaign of the winter of 1793–4 was notoriously violent, a crowd of women petitioned the administrators of the District of Corligny, claiming:

> qu'elles entendaient reprendre l'exercice de leur religion, qu'elles voulaient vivre et périr pour elle, qu'elles exigeaient la remise sur le champ de leurs cloches et ornements ainsi que le libre usage de l'église pour y faire célébrer, les jours de dimanche et de fête, les offices de la religion qu'elles professaient ... [*Charrier, 1926: I, 354*].

At Vidouville, in the Calvados, women were so ashamed of having received communion from the constitutional priests that they later had their tongues scraped [*Hufton, 1971: 165*]. The Seine-et-Marne was another peaceful region, yet even here, so joyful were the countrypeople to learn of the Convention's decree of December 1793 guaranteeing freedom of religion that they invaded the Jacobin club of La Ferté-Gaucher to retrieve confiscated religious objects. For roughing up a few astonished Jacobins in the process, no less than 800 were arrested and twenty were finally sent to a grim fate before the Revolutionary Tribunal in Paris [*Birdeux, 1953 : II, 154–79; cf. Gerbaud, Lamadon, et al., 1972: 34*]. Peasant communities also withdrew into themselves, showing their disgust at the religious reforms, not so much by petitions, demonstrations or violent outbursts as by refusing to have anything to do with public authority. This was particularly easy in lonely or mountain regions where the hold of the central government was weak and people could hear Mass in isolated houses, put on their Sunday best and ignore the national *fêtes* and *décadis*, organize eerie torchlight processions into the forests where refractory priests said Mass in secret, and have children baptized by recusants whilst 'forgetting' to record the birth in the civil registry. Worship could be carried on even when there were no priests. Thus in the lonely hills around Buxy in the Saône-et-Loire, people went quietly to deserted churches where, according to an official report, they 'récitent paisiblement et à voix basse ce qu'ils appellent des prières, le plus communément en langue latine' while, on other occasions, laymen conducted 'messes blanches', in which all the normal parts of the Mass were recited except for the prayers of Consecration.[7]

Reactions of this sort were quite consistent with what is known about the importance of liturgy and ceremony to the common people of the old regime. In this sense, the iconoclasm and disruption which the Revolution brought into people's lives deeply upset all rural communities, and so there is almost no story to tell. More serious disputes over religion came in regions where there were also more profound political conflicts. Local administrators knew this from the beginning. Those of the Ille-et-Vilaine hinted at it when they welcomed the Civil Constitution as a means of putting the clergy in their 'véritable place'.[8] The *procureur* of the District of Bayeux in the Calvados urged the prompt replacement of refractories by constitutional priests, otherwise, 'quel coup porté à la loi, à la Constitution, quel triomphe pour le parti ennemi!' [*Sévestre, 1924: II, 519*]. Accepting the religious settlement thus meant accepting the political, a point repeated by an official in the poverty-stricken Corrèze who warned the public against the agitation of recusants who wished to destroy 'cette Constitution qui assure votre bonheur, vous délivre de la dîme, abolit le régime féodal et allège vos impôts; songez à ce serment et vous verrez que les prêtres qui refuseront de le prêter, en cherchant à conserver leurs places, voudroient vous accabler et vous avilir'. [*Fage, 1890: 10*]. Undermining the refractory priests and supporting the constitutionals thus became a means of assuring loyalty to the revolutionary settlement. In September 1793, a Jacobin from Autun in the Saône-et-Loire blamed the defunct Legislative Assembly for not pursuing this policy vigorously enough with the inevitable result that the government was hard put to assure the loyalty of the citizenry.[9] Indeed this theme is so common by the end of the period that officials expected the mere appearance of a recusant in a region to bring about an increase in draft-dodging, tax-evasion, uprooting of liberty trees, attacks on the buyers of *biens nationaux*, harrassment and even murder of local revolutionaries. A show of disaffection over religious issues was considered, both by its perpetrators and by the Revolutionary authorities, as an expression of a whole range of discontents.

This can be seen most dramatically in the awesome risings in the West of France[10] (see map no. 2). In March 1793, no less than fourteen departments rose against the conscription of 300,000 men for the army. At the same time there were protests against the deportation of refractory priests in the previous August, against the Republic, against *la nation*, against *la patrie* and demands for the return of the King and the seigneurs. Almost every town of consequence which happened to be a seat of government was besieged by a rag-tag crowd of peasants angrily waving potentially lethal farm tools and home-made white flags. North of the Loire, except for defeats at La Roche-Bernard and Rochefort in the Morbihan, the National Guards and the army beat back the attackers, but south of the river, the greater part of the district capitals succumbed. Angers and Saumur were abandoned to the newly-created Catholic and Royal Army, while Nantes barely withstood a month-long siege. In October, some hundred thousand

Vendeans, as they were called, crossed the Loire, partly to stimulate further risings in Maine and Brittany and partly to receive arms from the British fleet off Granville in Normandy. They failed to take Granville and were subsequently badly beaten in battles around Le Mans and Savenay in November and December 1793. But this was not the end of popular counter-revolution. A few months later, on both sides of the river, bands of guerillas known as *chouans* began murdering constitutional priests and republicans, attacking buyers of *biens nationaux*, ambushing army patrols, stopping grain from reaching the towns and forbidding farmers to pay their rents. Indeed the *chouannerie* was more long-lasting and extensive than even the Vendean risings. The guerrilla war lasted until 1796 and there were fresh outbreaks in 1799–1801, 1815 and 1832. Chouannerie was the most popular of the popular movements of the Revolution.

There have been attempts to explain the revolts in the West, particularly those in the southern half of the Department of the Maine-et-Loire, by employing modernisation theory [*Tilly, 1964*]. This interpretation argues that the introduction of handkerchief manufacturing around Cholet in the course of the eighteenth century was profoundly disturbing in a region of subsistence agriculture. Greedy putting-out merchants and rack-renting estate stewards eventually aligned both rural weavers and peasants against the bourgeoisie, particularly when the latter assumed political power after 1790 [*ibid.*]. Unfortunately, weavers were prominent as supporters of the Revolution in other parts of the West, so that the emphasis on modernisation in the form of the recent introduction of textile manufacture may well be misplaced.

Instead of concentrating on these marginal folk in the countryside, it seems more useful to investigate the problems of the majority – the peasants. In fact, it can be shown that there was an extremely close correlation between *chouannerie* and areas of tenant farming, and we have argued elsewhere that the West was distinguished by a relatively higher proportion of medium-sized leaseholders than elsewhere. There was thus little room for the conflicts over engrossing of land, leases and commons which set the large tenant-farmers and peasant proprietors of the northern plains against their poorer neighbours. There was also a larger constituency of tenants to be satisfied, a constituency suffering from rents which in the 1780s had reached unprecedented heights. Conversely, there were scattered reservoirs of support for the Republic in the West wherever there were significant numbers of small peasant proprietors. On balance, as Alfred Cobban pointed out, proprietors of whatever sort did rather well out of the revolutionary land settlement. Peasant owners were immediately released from many seigneurial dues, and whatever the law said about the others, they soon found that they could avoid them as well. Furthermore, even if taxes rose as the revolutionary wars dragged on, this was more than compensated by the outright abolition of the ecclesiastical tithe. For tenants, the situation was considerably worse. In Brittany, although the Constituent Assembly transformed the hereditary tenure known as the *quevaise* into a redeemable quit-rent, it was completely baffled by the system of shared ownership and leasehold known as the *domaine congéable* which prevailed in the western half of the province. The politicians procrastinated when tenants demanded more secure tenure or the opportunity to buy out their landlords. Fluctuating and confused legislation throughout the period did little to satisfy these demands. Peasants working land under more conventional forms of tenancy in return for payments in cash, kind or labour and those on sharecropping leases were frustrated too. Depending on the type of calculation made, it is possible to show that the revolutionary legislation did nothing for them or that it increased their taxes and rents by up to forty per cent over what they had paid to King, Church, seigneur and landlord in the old regime. A crucial element was the disposition of the tithe. The Assembly had agreed in principle to abolish it on the famous night of 4–5 August 1789, but took until 1 December 1790 to decide that landlords could add the equivalent of the former tithe to their leases. In other words, tenants continued to pay the tithe in the guise of rent. One month later, the parish clergy was made to take its oath of loyalty to the Civil Constitution of the Clergy [*Le Goff and Sutherland, 1974, 1983; Le Goff, 1981; Sutherland, 1982; Cobban, 1964: 102–03*].

Until this time, there was no sign that peasant communities were much interested in the Civil Constitution. No doubt they were attached to their priests and were distressed at the possibility of having them eventually replaced if they refused the oath. No doubt, in regions of scattered settlements like the West the Church and religious observances played a greater socializing role than they did elsewhere, and thus made the issue more immediate to parishioners. But within the West, church-going provided a focus for people' lives in both counter-revolutionary and revolutionary zones. Only in regions where there was already considerable peasant discontent over other issues was there much trouble over the Civil Constitution. In fact, the priests did not have the opportunity to consider the oath freely. In most dioceses, the bishops, cathedral canons and seminary professors tried to persuade them to refuse. There was considerable pressure from the laity too, pressure which could be decisive. As the *curé* of Reviers in the Calvados claimed, 'Je me serais acquitté du serment de fidelité si je n'eusse trouvé des obstacles de la part de mes paroissiens qu'un faux zèle égare ou plutôt qui se laissent persuader par les discours séditieux de quelques fanatiques intéressés [*Sévestre, 1924: II, 331–2*]. The *curés* of Versou, also in the Calvados, refused the oath because they feared losing 'l'estime de leurs paroissiens' [*ibid.: 331–2*]. Those who took the oath lost this respect. As the municipal officers of Theix, in the Morbihan, wrote, 'Nous regardons...comme indignes de notre confiance les prêtres qui seraient assez lâches pour faire le serment' [*Cariou, 1965: 70*]. Constitutional priests thus came to be seen as the agents of the régime, just as refractories had the courage to oppose it. Almost everywhere, the agitation surrounding the implementation of the Civil Constitution which preceded the risings of March 1793 represented a manifestation of profound discontent over both religious and secular issues.

The course of events in the Department of the Nord, in the troubled frontier zone of north-eastern France, demonstrates, in its complexity, the way in which religious issues were bound up with a large number of conflicts within the peasant community and between the rural community and other groups, which the Revolution settled only in part. There were five basic conflicts in the Nord; two of them were social. First, there was the opposition of the mass of producers to the seigneurial regime and to the church tithe. This was a struggle all rural people could back, but it was over by 1791. Secondly, there were social conflicts within the peasantry: the opposition of rich and poor, large tenant farmer and smallholder or farm-labourer. The third line of cleavage passed between 'patriots' and 'aristocrats', that is, the supporters and opponents of the new regime; it tended to become confused, after the Allies occupied much of the Department between August and October 1792 and March 1793 and July 1794, with a division between those who had 'collaborated' with the occupying authorities and those, who, afterwards, denounced the collaborators. Finally, on top of this was the religious conflict; at first, between partisans and adversaries of the constitutional clergy; then between those who, after the dechristianising and persecution of 1793 and later, wanted a priest in their commune – any priest, recusant or constitutional, provided he was in Holy Orders – and those who did not. This religious division was partly a polarizing factor, that is, it made people choose between revolutionary and counter-revolutionary camps, but it also served to widen the gap between the two for people who had already made their choice on other grounds, by adding the venom of religious sectarianism to the bitterness of political partisanship. And, given the abundance of grievances against the new regime in the Nord, it helped put the mass of people on the side of the counter-revolution, albeit gradually [Lefebvre, 1924].

Certainly, there were great disappointments and provocations in a region where all groups in rural society competed for scarce resources and where the demands of the military were inordinately heavy. As elsewhere, the abolition of the tithe left the prosperous part of the peasantry divided into contented landowners who had picked up the clergy's former share of the crop and discontented tenants who had to add the value of the tithe to the rent which they paid their landlords. Once the war began in April 1792, rural communities were subject to a requisitioning policy which was designed to get from the countryside as much grain and animal stock as possible in order to allow the towns and fortresses to withstand long sieges. Peasants were expected to put their carts and horses at the disposition of civil and military authorities; soldiers and often ill-disciplined and poorly-equipped volunteers were billeted on them; and if they lived near the sea, a river or a canal, they might have their meadows flooded as a defensive measure [*Deschuytter, 1958–9*]. Nor were these extraordinary demands met with much sympathy. The deputies Lacoste and Ducos wrote that

> les habitants des campagnes aux quels la Révolution a prodigué ses premiers bienfaits, qui ne paient plus de dîme ni de cens, qui sont rédimés de la servitude et de tous les droits fiscaux et oppressifs... sont devenus en grande partie... des citoyens ingrats qui exposent leurs frères à manquer de pain, pour satisfaire un vil intérêt [cited *ibid.*: II, 117].

Whatever resentments peasants might have felt at bearing the brunt of the war were complicated by the application of the Civil Constitution of the Clergy, which split the countryside into partisans and opponents of the juring and non-juring clergy. Most of the *curés* of the Department refused the oath; but in the *région herbagère*, in the south of the Department, where peasants owned over half the cultivated land, the clergy tended to accept it. It seems likely that the satisfaction of the mass of peasants with the material results of the Revolution, in this case the abolition of the tithe, played some part in the decision of their clergy. [*Lefebvre, 1924: xii–xx, 20*]. The king's flight toward the frontier in April 1791 worsened the political and religious conflict in each village, though apparently the coastal and northern region, where the peasants tended to be tenants rather than proprietors, favoured the recusants more than did the *région herbagère*. [*ibid.: 790*]. The standard persecution followed, with the Department anticipating, as local administrators did so often elsewhere, the harsh deportation measures eventually ordered by the Legislative Assembly in August 1792. [*ibid.: 800*]. Finally, the law of 29–30 Vendémiaire Year II/20–1 October 1793 made it virtually impossible for the recusants to remain in France. Although there had been demonstrations in favour of the non-jurors in many parishes, the peasants eventually accepted the constitutional clergy, *faute de mieux*, rather than do without religious observances altogether.

It was at this point that the radical republican politicians truly earned their reputation for self-destructive folly, by making adherence to the Republic's anti-clerical policy the criterion for loyalty, and by making that anti-clericalism insupportable to the mass of peasants. In the panic engendered by the French army's retreat from the northern frontier in August 1793, republican authorities launched a violent campaign of repression against civilians behind the lines. Some of this took the form of dechristianisation, backed by the gangs of *armées révolutionnaires* or by the regular army, but more often, it was a matter of arresting civilians, usually on the pretext of having 'favoured the constitutional priest', the only clerical target left. Or it involved the iconoclastic destruction of crosses and statues in churches, cemeteries, crossroads and markets, or the rigorous enforcement of the republican calendar and the consequent arrest of those who observed Sundays, or the pillaging and closing of churches. The government's attempt to halt the dechristianisation campaign remained a dead letter here [*Peter and Poulet, 1930: I, 312–46*]. 'One way or another', says Lefebvre, 'the municipalities and terrorist committees alienated the vast majority of peasants from the Republic, and consequently from the Revolution, by arresting suspects more or less arbitrarily and abolishing religous services' [*Lefebvre, 1924: 839*]. These actions were reinforced by the full panoply of revolutionary legislation designed to impose support for the war effort, including of course conscription of young men in March 1793 – at which the peasants rebelled as they had in Vendée – the raising of emergency revenues by forced loans on the rich, and the compulsory victualling of towns and the Army by the countryside at prices set by decree. When the Thermidorean regime eased the persecution of the clergy with the law of 3 Ventôse Year III/21 February 1795, which allowed the free but unsubsidised exercise of religion, the priests who returned to the Nord tended to be either Belgian missionaries or the former refractories, neither of whom could be expected to counsel submission to the new regime. The final blow was the 'little' outbreak of official anticlericalism which followed the 'republican' coup d'état in Paris on 18 Fructidor Year V/4 September 1797. On the local level, its main effect turned out to be the arbitrary sale by the departmental authorities of two out of every three parish churches, on the condition that the purchasers demolish them – unless the commune bought off the purchasers. This was a form of fiscal extortion at which even the old regime would have blanched. By then, the peasants of the Nord, whether they had initially supported the Revolution or not, whether they had backed the constitutional clergy or the recusants, had become pretty solidly anti-Revolutionary, and the religious policies of Parisian and local administrators had been in large part responsible for this.

Unlike the West of France, however, the process of alienation from the Revolution had been much more drawn-out, and this raises the question of whether the way local social conflicts within the peasantry crystallised around religious issues was responsible for this more gradual shift. Here, at least, no one has yet advanced a version of modernisation theory as an explanation for this, and indeed, the Nord, traditionally one of the farming regions of France in which market orientation had long been established, is not very propitious terrain for such an undertaking. In a more empirical vein, Georges Lefebvre suggested that it is possible to detect certain tendencies of one side or another to have the backing of certain social groups in the Nord, or of regions characterized by a particular form of landholding. Thus, the initial supporters of the recusant priests tended to include those who felt hard done by as a result of the Revolution: well-off tenant farmers and large peasant landowners; the latter, presumably because they feared the day-labourers and cotters whom the local radicals affected to represent; the former for this reason too, and also because they had been deprived of the benefits from the abolition of the tithe. Conversely, the constitutional priests tended to get the support of the *menu peuple* in the countryside, especially in the southern part of the Department, which was characterised by the presence of many small peasant proprietors and where there was the smallest proportion of tenant farmers. It is at least arguable that a large part of the rural elite in the Nord was deterred from supporting the Revolution in its religious policies partly because the Revolution had done little for them (in the case of the tenants) and partly because, unlike the West, the social distance between the prosperous *laboureurs*, whether tenants or peasant proprietors, and the rest of the population was so great that the *laboureur* often feared instinctively the democratic tendencies of the Revolution even when he had profitted from it through the abolition of seigneurial dues and the tithe. On Christmas Day 1793, the constitutional *curé* of Haverskerque was reported as having preached that

> the rich had no religion, that only the common folk were religious, that they would defend their curé against armed force and that he was proud of his day-labourers because without them, all was lost. [*Lefebvre, 1924: 829*].

The 'rich' as it happened, did have religion, only of the wrong variety: they had backed the non-juring clergy. It is difficult to imagine such a frank admission of the social divisions which underlay religious conflict in the rural community in the mouth of Breton or Vendean *curé*; the society they lived in was of a different sort, with more attenuated contrasts between rich and poor, and in which elite behaviour differed less from that of the mass. In the Nord, however, it was only the horrors of war and the misplaced zealotry of the Republicans behind the French lines which finally drove together in hostility to the godless Republic the two rival groups of Catholics and the conflicting social strata they represented.

Despite their apparent complexity, the revolts in the West and the discontent and sporadic upheavals of the northern frontier appear disarmingly simple when the series of risings in southern France is considered. All through a zone shaped liked an inverted letter 'T', down the Rhône and throughout Provence to the south-east and across Languedoc to the south-west a series of violent clashes, both urban and rural, marked the history of the Revolution (see map no. 2). Some of these had little enough to do with religion itself: this was the case with the notorious 'federalist' insurrections of Lyon, Toulon, Toulouse and Marseille, followed timidly by many of the other towns of the South-East and South-West [*Riffaterre, 1912–28: II, 7–9, 22–3; Lucas, 1973: 54*]. These were protests against the radicalisation of the Republic, touched off by local and properly urban social conflicts. Nor was it the case with the great peasant *jacquerie* which swept across Languedoc and Provence in two great waves in the spring and autumn of 1792; this was in part a blow against the remnants of the seigneurial system which the 'abolition of feudalism' in 1789–90 had failed to abolish, in part a simple revolt against the rich and propertied, particularly against lawyers who, in Lower (eastern) Languedoc, often combined crooked litigation with an equally lucrative sideline in usury; partly, too, a way of intimidating the local nobility, which had been particularly active in counter-revolutionary plots. The more properly religious rural revolts were of two kinds. First of all, there were a series of clashes between Catholics and Protestants in the early years of the Revolution, specifically *méridional* in form and content. By the end of 1792, these had been put down and to a great extent superseded by the social uprisings just described. But after the fall of the war dictatorship of the Committee of Public Safety in the summer of 1794, there occurred a second series of revolts directed specifically against the religious policies of the Republic, in which the anti-Protestant element appears to have been of less importance than in 1790–92, and which affected primarily the western part of Languedoc.

The first series of disturbances, those between Catholics and Protestants, had their origins in town where the local Protestant bourgeoisie, now in full possession of civil rights thanks to the reforms of 1787–9, were sufficiently numerous to threaten the Catholic oligarchies which had dominated municipal and provincial government under the old regime. To redress the balance, the Catholic bourgeoisie and nobility called on Catholic peasants for help when they could; and the new Protestant ruling elite, to defend their conquests, appealed to their own peasants [*Wemyss, 1957*]. Obscure struggles occurred in many places in the South-West, but the main flash-points were the towns of Montauban, Nîmes and Uzès. At Montauban, the Protestants met the challenge quickly and efficiently with the help of National Guards from Bordeaux and the firm backing of the National Assembly [*Ligou, 1958: 217–63*]. Trouble never occurred there again, but the conflicts in Lower (eastern) Languedoc, particularly in the Department of the Gard and the southern half of the Ardèche proved more intractable. The incident which made urban politics into rural revolt was the 'bagarre de Nîmes', a five-day election riot beginning on 13 June 1790 in which Catholic peasants from the eastern suburbs of that town and the north-eastern part of the Department of the Gard, called in to support the threatened Catholic municipality of Nîmes, were soundly and bloodily routed by Protestant forces, whose bulk was drawn from the Protestant peasantry of the Cévennes, in the west of the Department.[11] Somewhat similar events in the town of Uzès, in the north of the Gard, led to a flight of Catholics into the countryside on the frontier with the neighbouring Department of the Ardèche early in the next year.

The rural response to these threats were the *camps de Jalès* – armed rallies of peasants organized by a cadre of Catholic nobles, bourgeois and clerics in the southern part of the Ardèche. Originally conceived as a variant on the 'Federations' of National Guards so popular in 1790, with the added intent of protesting against the ill-treatment of Catholics by the Protestants in Nîmes, the 1790, 1791 and 1792 camps became rallying points for armed insurrection, grouping at their height as many as 20,000 men and possibly even twice that number. All of these conspiracies failed through mismanagement, though the second and third of them, in 1791 and 1792, were considered real threats by the authorities, because of the danger that they might rally counter-revolutionaries all through eastern Languedoc, the Forez and Lyons to a giant army which could conceivably join up with the Bretons and Vendeans and march — why not? — on the capital [*Brugal, 1884–5; Jolivet, 1930: 196–252, 354–72; Rouvière, 1887–9: I, 309 n 1*].

In the South-West too, popular counter-revolution could be channelled into conspiratorial activity, although the risings here took the longest time of all to mature [*Lacouture, 1932; Hansy, 1936*]. The organizing role was performed by the *Instituts Philanthropiques*, which, as the name suggests, consisted of an array of front organisations concealing a central committee. Like the Masonic lodges on which they were probably modelled, only the fully initiated knew the real counter-revolutionary aims and strategy while their organizers enticed ordinary adepts into the Institutes by playing on whatever real or imagined wrongs they had suffered. Most of these discontents were real enough, for however much the local squirearchy was fighting, not for religion, but 'pour les parlements et les seigneuries', as some revolutionaries in the Tarn alleged,[12] the peasants who followed them had accumulated a large stock of grievances of a different sort. Although the State was officially neutral in religious matters after 1795, local authorities continued to take support for the constitutional priests as a test of loyalty to the regime. Even refractories who had returned to France legally were harrassed in dozens of petty ways. Yet the State was considerably weaker than it had been in 1794. Local officials were far from zealous, tolerating all sorts of subversive acts such as the erecting of public crosses, pilgrimages, draft-dodging and seditious cries. Even after the republican coup d'état of Fructidor Year V/September, 1797, when the administrations were purged of crypto-royalists, these things continued. The military situation was also far from favourable. After the Republic's disasters in Switzerland and Italy in 1799, the 1798 legislation on conscription was applied with vigour. Energetic conscription measures had always led to trouble. As early as August 1793 an attempt to round up draft dodgers around Pamiers provoked a rising of 600 young men who threatened to join the invading Spanish armies, kill all the 'democrats', disarm 'protestants' and establish Louis XVII in all his rights [*Arnaud, 1904: 410–12*]. In 1799, the result was much the same. It was said that there were already 6,000 deserters hiding in the Pyrenees and of 1319 young conscripts of the Ariège in the class of

1799, only eleven ever finally joined the armies. The military reverses of 1799 also forced the government to denude the region of troops. On the eve of the insurrection, the Ariège was policed by a mere 539 National Guards and there were only thirty troops of the line stationed in the entire Haute-Garonne.[13] If the conspirators were to strike, August 1799 was the time.

Like most of the royalists' grand designs, the insurrection of the Year VII turned out as low farce rather than chivalric adventure. Although it was supposed to break out simultaneously in about ten departments, one of its leaders, the Comte de Paulo, not only quarrelled with one of his fellow conspirators, the republican turncoat general Rougé, but started his part of the operations too soon. His peasants came pouring out of the Ariège hills ten days ahead of schedule shouting: 'Il faut tuer tous les enfants des huguenots, ensuite leurs mères, et ensuite leurs pères pour en voir la fin' [*Hansy, 1936: 31*]. Many insurgents heard Mass before going into battle. But such religious enthusiasm was to no avail. Weak as they were, the republicans eventually defeated a horde of 15,000 peasants at Montréjeau outside Toulouse on 3 Fructidor Year VII/20 August 1799. About 2,000 rebels were killed in this engagement, another 2,000 in mopping-up operations and around 1100 prisoners were taken.[14] Although the government released many soon after because it was convinced the peasants were misled, several hundred were still languishing in prison months later.

It is tempting to consider these risings of the South-West as inspired primarily by religious motives and hatred of conscription, but here, too, the local form of rural social structure and conflicts within peasant society seem to have had a strong influence on the shape and timing of the revolts. The rural societies of the Midi had, as everywhere in France, infinite variations, but authorities seem to agree on the widespread prevalence of a tripartite hierarchy, consisting of a mass of day-labourers, often cotters with a title to a small patch of land, at the base; a relatively small number of self-sufficient peasant proprietors in the middle; and, at the apex, a rural elite who were nearly always tenants, usually sharecroppers, working land belonging to bourgeois or noble landlords [*Brunet, 1965; Soboul, 1958; Bozon, 1956; 1963: 147–81; Frèche, n.d.: 147–210*]. The latter were often quite numerous, and the day-labourers depended on them for temporary and permanent employment. Keeping in mind the effects that have just been traced of the removal of the tithe and the partial abolition of the seigneurial system on the political attitudes of the peasantry in the West and North of France, it can be seen that the repercussions of these measures in the Midi were bound to be more complex and diffused. All indications are not only that the *métayers* in the South were left unsatisfied by the reforms of the Constituent and Legislative Assemblies, but that they saw their lot worsen as the Revolution passed through the radical phase of 1793–4 into the Thermidorean and Directorial periods [*Brunet, 1965: 363–81; Higgs, 1973: 33*]. Peasant proprietors, on the contrary, ought to have profited. When such men dominated rural society, they ought to have carried the day for the Revolution, especially as the mass of day-labourers were also landowners. But when the *métayers* predominated, the rural community was liable to be pulled in both directions, with the *métayers* exercising their influence against the Revolution among the day-labourers dependent on them.

Thus it is probably unwise to offer, as do Jean Sentou [*1967: 461*] and Jacques Godechot [*1961: 218–9*], a general explanation of the prevalence of religious and counter-revolutionary popular movements in the southern countryside as the result of the prevalence of *métayage* without a careful consideration of the local variants in social structure. Even within the limited context of eastern Languedoc, the complexity of the relations between social structure, economy and rural revolt can easily be oversimplified. In the Department of the Gard, a more sophisticated variant of the equation of *métayage* with counter-revolution has been attempted. Here, using Charles Tilly's equation of counter-revolution with rapid and uneven modernisation, James Hood [*1976: 259–63*] and Gwynne Lewis [*1973; 1978: 1–10*] have made much of the claim that the Catholic peasant supporters of the Catholic party in Nîmes were drawn from newly and imperfectly market-oriented *métayage* areas in the north-east of the Department, while the Protestants pulled in their forces from the thoroughly mercantile Cévennes, where rural industry, particularly the textile trade, was an old tradition. But the limited usefulness of both these explanations can be seen, even within the context of eastern Languedoc, when the support for the rural riposte to the Protestant triumph, the *Camps de Jalès* on the frontier of the Gard and the Ardèche, is considered.

Here, the evidence is overwhelming that the bulk of the peasants who flocked in 1790 to the defence of religion in the Ardèche and the Gard came from precisely those regions where they ought not to have, that is, from the Catholic mountain villages of the Cévennes, where the predominant pattern of land distribution was that of a *démocratie paysanne*. There was a relatively egalitarian distribution of land in small peasant-owned plots, an absence of *métayage*; and a thorough integration in a market economy, in the production of raw silk and wine, while paradoxically, the regions of the Ardèche characterized by the more typically 'aristocratic' tripartite rural social structure were largely uninvolved. Many of these parishes, which were to become the centre of the Jalès uprising, had already been active in the antiseigneurial riots of July and August 1789 [*Brugal, 1883; Jolivet, 1930: 135–42*]. The peasants who foregathered in the plain of Jalès in 1790 and 1791 appear themselves to have been aware of the anomaly of their conduct, and there are stories of how, at the camp of 1791, the peasants of Saint-André-Lachamp could only be persuaded to march by being reminded of their love for their religion [*Brugal, 1884–5: 107*]. As one of the rural mayors, Louis Heyrand of St-Sauveur, reported about this time

> The inhabitants of my commune recognize that the Constitution is right on several points, but not on religion, for example. They do not detest patriots in general: only those who support the Huguenots [*ibid.: VII, 349*].

Indeed, they went farther than this, for only four months before the third Camp de Jalès, planned by the Comte de Saillans and local counter-revolutionaries as a full-fledged military uprising, there took place all through the south the first of the great *jacqueries* of 1792, against nobles, counter-revolutionaries and the rich. What touched it off? Not, as local legend has it, the drowning of a detachment of patriotic National Guards in the Rhône in a suspicious-looking accident, but a revolt which had already started before this incident in the southern Ardèche and the north of the Gard. Several of the parishes which participated had been among those which went to Jalès to defend the true faith in 1790. Why should they have done so? Partly because local revolutionary administrators had encouraged them to revolt against the aristocrats in order to destroy the counter-revolution as a mass movement. Then, too, the Vivarais was a region in which the agents of justice and repression had intervened only sporadically under the old regime, and where, more than in most other areas, men were left alone to settle their quarrels. Resentment of lawyer-usurers was one of the main motivations of the rioters of 1792, and this was an old tradition in the Vivarais, having been the cause of the rising of the *masques armés* of 1783 [*Jolivet, 1930: 325–51; Chaumié, 1965: 90–9; Vovelle, 1968: 351–2; Mazel, 1886; Sonenscher, 1972, 1978; Castan, 1972; 1976; 1980: 63, 110–12*]. But the necessary condition for revolt here, as in Provence and the Languedoc lowlands, was the economic crisis. A series of hard winters hit the production of the wine and silk which the region exported and the grain crops and chestnut trees it depended on for much of its subsistence. No doubt the collapse of the Lyon economy by 1792 also helped. Meanwhile, direct taxes rose by over a quarter of what they had been in 1788, and widespread tax-evasion became normal [*Jolivet, 1930: 200–208, 325–40; Vovelle, 1968: 346–9*]. Just before the abortive royalist rising of February and the successful *jacquerie* of March, Colonel Durand of the 38th Line Regiment, stationed at the little town of Les Vans reported

> I have made a tour of the parishes of the canton of Vans . . . Nothing but poverty can be seen through the countryside I crossed. Most people are unable to pay their taxes. This poverty is dangerous. People are ready to follow any leader ('Les esprits sont disposés à se laisser entraîner') [*Brugal, 1884–5: VII, 296*].

Here, revolutionaries and counter-revolutionaries were bidding for the support of the same peasants, the former relying on the economic interest of peasant proprietors to carry the day and the latter on the mobilising force of religious feeling, particularly anti-Protestant sentiment. In 1790 and 1791, religious feeling won out; in 1789 and 1792, it was economic advantage. But running through all the political upheavals in the first four years of the revolution is the theme of economic hardship, for the crises of 1789–95 came in a region whose population had risen dramatically during the century without an equivalent increase in resources [*Molinier, 1980*]. Economic collapse could thus make counter-revolutionaries as well as revolutionaries out of desperate men, even in this area of 'peasant democracy'.

Where the more 'logical' link between *métayer*-dominated social structure and rural religious revolt took effect seems to have been in the western part of Languedoc, in the later and more widespread attacks on the Republic in 1798 and 1799. By then, it seems that the persistent economic difficulties of the period 1792–9, the resentment of requisitions by urban National Guards and troops, and, finally, a return to mass conscription in 1798–9 had taken their toll. The surviving lists of prisoners held after the uprisings of the summer of 1799 in the region around Toulouse show that the movement was heavily rural, that it represented all strata in rural society, and that it came from the communes along the valley of the Garonne, where sharecropping, often with bourgeois as landlords, was common.[15] In the insurgent region, both rural day-labourers, directly menaced by conscription, and their *métayer* employers, who had gained nothing and suffered much from the Revolution, joined in a massive uprising against the Republic and its religious persecution.

Thus the link between religion and rural revolt during the French Revolution can be seen to have been extremely complex, even if the historian limits himself to the analysis of the ties between religion and counter-revolutionary revolt alone. The unresolved problems and the deeply-entrenched conflicts of rural society lived on after 1791 and both fed and themselves were nourished by religious antagonism between supporters and opponents of the new Constitutional Church, and of religion itself. It would be agreeable indeed to conclude with some great unifying explanation which sees long-standing habits of modernisation and urbanisation as the cause of rural acquiescence in the political Revolution and disruptive, abrupt or non-existent modernisation and urbanisation behind the rural revolt against it. Though a useful hypothesis, applications of the theory to counter-revolutionary popular movements in the French Revolution can and have been shown to contradict the evidence too often to make it useful as a general model. Other explanations, such as those of Marcel Faucheux [*1964*] or Michel Vovelle [*1976*], which rely on the presence or absence of poverty, or a supposed 'dechristianisation' antedating the Revolution have the same defects.[16] A less ambitious but perhaps more realistic approach is, we would suggest, to put the emphasis on the dominant groups in rural society and the way in which they held their land. For when such men stood up for the

Revolution in their communities, they could carry most of the others with them, or at least defuse discontent on religious issues as well as on other questions.

But there was a large and unreliable element among these dominant groups: the tenant farmers. These men, whether small or large, can safely be said to have got no direct concrete benefit from the social policy of the Revolution and little reason to support it once the context of its social and religious policy became apparent. Indeed, when tenants dominated rural society as they did in the Nord, they often found themselves threatened by the democratic tendencies of the lower orders in the countryside, and came to sympathize with the recusants and royalists as a result. Only the extremes of Republican anticlericalism and repression in 1793–4 could put the small landowners and day-labourers on the same side as these *coqs de village*. But when, as happened in the West, tenants formed a numerous group, not too obviously richer than the rest of rural society, their own disappointment with the failure of the Revolution to better their lot merged with the general resentment of rural society against the economic hardships which the new regime inherited, in a worsened form, from the old. This resentment showed itself above all in opposition, often violent, to the religious policy of the Revolution from 1791 onwards.

Peasant proprietors, on the other hand, seem to have benefited from the Revolution, if they had enough land, or big enough tithes or seigneurial dues, that their abolition made a difference to their retained surplus. Consequently, these smallholders, particularly when they were grouped in semi-egalitarian *démocraties paysannes*, put up with the Revolution and its religious settlement, even if they did not actually like it. For such men, it took great pressures, such as those exercised by the combination of economic collapse and the reawakening of ancestral anti-Protestant hatreds as in the Ardèche, to put them, often against their own expressed better judgement, on the side of Church and King.

Notes

(1) The best introductions to the traditional historiography of this once dismal field are *Mitchell, 1968* and *Godechot, 1961*.
(2) The principal works are *Tilly, 1964, Lewis, 1973, 1978* and *Hood, 1971, 1976, 1979*; French and British scholarship has in the meantime applied more traditional techniques of social history to the analysis; see *Bois, 1960; Faucheux, 1964; Petitfrère, 1973; 1977: a–b; 1979; 1980* and *Sonenscher, 1972*.
(3) The best modern summaries are in McManners [*1969: 24–60*] and *Langlois and Tackett* [*1980: 245–51*].
(4) On this episode, the most recent synthesis is *Vovelle 1976*, but see the trenchant criticism of G. *Cholvy 1978*.
(5) Some of the troubles of the South-East and South-West, particularly in the Bouches-du-Rhône, Vaucluse, Var, Charente-Maritime and Gironde, have more to do with the 'federalist' movement of 1793, led by disgruntled revolutionaries with some help from

crypto-royalists, than with counter-revolutionary outbreaks proper; this was also the case in the Norman Departments of the Orne and the Manche. We have not dealt in this article with the White Terrors of 1795 or 1815 which, while often similar in origins to the activity described here, appear to have been more specifically political and vindictive in their overt aims.

(6) A.(rchives) N.(ationales), F^7 3679 1, petition of 20 September 1795.
(7) A.N. BB^{18} 720, commissaire du directoire executif to minister of Justice, 12 Pluviôse Year IV/ 1 February 1796.
(8) A.N. F^{1C} III Saône-et-Loire 6, report of St-Victor to Minister of Interior, 16 September 1793.
(9) A.N. F^{19} 430, letter to Minister of the Interior, 1 October 1791.
(10) There are dozens of narratives of the risings in the West. One of the best is Dubreuil [*1929–30*].
(11) The most recent treatment of these incidents are Lewis, [*1978: 18–25*] and Hood, *1971, 1975, 1979*.
(12) A.N. F^7 7602, administration municipale de Lavaur to Deputies of the Tarn, 20 Thermidor Year VII/7 August 1799.
(13) Cf. Hansy, *1936: 10–15*. A.N. F^7 7602, commissaire du directoire executif of the Haute Garonne to Ministre de la Police Générale, 21 Thermidor Year VII/8 August 1799.
(14) A.N. F^7 7602, Commissaire du Directoire executif . . . Haute-Garonne, 5 Fructidor Year VII/10 August 1799.
(15) A.N. F^7 7602 Etat nominatif des individus détenus dans les prisons . . . de Toulouse . . . 11 Pluviôse Year VIII/31 January 1800. Of the 71 surviving prisoners, there were 14 *brassiers* (day labourers), almost as many *laboureurs* (13), twice as many who were *agriculteurs* (27) and another five were *cultivateurs*. On landholding and form of cultivation see Frèche [*n.d.*]. We wish to thank Professor D. C. Higgs for providing us with this information.
(16) On the shortcomings of these, see Sutherland [*1982*] and Cholvy [*1978*] respectively.

References

Arnaud, G. 1904, *Histoire de la Révolution dans le département de l'Ariège (1789–1795)*.
Birdeux, F. 1953, *Histoire religieuse du département de Seine-et-Marne pendant la Révolution*.
Bois, P. 1960, *Les Paysans de l'ouest. Des structures économiques et sociales aux options politiques depuis l'époque révolutionnaire dans la Sarthe*.
Bozon, P. 1956, 'La Structure agraire en Haut Vivarais', *Revue de Géographie alpine*, XLIV.
Bozon, P. 1963, *La Vie Rurale en Vivarais: étude géographique*.
Brugal, S. (pseud. of F. Boissin) 1884–5, 'Les Camps de Jalès', *Revue de la Révolution*, IV–VII.
Brugal, S. (pseud. of F. Boissin) 1883, 'La Jacquerie dans le Vivarais, de 1789 à 1793', *Revue de la Révolution*, I.
Brunet, R. 1965, *Les Campagnes toulousaines. Etude géographique*.
Cariou, A. 1965, 'La Constitution civile du clergé dans le département du Morbihan', *Mémoires de la Société d'Histoire et d'archéolgie de Bretagne*, XLV.
Castan, N. 1972, 'Caractéristiques criminelles des hautes régions du Languedoc oriental de 1780 à 1790', *Vivarais et Languedoc. Fédération historique du Languedoc méditerranéenne et du Roussillon, XLIVe Congrès (Privas, 22–23 mai 1971)*.
Castan, N. 1976, 'Révoltes populaires en Languedoc au XVIIIe siècle', *Actes du 96e congrès national des sociétés savantes (Toulouse, 1971) Section d'histoire moderne et contemporaine*, II.
Castan, N. 1980, *Les Criminels de Languedoc. Les exigences d'ordre et les voies du ressentiment dans une société pré-révolutionnaire (1750–1790)*.
Charrier, J. 1926, *Histoire religieuse du département de la Nièvre pendant la Révolution*.
Chaumié, J. 1965, *La Réseau d'Antraigues et la contre-révolution*.

Cholvy, G. 1978, 'Religion et Révolution: la déchristianisation de l'An II', *Annales historiques de la Révolution francaise*, 233.
Cobban, A. 1964, *The Social Interpretation of the French Revolution*.
Deschuytter, G. 1958–9, *L'Esprit public et son évolution dans le Nord de 1791 au lendemain de Thermidor An II*.
Dubreuil, L. 1929–30, *Histoire des insurrections de l'Ouest*.
Fage, R. 1890, *Le Diocèse de Corrèze pendant la Révolution*.
Faucheux, M. 1964, *L'Insurrection vendéenne de 1793 Aspects économiques et sociaux*.
Frèche, G. n.d., *Toulouse et la région Midi-Pyrénées au siècle des lumières (vers 1670–1789)*.
Gerbaud, G., Lamadon, A. et al. 1972, *La Révolution dans le Puy-de-Dôme*.
Godechot, J. 1961, *La Contre-révolution. Doctrine et action 1789–1804*.
Greer, D. 1935, *The Incidence of the Terror in the French Revolution*.
Hansy, T. de 1936, *Contribution à l'histoire de l'insurrection royaliste de Thermidor An VII (Août, 1799) dans l'Ariège*.
Higgs, D. 1973, *Ultraroyalism in Toulouse From its Origins to the Revolution of 1830*.
Hood, J. N. 1971, 'Protestant-Catholic Relations and the Roots of the First Popular Counter-revolutionary Movement in France', *Journal of Modern History*, XLIII.
Hood, J. N. 1976, 'Patterns of Popular Protest in the French Revolution: the Conceptual Contribution of the Gard', *Journal of Modern History*, XLVIII.
Hood, J. N. 1979, 'Revival and Mutation of Old Rivalries in Revolutionary France', *Past & Present*, LXXXIII.
Hufton, O. 1971, 'Women in Revolution, 1789–1796', D. Johnson (ed.), *French Society and the Revolution, 1976*.
Jolivet, C. 1930, *La Révolution dans l'Ardèche 1788–1795*.
Lacouture, J. 1932, *Le Mouvement royaliste dans le Sud-Ouest (1797–1800)*.
Le Goff, T. J. A. 1981, *Vannes and its Region: A Study of Town and Country in Eighteenth-Century France*.
Le Goff, T. J. A. and Sutherland, D. M. G. 1974, 'The Revolution and the Rural Community in Eighteenth-Century Brittany', D. Johnson (ed.), *French Society and the Revolution, 1976*.
Le Goff, T. J. A. and Sutherland, D. M. G. 1983, 'The Social Origins of Counter-Revolution in Western France', *Past and Present*, XCIX.
Langlois, C. and Tackett, T. 1980, 'A l'épreuve de la Révolution (1770–1830)' F. Lebrun (ed.) *Histoire des Catholiques en France du XVe siècle à nos jours*.
Lefebvre, G. 1924, *Les Paysans du Nord*.
Lefebvre, G. 1933, 'La Révolution française et les paysans', *Etudes sur la Révolution francaise*, 1963.
Lewis, G. 1973, 'The White Terror of 1815 in the Department of the Gard: Counter-Revolution, Continuity and the Individual', D. Johnson (ed.) *French Society and the Revolution, 1976*.
Lewis, G. 1978, *The Second Vendée. The Continuity of Counter-Revolution in the Department of the Gard 1789–1815*.
Ligou, D. 1958, *Montauban à la fin de l'ancien régime et aux débuts de la Révolution 1787–1794*.
Lucas, C. 1973, *The Structure of the Terror. The Example of Javogues and the Loire*.
Lucas, C. 1978, 'The Problem of the Midi in the French Revolution', *Transactions of the Royal Historical Society*, 5th ser., XXVIII.
McManners, J. 1969, *The French Revolution and the Church*.
Mitchell, H. 1968, 'The Vendée and Counter-Revolution: a Review Essay', *French Historical Studies*, V.
Mazel, H. 1886, 'La Révolution dans le Midi. L'incendie des châteaux du Bas-Languedoc', *Revue de la Révolution*, VIII.
Molinier, A. 1980, 'En Vivarais au XVIIIe siècle: une croissance démographique sans révolution agricole', *Annales du Midi*, XCII.
Peter, J. and Poulet, C., 1930, *Histoire religieuse du département du Nord pendant la Révolution*

(1789–1802).
Petitfrère, C. 1973, 'Les grandes composantes sociales des armées vendéennes d'Anjou', *Annales historiques de la Révolution francaise*, 21.
Petitfrère, C. 1977a, 'Les Causes de la Vendée et de la Chouannerie Essai d'historiographie', *Annales de Bretagne*, LXXXIV.
Petitfrère, C. 1977b, 'Les Tables personnelles des rebelles de la Vendée', *Annales de Bretagne*, LXXIV.
Petitfrère, C. 1980, *Blancs et Bleus d'Anjou 1789–1793*.
Riffaterre, C. 1912–28, *Le Mouvement antijacobin et antiparisien à Lyon et dans le Rhône-et-Loire en 1793 (29 mai-15 août)*.
Rouvière, F. 1887–9, *Histoire de la Révolution française dans le Département du Gard*.
Rudé, G. 1964, *The Crowd in History*.
Sentou, J. 1967, 'Révolution et contre-révolution' P. Wolff (ed.), *Histoire du Languedoc*.
Sévestre, E. 1924, *Les Problèmes religieux de la Révolution et de l'Empire en Normandie, 1787–1815*.
Soboul, A. 1958, *Les Campagnes montpelliéraines à la fin de l'ancien régime. Propriété et cultures d'après le compoix*.
Sonenscher, M. 1972, 'La Révolte des masques armés de 1783 en Vivarais', *Vivarais et Languedoc. Fédération historique du Languedoc méditerranéenne et du Rousillon XLIVe Congrès (Privas, 22–23 mai 1971)*.
Sonenscher, M. 1978, 'Royalists and Patriots: Nîmes and its hinterland in the late eighteenth century', University of Warwick Ph.D.
Sutherland, D. M. G. 1982, *The Chouans. The Social Origins of Popular Counter-Revolution in Upper Brittany 1770–1791*.
Tilly, C. 1964, *The Vendée*.
Vovelle, M. 1968, 'Les Troubles sociaux en Provence (1750–1792)', *Actes du quatre-vingt-treizième congrès national des sociétés savantes. Tours 1966 Section d'histoire moderne et contemporaine*, II.
Vovelle, M. 1976, *Religion et Révolution. La Déchristianisation de l'an II*.
Vovelle, M. 1977, 'La Déchristianisation en l'An II. Sur le compte rendu de G. Cholvy', *Annales historiques de la Révolution francaise*, 233.
Wemyss, A. 1957, 'Les Protestants du Midi pendant la Révolution', *Annales du Midi*, LXIX.

Central and Eastern Europe 1525–1848

Preface

CHRISTOPHER R. FRIEDRICHS

Rural uprisings were an endemic feature of the *ancien régime* in central and eastern Europe. The great German Peasant War of 1525 has always been regarded as an event of European importance; it is increasingly recognized, however, that even after the 'defeat' of the peasants in 1525, rural disturbances continued to erupt in the German-speaking lands until the nineteenth century. Eastern Europe was no less affected by rural distrubances; Russia, in fact, experienced four massive rural revolts in the course of the seventeenth and eighteenth centuries.

Two questions in particular have perplexed recent students of these uprisings. First, to what extent can or should these disturbances be labelled 'peasant' revolts? In the Russian and Polish uprisings, for example, one must constantly take account of the role of the Cossacks, who can hardly be labelled 'peasants' in any traditional sense [cf. *Avrich, 1972; Kamen, 1971: ch. 10*]. In the Germanic lands the tacit or open assistance of townsmen, village elites or minor noblemen make it equally difficult to label these disturbances as 'peasant uprisings'. On the other hand, they would scarcely have had the impact they did without the willing and determined participation of large numbers of peasants.

A second question, and one which particularly concerned the contributors to this volume, involves the role of religion in rural uprisings. In some cases, as in the Peasant War of 1525, the role of religion has possibly been overstated by some historians. In other cases, as R. Wirtz suggests below in his discussion of early nineteenth-century Germany, it has perhaps been underemphasized. But a correct assessment of the role of religion in rural uprisings requires more than merely 'weighting' its relative importance; the essential question is how religious aspirations and values interact with the other factors that incite rural people to rebel against the accepted system of authority.

Four of the papers presented in this section offer broad interpretive surveys of the relationship between religion and rural discontent. G. Vogler considers Germany from the sixteenth to the eighteenth century, V. Buganov and A. Klibanov examine Russia in the seventeenth and eighteenth centuries, and R. Wirtz considers Germany in the so-called 'Vormärz' era – the epoch between the Congress of Vienna and the March Revolutions of 1848. All four authors concur on at least one important point: the capacity of the Christian religion to influence peasants' relationship with their social superiors in two different and sharply opposing ways. On the one hand, the transfer of hope and justice to another world can serve to reinforce peasant submission and obedience to legal and social order of this world. On the other hand, Christian precepts of human dignity and moral equality may serve to justify resistance to an oppressive social order. These opposing lessons of Christianity correspond, in fact, to the difference between the 'great tradition' and the 'little tradition' of religion which J. C. Scott [*1977*] has identified as a common feature of various cultural systems. The values of the 'great tradition' are typically espoused by the social and ecclesiastical elites; those of the 'little tradition', by contrast, find their clearest expression among the lower orders — especially in times of disturbance or distress.

This is not, however, the only dichotomous aspect of religion in its relationship to peasant aims and values. Vogler in particular draws attention to the fact that when religion contributes to rural unrest, it can do so in two different ways. On the one hand, religious values can supply aggrieved peasants with a set of values and concepts that justify rebellion against the existing social and economic system. On the other hand, when a clearly defined difference between two systems of religious belief and organization emerges, then the right to maintain the alternative, non-official religion can itself become the main object of an uprising. This happened from time to time during the Middle Ages, when heretical movements assumed a clear organizational character. It happened more explicitly after the Reformation, when Protestant liturgical and institutional systems arose in central Europe in competition to the older Catholic ones. A similar situation emerged in Russia in the seventeenth century, when Old Believers who resisted liturgical changes rejected the institutional leadership of the Orthodox authorities who had introduced them, or in the eighteenth when spiritual Christians opposed ritualistic Orthodoxy.

In some cases, then, religious ideas may provide theological validation for attempts to rectify social or economic grievances. In other cases, however, rebels may identify the right to worship in an alternative fashion as a major goal in itself. These two patterns, in fact, correspond roughly to the distinction drawn by P. Burke (*supra*) between religion as the 'means' or religion as the 'ends' of a rural revolt. No doubt Burke's vocabulary will strike some as being too simplistic. But to refer to the role of religion as the 'means' of revolt need not imply that one envisions a crass and conscious exploitation of religious ideas to justify explicitly 'secular' ends. It refers, instead, to situations in which a certain body of religious ideas and teachings is perceived as having a significant bearing on the social system in such a way that rebellion against the authorities is justified, or even required.

These considerations will be useful to bear in mind as one turns from the more general studies to the three case studies presented in this section. All, as it happens, deal with uprisings on the Alpine fringe of the Germanic lands. But the issues they raise and the contrasts they suggest are of general importance.

Of the three case studies, P. Broadhead's description of the St Gallen rising in 1529 offers the most straightforward example of religion being used as a means to validate or justify identifiably secular ends – in this case, the overthrow of the harsh seigneurial regime of the abbot of St Gallen. By espousing the Protestant cause, the peasants of St Gallen succeeded in adding an effective religious dimension to their long-standing economic grievances. The twist here is that the rebels had to turn for support to the powerful city-state of Zürich, which in dealing with the matter also used religion as a means towards secular ends – in this case, the extension of Zürich's imperials power into the St Gallen district. The ironic result was that the St Gallen rebels achieved the religious changes for which they had agitated but not the secular ends for which these religious changes had, to some extent, been only the means.

K.-H. Ludwig discusses disturbances in three Austrian mining districts which occurred contemporaneously with the great Peasant War of 1525. But only the uprising in the Styrian district of Schladming is treated in detail. Here, in contrast to St Gallen, we can see religious changes clearly identified as the 'ends' rather than the 'means' of an uprising: the miners agitated above all for the freedom to install and maintain a Protestant minister. The miners do appear to have had some inadequately formulated concept that freedom for Protestant preaching might bring in its wake some favorable social or economic transformation, but these ideas do not seem to have been sufficiently developed to allow for the articulation of social or economic grievances. Their only conscious aim was to change the religious situation of their community – and in this aim they, like so many rural rebels, were unsuccessful.

A substantially more complex model is presented by H. Rebel's description of the Upper Austrian uprising of 1626. To some extent, this great rebellion has been interpreted as a struggle over religious issues as such. It is certainly true that the uprising was initially triggered by Habsburg attempts to remove Protestant ministers and impose the Counter-Reformation on a substantially Protestant region. According to Rebel, however, the key issue was not merely the right to practice a preferred religion. What really mattered were the implications which religious changes would have for the social roles and self-perception of peasants, or more specifically of peasant householders, in the affected communities. These peasants, Rebel argues, had welcomed the gradual disintegration of communal life and communal interaction during the preceding century and the emerging role of peasants as independent, autonomous householders responsible not to their fellow-villagers but only to the state. By 1620, he argues, peasant householders believed that there existed an established consensus, not only about their opportunities and obligations within this system, but also about the limits of the system as well; above all they assumed, on the basis of the Habsburgs' hitherto lax religious policies, that certain spheres of life and activity were not encompassed within the state's purview. To Rebel, then, the Upper Austrian peasants of the 1620's, far from being reactionaries intent on preserving communal traditions, were 'modern men,' defined as such because they willingly accepted the decay of traditional communal values and accepted 'bureaucratic' roles within a modern state system, but also demanded certain spheres of autonomy – in particular, freedom of conscience.

This assumed consensus was rudely overturned in the 1620's, when the Habsburgs and their Bavarian allies adopted economic and religious policies which sharply reduced the degree of personal autonomy to which the peasant householders had become accustomed. The initial response was violence – but the rebellion of 1626, like most rural rebellions, was brutally crushed. Ultimately the peasants had to adopt other strategies for coping with the new situation, either by emigrating, or by converting, or by making an insincere conversion while remaining inwardly loyal to Protestantism.

Rebel's argument describes in a particularly sophisticated way how changes in the institutional aspects of religion can have social and emotional implications so threatening that they drive rural people to revolt. Yet two aspects of Rebel's argument may leave readers slightly dissatisfied. In the first place, while the backgrounds and motives of rebel leaders are fully explored, less is said about their followers. One can readily sense how Habsburg policy threatened the sense of autonomy enjoyed by economically active and socially ambitious rural leaders. One does wonder, however, if the issue of autonomy was quite so important for every modest *Hausvater* who joined the revolt. Secondly, Rebel's treatment of the problem of class is somewhat ambiguous. On the one hand, Rebel argues that class consciousness had declined along with the decay of the village communities, and that the individualistic peasant leaders of 1626 were actually less class-conscious than their communally-minded ancestors. At the same time, he uses the language of class – albeit rather hestitantly – in adopting the formulation of A. Hoffman that the peasant leaders of 1626 might be seen as 'socially mobile rural "bourgeois".' Capitalists they were, but unless one takes the position that the terms 'bourgeois' and 'capitalist' are to be used interchangeably, formulations of this sort are more likely to obscure than to clarify the issues. One may hope for a more precise treatment of the problem in Rebel's forthcoming book, whose title, suggestively enough, is *Peasant Classes* [1983].

All these papers, then, attempt to assess the role of religion in rural revolt. Yet none of them, it must be said, comes fully to grips with the complexity of peasant religiosity. This is, in fact, hardly surprising, for we still know very little indeed about the character of peasant religious experience in pre-modern Europe. It is increasingly recognized that the teachings of formal religion were not effectively communicated to the European peasantry, and that the Reformation made little difference in this respect [*Thomas, 1971; Strauss, 1978, esp. chaps. 12–13*]. In some areas, in fact, peasant ignorance of the tenets of formal religion persisted deep into the nineteenth century. In 1862, for example, a visitation of Bygdeå parish in northern Sweden showed that 97 per cent of the adult inhabitants were moderately to fully literate – yet less than one per cent were found to have 'good' comprehension of the Lutheran catechism, and only 9 per cent showed a 'passable' understanding of its teachings [*Johansson, 1979: 223–28*]. But it is easier to establish what peasants did *not* know about the Christian religion than to determine what, in fact, they did profess or believe. Even the invaluable compilation of material provided by K. Thomas' massive study of magical and other non-orthodox beliefs in early modern England has left many aspects of peasant religiosity still obscure [*Thomas, 1971*].

One thing, however, is clear: religious beliefs were not necessarily uniform within any social group or within any community. It would certainly be misleading to envision European communities in terms of a priest and a squire professing formal religion in the 'great tradition' on the one hand and a mass of untutored villagers loyal to their own 'little tradition' on the other. Each village sub-group, each family perhaps, arrived at its own syncretic *mélange* of orthodox and unorthodox beliefs. But if this was so, we must assume that the 'religious factor' in any given uprising may have been very different indeed for different members of any one group of rural rebels.

In particular, we must assume that in many such situations the religious values of 'leaders' and 'followers' may have been divergent. We know, after all, that all over Europe rural revolts and uprisings, though necessarily supported by peasants, were often led by persons of higher rank – by members of the gentry, by local seigneurs, or, as in the Upper Austrian revolt, by ambitious members of the local elite [cf. *Mousnier, 1970: Part I*]. Much has been learned about these rebel leaders, and much more still could be learned, for these are the people whose grievances, aspirations and excuses are most fully recorded. But surely future historians will increasingly try to detect the attitudes and motivations of peasant 'followers' – the silent people who, though not arrested, condemned and executed as ringleaders, in fact made every rural rebellion possible by their numbers and support.

References

Avrich, P., 1972, *Russian Rebels, 1600–1800*, New York.
Johansson, E., 1979, 'An Introduction to the Study of Literacy in Sweden,' E. Jackson and I. Winchester, eds., *Records of the Past: Exploring New Sources in Social History*, Toronto, 207–239.
Kamen, H., 1971, *The Iron Century: Social Change in Europe, 1550–1660*, London.

Mousnier, R., 1970, *Peasant Uprisings in Seventeenth-Century France, Russia and China*, trans. by B. Pearce, New York.
Rebel, H., 1983, *Peasant Classes: The Bureaucratization of Property and Family Relations under Early Habsburg Absolutism, 1511–1636*, Princeton, N.J.
Scott, J. C., 1977, 'Protest and Profanation: Agrarian Revolt and the Little Tradition,' *Theory and Society*, 4: 1–38, 211–49.
Strauss, G., 1978, *Luther's House of Learning: Indoctrination of the Young in the German Reformation*, Baltimore.
Thomas, K., 1971, *Religion and the Decline of Magic*, London.

Miners, pastors and the peasant war in Upper Austria 1524–26

KARL-HEINZ LUDWIG

I have already elsewhere [*Ludwig, 1978*] attempted to draw attention to the rôle of miners in the Peasant War. Recently the coalition of 'peasants, townsmen and miners' has been referred to in regard to the area around Salzburg [*Blickle, 1981: xix*]. It was in the eastern Alpine regions (see map no. 3) that mining communities exercised the strongest influence on the development of the Peasant War. In the following short sketch (derived from the conclusions of a paper read at the 1976 Innsbruck-Vill conference in memory of Michael Gaismair) I shall outline a pattern of events to highlight the question of religious and confessional elements in this conflict.

In the town of Schwaz in Tirol, which was at the time the largest mining district employing well over ten thousand workers, miners managed to obtain substantial concessions. On 5 February 1525 they presented their ruler, Archduke Ferdinand of Austria, with a list of twenty-one grievances. All were socio-economic matters. They had nothing to do with religious and confessional questions [*Ludwig, 1979*]. The large manufacturers, the owners of mines and foundries including the Fuggers and their agents remained Catholics.

As from late May 1525 mine-owners and mine-workers from the neighbouring Archbishopric of Salzburg put their weight decisively behind the fourteen articles of the Gastein mining district and allied grievances, which were based on an evangelical protest in confrontation with their traditional Catholic ecclesiastical state government. However, the rebels acted in a mainly political way. As a continuous mass movement Protestantism in Salzburg was not so much a cause as a consequence of the Peasant War. Mine-labourers were not directly involved in the complexities of tithe paying. Economic anticlericalism as motivation for the espousal of Reformation demands [cf. *Cohn, 1979*] thus had a particular cause. In Gastein and Rauris this was due to the increase in rent of mined ore from the owners of the mines. This rent was claimed to grow with the level of production as a result of technical innovations. This was completely new and against tradition. On the other hand those miners, willing to operate with mining-brotherhoods that were traditionally tied to the clerical system, had a chance to be owner and worker in one person. When the Counter-Reformation

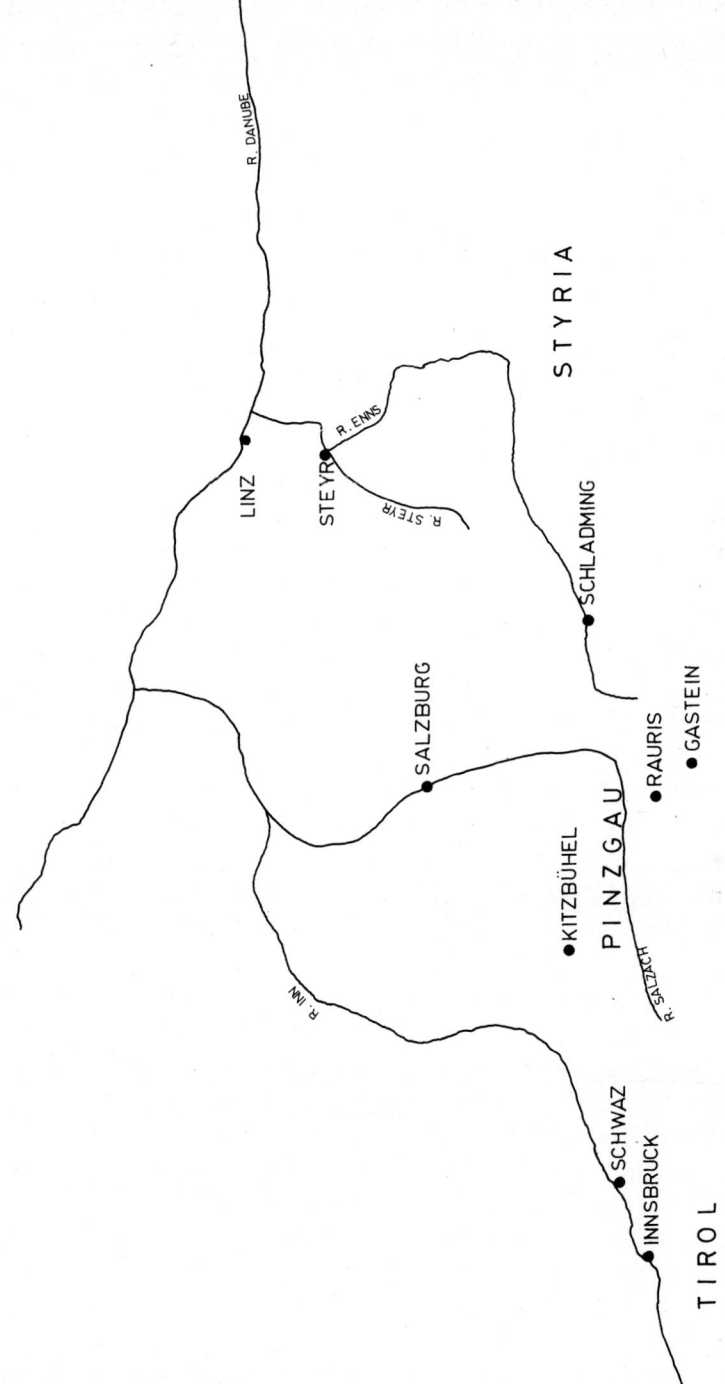

Map 3. Some mining communities in sixteenth-century Upper Austria

Catholic Church prohibited such economical activity of the brotherhoods since 1525/26, numerous small manufacturers were made dependent to the owners of the foundries.

In the Schladming district the religious question emerged above all as a main cause in the great peasant war. Schladming town in the Styrian Enns valley was the place where the rebels had their greatest military success when they routed the army of the Styrian nobility under its leader, Sigismund of Dietrichstein, on 3 July 1525. Three months later a second army under Nicholas of Salm burnt the town. 1500 rebel miners were subsequently hunted by victorious government forces as the main enemy [*Hutter, 1925: 20ff; Kunnert, 1927: 52, 63ff; Kunnert, 1929: 90f*]. Archduke Ferdinand repeatedly insisted that all the leaders and commanders who were active at Schladming be handed over to him [*Leist, 1887: 308*]. Schladming rebel miners heading for Kitzbühel or Schwaz regularly experienced difficulties with the authorities [*TLA, An die Fürstl. Durchl. II, 1525–6, fol 35*], who always regarded them as trouble makers. By December 1525 government hysteria reached such a peak that even miners' wives were interrogated by torture [*TLA, Codex 1874, fol 439^v – 440*]. These pitiable refugees only found somewhat safer shelter in the Salzburg mountains, especially in Pinzgau where they had nothing to lose in agitating for a second great rebellion of the Salzburg peasantry [*Leist, 1887: 310; Köchl, 1907: 73*]. After the rebels' military failure outside Radstadt in the summer of 1526, they were forced to flee this country too [*Leist, 1887: 392*]. Salzburg was placed strictly out of bounds and as late as 1528 their hometown of Schladming issued a mandate forbidding residence to all former rebel miners [*Kunnert, 1927: 71*].

In so far as they have not been swallowed up in the course of the military events and failures themselves, the deeper causes for the particularly radical behaviour of the Schladming miners are to be found in the field of religion. Schladming thus becomes a case directly for a third type of relationship between mining community and peasant war in the east Alpine region. Whereas religious theory failed to make any serious headway with the miners of Schwaz during 1525–6, and whilst it helped to unite mine-owners and mine-labourers in Gastein and Rauris politically and strategically against their ecclesiastical overlords, it was only in Schladming that religion seemed to influence the mining community directly through Reformation preaching.

Since the autumn of 1524 the common mining communities of Schladming had been locked in serious religious controversy. They clashed above all with the episcopal authority, a factor which, in contrast with the well worn theme of secular and landlord authority versus rebels, up to now has hardly been researched. In Tirol during the years before the peasant war, persecution and condemnation of heretical persons by the metropolitan see of Salzburg, notably the cases of Jacob Strauss, Stephan Agricola and Eustace of Heisterwang, had led to widespread anger. Unrest in Schladming was particularly strengthened by the relatively closed ties of the mining community in which it occurred.

In Schladming religious conflict was conducted only by the miners, from whom the burghers of the town kept aloof [*HKA, Innerö. Misz. Nr. 149*]. A variety of reasons, no less among which was an extremely profitable mining year for 1524, enabled mine-owners on the whole to keep out of the direct hostilities in which their workers were involved during the subsequent peasant war [*Kunnert, 1927: 60; Kunnert, 1929: 87f*]. A more detailed examination which would also include religious and confessional activities has still not been made. Yet at least those mine-owners who wished to reactivate the mines already towards the end of October 1525 had their credentials carefully investigated, since a number of them were under suspicion of having succoured and supported the rebels, and thus had to prove their innocence to the authorities.

By late 1524 mine-workers were above all enthused by the 'pure Gospel' and just treatment of a reforming preacher. The district court of Steyer reported the following from just before Christmas [*HKA, Innerö. Misz. Nr. 149; Kunnert, 1929: 86ff; Pferschy, 1976: 57–72*]. Led by Peter Klein, the mine-workers defended a dubious priest whom they called 'Herr Franz', since he alone had revealed to them the Holy Gospel. He had castigated especially the misuse of priesthood by rich priests and prelates. When the town judge imprisoned the preacher, the mine-workers forcibly freed and protected him. They then refused to hand him over to the ecclesiastical authorities in Salzburg, saying that such an act would be tantamount to delivering him into the slaughter-house.

The mine-workers wanted to discuss their spiritual needs with their true lord and ruler, Archduke Ferdinand, and not with the metropolitan authority in Salzburg. In the German-Austrian territorial state, the relationship between government and church authority was now tilted in favour of the former. When Schladming mine-workers overthrew their representatives' decision themselves to pay for the upkeep of the preacher for two months in order to allow for the establishment of a proper inquiry, the preacher himself more or less had to agree to his further imprisonment. His reasons were truly Lutheran: he wanted to prevent the miners from breaking the law just for his sake. Yet under no circumstances was he to be handed over to metropolitan Salzburg. On 18 December the mine-workers' associations wrote personally and directly to the viceroy and councillors of Archduke Ferdinand stating that they would rely solely on his authority and decision in ecclesiastical matters.

With considerable political acumen the mine-workers were calling upon their secular authorities for protection against the ecclesiastics. In four brief articles they refuted the verbal abuse that Vicar Wolfgang Mayr from Haus in the Enns valley had heaped upon them [*HKA, Innerö. Misz. Nr. 149, Anl.*]. They claimed that this representative of the Archbishop of Salzburg who may have been related to the Schladming mine-owner family of Mayr, had unfairly accused them of being heretics, and of having eaten forbidden flesh on fast-days. Thirdly, he lamented that 4,500 persons took communion at Easter, whereas only 2,700 had made confession. This shows that possibly more than one-third of the congregation were already Protestant. The fourth point concerned the demand for the pure Gospel and an end to further molesting of the poor. The mine-workers finally demanded proof of their guilt, failing which the Vicar should recant and pay the costs which they had because of the whole affair.

Official inquiries about the organisers who had temporarily freed the reforming preacher from prison failed to make progress. Schladming burghers declared that 'a whole rabble of mine-workers' invaded a meeting of the town council at which a woodman named Sigismund Kobolt was particularly vociferous. In the meantime he was no longer employed in the Enns valley but had taken himself off to work in Gastein or Rauris. Further information was denied the regional court for fear of reprisals from the mine-workers. The court complained bitterly about leadership at the mine, and especially against Klein himself. Since the mine had produced an extra profit of 2,000 gulden for the ruler's treasury in 1524, the court thought it highly unsuitable to browbeat the existing work-force with fines without suitable cognisance of their efforts. Klein, whom the mining-manufacturers still regarded as the best of the mine-workers, and 'who of all the Schladming miners finds the best ore', could always be prosecuted later. The reforming preacher remained in chains in prison until the following year.

It is significant that the Schladming records indicate a social structure whereby 'those who were permanent residents and who had sufficient property to fear its loss would like to have argued with the preacher if the ordinary mine-workers had allowed it': yet the 'common rabble was always opposed to it'. Equating miners with rabble was unthinkable in Schwaz during 1524–6, and there is equally no record of anything similar for nearby Gastein and Rauris. It seems that there really was a local east-west division which also applied to the social position of mine-labourers comparable to the economic situation of the peasants and even more to their politics. In the west in Tirol, rural courts had parliamentary representation, and there was the making of something remarkably similar in the Archbishopric of Salzburg. None of this was available to the eastern provinces. In Styria landlords exercised an almost exclusive control.

By December 1524 the Schladming miners' judge, Conrad Räustl, was no longer trusted by the government. He reported four days late to the regional judge and was not named as one of the three men trusted to report at once to the authorities any further signs of unrest among the miners. Less than half a year later Räustl was actually the commander-in-chief of the Enns valley rebels, having brought miners and peasants together on his side. After suffering a severe reverse at the battle of Schladming, the Lord-Lieutenant of Styria described Räustl as 'the greatest cause of this defeat' for the government troops, since he had obtained the support of the Salzburg rebels by convincing them that the Lord-Lieutenant was invading Salzburg territory in order to 'smash, burn and grind them down' [*HKA, Reichsakten Fasz. 78, rote Nr. 77, fol 442–442ᵛ*].

Even before the battle of Schladming, miners' leader Peter Klein had been captured [*Stülz, 1857: 139*] and although he claimed that Räustl was the ringleader, he was still tortured. Government officials in Styria had hired considerable numbers of mercenaries and other professional soldiers, and from this supposed position of strength they were in no mood to make concessions. Archduke Ferdinand's government here showed itself much more intransigent than in Tirol, where even workers' spokesmen were consulted in parliamentary negotiations. On 22 June 1525 the Lord-Lieutenant of Styria was ordered 'to spear, flay, quarter and subject to all manner of cruel punishment Peter Klein and all other rebel leaders and commanders' [*Leist, 1887: 280*].

No doubt these government actions further radicalised the miners. Yet the ensuing conflict, which reached its height with the government defeat at the battle of Schladming on 3 July 1525, lacked a wider political perspective, unless one generalises the main motive for the rebellion, as did Lord-Lieutenant Dietrichstein, possibly under reforming influence, when he accused the peasants of rebelling against ecclesiastical oppression [*Stülz, 1857: 137*]. Inner Austrian government sources also warn against 'a mood of conspiracy' (*ein pündtisch gemuet*) among miners and peasants, whose motive was presumably a general urge for emancipation perhaps aiming towards an equal political status for nobles, peasants and even miners [*Bucholtz, 1838: 627f, 633ff, 647f; Moltke, 1970: 311*]. In 1525–6 the ready conversion of Reformation theory into political opposition, which was later to be so characteristic of popular religion in the Alps, was still in its infancy [*Ludwig, 1976: 134f*].

The three Alpine mining districts that we have examined each had different motives in the way that their workers responded to the peasant war. Firstly, in Schwaz in Tirol there was a relatively well organised mining community which elected its own leadership to present workers' economic and political interests in negotiations with the mine-owners on the one hand, and the government on the other. Secondly, in Gastein and Rauris Salzburg miners had no officially recognised spokesmen, and they learned to oppose government interference by following the aims and methods of the owners of mines and foundries. Thirdly, in Schladming in Styria a mining community who had become evangelised by religion and who expected political reforms as part of a specific reform of the church attempted but failed to make the transition from religious to social reform – let alone to social revolution. The vital part played by miners in the Peasant War in the Alps now needs further close examination, for it was precisely in the mining communities that the boiling point came for social, political and religious movements which were widespread in the day to day life of the community at large.

References

Blickle, Peter, 1981, *The Revolution of 1525* ... Transl. T. A. Brady, H. C. E. Midelfort, Baltimore.
Bucholtz, F. B. von, 1838, *Geschichte der Regierung Ferdinand des Ersten*, vol 9, Vienna (reprint, Graz, 1968).
Cohn, Henry J., 1979, 'Anticlericalism in the German Peasants' War 1525', *Past and Present*, LXXXIII, May: 3–31.
HKA = Hofkammer-Archiv, Vienna.
Hutter, Franz, 1925, *Die Stadt Schladming*, Graz.
Köchl, Karl, 1907, 'Die Bauernkriege im Erzstift Salzburg 1525–6', *Mitteilungen der Gesellschaft für Salzburger Landeskunde*, XLVII.
Kunnert, Heinrich, 1927, Beiträge zur Geschichte des Bergbaues im Berggerichtsbezirk Schladming 1304–1616, Diss. phil. Vienna.
Kunnert, Heinrich, 1929, 'Aus der Geschichte des Schladminger Bergbaues. IV', *Blätter für Heimatkunde, Steiermark*, VII.
Leist, Friedrich, 1887, 'Quellen-Beiträge zur Geschichte des Bauern-Aufruhrs in Salzburg 1525 und 1526', *Mitteilungen der Gesellschaft für Salzburger Landeskunde*, XXVII.
Ludwig, Karl-Heinz, 1976, 'Ergebung und Widerstand im Zusammenhang mit dem Bauernkrieg von 1525–6', *Mitteilungen der Gesellschaft für Salzburger Landeskunde*, CXVI.
Ludwig, Karl-Heinz, 1978, 'Bergleute im Bauernkrieg', *Zeitschrift für Historische Forschung*, V: 23–47.
Ludwig, Karl-Heinz, 1979, 'Die 21 Artikel der Gesellschaften der Bergwerke 1525', *Der Anschnitt*, XXXI: 10–21.
Moltke, Konrad von, 1970, *Siegmund von Dietrichstein*, Göttingen.
Pferschy, G., 1976, 'Der Bericht Wolfgang Grasweins über seine Verhandlungen mit den Schladminger Knappen im Dezember 1524', *Mitteilungen des Steiermärkischen Landesarchivs*, XXVI: 57–72.
Stülz, Jodok, 1857, 'Bericht des Landeshauptmanns Sigmund von Dietrichstein an den Erzherzog Ferdinand über den Überfall zu Schladming am 3. Juli 1525', *Archiv für Kunde österreichischer Geschichtsquellen*, XVII.
TLA = Tiroler Landesarchiv, Innsbruck.

Rural revolt and urban betrayal in Reformation Switzerland: the peasants of St Gallen and Zwinglian Zurich

PHILIP BROADHEAD

In 1529 the people of the lands of St Gallen in Switzerland rejected the authority of their ruler, the abbot of St Gallen, and gave their allegiance instead to the neighbouring Protestant canton of Zurich [cf. *Spillmann, 1965; Blickle, 1980*]. Ostensibly this was a rural rebellion motivated by religious issues. It involved the rejection of both the traditional secular and spiritual power of the Roman Catholic Church, the secularisation of Church property, and the adoption of the Protestant faith by the people of the lands of St Gallen. Closer investigation reveals, however, the paramount role of secular forces in causing the rebellion amongst the subjects, and prompting the intervention of Zurich against the abbot. Religion, it will be seen, was a secondary, but nevertheless crucial factor in promoting this rebellion.

This rebellion was the culmination of many decades of unrest, complaint and opposition, which was rooted in a widespread hostility to the secular rule of the monastery. Central to this was a conflict over the status of the local peasantry; for in the early fifteenth century, during a period of weak rule by the monastery, the peasants had successfully freed themselves from many feudal controls over their lives and property, which had previously been exercised by the abbots. The peasants consequently considered themselves to be free tenants of the monastery (*freie Gotteshausleute*), rather than the feudal subjects of the abbot [*Blickle, 1980: 229*]. From 1463 under the energetic rule of Abbot Ulrich Rösch, the monastery had attempted to restore its political and economic control over the area and its people, by reviving, and wherever possible extending, the feudal rights of the abbot over the territory. The abbots aimed to restore their power through a re-imposition of serfdom which had been eroded in the early fifteenth century. In a situation of serfdom the abbot would have complete control in the area through his claim to own all the land and fix all the tenancies, his control of the local legal courts, and his insistence that the peasants were his bondsmen, without individual freedom. These objectives brought ruler and subjects into direct conflict as the peasantry was determined to consolidate and defend the concessions they had won earlier, against the onslaught of the abbots [*ibid., 265*]. There was therefore peasant unrest and opposition in St Gallen in 1489, 1525 and 1529 prompted by conflict over a number of recurring grievances. Peasants protested against innovations and new burdens imposed upon them by the abbot, especially increased death duties, entry fines, tithes and new laws. In 1490 their rebellion was squashed by joint action from the abbot's allies in Zurich, Schwyz, Glarus and Lucerne, who intervened to restore order and authority [*Spillmann, 1965: 13*]. In return, however, the abbot was forced to renew his alliance with them, giving considerable influence within his lands to a military official (*Hauptmann*) who was appointed in turn by each of these four protecting powers [*Blickle, 1980: 230*]. The influence of the *Hauptmann* was revealed in 1529 when the then incumbent, Jakob Frei, a nominee of evangelical Zurich, used his authority to enforce the secularisation of monastic property, and himself assumed the ruling functions of the abbot [*Egli, 1968: 620*]. Already in 1525 the instability caused by peasant revolt in Germany and the fear of war within the Swiss Confederation had given the peasants a golden opportunity to rebel against the authority of their abbot. They had hoped for support from amongst the abbots' enemies within Switzerland, notably Zurich, but when this failed to materialise, and with the example of the violent suppression of the rebellious German peasants before them, the revolt had ended in submission and punishment of ringleaders [*Kessler, 1902: 197*].

By 1529 the situation in St Gallen had changed considerably due to the opening rift between the four protecting powers (*Schirmorte*), Zurich, Glarus, Schwyz and Lucerne, who had, since 1490, largely dominated the wider external affairs of the territory. Their split was rooted in the ambitious foreign policy of Zurich, and was brought to crisis point by the Reformation in Switzerland [*Potter, 1976: 278*]. Schwyz and Lucerne remained staunchly Catholic, but Zurich and subsequently Glarus accepted the evangelical teachings of Zwingli. Zurich moreover did its utmost to encourage the spread of these doctrines in Switzerland, including St Gallen, which aroused the hostility of the Catholic cantons. These disputes ensured that concerted action by the four powers was no longer possible, and control of the strategic lands of St Gallen became a crucial issue in the divided political and religious life of Switzerland. In these circumstances the peasants of St Gallen found themselves in a strong position. Abbot, Catholic protecting powers, and evangelical Zurich competed against each other for peasant support in order to obtain effective dominance of the territory. Peasants played off the abbot against his rivals by offering their allegiance to any power that gave the best promise of satisfying their rural grievances. Popular opposition to the government of the abbot was strengthened by the negative attitude of religious reformers in Zurich towards monasticism. Attacks by Zwingli upon clerical celibacy, the Mass, and dietary restrictions

[*Finsler, 1918: 20–27, 52–60, 199–202*] left religious houses without function or Biblical justification in the view of his followers. These doctrines had been used successfully to justify suppression of monasteries and convents in Zurich [*Potter, 1976: 142–3*]. Zwingli also taught that spiritual and secular rule should be divided, and that temporal government should always be controlled by lay rulers and magistrates [*Finsler, 1918: 138*]. This amounted to a strong condemnation of the situation in St Gallen, where Zwingli's doctrines had won wide support by 1529. The doctrines of the Reformation, especially the condemnation of monasticism, provided for the first time a common bond between the peasants of St Gallen and the citizens of Zurich. Until then, the interests of town and country had always been divided: citizens aimed to maintain order and dominance over the countryside especially in marketing and manufacture, while the peasants struggled for rural independence and personal freedom. In 1490 and 1525 Zurich had acted to suppress peasant unrest in St Gallen, mainly out of anxiety that it would spread to its own rural subjects. In 1529 the call for religious reform with removal of the abbot gave, at least for a time, a unity of purpose. The peasants of Rorschach called upon Zurich to introduce and defend evangelical preaching in the area, for with it went a condemnation of the monastery. The peasants of the Rheintal asked Zurich for help in the fight against the rule of the abbot, and in defence of the Gospel [*Strickler, 1876: 126*]. In May Zurich justified its intervention against the abbot by saying it had acted at the request of the peasants to replace the abuses of the Roman Catholic Church with the teaching of the Gospel [*ibid., 166*].

For the first time the subjects of St Gallen had, in Zurich, a powerful and determined ally against the abbot. Already in January 1529 the leaders of the Zurich Council had decided that they should act to secularise the territories comprising St Gallen, and this instruction had been given to Jakob Frei, the *Hauptmann* appointed by Zurich [*Spillmann, 1965: 28*]. All that was needed was a suitable opportunity for action, and this presented itself with the mortal illness of the abbot, Franz Gaisberg, who along with a group of monks had left the main monastic buildings in St Gallen town for the greater seclusion and security of Rorschach. Zurich intended that on the death of Gaisberg no new abbot should be elected, and instead the monks should be promised pensions and persuaded to leave the house. This would leave the way open for secularisation, without bringing Zurich into open conflict with the monastery or its Catholic allies, a method which had been successfully applied in Zurich. In the event these plans went adrift as the monks suppressed the news of the abbot's death and fled from the control of Zurich to Rapperswil where they elected Kilian German as abbot [*ibid., 33*]. This complicated the process of secularisation for Zurich as St Gallen now polarised the conflict between Catholic and Protestant in Switzerland. In its efforts to remove the authority of the abbot, it was necessary for Zurich to win the cooperation and assistance of the monastic tenants. This process began in early April 1529, when Jakob Frei persuaded subjects of the abbot in Rorschach not to swear fealty to him, and a similar denial, again instigated by Zurich, took place in the Rheintal [*Egli, 1968: 372*]. Thereby Zurich tried to annul and invalidate the election of Abbot German, but this outside attack on the authority of the abbot created an ideal opportunity for resurgence of peasant grievance and unrest at home. Meeting at Lömmenschwil on 23 April, the representatives of all the local districts in the territories of St Gallen were encouraged by Zurich to refuse to accept German or any other individual as abbot, unless he had first the approval of Zurich [*Strickler, 1876: 113*]. This measure formed a significant break with the past for it united the native rural movement of peasant resistance with the outside evangelical campaign against the monastery waged by urban Zurich. It also established the political control of Zurich over the lands of the abbot by tacit consent of his mainly peasant subjects. It seemed at first to give the peasantry the victory that they had been seeking for over a generation and more, namely, to secure a means of appeal against the feudal authority of the abbot, by which it would be possible to by-pass, and consequently drastically weaken his power over them. Above all, it seemed to give peasant rebels protection against the abbot, and it also provided Zurich with a pretext for religious interference combined with territorial aggrandisement. On the strength of this, the forces of Zurich occupied the territory of St Gallen with the assistance of the native tenants, and following the flight of the abbot, Jakob Frei assumed ruling power on behalf of Zurich.

Peasant support for Zurich had been given in the belief that removal of monastic power would open the way for the redress of their grievances. Instructions from Zurich to its representatives in St Gallen make it clear that in May 1529 the peasants were promised, albeit only in the most general of terms, an improvement in their circumstances and removal of all 'unjust burdens' [*ibid., 184*]. Peasants had rejected their abbot in expectation of better conditions for themselves, and the nature of the reforms which they envisaged became apparent during the summer of 1529. The representatives of Wil made it clear to Zurich that they wished all the political and economic impositions of the abbot to be removed; they wished to live according to the guidance of the Bible, and to follow all their old customs and rights as observed before the abbots tried to reassert their authority. They wanted self-government without outside interference [*ibid., 345*]. In September, Zurich was presented with a major set of peasant demands that were the culmination of sixty years of accumulated unrest. They called for political autonomy for the area, and replacement of the abbot's feudal lordship, with an administration formed from locally elected representatives. The exercise of law and justice, which had formerly been in the hands of the abbot at home and underwritten by the *Hauptmann* externally, should be vested instead in a popularly elected official, called a *Landammann*. His courts would be sovereign courts, subject to none, and from which there was to be no right of appeal. In each locality the law was to be administered by judges and councillors who were responsible to the *Landammann* [*ibid., 366*]. The peasants envisaged a state which was not subject to any feudal power or outside authority, which would be independent and run by its own elected officials. The cohesion of this state, the authority of its rulers and its independence were to be guaranteed by the swearing of a territorial state oath, which would guarantee the loyalty of the natives of St Gallen to their own government. This oath was a declaration by the inhabitants of the independence and self-determination of their territory [*Spillmann, 1965: 43*]. As a corollary to this the peasants demanded abolition of all feudal dues, taxes, and Church tithes. It all amounted to a new economic and political order in St Gallen and one for which the peasants believed they had full Scriptural support, an evangelical Christian peasant republic. Following the precedent of the rebellion of 1525, the peasants called upon the Bible as the highest authority to refute the charters and pretentions of the abbot [*Strickler, 1876: 366*]. This was a manifesto founded on demands for political and economic change, for the peasants had found in Zwingli's doctrine of the primacy of Scripture a means to circumvent the secular legal authority of the abbot. But would their new masters in urban evangelical Zurich accept this St Gallen peasant point of view?

The peasants had not demanded abolition of the post of *Hauptmann*, but with supreme authority passing to the elected *Landammann* and his local officials, the *Hauptmann* would be little more than a powerless figurehead from outside. The response of Zurich to these demands revealed the gulf between the aims of the peasants and the intentions of the protecting power. Zurich had not acted against the abbot in order to establish a free territory, albeit a Zwinglian one, over which it had no control. On the contrary the Council of Zurich showed that it was determined to maintain its authority in St Gallen for political reasons of its own. The substitution of rule by Zurich and Glarus in place of the abbot at St Gallen had significantly altered the balance of power in eastern Switzerland in favour of the Protestant cantons. The absorption of these strategic lands had made Zurich the dominant political and military power of the region, and increased its ability to blockade its Catholic enemies in the central cantons. Zwingli repeatedly warned the Council of Zurich that it should act permanently to eliminate the power of the monastery, which was otherwise a major strategic threat to the security of Zurich and with it the Swiss Reformation itself. He saw coexistence with the Catholics as impossible, and fully supported any interference in St Gallen as a necessary preemptive, defensive act. Thus Zurich Council was not prepared for its own political reasons to concede peasant self-government within St Gallen, for this would create a vulnerable state in which the Catholic powers, particularly Schwyz and Lucerne, would have a ready pretext for intervention. After half a year's delay a committee of the Council was formed in Zurich half-heartedly to respond to the constitutional issues raised by the peasants, despite Zwingli's own appeals for urgency [*Egli, 1968: 357*]. By then it was already October, and it was apparent that confrontation between the former allies, urban Zurich and peasant St Gallen was unavoidable [*Spillmann, 1965: 54*].

Peasant political radicalism far exceeded what was acceptable to the urban evangelical rulers of Zurich, who perceived in it a rural attack on established secular authority. Jakob Frei believed that the unrest was caused by dissidents (*Widerwärtige*) and Anabaptists, [*Strickler, 1876: 404*], extreme religious sectarians who were opposed by Zwingli and other Protestant leaders. Anabaptists insisted that their members accept re-baptism as an outward sign of spiritual renewal and membership of the sect. Frequently they refused to accept the authority of secular governments, and they denied the authority of both the Protestant and Roman Catholic Churches. Instructions sent by Zurich to its agent in St Gallen in October 1529, show that the Council also saw in the demands of the peasants for self-government a motivation by political extremists and religious sectarians, who, '... in the Anabaptist way (wish) to be their own lords and shake off all authority which they find burdensome' [*ibid., 405*]. The agent was instructed to reject these demands and remind the peasants of their Christian duty to be obedient. He was also to indicate to them that it was in the interests of the peasants to accept his instructions, for if Zurich withdrew its protection from them there would be nothing to prevent the restoration of the abbot. The subsequent actions of Zurich in this dispute emphasised the conflicting interests and motives of both parties in their opposition to the abbot. In reply to the demand of the peasants for political independence, the abolition of all feudal dues, and a government formed from locally elected officials the answer of Zurich was a final uncompromising refusal [*Spillmann, 1965: 53*]. The *Hauptmann* was to retain his control of the government, and the only concession to the peasants was that some minor legal officials were to be chosen locally, although these were to remain under the orders of the *Hauptmann*. Any moves towards autonomy were firmly blocked by Zurich, to which all St Gallen local communities were to be subject. Thus the peasants were disappointed in their demands for significant improvement in their feudal status and burdens. As their ruler they had merely succeeded in replacing a Catholic abbot by a Protestant city council after April 1529. No fundamental change in their political and social status occurred, as they had been led to hope for. Zurich was prepared merely to consider removal of some recent fiscal innovations imposed by the abbots, but no orders were given for the total removal of feudal restrictions and burdens [*Strickler, 1876: 467*]. Zurich justified this in December 1529 by maintaining that such fundamental changes would affect the interests of the four protecting powers and could only be achieved by agreement between them all [*Spillmann, 1965: 56*]. This was in fact placing impossible preconditions on change, for it was inconceivable that Catholic Lucerne and Schwyz, as allies of the abbot, would accept the destruction of his authority and control in favour of Zurich. It was only in matters directly to its own advantage that Zurich was prepared to introduce constitutional changes which infringed the rights of the other protecting powers, as for example when Zurich decreed that only a Protestant could serve as *Hauptmann*, and when it extended the period of office for Frei for an unconstitutional second term of two years [*Egli, 1968: 621*].

When Zurich and Glarus presented their commands to the *Landsgemeinde* of the territory of St Gallen in Wil in December 1529, the locals rioted. Former allies in the struggle against the abbot had now become enemies. Zurich and Glarus had promised to consider peasant grievances, but decisions fell far short of peasant expectations. The local population was to be allowed to elect their pastors, but their choices had to be vetted by Zurich. Some minor administrative posts were to be filled by local men, but under the control of the *Hauptmann*. He retained supreme authority; he had the disposal of the power and possessions of the monastery, and the tenants were to swear their loyalty to him [*ibid., 630*]. No proposals were made for removing the feudal burdens of the peasantry, whom it was insisted should continue to pay taxes and tithes as before [*ibid., 625*]. The peasants found themselves subject to the forces of Zurich and Glarus, cheated of their hopes of change, and part of a satellite state of Zurich. The rioting in Wil was the immediate result of the ultimatum, and the representatives of the two cantons had to seek refuge in the local fortress until they were rescued by their own forces. When constitutional reforms were eventually imposed in St Gallen in May, the only concession made to the natives was the setting up of a twelve man council of locals to advise, but not to direct the actions of the *Hauptmann* [*Spillmann, 1965: 100*].

Peasants could after all expect little sympathy from the rulers of Zurich, whose city council contained landowners and *rentiers*. Zurich city itself was a rural landowner, and there was no desire to encourage or support peasant discontent whether at home or abroad [*Birnbaum, 1959: 30*]. The Council would hardly have given its support to the growth of the Zwinglian Reformation in Zurich or to its spread within Switzerland, if it had believed that it constituted a threat to the duly constituted secular authority, property and influence of the canton or its rulers. On the contrary, the support given by the Council to the Reformation indicates that it was seen as a means of enhancing its authority and prestige both at home and abroad. The peasants had been mistaken finally in their belief that political change would be introduced into St Gallen by Zurich, but had they been equally misled when they had originally given their support to Zwingli and the Zurich Reformation? On a number of crucial issues the peasants were deluded and deceived in their expectation of support from Zwingli for their aims. Zwingli was certainly a consistent opponent of the abbot, and he recommended the secularisation of monastic property with or without the cooperation of Schwyz and Lucerne. Zwingli believed that in the interest of its own security, Zurich should replace the authority of the abbot in St Gallen. To this end he believed that it was vital for Zurich to win the support of the St Gallen peasants, and consequently he advised the Council to support the rural opposition to the abbot [*Egli, 1968: 356*]. He also believed that Zurich should make clear to the native peasants that the city was the only powerful ally prepared to assist them with constitutional reform, but only in return for their firm allegiance [*ibid., 400*]. In a further memorandum to the Zurich Council Zwingli made it clear that these measures were little more than a subterfuge designed to pacify the peasantry. As a son of a peasant from the lands of the monastery in Toggenburg, Zwingli was well aware of the political aims of the peasantry and the resentment caused by feudal burdens, but he made it obvious to the Council that he opposed the dismemberment of feudal authority in St Gallen and the handing over of political and legal power to the inhabitants [*ibid., 398–9*]. Zwingli supported a policy of secularisation, but only if the benefits passed to Zurich and not to the peasants. This advice to the Council shows that the major concerns of Zwingli were the advance of his religious doctrines and the security and power of Zurich, for in his mind the two were inseparable. Only when these had been safeguarded could the interests of the inhabitants of the lands of St Gallen be considered.

The attitude of Luther towards peasant insurrection had been made clear in 1525, when he urged the German princes to use force to suppress rebellion amongst their subjects [*Borcherdt and Merz, 1964: 148–152*]. Zwingli did not make such a violent response, yet he also believed that peasant rebellion should be resisted, and order and authority upheld in the countryside. The peasants may however have been encouraged by initial ambiguities in Zwingli's attitude towards serfdom, for he had maintained in 1525 that serfdom should be abolished [*Egli, 1927: 346–7*]. At the same time, however, he informed the Council that serfdom had the sanction of God [*ibid., 355*]. It was the second view which accorded with the attitude of the rulers of Zurich, who were determined to maintain feudal authority within their lands and, like them, Zwingli saw serfdom as a useful means of maintaining order and control over the peasants. Zwingli was as hostile as Luther to efforts by subjects to overthrow the authority of secular rulers and magistrates. His tract, *Of Divine and Human Justice*, written in 1523, considered the secular ruler to be the servant of God, appointed by Him to prevent war, disorder and rebellion. Because secular authority had divine sanction it was to be obeyed by all [*Finsler, 1918: 357*]. The peasants may have been encouraged by his insistence that secular authority should not be exercised by clerics, which would apparently remove divine sanction from the rule of the abbot of St Gallen. This was not, however, a licence for rebellion, for Zwingli believed that the former authority of the abbot devolved not on his subjects but on Jakob Frei, as the representative of those external secular governments bound by treaty to protect the lands of St Gallen [*Egli, 1968: 395*]. If the peasants saw in the attacks of Zwingli upon clerical abuse of the tithe a justification for their own complaints against payment of those very tithes, then they were sadly mistaken, for in 1525 Zwingli had declared that peasants were still bound to pay their tithes, despite the removal of the authority of the Roman Catholic Church [*Egli, 1927: 352–9*]. In 1524 Zwingli had also condemned those who supported the call for religious reform from a desire to seize the wealth of the Church, out of hatred of the clergy, or because they hoped to avoid the payment of taxes and tithes [*Finsler, 1918: 445–6*]. These motives, he believed, harmed the cause of religious reform, which needed the protection of the ruling secular authority to ensure that all was done for the Christian well-being of the community: subjects should obey, and rulers continue to rule, quite irrespective of what was to happen to ecclesiastical power. Against this background the peasants could not expect Zwingli to champion their demand for political freedom and the abolition of feudalism. Zwingli, on the contrary, believed that it was necessary for Zurich to rule and uphold order in St Gallen, for he appreciated the dangers which both the abbot and his Catholic allies posed to the Reformation in the area [*Egli, 1968: 376*]. Zwingli was also alarmed by the rising support for the Anabaptists within St Gallen [*ibid., 614*], and he believed that the best protection against these threats lay in control of the area by Zurich. The Council had already shown in Zurich that it shared Zwingli's view that the growth of heterodox religious opinions would lead to social and political disorder, and it had committed itself to the use of force to uphold orthodox Zwinglian views and the authority of the reformer [*Potter, 1976: 186*]. In order to combat religious radicalism in St Gallen, Zwingli believed Zurich must exercise full authority in the area and resist demands for political autonomy. There was therefore little support for the demands of the peasants either from Zwingli or the government of Zurich.

Secular motives dominated the rebellion in St Gallen; on the part of Zurich the desire for political power, security and territory, on the part of the local inhabitants the desire for personal freedom and political autonomy. This conflict of aims made any permanent alliance unlikely, once the abbot had been dislodged. Yet despite these secular considerations, the religious reforms of Zwingli were essential components of resistance to the abbot, both for Zurich and the inhabitants of St Gallen. Zurich was no theocracy and the Council was not bound to accept the advice of Zwingli, but in justifying its actions against the abbot, the arguments of Zwingli were indispensable. It allowed the Council to explain its intervention against the established authority of the abbot and the seizure of his lands. This could not be done by an appeal to existing secular or canon law, which favoured the abbot, but it could be done from Zwingli's teaching that the authority of the Bible took precedence over any other law. Zwingli claimed that as a cleric the abbot had no title to secular rule [*Finsler, 1918: 357*], and he also insisted that the abbot should defend and justify monasticism with evidence from the Bible, before Zurich or any of the subjects of St Gallen should accept his authority [*Spillmann, 1965: 41*].

Zwingli believed that Zurich had a Christian duty to spread the doctrines of the Reformation in Switzerland in opposition to the Roman Catholic Church, and in fulfilment of this mission Zurich was empowered by God to intervene in St Gallen. Finally, Zwingli justified intervention in St Gallen by claiming that the election of Abbot German was uncanonical and invalid [*Egli, 1968: 354–5*]; that the abbot was seeking to usurp power, which it was the duty of Zurich to resist. This policy provided Zurich with the semblance of legality for its action. Yet the inhabitants of St Gallen believed that they had found in the doctrines of Zwingli justification for their rebellion. Günther Franz [*1956: 87*] and Peter Blickle [*1975: 141*] have shown that the peasants for their own political purposes seized upon the doctrine advanced by the religious reformers that the Bible was the ultimate source of authority, and that in any conflict between secular and Biblical authority, the law of God exceeded that of man. During the Peasants' War of 1525 the peasants had insisted that, although serfdom had the sanction of secular law, it could not be justified by Divine Law. As serfdom and a feudal organisation of society were not prescribed by the Bible, they must be a human invention, which should be swept aside in favour of a more Christian ordering of society. This popular attitude involved a much wider interpretation of the ideological attitude of 'justification by faith alone' or *sola scriptura* than either Luther or Zwingli had intended, and if it were not opposed by the existing ruling authorities, then the common people would themselves use this notion of Divine Law to usher in major social and political change.

In 1525 the peasants of Gossau in St Gallen had demanded abolition of the tithe, since it was 'contrary to God and against His Holy Word and Gospel' [*Gmür, 1903: 374*]. The peasants saw in the doctrines of the Reformation an opportunity to improve their own legal and economic position against the abbot [*Blickle, 1980: 275–80*]. Consequently they used the support of scripture for their secular claims in order to overrule the temporal authority of the abbot. In this they expected Zurich to support them. In August 1529 the peasant leaders of Wil declared that in establishing their own government and restoring old laws and customs, they were following the guidance of the Bible [*Strickler, 1876: 345–6*]. Similarly, when the peasants presented their reform programme to Zurich in September 1529 which included abolition of tithes, secularisation of monastic lands, and establishment of political and legal independence, they gave as their ideological justification that it was the will of God solely from the Bible [*Spillmann, 1965: 43*]. Scriptural authority was the only means which the peasants could use to justify their opposition to the feudal demands which Zurich was attempting to enforce. Luther and Zwingli had advocated the primacy of Biblical authority, but had never intended that it should be used to support revolution or heterodox religious views. As a result Zwingli rejected as false any interpretation placed upon the Bible but his own. In 1527, in his disputes with the Anabaptists, he declared that authority did not necessarily need Biblical support to be binding upon people, for all that was correct Christian practice had not been committed to writing within the Bible [*Jackson, 1972: 141*].

The events of 1529 brought to a head the political differences between the city council of evangelical Zurich and the equally evangelical peasants of St Gallen. Both welcomed the opportunity to overthrow the authority of the abbot, but in the subsequent reorganisation of the territory their aims were totally opposed. The catalyst for rebellion, which governed its outbreak and direction, was the development of the Zwinglian Reformation in Zurich, for this provided a unity of purpose and justification for an attack upon the monastery. The peasants saw in the Zwinglian Reformation a promise of social and political, as well as religious autonomy but by 1530 they had been disillusioned. Instead they found this type of religion to be a force which served the political interests of Zurich city council, and to be ultimately unresponsive to demands for political freedom of subjects and neighbouring peasants. The peasants had required the support of the Reformation in their conflict with the monastery, but found that this could be achieved only by accepting the domination of Zurich, whose policies were the negation of the aspirations of the inhabitants of St Gallen. Zurich would not consider granting political and economic freedom to peasants, but insisted instead on imposing its own feudal control over the area. In this it had the full support of Zwingli, for the success of his Reformation relied upon the support of the rulers and citizens of Zurich and the strength of the state of Zurich. Political opposition to Zurich and religious opposition to Zwingli were therefore suppressed, and the peasants of St Gallen found their calls for reform were rejected and their aspirations ignored.

References

Birnbaum, N., 1959, 'The Zwinglian Reformation in Zurich', *Past and Present*, XV.
Blickle, P., 1975, *Die Revolution von 1525*, Munich, (English translation; Baltimore 1981).
Blickle, P., 1980, 'Bäuerliche Rebellionen in Fürststift St Gallen', *Aufruhr und Empörung*, Munich.
Borcherdt, H., and Merz, G, (eds.), 1964, *Martin Luther, Ausgewählte Werke*, IV, Munich.
Egli, E., *et al*, 1927 and 1968, *Huldreich Zwinglis sämtliche Werke*, (*Corpus Reformatorum*), IV; VI/ii, Zurich.

Finsler, G., et al, 1918, *Ulrich Zwingli. Eine Auswahl aus seinen Schriften*, Zurich.
Franz, G., 1956, *Der deutsche Bauernkrieg*, (4th ed), Darmstadt.
Gmür, M., 1903, *Die Rechtsquellen des Kantons St Gallen*, I, Arau.
Jackson, S., 1972, *Ulrich Zwingli: Selected Works*, Philadelphia.
Kessler, J., 1902, *Johannes Kesslers 'Sabbata'*, St Gallen.
Potter, G., 1976, *Zwingli*, Cambridge.
Spillmann, K., 1965, 'Zwingli und die zürcherische Politik gegenüber der Abtei St Gallen', *Mitteilungen zur vaterländischen Geschichte*, XLIV.
Strickler, J., 1876, *Die Eidgenössischen Abschiede aus dem Zeitraume von 1529–1532*, IV, Zurich.

Religion, confession and peasant resistance in the German territories in the sixteenth to eighteenth centuries

GÜNTER VOGLER

In his *Special Treatise on the Uprising of Subjects against their Rulers and Superiors*, published in 1633 in Jena, the Saxon nobleman, Johann Wilhelm Neumair von Ramsla, discussed the causes that may move subjects to rise against the authorities. The first of the carefully documented forty-five motives was 'that the subjects are forced into another religion or church service or otherwise persecuted and harrassed in this matter or changes are introduced' [*Neumair von Ramsla, 1633: 8*]. His examples for this case include the uprisings of the Salzburg miners of 1525 and of the peasants of Upper Austria in 1626 'as they had said they were oppressed and persecuted because of the religion' [*ibid. 11*].

The connections between religious beliefs and rural (or other social) resistance noted here was in fact not a rare phenomenon in the course of history. Still, only very few studies have been written on these correlations in regard to the territories of the Holy Roman Empire of the German Nation. Interest has been focussed on the religious and confessional factors in peasant working life, in rural customs and in peasant mentalities in general, above all by ethnographers. Little has been done, at least systematically, to elucidate the function of religion and confession in conflict situations of rural society and in acts of resistance in the countryside. Most of the relevant studies concentrate, of course, on the German Peasant War of 1524–25 when the correlations between the Gospels and the uprising could not be overlooked, particularly when the rôle of the Bible as legitimation of peasant demands and actions was to be ascertained [e.g. *Blickle 1981: 140–9, 237–44; Maurer, 1979: 273–7*]. These studies have supplied insights into the mutual relationship between religion and revolt and into the frame of reference regarding ideology and socio-political struggles. It is, however, legitimate to ask, whether the recourse to the Gospel was an exceptional event in 1524–25 or rather whether it is a typical feature of social and political behaviour in peasant riots, rebellions and wars.

For our seventeenth century Saxon author the topic was reduced to the case where subjects were forced to attend a church different from their own. If one would limit the inquiry to this theme alone, many aspects of the problem would be missed. Even though only a few of them will be discussed here, we have to be aware of the multifaceted character of the issue. We are, unfortunately, limited even in posing all the appropriate questions for such an inquiry, due to the lack of elaborate research on the mentality and the development of social consciousness among peasants in the German lands. There are no studies comparable to the French works on *religion populaire* [e.g. *La religion, 1979; Davis, 1974*]. Some research was done on 'popular piety' in pre-Reformation Germany [*Moeller, 1965*] and on peasant mentality especially in Bavaria [*Hörger, 1975, 1978; Phayer, 1970; Wunder, 1975*] but they do not add up yet to a solid foundation for a general picture [cf. *Schieder, 1977: 291–8*]. Thus no more can be attempted here than suggesting some avenues for future research on the rôle of religion and confession in the German territories' rural resistance from the sixteenth to the eighteenth centuries and raise the question of their gradual decline in conflict situations.

It may be useful to state that when we refer to religion we mean Christianity. However, it should be borne in mind that with the Reformation, a part of that early-bourgeois revolution that began in 1517 and included the peasant war [*Laube-Steinmetz-Vogler, 1974*], a new situation emerged. As the split in the church became gradually petrified, the significance shifted from Christian religion to the different confessions that came to be established and increasingly differentiated among each other. Thus, besides the general factor, religion, the social conditions and their conflicts were also defined by the particular factor, confession. Both of these had their rôle in rural society and its struggles.

Without wanting to discuss here the details of the different definitions of religion [*Klaus-Buhr, 1975*] or the Weberian theses about capitalism and Protestantism [cf. *Seyfarth-Sprondel, 1973*], let us recur to a comment of the young Marx (in his *Contribution to the critique of Hegel's philosophy of law*) where he called religion 'the self-consciousness and self-esteem of man who has either not yet found himself or has already lost himself again' [*Marx-Engels, 1975: 175*]. State and society, Marx continued,

> produce religion, which is an inverted world consciousness, because they are an inverted world.
>
> Religion is the general theory of that world, its encyclopaedic compendium, its logic in popular form, its spiritualistic *point d'honneur* [point of honour], its enthusiasm, its moral sanction, its solemn complement, its universal source of consolation and justification [*ibid.*].

Both the dependence of man lacking self-fulfilment and the encyclopaedic character of religion is important in these passages.

Peasants 'encounter' religion in many ways. Social conditions and norms of feudal society place them into an ecclesiastical community by birth, without any option. From this personal bond and the belonging to the village community several duties derive which refer to work, customs, ethical norms and cultic acts. No village is imaginable without a church that was not only the centre for the cult but for social life as well.

> For the peasant of the late Middle Ages the church was the mediator of religious grace, the road from the toilsome life on earth to the eternal one. But the local church, near to every-day life, was also a place for festive acts, starting point for processions to the fields and beating of the village bounds. The churchyard was a refuge in a very practical way as well. Its walls offered protection from feuding knights and as a last resort the fortified church tower served as sanctuary. It was also the place for court- and village-moots, especially if there was no tavern or 'play-house' available next to the village oak ... [Bader, 1962: 195f].

Peasants encountered the church also in another very tangible way, when the material foundations of the ecclesiastical order imposed on the serfs particular burdens, beyond the usual sacrificial offerings. These, too, were seen as founded in the Gospel, whence the command of tithing could be quoted. In this aspect immediate relations existed between the church and the social order, especially when clercs or ecclesiastical institutions featured as landlords and unequivocally connected the feudal system of lordship and expropriation with the religious one.

All these aspects explain the fact that as long as the intellectual life of a society is not or not completely secularised, perceptions of social conditions and motivations for social action will be defined by religious ideas. This seems to be more true and lasting longer among the peasantry than among other classes. Rudolf Endres [1980] goes as far as to state that a religiosity based on the closed connection with nature and the annual cycle was until the technological and secularising impact of modern times a 'specific characteristic' of the peasantry. In the countryside traditions about family, work, leisure and life in general, that had developed during the long centuries of feudalism, often survived the social conditions in which they were originally rooted.

If religion was thus constitutive for daily life, it had to have a major significance and function in the peasants' actions in class conflicts as well. Our task is to inquire to what extent and in what form religious thought has informed and influenced rural resistance against feudal lordship and exploitation in general and in its various aspects in particular. A point of departure is offered by the fear men felt owing to their dependence upon nature on the one hand, and of the obscurity of social relations on the other [Kuczynski, 1980: 124–45; Hörger, 1975: 248, 284; Frey, above]. An escape route existed into superstition but there was also a road to consolation in religion.

Religion is supposed to offer solace, in contrast to superstition; solace not only in daily troubles, whether the harvest will be sufficient, whether there will be enough to eat, but also solace against the furies of war and pestilence – and solace, indeed, against all social ills and oppressions [*Kuczynski, 1980: 133*].

These words, however, describe only one side of the coin: religion could, under certain circumstances, also become a mobilising factor, exactly in the context of peasant resistance against feudal exploitation. While religion could enforce discipline and subjection, it could also offer strength to those who wanted to contradict and resist. This fact can be best observed in the German Peasant War.

The growing anti-clericalism of the late fifteenth century, which became an open issue during the Peasant War has been amply demonstrated [e.g. *Cohn, 1979; Goertz, 1980: 40–8*]. Owing to the close bonds of religion and church with peasant existence even the 'common man' was confronted with the entire crisis of late medieval church already before the Reformation [*Baumgart, 1975: 190*]. By doing so, it became possible to challenge the entire scriptural legitimation of the feudal exploitation – and that is exactly what happened. The growing opposition to rendering the tithe was not only based on its having been an unreasonably high taxation, but its Biblical basis was also questioned [*Vogler, 1982; Buck, 1973*]. The slogan about 'divine law', that has found resonance in several German lands well before the Reformation and the Peasant War (e.g. in the movement of Hans Böheim in Niklashausen in 1476 or in the Bundschuh of 1502) [*Becker, 1975; Wunder, 1976*] demonstrates in a concentrated form this new attitude. During the Peasant War this slogan became a mobilising force across many a German territory, informing a mass movement.

Religion served during the Peasant War essentially three functions: namely to legitimate, to integrate and to aid in the formulation of a programme. Peasant complaints and demands were legitimated from Scripture as being in harmony with the Gospels, witness the Twelve Articles of the peasants of Swabia. Recourse to the Bible allowed different local movements to merge into a super-regional movement, by establishing a common ideal denominator. The Gospel was thus basic to the peasants' programme and its articulation. The villagers of Äpfingen presented their demands with these words in February 1525: 'That which is from God, we wish to retain, but that comes not from God, we shall not keep' [*Franz, 1972: 149*]. The programme of the Taubertal *Haufen* similarly states that 'whatever is raised up in the holy Gospels shall remain upright, and whatever has been cast down shall be left there' [*Franz, 1963: 368*]. The aim was quite simply to fulfil the 'divine law', and this paramount idea defined the mutual relationship between religious thought and socio-political uprising.

The prerequisite for such a function of religion was a re-interpretation of the Gospel by Martin Luther and other theologians of the Reformation [*Blickle,*

1981: 239–44]. It was crucial that this interpretation be spread abroad by preachers and laymen, and that 'these sermons did not remain mere theories but clamoured for practical application' [*Fuchs, 1980: 206*]. The particular aspects of this *praxis* are worth special inquiry, which would throw light on the actual use to which the Gospel has been put. Let us look at some of the contemporary evidence.

It is known that Thomas Münzer ordered a huge banner to be made from thirty ells of white fabric, displaying a rainbow and inscribed with the words *Verbum domini maneat in eternum* [May the Lord's Word last in eternity], plus a rhyme to signify that this was the symbol of the eternal pact with God [*Gess, 1917: 109*]. The divine covenant was understood as a revolutionary community, and the rainbow as its sign. Its impact can be gauged from a report describing the events in May 1525 when the peasant army had to face the superior forces of the princes at Frankenhausen. According to Hans Hut, Münzer preached that they should not trust the authorities

> and that God is with them, because the peasants had painted a rainbow on all the flags they carried with them. Münzer said that this was the covenant of God. And as Münzer preached ... for three days in a row the peasants could see a rainbow from all sides, all around the sun. Münzer pointed to this rainbow, consoled the peasants and said to them, that as they now could see the rainbow, so it was with the covenant as the sign that God was on their side. They should fight bravely and defiantly [*Franz, 1963: 523*].

This was not the only reference to a rainbow as the sign of divine revelation during the peasant war. The abbess of the Bamberg Poor Clares reported in a letter, that when the peasants' war broke out in their area, the guards of the convent saw two beautiful rainbows in the sky 'locked in a cross above our monastery, at which they were mightily surprised. Thereby, in our great oppression we have the good hope that our Lord God has given us this sign that he shall not forsake us' [*Franz, 1963: 408*].

It would be totally unfair to explain this fundamentally different interpretation of a celestial phenomenon as a divine sign by ascribing religious feeling to the latter case and demagogical intents to the former. The very same kind of natural appearance was articulated by the revolutionary preacher as a witness of God's support for the peasants' struggle against their lords, and by the orthodox abbess as a proof of divine protection for an ecclesiastical institution against the rebellious rustics. The question is – how is it possible that a 'sign of God' could be understood in such opposite ways?

Before we try to answer this, let us adduce one more example. When the peasants of Upper Swabia prepared their 'Basic and correct major articles of the entire peasantry' to be presented to the lords of the Swabian League, the text of their Twelve Articles had been augmented with biblical references in the margin, which sought to demonstrate that all these demands were based on the Gospel. Luther took issue with this procedure in his writing against the Twelve Articles. To him the author was not a pious and honest man,

> because he had noted many chapters from Scripture in the margin on which the articles seem to be founded, but he was unable to swallow the gruel and comprehend the meaning of the sayings; it was only to pretend [legitimacy] to his viciousness and your enterprise, to mislead you and bring you in danger ... He must be a rotten prophet, who attempts to use you for his arbitrary dealings with the Gospel – may God hinder that and protect you from him [*Laube-Seiffert, 1975: 215f*].

The peasants' concern was to identify their Twelve Articles with what they saw as 'divine law'. Luther's aim was to denounce their author as a demagogue. Luther's unwillingness to follow the social-revolutionary interpretation of the Gospel is also demonstrated by his comments on individual grievances. For example, the third article states that

> ... it has until now been the custom for lords to assume that we are their serfs. This is detestable, seeing that Christ by the shedding of His precious blood has redeemed and bought us all, the shepherd equally with the highest, no one excepted. Therefore it is proven from Scripture that we are free and wish to be free [*Cohn, 1975: 15f*].

This demand did not deny due subjection to authority; only servitude was to be abolished. Luther refused to follow this argument:

> This makes Christian liberty into a matter of flesh. Have Abraham and the other patriarchs not had serfs? ... Therefore this article is straight against the Gospel and a robbery because by this any one who became a serf robs his lord of his body; while a serf can be a Christian and live in Christ's freedom, just as a captive or a sick person can be a Christian even though not free [*Laube-Seiffert, 1975: 218f*].

Clearly, the difference between the authors of the articles and Luther rests on their different understanding of the 'Christian freedom'. This concept could be interpreted in opposing ways just as the rainbow could be seen as a sign of opposite messages from God.

These examples suggest that we have to see Christianity not as a monolith, but recognise its internal differences with all the possibilities of variant interpretations of its teachings from within itself. Besides, Christianity was always changing during the course of its long centuries of existence. The function of Christian religion cannot be understood without considering those who refer to it, because 'religion can be utilised in an ambivalent way' [*Bücking, 1978: 135*].

It is here where we can recognise a connection to the origins of Christianity as 'a movement of oppressed people'. The original message of salvation for the oppressed was, however, transformed under the impact of the feudalisation of society, whereby Christianity was 're-functionalised' to become a religion suitable to the interest of the new rulers. In this form it was taught and preached by the church, whilst the memories of its oppositional origins remained alive only in heretical movements. About this kind of Christianity Marx wrote that:

> The social principles of Christianity justified the slavery of antiquity, glorified the serfdom of the Middle Ages, and are capable, in case of need, of defending the oppression of the proletariat, even if with somewhat doleful grimaces [*Marx-Engels, 1976: 231*].

But the origins were not entirely forgotten and thus the original meaning of the Gospel could be 'rediscovered'. Reference to the past was a way of opening the road to a new perception of the faith, which was above all one that ignored the interests of feudal authorities, and finally turned against them. The interpretation remained, however, equivocal: the Gospel could be used both for and against the peasants, for the justification of either oppression or resistance to it. During the German Peasant War the interpretation of the crucial passages on authority in Romans 1:13 depended on the given situation and the constellation of the moment [*Schneider, 1980: 261–9*]. Yet, even though the lords claimed to act in the spirit of God's will, the prevailing understanding of the Gospel in 1525 was the revolutionary one.

The picture changes definitely after the defeat of the Peasant War. While there was no comparable uprising of peasants for several centuries in the German Empire, revolts and rebellions occurred intermittently in many territories and even with frequency in some of them. Peter Bierbauer [*1980*] was able to list sixty-six peasant revolts in German territories between 1525 and the French Revolution of at least regional significance. Considering the additional incidents of class conflict of a minor sort, and of the increasing number of law suits against landlords, one cannot ignore the continued importance of rural conflict during these centuries [*Heitz, 1977: 199ff*]. Nevertheless, all these conflicts were limited to the local or at most regional level in contrast to the nationwide uprising of 1524–26.

Otto Schiff already explained these changes as the lack of recourse to 'divine law' and the absence of Bibilical justification for peasant demands: 'It was not fear that restricted the movements to local dimensions but rather the lack of an ideal influence, of a social teaching that would have justified and mobilised them.' Even though this explanation remains one-sided, the observation that religion played a different rôle is none the less worth noting. If one surveys the causes of the single revolts and the demands that have been put forward, they prove to be overwhelmingly defined by social and economic interests and relations. They frequently concentrate on the refusal to perform additional labour services. They object to the increased demands of new or additional taxes imposed by the growing bureaucracies of the territorial principalities. For example, religious issues were only of marginal importance to the peasant revolt of Lower Austria in 1596–7, and religion became more relevant in the Upper Austrian one only 'where Counter-Reformation measures were particularly ruthlessly enforced' [*Reingräbner, 1975:76; Rebel, below*].

Even when religious issues appear in these movements, they never do so exclusive of other complaints and demands. But even where they are mentioned with emphasis, their character is different from that in the Peasant War. This is even clear from the case of the Upper Austrian revolt of 1626 despite the significant rôles played within it by the Counter-Reformation and the Bavarian occupation, as summarised by the contemporary song: *Weil es gilt die Seel und auch das Gut!* (It's about the soul and the property!)

In this period the religious element did not feature any more in the form of a Biblical justification, as a legitimating, integrating and programmatic factor based on Scripture, but as a specific demand in defence of a particular confession – Protestantism. After the mid-sixteenth century the relationship between religion and revolt generally shifted from Biblical legitimation to an emphasis upon confession. At least partially, uprisings were aimed at the defence of religious liberty for a particular confessional observance.

An episode from the Upper Austrian revolt offers a rather drastic example of what was at issue. It has been recorded that the rebels got hold of a consecrated host in a Catholic church which they fed to a small, weak dog, while they gave a big, husky dog a Lutheran consecrated host. They said, they wished to find out

> which sacrament is stronger and which of the animals will overpower the other: that confession shall be the winner. So they set the two dogs upon each other. The small beast bit the big Lutheran one dead on the spot. Although this has frightened the peasants, it also made them fiercer' [*Czerny, 1876: 70f*].

This weird story draws attention to the contrasting positions in this early seventeenth century event. Whereas a hundred years previously the confrontation had been mostly between divine law and secular customs, this time it was between two confessions. Scriptural justification for peasant demands hardly ever plays a rôle. References to Biblical passages are rare, and at best a general outcry against 'ungodly' or 'un-Christian' behaviour of the superiors whose oppressive demands are seen to be 'against God's will'. Jürgen Bücking [*1978: 137*] summarised this changed rôle of religion in the seventeenth century thus: 'While it had been the integrating and saving force of a movement of the oppressed, it became now, in the context of a general secularisation, merely a decorative element.'

The Gospels are still referred to occasionally, and some revolts are strongly gripped by confessional confrontation. But it is significant that such features mostly originate in the missionary zeal of individuals, such as the miller and ex-Landsknecht Bartholomaus Dosser, who in 1561–2 in Tyrol agitated for an uprising in which all monks and parsons should be robbed and strangled, all lords killed and the Council in Trent attacked [*Ladurner, 1866*]. The movement in the Austrian Marchland between 1632 and 1636, led by Martin Laimbauer had similar features: Martin claimed to have a personal divine mandate as a 'Christian Soul-Recruiter' to guide back to evangelical Christianity the peasants who under the pressure of the Counter-Reformation had become Catholics. He acted as a priest, produced magic signs and visions, and pretended to have communion with otherworldly powers [*Burgstaller, 1973*].

However, these incidents cannot be regarded as typical for the majority of revolts and rebellions. In the course of the eighteenth century not only religion in general but also confessional conflicts in particular lost much of their importance, without fully vanishing from the scene. In the great Bohemian peasant revolt of 1775 the main issue was beyond doubt the *robot* or labour service as the most resented of feudal burdens [*Petrán, 1973; Válka, 1975*]. Still, besides the complaints about the *robot*, confessional matters were also raised. The rebels fought for the freedom of Protestant faith against religious intolerance and hoped to receive help from Frederick II of Prussia. They maintained that the Catholic clergy would treat them as wolves treat the sheep

> for no other reason than that we through inner enlightenment have been sufficiently convinced of the grave errors in a religion which runs counter to the apostolic laws and the true God, and that we do not wish to be led into the hellish den of wolves and have our soul corrupted utterly (as, alas dear Lord, has already occurred) by the above false prophets [*Toegel, 1975: 25*].

The Bohemian conflict merged confessional conflict with economic grievances. It occurred in a region where Protestant churches were oppressed by intolerant authorities. Although some contemporary reports maintained that the robot was only an excuse; that the real ground for rebellion was religion [*ibid. 37*], and that frequent reference was made 'only to a war of religion' [*ibid. 38*], in fact the confessional issue faded into obscurity during the course of the uprising. Hence even this example suggests the profundity of changes to the rôle of religion in rural revolt.

The developments we have outlined fit into the chronology of early modern times. The Reformation was followed by the Counter-Reformation. The former had released the potential for a revolutionary interpretation of the Gospel, that is for an understanding that could serve as a motivating and legitimising force for the peasants, even though Luther protested against this 'misunderstood' perception of his teachings. With the Counter-Reformation the pressure on the new confession increased and religious issues became focussed on the defence of freedom of worship. The few peasant revolts that erupted as a response to territorial authorities' often violent imposition of a certain confession in the Empire were exclusively fought by Protestants whose church was attacked, hedged in, and even eliminated by Counter-Reformation rulers, and never by adherents of the old faith against Protestant princes. Confessionally motivated peasant resistance was centered in the territories under Habsburg rule, where the Catholic princes attempted to restore the unity of the old church.

To summarise, religion could play a significant role in the life of early modern German rural society in three basic ways. Firstly, Christian teachings served essentially to uphold the social status quo which was identified with divine order. According to Romans I: 13, all authority was from God and all Christian religions subscribed to this tenet. Hence Christianity could be used against anti-feudal, anti-seigneurial movements. It could be called upon as divine sanction for subjection and discipline, thus the ruling classes had in the Gospel an ideologically powerful means at their disposal to dampen and restrain its challengers in social conflicts.

Secondly, due to their ambivalence, biblical norms could be used as well to motivate social and political resistance, especially in times of high tension. The prerequisite for that was an interpretation which differed radically from the norms of the feudalised official church. Such norms prefigured in some of the late medieval heretical movements, and became widespread after the Reformation. The new teachings were carried to the peasants by preachers and laymen. Peasants were then convinced that their uprising was justified by God, and that their demands were legitimate, since they were based on the Gospel.

Thirdly, with the development of different Christian confessions, subjects ceased to be born automatically into a faith. Instead, they were faced with a religious choice, unless they were disinterested and apathetic. But when territorial rulers acquired the right of *cuius regio eius religio* that is, when they could dictate their own choice of confession upon their subjects, religious tolerance became a rare thing. Authorities now made serious attempts, to build monoconfessional states. These policies created further potential for new conflicts. Resistance against religious pressure meant now the defense of a personally chosen faith against the imposition of a confession that appeared to be false, alien and had been rejected by the individual or at least his or her family and peers.

Finally let us attempt to sketch a few theses, subject to modification by further detailed research, regarding the gradual weakening of religious and confessional elements in peasant resistance movements over the course of the early modern centuries.

1. The Reformation and in particular its interpretation of the Gospel triggered such a unique intellectual activity and theoretical debate that, in the context of a

high tide of class struggle, a revolutionary interpretation of Biblical norms became possible and, indeed, widely accepted. Thus a close correlation developed between the social-revolutionary understanding of Scripture and open class warfare, without, however, fully eliminating the possibility of authoritarian use of the Bible.

2. The situation changed considerably, when, due to the split in the church, the development of different confessions led to the establishment of various Protestant theologies and churches. With the growth of dogmatic rigidity in these theologies and the emergence of new orthodoxies the space for a revolutionary interpretation of the Gospel became again limited. Also, the theoretical elements supporting feudal and feudal-absolutist lordships gained strength and became institutionally embedded in the Protestant churches of the different German territories, often with the prince at their head and the local lords as patrons in the parishes.

3. Division in the church and confessional divergence seem to have caused widespread disinterest and insecurity among the people. It was not easy to decide which faith was the true one in the face of a barrage of theological and exegetical confessional arguments. Distinctions between the confessions tended to emerge very slowly, and it was not easy for the laymen to distinguish between Catholic and Protestant rituals and ceremonies [*Zeeden, 1965*]. Abstract dogmatic debates and intricate theological disputations were certainly not understood by the peasants [*Hörger, 1978: 285f*]. The 'irreligiosity' recorded by many in these times may have originated in these factors [cf. *Schulze, 1980: 125; Kamen, 1971: 252*]. Thus it could be stated correctly that in the seventeenth century 'fewer and fewer men died for their beliefs, a phenomenon not unrelated to the decline of witchcraft executions' [*Rabb, 1975: 80*].

4. Recently, the increased 'legislation' (*Verrechtlichung*) of peasant-lord conflicts after the sixteenth century has been extensively argued [*Schulze, 1975, 1980*]. As territorial states developed, so 'institutional possibilities for solving incipient conflicts emerged or increased' [*Schulze, 1975: 283*]. Hence legal means were found more often than before, for eliminating conflicts. This can be measured for example on the number of suits brought to the *Reichshofrat* or of the establishment of imperial commissions of arbitration [*Press, 1980: 101–5*]. When villagers took their case to court or got otherwise involved in a law-suit they not only had to become familiar with legal norms but had to supply evidence that would stand up in court. Justification was possible by charters, records, agreements, even testimonies and inquisition, but certainly not by the norms of the Gospel. The rôle of religion and religious ideology was necessarily undermined by these experiences.

5. An additional element of change was the spread of natural law. When social order was seen as an outcome of a natural state and theories of contract were

discussed, even if the social order was still regarded as divine creation, the situation was an entirely new one. 'Henceforth superstition, injustice, privilege, oppression, were to be superseded by eternal truth, eternal right, equality based on nature and the inalienable rights of man.' [*Engels, 1975: 502*]. The enlightened – or to be enlightened – peasant became the ideal, even if rarely the existing norm [*Gagliardo, 1969*].

6. Wherever religious tolerance was introduced, and this was increasingly done for economic, fiscal and military considerations [*Hassinger, 1958*], the ground for religious or confessional resistance ceased to exist. Religious freedom was, however, by no means widespread, and in particularly intolerant régimes religious motives still played their part alongside other grievances in revolts and uprisings, and they often stimulated mass emigration, such as that from Bohemia and Slovakia to Germany in the seventeenth–eighteenth centuries [*Winter, 1955*].

7. On the other hand Christianity also continued to support absolutist rule. Maria Theresa [*Walter, 1968: 408*] put it quite bluntly in her polemic against her son's attempts to introduce religious freedom: 'Nothing is so useful and healthy as religion. Do you want to see that everyone follows his own phantasies? What should become of us without a firm cult, without subjection to the church?' In a sermon in 1797 Franz Volkmar Reinhard, professor of theology at Wittenberg, since 1792 court preacher in Dresden, emphasised the disciplinary function of Christianity:

> The common people become either despairing and resigned, or unfettered and wild; either unhappy and miserable or rowdy and intemperate in their enjoyments, unless they are enlivened with friendship; guided with goodness; governed with force; and consoled with love: Christianity is well made to perform all these tasks [*Reinhard, 1831: 99*].

In the German Peasant War, at the start of the early modern epoch, the Gospel acted as an impulse for a social-revolutionary movement; at the end of the epoch, its system-preserving function prevailed. 'From the point of view of the nobility, religion was for the people and it was good for the people, because it acted against the spirit of rebellion' [*Schlingensiepen-Pogge, 1967: 42*].

Our observations should act as a spur to additional research into the details and regional variations of the relationships between religion, confession and rural resistance in the German lands. There is also need for comparative studies to explore the similarities and differences between the religious elements in movements within the boundaries of the Holy Roman Empire and without. The scale of comparison becomes apparent when one confronts, for instance, the Hungarian peasant war of 1514 [*Szücs, 1977: 157–87*] or the 1536 English

'Pilgrimage of Grace' [*Davies, 1968: Dickens, 1967*] with the German Peasant War of 1525. It becomes clear that the secret of religious history is social history. Yet religion at the same time casts its own unique light on society' [*Obelkevich, 1976: IX*].

New studies that will check the validity of these theses should consider that the problems of religion and rural resistance can fruitfully be treated only in the wider context of all types of peasant resistance in the epoch of transition from feudalism to capitalism [cf. *Heitz-Vogler, 1980; 1980a; Gutnova, 1966; 1975*]. It has also to be understood that trends discernable in feudal rural society may very well remain significant in times, when their social foundations have long ago perished. That is why these topics are of signal importance to those regions and societies, where contemporary struggles for social progress are steeped in historical traditions and past experience.

References

Bader, K. S., 1962, *Dorfgenossenschaft und Dorfgemeinde*, Weimar.
Baumgart, P., 1975, 'Formen der Volksfrömmigkeit – Krise der alten Kirche und die reformatorische Bewegung', in: P. Blicke, ed. *Revolte und Revolution in Europa* (*Historische Zeitschrift*, Beiheft 4) 186–204.
Becker, W., 1975, 'Göttliches Wort', 'Göttliches Recht', 'Göttliche Gerechtigkeit'. Die Politisierung theologischer Begriffe', in: Blickle, *Revolte*, 232–63.
Bierbauer, P., 1980, 'Bäuerliche Revolten im Alten Reich. Ein Forschungsbericht', in: Blickle et al. eds., *Aufruhr und Empörung? Studien zum bäuerlichen Widerstand im Alten Reich*, Munich: 1–68.
Blickle, P., 1981, *The Revolution of 1525*. Tr. T. A. Brady and H. C. E. Midlefort, Baltimore.
Buck, L., 1973, 'Opposition to Tithes in the Peasants' Revolt. A Case Study of Nuremberg in 1524', *The Sixteenth Century Journal* IV (1973) 2: 11–22.
Bücking, J., 1978, *Michael Gaismair: Reformer – Sozialrebell – Revolutionär. Seine Rolle im Tiroler 'Bauernkrieg'* (*1525/32*), Stuttgart.
Burgstaller, E., 1973, 'Martin Laimbauer und seine machländische Bauernbewegung 1632–1636', *Kunstjahrbuch der Stadt Linz*, 3–30.
Cohn, H., 1975, 'The Peasants of Swabia, 1525', *Journal of Peasant Studies*, III: 10–28.
Cohn, H., 1979, 'Anticlericalism in the German Peasants' War 1525', *Past and Present*, 83: 3–31.
Czerny, A., 1876, *Bilder aus der Zeit der Bauernunruhen in Oberösterreich, 1626, 1632, 1648*, Linz.
Davies, C. S. L., 1968, 'The Pilgrimage of Grace Reconsidered', *Past and Present* 41: 54–76.
Davis, N. Z., 1974, 'Some Tasks and Themes in the Study of Popular Religion', in: C. Trinkaus, H. Oberman, eds., *The Pursuit of Holiness in the Late Medieval and Renaissance Religion*, Leiden: 307–36.
Dickens, A. G., 1967, 'Secular and Religious Motivation in the Pilgrimage of Grace', in: G. J. Cuming, ed., *Studies in Church History*, IV: 39–64.
Endres, R., 1980, 'Bauerntum', *Theologische Realenzyklopädie*, Berlin, V: 338–45.
Engels, F., 1975, *Anti-Dühring*, 6th ed., Moscow.
Franz, G., 1963, *Quellen zur Geschichte des Bauernkrieges*, Darmstadt.
Franz, G., 1972, *Der deutsche Bauernkrieg. Aktenband*, Darmstadt.
Fuchs, W. P., 1980, 'Der Bauernkrieg in Mitteldeutschland', in: *Nachdenken über Geschichte* (G.

Berg, V. Dotterweich, eds.), Stuttgart: 199–220.
Gagliardo, J. G., 1969, *From Pariah to Patriot: The Changing Image of the German Peasant 1770–1840*, Lexington, Ky.
Gess, Felician, 1917, *Akten und Briefe zur Kirchenpolitik Herzog Georgs von Sachsen*, II, Leipzig.
Goertz, H. J., 1980, *Die Täufer*, Munich.
Gutnova, E. V., 1966, 'Nekotorye problemy ideologii krest'yanstva epokhi srednevekovya' [Some problems of the ideology of the peasantry in the medieval period], *Voprosy istorii*, 52–71.
Gutnova, E. V., 1975, 'Srednevekovoe krest'yanstvo i eresi' [Medieval peasantry and heresies], *Srednie veka*, XXXVIII: 28–38.
Hartweg, F., 1980, 'Die Schriftbeweise der 'Zwölf Artikel' der Bauernschaft und ihre Widerlegung durch Johann Brenz', in: S. Hoyer, ed., *Reform – Reformation – Revolution*, Leipzig: 193–211.
Hassinger, E., 1958, 'Wirtschaftliche Motive und Argumente für religiöse Duldsamkeit in 16. und 17. Jahrhundert', *Archiv für Reformationsgeschichte*, XLIX, 226–45.
Heitz, G., 1977, 'Bäuerliche Klassenkämpfe im Spätfeudalismus', in: G. Brendler, A. Laube, eds. *Der Deutsche Bauernkrieg 1524/25. Geschichte – Traditionen – Lehren*, Berlin: 199–224.
Heitz, G., and G. Vogler, 1980, 'Bauernbewegungen in Europa vom 16. bis zum 18. Jahrhundert', *Zeitschrift für Geschichtswissenschaft*, XXVIII: 442–54.
Heitz, G. and G. Vogler, 1980a, 'Agrarfrage, bäuerlicher Klassenkampf und bürgerliche Revolution in der Übergangsepoche vom Feudalismus zum Kapitalismus', *Ibid.* XXVIII: 1060–78.
Hörger, H., 1975, 'Dorfreligion und bäuerliche Mentalität im Wandel ihrer ideologischen Grundlagen', *Zeitschrift für bayerische Landesgeschichte*, XXXVIII: 244–316.
Hörger, H., 1978, *Kirche, Dorfreligion und bäuerliche Gesellschaft*, Munich (Strukturanalysen zur gesellschaftsgebundenen Religiösität ... I).
Kamen, H., 1971, *The Iron Century: Social Change in Europe 1550–1660*, New York.
Klaus, G., and M. Buhr, eds. 1975, *Philosophisches Wörterbuch*, 11th ed., Berlin.
Kuczynski, J., 1980, *Geschichte des Alltags des deutschen Volkes* I, Berlin.
La religion populaire, 1979, (Colloques internationaux du Centre de la recherche scientifique), Paris.
Ladurner, J., 1866, 'Bartholmä Dosser von Lüsten oder der projectirte Bauernrebell im Jahre 1561–1562', *Archiv für Geschichte und Altertumskunde Tirols*, III: 261–304.
Laube, A., M. Steinmetz and G. Vogler, 1974, *Illustrierte Geschichte der deutschen frühbürgerlichen Revolution*, Berlin.
Laube, A., and W. Seiffert, eds., 1975, *Flugschriften der Bauernkriegszeit*, Berlin.
Marx, K., 1981, 'Zur der Hegelschen Rechtsphilosophie. Einleitung', *Marx-Engels Werke*, Berlin, I: 378–91.
Marx, K., 1980, 'Der Kommunismus des "Rheinischen Beobachters" ', *Ibid.* IV: 191–203.
Marx, K., 1975; 1976; Marx-Engels, *Collected Works*, Moscow, III–IV.
Maurer, H. M., 1979, 'Der Bauernkrieg als Massenerhebung', in: *Bausteine zur geschichtlichen Landeskunde von Baden-Württemberg*, Stuttgart: 255–95.
Moeller, B., 1965, 'Frömmigkeit in Deutschland um 1500', *Archiv für Reformationsgeschichte*, LVI: 5–30.
Neumair von Ramsla, J. W., 1633, *Von Auffstand der Vntern wider ihre Regenten und Obern sonderbarer Tractat*, Jena.
Obelkevich, J., 1976, *Religion and Rural Society: South Lindsay 1825–1875*, Oxford.
Petrán, J., 1973, *Nevolnické povstáni 1775. Prolegomena edici pramenů* [The Uprising of 1775: Introduction to its sources], Prague.
Phayer, F. M., 1970, *Religion und das Gewöhnliche Volk in Bayern in der Zeit von 1750 bis 1850*, Munich.
Press, V., 1980, 'Von den Bauernrevolten des 16. zur konstitutionellen Verfassung des 19.

Jahrhunderts', in: H. Weber, ed. *Politische Ordnungen und soziale Kräfte im Alten Reich*, Wiesbaden: 85–112.
Rabb, Th. K., 1975, *The Struggle for Stability in Early Modern Europe*, New York.
Reingräbner, G., 1975, 'Religiöse Aspekte des niederösterreichischen Bauernaufstandes 1596/97', in' P. F. Barton, ed. *Sozialrevolution und Reformation*, Vienna: 73–84.
Reinhard, F. V., 1831, *Predigten*, V., Sulzbach.
Schieder, W., 1977, 'Religionsgeschichte als Sozialgeschichte: Einleitende Bemerkungen zur Forschungsproblematik', *Geschichte und Gesellschaft*, III, 3: 198–209.
Schlingensiepen-Pogge, A., 1967, *Das Sozialethos der lutherischen Aufklärungstheologie am Vorabend der Industriellen Revolution*, Göttingen.
Schneider, A., 1980, 'Zur Argumentation in den Flugschriften der Bauernkriegszeit', *Jahrbuch für Geschichte des Feudalismus*, IV: 259–88.
Schulze, W., 1975, 'Die veränderte Bedeutung sozialer Konflikte im 16. und 17. Jahrhundert', in: H. U. Wehler, ed. *Der deutsche Bauernkrieg 1524–26*, Göttingen: 277–303.
Schulze, W., 1980, *Bäuerlicher Widerstand und feudale Herrschaft in der frühen Neuzeit*, Stuttgart.
Seyfarth, C., and W. M. Sprondel, eds., 1973, *Religion und geschichtliche Entwicklung. Studien zur Protestantismus-Kapitalismus-These Max Webers*, Frankfurt/M.
Sturmberger, H., 1976, *Adam Graf Herberstorff: Herrschaft und Freiheit im konfessionellen Zeitalter*, Munich.
Szücs, J., 1977, 'Die Ideologie des Bauernkriegs', G. Heckenast, ed. *Aus der Geschichte der ostmitteleuropäischen Bauernbewegungen im 16.–17. Jahrhundert*, Budapest.
Toegel, M. et al., 1975, *Prameny k nevolnickému povstání v Cechách a na Morave v roce 1775* [Sources on the serfs' uprisings in Bohemia and Moravia in 1775], Prague.
Válka, J., 1975, 'K problému sociálního myslení a ideologie nevolníků 1775' [contributions to the problems of social thought and ideology in the 1775 revolt], *Povstání poddanského lidu 1775 v severovýchodních Cechách* [The 1775 uprising of the servile population in northeastern Bohemia], Prague: 161–82.
Vogler, G., 1982, *Nürnberg 1524/25. Studien zur reformatorischen und sozialen Bewegung in der Reichsstadt*, Berlin.
Walter, F., 1968, ed., *Maria Theresia. Briefe und Aktenstücke in Auswahl*, Darmstadt.
Winter, E., 1955, *Die tschechische und slowakische Emigration in Deutschland im 17. und 18. Jahrhundert*, Berlin.
Wunder, H., 1975, 'Zur Mentalität aufständischer Bauern. Möglichkeiten der Zusammenarbeit von Geschichtswissenschaft und Antropologie, dargestellt am Beispiel des Samländischen Bauernaufstandes von 1525', in: H. U. Wehler, ed. *Der Deutsche Bauernkrieg 1524–1526*, Göttingen: 9–37.
Wunder, H., 1976, ' "Old Law" and "Divine Law" in the German Peasant War', in: J. Bak, ed. *The German Peasant War of 1525*, London: 54–62.
Zeeden, W., 1965, *Die Entstehung der Konfessionen. Grundlagen und Formen der Konfessionsbildung im Zeitalter der Glaubenskämpfe*, Munich.

Bureaucratic tenure, peasant leadership and politiques during the Austrian Counter-Reformation

HERMANN REBEL

Early in the sixteenth century there occurred, for both theoretical and political reasons, a revolution in the Habsburgs' administration of public finance. With the exception of the *Salzkammergut*, royal properties in Upper and Lower Austria became 'public' properties as they came increasingly under the state-regulated administration of the crown's creditors. A case study of the social impact of the changes in Upper Austria has revealed that the funds that flowed from these pawn arrangements and lien administrations (*Pfandherrschaften*) produced a fiscal revolution at the estate level [*Rebel, 1983*]. The royal administration had taken the lead in changing the conditions of and incomes from peasant tenure on crown estates, in converting *Robot* service to cash payments, and in integrating peasant family, house and community institutions into estate administration – thereby rendering crown estate management more uniform, profitable and attractive to potential creditors and lien administrators. These latter in turn found it to their advantage to bring the administration of their own estates into line with that of the royal estates in their control; they realized increases in cash flow that enabled them to finance new economic and social enterprises. By the early seventeenth century there had developed a new kind of estate management, whose chief sources of income derived both directly and indirectly from the state's new fiscal arrangement. Under the direction of this new private and crown estate management the traditionally political and social institutions of the feudal state, the peasant family, the village commune and the territorial Estates, were left in place but their character changed as they became a part of a bureaucratic state apparatus consisting of peasant houses, village and parish guilds, estate magistracies and regional and state authorities.

One of the first acts toward this new fiscal state was the crown's assertion of control over and elimination of the partibility of peasant holdings on pawned estates. The lien contracts required the creditors to adhere to the Roman law principle of emphyteusis whereby they could act for a contractually specified time as if they were owners but had to return the property without having in any way diminished it. This meant that the lien administrator had to pay strictest attention to and stop the peasants' tendency to break up their holdings for inheritance or sale. If he didn't, agents of the crown would do it for him. This revolution in estate management extended, moreover, beyond a mere coerced impartibility which became, in time, a fundamental aspect of peasant tenure in Upper and Lower Austra and Bohemia; it changed the very nature of peasant property ownership and family life itself. Because peasant holdings now functioned as units in the state's and the estates' finances they were not only made impartible but were also reduced or, in some cases, upgraded to uniformly inheritable leaseholds whose administration was in the hands of tenants whose qualifications and competence, in turn, were no longer matters for village and parish scrutiny but were wholly subject to the judgment of estate officials. Not suprisingly, those officials applied standards of emphyteusis (determined by means of a property inventory taken at a tenant's death) similar to those to which the state's lien holders were also subject.

Under the new conditions of ownership the focus of the rural household economy shifted away from the traditional cycles of agricultural production and family development and toward the tenured peasant's fiscal and personnel management requirements as head of a house. The peasant holding functioned increasingly as both a 'farm' and as an adjunct to the bureaucratic order. For the head of a house to fail in either capacity meant a loss of tenure and he was increasingly required to manage both his properties and his family strictly for the benefit of maintaining his official position. The rules and contracts governing the devolution of property and the evolution of family and household relations were altered and standardized by the state to assist the heads of families. The settlement of the Upper Austrian peasant rebellions concerned with these changes in 1597 by royal mediation and by the publication of negotiated guidelines by the state (Rudolph II's Interim of 1597) marks the turning point by which this new system combining bureaucratic tenure with family management became public law.

The onset of the Counter-Reformation around 1600 produced a crisis of tenure for the housed peasants of Austria. Though threatening since the last decades of the sixteenth century, the change in religious regime did not begin in earnest in Upper Austria until 1625. After an initial failure, the Emperor's *Reformationskommission*, headed by the Bavarian lien administrator, Adam von Herbersdorf, tried to install a Catholic priest at the estate Frankenburg, where they could count on the cooperation of the estate's absentee owner, Franz Christopher Khevenhüller, and his chief manager, Abraham Grünpacher, both of whom were, like Herbersdorf himself, *politique* converts to Catholicism. This time, when they met with resistance, the authorities retaliated harshly. With the peasant crowd dispersed, Herbersdorf asked the estate bailiffs, village councillors, and parish guildmasters to step forward and assemble. He berated them severely for allowing such criminal behaviour to occur and concluded that, since the perpetrators had escaped, they would have to suffer criminal punishment instead. These men paired off, and were made to roll the dice against each other. Those who lost were bound and executed. Their bodies were left to hang for three days and then impaled on pikes alongside the Imperial road near the market at Vöcklabruck [*Stieve, 1904, 1: 60–64; Strnadt, 1926: 42–46*].

Herbersdorf's actions have been explained, if not excused altogether, as the normal procedure of military discipline in the era of the Thirty Years' War. One could maintain, moreover, that the cruel rolling of the dice not only allowed half of the 'guilty' to escape but introduced an element of chance that brought into play the ancient theory of trial by ordeal, according to which an evil act entered the world again to strike the evildoer. Herbersdorf was acting as the head of an occupying army, and precedents dating from the Romans to current seventeenth-century practice indicated that the principle of decimation decided by lot was often called on to deal with massive mutiny among soldiers, when it was expedient to have only a few experience the punishment of all. In this view, the 'dicing' at Frankenburg, an event that has retained a prominent place in Austrian popular history and mythology, did not warrant the outraged reaction of the peasants to what appeared as the infernal cruelty and tyranny of Herbersdorf's regime, since this action was a 'normal' part of military life [*Sturmberger, 1976: 242–246*].

This is, however, to forget that the parish leaders and peasant officeholders who were singled out at Frankenburg were not soldiers and that they represented not mutineers but, at worst, a more or less active opposition to the coerced transformation of parish organization and ministry. We cannot simply assume that the peasants were only capable of an emotional reaction to what they perceived as cruel and unjust punishments; there were cooler heads among them for whom the legal and social implications of the bizarre events at Frankenburg were perfectly clear. It was they who would be the targets of discipline in the state's new religious order. Not only was the new regime not punishing the recalcitrant and particularly rebellious individuals; it ignored them. Instead, it directed itself against those who had achieved the highest offices and positions of esteem and respect among their fellow subjects and parishioners and threatened them, first, with the loss of tenure if they did not comply with the order to assemble. Then, by executing men who were not personally responsible for the resistance, Herbersdorf was flinging the gauntlet in the face of the peasantry's leading groups and persons, and holding in opposition to their demands for religious self-determination his authority to deny them even the most fundamental processes of civilian law. Under the Counter-Reformation the new bureaucratic order for tenants and estate officers was enforced by military rules backed by the powers of the absolute state. It was this essential 'lawlessness' of the Counter-Revolution process that appeared to contradict as we shall see in a moment the recently achieved bureaucratic regulation of tenure.

With the peasantry of Frankenburg temporarily pacified and the installation of Catholic priests slowly gaining momentum in the other rural parishes, the *Reformationskommission* felt sufficiently secure to let the other shoe drop; on 10 October 1625, they published a *Reformationspatent* whose nine articles did not threaten the peasantry with merely religious but also with social reprisals, [*Stieve, 1904, 1: 38–39; Strnadt, 1926: 46–49*]. According to this patent, the parishes were required to give up immediately their Protestant clerics, key figures in the social life of the parish, as well as their control over the endowments and treasuries of the parish churches [*Stieve, 1904, 2: 37n. 3*], which had been a vital part of each rural parish guild's banking and commercial functions and had also supported the parish schools and their teachers. The Counter-Reformation state clearly aimed to bring under control the peasantry's 'independent' communal organizations and politics. Also in the area of education, the *Reformationspatent* forbade the keeping of private tutors, disbanded the women's social circles that had formed to read and interpret sermons, attacked the sale and ownership of proscribed heretical literature, and, finally, forbade the education of children in schools outside Upper Austria. All of these were important institutions and practices serving both peasantry and townsmen. Furthermore, the commercial, craft, and labor guilds were required to participate in their parish's Corpus Christi parade and were otherwise required to participate in the Catholic liturgical year. The most serious clause in this new religious order was, however, directed at the broad mass of the rural subject population. Everyone in Upper Austria had until Easter of 1626 to do one of two things: they could either convert to the Roman Church and display, when required, the documents proving they had attended confession, or they could choose to leave Upper Austria, after paying the customary 10 percent *Freigeld* as well as a further 10 percent on their assessed properties. Such *Beichtzettel* or *Absolutionsscheine*, as these documents were called, were introduced in 1598, after the pacification of the peasant uprising. [*Strnadt, 1926: 47–48*]. A three-time offender against the forced attendance of confession could lose his farm as early as 1598 but this was not enforced until after 1625 [*Czerny, 1890: 6*].

This clause of the *Reformationspatent* confronted the peasant householders with a frustrating dilemma. On the one hand, if they chose emigration and exercised a tenant's 'freedom' to move, they took a bad financial beating; according to the grievances of June and July of 1626, under Herbersdorf's administration of the *ius emigrandi*, other charges were imposed on top of the two 10 percent fees so that by the time a tenant received his permission to leave and his passport, he had often forfeited over 50 percent of his properties [*Stieve, 1904, 2: 252, 263–264*]. In other words, they not only gave up tenure and the social position they had built in Upper Austria but their chances of getting away with enough to purchase and maintain tenure elsewhere were not good. On the other hand, if they took the *politique* course as Abraham Grünpacher and others had done, and changed their religion to retain their tenured status, they denied many of the collective political and legal gains they appeared to have made since the latter decades of the sixteenth century, most notably, that no authority could determine *directly* a subject's religious choice [*Hantsch, 1968, 1: 320*] and that the maintenance of tenure over several generations guaranteed a kind of 'residency' that even the terms of emphyteusis could not touch [cf. *Hohberg, 1715: 13*].

The *Reformationspatent* of 1625 triggered an ill-fated peasant revolt that lasted through the Spring and Summer of 1626 because it constituted the culmination of the state's long policy to gain control over the terms of tenure and over the bureaucratic duties imposed on and the privileges dependent on tenure; it overthrew once and for all any illusion that the authority behind the position of the tenured class carried any kind of feudal or Estate-derived legality, and clearly demonstrated that it rested rather on bureaucratic rationality that was in turn wholly subject to the charismatic authority of the prince and his state. We can develop this theme by examining, first, the social position and the activities of the peasant leaders who organized the resistance of 1626 and, second, the peasant grievances that were sent to the Emperor in July of 1626.

Stefan Fadinger and Christoph Zeller led the Upper Austrian peasantry in the early phase of the war of 1626 and Achaz Wiellinger held the high command until the end of the rebellion. Fadinger and Zeller became the elected leaders of the peasant army that formed after an initial peasant victory at Peuerbach on 21 May, 1626. Stefan Fadinger was, like so many other peasants of his day, the subject of several authorities. The original owner of his tenancy was the Protestant *Freiherr* Johann Karl Jörger who lost his properties and life for the role he played in the 1620 fronde. Fadinger's new landlord, after 2 June 1622, was Count Carl von Harrach, one of the chief executors and beneficiaries of Ferdinand II's Counter-Reformation [*Fattinger, 1965: 49–52*]. Fadinger's tenancy is invariably described as the 'handsome estate' Fatting am Walde [*Stieve, 1904, 1: 73n. 3, 315n. 2*] and had been, significantly, in the hands of his family since the days of his great-grandfather in the early sixteenth century, when the family was subject to the estate Schaunberg. Stefan, the youngest of three sons, took it over in 1616/17 from his father Paulus. His brothers Moritz and Hans appear not to have been active in the 1626 uprising; the latter was deeply involved in the textile trade and died in 1637, a moderately wealthy man [*Fattinger, undated: 72–74*]. The fixed property of Stefan's tenancy was assessed at 800 fl and his indebtedness after his death amounted to 1,300 fl; the value of his movables and outstanding loans must have been quite high, for his inventory showed a surplus of 174 fl [*Stieve, 1904, 1: 74n. 12*]. The question of Stefan's occupational status is problematical. His wealth, his indebtedness, and, as we shall see, his overall social status were completely out of character with that of the 'simple' farmer that Stieve sees [*1904, 1: 73n. 6*]. Perhaps most telling in this regard is the actual size of his farm which at about 17 acres arable, 8 1/2 acres of meadowland, and a little more than 7 acres of woods, [*Fettinger, n.d.: 72*] was modest for a farmer of this period and could certainly not have accounted for his wealth and social status.

Although little remains in the archives concerning Fadinger, there is one fragment of evidence that places him squarely among the most legally privileged members of the tenant class. When the Steyr lawyer and manager of the Polheim estate Parz, Lazarus Holzmüller, was interrogated after the peasant war, he claimed that he, together with Wolf Madlseder (a magistrate of Steyr and, as we shall see, connected to Achaz Wiellinger as well) and Johann Grenner (the estate manager of Peuerbach) had helped to direct the peasant war and that the latter had held Fadiner's signet ring [*Stieve, 1904, 1: 113n. 3, n. 6, n. 7*]. Among the Upper Austrian peasantry of this period signet rings (*Petschaften*) were complex instruments not only of personal and public correspondence but also of commerce [cf. *Grüll, 1969: 6*]. They were exchanged as signs of mutual trust between parties engaged in private commercial and credit transactions as well as in official affairs. In their correspondence and even in estate documents, the highly placed and commercially active subject tenants were identified by such respectful terms of address as noble (*ersam*) and steadfast (*vest*), qualities that were of utmost importance in a cosmopolitan rural society where the wheels of commerce moved on hubs of trust, loyalty, and rank – and it was the use of personal signet rings that backed up these forms of address and that identified their bearers and holders as men of particularly good reputation involved in important commercial and public affairs. To 'hold' another man's seal, as Johann Grenner held Fadinger's, permitted the holder to affix that seal to an official document. Signet rings functioned as bureaucratic instruments denoting chains of authority and privilege. With his signet ring in the hands of the estate manager of Peuerbach, Fadinger was clearly not the simple peasant farmer that Stieve imagined but was rather an ally of a significant commercial and political figure. He stood above the common tenant farmers and had moved to the highest position of legally privileged occupational status to which a subject could aspire.

Stefan Fadinger's brother-in-law and second-in-command, Christoph Zeller, led the peasants from north of the Danube (even though he too lived south of the Danube in the parish St Agatha and was a subject of the estate Stauf). He was an innkeeper in the town of Haibach, a Protestant center and a focal point of the

1595–1597 rebellion [*Stieve, 1904, 1: 40*]. There is little information concerning Zeller's economic position, but it must have been quite high since the tavern alone, in two transfers during the late sixteenth century, was valued at 1,400 fl. The earliest Zeller incumbent of the tavern at Haibach was Christoph's great-uncle Michael who appears in 1530; Christoph's father, Siegmund Zeller, was the tenant innkeeper of a tavern at Haichenbach. Christoph's brother George held tenure on the Haibach tavern during the first two decades of the seventeenth century and Christoph himself took it over when it was sold by Peuerbach to the estate Stauf [*Stieve, 1904, 1: 73 n. 5; Fattinger, 1965: 55*]. According to the estate protocols, Zeller was a moneylender. He appears there also eight times, with three requests to hold a ceremonial feast (*Zehrung*), with four marriage sponsorships, and once as holder of a wardship [*Fattinger, 1965: 56*]. The most telling document concerning Zeller is a description of him by the Upper Austrian knight Erasmus von Rödern who claimed to know Zeller very well. Somewhat witheringly he identified Zeller as the former innkeeper at Haibach who now liked to be called 'Your Honor' (*Ir Gnaden*). He described him also as an equestrian sort ('*ein reiterischer Kerl*') and a teamster [*Stieve, 1904, 1: 113*]. The most significant piece of information in Erasmus' description of the rebel chief is that the latter had been under the special patronage and in the administrative service of one Hieronymus Schluchs at Grueb and Haglau, a *Ritter* whose seat Grueb was near Kirchberg in the *Mühlviertel*. It was as a member of Hieronymus's personal retinue that Zeller travelled in Upper and Lower Austria when the former performed his duties as provost in charge of rents and tenancies (*Lehensprobst*) for the Starhemberg family [*Fattinger, 1965: 56*]. This connection with Schluchs places Zeller in the same privileged occupational group as Fadinger, and, as we shall see, Achaz Wiellinger. After Schluchs' death in 1603, Zeller, according to Erasmus, went into military service, and that is all we know of him until he turns up as innkeeper in 1618 and as military organizer and peasant leader in 1626. In the course of the rebellion itself he appears to have been a ruthless and self-serving extortionist who used his status as supreme military commander to confiscate livestock, grains, linens, and properties of Catholic priests in order to sell these for personal profit [*Ottensheim, 1626–27: fols. 333–335*].

The Wiellinger family appears as incumbent on the Gatringerhof near the estate Starhemberg and the market town of Haag in 1480. In the course of the next century, members of the family achieved several positions of prominence and, in the case of his father, knighthood. Despite these favorable signs, the marriage into a noble house, the achievement of noble status eluded Achaz and it is around this failure that much of his story seems to turn.

When word reached Upper Austria on 15 July 1620, that a Bavarian invasion army was massing at the town of Ried in the nearby Inn quarter, over five hundred peasants from the parish Gaspoltshofen, led by a blacksmith and religious fanatic named Sebastian Stix and his brothers, [*Haag, n.d. 'Bayerischer Einfall, Verhör der Bauern'; Stieve, 1904, 1: 68*] appeared at the Gatringerhof, where Wiellinger organized them into military order. From there they staged a raid on the Bavarian border and damaged and closed the access roads. On their return they raided castle Starhemberg, a property of the bishop of Passau, where they committed extensive thefts and other damage. As part of the investigations that followed, Achaz Wiellinger was arrested in September of 1621 along with a number of other suspects and interrogated. In order to secure his release, he invoked a claim to nobility and protested his innocence and maltreatment through his solicitor and attorney, a Hans Bernhard Adler of Linz, to *Statthalter* Herbersdorf, who in turn reprimanded the Starhemberg estate manager Fink and ordered Wiellinger released. Fink held Wiellinger while she consulted further with Passau and finally released him on his own recognizance on 6 October 1621 [*Haag, n.d. 'Verhaftung des Achaz Wiellinger': fol. 42*]. In the course of these proceedings Passau issued a request to Fink to furnish some precise information concerning Wiellinger's actual legal status and privileges [*ibid.: fols 20–21*]. The description Fink gave of Wiellinger is enlightening. She identified the Gatringerhof as a former Hohenfelder peasant tenancy (*'ain plosses Bauerngut'*) under the estate Aistersheim. Achaz's father, whom she identified only as 'old Wiellinger', was the owner of the tenancy and she could affirm that he had achieved admission to the *Landtafel*, i.e., that he had achieved Estate status. When Achaz took over the tenancy he bought only the usual tenant rights from Ludwig Hohenfelder for 1,000 fl, but he did not acquire his father's legal status – although it was assumed by some that he did. As far as she knew, he had no noble seat, nor a noble estate, nor did he have any subjects of his own.

Achaz was probably not the nobleman he claimed to be, but he was extremely well connected. Fink's letter also contained the following information concerning Wiellinger's occupation and personal affairs: he was a traveller and dealer who counted among his contacts the *Pfarrer* at Hofkirchen; he served, in addition, on the administrative staff of his brother-in-law, one Wolf Gästelsperger, who was the *Bestandinhaber* (a type of manager cum lien administrator) for Helmhard Jörger's seat at Groebming and was a dealer in grains and linens [*Haag, n.d. 'Verhaftung': fol. 10*]. One can add to this evidence of high occupational status the following: a letter from Abraham Grünpacher, the Khevenhüller chief manager, to Maria Fink interceding on Achaz's behalf as the brother-in-law of Wiellinger's wife; [*Haag, n.d. 'Verhaftung': fols. 41–42*]. Wiellinger's own testimony that he had served in the administrations of the Lady von Königsberg and of Helmhard Jörger [*Stieve, 1904, 1: 55*] and the personal support that Wiellinger received in order to become the supreme commander of the Weiberau camp from the Steyr *Stadtrichter* and *Rathsbürger* Wolf Madlseder [*Stieve, 1904,*

1: 154 n. 8]. All of these facts together also place Wiellinger in the highest social circles among the Upper Austrian peasantry. At the same time, however, Wiellinger had not managed to sustain his father's leap across Estate boundaries and, though he sought treatment as a nobleman, his aspirations to become legally 'resident' (*landsässig*) remained frustrated.

The leaders of the 1626 uprising offer to the analyst an interesting combination of economic and social characteristics. Why should these men, who had achieved high social status, lead a rebellion? It has been suggested that their motives were those of a group of socially mobile rural 'bourgeois' with 'rising expectations' who were trapped in the incongruities arising from their attachment to 'feudal' institutions that on the one hand gave them the authority that allowed them to advance economically but that also blocked their full political emancipation and self-determination [*Hoffmann, 1976: 19–20*]. In the light of Fadinger's, Zeller's and Wiellinger's careers and of the Twelve Articles of 1626, which included peasant demands calling for the displacement of the clergy as an Estate and the installation in their stead of the peasants in some official capacity to 'protect' the territory, this interpretation seems plausible. The Twelve Articles of 1626 supply the archaic and reactionary side of the peasant leaders' apparently paradoxical position. And yet, while they may indeed have been upwardly mobile subjects whose movements had stalled, it is precisely with the latter point, concerning their apparently reactionary stance, that our analysis must contradict this initially attractive interpretation.

We know that the feudal appearance of Estate institutions was, since at least the latter half of the sixteenth century, increasingly mere appearance, and that Estates no longer represented erstwhile provincial corporate liberties but were rather a part of the state's apparatus for assigning positions to fulfill bureaucratic prescriptions and administrative needs. The interpretation that sees the peasant leaders only as feudal reactionaries defending and seeking to enlarge their vested status denies them any understanding of their actual position in the state. It also places them outside the liberal traditions of Central Europe by assigning to them a role of reactionary opposition to a state that is perceived to be moving ultimately toward emancipation and citizenship [*Hoffmann, 1976: 20*]. The fact of the matter is that the peasant leaders understood their position fully and their political demands, far from being reactionary, were fully appropriate to the existing institutions and implicitly envisioned a path of development that was at least politically, if not socially, progressive.

Their actual grievances (some 138 items alone in the *gravamina* sent to the emperor in July 1626) were couched in the terminology of established state law and, lapsing only occasionally into emotionally charged and indignant language, demanded that the state authorities obey the laws, follow procedures of accepted administrative practice and adhere to the terms of the Imperial religious constitution of 1555 on which the *Reformationspatent* of 1625 itself was explicitly founded. They did not challenge the existing structure of authority in any way whatsoever but repeatedly stressed their obedience to the emperor, and this not in the general terms common to many peasant rebellions, but specifically asserting that they rebelled not because they did not wish to remain subjects ('zwar nicht zu dem ende... das wir im stande der untertanen nit verbleiben') nor to seek another Estate ('keinen andern stant suechen') [*Stieve, 1904, 2: 254–266*]. They rebelled because the *Reformationspatent* not merely assured the failure of Protestantism but would unleash a chain reaction of dangerous and incongruous administrative turmoil in connection with the official, household, and family affairs of the tenured. They wished it known that their grievances referred to a specific time, beginning with the publication of the *Reformationspatent* in the previous year, and their chief complaint ('*hauptbeschwer*') was that to adhere to their religion meant that they had to forfeit their social position and that even after such renunciation, their departure from the province was being obstructed and exploited by the present regime acting contrary to law [*Stieve, 1904, 2: 256, 266*].

Their stress on the *Reformationspatent* and its many consequences suggests that bourgeois social and reactionary political motives were not really what were at work. The peasant leaders' objections to the specific changes in the religious regime have to be accounted for. In addition, many of the tenants who participated in the war represented a group who had not even gained a foothold among the occupationally privileged subjects who made up the leadership. The peasant followers of Fadinger, Zeller and Wiellinger were certainly not upwardly mobile feudal entrepreneurs. In order to explain as fully as possible the mixture of religious, political, economic, and social grievances that brought together the rebels of 1626, we must first consider whose problems the *gravamina* of 1626 expressed.

One explanation (a corollary to the 'entrepreneur' thesis) that might serve to link Fadinger, Zeller, and Wiellinger to their following has been developed in recent years by anthropologists studying the function of certain 'mediators' or 'brokers' who link peasant society to the larger units of civilization of which they are a separate and only partially congruent part [e.g., *Redfield, 1956; Wolf, 1956; Tilly, 1964; Silverman, 1965*]. We might perhaps be tempted to see the leaders of 1626 as *mafiosi* functioning as links between the subjects and the state authorities. Thus, for example, Professor Anton Blok's *mafiosi*

> emerged in the early 19th century when the Bourbon state tried to curb the power of the traditional landowning aristocracy and encouraged the emancipation of the peasantry.... The gradual emergence of what came to be known only later on as '*mafia*' can be understood in the context of this development in which the central government, the landlords, and the peasants arranged and rearranged themselves in

conflict and accommodation. I have referred above to this pattern as *modus vivendi*, in which mafiosi were recruited from the ranks of the peasantry to provide the large estate owners with armed staffs to confront both the impact of the State and the restive peasants, especially in the inland area of the island where the Bourbon State failed to monopolize the use of physical power [*1975: 10–11*].

While such characters as the Stix brothers who had raided the Bavarian border in 1620 and the innkeeper Zeller probably were 'violent entrepreneurs' who no doubt employed their public and quasi-public authority to use force both against outsiders and locals for their personal advantage, this does not explain why the Austrian peasant leadership as a whole would mobilize a large number of the tenants against the state, especially after the 'resistance' of the nobility was broken.

The comparison does, however, help to explain the connection of the events of 1626 to earlier developments in the Habsburg heartland. By 1600, the progress of bureaucratization in Austria had eliminated one of the conditions that characterize a society where mafiosi can 'exploit the gaps in communication between the peasant village and the larger society' and 'ensure and buttress their intermediate position through the systematic threat and practice of physical violence [*Blok, 1975: 8*]. The peasant leaders were themselves members of the tenant class that did not make up a separate society, representing purely localized part-systems of the whole state, but rather functioned as the lowest level of a statewide system of administration in which the lines of authority, while still defined by the institutions and language of part-societies, i.e., of Estates, flowed in one continuum from household to estate to state bureaucracy. The one thing the peasant leadership had in common with their followers was that they all held tenures as state posts on terms controlled, ultimately, by state authority. Seen in this context, the peasant leaders of 1626 and their followers were not engaged in a class struggle of the tenants as a class against, say, the noble estate owner class (as they had been in 1525 and 1595). Now they were members of a bureaucratic hierarchy objecting to changes in state administration.

Ralf Dahrendorf's further remarks on Max Weber's conceptualization of bureaucracy help to clarify what this view of the relationship between the leaders of 1626 and their tenant followers means in terms of social conflict:

> ... whereas industrial organizations are ... dichotomous, bureaucratic organizations typically display continuous gradations of competence and authority and are hierarchical. Within dichotomous organizations class conflict is possible; within hierarchical organizations it is not.... This means that all incumbents of bureaucratic roles in the association of political society belong to the same side of the fence that divides the positions of dominance from those of subjection.... Bureaucratic roles are roles of political dominance.... Nobody in particular seems to exercise the authority and yet authority is exercised, and we can identify people who do not

participate in its exercise. Thus the superficial impression of subordination in many minor bureaucratic roles must not deceive us. All bureaucratic roles are defined with reference to the total process of the exercise of authority to which they contribute to whatever small extent [*1958: 296–297*].

To be sure, some of the peasant leaders were involved in social conflicts that separated them from their poorer followers. Achaz Wiellinger's struggle for the recognition of his 'nobility', for example, demonstrates what personal conflicts happen when 'there are in a bureaucratic hierarchy several points of entry which divide the total career into subsections separated by insurmountable barriers' [*Dahrendorf, 1958: 296*]. His was a personal crisis, a product of his 'family's' specific social mobility that none of his fellow leaders, let alone his followers, shared. What Wiellinger did share with Fadinger and Zeller and the other poorer tenants who arose in 1626 was a position in a bureaucratic order under pressure to conform to an abrupt change at the top levels of state. Far from being conservative entrepeneurs or violent *mafiosi* exploiting the synapses between a tenant class and the state, the leaders who arose in 1626 stood at the head of a party within the administrative hierarchy of the Habsburg state, a party of tenants that sought 'to influence the existing dominion' [*Weber, 1958: 195*] in order to prevent or at least ameliorate what it saw as the imminent downward mobility of a good number of its members; it was a party of quasi-bureaucrats who objected to radical changes in the rights of incumbents and who protested that the responsibilities of office could not be carried out under the new conditions.

A more detailed examination of the July grievances bears out this view of the peasant rebels of 1626 as a political party acting in the defense of a particular vision of the bureaucratic state. The picture that emerges there of what was on their minds contradicts sharply any notions that we are dealing with an illiterate mass of simple peasant farmers, conservatively and inflexibly committed to feudal values and to a particular confessional orthodoxy. Their sole objection to the Counter-Reformation that reveals any kind of connection to traditional agricultural production is that the authorities' insistence on the observation of the hours of mass on feast days was interfering with such essential work and marketing processes as the delivery of milk and the milling of grains [*Stieve, 1904, 2: 262–263*]. But this was a minor aspect of the many objections to the *Reformationspatent* of 1625. Of primary importance was the disruption it caused in the province's good government and welfare ('*zerruettung gueter polizei*') and this disruption was blamed on the fact that the Counter-Reformation state placed the eradication of Protestantism above the efficient conduct and continuity of administrative processes. Their primary evidence for this was that experienced administrators were removed from office, their desks and papers ransacked, some put under house arrest in their places of office or in their homes and others publicly chastised (or even unjustly murdered, as at Frankenburg). There was, significantly, also objection raised that their replacements had not previously held tenure on a house or farm ('*unbegueterte*') and were therefore, according to the accepted rules, unqualified to hold office [*Stieve, 1904, 2: 259–260*]. Particularly objectionable was the incompetent and tyrannical administration by the new Catholic clergy of parish schools and churches [*Stieve, 1904, 2: 260*]. They noted that these unheard-of procedures ('*unerhörte procedere*') could be resisted better in the towns and cities but that the rural population was an easier victim of this administrative disjunction [*Stieve, 1904, 2: 265*]. Finally, administration of the courts suffered under the new regime: those plaintiffs who had not converted to Catholicism and had experienced harassment by occupying troops could not get their cases heard in court while cases in which Protestants were the defendants were expedited [*Stieve, 1904, 2: 260*].

Taken altogether, such protest amounts to much more than what one might expect from traditional peasant rebels. There was, for example, a considerable difference between the July grievances of 1626 and the Twelve Articles of 1525 in that the former no longer expressed the point of view of the tenant class as a village commune [cf. *Sabean, 1974*] but rather as individuals and groups singled out for bureaucratic harassment. Those who bore the worst of these torments were those Protestants who tried to exercise their right to emigrate. The July grievances not only present a detailed account and numerous examples of the treatment of these would-be migrants, they also place the difficulties of the emigres in a context of constitutional law and administrative regulation. The Catholic state authorities, preferring conversion to emigration, apparently obstructed the process of emigration as much as possible. Potential emigres had trouble getting passports; they were subject to verbal and physical abuse, and were occasionally imprisoned until they converted. The items inventoried in the migrants' liquidation assessments often included personal and other goods declared exempt by the 1597 Interim. Aside from placing numerous extra charges and taxes on the liquidated assets, the authorities often refused to accept the debased legal tender for which the migrant had agreed to sell his properties – and which the state itself had authorised and issued. Most troubling of all was that the way the state administered *ius emigrandi* violated administrative regulations securing the self-rule of families and households. If an emigre was single (and therefore 'unhoused') the authorities took this as an occasion to investigate the holdings of housed kin, ostensibly to determine the full value of all the emigre's assets; children were occasionally not allowed to leave with their parents and this, the peasant leaders claimed, violated the constitution of 1555 according to which husbands held authority over wives and parents over children. The state's violation of this house authority on occasion went so far that the wives of those migrants who had gone ahead to establish themselves elsewhere were forced into marriages with converts [*Stieve, 1904, 2: 261–264*]. In other words, the subject tenants objected strenuously to the *Reformationspatent* not on religious grounds as such but on the grounds that in practice it contravened many rights concerning inventory-taking, inheritance portions and children, and over family relations, generally, that the tenants had achieved during the sixteenth century through state intervention and bureaucratisation.

It is to this increasing insecurity of the individual's tenure that the complaints against the *Reformationspatent* make, finally, their most deeply cutting objection. No longer free to argue as members of a parish or village community, the tenured peasants pointed instead to their years of service as tenants (claiming not only individual terms of tenure lasting from thirty to over sixty years but also terms lasting through several generations of a family) and to their assistance to the House of Habsburg in the 'building' of the territory. They claimed this entitled them to some security as resident 'members of the state' ('*lantsmitglieder*'). They claimed also the rights of private persons ('*privatpersonen*') [*Stieve, 1904, 2: 257*] and remonstrated that because it was not possible for some to renounce their religious beliefs they should not be penalized with loss of tenure and status. They demanded a free conscience ('*freistellung des Gewissen*') and rejected the *politique* alternative [*Stieve, 1904, 2: 256, 266–267*].

But, as in Habsburg and Bourbon territories everywhere, [*Lockyer, 1974: 33–339*] it was the age for *politiques* like Wiellinger's in-law Abraham Grünpacher, a peasant tenant who had advanced in the bureaucratic hierarchy (much like Fadinger, Zeller and Wiellinger) to become Francis Khevenhüller's highest estate official. In their belief that they could base their rights to tenure on administrative law and on proven records and seniority of service, the peasant rebels of 1626, both leaders and followers, fell victim to an illusory perception of their position in the state. Once the tenant class had submitted to uniform subject status, had been forced to accept, by 1600, the state's maintenance and regulation of property and family life, and had been required to assume and use for their own purposes administrative functions and roles, they also had to accept, knowingly or not, the logic of bureaucratic politics. They had accepted dominant roles and belonged 'to the ruling political quasi-group. However, being a reserve army of authority, the bureaucratic members of this quasi-group are not potential members of an interest group of those in power. . . . The bureaucratic reserve army of authority is a mercenary army of class conflict; it is always in battle, but it is forced to place its strength in the service of changing masters and goals' [*Dahrendorf, 1958: 301*]. Far from being reactionary entrepreneurs in a distant time and place, the Austrian peasant rebels of 1626 were the first modern men, fighting one of the first battles in a political struggle that has lasted into and flowered profusely during this so-called 'post-capitalist' period of Western history. They wanted an ongoing separation between conditions of tenure and such private rights as freedom of conscience and an independent family and household life.

The faith they professed in the legal-rational practices of their system and in the rights that such major constitutional documents as the Interim of 1597 guaranteed them was seriously misplaced. We cannot fault them for misunderstanding their position or for maintaining 'bureaucratic' and legal-rational values in the face of a victorious state; the fact that the regulations governing station, competence, equality, and rationality of advancement present an illusory security for those required to play bureacratic roles often is not understood even in the present day [cf. *Redford, 1969: 132–264; Hirschman, 1970: chap. 7; Kariel, 1971*]. The legal-rational appearances of administrative institutions and processes are at all times subject to the reason of hierarchy and domination and are ultimately subject 'to an extra- and superbureaucratic power – to an 'unbusinesslike' power. And if rationality is embodied in administration, and *only* administration, then this legislative power must be irrational. The Weberian conception of reason ends in irrational *charisma*' [*Marcuse, 1968: 217*]. By appealing to the young legal and bureaucratic traditions of the Habsburg state, the peasant rebels of 1626 took the only path open to those tenants who did not wish to convert and whose emigration was beset by chicanery and by violations of law pretending to be administrative practice. The irony of their position was that their new prince, intent 'on creating a new kingdom that conformed to his image of royal prerogative and Christian duty,' [*Hantsch, 1968, 1: 340*] had at his disposal the same bureaucratic apparatus, created by his forebears during the previous century in negotiations with peasants and nobility, that now allowed him to realize his values and make them a reality in every house of the province. In this situation, the theories of magisterial resistance and even tyrannicide, which had seriously occupied some Austrian peasant rebels in 1511 and 1525 and whose formulas cropped up again in 1626, were almost entirely irrelevant.

The victory of the Counter-Reformation by no means meant a suspension or alteration of the nature and direction of development of the Austrian state. The legal-rational rules of calculable emphyteusis and house administration that, by 1600, had given rise to new patterns of family life and mobility all remained intact and continued to furnish the basis of rural economic and social life until the modern era. What happened in the 1620s was that the prince had asserted the prerogatives of his charismatic authority and had added a religious condition to the holding of tenure. Once that revolution was completed and only genuine Catholics or *politiques* held tenure, the state returned to its 'normal' legal-rational operations. Given the continuation of secret Protestant meetings, of the administration of the sacraments by itinerant and lay preachers and of the need for state censorship of both religious and secular works, [*Klingenstein, 1970*] we must assume that many of these conversions were *politique* conversions done for the sake of maintaining the convert's position as tenant or officeholder in a state that had not, after all, changed that much.

Although the term *politique* was born in the context of the French religious wars to signify someone for whom the 'primacy of the demands of the state over those of religion' was self-evident and was part of a necessary 'disentanglement of religious and political dissent' and a release from the 'nonsense of civil war', [*Koenigsberger, 1971: 198; Lockyer, 1974: 333; Koselleck, 1973: 14*] it is worthwhile to take it out of its context of origin in political and intellectual history and to consider it briefly from a social historical perspective as an element of the social relations of Austrian absolutism. At the outset we must keep in mind that because the Austrian state had managed to penetrate the peasant house and family even before the Counter-Reformation could be implemented, the *politique* type (in Austrian: *Konvertit*) was a mass phenomenon and not merely someone who appeared among the governing nobilities and patriciates of early modern Europe. How are we to judge the effects of widespread *politique* behaviour on social life? Reinhard Koselleck, following Hobbes' lead and starting from the necessity to end civil war by excluding religious morality from political action, has suggested that the *politique* choice signified a shift in the burdens of guilt and responsibility that amounts finally to a general unburdening of the individual. The state, guiltless because it acts on the basis of secular morality alone, claims a monopoly and assumes responsibility for the consequences of political action, and the only burden of guilt the subject is required to bear is that of acting against state authority or of withdrawing from participation in public life [*Koselleck, 1973: 15–16*]. In this view subjects are no longer required to act morally at all in the political sphere except to follow the state's mandates; the state takes responsibility for secular morality and religious morality was in any case inadmissible [*ibid. 30–31*]. Here we are looking at the beginnings of the separation of the public from the private individual and of the state from society. Whatever price individuals had to pay for enduring this split, they were rewarded by public religious and moral peace and by the benefits of the progress of the state [*ibid. 29–33*]. This view fits the claim that any discomforts that results from *politique* dualism were, in terms derived from Gerhard Oestreich's functionalist view of the absolute state, only one aspect of the 'social discipline' necessary to drive early modern rural populations away from their self-indulgence and toward modernity and rationality [*Oestreich, 1969*; cf. *Klingenstein, 1970: 48*].

We must reject this version of the social effects of *politique* behavior in the absolute state both on general theoretical grounds and on the basis of our investigations into Austrian rural society. Elsewhere we have followed Ralf

Dahrendorf's lead and explicitly rejected any analysis of roles that sees an independent and integrated person 'within' each individual's role complex [*Dahrendorf, 1968; Rebel, 1983, chap. 7*]. The *politique* rationalization in which a person is 'secretly free' and 'only in secret human' [*Koselleck, 1973: 30*] is the door by which the repression of publicly inadmissible conflict enters the private world and becomes the burden of each individual who wishes (or is required) to participate in public life. It is the officially prescribed role complex and not the person that is integrated and it is the former that governs a person's decisions and choices according to its necessary interplay of dominant and secondary values – and the suppressed conflicts and incongruencies of the role complex then split the person so that the state may be 'free' of conflict.

In early modern Austria, after the Counter-Reformation's victory over the peasantry, the problematical aspects of the *politique* solution to role conflict in a bureaucratized state were especially evident. There the necessity to convert, whether one wanted to or not, was intimately bound up with the private sphere of home and family. The state, unwilling to tolerate religious conflict, expected individuals to repress that conflict within themselves as a precondition of participating in the state – and to have any kind of family or successfully mobile social life one had first to participate in the state as tenant householder. Here the burden of repressed values conflict is not removed from the subject and placed on the state, as Koselleck has suggested, but quite the reverse occurs. The state, having penetrated the peasant family and indeed, the subject individual, by acquiring control over key institutions of property, family, and welfare could now shift the burden of religious conflict downward. The Counter-Reformation that followed the victories of the Habsburg state in the 1620s was not a radically discontinuous change but merely another step, albeit an important one, in the further bureaucratization of the peasant family. The subject population had long ago acquiesced in the state's invasion of family life. Where the rigors of tenure, emphyteusis, and social mobility for the tenured had required for some time a repression of personal and familial needs in favor of the state-controlled norms, the acquiescence in *politique* behavior during the 1620s was not, once initial objections to procedural changes had been overcome, a great issue. The tenant class, long helpless against the invasion and incorporation of family life by the state, understood and accepted that one simply had to endure the internal split that was covered over by *politique* behavior not only to participate in a limited public sphere as subject or state official but to play even those most elemental and private social roles of spouse and parent.

References

Blok, A., 1975, *The Mafia of a Sicilian Village, 1860–1960*, New York.
Czerny, A., 1890, *Der Zweite Bauernaufstand in Oberösterreich, 1595–1597*, Linz.
Dahrendorf, R., 1958, *Class and Class Conflict in Industrial Society*, Stanford.
Dahrendorf, R., 1968, *Essays in the Theory of Society*, Stanford.
Fattinger, H., 1965, 'Stefan Fadinger und Christoph Zeller. Ihre Familie und ihre Heimat,' *Oberösterreichische Heimatblätter* 19.
Fattinger, H., n.d. *Unsere bäuerlichen Vorfahren*. Typescript. Upper Austrian State Archives, Linz.
Grüll, G., 1969, *Der Bauer im Lande ob der Enns am Ausgang des sechzehnten Jahrhunderts*, Vienna.
Haag, n.d. 'Bayerischer Einfall,' 'Verhör der Bauern,' 'Verhaftung des Achaz Wiellinger.' Manuscripts. Haag Estate Archive, Haag-am-Hausruck, Upper Austria.
Hantsch, H., 1968, *Die Geschichte Osterreichs*, Graz.
Hirschman, A. O., 1970, *Exit, Voice and Loyalty*, Cambridge, Mass.
Hoffman, A., 1976, 'Zur Typologie der Bauernaufstände in Oberösterreich' *Der Oberösterreichische Bauernkrieg; Ausstellung des Landes Oberösterreich*, Linz.
Hohberg, W. L. von, 1715, *Georgica Curiosa*, 5th ed. Nuremberg.
Kariel, H., 1971, *The Decline of American Pluralism*, Stanford.
Klingenstein, G., 1970, *Staatsverwaltung und kirchliche Autorität im 18. Jahrhundert*, Munich.
Koenigsberger, H., 1971, *The Habsburgs in Europe, 1516–1660*, Ithaca.
Koselleck, R., 1973, *Kritik und Krise: Ein Studie zur Pathogenese der bürgerlichen Welt*, Frankfurt.
Lockyer, R., 1974, *Habsburg and Bourbon Europe, 1470–1720*, London.
Marcuse, H., 1968, *Negations: Essays in Critical Theory*, Boston.
Oestreich, G., 1969, 'Strukturprobleme des europäischen Absolutismus,' *Vierteljahrschrift für Sozial – und Wirtschaftsgeschichte*, 55.
Ottensheim, 1626–1627, *Briefprotokolle, 072a*, Upper Austrian State Archives, Linz.
Rebel, H., 1983, *Peasant Classes: The Bureaucratization of Property and Family Relations Under Early Habsburg Absolutism, 1511–1636*, Princeton.
Redfield, R., 1956, *Peasant Society and Culture*, Chicago.
Redford, E. S., 1969, *Democracy in the Administrative State*, New York.
Sabean, D., 1974, 'Family and Land Tenure: A Case Study of Conflict in the German Peasants' War (1525)' *Peasant Studies Newsletter*.
Silverman, S., 1965, 'The Community-Nation Mediator in Traditional Italy,' *Ethnology*, 4.
Stieve, F., 1904, *Der Oberösterreichische Bauernaufstand des Jahres 1626*, 2, Linz.
Strnadt, J., 1924, *Der Bauernkrieg in Oberösterreich im Jahr 1626*, Wels.
Sturmberger, H., 1976, *Adam Graf Herbersdorf: Herrschaft und Freiheit im konfessionellen Zeitalter*, Munich.
Tilly, C., 1964, *The Vendée*, Cambridge, Mass.
Weber, M., 1958, 'Class, Status, Party,' in *From Max Weber*, H. H. Gerth and C. Wright Mills, eds., New York.
Wolf, E., 1956, 'Aspects of Group Relations in a Complex Society: Mexico' *American Anthropologist*, 58.

Religious ideologies in Russian popular movements in the seventeenth and eighteenth centuries

VIKTOR I. BUGANOV

The establishment of an essentially feudal state in ancient Rus and the introduction of Christianity were almost simultaneous events. The former began in the ninth century and the latter was officially adopted in 988 A.D. The rôles and functions of Christian religion were manifold and contradictory. On the one hand it has supplied the feudal lords from the very beginning with a powerful ideological weapon for the enslavement and exploitation of the lower classes, for the repression of protest and class conflict, for the clouding of the peoples' consciousness. On the other hand, it enhanced the growth of civilisation by introducing and spreading literacy, encouraging the writing of chronicles, annals, legends, saints' lives, by sponsoring architecture, painting and the decorative arts. Religion also offered the lower classes a possibility to express in theological terms their views and ideals, the demands of their class or estate, their anti-feudal ideas and dreams about equality, truth and justice. This double-faced rôle of religion as the world view of medieval men and women affected everyday life as much as specific popular movements, uprisings, heresies and religious reform.

Christianity's resonance among the masses can be traced back to its genesis in the late Roman Empire, when it was regarded as the religion of the oppressed. The Christian God appeared as a god of good-will, truth and justice, an avenger of evil and falsehood and a defender of the family and its foundations – property, thrift, respect for age, dignity, honesty, work and temperance. The social, political and ethical norms, views and yearnings of common men in town and country were necessarily clad in a cloak of religion. At the same time, religion taught not to stand up against evil, to honour all authorities even if they were unjust. In this manner Christianity on the one hand sanctified the existing system of exploitation and coercion, on the other reminded people of such lofty ideals as brotherhood, equality, and the striving for a good, just world [*Tserkov', 1967; Kartsov, 1971: ch. I*].

However, the ecclesiastical establishment, the writings of the Church Fathers and the sermons of thaumaturges and priests distorted the ideas of primitive

Christianity, while many of the clergy and the monks were not exactly models of Christian humility, integrity and respectability. Mockery of the clercs' vices is a frequent subject of popular satirical tales and proverbs. The 'critique' of this religious system did not remain confined to the ideological realm, but was also expressed in different forms of protest, including rural and urban revolts and uprisings, and finally, in the seventeenth and eighteenth centuries, in mighty peasant wars.

In feudal Russia, just as elsewhere, class struggle was fought in the economic, political and ideological — that is religious — spheres simultaneously. Clearly, not every movement's slogans and programmes contained directly religious elements. But even if the resistance manifested itself in the refusal of increased labour services and taxes; by setting fire to the nobility's houses; in stealing wood; encroaching on seigneurial pastures; and attacks on the *pomeshchik*-gentry, the boyars, monks, merchants and officers of the local and central administration, the consciousness of the fighters was basically a religious one. Their acts were based on concepts of justice and injustice, good and evil, that were not only the results of the life experience of many generations, but were also hallowed by the dogma of the orthodox church, augmented — particularly among the urban strata — by reforming teachings and by remnants of non-Christian beliefs that had survived from pagan times.

The seventeenth-eighteenth centuries, the age of the great peasant wars in Russia coincided with the beginning of a new epoch in the country's history. At this time, when the power of the centralised state approached absolutism and serfdom was flourishing, the tremendous pressure from feudal lords, the church and the state made the living conditions of the lower classes particularly harsh. Four major peasant wars plus a number of rural and urban uprisings which included peasants, serving elements (*streltsy*-soldiers) and the proto-proletarians of Central Russia and the Ural, were fought. At the very same time the broad masses of the Russian people broke with the pravoslav official orthodox church in the great schism.

In one form or another, these movements produced a religiously motivated programme of protest. Some had a more retrospect aspect, insofar as the ideals of their members lay in the ancient prefeudal past, and the disregard of the traditional ethical norms by their contemporaries appeared to them as Paradise Lost. Others had a more future oriented perspective, fighting for a coming Eden against the state and all churches, orthodox as well as Old Believer [*Klibanov, 1977: 83–959*].

In early seventeenth century peasant wars we detect the firm belief in a 'good Tsar' who would come to replace the 'bad and evil Tsar', namely Boris Godunov and later V. I. Shuisky. Many attempted to play the rôle of these 'good Tsars' — the two False Dmitrys, 'Tsarevich Peter' during the Bolotnikov uprising, and a few others. According to the naive hopes and imaginations of the rebels, this ideal ruler would follow godly law and godly truth, remove 'evil boyars and nobles', and relieve the oppressed of their many burdens. In areas where an uprising established control, fighters put these ideas into practice. They established a new order of secular self government modelled on Cossack communities where decisions were passed by general meetings and implemented by elected officials. They stopped to pay taxes or to work for the lords, whose property they confiscated and re-distributed among themselves. Religious ideas about a peaceable and egalitarian community grew increasingly into clearly anti-feudal programmes and actions [*Smirnov, 1951; Koretsky, 1975; Buganov, 1976: ch. 1*].

In the middle of the seventeenth century the Russian church was split by the reforms of Patriarch Nikon, who changed certain rites of divine service and corrected the liturgical books, and by the synodal decrees of 1655–6. This schism separated the official 'Nikonian' church from the dissenting Old Believers, who were ruthlessly persecuted. After this date religious dissent acquired ever more an anti-feudal character which considerably influenced popular movements. During the Solovetsky-uprising (1668–76) armed fighters against Tsarist power and the official church included not only monks of the Solovetsky monastery (in the White Sea), but also peasants of the area with some others who found their way to the north, even Don Cossacks. Enserfed peasants, urban craftsmen and traders, soldiers and Cossacks gathered under the flag of Old Belief. They rose not only against the enemies of their confession but also against that secular government which was supported by the official church. They confronted the whole oppressive feudal system; the nobles, the merchants, the Nikonian clergy, and all those whom they saw as rich men and exploiters.

Religious motives also played a significant part in the Second Russian Peasant War of 1667–71, fought at the same time as the Solovestky uprising [*Stepanov, 1966; Buganov, 1976: ch. 2*]. Official documents, followed by aristocratic and bourgeois historiography, tended to depict Stenka Razin and his comrades as enemies of church and religion. True, they made short work not only of the nobility but also of priests who had actively opposed the uprising, as for example when they executed Archbishop Iosif of Astrakhan. Razin expressed his contempt for ecclesiastical ceremonies, when for instance, he forbade his soldiers from marrying in church, suggesting that instead of a clerical wedding they should just act: 'Go round and into the willows, and the matter is settled'. Yet this does not prove that Razin and 'his boys' did not believe in god or that they rejected religion. Just to the contrary, their appeals contain explicit references to the defense of Christian ideas. As a twenty-year old in 1652 Razin went on pilgrimage from the Don to the Solovetsky monastery. He repeated this a decade later. His camp 'chaplain' was a certain popa Theodosius. Many of Razin's fellow participants were just as religious, and kept priests among their troops who read the offices for the dead. Some of these priests, being literate, produced those 'charming letters' which were a kind of agitational writing, calling on Russian people to support the uprising.

Apart from the supporters of the official orthodox church, the movement could also count on a fair number of Old Believers from the Don and Volga regions. In the district of Temnikov dissenting priests were among the rebels and they even fought in battles against the Tsar's army. Such were the priests Sabba, and Pimen and others. From this district, the famous *staritsa*-nun, Alena, led many thousand men in the uprising and repulsed several punitive expeditions. When her troops were finally defeated, Alena was captured and burned at the stake just like another Jeanne d'Arc. As she was led to her death in Arzamus at the headquarters of Prince Iury Aleksandrovich Dolgoruky, who was commander of the Tsarist troops, this fearless and unbroken woman – most probably an Old Believer – exclaimed: 'Had everyone been fighting as I was, then Prince Iury would have had to have taken to his heels!'

In districts and towns along the Volga local clergy appears not only as participants but also as leaders of this peasant war. After its defeat, many Old Believers chose to burn themselves or to escape into some inaccessible corner of Russia [*Kartsov, 1977*]. The leader of the uprising, Stepan Timofeevich Razin was beheaded on the Red Square in Moscow. By way of reprisal the troops of the Tsar may have killed about a hundred thousand rebels. Many of the survivors joined subsequent popular movements, such as the Solovetsky uprising, the Moscow uprising of 1682, and the rebellions on the Don during 1688–89.

In the Moscow rising, the Old Believers were reported to have preached openly to the crowds. Silvestr Medvedev, the contemporary chronicler of the official church, noted that 'common people were taught not to go to holy church'. He stated that the muzhiks listened with sympathy to the schismatics, but they attacked their opponents mercilessly. The same Old Believers, both lay and clerical leaders, such as the defrocked priest, Nikita, called for a public disputation in the Kreml with the official, Nikonian clergy. Under the conditions of the uprising, when about fourteen thousand rebellious *streltsy* were holding the capital, of whom one half were probably Old Believers, they were able to dictate the terms. The government was forced to agree to the public disputation which caused them and the official church a considerable humiliation. This having been a significant event in the uprising, it has often been called the 'Raskolnik rebellion' [*Buganov, 1969: 210–35*].

The Don uprising of 1688–89 included many of Razin's former supporters and lieutenants alongside former participants from the Moscow rebellion. It was lead by the Old Believer, Kuz'ma Kosoy, a former blacksmith from Elets who had joined the Cossacks in 1667, when they fought under Stenka Razin. Kosoy attempted to organise rebellion already during the late 1670's. He dreamt of a common action of peasants, Cossacks and *streltsy*. He assembled all kinds of fugitives in the Medveditsa river region, and encouraged them to march on Moscow, with the avowed intention of 'clearing the land and smiting the dishonest with the sword'. He predicted that among those who will reach Moscow, there would arise a certain Tsar Michael, 'a saviour sent by God', or a man 'by his good deeds pleasing to God', who would liberate all the Old Believers, Kuz'ma expected that he himself would be this Messiah, who would set about delivering the oppressed from violence and persecution.

During the early autumn of 1687, Kuz'ma Kosoy was captured and subsequently tortured to death in Moscow. The peasant and poor Cossack Old Believers from the Medveditsa region rose in rebellion and held out for two years before being defeated. In this movement eschatological and millenarian religious ideals seem to have been the major forms of ideology. The struggle for true belief meant for them a fight for secular truth. Their aim was to establish the kingdom of God on earth. These abstract concepts served as motives and justifications for the struggle against very real oppressors, and for a better social order here and now [*Klibanov, 1977: 114–23*].

Both orthodox and schismatic Christians participated in the Astrakhan uprising of 1705–6, which set an example in establishing a social system based on their views of right and justice. It was led by the trader Yakov Nosov, an Old Believer. In their area of control, the rebels set up a republican government which united autonomous communities of towns, centered on Astrakhan. Legislative and judicial power rested with a general assembly of all Russians and non-Russians in the community. The executive and military command was elected, by civilians and soldiers respectively. Serfs and slaves were liberated. The property of the landowners was confiscated, partly re-distributed among the members of the communities, and partly retained as a communal fund. Abuses of power, such as miscarriage of justice, bribery and other offenses were severely punished [*Golikova, 1975; Klibanov, 1977: 97–100*]. Even though the Astrakhan federation was soon destroyed in a massacre perpetrated by Tsarist troops, this communal movement, not dissimilar to those in medieval feudal Western Europe, provides evidence of the strength and continuity of peasant traditions of autonomy, freedom and equality. Had this experiment lasted longer, it might have shown what possibilities were inherent in such a structure for the development of the forces of production in agriculture, industry and commerce. It might have demonstrated, what kind of achievements in the growth of culture could have been realised by the work of free men and women. Yet, in the long run such communes would have led to the emergence of bourgeois power, and become the source of new equalities – no longer feudal but capitalist. Examples of such development may be seen in those Old Believer 'communities' which existed in the eighteenth and nineteenth centuries, in which rich merchants, usurers and capitalists took advantage of their less fortunate brethren. None the less, the direction in the development of social creativity of the masses, exemplified by the federation of Astrakhan in the early eighteenth century would have been unequivocally progressive had it been allowed to survive. It was, however, as with so many other trends, nipped in the bud by autocracy.

During 1707–10, in the Third Russian Peasant War, which was fought in the lower Volga region, across several south Russian districts and in parts of the Ukraine, defence of the Old Belief reappeared as one of the slogans, just as in Astrakhan. The strange appeal 'for beard and moustache' was a response to Tsar Peter I's well known order abolishing traditional Russian hairdos. Many of the rebel rank and file for example from the tributaries of the Don (Medveditsa, Khopra, Buzuluka) and a number of their leaders, such as ataman Ignat Nekrasov, Nikita Golyy, possibly Khokhlach and supreme commander Kondraty Bulavin, were Old Believers. To them, Tsar Peter's modernising autocracy was an attack on supreme tradition and divine command – an affront to the old faith. Their defence of custom and religion thus masked the wider struggle against material oppression and served as a justification for rebellion against injustice [*Pod'yapolskaya, 1962; Buganov, 1976: ch. 3*].

Naturally, religious opposition was not the common general ideology of this peasant war or of any other uprising in pre-modern Russia. Essential demands stemmed from secular, social conditions and referred to the abolition of serfdom and noble oppression. The fighters came from different religious backgrounds, Russian Orthodoxy as well as Old Belief. In these wars against the state and feudal oppression many Muslims (Tatars, Bashkirs, Kazakhs), Buddhists (Kalmyks) and pagans (Mari, Man'si, Chuvash and so on) fought side by side with Christian Russians. Therefore, in the army of Razin as in the later peasant wars the principle of religious tolerance and equality of all faiths was of great significance [*Klibanov, 1977: 133f*].

This element of tolerance was particularly pronounced in the last of the great popular movements, – the Pugachev uprising of 1773–5. This Fourth Peasant War was sparked off and preceded by the Yaik Cossack uprising, among whom the majority were Old Believers. After its suppression, many of its participants joined the uprising led by the Don Cossack, E. I. Pugachev, which began a year later. Some of the main centres of this war, in the Ural and on both banks of the Volga, were also the very areas where Old Belief had its deepest roots. Pugachev, before he became the leader of a movement covering an enormous territory in south-west Russia (Yaik, Orenburg, the Ural and Volga regions and Western Siberia), had visited many of the major centres of religious dissent, such as Vetka in Bielorussia, the one at the River Irgiz (in the Trans-Volga region) where he conferred with Old Believers as well as meeting others from the Ukraine, the Don, the Yaik and Kazan'. Old Believers helped him out of many a dangerous situation well before the uprising, and they may have been the ones who suggested to him the idea of presenting himself as a pretender. As is well known, Pugachev declared himself Emperor as Peter III Fedorovich, who in 1762 was killed by the palace guards.

In Pugachev's manifestos to the Russian and non-Russian people religion appears essentially as an appeal for tolerance and for the acceptance of the equality of all beliefs. The authors of these documents based their appeals on the principle that people should believe in a god of their own choice and worship the way that they wished. Many of Pugachev's flags, under which the rebel army fought, displayed the triple cross of the Old Believers. In his proclamations, one of the ideological leaders of the movement, ataman Ivan Gyazov, expressed well this oppositional thought not only against the social order but also the established church. The fight for Old Belief also appealed to the non-Russians, because in its social implication it entailed the abolition of serfdom and other forms of feudal oppression. The call for the 'return to the old ways' which characterised the Pugachev uprising, was nothing else but a long standing expression of popular dreams about a world without servility and oppression, a social order which was free of arbitrary taxation and exploitation. That world, which may also have implied religious tolerance, appeared to be a 'divine' order worth fighting for [*Klibanov, 1977*: 136–62; *Kartsov, 1977*: 23–73; *Buganov, 1976*: ch. 4; *Krest'yanskaya...*, 1961–70].

While those programmes of the Pugachev revolt and other popular movements that reflected the ideas of the participants in terms of a new social order had the greatest resonance among the masses, there were frequently also religious motives. The main thrust of these movements was against serfdom, against the nobility, the powerful and the rich, in a word: against oppressors and exploiters. But the declaration of religious tolerance, the rejection of confessional fanaticism and the freedom to pursue one's chosen faith proved to be significant elements in developing a cohesion, a solidarity and a mutual trust among the participants of these uprisings especially because of the multinational character of the country in which they were fought.

As we have seen, religion and religious ideas supplied a common denominator for popular movements in Russia during the seventeenth and eighteenth centuries. They were the guise in which the hopes and expectations of participants were expressed, a general feature of all mass movements in the feudal era. After all, it was institutionally organised religion that sanctioned the existing order and in turn the ruling classes and their state supported organised religion. Yet Christianity meant more than this. It also offered possibilities for the lower classes. The peasants and the poor were of course believers, informed by religious dogma – that is, by norms that derived from primitive Christianity, and supplied them with a frame of reference in formulating their yearnings for the reduction or elimination of feudal oppression, for law, justice and equality.

Religion played this contradictory, double-faced role over many centuries. It conserved and consolidated that side of popular consciousness which called for submissiveness, penitence and fast in face of adversity, and rejected open resistance to evil. From it, elements of mass ideology and psychology flourished until very recent times. One may recall the populist views of Tolstoy based on a world view of the Russian peasantry, which grew out of popular religiosity and still bore its backward looking character. Thus religious norms, going back to late Antiquity, could give food for thought to the oppressed and serve as ideological masks for their hopes and expectations about a good and just social order for century after century. Notwithstanding the utopian character and the impracticability of these ideas, they were forces that, among many others, contributed to historical progress.

It was only in the early twentieth century that it became clear to the masses that religious factors do not point the way to the solution of the needs of society and the tasks of the working classes. Religion proved not to be useful in intensifying class struggle and revolutionary movement. That struggle and that movement had to move away from the road of religious consciousness toward a scientific theory. This task was fulfilled by the Russian progressive movements of the nineteenth and the three Russian revolutions of the early twentieth.

References

Buganov, V. I., 1969, *Moskovskie vosstania kontsa XVII v.* [The Moscow uprising in the late 17th C.] Moscow.
Buganov, V. I., 1976, *Krest'yanskie voyny v Rossii XVII–XVIII vv.* [Peasant wars in Russia in the 17th–18th C.] Moscow.
Golinkova, N. B., 1975, *Astrakhanskoe vosstanie 1705–1706 gg.* [The Astrachan uprising of 1705–6] Moscow.
Krest'yanskaya ..., 1961–70, *Krest'yanskaya voyna v Rossii v 1773–75 godakh: Vosstanie Pugacheva* [Peasant war in Russia in 1773–5: The Pugachev uprising] 3 vols. Leningrad.
Kartsov, V. G., 1971, 'Razintsy i raskol'niki' [Razin's men and Old Believers] *Voprosy istorii*, no. 3, 121–31.
Kartsov, V. G., 1977, *Religioznyy raskol kak forma antifeudal'nogo protesta v istorii Rossii* 1 [Religious schism as a form of anti-feudal protest in Russian history] Kalinin.
Klibanov, A. I., 1977, *Narodnaya sotsial'naya utopiya v Rossii. Period feodalizma* [Popular social utopia in Russia: The feudal period] Moscow.
Koretsky, V. I., 1975, *Formirovanie Krepostnogo prava i Pervaia krest'yanskaya voyna v Rossii* [The development of serfdom and the First Russian Peasant War] Moscow.
Pod'yapol'skaya, E. P., 1962, *Vosstanie Bulavina 1707–1709* [The Bulavin uprising in 1707–9] Moscow.
Smirnov, I. I., 1951, *Vosstanie Bolotnikova 1606–1607* [The Bolotnikov uprising in 1606–7] Moscow.
Stepanov, I. V., 1966, *Krest'yanskaya voyna v Rossii v 1670–1671 gg.: Vosstania Stepana Razina* [Peasant War in Russia in 1670–1: The uprising of Stepan Razin] Leningrad.
Tserkov' ..., 1967, *Tserkov' v istorii Rossii* [The Church in Russian history] Moscow.

'Irreligiosity' in seventeenth and eighteenth century peasant uprisings in Russia

ALEKSANDR I. KLIBANOV

Religion and rural revolt is a topic of both scholarly and actual significance. Their connection can and should be studied in a wide chronological frame, including the rural movements of contemporary 'underdeveloped' societies. The scope of this study has to include the history of peasantries, the evolution of religion and the particular ethnic and regional traits of religious beliefs as well as of peasant uprisings. The interaction of religion and resistance or revolt is very diverse, as I have tried to show in my studies on the rôle and character of religious beliefs in Russian popular movements [Klibanov, *1960; 1965; 1977; 1978*].

Religious conviction of different levels and varied patterns was a constant element in the mental life of medieval people. In Western Europe anti-feudal peasant uprisings were generally connected with one or another heretical movement, such as the Bogomils, Valdensians, Albigensians, Flagellant, Lollards, Taborites, Anabaptists etc. However, while the mass rebellion of the 1358 *Jacquerie* did not display any religious motivation, the great French rural uprising of 1702–5 did just that. The peasant wars in Sung China (tenth–thirteenth centuries) were closely linked with heresies, such as the White Lotus, but the great rising of Chinese peasants in 1628–45 seems to have had no religious motives whatsoever. In this volume here, many authors explore the necessary and sufficient conditions under which peasant revolts include anti-ecclesiastical programmes or even focus on such issues. The study of these conditions is particularly important for historians of Russian rural anti-feudal movements. From the Bolotnikov-rising (1606–7) to the Pugachev rebellion (1773–5) we find a peculiar ideological trait that might be called 'irreligiosity', although at the same time several sects existed among the Russian peasantry, constituting a wide spectrum of anti-ecclesiastical opposition. Participants and many leaders of peasant uprisings came from among religious dissenters, suggesting that there was something common in the social discourse of religious opposition and rural revolt. None the less, the language (concepts, images and symbols) of the religious opposition did not in Russia become the widely accepted medium for the mass rural uprisings.

One reason for this seems to be that the 'dialects' of the anti-ecclesiastical circles were too numerous and hence difference rather than unity characterised the dissenting religious movements. Furthermore, the social character of the Russian Orthodox church defined to a great extent the 'ireligiosity' of peasant revolts. In contrast to the (Roman) Catholic, the Russian Orthodox church was not the only centre of Orthodoxy. It has never enjoyed such power and independence as the Western church; since the times of Ivan III (1462–1503) ecclesiastical landed property, trade and commercial activity as well as the legal-political immunity of the Russian Orthodox church were subject to secular regulation and challenged by the opposition of powerful secular lords. While the church, as the greatest landowner, in fact exploited peasants, burdened them with numerous taxes and dues and, by extending its jurisdiction to matters of family, property and inheritance, interfered with their lives, it was still not regarded by wide strata of the society as the main source of social ills, hardships and vices. Surely, during the peasant uprising many a score was settled between serfs and ecclesiastical landlords, but there was always a considerable difference between the position of and the attitudes to the Russian Orthodox and the Western Catholic church. This essential difference is to be born in mind if one wants to understand why peasant uprisings in Russia were 'irreligious'.

The multinational character of the mass revolts, especially Razin's and Pugachev's, should also be considered. Many of their participants were Muslims, Lamaist or followers of 'natural' cults. Some of the latter were regarded as Orthodox Christians, having been baptized by missionaries, but actually held on to their traditional cults, identifying ancestral devotion with the preservation of ethnic identity and with resistance to feudal oppression.

This helps us to understand why the popular mass uprisings of Russia, comprising both rural and urban lower classes, expected their participants to 'lay aside' their religious differences, emphasizing the integrating rather than the divisive factors. Of course, while noting the apparent lack of religious issues in the uprisings, one should never assume that the participants were in any way 'irreligious', be they of the old guard of anti-ecclesiastical movements, such as the sectarians and Old Believers, be they Muslims, Lamaists, pagans or Orthodox Christians.

Heresies appear in the feudal period essentially at two historical junctions. First, when popular beliefs first encounter Christian teaching, and second, when popular religiosity, having tasted the fruit of Christianity's tree of knowledge, begins to break with that doctrine. The former was characterised by a nostalgic anti-ecclesiastical idealisation of the free peasant community (*obshchina*). The latter was the anti-ecclesiastical protest of serfs, urban poor and burghers, anticipating a social order that would replace the feudal system.

An example for the first type was, to my mind, Bogomilism in its eastern and western versions. Numerous uprisings of the *smerdy* dependant peasants in eleventh century Suzdal, Rostov and Novgorod were rooted in the popular faith and led by a hierarchy of papagan priests (*volkhvy*). These uprisings incorporated some elements of Bogomil comsology and gnostic-dualistic ideas [*Kazachkova, 1958: 238–314; Angelov, 1969: 431–8*]. This tradition did not, however, survive beyond the first third of the twelfth century. The last mention of the *volkhv* as an element dangerous to the existing order is an entry in the First Novgorod Annals for 1227 A.D., which records that four of them were burnt at the stake in Novgorod [*Grekov, 1953: 267*].

The absence of any later reference to the activities of *volkhvy* suggests that among the Russian population the first stage of Christianisation had been completed already before the end of Old Rus. Thereafter the Orthodox clergy was under no serious threat from the hierarchy of pagan priests. Yet there is evidence for a long drawn-out confrontation between Orthodox missionaries and pagan priests of the non-Russian peoples. The *Life of Stephen of Perm*, written in the late fourteenth century by Epifany the Wise (who died c. 1420), includes a chapter entitled 'On the debate with the *volkhv*'. It gives a description of Pam, the chief priest of the Permian Komi people, a figure presenting the 'type' of pagan priest, analogous to the *volkhvy* of the Slavs. The words that Epifany puts into the mouth of Pam illustrate well the kind of ideas that lie behind the resistance to Christianisation:

> Brethren, men of Perm, do not forsake your paternal gods, do not forget the sacrifices due to them, nor the old rights and customs. Do not abandon your ancient faith!... Listen to me, and not to Stephen, the newcomer from Moscow. What good can come from Muscovy? Do not our hardships and heavy burdens, the violence, the commanders, overseers, tax-collectors all come from there? [*Povest', 1862: IV, 138*].

The hagiographer presents us with a pagan priest who debates with Bishop Stephen in the name of the 'men of Perm' and equates the defence of ancient faith with opposition to exploitation ('hardships', 'burdens') and to feudal lordship ('commanders, overseers, tax-collectors'). This text usefully demonstrates the social motives that went with confrontation between adherents of traditional cults and Christian missionaries. To my mind, these motivations can very well be assumed to have been also those of eleventh century *smerdy* led by their *volkhvy*. The words ascribed to Pam concerning the tribal gods are worth quoting more fully in order to highlight these motives:

> It is they who grant us all the game, and all that is in the waters, and all that is in the sky, and all that is in the forest; in the woods; in the clearings; in young growth; among the willows; and among the poplars; and among the trees around the fields; and all that is in other kinds of woodland as well as that which lives on the trees of the

forest; the squirrels; the sable; the marder; and all the other beasts for our hunt. All that we bring home, all that comes from our gods and it goes to enrich your dukes; your boyars; and your nobles, who are dressed in those coats with marvellous fur trimmings, and who parade before the common people, who have produced these, and who have enjoyed these riches in great abundance for many years. Is it not our prey that is being sent to the [Mongol] Horde, where it is received by their so-called Emperor? And to Constantinople, and to the West, and to Lithuania, and to other towns and countries and distant lands? [*Ibid., 141*].

These words of Pam have an authentic ring even though they reach us through ecclesiastical transmission. They describe the land of Perm as an earthly Paradise that had flourished for uncounted centuries down to those very days of tragic confrontation with the missionary. In the debate with Stephen, Pam is fighting for this Garden of Eden, granted and maintained by the tribal gods of the Komi. Reporting the counter-arguments of Stephen, Epifany totally disregards any connection between the traditional beliefs of Permians on the one hand and their material well-being and freedom from alien and hostile lords on the other. The missionary, endowed with the superior art of rhetoric, of course, victoriously carries the day.

Sources on the conversion of non-Russian people, such as the Chuvash, the Mordva and others also indicate that there was a close correlation between the defence of tribal cults and of the free communities. The outside threat of a Christian mission with its attendant feudal oppression smoothed internal tensions that had eroded tribal communities, social differentiation and the emergence of lordship within the community. The arguments of Pam, as recorded in Epifany's narrative, did not reflect existing realities but rather glorified in religious terms a distant patriarchal past.

The lack of mention of *volkhv*-activity among Russians after 1227 is more than balanced by ecclesiastical writings of the twelfth–fifteenth centuries against pagan religious practices and popular beliefs with their rites, calendar festivities and soothsayings [*Gal'kovsky, 1913*]. The canons of the Synod of Stroglav (1551) emphasized the importance to fight against them. Simeon of Polotsk in the 'Sermon on false beliefs and superstitions' (included in his collection of sermons published in 1681) criticised the whole roster of customs and omens based on popular belief. That popular version of Orthodoxy that existed throughout the feudal period – and in fragments up to our own century – has been called 'dual faith' or 'everyday Russian Orthodoxy'. Gradually, 'dual faith' became synchretistic: its pagan and Orthodox components interacted with each other rather than existing side by side. The two initially antagonistic beliefs formed a dynamically balanced system in which Christian Orthodoxy began to predominate, though never fully gaining the upper hand.

The critical turn-about was reached some time in the first half of the seventeenth century. It can be dated by comparing the synodal canons of 1551 with the decrees of the Assembly of 1649 (*Sobornoe ulozhenie*). While the former still devotes great attention to the repression of popular religious practices, the latter tells us hardly anything about them. The first canon of 1649 is styled 'Against the blasphemers and enemies of the church', and is devoted to the protection of ecclesiastical institutions, the sanctity of clergy, behaviour in church, and the basic tenets of Orthodox faith: belief in Jesus Christ; in the Mother of God; in the Holy Cross and the saints. This canon is not aimed at the remnants of popular pagan belief, but rather, as suggested by its title, at those members of the church who defy its commands or openly express their opposition. Although as early as the late fourteenth century urban heresy had been referred to by Bishop Stephen as prevalent in the towns of Pskov and Novgorod, by the seventeenth century dissenting movements seem to have reached the countryside as well. By the third decade of the century Old Belief had clearly began to emerge. It was to grow by the end of the seventeenth century into a large movement with several branches, which shook the entire edifice of the official church. Russian Orthodoxy was now opposed on its own grounds.

As far as we can judge from the scant evidence in the early sources of Old Belief, it was linked with apocryphal writings and with texts that had been placed on the index. Old Belief was heretical from the outset, as it stood in opposition to the established church and its canon of texts. Old Believers (*raskolniki* = 'splitters') absorbed from popular belief above all aspects of a mythical, epic and folkloric perception of the world, rather than ideological and cultic elements. This can be seen in the transformation of abstract Orthodox teachings into more down-to-earth and concrete forms, in the attempts at translating the numinous language of Christianity into a phenomenal one and in weakening the church's personal principle in favour of collectivism [*Klibanov, 1973*]. A view of Old Belief 'from inside' proves that their devotion to cultic objects and religious rituals does not make their religion one of forms and rites. It rather marks their belonging to a historical form of consciousness, not dissimilar to that represented by Pam against Stephen, characterised by extroversion. *Protopop* Avakum urged his co-believers to die for a single *az* of Old Belief. *Az*, that is the first letter of the alphabet, denotes here the slightest particle [we might say – an iota – Transl.] of their social and spiritual values. The focus of these values was the ideal of a free peasantry: and in the defence of this *az* thousands of raskolniki risked their lives. It was the symbol of a religious utopia, a world of freely working inhabitants in a god-given earthly Paradise, where rivers, woods and forests reward all men and women with rich yield. An utopia of patriarchal character, to be sure, and – as is typical for utopian dreams – totally abstracted from existing realities in which the conditions of such an ideal world were long ago lost. But this utopia was seen as the 'ancient blessedness' in contrast to 'present evilness' as incorporated in the established church.

A late parallel to Pam's speech can be found in the writings of a soldier-deserter, Evfemy, a contemporary of Pugachev. In his view [Emperor Peter I] 'destroyed the people by dividing them into ranks (*chin*), by levying tax on every soul, and then enclosing the fields and splitting of the traders'. The result, according to Evfemy, was that 'people became, as it were, pagans pitched against one another as in a war, they drew borders among the lands and everybody said 'this is mine'. This word 'mine' was, however, called by Saint Chrysostomos as being of the devil, since all that God created is in common' [*Klibanov, 1977: 257*]. Private property is seen as having created conflict among men and this contributed to the general decline of morals:

> And then the Adversary made men cling to their property. Hence began all falsehood, false measure and unjust weight, and everything got mixed up with base matter. Oaths and promises began to appear and people were jealous of each other's property. Jealousy, hatred and conflict predominated. Violent feuds were fought, and much harm was done through robbery. And all this was the consequence of those new divisions and prohibitions [*Ibid., 208*].

In spite of the four centuries that separate them, the statements and accusations of pagan priest Pam and Old Believer Evfemy are impressively similar. Evfemy might even be seen as a version of the former, merely improved upon in the spirit of Old Belief and amplified by reference to the church father.

Evfemy had very definite ideas about the struggle against the unbearable burdens imposed by imperial and ecclesiastical authorities. They differed from those of Pugachev, but the social preaching of Evfemy found an echo in the uprising's manifestoes and edicts. If we had more contemporary evidence on the ideological bases of the *volkhv*-led uprisings of the *smerdy* we might also find further parallels between the eighteenth and the eleventh century. For those very layers of social consciousness, which informed the peasant uprisings of the seventeenth and eighteenth centuries had their roots in a far remote past. Although the formulations and the references to the actual realities had changed, essence remained very much the same from the time of Pam to that of Evfemy, if not from an even more ancient past.

Almost simultaneously with the emergence of Old Belief, other religious movements arose in both urban and rural surroundings, which can be called 'new belief'. I am not referring to that new religion which was introduced in the mid-seventeenth century by the Nikonian reforms and attacked as novelty by the Old Believer, Avakum, in the late eighteenth. First of all I have in mind the teaching of Danila Filippov in the districts of Kostroma, Vladimir and Nizhny-Novgorod. He represents the earliest known forms of 'spiritual Christianity' and his followers called themselves 'devotees of Christ's faith'. Official church literature later referred to this sect as *Khristovshchina* or *Khlystovshchina*, the latter meaning flagellants.

Scholars, including myself, usually regarded Danila Filippov as a hero of folklore in the tradition of the 'devotees of Christ's faith', but he seems to me now to have been a real person. He began preaching some time in the 1620s[1]. According to a tradition of this sect, which was recorded as early as the eighteenth century, Danila threw his ecclesiastical books, both new and old, into the River Volga, thereby signalling that he was going to go his own way. The paramount command of his teaching was 'Thou shalt listen to the Holy Spirit', that is to the live, spoken word, instead of the dead letter of books. He also prescribed strict asceticism in matters of sex and drink, and the avoidance of religious family festivities such as baptisms, weddings and other entertainments.

The 'devotees of Christ's faith' constituted homogeneous communities and believed in becoming 'Christ-like'. Their cult was ecstatic; exhausted by severe fasting, they held secret meetings behind closed doors, with dancing in circle, chanting, praying and hearing prophesies from those members who felt to be 'visited by the spirit'. They interpreted Scripture in an allegorical way, 'in spirit and truth', and emulated Christ and his disciples by their own 'saviours' and 'apostles', following the words of the Gospels. They did not oppose attendance at Orthodox divine service, and did not remove the icons from their homes. Their main prayer was a short, silent 'prayer of Jesus', which was widespread among the Old Believers. These were hardly tactical moves to deceive or placate the official church, but rather a farewell tribute to Orthodoxy by those who came to believe in a 'salvation by faith'. Thus began the development of a personalized form of social consciousness among the Russian peasantry.

In the course of the eighteenth century spiritual Christianity spread and soon developed new forms, such as the Dukhobors and Molokans. They were characterized by a final and complete break with Russian Orthodoxy. In contrast to the 'devotees of Christ's faith' these movements abandoned ecstatic cults and religious mysticism. It was their social ideal to denounce all forms of human domination over men, and also of any state and church power. The category, man, receives an almost divine standing, since these sects believe firmly in the sovereignty of the individual. However, spiritual Christianity began to involve a kind of Christian rationalism. It was an introverted form of social consciousness which consistently rejected Russian Orthodoxy as external, formal and ritualistic. This spiritual religious life came to replace that traditional world-view which has been entrenched in the minds of most of the peasantry for quite a long period. This new world view was in its logical core not dissimilar from the one discussed by Immanuel Kant as 'true' or 'pure moral' religion in contrast to different 'ecclesiastical faiths' [*1934: esp. 98ff*].

Spiritual Christianity was a symptom of profound transformations which the peasantry experienced in the course of contradictory socio-economic and cultural developments in seventeenth and eighteenth century Russia. Such transformations were uneven due to the regional differences in the vast Russian Empire. These unevenesses and contradictions explain, why religious opposition, although very widespread, did not become unified enough to develop an alternative ideological language. During the territorially restricted peasant uprisings from the Solovetsky in 1668–76 to that of Bulavin in 1707–9, the rôle of religious opposition became increasingly significant as both an ideological and an organisational element. That is also true, albeit to a lesser extent, for the 'national' uprisings of Razin and Pugachev. Here we are dealing essentially with an Old Believer opposition, which is significant, as it shows that traditionally oriented consciousness remained deeply rooted among the peasantry even in the period when the first steps toward a capitalist development were being taken within the serf-owning society.

The peasant wars of the seventeenth–eighteenth centuries mobilised adherents of several religions, from spiritual Christians to pagans. Each of them legitimated their own struggle against feudal oppression in a particular spirit, so that they were able to fight together while walking different (religious) paths. It is in this sense that we can speak of the 'irreligiosity' of these uprisings. As in any popular uprising, so also in the Russian peasant wars, psychological motives played a significant part, but we shall bracket their discussion for this time.

The question remains, whether these 'irreligious' revolts were bereft of all ideological language, that is, whether they got beyond some kind of personalised, psychological gut-reaction. The non-sectarian character of the movements does not imply that participants were necessarily irreligious men and women. Equally, religious tolerance among both leaders and common participants was in itself a highly significant ideological fact. Finally, the necessity to eliminate the religious ideas made these rebels more aware of the need to state their general social programme as forcefully as possible, in order to achieve unity of purpose. The common programme, the fight for a system of free producers who would own and control the rich resources of nature, thus emerged all the more clearly.

The participants of these uprisings had different ideas about what that system would be like, as they represented very varied levels and segments of social consciousness. But this was not perhaps the main point. For the oppressed people the central issue was to achieve independence for a life based on equality and work. There were different types of recourse to a higher *in nomine*, by which the rebelling peasants legitimated and enforced their appeal and drive. Whether this 'in the name of' was an echo of a distant patriarchal past or an appeal to a future which was still to be achieved – this question had to be postponed by the fighting peasants.

Note

1. This emerges from a sentence passed by the provincial ecclesiastical court of Kostroma in 1747 against the 'devotees of Christ's faith' Anna Stepanova and Dar'ya Vasil'evna, granddaughters of the late Danila Filippov who died at an advanced age around 1700. Tsentral'ny gosudarstvenny arkhiv, Fond 796, Inv. 28, Coll. unit 213 (chancery of the Synod).

References

Angelov, D., 1969, *Bogomilstvoto v Bulgariya* [Bogomilism in Bulgaria] Sofia.
Gal'kovsky, I. M., 1913, *Bor'ba khristianstva s ostatkami yazychestva v drevney Rusi* 2 [The struggle of Christianity with the remnants of paganism in Old Rus] Moscow.
Grekov, B. D., 1953, *Kievskaya Rus'* [Kievan Rus] Moscow.
Kant, I., 1934, *Religion within the limits of reason alone*, Transl. T. M. Greene, and H. H. Hudson, Chicago-London.
Kazachkova, D. A., 1958, 'Zarozhdenie i razvitie antitserkovoy ideologii v drevney Rusi XI v.' [Origins and development of anti-ecclesiastical ideology in Old Rus in the 11th C.] *Voprosy istorii religii i ateizma* V: 283–314.
Klibanov, A. I., 1960, *Reformatsionnye dvizheniya v Rossii v XIV-pervoy polovine XVI vv.* [Reformational movements in Russia from the 14th to the first part of the 16th C.] Moscow.
Klibanov, A. I., 1965, *Istoriya religioznogo sektantstva v Rossii* [The history of religious sectarianism in Russia] Moscow (Engl. transl. by E. & S. P. Dunn, London, 1982).
Klibanov, A. I., 1973, 'Protopop Avvakum kak kul'turno-istoricheskoe yavleniya' [The protopope Avvakum as a cultural-historical phenomenon] *Istoriya SSSR*, 76–98.
Klibanov, A. I., 1977, *Narodnaya sotsial'naya utopiya v Rossii*, t. I [Popular social utopia in Russia] Moscow.
Klibanov, A. I., 1978, *Idem*, t. II, Moscow.
Povest' . . . 1862, 'Provest' o Stefane, episkope Permskom' [The Story of Stephen, Bishop of Perm] *Pamiatniki starinoy russkoi literatury* IV, St Petersburg.

Religious patterns of interpretation and mobilisation in Vormärz Germany

RAINER WIRTZ

> What God has created in this world
> Is of good and just report
> Only use it wisely,
> According to His design ...
> [*Noth- und Hilfsbüchlein, 1788: 122*][1]

During the decades preceding the 1848 Revolution religion caused mass movements and unrest in Germany. The emotional and active elements of religion worked themselves out in various ways. At times pilgrimages mobilised hundreds of thousands, and at others, as for example after the appearance in 1835 of David Friedrich Strauss' book on the life of Jesus, German educated opinion was more upset than any revolutionary manifesto could have achieved. Myth-killing enlightened theology, rationalism, naturalism and its supernatural superlatives forced their way into a worn-out religion administered by the official church. Religion and church were no longer the indisputable norms determining the world of rank and order in society: they were wide open to debate.

The newly ultramontane orthodoxy centred on Rome opposed enlightened tendencies in theology. The Roman Catholic official church saw itself seriously challenged by manifold creations of German Catholic congregations. It was just as impossible to keep nationalist ideas out of church and religion as it was to excise liberal and socialist influences. There was basically no split between politics and religion. Religious questions were political matters, and political questions were religious matters.

After 1848 it became clear that the previous years of unrest had been instrumental in creating a bourgeois state power and justice. Yet historians have tended to stress legal, institutional and narrative aspects rather than making religion the central theme of this transformation [Cf. *Mayer, 1969: 7–107*]. Economic and political crises characterised this transition to 'modernity'. The relationship between state and society was redefined.

It was first discussed in religious language but over and above the appeal to religious thought an attempt was made to influence people to think and act in a newly understood secular manner. A well-known example is Wilhelm Weitling, organiser of a 'communist' movement among Swiss journeymen, and member of the League of the Just whose concepts of justice and equality were so firmly based on quotations from the Bible that he and his followers were sometimes still classed as religious sectarians within the utopian socialist movement [*Weitling, 1907*]. According to Schieder [*1963*], craftsmen were not to be politicised without resort to religious form and content in the agitation used. This was even reciprocated at the level of the more highly educated middle-class who were often in personal agreement with political liberals in opposing the new ultramontane tendencies in official church circles as well as nonconformist and German Catholic congregational ones. Conflicts over religious exercise and freedom were aired in press and public more vigorously than 'merely' political matters. Among the lasting counter-demonstrations to the great assembly of democrats and liberals at Hambach in 1832 was a pilgrimage to the Holy Shroud of Trier in 1844 with 200,000 participants, demonstratively also a military display of the reactionaries [*Schieder, 1974; Korff, 1977*]. Religion contained emotional and active forces which could be mobilised for a great variety often of mutually contradictory causes.

Political tension between reactionary and progressive forces was largely created by resort to religion. Hans Rosenberg [*1930: 516*] saw the repressive policies of Metternich's Europe 'as creating indirectly through religious, ecclesiastical, theological, philosophical and literary controversies the successful development of political parties in Germany'. To simplify, one may regard religion as providing a substitute for war, when reaction allied itself with official church orthodoxy, and when emerging political liberalism took the side of rational theology. Predominant attitudes to exercise of power had not broken away from religious form and content, which was achieved only very gradually, since without resort to religion no secular models of society could be popularised.

These conflicts were fought in pamphlets and newspapers as well as in the discussions of local assemblies, treasuries and parliaments. In clubs and political meetings all the problems of the world were debated. In the southwest German state of Baden the key issues before 1848 were control of local government, Jewish emancipation, discharge of tenants' obligations to former landowners, loosening of restrictions on business and manufacture, and the correct relationship between state and church [*Fischer, 1962: 156ff*]. This was the stage upon which growing civic awareness found elbow-room for manoeuvre against reactionary government censorship. The new political culture was essentially middle-class and therefore severely limited in its aspirations. Before 1848 in Germany this culture was dominated by the traditional towns who exercised their power hegemonically over at least 75% of the total population. These were the peasants who lived in the surrounding countryside and who were first to be educated, enlightened and trained to espouse 'correct' views and attitudes [*Hobsbawm,*

1962: 266ff].

How was this rural population to be involved in political activity when its view of the world was in no way akin to that of liberal and radical movements? For the peasants the victories of Napoleon were the actions of the antichrist, and the famines of 1817 and 1847 were seen to be God's punishment. For liberals and radicals resistance to Napoleon was a conscious national act, and the famines, when tied to the crisis of redundancy among traditional journeymen, were seen as part of the economic transformation towards liberal laissez-faire capitalism. A religious view of the world was much more fatalistic. It implied obedience and subservience which in turn promised a better life in the hereafter. To cope with everyday existence this side of religion was used as an opiate to get through this vale of tears on earth. Sayings in almanacs, pleas in front of votive altars, and publications like the Noth- und Hiffsbüchlein (Good Advice and help for peasants in need), from which we have cited a ditty at the beginning of this essay, were also regarded as concrete aids to life, and they were internalised as such by many individuals. The religious influence of such works was not merely felt through passive acceptance of what they had to say, but it also limited popular aspirations and regulated the relationship between work and leisure. The rhythm of work and the yearly cycle were controlled by the religious customs surrounding Sundays and holy-days. Rites of passage were celebrated with specialised activities for men and women, young and old. Especially the cults of Catholic rural communities, such as the blessing of sick animals, pilgrimages, and the handling of relics, provided at one and the same time the popular medicine and the prophylaxis of an animistic world. The decline of magic altered the position of church and parish priest more than it did that of popular belief or superstition as for example in the seventeenth and eighteenth century reduction of the number of church holidays due to new economic forms of work and life [Cf. *Thomas, 1971; Meyer, 1900: 480ff, 518ff; Scharfe, 1980*]. Religion was an aid to life and survival. As such it was institutionalised and used to legitimate the ruling class.

In the first half of the nineteenth century the position of enlightened parish priest became harder to uphold. It was his task to teach his flock that the prince was their fatherly ruler by the grace of God as biblically expressed in Romans 13.3 [Cf. *Jeggle, 1977: 55ff, 66ff*]. At the same time this priest was a member of the local society for agricultural improvement, where he attempted to induct his parishioners into the blessings of modern manuring and field cropping. As the predominant, fashionable spiritual trend of the times, rational theology had to serve two masters. On the one hand it had to find Christian legitimation for obedience to the reactionary rulers of the Holy Alliance down to local territorial princely powers. On the other hand it had to represent the world as personally changeable, if not exactly conquerable by man, provided one became educated enough for the task. The possibility of planning your own future, which was not necessarily tied to any collective policy of the community, also provided quite another tie with the existing order of state and society, whereby some individuals were able to develop an attitude which was not catered for in God's traditional natural world order.

Contradictions within rational theology were also apparent in the exercise of power, where government supported tendencies towards enlightenment and natural rights, tolerating theologians as long as they restricted their discussions to the Kingdom of God. Yet it was no big step from criticising those who misused God's wisdom and almightiness to criticising those who misused the power of the state, since both were mediated through the person of the ruling prince.

Social movements were embedded in a dual society which partly depended on political domination, property, education and participation in urban life, whilst the other part consisted of the rural masses who were subordinated to the technological, economic and political innovations of the former [*Scott, 1977: 102ff*]. The two parts naturally overlapped. The focal point of such a dual society lay in religion which hinged the new hegemonic aspirations of the rising middle-class with the social thought of the rural population. With its allegories and through its local networks religion provided a channel of communication to link both parts by analogy between the biblical past and current affairs. Religion was thus capable of being latently socio-critical, especially when biblical quotations were believed literally. The same religion could equally legitimate and stabilise the existing reactionary political authorities. The conflict between liberalism and reaction did not obliterate the continuation also into the nineteenth century of religion as a vital component of a little tradition, which in the make-up of everyday culture provided rural inhabitants with an autonomous set of values [*Scott, 1974*]. Religion was an emotional reservoir both for semantic excesses perpetrated on verbal battlefronts, and also for uniting within itself significant contradictions of the times. The important contradiction must be stressed that religion was both the mode of linguistic communication whilst at the same time it was the object of conflict.

> Thoroughly examine the reasons for every piece of evil,
> And you will appreciate that not the Devil but God imposes it,
> In order to make you a better person.
> So use what is yours as best you can,
> And you will always find the comfort that you need
> [*Noth- und Hilfsbüchlein, 1788: 476*]

The famines of 1817 and 1847 thus came from God, according to simple religious wisdom. They were a test imposed willy-nilly to strengthen and improve the faith of those who suffered. This view of society was upheld to strengthen patient obedience and suffering in the here-and-now in order to find reward in the after-life. To take your own measures against this inevitable punishment was unthinkable. And yet after 1847 rural protests began to be organised in letters and threats of rebellion. In March 1848 there were peasant revolts in Saxony, Hesse and Baden. A pamphlet from North Baden called upon

> Brothers and fellow citizens of the state of Baden! The time has come by God's chosen hand that we use our physical strength to secure our own freedom which he gave us when he made the world, and which he wishes to give back to us, if we now follow him. That is why God has inflicted famine to awaken the German people and call upon them to fight for each other in unity and brotherly love. Let us tell you why this revolution must take place. Firstly, the nobility must be exterminated; secondly, Jews must be expelled from Germany; thirdly, that all kings, dukes and ruling princes be abolished and Germany made into a free state like America; fourthly, all government officials must be murdered. Good times will then return to Germany. The day of the revolution is fixed for 12 April of this year, when all men and youths capable of bearing arms living in the local districts shall assemble with guns, swords or straightened scythes. And each place will elect its own leader. Signed by the Friends of the Fatherland [*Generallandesarchiv Karlsruhe, Abt. 236, Fasz. 8492; cf. Lautenschlager, 1915*].

According to the pamphlet a famine had been sent by God, only with the twist that this calamity was a sign for the German people to unite and overthrow their landlords and rulers. For the very God who sent these calamities had at the beginning of the world also given mankind freedom, which then had been usurped by nobles, Jews and officials. A residual belief that the earliest Christians were free was here linked with a nationalistic desire for common action by the German people – residual because the notion of a just king-emperor was retained. Local grievances, such as those against a noble landlord who insisted on his feudal privileges; against officials who rigorously taxed the peasants and prosecuted their actions at law; against Jews who were supposed to have control either of cattle markets and rural money-lending, or as paupers outside the village community to have become a burden upon totally inadequate local charity funds, were not even named, since they were regarded to be self-evident. It was sufficient to name the type of person, such as the official, who then personified the grievance itself.

Using actual need as background, axioms about God's help, an original state of freedom, and location of crisis in specific rural districts, all were merged into a sure sign from on high. Biblical notions were thereby presented to motivate and to legitimate concrete action, whose aim in an alliance with an ideal of national unity was to overcome the supposed causes of the original calamity. This alliance was new and it came partly from national feelings stirred up by the wars of liberation against Napoleon, and partly in reaction to the absence, since the collapse in 1803 of the Holy Roman Empire, of judicial systems of appeal against territorial state governments, thirty-two of whom survived to operate as newly sovereign entities after 1815. The appeal back to God was an attempt to find the immediate legitimation that would convince the peasants, to whom the pamphlet was addressed, of the righteousness of the rebel cause. Authorship was ascribed to a soap-seller who distributed the pamphlet along with his product. He must have known his clients well enough to appreciate that religious attitudes and beliefs were tied in their minds directly to wordly matters, whereby there was no fundamental distinction between politics and religion. The author himself could equally just as well have held the same rural politico-religious views.

Many illegal pamphlets circulated in Germany during the 1830s and 40s, condemning the European system set up by the Congress of Vienna, and taking issue with various aspects, such as its sham parliaments and lack of press freedom. But this was of little interest or concern to the peasantry. On 3 April 1833 there occurred an attack on the Frankfurt city militia, which was supposed to have given the signal for a general uprising, but this conspiracy was betrayed and made unrealistic by its narrow appeal mainly to students. Thereafter, people like the theologian Friedrich Weidig and the playwright Georg Büchner realised that a handful of undisciplined, urban liberals could not make a revolution, and so they began to direct their attention to the peasantry. An attempt was then made to win support with pamphlets directed towards an audience of small-peasant and rural craftsmen, of which Büchner's famous tract, the *Hessische Landbote* [Hessian Rural Messenger], was an example in an attempt 'to unite the material interests of the people with those of the revolution' [*Noellner, 1844: 114*]. Here we are not concerned with discovering what part each had in writing the *Landbote* [*cf. Mayer, 1976; Mayer, 1981*], but rather we shall explore how these types of argument utilised religious content and to what extent they were effective or not, although it is obvious that most of the Bible quotations came from the theologian, Weidig [*Noellner, 1844: 99*]. To the social problems of his time he thought that the Bible could give a direct answer which was not contradictory to the aims of liberalism but rather it could even legitimate demands for national unity.

The *Landbote* starts with the Biblical myth of creation, which is then pressed into service as an attack on ruling princes. It states [*Büchner, 1958: 333*] –

> In the year 1834 it looks as if the Bible will be punished for lying. It looks as if God made the peasants and workers on the fifth day, and ruling princes and other fine folk on the sixth, telling the latter to rule over all animals that crawl on earth, as if he had included peasants and citizens among the crawlers.

In Büchner's draft the word 'rich' replaced 'fine folk', which was due to the fact that he did not wish to exclude urban citizens who may have been wealthy but who were, in contradistinction to the ruling princes, definitely not 'fine folk'. Büchner imitated the language of an Old Testament prophet, whereby he clearly told his readers that Godly law had been broken, and that the 'original' situation had to be restored, for the Bible, surely, could not lie. Here there are parallels with arguments used during the much earlier German Peasant War of 1525, where God's justice was used not only to condemn particular material abuses but also built into wider plans to reshape the whole of political, social, economic and religious life as confirmed by stringing together select quotations from the Bible [*Wunder, 1976: 55*].

If we ascribe these parts of the text to Weidig, then we begin to make him into the prophet of 1834, who based himself on quotations from Micah, Ezekiel and Isaiah. This was similar to developments in Britain, where, according to Oliver [*1978:12*], it

> would reveal either a considerable interest in the detailed fulfilment of biblical prophecy, or a readiness to employ prophetic concepts to convey their message. Such, however, can be shown to be perfectly reasonable expectations in early nineteenth century England.

Analogies were intuitively applied to current situations in a manner that was as yet still strange to the historico-scientific theological method of the day. These prophets seemed to fit as critics into the current social situation which, like the German Federation of 1815 itself, was seen to have destroyed the popular community of ancient myth and replaced it with a monarchy and an urban middle class, who were tied to a world of commerce. To the common needs of the whole populace these prophets tried to apply the ancient Godly law from which was derived the rights of widows and orphans, peasants and small craftsmen and shop-keepers by literal reference to the words of God in the Old Testament, as in the very imitation practised in the introduction to Büchner's *Landbote*.

The analogy of using Old Testament prophecy to influence events in the coming year of 1834 formed the basis for an impressive polemic against ruling princes and their governments. Prophetic argument was concretised and strengthened by actual examples of bad monarchic rule in order to show that these rulers were not sanctioned by God. As Büchner [*1958: 339*] said

> You put up with all this mismanagement because scoundrels tell you that this government is from God. This government is not from God but rather it is the father of lies. These ruling princes do not exercise just authority, and for centuries they have scorned and betrayed the office of German emperor, who long ago used to be elected freely by the German people. German princes derive their power from betrayal and perjury, and not because they have been chosen by the people. That is why the existence and actions of these princes are damned by God!

The state was compared to a vicious animal as in Revelation 13, where its Godly legitimation was questioned. From the New Testament, Romans 13 was used polemically also to denote exercise of power in an unchristian manner. Büchner [*ibid., 340*] again

> But the empire of darkness is coming to a close. Very shortly now Germany will flay the princes and arise a free state with a popularly elected government. The Holy Script says, render unto Caesar that which is Caesar's. But what acrues to these treacherous princes if not the rewards of Judas!

Büchner and Weidig then alleged that just as Judas' treachery was worth thirty pieces of silver, so the original betrayal of the people's emperor was perpetuated by thirty German princes. The rootless and captive situation of the German people was then compared with that of the Israelites. By analogy the Bible is here alluded to indirectly in Büchner's vivid words.

> The Lord gave the beautiful land of Germany, which for many centuries was the grandest empire on earth, into the hands of foreign and native butchers, since the hearts of German people had turned away from the freedom and equality of their ancestors and from fear of God, towards worship of many little lords, dukes and kinglets.

Napoleon was thereupon slipped into the pastiche:- 'The Lord, who has broken the stick of that beater, Napoleon, will also topple the idols of our native tyrants with the hands of his own people' [*ibid., 343*]. Here Weidig used the biblical history of the royal house of Israel (2 Kings: 17ff), whereby Napoleon became another Nebuchadnezzar as the tool of a wrathful God (2 Kings: 24), making the now hopefully rebellious people into the executors of divine will. Even within a single sentence the context steers implicitly from present to distant biblical past so that the reader has no need to complete the parallels and analogies for himself. Current political circumstances made the comparisons and contrasts self-evident. Time shrank to let the biblical become the present, and current time in turn became biblical.

How were the tactics of Büchner and Weidig, who used religious material for seditious propaganda purposes, regarded? Was it really all that skilful when that soap-seller twisted God's biblical wrath into a programme for popular action? State authorities were naturally unimpressed. To them the Bible was being misused in order to set poverty against wealth, and the small man against the propertied, similar to all those *paroles d'un croyant* which also misappropriated biblical language [*Ilse, 1860: 350*]. Reference was soon made to the widely circulating work of the Frenchman, Lamennais [*1838*], who equally interpreted his times by direct resort to the Bible in order to lambast the Catholic state church.

In Lamennais many of those who were opposed to existing society found a model to offer them biblical justification for their fears and hopes. Demands for freedom and equality were not only rationally argued from natural law but also derived from the Bible. Schieder [*1963*] shows that this curious alliance of arguments was particularly fashionable among craftsmen and it seems that Lamennais' work was very popular in the Germany of the later 1830s in that it helped many to move with greater ease from biblical radicalism to radical-democratic and utopian-socialist views [*Obermann, 1967: 107; Vester, 1970: 239*]. By resorting back to the Bible and especially to its Old Testament, whether systematically as in the *Landbote* or crudely as in the pamphlet from which we have already quoted, an attempt was made to understand the current crisis by explaining to others that it could only be solved through a transformation of society. For many the Bible became a last resort for reordering the world precisely because official churches were becoming more and more integrated into secularised state systems. As society became bourgeois and secular, so the more meaningful of the old links between it and religion were broken [*Dülmen, 1980: 45*].

The rural world in pre-1848 Germany was no longer a healthy one, even if the church continued to remain in place at the geographical centre of the village. Many new political boundaries were drawn and they demanded new loyalties. Local government in the countryside was now riddled with middle-class legal values. Agrarian markets were reorganised according to new customs duties around new commercial centres. Integration into new markets and new productive processes broke down existing subsistence economies with their dependant work-norms. More intensive exploitation of forest and field resources cut down existing common rights, which themselves became ever more important to the survival of ordinary people as the overall economic pressure on the countryside increased.

These secular trends which are usually labelled in terms of the triumph of capitalistic productive processes by the bourgeois state, were characterised by regular agrarian and more general economic crises [*cf. Bergmann, 1976*]. Rural life and culture was wide open to coercive forces which it could no longer comprehend. How then could these threats have been interpreted other than via religious ideas? After all, the everyday struggle for existence was hedged about with religious symbolism. Despite his reactionary idealisation of the German peasant, Riehl understood this interdependency when he wrote that 'religion was peasant habit just as much as habit was peasant religion'.

In the period up to 1848 peasant resistance was directed above all against those specific property relations which had been created according to bourgeois principles of justice. Most common were cases of poaching and breaking of the forest laws. In areas of particularly feudal and noble jurisdiction tithe barns and even manor houses were stormed. The slogan of emancipation especially as regards full legal equality for Jews provided an excuse for persecution of Jewish cattle-dealers and the Jewish village poor. Peasant demonstrations usually coincided with church festivals, such as during Carnival, at Ascension, Easter, Whitsun and Martinmas. They were traditional occasions for censure, communal meetings, or quarter days for paying rent and tithe, when common action was easy to organise. They were often times of natural tension, as at Martinmas when rents were always due for payment. Peasants rarely rebelled against their more distant central governments, represented in the person of the ruler, but when they did, then it was done in a drastic manner, as shown in the *Landbote* as total rejection with the words – 'this ruling authority has not come from God' – which did not preclude the demand for substitution of a just alternative. Mayer [*1981: 78f*] has now shown how popular the *Landbote* was with the Hessian peasants who read it and discussed its ideas precisely because it was written not for the so-called educated urbanites, but for plain country folk in a language analogous to religious imagery that they could understand. On the whole this meant that intermediate government authorities such as the local nobility, official bailiffs and even parish priests were the real object of peasant violence. A curious attitude towards the ruler as a godfather figure was still prevalent in the 1840s [*Scharfe, 1976: 190*], when a number of peasant revolts started with a shout in praise of the ruler, followed by a cry to burn all aristocrats, hang all officials and clergy. In conscious imitation of the German Peasant War of 1525, grievances were presented in the form of Twelve Articles. Some people took part in the peasant demonstrations of the 1840s dressed in sackcloth with ashes on their head. Particpants generally demanded a form of justice which had nothing in common with bourgeois legal principles. Justice was to be carried out according to ancient custom, which meant anything from pre-1800 to the time of Adam and Eve. Yet resorting to ancient custom as law meant losing one case after another, for the earlier process of legalisation, which Schulze [*1980*] has sought to analyse, was subsequently regarded by peasants as less than equitable. Legislation no longer seemed to regulate social and material injustices in the interest of fair rents for reciprocal services. Hence formerly freely accessible common meadows and woodlands were 'liberated' by means of peasant self-help. In the general crisis of the 1840s the fiction of ancient custom was equated with Godly law but in reality the new secular authorities no longer accepted custom as actionable at law [*Scharfe, 1876: 188; Wirtz, 1979: 98*].

In a number of peasant uprisings sharing with others and even its mere expectation was of fundamental importance [*Wirtz, 1979: 81–104*]. It was of course important to know that the contents of a confiscated tithe barn would be shared among the whole community, and that often implied rigorous adherance to equal shares all round. This approach to establishing equality was inseparable from a fundamental yearning for freedom. Freedom meant the use of nature open to all, as well as the liberation from all existing authority, which at that time had been seen to be mere economic coercion to obtain taxes and rents without offering subjects any government services in return. These basic concepts of freedom and equality, which were central to the upheavals of the 1840s, led to considerable misunderstanding especially among the peasants, who thought that the very same words that a constitutional monarchy or republic used, would be identical to the very understanding of these fundamental rights [*ibid.*]. Peasant misconception of civil liberty sometimes served merely to strengthen their belief in what God was supposed to have granted as freedom and equality, and it could act as the last straw that broke the camel's back.

Freedom and equality with their allied notions of law and justice are complementary parts of a view of society which drew its strength from religion and which gained momentum the more that peasants felt their own way of life to be drastically threatened by novel political, social and economic developments. The greater this threat, so the more desperate was the resort to fundamental beliefs, for peasants basically had no alternative but their religion to fall back upon. At that point the educated rebels, Büchner and Weidig with their *Landbote*, joined forces with the uneducated soap-seller and his cruder call to revolt analysed in the above pamphlet. What difference was there after all between a community in which all resources are shared in common, and a state built upon an early Christian legitimation of freedom and equality? It was not just a question of economics, for in the 1840s a whole rural world had collapsed under the onslaught of secularisation, bourgeois legislation and capitalist methods of production, phenomena which not only threatened the social cohesion of the village community, not only its chances of survival, but also each and every aspect of traditional life.

The use of biblical and especially prophetic sayings as a direct guide and fundamental justification for rebellion is not an isolated phenomenon to be ascribed merely to a decaying rural population in 1840s Germany. Similar arguments were used by journeymen in England, as has been shown by Oliver [*1978*] and Harrison [*1979*], and they also apply to the German urban scene as shown by Graf [*1978*]. Societies in transformation usually seem to fall back on specific religious beliefs which take hold of different groups and sections with varying degrees of intensity [*Dülmen, 1980: 55*]. For some, a wide discrepancy appears between their view of the world and its rapid development in reality, which can become unbearable and lead to dearth, misery, loss of status, psychic and emotional damage. For others, this process may lead to upward mobility and a new-found wealth and status.

Most people could only reduce or abolish these rifts by seeking to return to an earlier state of affairs which was supposed to have been more equitable. In the 1840s that meant sticking to old rights and privileges, however defined, or even seemingly destroying something in order to restore the ancient way of doing things. For those who could, reform and adaptability also offered an opportunity to overcome the loss of old ways. Although this is too schematic a description, for it leaves little room for variation and difference within the essential dualism of a religious attitude to society on the one hand, and actual development of that society on the other, we are led beyond it to the categories of the 'little tradition' and of the 'great tradition' which James Scott [*1977*] has demonstrated in non-European and non-Christian cases, making it into an essentially world-wide problem of religion and rural revolt. When these categories are applied, then the boundaries between rural peasant and urban middle-class society, between little and great tradition, are loosened and made more realistic. For rural society was being continually eroded by the great tradition with its new capitalist forms of economic production and political domination. Briefly said, capitalist culture first attacked the economic and political apparatus of state power in the urban centres, and from there the surrounding countryside. Here Scott's notion of the wider society that takes over and strangles the rural countryside has been extended into an apposite, creeping *société englobante* [*Mendras, 1972*].

Religion was a link between the great and little tradition in that it legitimised power in the eyes of ruler and ruled alike, making communication between the two possible and, at least in an ideal-typical manner, regulating duties and privileges. It was precisely here that the importance of Büchner's *Landbote* lay, for it argued at the level of a little tradition in order to combat and seek to overcome the presumptions of the great tradition. Thereby traditional attitudes to justice were called upon to provide a basis for action in order to create a new system justified by God, which lies beyond Scott's interpretative model. In other words, the *Landbote* was using the drastic discrepancy between rural consciousness and the new social and political hegemony in order to overcome the disturbing social relations that had been created by that very discrepancy. Religion was a stabilising factor through its general ties with the existing world order. Yet in the secularisation of the first half of the nineteenth century official churches increasingly became part of the great tradition, whereas previously they had always been at least closely linked with the world of little tradition. Hence religion and church lost their more general, public validity and rival belief systems got a grip above all in the towns. In this situation the official church tried to retaliate by resorting to stricter doctrinal purity as seen in the content of its sermons and other cultural activities, in order to keep out more critical and doubtful elements. The 1844 Pilgrimage of Trier, which has already been mentioned, was instigated as an immunisation against 'communism' [*Schieder, 1974: 453f*]. After its secularisation the official church strengthened its position again by playing its part in 'stabilising' the modern capitalist state. If we look outwards from the 1840s in Germany, then we can see already the roots of future conflicts between state and church, especially in the so-called *Kulturkampf* of the 1880s between Bismarck's state and the Roman Catholic hierarchy, and also in some of the ceremonial practises of the future working-class movement, as for example the so called Joseph-cult or that around Lasalle [*Korff, 1973; Grote, 1968*].

Scott's categories allow for long-term comparisons; for a clearer understanding of periods of transition, and they also bring more into the foreground the socio-cultural and anthropological dimensions of religion. Without these dimensions we could not understand the religious arguments in the *Landbote* and in the pamphlets produced by agrarian rebellions in the first half of the nineteenth century in Germany. Religion as a component of the little tradition still provided the framework of experience and consciousness for most rural inhabitants, within which they could comprehend social change. Within their view of religion there was an answer to everything, and it included what we would understand as an anthropology, a view of the past and present world which came before any rival philosophies and beliefs had established themselves. This closed world view without alternatives could still make religion an active force in the 1830s and '40s by letting biblical analogies reveal the state of society by either leading the way to change or making its acceptance possible. The thesis of Peter Berger [*1973: 122; cf. Dülmen, 1980: 42*] which lets religion appear historically not only as setting up the world by giving it meaning, legitimising and sustaining it, but also as world-shattering or revolutionary force, is certainly generally applicable to agrarian unrest in pre-1848 Germany, where we have found all these different uses of religion simultaneously. But it seems to be even more important to note that religion was taken very literally in certain real situations in the past, where it was capable of providing concrete advice for immediate action.

The German rural crisis of these years was not only an economic one, it was also a time when the old social and legal systems that had been developed laboriously during the seventeenth and eighteenth centuries were put out of action [*cf. Schulze, 1980; Blickle, 1980*]. For the peasants who were caught up in them, the changes were so far-reaching that legal system, village community and not even church were able to stop them. Only biblical prophecies remained as a very last resort to close the gap yawning between consciousness and reality. Those who called for rebellion and who then actually did revolt fell back above all upon the Old Testament which contained cases of resistance to unjust authority, a form of argument which was also used in fifteenth and sixteenth century Germany. So it seemed that the late middle ages still lay very close to the 1840s: the 'modern' future, however, was very distant indeed.

Note

1. This tract for peasant edification had a print-run of about 400,000 by the year 1800, making it just about the most widely circulated secular book.

References

Berger, P. L., 1973, *Zur Dialektik von Religion und Gesellschaft*, Frankfurt-am-Main.
Bergmann, J., 1976, 'Ökonomische Voraussetzungen der Revolution von 1848', *Geschichte und Gesellschaft, Sonderheft*, II: 254–87.
Blickle, P., 1980, *Aufruhr und Empörung? Studien zum bäuerlichen Widerstand im Alten Reich*, Munich.
Büchner, Georg, 1958, *Werke und Briefe. Gesamtausgabe*, Wiesbaden.
Dülmen, Richard van, 1980, 'Religionsgeschichte in der historischen Sozialforschung', *Geschichte und Gesellschaft*, VI.
Fischer, W., 1962, 'Staat und Gesellschaft Badens im Vormärz', Conze, W. ed., *Staat und Gesellschaft im Vormärz*, Stuttgart.
Graf, F. W., 1978, *Die Politisierung des religiösen Bewusstseins*, Stuttgart.
Grote, H., 1968, *Sozialdemokratie und Religion, 1863–75*, Tübingen.
Harrison, J. F. C., 1979, *The second coming of popular millennarianism, 1780–1830*, London.
Hobsbawm, E. J., 1962, *The Age of Revolution*, London.
Ilse, L., 1860, *Geschichte der politischen Untersuchungen zu Mainz und zu Frankfurt, 1819–27; 1833–42*, Frankfurt-am-Main.
Jeggle, U., 1977, *Kiebingen – eine Heimatgeschichte*, Tübingen.
Korff, G., 1973, 'Heiligenverehrung und soziale Frage', Wiegelmann, G., ed. *Kultureller Wandel im 19. Jahrhundert*, Göttingen.
Korff, G., 1977, 'Formierung der Frömmigkeit', *Geschichte und Gesellschaft*, III: 352–83.
Lamennais, F. de, 1838, *Le livre du peuple*, Paris; German version, 1837, *Das Volksbuch*.
Lautenschlager, R., 1915, *Die Agrarunruhen in den badischen Standes und Grundherrschaften*, Mannheim.
Mayer, G., 1969, *Radikalismus, Sozialismus und Demokratie*, Frankfurt-am-Main.
Mayer, T. M., 1976, 'Büchner und Weidig', *Text und Kritik, Sonderband, Georg Büchner, I und II*, Munich: 16–298.
Mayer, T. M., 1981, 'Die Verbreitung und Wirkung des Hessischen Landboten', *Georg Büchner Jahrbuch*, I: 57–99.
Meyer, E. H., 1900, *Badisches Volksleben im 19. Jahrhundert*, Strasbourg.
Mendras, H., 1972, 'Un schema d'analyse de la paysannerie occidentale', *Peasant Studies Newsletter*, I: 79–93; 126–44.
Noellner, F., 1844, *Actenmässige Darlegung des wegen Hochverraths eingeleiteten Verfahrens gegen Pfarrer Dr. Friedrich Ludwig Weidig*, Darmstadt.
Noth- und Hülfsbüchlein für Bauersleute/oder lehrreiche Freuden-und Trauergechichte des Dorfes Mildheim, 1788, Leipzig (reprint, 1980, Dortmund).
Obermann, K., 1967, *Deutschland von 1815–49*, Berlin.
Oliver, W. H., 1978, *Prophets and millennialists*, Oxford.
Rosenberg, H., 1930, 'Theologischer Rationalismus und vormärzlicher Liberalismus', *Historische Zeitschrift*, CXLI.
Scharfe, M., 1976, 'Die Erwartung, dass nun alles frei sey', K. Köstlin, and K. D. Sievers, eds., *Das Recht der kleinen Leute. Festschrift für K. S. Kramer*, Berlin.
Scharfe, M., 1980, *Die Religion des Volkes*, Gütersloh.
Schieder, W., 1963, *Anfänge der deutschen Arbeiterbewegung*, Stuttgart.
Schieder, W., 1974, 'Kirche und Revolution', *Archiv für Sozialgeschichte*, XIV: 419–54.
Schulze, W., 1980, *Bäuerlicher Widerstand und feudale Herrschaft in der Frühen Neuzeit*,

Stuttgart.
Scott, J. C., 1977, 'Revolution in the Revolution: peasants and commissars', *Theory and Society*, VII: 97–134.
Scott, J. C., 1974, 'Protest and profanation: agrarian revolt and the little tradition', *Theory and Society*, IV: 1–38; 211–46.
Thomas, K., 1971, *Religion and the decline of Magic*, London.
Vester, M., ed., 1970, *Die Frühsozialisten*, I, Hamburg.
Weitling, W., 1907, 'Autobiographie', H. Schlüter, ed., *Die Anfänge der deutschen Arbeiterbewegung in Amerika*, Stuttgart.
Wirtz, R., 1979, 'Die Begriffsverwirrung der Bauern im Odenwald', D. Puls, ed., *Protestverhalten und Wahrnehmungsformen*, Frankfurt.
Wunder, H., 1976, 'Altes Recht und göttliches Recht im deutschen Bauernkrieg', *Zeitschrift für Agrargeschichte*, XXIV.

Middle East and Africa

Preface

HANS G. KIPPENBERG

It is almost a commonplace in studies about Islam that religion determined social life:

> Islam ... has no words to distinguish between sacred and profane, spiritual and temporal, for it does not accept or even know the dichotomy that these pairs of antonyms express — the cleavage and clash of Church and State, of Pope and Emperor, of God and Caesar .... Orthodoxy meant the acceptance of the existing order, heresy or apostasy its criticism or rejection ... Whenever a group of men sought to challenge and to change the existing order, they made their teachings a theology and their instrument a sect, as naturally and as inevitably as their modern counterparts make ideologies and political parties [Lewis, *1953: 62*].

The studies presented here do not corroborate this view. 'Muslims could and in fact did distinguish between secular and "religious" revolts' as Daniel [*1978: 518*] has pointed out. A careful analysis of chiefly religious movements highlights the religious factor in social processes. We cannot remain satisfied with Lewis' statement. A comparison between three types of Iranian peasant movements should clarify what is meant here. These were purely political movements and two kinds of religious movements: those in which leaders defended the Islamic law and those in which holy men abrogated the Islamic law.

Compared with political movements such as Mazyar's, who led the native Iranian peasantry in the fight against the colonial landholding class of the Arabs in ninth century Tabaristan [*Daniel, 1978: 490*], the religious revolts were more radical. As a rule they do not attempt to use the existing political institutions for their own ends but radically dismiss the existing order as illegitimate. Moqanna' and Babak who led religious movements against the Arabs represented similar social interest of peasants as Mazyar did. The difference between these movements lay rather in the way they represented these social concerns. The religious leaders fought for rural interests as part of a true and just order. This had two consequences. First the appeal to religion transformed the models which Iranian rural communities had of their internal relations into a divine order which had become manifest by the true leader. Religion was to objectify social needs, that exceeded existing possibilities. Second, the reference to religion made the standing of the leader absolute. It implied a certain independence of the leader and facilitated the rise of a state. In short: the appeal to a true and just order manifest in the leader was the turning point in the development from an Iranian peasant culture to a state ratifying beliefs and actions inherent in this culture.

There were many religious movements in Iran that rose to defend Islamic law. Their aim was puritanism [*Gellner, 1981*]. They did not claim, of course, that their leader was superior to this law. The movements Bruinessen and Grevemeyer describe fit into this type: puritans, leaders of a Sufi order (the Nakshbandi), fought for the Islamic law. In cities such movements were mostly led by the Ulama, the Shi'i clergymen. These puritan movements could also appeal to Mahdist ideas. For example the Ulama who led the Tobacco Protest in Iran in 1891/92 against the selling of the Iranian concession to an Englishman blamed the Shah for injustice. And their *marja'e taqlid* ('source of emulation', the highest rank among the Shi'i clergy), Hajji Mirza, Hasan of Shiraz, edited a *fatva* (an authoritative opinion issued on a matter of law). 'In the Name of God, the Merciful, the Forgiving. Today the use of *tunbaku* and tobacco, in whatever fashion, is reckoned against the Imam of the Age (may God hasten his glad event)' [*Browne, 1910: 22 n.1; Keddie, 1966*]. The revolutionary movement which in 1978/79 succeeded in overthrowing the regime of the Shah, fits also into this category. Although there were people expecting Khomayni to be Imam Mahdi [*Algar, 1980a: 43*], the revolutionary leaders, Ulama and laymen alike, interpreted street fighting as reenactment of the battle of Kerbala in 680 A.D. in which Hosayn had been killed for the sake of the true Islamic order [*Fischer, 1980: 136–231; Kippenberg, 1981*]. Article five of the constitution of the Islamic Republic of Iran declares the leader of the Shi'i Ulama as deputy of the Hidden Imam:

> During the Occultation of the Lord of the Age (may God hasten his renewed manifestation!), the governance and leadership of the nation devolve upon the just and pious *faqih* [i.e. Muslim jurisprudent] who is acquainted with the circumstances of his age; courageous, resourceful, and possessed of administrative ability; and recognized, and accepted as leader by the majority of the people [*Algar, 1980b: 29*].

The defence of regional autonomy of rural populations, whose way of life was embedded in and sanctified by Islam, against modernising and secularising central authorities would be a version of this type of rising. The active participation of the Nakshbandi Sufi order in the revolt of Eshaq Khan and of Shaykh Said was based on the similar interests of local clergy and local networks in opposition to Kabul or Ankara. Religious appeal was above all organisational. Relatively weak regional solidarity was enhanced and enforced by the religious discipline of the Shaykhs and their followers. The drive of restoring Islamic law, without Mahdist expectations, characterizes these movements.

Compared with movements establishing the Islamic law as obligatory, the essential characteristic of the movements that Greussing and Kippenberg deal with, is summed up in the term *qiyama*, meaning 'rising'. It is a word connected with the messianic Qa'em ('He who will arise [with the sword]'). The Isma'ilis gave it a special meaning as removal of dissimulation and abolition of the 'outer law' [*Hodgson, 1955: 299–307*]. The authority of the divine law is replaced by that of the divine man. The ethic of rule observance is replaced by an ethic of loyalty [*Gellner, 1981: 41*]. This replacement is a characteristic of Mahdist movements in Iran and the surrounding countries. It has been mentioned in accounts about the Nusairis during fourteenth century A.D. [*Gibb, 1958: 111–113*]; fourteenth to fifteenth century Eastern Turkey, where Bedr od-Din rose as Mahdi [*Babinger, 1921*]; and the Roshaniyah, an Afghan movement in the sixteenth century [*Leyden, 1810*]. This recurrence of a similar idea need not be explained by diffusion. It is much more likely that this ethic of loyalty originated in the concepts of legitimacy of social relations among peasants, artisans and tribesmen. They valued loyalty and reciprocity higher than the observance of abstract laws.

Montgomery Watt characterised these movements with the term 'absolutism' [*1973: 174f*]. They surely were absolutist in the leaders' demand for loyalty. But on the other hand they also succeeded in establishing social relations based on reciprocity between leaders and supporters. Evidently such terms as absolutist versus constitutional do not fit these movements. Neither do conventional categories of Marxian analysis. These movements were not class struggles promoting economic development, but it would be wrong to describe them therefore as reactionary. There is no continuity between the social and political movements familiar to us and the so called messianic movements [*Bastide, 1968: XIVf*]. It is this very discontinuity that we tried to exemplify in the case studies from the Middle East and North Africa.

Editors' note

The references to this preface are included in those to H. G. Kippenberg's article. Non-Islamic Africa being represented by a single article, no comparative preface could be provided here.

Limits of Islamic civilisation: Mahdist movements in Abbasid Iran

HANS G. KIPPENBERG

> The common people who make claims with respect to the Mahdi and who are not guided in this connection by any intelligence or helped by any knowledge, assume that the appearance (of the Mahdi) will take place in some remote province at the limits of civilisation, since these regions are not under the control of (ruling) dynasties and out of the reach of law and force [Ibn Khaldun: Rosenthal, 1958: 196f].

The well known vizier of the Saljuqs, Nezam ol-Molk, who devoted his life to fight heretics and was killed by an Isma'ili self-sacrificing assassin in 1092, described his enemies in his *Siyasat-nameh* (Book of Government). One of them, a certain Khalaf, had been sent out as a missionary and visited the city of Rayy:

> In the district of Pashapuya there is a village which they call Kolayn; there he stayed and practised embroidery, at which craft he was expert. He remained there some time without being able to reveal his secret to anybody, till at last by dint of a thousand wiles he managed to suborn a suitable person, and began to instruct him in the religion; he made out that the religion was that of 'the people of the house' and had to be kept hidden; and said: 'When the Qa'em (Mahdi) appears, the religion will be revealed, and the time of his coming is near. It behoves you to learn now, so that when you see him you will not be ignorant of the religion'. So the people of this village secretly began to learn the religion. One day the headman of Kolayn was passing outside the village when he heard a voice coming from a ruined mosque. He approached the mosque and listened. This Khalaf was expounding his religion to one of the people. On returning to the village he said: 'O people destroy his embroideries. Do not go near him. Judging by what I have heard, I am afraid that our village may suffer through his activities ... I heard him say (in broken Arabic): 'The hidden meaning of this chapter is mercy'. When he knew that he had been discovered, he fled from Kolayn to Rayy where he died. He had converted a few inhabitants of Kolayn, men and women, and his son Ahmad ibn Khalaf took his place and continued to foster his father's religion [Darke, 1978: 209; Stern, 1960: 57–60].

This report, as good an example of a Mahdist movement as any, offers a good chance to clarify a theoretical issue. A movement like this one can be described in Marxian terms as a protest movement in which religion serves as an expression of social distress and as a protest against it. But it can also be conceived in the terms of Max Weber as a generator of loyalties. The two views are not mutually exclusive. Common distress often engenders deep loyalties. However, the category 'protest' does not explain several typical details in Khalaf's story. Missionaries like him established loyalties of hundreds of years standing before actual public protest emerged, if at all. Their mission resulted first and foremost in creating a secret religious network. A great number of village communities and estates constituted such a network, but these loyalties were kept hidden for many generations [*Kohlberg, 1975; Meyer, 1980*]. Protest then was in fact the suspension of this dissimulation (*taqiyah/ketman*) and a turn to open fight for long existing loyalties. I propose to study the protest movements in the context of these loyalties.

The entire history of Shi'ite Islam was characterized by faction and conversion. The salient point was always the identity of the Mahdi. An early example, repeated in innumerable versions, was the division in the party (*shi'ah*) of Ali. After the death of Hosayn, slain in Kerbala in 680 A.D., Mohammad ebn ol-Hanafiyah was recognized as chief of the clan of Mohammad – the 'people of the house', as Nezam ol-Molk put it. A protest movement in Kufa, directed against the Umayyad caliph in 685–687 A.D. proclaimed his *mahdi*; that means the one who is rightly guided (by God). It is the first time the title *mahdi* (derived from *hada* = to guide) is used. After the defeat of this protest the surviving adherents of Mohammad ebn ol-Hanafiyah (d. 701), called the Kaysaniyah after their leader Abu Amra Kaysan, split in two groups. The one expected his return from Razwa Mountain, the other regarded his son as his successor [*Laoust, 1965: 30f*]. This latter maintained the continuance of the Imamate, while the former stopped with the Imamate and expected the return of the last Imam as Mahdi.

This pattern of division has been reiterated later many times. While some scholars ascribe to the former group political quietism in contrast to political activism of the latter [*Sachedina, 1981: 54*] the history of Mahdist movements does not confirm such a clear dichotomy. Still there are some connections to political activism. Groups that had left the Kaysaniyah replaced the idea of return (*raj'ah*) of the concealed Imam by that of the reincarnation of his spirit in another body (*tanasokh*) [*Laoust, 1965: 31*]. By this they abandoned the principle of conferring the Imamate only on descendants of the clan of Mohammad. We shall see how Iranian leaders used this principle for claiming supreme authority. Another idea linked with political activism was the designation of the leader as *qa'em* = 'he who will arise (with the sword)' [*Sachedina, 1981: 60–64*]. This title was known in pre-Islamic times and maintained its own meaning even when combined with that of Mahdi. Tradition reports that Mohammad ol-Baqer said:

When ol-Qa'em from the family of the Prophet will rise he will distribute equally among the people and will establish justice among his subjects. Thus those who obey him will obey God and those who defy him will defy God; but he will be called al-Mahdi, the one who will guide, since he will guide to the secret matters [*Sachedina, 1981: 61*].

Shi'is associated with the Qa'em revolt and with the Mahdi esoteric guidance. Many a revolutionary movement was fought under the flag of the Qa'em, as late as the nineteenth century, when Mirza Ali Mohammad, the Bab, declared himself Qa'em [*Greussing*, below].

In the sense of these notions, I propose to look at movements of peasants and craftsmen which originated or ended in religious factions, which were kept hidden by the participants and were led by men considered divine or holy. In the history of Iran such movements were significant between the eighth and the twelfth centuries and later, in the fourteenth to sixteenth centuries. These two periods were divided by the Mongol invasion which shattered the whole Iranian society, hence they should be studied separately. I chose to concentrate on the earlier period, during which the following movements among peoples speaking Iranian languages fit our description and are relatively well documented: the Abbasid revolt led in Khorasan by Abu Moslem (747–755); the Moqanna'-movement in Transoxiana (775/6-782/3); the Babak-movement in Azerbaijan (816—838) and the Qarmatis and Isma'ilis in different parts of Iran (before 874/5 until the twelfth century). Our analysis shall be first and foremost concerned with the loyalties in these movements. This demands a minute analysis of a few movements. The results are of course only valid for these movements and not for all. Nevertheless it shall become evident, that these movements, as specific as they might have been, point to the limits of Islamic civilization: they were ratifying social relations, which existed in Iranian society but had been excluded from Islamic public order.

The heresy of the Khorramdinites as a peasant culture

Some of them maintain that religion means these two things: to recognize the imam and keep fidelity; he who had attained both has reached perfection and is beyond all legal restrictions [*Shahrastani, 1850: 173*].

When Arabic armies conquered the Middle East, they saw themselves confronted with socio-geographical conditions that were unfavourable to an effective government. First of all the imposing size of the area limited such efforts. The Arabs did not succeed in penetrating the highlands of Iran. A map in the book of Planhol [*1968b: 214*] indicates, how many parts of the Turko-Iranian world managed to withdraw from Islamic control, including densely populated areas around the Caspian sea and Transoxiana.

The internal organisation of villages that were hotbeds of revolutionary activities is significant. Today we discern three historical types of villages in Iran [*Planhol, 1968a: 418–432*]:

a) ancient settlements in mountain areas, where even if rainfall would be sufficient for cultivation, the position of the village is defined by an irrigable area and hence the resource of water serves as a focal point for the community;

b) loosely knit villages in the areas of heavy rainfall along the Caspian sea;

c) fortified villages (*qal'ah*), settlements on the open plains; this type is extremely old and goes back to clan-communities.

Although there is little information on pre-Islamic village structures, certain communal organisation existed at the time of Islamic conquest or was created in the centuries immediately following it, since the Muslims normally dealt with conquered peoples in groups [*Lambton, 1969: 2f*]. Conflict between tens of thousands of village-communities and the Islamic conquerors was favored by these socio-geographical conditions, but it was generated by other circumstances.

When Islam was imposed on the Middle East, a development that began in the eastern cities of the later Roman empire came to an end. Community life was shaped by religion and religious communities received their distinct legal institutions [*Liebeschütz, 1972: 265; Morony, 1974: 113*]. Islamization was in the first place the introduction of Islamic jurisdiction on all people with the exception of Jews and Christians.

The two major anti-Islamic revolts of Moqanna' and Babak were based on religious networks that predated Islam. Moqanna' had been supported by the so called 'White Raiments' [*Daniel, 1979: 132/140*]. After his defeat, his followers were divided into those who expected the return of Moqanna' and those who remained part of the religious network called 'White Raiments' [*Browne, 1902: 322f; Frye, 1954: 75*]. The same happened to Babak: Khorramdinites accepted him as leader but split after his defeat [*Sadighi, 1938: 278f*].

The 'White Raiments' and the Khorramdinites were related and, according to Shahrastani, advocated the same ideas:

> The heretical doctrines of the ultra-Shi'ites are four: anthropomorphism, change of (Divine) purpose, return (*raj'ah*) and metempsychosis (*tanasokh*). In every land they bear different names: in Isfahan they are called Khorramiyah and Kudiyah, in Rayy Mazdakiyah and Sinbadiyah, in Azerbaijan Zakuliyah, in some places Mohammirah (wearing red as their badge) and in Transoxiana Mobayida (wearing white as their badge) [*Browne, 1902: 311*].

Although most Islamic historians deal with these groups essentially as heretical circles they fulfilled important function in the social life of peasants. We owe an excellent report on these to Motahhar ebn Taher ol-Maqdisi. It is based on his personal acquaintance with members of the sect and his reading of some of their books.

> They are divided into various sects and sorts, but all agree on 'return' (i.e. transmigration), asserting, however, that names and bodies are changed. They maintain that all the Apostles, though their codes and religious systems differ, are inspired by one spirit; that revelation never ceases; and in their opinion every adherent of a religion is right, so long as he hopes for reward and fears punishment. They do not approve of defaming such a person or harming him, providing he shows no desire to injure their own community or attack their system. They strenuously avoid bloodshed except when they are in open rebellion. They highly esteem Abu Moslem and curse ol-Mansur for having put him to death. They frequently implore the divine favour for Mahdi ebn Firuz owing to his being a descendant of Abu Moslem's daughter Fatemah. They have *imams* to whom they have recourse in legal matters, and Apostles who go on circuit among them, and whom they call by the Persian name *fereshtah* (angel). Wine and liquors are in their opinion more fortune-bringing than all other things. The basis of their system is Light and Darkness. Those whom we have met in their homes . . . were found by us to be most scrupulous about cleanliness and purity and most anxious to win people's favour by spontaneous acts of kindness. Some of them, we found, permit promiscuity where the women consent, and indeed the enjoyment of anything craved by the natural mind, provided no injury results to any one therefrom [*Margoliouth, 1961: 258*].

What from the point of view of Islamic civilization resembles a heresy is in fact a peasant culture: a model for and of a peasant society, which has its own traditions of action and thought, and is able to regulate its internal relations with the help of its own élite of holy men. The idea of transmigration of the divine spirit in holy men is the focal point: it assures the village communities' independence of urban scribes and scholars. The truth needs no mediation by officials, but is embodied in persons, coming from the peasant society itself. Salvation depends on loyalty, not on fasting, praying, pilgrimages.

The revolt of Moqanna' in Transoxiana (775/6–782/3)

The movement of Moqanna' used this religious network, while transforming it. Moqanna' was a villager from the vicinity of Merv. He was first a bleacher, later a master in conjuration and magic, and served as captain in the army of Abu Moslem. After an imprisonment in Baghdad he returned to Merv and declared himself God.

> 'I call myself by whatever name I wish. I am the one who showed myself to people as Adam, then in the form of Noah, also in the form of Abraham, Moses, then in the guise of Jesus, Mohammad the prophet, in the guise of Abu Moslem, and now in the guise which you see'. The people said: 'Others considered themselves prophets, but

you pretend to be God'. He replied: 'They had a soul, but I was the spirit in them. I have the power to be in any guise I wish to show'. He wrote letters to every district and gave them to his missionaries [Frye, 1954: 66; Schefer, 1892: 64f].

This mission succeeded in rural parts of Transoxiana.

> The first village which joined Moqanna' and proclaimed his faith was a village of Kesh called Subakh. Their headman was Omar Subakhi and they raised a revolt. Their *amir* was a pious Arab and they killed him. In Soghd most of the villages accepted the faith of Moqanna'. Many of the villages of Bokhara turned to infidelity and made manifest their infidelity. This evil increased and the afflictions on the Moslems became severe. They attacked caravans, pillaged villages, and caused much devastation [Frye, 1954: 67; Schefer, 1892: 65].

On account of his success, Moqanna' crossed the Oxus river and settled in a very strong fortress in the district of Kesh. Moqanna' started as a representative of a traditional village religion but became the head of a political faction (*ta'ifah*) [Frye, 1954: 68; Schefer, 1892: 66; Mottahadeh, 1980: 159]. After his arrival in Transoxiana he contacted Turkish tribes.

> Moqanna' invited the Turks and permitted them (to take) the life and possessions of the Moslems. Many troops came from Turkestan in the hope of plunder. They pillaged the districts and carried the women and children of Moslems into captivity and killed (others) [Frye, 1954: 68; Schefer, 1892: 66].

Moqanna' acted as a sovereign, making political decisions on his own responsibility, and could count on a group of men who were bound to enforce his orders [Frye, 1954: 71, 73; Schefer, 1892: 69, 72; Mottahadeh, 1980: 115f].

The Turks joined Moqanna' for obvious reasons. But adherents of the 'White Raiments' did not follow him for his religious doctrines either. Moqanna' declared himself the spirit, which had earlier appeared in the guise of Abu Moslem, but the 'White Raiments' had never been devoted followers of Abu Moslem. On the contrary! One of the strongholds of the 'White Raiments' during the Moqanna'-revolt was a fortified village of the *qal'ah*-type near Bokhara [Frye, 1954: 68f; Schefer, 1892: 65]. The head of this village was a woman whose husband had been killed by Abu Moslem. After the victory of the Moslems she was asked by one of the Moslem leaders, to pardon Abu Moslem. 'She replied: "Abu Moslem is called the father of the Moslems. He who killed my husband cannot be the father of the Moslems" ' [Frye, 1954: 71; Schefer, 1892: 69].

Before we try to elaborate the common interest between the different groups supporting Moqanna' we must mention the *dehqans*. They were the local nobles, who owned estates and who functioned as middlemen for the peasants: they recruited soldiers and collected taxes [Daniel, 1979: 17; Frye, 1954: 8, 30,

71]. These *dehqans* had only in the time of Abu Moslem converted from Zoroastrianism to Islam [*Vloten, 1894: 67*]. Some of them were apparently engaged in the revolt of Moqanna'. We are told, that Moqanna' had one hundred daughters of the *dehqans* of Soghd, Kesh and Nakhshab with him in his fortress [*Frye, 1954: 73; Schefer, 1892: 71*].

Thus Moqanna' was the leader of a coalition which consisted of village-communities belonging to the 'White Raiments', of *dehqans* who functioned as patrons for peasants and of Turkish tribes that invaded the plains of Transoxiana. What were the common interests between these different groups? We remember that the revolt of Moqanna' started with the assassination of a local Arab *amir* and that the insurgents attacked caravans and pillaged villages. When the 'White Raiments' of Narshakh had been defeated for the first time, they were forced by the notables (*a'yan*) of Bokhara to sign a treaty. 'Provisions were made forbidding them to molest the roads or to kill Moslems and for them to disperse to their villages and obey their *amir*. They confirmed their faith in God and His Prophet' [*Frye, 1954: 69; Schefer, 1892: 67*]. This treaty indicates the intentions of their adversaries, the notables of Bokhara. These *a'yan* were the most eminent men, to some extent surely belonging to the *dehqans*. They represented their local community vis-à-vis the government [*Mottahadeh, 1980: 123–129*]. Together with the *qazi*, the Islamic judge, they backed the local officer (*amir*) who established Islamic authority at village level. The treaty with Bokhara suggests attempts at enforcing an Islamic order beyond the confines of the city. This implied the replacement of village self-government by an extraneous administration. The communities, the *dehqans* and the Turks had all their reason to oppose this.

Just as the notables of Bokhara had economic reasons for supporting the Islamic order so had the followers of Moqanna' for rejecting it. In his 'History of Bokhara' Narshakhi mentions villages that subsisted not on agriculture but on trade and handicraft [*Frye, 1954: 12–19*]. Logically villagers engaged in commerce were not likely to attack caravan routes and convoys, thus disrupting trade. Therefore Moqanna's supporters must be sought in those villages and estates that were essentially self-sufficient and uninterested in trade.

Thus the movement of Moqanna' – and, we may add, that of Babak as well [*Daniel, 1978: 443–477*] – established social relations which were contrary to the Islamic order that subordinated the ruler as well as town and country to divine law and its officials [*Cahen, 1958*]. Since pre-Islamic times there existed in Iran rural communities which regulated their internal affairs without civic officials. They objectified their autonomy by means of the idea that salvation depends on obedience to an aristocracy of holy men. Moqanna' and Babak integrated this peasant culture and tried to transform it into a political order.

The expectation of a Mahdi

Moqanna' and later Babak were regarded by some of their former adherents as Mahdis who would return. Bar-Hebraeus in the thirteenth century recorded that Moqanna' 'had promised his followers that his spirit would pass into the form of a grizzled-headed man riding on a grey horse, and that he would return unto them after so many years, and cause them to possess the earth' [*Browne, 1902: 323*]. This idea of the imminent return of a concealed Mahdi spread like wildfire in ninth century Iran. The afore mentioned Khalaf, one of the early Qarmati missionaries, announced the return of Mohammad ibn Ismail [*Madelung, 1978b: 661*]. Islamic theologians transmitted this expectation as a tradition deriving from Mohammad. In the fourteenth century Ibn Khaldun collected these traditions and investigated their authenticity. For example Fitr ibn Khalifah (d. 770 A.D.) transmitted as a tradition from the Prophet: 'If only one day of the whole duration of the world remained, God would send a man of my family who will fill the world with justice (*adl*) as it had been filled with injustice (*zolm*)' [*Rosenthal, 1958: 162f*]. Ibn Khaldun rightly doubts this ascription [*Margoliouth, 1915–16; Snouck Hurgronje, 1923*], but there is no doubt that this expectation existed already in the eighth century. It was an old, pre-Islamic hope for a savior who would come and remove injustice. Again and again the lack of protection was the salient point. The eschatological saviour was considered as a just ruler who protected the poor and the weak against the violence of the nobles [*Darke, 1978: 39; Bidez-Cumont, 1973: 370–372; Browne, 1920: 465–470*]. Especially the state officials tried to improve their power position by reckless exploitation of peasants and artisans. This experience nourished the expectations of Iranians. The Qarmati announcement of the Mahdi appealed to such social wants, and found great resonance among artisans of urban areas.

The village Kolayn where Khalaf announced the appearance of the Qa'em, was situated in one of the four districts of the city of Rayy [*Stern, 1960: 57–59*]. The Qarmati mission aimed at urban areas and was supported by the common people there. It was not by chance, that Khalaf was a tradesman. There are other indications, that the Qarmatians gained influence especially over the guilds of artisans. L. Massignon [*1920 and 1934*] even supposed, that the rise of guilds at all was connected with the Qarmati missions. Although this thesis has been challenged, the fact remains, that Iranian guilds had a culture of their own, and that the expectation of eschatological justice was part of it [*Massignon, 1969*]. The Qarmati concern for urban areas achieved remarkable success: they were able to organize an urban society according to their principles. This state was situated south of Persia in Bahrain, a district along the Persian or Arabic gulf between Basra and Oman [*Schefer, 1881: 230 note 1*].

Of course we are curious how Qarmatis would organize a society provided they had the chance to do so. This curiousness was also felt by Nasir-e Khosrou, an important Persian writer who belonged to the Isma'ilis. He was born in a small town in the neighbourhood of Balkh in North Afghanistan [*Corbin, 1975: 531*]. His shrine in Badakhshan has been a highly venerated place of pilgrimage [*Dupree, 1976: 9f*]. During a long journey in Near East in 1047 he visited Egypt, where the Fatemids, a branch of the Isma'ilis ruled. Nasir-e Khosrou, himself a former civil servant, was impressed by the wise administration of the Fatemid caliph and joined the Isma'ilis [*Browne, 1906: 221f*]. On his way back to Khorasan, where he arrived in 1052, he visited Lahsa, the capital of the Qarmati state of Bahrain. His detailed account in his *Safar-nameh* is a unique source based on personal observation and without the usual prejudice against the Isma'ilis.

When Nasir-e Khosrou visited Lahsa in 1051, the Qarmati state was some 150 years old. In the years 899–903 the Qarmati missionary Abu Sa'id succeeded at first to conquer parts of Bahrain and finally the old capital Hajar, probably supported by remainders of a slave rising in Iraq [*Goeje, 1886: 37–46*]. The population was above all Persian and Jewish. The Bedouins in the surrounding steppe and desert also refused the numerous Islamic obligations [*Goeje, 1886: 36*]. All in all the message of Abu Sa'id met favourable conditions. At the time of Nasir-e Khosrou's visit more than 20,000 male inhabitants able to bear arms still remembered him. 'They said that the Sultan of the place was a *sharif* and this man had turned the people away from Islam. He told them that he had freed them from prayer and fasting and he preached to that people that they should have no recourse (*marja*') to any but him' [*Lewis, 1974: 65; Schefer, 1881: 82*]. After his assassination in 913 they built a fine tomb over his grave and expected there his return. So he became a Mahdi of his own, who joined the Mahdi he himself had expected [Mohammad ebn Abd-Allah ebn Mohammad ebn al-Hanafiyah, in: *Madelung, 1978b: 661*]. Nasir-e Khosrou tells us:

> In his final instructions to his sons he said: 'Let six of my descendants always hold and conduct this government, and protect this people with justice and equity (*adl* and *dad*) and without opposing one another until I return' [*Lewis, 1974: 66; Schefer, 1881: 82*].

Abu Sa'id wished the rule of his descendants to be an anticipation of the rule of the Mahdi. His words do not only repeat the key terms of the Mahdi expectation but also corroborate that the Qarmati expectation of a Mahdi answered social wants for protection. The report of Nasir-e Khosrou testifies, that the six Sultans of Bahrain took measures which assured their subjects (*ra'iyat*) a privileged position:

> At that time they had 30,000 Zanji or Ethiopian slaves, bought for money engaged in agriculture and gardening. They take no tithes or taxes from the people. If anyone

becomes destitute or falls into debt, they look after him until his affairs go better. If anyone lends money to another he asks for nothing beyond the principle. If a stranger, knowing a trade, arrives in that town they give him enough capital to set him up, so that he can buy the materials and tools of trade and, when he is ready, return the exact sum which had been lent to him. If any property belonging to one of the owners of property and appurtenances is ruined and he lacks the means to restore it, they send some of their own slaves to make good the ruined property and appurtenances and ask nothing from the owner. There are mills in Lahsa which are the property of the government and in which they turn wheat into flour of the people without taking any fee. They pay for the upkeep of these mills and the wages of the millers from the money of the government.... They buy and sell in this town with lead, which is kept in baskets, each weighing 6,000 dirhams [= 18 kg]. When they make a transaction, they count baskets and take them away. Nobody exports this money [*Lewis, 1974: 66f; Schefer, 1881: 82f*].

The Sultans acted as patrons, controlling the flow of goods and services among their subjects. They disposed of the slaves needed in the fertile date domains in Bahrain. Besides the gains made by these domains they disposed of other substantial sources of revenue [*Goeje, 1886: 153–155*]. The Sultans used these funds, to favour their people in the city: the artisans and citizens who belonged to the Mo'menin i.e. the believers [*Goeje, 1886: 151*]. The goods and services which the Sultans granted their clients imposed obligations on them [*Scott, 1977*]. All citizens were obliged to military service, somewhat similar to that of ancient *hoplites*; and the artisans and cultivators of corn had to offer their goods conforming to a fixed rate. The use of lead money in place of silver or gold indicates that the prices were lower than in the surrounding states. Money in Bahrain seems to have served the equal distribution of necessities of life among the citizens.

Orthodox Moslems reproached the inhabitants of Lahsa as being 'without religion' [*Schefer, 1881: 233, 84*]. Abu Sa'id had freed them from prayer and fasting. In an earlier period of their history the Qarmatis of Bahrain made terrible wars against the Moslems, but later they pursued a more peaceful policy. And at the time of Nasir-e Khosrou they even tolerated an orthodox Moslem, who had built a mosque in Lahsa and took care of pilgrims who arrived in the town [*Lewis, 1974: 66f; Schefer, 1881: 83*]. This change in attitude corroborates, that the central issue regarding Islam was not a theological but a social one. The loyalty to leaders who governed in the name of the hidden Imam was valued higher than the subjection to the divine law. This reversal of values was itself a means of creating a distinct social order not governed by the same classes that dominated the Islamic empire.

At the time of the Qarmatis' expansion, the social relations in this empire changed. The *dehqans*, the local landlords disappeared. The institution of *hemayah* (protection) which, similarly to the late Roman *patrocinium*, functioned as a protection of peasants and artisans also vanished. It was replaced by the Iqta – system: the state assigned the right to collect revenue to provincial military commanders as payment for their services. The needs which gave rise to this institution were not protection but the need of the state for money [Lambton, 1967; Cahen, 1957 and 1971]. The social order of Lahsa should be compared with these institutions. In Bahrain in place of a military aristocracy claiming the state revenues as payment for services the citizens served as warriors. To make this possible the state supported them. To realize such an order the Qarmatis had to leave the Abbasid empire. Under the favorable conditions of Bahrain they were able to establish a system which was advantageous for urban producers. The mahdism of Bahrain represented a type of social relation which was outside Islamic civilization.

Conclusion

In the social history of the Near East Islam served as both an instrument and an argument for bureaucratisation. Divine law was to be imposed on cities, villages, towns just as it was on rulers, officials, tradesmen and theologians. The movements in which holy men reduced the duty of obedience to Islamic law to the second place have to be understood in this context. Ethics of loyalty preempted ethics of rule-observance. Loyalty was preferred always by such groups that refused to subordinate their lives to Islamic bureaucracies. So-called Shi'ite extremism with its deification of men has therefore not only a theological but also a political edge. It represented ways of life that rejected central authority, abstract law and urban bureaucracy. The movement of Moqanna' is a good example for the significance of rural needs of autonomy in accepting a leader as god. Similarly, the Qarmatis exemplify how inhabitants of urban areas were able to found a republic of free citizens in the name of Abu Sa'id, as their refuge. Hence Mahdism or anthropolatry became both an instrument and an argument for primordial loyalties against bureaucratization of lordship.

References

Algar, Hamid, 1980a, *The Islamic Revolution in Iran*, ed. by K. Siddiqi, London.
Algar, Hamid, 1980b, *Constitution of the Islamic Republic of Iran*, Berkeley.
Amoretti, B. S., 1975, 'Sects and Heresies', *The Cambridge History of Iran*, (ed. by R. N. Frye) Cambridge, 481–520.
Babinger, Franz, 1921, 'Schejch Bedr ed-Dīn, der Sohn des Richters von Simaw', *Der Islam* 11, 1–106.
Bastide, Roger, 1968, Preface à M. I. Pereira de Queiroz, *Réforme et révolution dans les sociétés traditionelles*, Paris.

Bidez, Joseph – Cumont, Franz, 1973, *Les Mages Hellenisés*, II, Paris.
Browne, Edward G., 1902 and 1906, *A Literary History of Persia*, 2 vols., Cambridge.
Browne, Edward G., 1910, *The Persian Revolution of 1905–1909*, Cambridge.
Browne, Edward G., 1920, *A History of the Persian Literature under Tartar Dominion (A.D. 1265–1502)*, Cambridge.
Cahen, Claude, 1957, 'Notes pour l'histoire de l'himaya', *Mélanges Louis Massignon*, Paris, 287–303.
Cahen, Claude, 1958, 'Zur Geschichte der städtischen Gesellschaft im islamischen Orient des Mittelalters', *Saeculum* 9, 59–76.
Cahen, Claude, 1963, 'Points de vue sur la "Révolution abbaside"', *Revue Historique* 230, 295–338.
Cahen, Claude, 1971, 'Himāya', *Encyclopedia of Islam* (2. ed.) 3: 394f.
Canfield, Robert Leroy, 1973, *Faction and Conversion in a Plural Society: Religious Alignments in the Hindu Kush*.
Corbin, Henry, 1975, 'Nāṣir-e Khusrau and Iranian Ismāʾilism', *The Cambridge History of Iran*, 4 (ed. R. N. Frye), Cambridge, 520–542.
Daniel, Elton, L. 1978, *Iran's Awakening: A Study of Local Rebellions in the Eastern Provinces of the Islamic Empire*, Ann Arbor, Mi.
Daniel, Elton L., 1979, *The Political and Social History of Khurasan under Abbasid Rule 747–820*, Chicago.
Darke, Hubert, 1978, *The Book of Government or Rules for Kings: The Siyar al-Muluk or Siyasat-nama of Niẓam al-Mulk*, London.
Dupree, Louis, 1976, *Saint Cults in Afghanistan*, Hanover.
Fischer, Michael M. J., 1980, *Iran. From Religious Dispute to Revolution*, Harvard.
Frye, Richard N., 1954, *The History of Bukhara*. Translated from a Persian Abridgment of the Arabic Original by Narshakhī, Cambridge (Mass.).
Gellner, Ernest, 1981, *Muslim Society. A Sociological Interpretation*, Cambridge.
Gibb, Hamilton A. R., 1958, *The Travels of Ibn Baṭṭūta A.D. 1325–1354*, I, Cambridge.
de Goeje, M. J., 1886, *Mémoire sur les Carmathes du Bahraïn et les Fatimides*, (2. ed.) Leiden.
Hodgson, Marshall G. S., 1955, *The Order of Assassins*.
Keddie, Nikki, 1966, *Religion and Rebellion in Iran. The Tobacco Protest of 1891–1892*.
Kippenberg, Hans G., 1981, 'Jeder Tag 'Ashura, jedes Grab Kerbala. Zur Ritualisierung der Strassenkämpfe in Iran', K. Greussing (ed.), *Religion und Politik im Iran*, Frankfurt, 217–256.
Kohlberg, Etan, 1975, 'Some Imāmi – Shīʾī Views on Taqiyya', *Journal of the American Oriental Society* 95, 395–402.
Lambton, Ann K. S., 1967, 'The Evolution of the Iqṭāʾ in Medieval Iran', *Iran* 5, 41–50.
Lambton, Ann K. S., 1969, *Landlord and Peasant in Persia. A Study of Land Tenure and Land Revenue Administration*, (2. ed.) London.
Laoust, Henry, 1965, *Les Schismes dans l'Islam*, Paris.
Lewis, Bernard, 1953, 'Some Observations on the Significance of Heresy in the History of Islam', *Studia Islamica*, 1, 43–63.
Lewis, Bernard, 1974, *Islam from the Prophet Mohammad to the Capture of Constantinople*, II, New York.
Leyden, J, 1810, 'The Rosheniah Sect and its Founder Bayezid Ansari', *Asiatick Researches or Transactions of the Society Instituted in Bengal* 11: 363–428.
Liebeschütz, J. H. W. G., 1972, *Antioch: City and Imperial Administration in the Later Roman Empire*, Oxford.
Madelung, Wilfred, 1978a and b, 'Ismāʾiliyya' and 'Karmatī', *Encyclopedia of Islam*, 4: 198–206, 660–665.
Madelung, Wilfred, 1980, 'A Treatise of The Sharīf al-Murtadā on the Legality of Working for the Government', *Bulletin of the School of Oriental and African Studies*, 43: 18–31.
Margoliouth, David S., 1915–1916, 'On Mahdis and Mahdiism', *British Academy Proceedings*

7: 213–233.
Margoliouth, David S., 1961, 'Khurramīya', *Shorter Encyclopedia of Islam*, 257f.
Massignon, Louis, 1920, 'Les Corps de Métier et la Cité Islamique', *Revue Internationale de Sociologie* 28: 473–489.
Massignon, Louis, 1934, 'Sinf', *Enzyklopaedie des Islam*, 4: 468f.
Massignon, Louis, 1969, 'La "futuwwa", ou "pacte d'honneur artisanal" entre les travailleurs musulman au Moyen Age'. *Opera Minora* 1: 396–421, Paris.
Meyer, Egbert, 1980, 'Anlaß und Anwendungsbereich der taqiyya', *Der Islam* 57: 246–280.
Morony, Michael G., 1974, 'Religious Communities in Late Sasanian and Early Muslim Iraq', *Journal of the Economic and Social History of the Orient* 17: 113–135.
Mottahadeh, Roy P., 1980, *Loyalty and Leadership in an Early Islamic Society*, Princeton.
de Planhol, Xavier, 1968a, 'Geography of Settlement', *The Cambridge History of Iran*, 1: (ed. W. B. Fisher) 409–467.
de Planhol, Xavier, 1968b, *Les Fondements géographiques de l'histoire de l'Islam*, Paris.
Rosenthal, Franz, 1958, *Ibn Khaldûn. the Muqaddimah*, 2 vols, New York.
Sachedina, Abdulaziz A., 1981, *Islamic Messianism. The Idea of Mahdi in Twelver Shi'ism*, Albany.
Sadighi, Gholam H., 1938, *Les mouvements religieux iraniens au IIe et au IIIe siècle de l'Hégire*, Paris.
Schahrastani, 1850/51, *Religionspartheien und Philosophen-Schulen*, transl. T. Haarbrücker, Halle.
Schefer, Charles, 1881, *Nāsir-e Khusraw, Safar-Name*, Paris.
Schefer, Charles, 1892, *Description topographique et historique de Boukhara par M. Nerchakhy*, Paris.
Scott, James, 1977, Patronage or Exploitation? E. Gellner – J. Waterbury, eds., *Patrons and Clients in Mediterranean Societies*, 21–39, London.
Snouck, Hurgronje, C., 1923, 'Der Mahdi', *Verspreide Geschriften* 1: 145–181.
Stern, S. M., 1960, 'The Early Ismā'īlī missionaries in North-West Persia and in Khurāsān and Transoxiana', *Bulletin of the School of Oriental and African Studies* 23: 56–90.
Van Vloten, G., 1894, *Recherches sur la domination arabe, le chiitisme et les croyances messianiques sous le khalifat des Omayades*, Amsterdam.
Watt, Montgomery W., 1973, *The Formative Period of Islamic Thought*, Edinburgh.

The Babi movement in Iran 1844–52: from merchant protest to peasant revolution

KURT GREUSSING

The spectre that haunted Europe also spooked the Middle East. All powers of old Iran came together in an attempt to exorcise that very spectre. They comprised the Shah and local potentates, ministers and mollas, British diplomats and Russian consuls. The Iranian spectre was also conjured up by people who preached 'the abolition of property' and could be 'compared in their political aims with the Communists of Europe', according to a despatch of September 1852 from the Russian ambassador in Tehran [*Ivanov, 1939: 159*]. The wife of his British counterpart complained: 'Under the disguise of a new revelation, socialism and communism have made advances in Mazenderan, Yezd, Fars and Zenjan, which would leave nothing to wish for in the aspirations of the reddest republican' [*Sheil, 1856: 176*]. The master of this Iranian spectre 'was noted as a person of irregular and eccentric habits, possessing somewhat indefinite ideas of "meum" and "tuum", and consequently better known than trusted ... a religious demagogue' [*Binning, 1857: I, 404*]. S. G. W. Benjamin, the first ambassador of the United States to Persia, also was able to report that the religious doctrine of this new teaching was augmented by a socialism 'which formulated the equality of all, sweeping away social classes and distinctions, and ordaining a community of property, and also, at first, of wives' [*Benjamin, 1887: 354*].

All the accusations hurled against the Communist movement of the nineteenth century, to which Marx and Engels replied with a unique mixture of irony and analytical wit in their *Communist Manifesto*, were raised against the Babi movement as it shook the secular and spiritual powers of Iran with a series of uprisings between 1848–52. How threatening to some Western conservatives of the time the parallels between these revolts and the European working class movement had been, can be gauged from a comment of a German Orientalist writing in 1879.

> The Persian state is so unstable and the situation of the lower classes, especially in the countryside, so pitiable, that a renewed uprising of the sect could sweep away everything. It would surely seek to use even a partial victory to introduce basic social changes, and the hapless country would thereby become even more unhappy. There is much praise here for religion as a remedy against socialism, for good reason. But one

can see that there is another side to the coin. If our socialist leaders were ever to combine their European efficiency with the tremendous force of religious enthusiasm of these Asians, or even only with firm religious convictions, then our entire civilization [*Bildung*] would have to fear them greatly [*Nöldeke, 1879: 291*].

However, the early European and Iranian Socialism of those times had little more in common than the mere fears and prejudices that were mobilised against them. Whereas the west European working class movements developed from the social experience of subjection to the capitalist machinery that had dissolved the peasant world, the resistance movement of mid-nineteenth century Iran was based on markedly different conditions. It was at first a religious-innovatory movement, very much in concert with a reforming Shi'ite Islamic learned tradition. But its ideology had been influenced also by the dissolution of traditional social conditions through merchant capitalism. With the inclusion of the urban poor and the peasantry, chiliastic beliefs of Shi'ite Islam were conjured up, and this led to political radicalisation of the movement and its social ideas.

Iran in the early nineteenth century: foreign capital and economic crisis

In 1796 the Qajar took power in Iran under well-nigh civil war conditions. At the same time, the colonial interests of the two rival powers, Britain and Russia, began to clash in the region. Already by 1809 and 1812 the Qajars were promised assistance from Britain in struggles for the throne and against the neighbouring Afghans. Russia beat Iran in open battles, which led to the loss of northern territories and to granting forced commercial privileges by the treaties of Golestan (1813) and Turkmanchai (1828). The British secured their definitive influence through the Anglo-Persian Commercial Treaty of 1841, which opened up all fields of trade to foreigners.

Both colonial powers, however, remained satisfied with Iran's semi-colonial status, while the Iranian monarchy managed to stabilise its position in the country through granting new concessions to the rival powers. The country was hence only commercially 'colonised', to the great advantage of the government as it thereby filled its regularly empty coffers through the payments for privileges, but equally only at the expense of Iranian local trade and industry. Still, this arrangement meant that Iran was not exposed, as many other Islamic countries, to the politically always problematic presence of 'unbelievers'. Around 1857 there were less than a hundred Europeans (including Russians) in the country: a few merchants, doctors, missionaries and mechanics [*Blau, 1858: 38*].

Foreign trade played an increasing part in the social and political change of nineteenth century Iran. While until the fifties Iran's international balance of trade remained, by growing volume, fairly balanced, denoting no obvious economic drain, the qualitative and regional imbalances in commerce had grave consequences. The pressure of foreign commercial capital was particularly felt in the north. In Tabriz imports between 1833 and 1847 totalled ca. 241 million assignat-rubles, whilst exports were worth barely 90 million [*Ivanov, 1939: 167*]. Particularly overwhelming were imports of textiles. During the years 1850–57 out of an average total import volume of nearly 21 million thalers (= about £3 million) just over 13 million were manufactures, while out of a total export of 21 million less than 6 million thalers came from silk, wool and cotton fabrics [*Blau, 1858: 167f*].

While in the first half of the century commerce in general remained in Persian hands, foreign trade in the major emporium of Tabriz had already by the 1830's fallen into Russian hands [*Berezin, 1852: 59, App. 19*]. Imports via the Caspian ports and Tabriz adversely affected Iranian trade and manufacture in the north. In 1844 the British consul, K. E. Abbott, wrote: 'A memorial was presented to His Majesty the Shah by the traders and manufacturers of Cashan praying for protection of their commerce which they represented as suffering in consequence of the introduction of European merchandise into their country...' From Tabriz a British diplomat reported that the merchants had petitioned the crown prince to prohibit European imports 'on the ground principally of the ruin Persian manufactures are reduced to by the constant and immense importation of foreign goods'. In 1849, Abbott reported from Kashan that 'the manufacturers have ... rapidly declined for some time past in consequence of the trade with Europe which has gradually extended into every part of the Kingdom to the detriment and ruin of many branches of native industry' [*Issawi, 1971: 258f*].

Not all Iranian merchants and small entrepreneurs were equally affected by these developments. Since commerce remained to a great extent in Persian hands, the faction that cooperated with foreign capital profited from the increased volume of imports and exports. But the merchants connected with the bazaar-craftsmen and with village production in the surroundings of the cities were badly hit. They lost markets as their domestic production became uncompetitive, worsened by fiscal and legal disadvantages. Because

> foreign merchants, whose countries have a commercial treaty, pay five per cent entry customs; domestic merchants pay less, but they have to pass customs in every city on their way, and are thus incomparably worse off than the foreigners; they are forced to order supplies under a foreign firm, which leads to constant conflicts and litigation [*Polak, 1856: II, 189f*].

At the same time international treaties with powers like Britain and Russia assured foreign merchants of complete recompense through consular jurisdiction in the case of bankruptcy, while Persian dealers under the same rules went empty-handed [*Anonymous, 1842: 303*].

Foreign commercial activity in the cities affected the trade and economy of the peasantry in the rural hinterland. Iranian cities were always characterised by close connections with their surrounding countryside [*Ashraf, 1974: 11, 47*]. A substantial division of labour between villages increased the importance of nearby cities as central places for exchange and service. Town and country relations were basically defined by two different processes: by the economically more significant expropriation of rural surplus in form of rent paid to city-dwelling landlords and tax farmers, and by economic exchange. The latter consisted not only of the exchange of agrarian for manufactured goods, but, more significantly, of a village cottage industry, in effect a putting-out system controlled by urban merchants [*Ehlers, 1978: 133f*].

It was the expansion of foreign trade which essentially transformed these relations. Villages fell prey to the impact of merchant capital both in the economic sphere and in that of extra-economic coercion. The former manifested itself in the urban merchants' reorganising, expanding or abandoning the cottage industries under the new conditions of international economy. When rents in kind were turned into money payments during the course of the nineteenth century, agrarian production proper was reorganised forcibly towards cash crops. This change was also enhanced by changes in the system of social and political (extra-economic) coercion.

In the traditional Iranian system, high administrative and military officers were granted the dues of certain villages. Generally, it came to two-fifths of local agrarian production, based on a theory that the state-owned factors of production, land and water resources, were worth this amount. The remaining three fifths were distributed among the immediate producers according to their ownership of the productive factors – labour, seed and tools, and draught animals. This system was abandoned when the state began to pay officials' salaries from a central budget made up from taxes levied on great landowners and increasingly on immediate producers as well. However, since the Persian state in the nineteenth century did not have as yet the administrative resources to collect these revenues, it turned to tax farming or sold crown lands to wealthy merchants and bureaucrats. Tax farmers paid the amount calculated for a region in advance and then recouped the surplus from producers assigned to them by the government. The growing financial need of the court, that had triggered the sale of privileges and crown domains also put increasing pressure on the peasantry, mediated by the tax farmers. These in turn tried to extort ever increasing amounts from the peasants which included forcing them to change to cash crops. *Olson* has documented these developments for southern Iran where state taxation grew at such a pace that in the course of the first half of the nineteenth century the increase was from one-tenth to one-third of the harvest [*1981: 175f*].

The extent of ruthless exploitation to which this system led was impressively described by Polak. By the mid-nineteenth century the office of provincial governor, for which a considerable sum had to be paid to the court, was held always only for one year,

> therefore tax-payers would prefer to have a bad governor stay in office for longer, since even if a better were to replace him, he would not be 'full' yet. One may guess at the sums extorted by governors from the fact that in the course of several years Issa Khan and Amir Aslan Khan, two uncles of the Shah, managed to amass a fortune of about one million Tuman each, over and above paying the representative expenses of their office as governors. [1 million Tuman was – according to Binning, *1857: II, 46; II, 297* – roughly the price of 250,000 yokes of oxen or the cost of 330,000 peasant mud houses, or one-third of the entire annual state revenue.] The Shah was well aware of this but thought that he was quite unable to change matters. He instructed the successor of Issa Khan, in my presence, as he was about to leave for the province of Khamseh with these words: 'My uncle was rather hard on the province; take care that the people can still make a living, for they are poor and patiently quiet...' None the less the same Issa Khan was granted the governorship of another province and the patent printed in the official gazette stated: 'Considering the merits acquired by Issa Khan through the good treatment of the rayets [*ra'iyat*: herd, peasants, subjects] and the care for the country's culture, we named him governor of Ispahan so that he can in the same way advance the well-being of this province' [*1865: II, 127f*].

From the 1830s onwards these drastic changes were accompanied by major price increases in cereal foods and fodder. This onslaught on the rural economy caused mass migration into the towns and was worsened by disease and epidemics. In September 1848, on the eve of the first major Babi uprising, the Russian consul of the Caspian province of Gilan described the residential areas as 'to a very great extent ruined and impoverished' and saw 'the threat of poverty and decay' all around him [*Ivanov, 1939: 54*].

These pressures on the urban and rural economy spread outwards from the main trade routes. But on these routes not only caravans with foreign goods and the surplus expropriated from the peasants could travel, but also those political-religious ideas that were to make the economic crisis into a wide, socio-political issue through the Babi uprisings. All the centres of this revolt lay along the trade routes.

Babism: a religious innovation of the nineteenth century

Shi'ite Islam holds the chiliastic tradition that the twelfth successor of the Prophet, the hidden Imam Mahdi will emerge from his concealment and make an end to oppression and tyranny in the world. With the establishment of the Shi'ah as the state religion in sixteenth century Iran the Shi'ite clergy received important political functions. In the following centuries some of them attempted, not without success, to claim absolute monopoly for the interpretation of divine law and to become interim leaders of the community, until such time as the Mahdi would arrive. Yet this claim to an 'official' clergy was continuously challenged by various groups who maintained that the community had immediate contact with the Mahdi and hence direct access to divine wisdom through a physically present, divinely inspired person.

One of these groups was the sect of Shaykhis under the leadership of Shaykh Ahmad Ahsa'i (1753–1826), a religious precursor of Babism. In 1843, after the death of the sect's leader Sayyed Kazem Rashti, the group split into three factions. The leader of one of them, Sayyed Ali Mohammad of Shiraz declared himself in 1844 a divinely inspired person who represented the 'gate' (*Bab*) to the Imam Mahdi. That this happened in the 1260. year of the Hejrah had profound significance for the Babis: it was exactly one thousand (lunar) years after the inauguration of the Imam Mahdi of the Twelver Shi'is (873/74 A.D.=260 A.H.). The manifestation of Ali Mohammad as Bab seemed to mark the end of the millennial concealment of the Mahdi, and to signal his imminent second coming. As a matter of fact, the Bab soon began to call himself not the 'gate' to the hidden Imam, but as the Imam himself: *Qa'em*, i.e. 'he who emerges', or *Noqteh-ye bayan* – 'the point of revelation' [*Browne, 1891: 290–5*].

In the early phase of the movement, till mid-1848, the Babis saw themselves as a religious reform movement trying to spread their creed among the secular and spiritual élites [*Ivanov, 1939: 61–3, 80*]. With his self-proclamation as Bab, however, Ali Mohammad had inevitably alienated the higher Shi'ite clergy, for he had thereby declared the traditional revelation of the Prophet to be obsolete. Thus he spent most of his short career in jail and house arrest, which, however, did not prevent him from keeping touch with his followers. A growing concern for social matters is conspicuous in the development of the ideas of the Bab, who himself coming from a family of textile merchants in Shiraz, had for five years been active in that trade. In his last writing from probably 1847, the *Bayan-e farsi*, the social programmes of the new order are primarily focussed on the interests of merchants. He distinguished four strictly separated social classes: higher clergy, higher civil servants, great merchants, and finally the fourth estate as 'other employed persons in their manifold ranks'. About them, who were to include bazaar traders, craftsmen and peasants, he had little to say [*Bab, n.d.: 246*].

Commerce seems to have been the highest profession in the Bab's eyes. Most of his demands could be summed up as calls for 'modernisation' under the given conditions: the post should be improved to the standards of Europe [*ibid. IV: 16*], unauthorised persons should not open letters and commercial correspondence [*IV: 18*], the exchange rate between gold and silver should not be allowed to fluctuate [*V: 19*], debtors should be forced to repay loans [*VII: 3*], and so on. While all non-believers, that is non-Babis, shall be expelled from the realm of the new order and their property confiscated, merchants, including foreign Christians, were to be allowed to pursue their business with profit [*VII: 16*]. The Bab permitted trade with all people including slaves, and he justified, in the fine spirit of commerce, the collecting of interest [*V: 18*].

Thus the Bab did not intend any essential break with existing property and other social relations, but rather he wished for a legal reform of the political superstructure as to eliminate despotic irregularities including foreign merchants' privileges and to protect individual rights. The abolition of private property, as preached by the more radical wing after 1848, was not foreseen by the Bab. For him, only the confiscated property of non-believers was to be distributed equally among the members of his community [*V: 6*].

Radicalisation of religious ideology and revolutionary mobilisation

In the beginning Babism was a reaction to orthodox Shi'ite Islam. Therefore the Babist sources that have come down to us are mainly concerned with separating themselves from orthodoxy by formulating a new religious creed. Babis saw the history of revelation as a series of ever more complete prophetic cycles. Whereas in Islam Mohammad counts as the last of the prophets and their 'seal', with his book, the Qoran and his personal practice, as the final form of divine revelation, Babis believed in the appearance of new prophets who would finally end the existing revelatory cycle. This belief even permitted them to formulate social demands that stood in opposition to existing teachings and social conditions.

Conflicts naturally started as altercations between orthodox clergy and those of their colleagues who had turned into Babis. We read in the memoirs of an orthodox Shi'ite about Babi leader Molla Mohammad Ali Barforushi, who began his agitation in his home town of Barforush – present day Babol – in Mazanderan by

> seducing people who came frequently and gladly to see him [telling them]: 'I am the man of God. I am the representative of the Lord of the Time [the Mahdi]. Whatever I say, harken unto me: These mollas of ours, whatever they say, is a lie. [But] what I say is the truth.' And they replied: 'Whatever you say, is the truth' [*Shaykh ol-Ajam, 1866: 205*].[1]

In the course of the debates the Babi leaders turned increasingly to a lower class audience, by which token new social interests became involved in their message and social-radical aspects surrounding the expectation of the Mahdi gained strength. During the armed conflicts, then, these elements became even more important.

In the second half of 1848 some three hundred Babis, probably mostly lower clergy and merchants, gathered in the village of Bedasht near the border of the northern provinces Mazanderan and Khorasan. The trigger was the arrest of the Bab in Maku, which may have led them to discuss plans for his liberation. In this meeting the social concerns of the lower classes, which did not feature at all in the Bab's original message, were vehemently argued above all by Molla Mohammad Ali of Barforush, who himself came from a peasant family. His chiliastic appeal was couched in a language that reflected the social experience of the urban and rural poor:

> When therefore men will perceive that he who has power over all their property is the Lord of the Time, and when they will have given up the control of their property which is really control over violently appropriated [things], then all the statutes of *khoms* and *zakat* [religious taxes] will be annulled and the reign of the family of Mohammad [the Twelfth Imam] will begin ... What concerns that command holds true for all other commands of the law of the Prophet. Since these are merely the prescriptions for the homebound road, so it is that when the traveller has reached home, the laws of travel shall not apply to him any longer. Or regard the example of the peasant. The melon seed that he plants into the earth is expected to turn into a melon. As long as the melon has not ripened, and is still hidden in the secret of its bloom, its leaf, branch, stem and root, the peasant will take care to water and weed it, and follow all the other prescriptions ... But when the melon has matured and he has picked it, then all the commands for the care of the plant have lost their meaning. Therefore shall the *shari'ah* [the religious law; but also 'a straight and even road'] of His Holiness the Prophet of God becomes obsolete, because its commands were there only for starting out on the road [*Mirza Jani, 1919: 150f*].

Mohammad Ali of Barforush drew from his messianic beliefs more radical social consequences than the Bab himself – above all, the abolition of private property.

> [Certain] traditions teach us that in the realm of the Qa'em [the Mahdi], people will ... go to the bazaar, say prayers and take whatever they want from the shops. Should someone do such a thing in our times, his hand would be cut off according to the law of the Prophet of God. In short, the religious commands of the Qa'em – peace be upon Him – are those of unity. All property is His property; all males are His man servants and all females His maidservants [*Mirza Jani, 1910: 151*].

This chiliastic programme goaded into action that other, especially culturally oppressed group – women, whose speaker, alongside Mohammad Ali Barforushi at the Bedasht meeting was the legendary woman, Qorrat ol-Ayn ('Brightness of the Eye'). Whilst addressing the crowd she demonstratively took off her veil. She spoke of emancipation from existing burdens and behests and said, 'all women are common to you, all goods are yours in common', which split the meeting into 'Moslems who promptly gave up Babism and into those with neither goods nor women, who thereupon gave up Islam' [*Nicolas, 1905: 280f*].

The meeting of Bedasht ended in schism [*Mirza Jani, 1910: 153f*]. One group of Babis went to Barforush, and after they had been expelled, barricaded themselves at the tomb of Shaykh Tabarsi, to the south-east of the city. The Russian ambassador to Tehran reported in January 1849 that in Mazanderan two thousand members 'of various tribes and other lower social classes' had stood up against the state [*Ivanov, 1939: 144f*]. The Babis held the fortress of Shaykh Tabarsi for more than half a year against the imperial troops. At times more than seven thousand men and women were reported to have congregated there. They were finally starved out and had to give up. Including Mohammad Ali Barforushi, they all were either summarily murdered or publicly executed in the following days [*Shaykh ol-Ajam, 1866: 211*].

After the Bedasht meeting Babi resistance grew into a mass movement. In February 1849, grand viser Amir-e Kabir told the Russian ambassador, Dolgorukii, that in the southern provinces, in Tehran and Azerbaijan already some 100,000 people might be in open rebellion against the government [*Ivanov, 1939: 146*], in a country of not more than 8 million inhabitants [*Binning, 1857: II, 297*]. Diffuse and local anti-government movements and Babi-uprisings then began to merge across the whole country. Execution of the Bab in Tabriz in July 1850 did by no means decrease the spread of the rebellion.

In the northern town of Zanjan Babis were in open revolt from May, 1850 to the end of the year. During that summer rebellion broke out at Nayriz in the south, after another Babi-rising in Yazd [*Watson, 1866: 385–94; Muhammad, 1927: 464*]. In Zanjan the uprising started with an attack on the orthodox clergy. Following the Bab's orders, Mohammad Ali Zanjani, the future leader of the revolt, prevented mollas from leading the communal Friday prayers [*Mirza Jani, 1910: 230*]. When about a thousand of his adherents frustrated his arrest and deportation to Tehran, the imperial troops intervened. But 'the host of vileness' – as the contemporary Babi-chronist styled the government soldiers – had no chance against the Babis who barricaded themselves and soon occupied more than half the town [*ibid. 230f*]. A barricade was thrown across town, dividing even the bazaar [*Abdu'l-Ahad, 1897: 792f*]. In the ensuing struggle three groups played major parts: members of the urban lower strata; villagers from the surrounding countryside; and women. Molla Mohammad Ali Zanjani must have had a considerable following among the urban poor, even before he became a Babi. Many years later a diarist remembered:

> The manner in which these people disposed themselves in the Mosque was as follows: the poor sat on the right side of the pulpit [i.e. in the place of honour] and the rich on the left side; and I myself repeatedly beheld in my childhood that His Holiness [i.e. Mohammad Ali Zanjanai] when preaching, ever turned his face towards the poor, only at times glancing towards the rich [*Abdu'l-Ahad, 1897: 779*].

Informers of the British ambassador reported that when armed struggle broke out, support came 'from the adjacent villages and districts' [*FO 60/152, Sheil to Palmerston, June 25, 1850, fol. 130*]. During the fighting the courage and quality of military leadership displayed by the women was repeatedly emphasised [*Abdu'l-Ahad, 1897: 802f; FO 60/153 Abbott to Sheil, Aug. 30, 1850, fol. 138*]. The armed conflict significantly helped to radicalise the social programme of the rebels. 'Among Babees property ought to be in common; no man ought to be richer than another', wrote Sheil to Palmerston, referring to specific information he had from a disciple of the Bab [*FO 60/152, June 21, 1850, fol. 80ff*]. In Zanjan, Mohammad Ali 'commanded his followers that they should all be as one family and one household, and that all things, from eatables to clothing, whatever there was, should be divided for use' [*Abdu'l-Ahad, 1897: 793*]. Only after their leader had been fatally wounded and the Babis' control reduced to a few houses, could the uprising be repressed with a bloody attack by government troops [*FO 60/158, January 6, 1851, fol. 14f*].

Rebel agitation was different but probably not a-typical in Nayriz. The leader of the uprising, Sayyed Yahya of Darab, had opened a Babist propaganda campaign in the villages and small towns surrounding the central city and come into conflict with orthodox clergy. Expelled first from Fasa and then from Estahbanat, he went to Nayriz with a following of five hundred from Fasa alone [*Lesan ol-Molk, 1860: fol. 302b*]. In Nayriz he made contact with an urban faction, which was already opposed to the Qajar government.

> These evildoers rebelled against their governor Hajji Zayn ol-Abedin Khan. Sayyed Yahya made friends with the evildoers and made his intentions perfectly plain in public. All evildoers, numbering about five hundred persons, accepted his teaching. He negated all the commandments of the Moslem religion, and his reputation grew day by day [*Hasan-e Fasa'i, 1896/7: 304*].

The Babi-fighters' numbers grew allegedly to more than three thousand [*Busse, 1972: 291f*], but their uprising also ended in bloody repression. In the summer of 1852 another rebellion in Nayriz failed [*Browne, 1891: 258f*]. Attempts had been made also in Barforush during the spring of 1852, in Zanjan, and in Azerbaijan among other places. All were unsuccessful [*Ivanov, 1939: 127*].

The ceaseless bloodletting finally exhausted the energies of the Babis. Most of their leadership had either fallen in battle or had been executed. When the remaining leaders assembled in Tehran during August 1852, some younger members made an amateurish attempt to assassinate the Shah. The systematic persecution that followed, was in fact little less than a massacre organised by the state [*Sheil, 1856: 278–81; Nicolas, 1905: 437–45*]. It forced the few last survivors to emigrate, first to Baghdad and finally into Turkey. There the movement split into two factions. The small, uninfluential splinter group of the

Azalis tried to sustain the revolutionary image. The more powerful faction of the *Baha'is* gave up any resistance to secular power and founded a new, quietist 'world religion'. Babism as a social movement ceased to exist.

Summary

The Babi movement provided one of the largest and most important popular uprisings in nineteenth century Iran. As a religious movement it has been more amply documented than almost any other aspect of Persian history in the last century [e.g. *Browne, 1889; 1891*]. But as also a social movement it has been much less extensively explored. The pioneer work of Ivanov is still the most informative. He saw Babism as a radical, democratic, anti-feudal and anti-imperialist mass movement, with elements of disunity typical of traditional peasant uprisings, even though the fighters counted among them many urban poor, craftsmen, small tradesmen and lower clergy. For him it was an immature anticipation of Communism, doomed to failure [*Ivanov, 1939: 137–41*]. N. R. Keddie [*1961/2: 267–73*] emphasised the millenarian character of the movement and saw its conflicts with orthodox clergy as more significant than those with the government. She pointed out that its millenarian concepts were already intermingled with new ideas about social and cultural reform, which then became significant in the national-democratic movement around the turn of the century. *M. R. Feshahi* described the Babis as 'the last movement of the feudal Middle Ages' [*1977: 1*], in which the peasants represented the old feudal world, whereas the participation by merchants already hinted at a transition to a modern one. *F. Kazemi* [*1973: 131*] placed the movement, on the basis of its clerical and urban based merchant leadership, into the context of urban conflicts. He admitted, though, that through its messianic overtones, Babism also found resonance among impoverished peasants and other disenfranchised elements.

These attempts at a social explanation are probably too diffuse. They do not explain the transformation of Babism from a religious reform movement without radical social content into a genuine social revolutionary one. True, a more detailed analysis is also hindered by the lack of sources, as the successors of the Babis, the quietist *Baha'is* soon began to censor, falsify or destroy much of the evidence regarding the radical phase of the movement [*Tumanskii, 1899: ix*].[2]

Babism began as a religious reform movement among urban élites in a frame of Mahdist-imamite tradition. This led to conflicts with the higher clergy and hence rather soon to confrontations with secular powers. But it also took place in a new political and social context overshadowed by the economic crisis caused by influx of foreign commercial capital which affected not only merchants but also urban craftsmen and rural primary producers. For the peasantry the crisis was enhanced by an increased expropriation of surplus by landlords and the state. This process in turn was accelerated by an expansion of international capital tying Iran increasingly into the network of colonial interests.

This crisis did not spread over the country in an even and synchronic manner. The cities and their rural surroundings along the trade routes were hit first and foremost. The social potential that radicalised the 1848 movement was developed in these specific parts of the country. It was only after their religious propaganda failed among the élites that Babi activists took their message to the urban and rural lower classes. They themselves were neither peasants nor poor townsmen, but they became what is called 'agents of articulation' in rural social movements. As representatives of the people living in the central places along the caravan routes, they funnelled the crisis experience of these most affected strata into a politically active movement. The movement's transformation followed two lines. In the religious teachings the radical aspects of Mahdi-expectation gained influence, whilst in the social and secular field merchant interests were gradually replaced by millenarian ideas about common property of goods and equality of women.

Although the uprisings broke out in various places almost simultaneously, there was no overall strategy. The struggle was defensive, but not necessarily disorganised. The Babis seem to have had a relatively uniform and efficient propaganda machine all over the country. Understandably, their influence was strongest in areas near trade routes, in those cities and adjacent villages, that were heaviest hit by the economic crisis. In more distant parts of the country and among the nomads, who made up a quarter to a third of the population, Babism did not produce a following.

The essentially defensive character of the uprisings, and the lack of major military campaigns aimed at the overthrow of the central government, were mainly the result of logistic difficulties and not of any alleged basic inability of peasants to unite in great movements. To conduct such a campaign, Babis would have had to plunder fellow peasants in order to supply their army, a method widely used by their enemies, the imperial troops [*Binning, 1857: II, 296*]. The religious matrix of the movement also played its vital part here. At the outset, Mahdist-chiliastic movements rarely have long term strategic plans. They expect an immediate diachronic break with the existing order and a swift, painful transition to the realm of eternal justice. They are essentially an extravagant, catastrophic expectation of a new society.

In the context of the prevailing social, political and cultural conditions of nineteenth century Iran, Babism was certainly a revolutionary movement. However, its radicalism contributed not only to an immediately successful short-term mobilisation and military organisation of the urban and rural poor, but also to their final defeat. The world in which the Babis acted was *economically* definitely ripe for radical changes; not so *politically* and *culturally*, where there were no past political experiences that could have mediated between chiliastic expectations and a realistic programme to implement a transformation of society. This was accomplished only later, to a great extent under cultural influences from abroad, by the Iranian Constitutionalist Movement of 1905–11. The Babis' 'anticipation of Communism' was not 'immature' – it was too early.

Notes

1. More attention and credence has to be given to a manuscript acquired by B. Dorn in 1860 in Barforush, written by Shaykh ol-Ajam in the Mazanderani dialect. *Mirza Karzem-Beg [1866a: 332, 334]* held it to be a history of the Bab, and hence 'full of mistakes', 'without any historical value'. This misjudgment had been broadcast without further research by both Browne *[1891: 205]* and Ivanov *[1939: 22]*. In fact the text is about 'Memedali', i.e. Mohammad Ali (of Barforush) and his story tallies with other sources.
2. This holds also true for the main source on the Babis by *Mirza Jani [1910]*, a Kashan merchant, who was executed after the defeat of the uprising in 1852 in Tehran. His account from 1851 is our only source by a contemporary Babi on the radical phase following the meeting in Bedasht. A manuscript, edited by E. G. Browne in 1910, was originally acquired by Count Gobineau in 1862–63 at Tehran, during a time, before the remnant Babis had split, and thus before 1864 when the *Baha'is* began to eradicate the revolutionary roots of their movement. *Baha'i* claims that the 'heretical' text is a forgery of an earlier, lost original *[Balyuzi, 1970: 70, 88]* cannot be accepted, even if the manuscript should not be Mirza Jani's autograph.

References

Abdu'l-Ahad-i-Zanjani, 1897, 'Personal Reminiscences of the Babi Insurrection at Zanjan, written in Persian by Aqa Abdu'l-Ahad-i-Zanjani, and translated into English by Edward G. Browne', *Journal of the Royal Asiatic Society*, XXIX: 761–827.
Anonymous, 1842, 'O torgovle v Tavrise v 1841 godu' [On the trade in Tabriz in 1841], *Zhurnal manufaktur i torgovli*, ch. 2, No. 5: 297–313, St Petersburg.
Ashraf, Ahmad, 1353/1974, 'Vizhegiha-ye tarikhi-e shahrneshini dar Iran – doureh-ye eslami' [Historical characteristics of Iranian cities in the Islamic era], *Olum-e ejtema'i*, I, No. 4: 7–49 (Tehran University, Tehran).
Bab (Ali Mohammad Shirazi), n.d., *Bayan-e farsi*, Tehran(?) (ca. 1960, British Museum OMPB 14178.e.10); *Le Béyan Persan*, traduit du Persan par A.-L.-M. Nicolas, 4 vols., Paris 1911–1914.
Balyuzi, H. M., 1970, *Edward Granville Browne and the Bahá'í Faith*, London.
Benjamin, S. G. W., 1887, *Persia and the Persians*, London.
Berezin, I., 1852, *Puteshestvie po severnoi Persii* [Journey to Northern Persia], Kazan.
Binning, Robert B. M., 1857, *A Journal of Two Years' Travel in Persia, Ceylon etc.*, 2 vols., London.
Blau, Otto, 1858, *Commercielle Zustände Persiens. Aus den Erfahrungen einer Reise im Sommer 1857*, Berlin.
Browne, Edward G., 1889, 'The Bábí's of Persia', *Journal of the Royal Asiatic Society*, XXI: 485–526, 881–1009.
Browne, Edward G., 1891, *A Traveller's Narrative to illustrate the episode of the Bab* (vol. II), Cambridge.
Busse, Heribert, 1972, *History of Persia under Qajar Rule. Translated from the Persian of Hasan-e*

Fasa'i's Farsnama-ye Naseri, New York/London.
Ehlers, Eckart, 1978, 'Rentenkapitalismus und Stadtentwicklung im islamischen Orient', *Erdkunde*, XXXII: 124–142.
Feshahi, Mohammad Reza, 1356/1977, *Vapasin-e jonbesh-e qorun-e vasetayi dar douran-e fe'udal* [The last movement of the middle ages in the feudal era], Tehran.
Hasan-c Fasa'i, 1313–14 A.H./1896–97, *Farsnameh-ye naseri*, vol. I, Tehran.
Issawi, Charles, ed., 1971, *The Economic History of Iran 1800–1914*, Chicago/London.
Ivanov, M. S., 1939, *Babidskie vosstaniya v Irane (1848–1852)* [The Babi uprisings in Iran, 1848–1852], Moscow/Leningrad.
Kazemi, Farhad, 1973, 'Some Preliminary Observations on the Early Development of Babism', *Muslim World*, LXIII: 119–131 (Hartford, Conn.).
Keddie, Nikki R., 1961–62, 'Religion and Irreligion in Early Iranian Nationalism', *Comparative Studies in Society and History*, IV: 265–295.
Lesan ol-Molk, Mohammad Taqi Sepehr, ca. 1860, *Nasekh ot-tavarikh-e qajariyeh* [The best of histories of the Qajar rule], vol. III, Tehran.
Mirza Jani Kashani, 1910, *Ketab-e noqtat ol-Kaf* [The book of the point of K], ed. from the unique Paris M. S. Suppl. Persan 1071, by E. G. Brown, Leyden/London.
Mirza Kazam-Beg, 1866a/b, 'Bab et les Babis ou Le soulèvement politique et religieux en Perse, de 1844 à 1852', *Journal Asiatique*, sér. 6, VII: 329–384, 457–522; VIII: 196–252, 357–400, 473–507.
Muhammad, Khan Bahadur Agha Mirza, 1927, 'Some New Notes on Babism', *Journal of the Royal Asiatic Society*, 443–470 (London).
Nicolas, A. L. M., 1905, *Seyyèd Ali Mohammad, dit le Bâb*, Paris.
Nöldeke, Theodor, 1879, 'Orientalischer Socialismus', *Deutsche Rundschau*, XVIII: 284–291.
Olson, Roger T., 1981, 'Persian Gulf Trade and the Agricultural Economy of Southern Iran in the Nineteenth Century', M. E. Bonine and N. R. Keddie, eds., *Modern Iran. The Dialectics of Continuity and Change*, 173–189, Albany.
Polak, Jakob, 1865, *Persien, das Land und seine Bewohner. Ethnographische Schilderungen*, 2 vols., Leipzig.
Shaykh ol-Ajam Mazanderani, 1866, 'Men kelam-e Shaykh ol-Ajam Mazanderani' [From the account of Shaykh ol-Ajam of Mazanderan], B. Dorn, 'Nachträge zu dem Verzeichnis der von der Kaiserlichen öffentlichen Bibliothek erworbenen Chanykov'schen Handschriften ...', *Bulletin de l'Académie Impériale des Sciences de St-Pétersbourg*, IX: 202–231.
Sheil, Lady, 1856, *Glimpses of Life and Manners in Persia*, London.
Tumanskii, A. G., 1899, *Kitabe Akdes – 'Svyashtshenneishaya Kniga' sovremennykh babidov* ('The Most Holy Book' of the contemporary Babis), Mémoires de l'Académie Impériale des Sciences de St-Pétersburg, VIIIe série, classe historico-philologique, vol. III, No. 6.
Watson, Robert Grant, 1866, *A History of Persia from the Beginning of the Nineteenth Century to the Year 1858*, London.

Manuscript source

Public Record Office, Foreign Office Archives, London: FO 60, despatches from and to Persia.

The revolt of Eshaq Khan in Afghan-Turkestan in 1888: peasant mobilisation and re-formation of patron-client relationships

JAN-HEEREN GREVEMEYER

One of the greatest rebellions against the central authority of Amir Abdorrahman Khan (1880–1901) broke out in Afghan-Turkestan in 1888, headed by a religious charismatic leader. According to Ghobar [*1967: 664*] it was an 'anti-centralist' movement which mobilised 'peasants, herdsmen, government agents and provincial officers' to challenge the reforming policies of the young Afghan state. This revolt, which, initially at least, had genuine popular support [*Khalfin, 1958: 260*], eliminated Kabul's control of the whole nothern part of the country for a few weeks.

Ghobar [1967] and *Khalfin* [1958], Afghani and Russian authors respectively, characterised the movement as an 'anti-centralist', 'popular' and 'peasant' uprising; in other words, as a typical rural revolt in the context of social crisis. However, to describe this uprising as a popular movement suggests a revolt of peasants pursuing their own interests, which was not the exact case. The coalition of local tenants and landlords that rose against the centralising efforts and 'internal imperialism' [*Dupree, 1973: 418*] of King Abdorrahman Khan defies the definition of popular movement *tout court*.

If we wish to understand the historical situation and also the contemporary conditions in Afghanistan, we must abandon those views that derive their justification, *inter alia*, from Engels' analysis of the German Peasant War, namely, that the resistance of peasant classes, whatever the concrete social outcome of their struggles, contains an element of 'anticipation of communism' [*Engels, 1956: 60*]. Such linear concepts of progressive liberation from oppression and exploitation suffer, among other things, from an exclusively Eurocentric frame of reference. In the history of Afghanistan no such process can be detected, and there is absolutely no evidence for a class-specific organisation of peasants in an uprising against the upper strata in either village or region.

The Communist Khalq-Parcham Party that came to power in 1978 attempted to apply a Marxist-Leninist class analysis to Afghan society and to transform it through the emancipation of the socially and economically oppressed masses.

When the Taraki government (1978–79) tried to realise this programme through an agrarian reform, they failed, precisely because Afghan society was not amenable to being forced into the Procrustian bed of orthodox concepts on class-antagonisms. Rural Afghanistan is in fact still defined by effective patron-client relationships which cross class barriers. This system does not imply only exploitation of peasants, but also imposes a number of obligations on the so called feudal lords, usurers and exploiters. These mutual relations which counteract political mediatisation and economic exploitation are essential for the survival of a population living on the edge of subsistence.

In the last two decades these conditions were somewhat altered through migration for work into Iran, through the intermittent market oriented agriculture of some estates (e.g. in Herat), through the famines of the 1970's and through the expansion of education and its concomitant effects on social mobility. But even these did not dissolve the system of clientèle and did not lead to a class-oriented organisation of dependent producers. In 1979 the dependent peasantry that was to be the beneficiary of the agrarian reform rose together with the expropriated landowners against the government. The subsistence of the peasantry seemed to be still best ensured through the client-patron relationships [*Grevemeyer, 1980; Tabibi, 1981*].

Just as present resistance brings new social transformations, so the movement of Eshaq Khan stood also at the crossroads of social changes. Then, as now, the target is not simply one of emancipation from existing domination and exploitation, but adjustment of the system of clientèle to new demands and conditions. Just as the Taraki/Amin/Karmal governments failed in their efforts to create a class of small-holders responsible only to the state, so, in the last analysis, King Abdorrahman failed to establish a stratum of *citoyens* subject only to the crown.

The outcome of the present upheaval is still undecided. The uprising of Eshaq Khan with his allies from the élite and their clientèle collapsed after a few weeks. But the defeated revolt of 1888 forced the upper strata to form themselves anew, which they accomplished by adjusting their interests to the village level. This gave the clientèle system a new foundation and, at the same time, a new basis for survival of immediate producers. When Abdorrahman Khan died in 1901, Afghanistan entered the twentieth century as a politically united state. However, below the level of government administration, the nation was composed of villages which were virtually autonomous, economically and politically.

The dominion of the Afghans

The Empire of the Pashtuns (also called Pathans, Afghans) had been founded around the middle of the eighteenth century by King Ahmed Shah and comprised an area from Delhi in the east to Mashhad in the west, from the River Amu-Darya in the north to the Indian Ocean in the south. This move was very much in the tradition of Central Asian empire building: an able soldier and a clever diplomat had gradually increased his retinue from what had begun as a small group of loyal followers into a major empire. After two generations, however, it was again so much divided along geographical, linguistic, ethnic and religious lines, that when the colonial powers, Russia and, above all Britain, became interested in the area, it seemed likely that Afghanistan would fall pray to them sooner rather than later.

But two expensive wars in 1838–42 and 1878–80 convinced the British to seek political arrangements with the Afghan rulers. The British Governor General, Lord Ellenborough, had already proposed after the first Anglo-Afghan war to 'leave it to the Afghans themselves to create a government amidst the anarchy which is the consequence of their crimes' [Khan, 1963: 72]. Within a few decades of his utterance the British and Russians had made Afghanistan into a buffer state with definite borders. Decisions on internal matters were left to the Afghan regents, but the country's foreign affairs were in the hands of the British. Britain approved King Abdorrahman Khan and supported his government with money and arms in order to centralise the country.

With this international backing, Amir Abdorrahman Khan was able to attempt to subject areas never before controlled by the Afghans, such as Kafirestan (today: Nurestan) and other, half-autonomous regions. His autobiographical justification for violent action is much influenced by a British view of Afghan society:

> Taking into consideration that the boundary lines made a strong wall around the country, shaping it, as it were, into a house, it was necessary to clear that house of all the injurious scorpions existing in it... To explain myself: I mean that I had to put in order all those hundreds of petty chiefs, plunderers, robbers, and cut-throats... This necessitated breaking down the feudal and tribal system, and substituting one grand community under one law and under one rule [Mir Munshi, 1900: II, 176f].

From empire to state: Afghan–Turkestan's experience

The 'petty chiefs' and others described in these not exactly flattering terms by the king were that traditional political élite whom both the ruler and his British protectors wished to make powerless. Their common interest was to stablise Afghanistan by eliminating the danger of political fragmentation from within and imperialist encroachment from without.

The English-Russian border treaties of 1873 and 1879 defined Afghanistan's northern frontier with the Russian vassal state of Bokhara thus declaring the northern regions an integral part of the Afghan state. This, however, could not yet assure the Kabul government's effective control of that area nominally under its rule since the mid-nineteenth century. Communication across the Hindukush was very difficult, even in the summer. There was only a very small presence of Afghan military and administrative staff to protect the interests of the kingdom. The Afghan governors, vice-governors and officers had to count on the cooperation of the notables for tax collection and defence.

The French traveller, Ferrier, who visited the area a few years before its incorporation into Afghanistan, described these autonomous Uzbek lords who had been accustomed to rule their own country since the sixteenth century, despite their nominal acceptance of the overlordship of some far away authority:

> The amount of rivalry and intrigue that exist amongst the petty Khans of Turkistan is perfectly incredible. [. . .] The certain consequence is a permanent state of warfare. [. . .] They recognise the suzerainty of the princes of Herat, Bokhara, or Khulm, only because they have not sufficient power to throw it off; or, that occasionally it happens to be to their interest to acknowledge it. They will change their protectors as often as it suits them. [. . .] If they furnish him a contingent for a war they receive an indemnity from him, and are otherwise repaid by a portion of the plunder taken [*Ferrier, 1857: 204*].

At first, the position of these Khans as petty rulers was not affected unduly by Kabul. They received the usual privileges for their services and were included in the retainer- and loyalty system of the Afghans. Yet these privileges were of limited political value. With one exception, the eight regional governments were in the hands of Afghan civil servants and military officers. When Eshaq Khan became the governor of Afghan-Turkestan in 1880, the traditional upper strata had already been to a considerable extent removed from leading positions, although they still enjoyed social influence of some importance. Regular Afghan troops were augmented usually by militias and auxiliaries of Uzbeks, Hazarahs and Turkomans under their own commanders. [*Yate, 1888: 274, 284*]. In spite of an Afghan settlement drive, the area counted only 12,000 of them in contrast to 640,000 Uzbeks, Tajiks, Turkomans and Hazarahs [*Khalfin, 1958: 254f*].

When Yate visited the court of Eshaq Khan in 1886 he noted at a meeting with the governor, his son and the court dignitaries: 'A very heterogeneous lot they were, . . . with not a thoroughbred-looking Afghan amongst them', and he remarked that the governor had granted all influential posts to young nobles [*Yate, 1888: 278*]. One may assume that these 'nobles' were members of the Uzbek élites, integrated into the Afghan military administration. Yate also knew that 'the local mirs have almost all been ousted' [*ibid., 319*], indicating considerable changes that had occurred in the forty years since Ferrier saw the country.

The coalition of some local nobles with the Afghanis who came from Kabul did not provide a better centralised state control of the region. The opposite was the case, since association of Afghan governors with local élites gave those satraps great personal power, enabling a man such as Eshaq Khan to see himself as a relatively autonomous agent of his own interests. Such a separation of Afghan governors from the central authority was no novelty in Afghan-Turkestan [*Wheeler, 1869: 112*], and could be seen as a version of the earlier independence of Uzbek local rulers. Therefore, when Abdorrahman Khan started seriously to implement his centralising reforms, the entire political system of gradual autonomy and its socio-economic parallel in clientism and subsistence maintenance was threatened.

Centralisation and traditional coalitions: the reforms of Abdorrahman Khan and the resistance of Eshaq Khan

The policies of Abdorrahman Khan can be summarised under two headings: the establishment of a new taxation system and of an army which was to be loyal only to the king. Although there was no conscription in Afghanistan, every eight inhabitants were required to supply one soldier. The standing army counted about 100,000 men to which were added the 'tribal levies' and the militias (police, borderguards). The soldiers received regular pay and were stationed as a rule outside their home districts [*Ghobar, 1967: 644f*]. To finance this armed force, the king introduced a series of new taxes and markedly increased the rates of existing ones. Ghobar [*ibid.: 647*] estimated that in the course of a few years the annual revenue of the state was doubled. The tax reform and the concomitant monetarising of many dues not only endangered the existing system whereby surplus was appropriated and redistributed via the upper classes, but disturbed the entire edifice of expropriation and distribution embedded in rural social conditions. The due levied on the lords, whose income originated mainly from animal husbandry, was doubled and the taxes of the peasantry on land and agrarian produce also rose steeply. A substantial part of the surplus that had been redistributed at the village level was now to be transferred to the state, and hence the resources for winning a local clientèle, indeed, even for the maintenance of clients, were sharply reduced.

The monetarisation of revenue included an additional increase of burdens for both producers and lords, as cash was in short supply. The historian Vambéry reports that when he tried to sell some goods in the bazaar of Andkhoi he received 'in exchange only fruit and bread instead of money' [*Vambery, 1970: 279*]. The necessary cash could be obtained only on the superregional markets, to the advantage of traders and commercial agents. Considering the shortage of money, the lack of an extensive system of bazaars (with the exception of a few minor ones) and the control of the trade in the two major markets in Mazar-e Sharif and

Tashqorghan by non-local Afghans, Indians and Jews, a strict monetarisation of taxes would have quickly subjected even the upper classes to the bazaar and deprived them of the control of their clientèles. The central authorities did not have the resources to develop a marketing system, and other than the rather primitive rural crafts the peasants had no way of earning cash. This level and mode of taxation was about to ruin the subsistence economy of the entire dependent rural population.

Elias [1886: 64f], comparing the taxation system in the Afghan province of Qataghan-Badakhshan with that of the Uzbek, called the former simply 'oppressive and unjust'. The Uzbek system levied half a rupee on every house, which could be raised to two rupees for shops; one of every forty sheep had to be given in tax and the dues on cereal crops were a tenth of the harvest. Beyond these only minor additional dues were levied. The Afghan government, in contrast, now levied 4.33 rupees as house-tax, 10.33 rupees on a pair of oxen, and 10 rupees on every 100 sheep (equal to the price of about 5 sheep – [*Ghobar, 1967: 644*]). Additionally, the dues on agrarian products remained in force and new taxes were levied on these at the time of their sale in the bazaar.

In practice all of this amounted to ratios of taxation that endangered the survival of the producers. In 1836 in the bazaar of Konduz a rupee bought 15–20 kg wheat [*Burnes et al. 1839: 143*]; the harvest of a small peasant family amounted to 2–2500 kg out of which the house-tax took 220–300 kg, another 10–20% went as dues in kind, and additional levies were paid at the mill and from sales in the bazaar. Simultaneously, goods that had to be bought for cash became more expensive because of increased bazaar taxes. While land was not a limited resource, due to the considerable losses of men during the wars of the nineteenth century [*Yate, 1888: 267, 339*], a peasant family of five could not cultivate more than ca. 2-2.5 ha. Had the tax reforms been strictly implemented, many families would have fallen below the subsistence level[1].

There were only two options open for the peasants: to turn to the state and ask for remissions or to take recourse to the traditional client-relationships and request help from the patrons. The latter alternative seemed inevitable, as the state, that is Kabul, was regarded as a perpetual menace to the lives of all inhabitants of the step [*Khafi, 1336/1957: II, 160f*]. It was at this moment that Eshaq Khan entered the picture.

The politics, origins, religious piety and social status of Eshaq Khan characterise him as a typical representative of traditional lordship. Although he was the son of a former Afghan king and close relative of Abdorrahman Khan, he regarded his office as a position from which to pursue a politics independent of Kabul, just as his Uzbek predecessors had always done. Eshaq Khan did not stand out during the first years of his governorship, for he acknowledged the authority of Kabul, had the Friday prayer read for Abdorrahman Khan [*Khafi*

1336/1957: II, 160] and received the usual support of arms and men from the king [Mir Munshi, 1900: I, 262]. In the recruitment of soldiers and militias he stuck to the tribal levies and left local lords in command. He also used the mirs as his middlemen in the administration. His taxation policy centered on accepted practice to provide him with the usual quotas. He did not interfere with the internal affairs of the villages, which were administered by the local clergy or the leading men [Khafi, 1336/1957: II, 165; Kakar, 1971: 143].

The coalition between the Afghan governor and the domestic élite was strengthened by an additional tie: probably during his exile in Samarkand, Eshaq Khan had come under the influence of a Sufi order, the Naqshbandis [Kakar, 1971: 141]. The adherents of this order were known for the strict submission of the disciples (*morid*) to their leaders (*shaykh, pir*). Many regions, including Afghan-Turkestan, were included in the network comprising retainers of leaders of the order. Naqshbandis were active in several rebellions against Abdorrahman Khan [Jäkel, 1977: 27].

All sources agree that the newly appointed Eshaq Khan was extremely pious and that he associated himself closely with the clergy, [Khafi, 1336/1957: II, 160; Elias, 1886: 88ff; Mir Munshi, 1900: I, 263ff]. He insisted on being addressed as *faqir* (common man, with no material aspirations), or *molla* (clergy), instead of governor, and spent most of his days in devoted prayer [Kakar, 1971: 143f]. This conspicuous piety gained additional significance because his residence, Mazar-e Sharif, was an important religious centre with a great mosque.

The orientation of Eshaq Khan towards the clergy, his self-styling as *faqir* and *molla* suggest the position he intended to take vis-à-vis this powerful group. He wanted to be one of them, and to represent their interests. The clergy had no formal hierarchy [Elphinstone, 1839: 1,286]. As owners of land and cattle, they were part of the traditional ruling class. As administrators of justice and middlemen, as supervisors of ethics and representatives of cultural concerns (including guardianship over the mandatory mutual assistance of Moslems), they enjoyed a highly significant place in the informal organisation of society and the mobilisation of followers. Any open attack on their status and privileges was due to provoke vehement resistance. And this precisely was done by Abdorrahman Khan, who regarded the clergy as his arch enemies. He styled them as 'these numberless robbers, thieves, false prophets and trumpery kings', complaining that 'nearly half the revenue of the whole kingdom was given by the Government as allowances' to them [Mir Munshi, 1900: I, 218, 252]. In order to confront these groups 'all the land and property, as well as money, which used to support the Mullahs, is transferred to the government treasury' [ibid. II, 205]. Thus, clergy were as seriously hit by tax reform as secular lords and their clientèle, and they feared for their privileges and power.

Eshaq Khan resisted the orders of the king and left the property of the clergy untouched. This provoked the open hostility of Abdorrahman Khan, who now condemned him as a 'false prophet' in these words:

> All this time Ishak was collecting gold and guns, making secret preparations, and intriguing against me. He posed before the people of Turkestan as a holy saint and a very virtuous strict Mahomedan. . . . The second deceit that Ishak practiced upon the uneducated Mahomedans was that in addition to being an ecclesiastical leader and mullah, he entered into the group of the disciples of one of the Dervishes of the Nakhshbandis. . . . As the Turkomans are specially devoted to this sect, Ishak Khan joined them to curry favour with the Turkomans who were under his governorship. The false Pirs of Mazar-i Sherif told Ishak that . . . Nakhshband had bestowed the throne of Kabul upon him. Ishak believed this, and publicly proclaimed himself Amir of Afghanistan [Mir Munshi, 1900: I, 263–5].

The refusal of Eshaq Khan to confiscate religious endowments for the crown gave rather undramatic events a sudden turn. The king ordered the governor to present himself at court in Kabul. Eshaq's followers feared, hardly unfounded, that he would never return from there [Khafi, 1336/1957: II, 168]. At this point a decision for the uprising was made, and the subsequent mobilisation proved that almost all strata of the population were ready to rise against Abdorrahman Khan. According to social hierarchy, first the 'great men at court, the decisive office holders, the army officers, the district governors and the whitebeards agreed to fight' [ibid.]. Soon thereafter Eshaq Khan was crowned rival king which gave the movement its traditional legitimation. At this time something novel was introduced. In order to assure the support of everyone, the gathering of the leading men decided that all members of the retinues must personally swear an oath of loyalty to the cause. It may have been modelled on the procedures of the Sufi order. It was an unusual step to mobilise every retainer individually. The chronicler of the movement described the events as follows:

> All officers of the army and of the militias swore their oaths in the town of Shadian and committed themselves to a contract. Then the officers were charged to mobilise all the common people in the army against the officer Mohammad Hoseyn Khan (who had been absolutely unbearable), and also have them swear and sign the proclamation. They should appeal to the men in their own words and miss no measures against the life, limb and property of that man. The great men of the land were also charged to move their common men to swear and join the compact so that within fifteen days all soldiers and common men take the oath on the agreement. How the masses were won for this agreement, and how this plan was indeed carried out! It is told that not a single beggar on the corner or in the bazaar was spared unless he joined the alliance and swore on the holy Qoran. . . . If anyone was seen to hesitate or take too much time, a cry was immediately raised that he be killed or robbed, and so he hastened to swear the oath under duress [Khafi, ibid. 170].

This novel attempt at mass mobilisation overriding traditional retainer and loyalty systems proved only partially successful. Holy War was declared against King Abdorrahman Khan. Eshaq Khan's army began its march on Kabul. In Maimaneh, the Afghan general declared himself for Eshaq, only to be arrested by his garrison officers cooperating with local Uzbek potentates. The same happened in Andkhoi and Daulatabad. In each centre the Uzbek leaders came out against Eshaq Khan [*Kakar, 1971: 149*]. However, when Eshaq Khan's troops reached the centre of Qataghan-Badakhshan, Khanabad, the local garrison joined them, enabling former lords of the neighbouring Badakhshan and Qataghan, who had served as sub-governors there, to support the rebellion. These two provinces fell into the hands of Eshaq Khan [*Khafi, 1336/1957: II, 173–6*], but as soon as the first rumours of the approach of the Kabul army reached the rebels, the new followers quickly changed sides.

The decisive battle was fought on 27 September 1888 near Ghaznigak, south of Tashqorghan. Although the chances for a rebel victory were initially good, false information led Eshaq to decide to flee. The abandoned army was soon defeated. Abdorrahman Khan had no qualms in finally taking away all power from the local upper classes and demanding considerable reparations from the region. In the following two years some thousand people were executed [*Kakar, 1971: 155*].

Conclusions

Eshaq Khan returned to exile and a new governor came to Afghan-Turkestan to implement Abdorrahman Khan's reforms. His attempts at enforcing the new tax system in fact led to the ruin of hundreds of peasant families, many of whom fled to Bokhara or to Russian Turkestan [*Kakar, 1980: 87*]. The upper classes, having recovered from the bloody reprisals of the new government, gradually realigned themselves and their clientèles. The central authorities, always short of manpower to build up an efficient local administration, thereby were still forced to cooperate with the upper classes of the region. Although they were definitively eliminated from regional positions of political decision making, their hold on the villages became correspondingly stronger. From this base they were able to sabbotage the reforms of the centralised state, as its administration depended on them as local middle-men. The state needed their knowledge and assistance in collecting taxes and recruiting soldiers. Having changed their base to the village, they were also forced to build up a clientèle on the village level.

The reconstruction of the patron–client relationships was forced into new channels. Bereft of their political-military power, the lords had to build a system based on economic coercion. They did so through rental tenancy arrangements; investments in the bazaar; and mechanisms of debt, manipulated through the rental system and bazaar interests. A good part of that surplus which the state intended to appropriate thus remained in the hands of the village upper strata. They were able to use this in an intra-village redistribution for the establishment and maintenance of a new system of clientèle, which has secured their power, up to our very times. This dynamic development was indeed an unforeseen result of a social movement the intial aim of which was to preserve the old conditions.

The movement of Eshaq Khan certainly cannot be described as a peasant movement in the strict sense of the term. Rather, it should be viewed as an uprising of a traditional rural collective and a rural region against that arch enemy, the centralised state. Attempts to establish an efficient state machinery with a standing army and a necessary tax-base meant confrontation of the bureaucratic centre with traditional upper classes, including the clergy. The knock-on effect of all this made the life of the lower classes unbearable. Under these conditions a religious appeal was able to mobilise those forces transcending class lines that were ready to fight the central authority. Yet it was not essentially a chiliastic appeal, nor a promise for a society without oppression and exploitation, as were the tradition in neighbouring Shi'ite Iran. Religious ideas were not the prime movers, but factors that triggered the conflict, spreading it ideologically and thus allowing for the mobilisation of wider groups of people. They served as an important enforcement to primordial loyalties that for many centuries guaranteed the survival of peasant populations and that were now threatened by the intervention of the modern state.

The revolt of Eshaq Khan was therefore very typical for Afghanistan. Not a peasantry 'as a class', but rather a hierarchical rural collective in its entirety resisted the threat to its existential base in a 'country' versus 'court' pattern. This set-up did not change to our days, until the recent Soviet intervention. But continuity did not imply stagnation. These collectives were forced by the context of the modern world with its colonialisms, capitalisms and imperialisms, to change their structures and remain flexibly operative. They indeed adapted the 'traditional', 'feudal' rural social system, together with its religious milieu, to the internal as well as external fight against imperialism enshrined in the overbearing power of a centralised state.

Note

1. For comparisons see the study on Iran [*Research Group, 1968: 129, 145*]: A five-person-household needs annually ca. 1900 kg wheat for bare subsistence. If we assume that such a family in Afghan-Turkestan cultivated 2–3 ha land and brought in a harvest of 2250 kg wheat, it had to render dues, in the best case, of at least 225 kg, state taxes would have amounted to another 260 kg and other taxes and dues, of ca. 5%, 115 kg more. Only 1650 kg would have remained for consumption, i.e. 87% of the minimum necessary for subsistence.

Religion and rural revolt

References

Burnes, A., et al., 1839, *Reports and Papers, Political, Geographical and Commercial, submitted to Government*, Calcutta.
Dupree, Louis, 1973, *Afghanistan*, Princeton.
Elias, N., 1886, *Report of a Mission to Chinese Turkestan and Badakhshan in 1885–1886*, Calcutta (in: Political and Secret Department Library, India Office Library, London, L/P+S/20).
Elphinstone, Mountstuart, 1839 (3rd ed.), *An Account of the Kingdom of Caubul*, London.
Ferrier, J. P., 1857, *Caravan Journeys and Wanderings in Persia, Afghanistan, Turkistan, and Beloochistan*, London.
Ghobar, Mir Gholam Mohammad, 1346/1967, *Afghanestan dar masir-e tarikh* [Afghanistan in the course of history], Kabul.
Grevemeyer, Jan-Heeren, 1980, 'Afghanistan: Das 'neue Modell einer Revolution' und der dörfliche Widerstand', K. Greussing and J.-H. Grevemeyer, eds., *Revolution in Iran und Afghanistan*, 140–176, Frankfurt.
Grevemeyer, Jan-Heeren, 1981, 'Im Windschatten des Widerstands – Zentralstaatsbildung und koloniale Intervention in Afghanistan' in J.-H. Grevemeyer, ed., *Traditionale Gesellschaften und europäischer Kolonialismus*, 82–104, Frankfurt.
Jäkel, Klaus, 1977, 'Reform und Reaktion in Afghanistan: Notizen zu Aufstieg und Fall Amanullahs', *mardom nameh – Hefte zur Geschichte und Gesellschaft des Mittleren Orients*, No. 3, 24–57.
Kakar, M. Hassan, 1971, *Afghanistan. A Study in International Political Developments 1880–1896*, Kabul.
Kakar, Hasan Kawun, 1980, *Government and Society in Afghanistan: The Reign of Amir 'Abd al-Rahman Khan*, Austin/London.
Kateb, Faiz Mohammad, 1331–1333/1952–1954, *Saraj at-tavarikh* [The lamp of history], 3 vols., Kabul.
Khafi, Mirza Yaqub Ali, 1336/1957, *Padeshahan-e motakher-e Afghanestan* (Recent kings of Afghanistan), 2 vols., Kabul.
Khalfin, N. A., 1958, 'The Rising of Ishaq Khan in Southern Turkestan (1888)', *Central Asian Review*, VI, No. 3: 253–263a.
Khan, Munawwar, (1963), *Anglo-Afghan Relations 1798–1878*, Peshawar.
Mir Munshi Sultan Mahomed Khan, ed., 1900, *The Life of Abdur Rahman, Amir of Afghanistan*, 2 vols., London.
Research Group, 1968, 'Nutrition in Iran', *tahqiqat-e eqtesadi*, V, No. 13–14: 125–148 (Tehran).
Tabibi, Latif, 1981, *Die afghanische Landreform von 1979: Ihre Vorgeschichte und Konsequenzen*, Ph.D. Dissertation, FU Berlin.
Vambery, Arminius, 1970, *Travels in Central Asia*, New York.
Wheeler, J. T., 1869, *Memorandum on Afghan-Turkestan*, Calcutta.
Yate, C. E., 1888, *Northern Afghanistan or Letters from the Afghan Boundary Commission*, Edinburgh/London.

*Popular Islam, Kurdish nationalism
and rural revolt:
the rebellion of Shaikh Said in Turkey (1925)* *

MARTIN VAN BRUINESSEN

In February and March 1925 the young Republic of Turkey was shaken by a revolt of Kurdish peasants that rapidly spread over a vast part of its Eastern provinces [*Bruinessen, 1978; cf. Firat, 1970; Cemal, 1955; Toker, 1968; Olson & Tucker, 1978*]. Bands of primitively armed peasants, led by religious and tribal chiefs, invaded one by one the towns, establishing their own rudimentary administration and chasing away all military and civilian officials that remained loyal to the central government. The rebels' movements were coordinated by a popular leader of a dervish order, Shaikh Said, while other shaikhs of the same order similarly took leading positions in the revolt. The ostensible aim of the revolt was to halt the secularising reforms initiated by the Turkish government. Afterwards, however, the leaders were accused of having attempted to establish an independent Kurdish state. It cost the government over two months' time and the deployment of the air force beside 35,000 land troops to put down the revolt with much bloodshed. In the process, much of Turkey's tenuous democracy was sacrificed as well.

The revolt provided occasion for the assumption of dictatorial powers by Mustafa Kamal (Ataturk) and Ismet (Inönü). The relatively liberal government of Fethi Bay (Okyar) was forced to step down through a coup within the ruling party, and the severe Ismet, who was strongly disliked by the 'liberal' and conservative opposition, returned as Prime Minister. Two weeks after news of the revolt had reached Ankara he presented his new cabinet. The next day he had the Turkish National Assembly pass a law on the re-establishment of order, which gave the government virtually unlimited powers. Special tribunals, established under this law, were to try and condemn to death leaders of the Kurdish revolt, and consecutively many other political opponents as well. Due to the

---

* The interviews on which this article is partially based, and a perusal of the relevant material in the Public Records Office in London were part of a wider research project sponsored by the Netherlands Organisation for the Advancement of Pure Research (ZWO).

government's dictatorial powers, kemalist reforms could be carried through with increasing speed and ever less regard for the opposition. One of these reform measures, directly connected with the revolt, was the suppression of all dervish orders — those repositories of popular Islam. Another consequence was the government's subsequent policy of forced assimilation of the Kurds and of denial of cultural rights to them.

The latter policy, although pursued for several decades, has failed to achieve its apparent objective of extirpating Kurdish separatism. During the 1970s an increasingly militant Kurdish nationalism found a seemingly broad popular base both in the towns and in the villages of Eastern Turkey. Although many of today's Kurdish nationalists brand Shaikh Said's rebellion as reactionary, its memory is kept alive, and many others speak about it with obvious pride. Several Kurdish journals devoted lengthy articles to it. The rebellion has grown into a symbol for both Kurdish nationalists and their opponents.

Background

The most obvious reason for the revolt was the programme of secularisation that the republican government had inaugurated. Abolition of the sultanate in 1923 was followed a year later by that of the caliphate, which created much resentment in more conservative circles at home and abroad. Especially among the Kurds, the caliphate had been held in high esteem. When, at the outset of the First World War, the Sultan in his capacity of Caliph or supreme leader of all orthodox muslims proclaimed a *cihad* (holy war), most Kurds rallied to the call. The large sums that had been spent by Russians in an attempt to buy some Kurdish chiefs' loyalties were of no avail, nor could emotional appeals by Kurdish nationalists compete against the Caliph's word. To many, the caliphate was the very embodiment of Islam, and its abolition seemed a blow dealt to Islam itself. The first educational reforms similarly seemed to strike at religion, since the traditional centres of religious training (*medreses*) were abolished and replaced with modern, Western-type schools. Immediately prior to the revolt Shaikh Said held several sermons in which he vehemently condemned these measures. Later, during his trial, the shaikh gave the following summary of one of these speeches, held at Piran, where the revolt broke out prematurely:

> The *medreses* have been closed down. The Ministry of Religion and Pious Foundations has been abolished. In the newspapers a horde of irreligious writers wantonly insult religion and besmirch the name of our Lord the Prophet. I shall this very day, if only I can, start struggling and become one of those who contribute to the saving of religion [*Cemal, 1955:24; Toker, 1968:38*].

Once the revolt had broken out, he continued to use these arguments to recruit more support. Resistance against the kemalists' secularist programme was thus one important aspect of the rebellion. Yet, the first preparations for revolt had been made by a clandestine organisation of educated Kurds, whose aims were not religious at all but purely nationalist. They had approached Said and the other shaikhs because the latter had the necessary influence that these nationalists still lacked. Before going more deeply into their role, a few words should be said about the actual participants of the revolt, and the reasons why the shaikhs wielded so much influence among them.

Socio-economic conditions of the rebellious area

The central area of the revolt — the area where it started and which provided most of the peasants recruits — was the mountainous region to the north of Diyarbakir (see map no. 4). Sporadic outbursts of violence occurred further afield, and people also came from outside to join the revolt. Yet only in this area was participation massive. Most of the Kurds living in this area speak *Zaza*, an archaic Iranian language rather different from Kurdish proper or *Kurmanci*. Some of the Zaza-speaking tribes, notably those of the Dersim district, belong to the heterodox *Alevi* sect, others are orthodox Sunni muslims. It was only the latter who participated in the revolt.

The economy of the Zaza villages was, and to a large extent still is, a closed one. Virtually every villager owned a small plot of land and some animals, only allowing a frugal existence. What he did not produce himself he tended to acquire by barter rather than sale. The exception was tobacco, grown in some of the villages and sold, at low prices, to the state monopoly. Due to the scarcity of land, young Zazas regularly left their villages for the regional towns or one of the big cities. Diyarbakir, Elazig and Istanbul had significant numbers of immigrants from these villages, which was to prove an important factor during the revolt. Most Zazas were sedentary cultivators, without a recent nomadic history; their villages had a strong tribal organisation. Each of their small tribes comprised one or a few villages only, led by a chief only marginally richer than the commoners. Decisions on matters concerning the whole tribe, such as defence of tribal territory, feuds, and also the present revolt, were made after deliberations in a council consisting of the chief (*aga*), the most important elders or greybeards (*ri spi*), and the village headmen (*muhtar*). Commoners of the tribe usually complied without questioning these decisions.

The northernmost part of the rebellious area, with its higher mountains and richer pastures, was inhabited by the large, Kurmanci-speaking Cibran tribe. Like its neighbours, the Hasanan and Haydaran, sections of which were also to join the revolt, this tribe had previously been nomadic, but by 1925 it was largely settled. Commoners combined simple agriculture with moderate shepherding, but

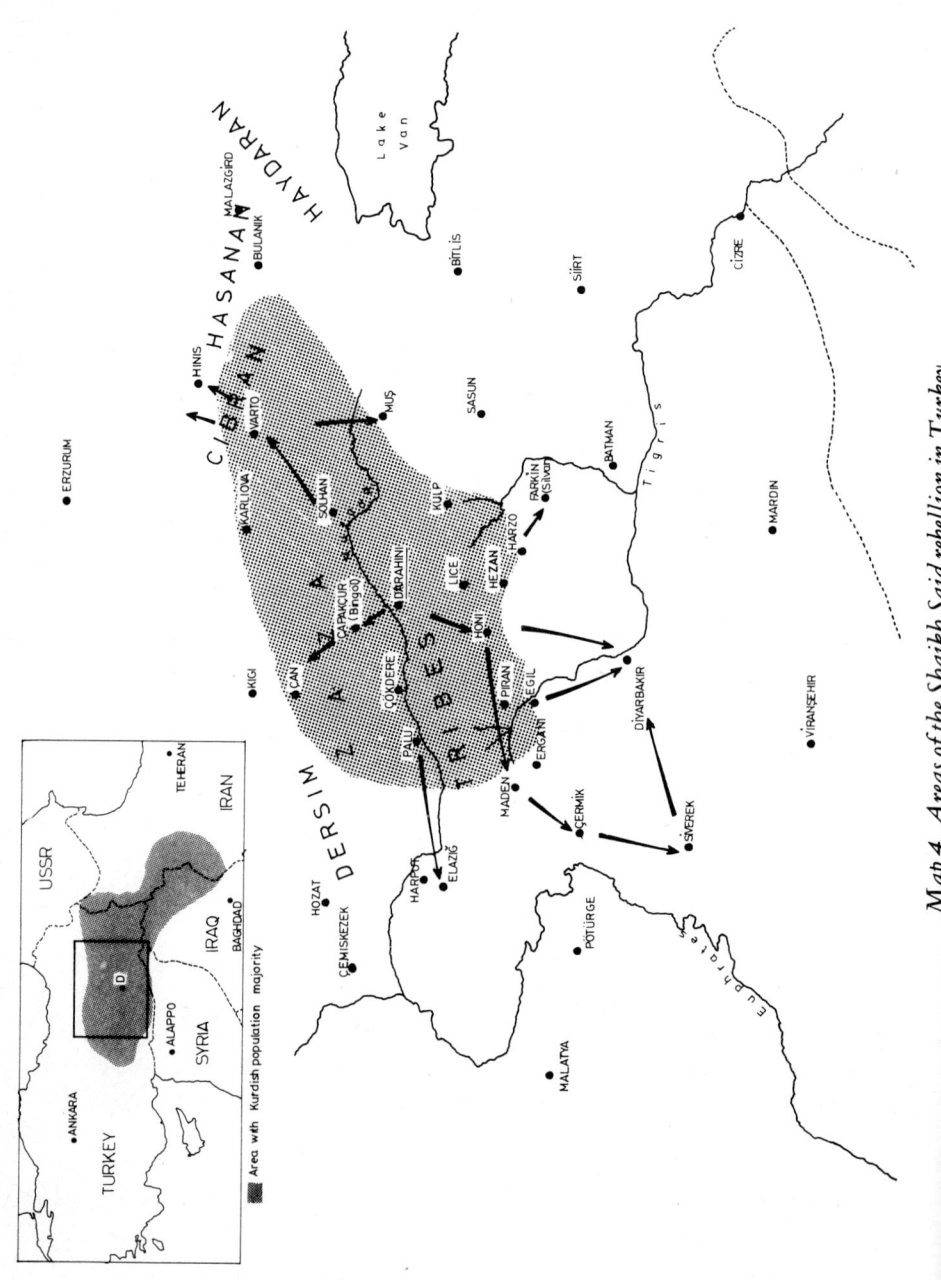

Map 4. Areas of the Shaikh Said rebellion in Turkey

leading families with branches living in, and ruling over Karliova, Varto and Bulanik, owned large flocks. So did Shaikh Said, who had not been born into any of these tribes, but who had married into the leading family of the Cibran. He had moved to Hinis from his native Palu in order to accommodate his flocks on better pasture, and to extend his spiritual and political influence among Kurmanci speakers as well. The Shaikh and his sons were involved in the wholesale trade of live animals, which brought the latter frequently to big cities like Istanbul and Aleppo. Apart from this, there seems not to have been much trade in the area. The small towns were administrative rather than commercial centres.

Most villagers in the mountains were independent subsistence farmers, in contrast with those of the fertile plains around Diyarbakir and Farkin (Silvan). In the latter wheat-growing districts, large holdings predominated, and most villagers were poverty-stricken sharecroppers or tenants, lacking tribal organisation and dependent on the absentee landlords. Such villagers do not seem to have taken an active part in the revolt.

The shaikhs

The top leaders of the rebellion were not tribal chiefs but *shaikhs*, religious leaders. These are the heads of sufi or dervish orders, in this particular case the *Naksibendi* order, very popular in Kurdistan [*Cf. Algar, 1976; Hourani, 1972; Bruinessen, 1978*]. It was the dervish orders rather than the official religion of the mosque that satisfied the villagers' emotional and devotional religious needs. However, unlike many other situations there was not a clear-cut distinction here between official and popular religion. Each supplemented the other, they were not seen as rival traditions but as parts of the same complex. More than the other orders, the Naksibendi order stimulated mosque attendance and strict performance of religious duties. The mosque personnel on the other hand showed great respect to most Naksibendi shaikhs. Nevertheless, a whole complex of unorthodox religious beliefs and devotional practices had accumulated around this otherwise perfectly orthodox order. To many of their followers, the shaikhs were not simply pious mystics but miracle-working saints whose hand-written amulets warded off danger and evil influences, and whose spittle was an unfailing medicine. By supernatural means they would help those of their followers who were in trouble. Some even claimed that on the Day of Judgment they would take their followers across the bridge into the abode of eternal bliss.

In many parts of Kurdistan it was thought essential for a believer to be attached at least nominally to a shaikh. From elderly people one may still hear the saying there that 'if you don't have a shaikh, the devil will act as yours'. 'Having a shaikh', however, meant different things to different people. The majority of any shaikh's followers were only nominally his disciples. They visited him once or twice a year to kiss his hand, bring him presents and receive his blessings, sometimes after having done repentance. Furthermore they would go to the shaikh for such diverse problems as disease, a wife's barrenness, a family quarrel or a feud, questions of doctrine, the request of a talisman or wise counsel on matters private or public. The greater a shaikh's reputation for saintliness and miraculous powers, or the more cleverly he solved people's conflicts and other problems, the larger the flock of his followers became. Great shaikhs made annual tours to give their followers wide opportunity to listen to their sermons, and to collect small and large gifts.

Stricter followers participated in weekly or more frequent meditation sessions led by the shaikh or a deputy (*halife*). Each order has its own distinctive spiritual exercises, which should induce in a practising disciple ecstatic states leading to direct experience of the Divine. Such exercises are usually practised communally. The shaikh's physical or spiritual presence is essential for the success of such exercises, especially in the Naksibendi order, since it is through the shaikh's mediation that relations with the Divine are established. Thus a shaikh's practising disciples develop extremely strong ties of loyalty to him. They are his staunchest supporters and propagandists, broadcasting his spiritual achievements. A shaikh rarely has more than a hundred at most of these disciples. Unlike the other orders, which are generally associated with the traditional urban middle classes, many Naksibendi disciples in Kurdistan are villagers, often poor ones. Two special types of followers are the usually elderly men who have given up worldly life for one of spiritual discipline in the shaikh's immediate surroundings and, more important in the present context, the shaikh's retainers. The latter are armed men acting as his bodyguards, or in some cases as his law-enforcers. Their presence has to do with the political and economic roles shaikhs have come to play in many parts of Kurdistan.

In most cases, shaikhs do not live in the area of their birth, and so they tend not to belong to any local tribe. This, combined with their presumed saintliness, makes them ideal intermediaries in tribal conflicts. This gives an enterprising shaikh considerable political influence and wealth. The most powerful shaikhs often live in areas lacking big tribal chiefs strong enough to resolve conflicts, such as in the Zaza districts with which we are concerned, where there were frequent rivalries and feuds between many petty chiefs. Shaikh Said of Palu, Shaikh Serif of Gökdere, and a number of other shaikhs, had succeeded each in becoming more powerful than any of the local Zaza tribal chiefs. These shaikhs were anything but introverted, other-worldly figures as some Naksibendi shaikhs elsewhere were. Equally at ease in the saddle as on the prayer mat, they handled guns as expertly as rosaries. Their reputation for saintliness was matched by that for physical prowess. One of them, Shaikh Serif, had been the commander of an irregular regiment of Zaza Kurds during the First World War. Not all tribes accepted shaikh authority. Around our area a number of tribes subscribe to heterodox Shi'i (Alevi) beliefs. Alevis and Sunnis (the Naksibendis are especially staunch Sunni muslims) are contemptuous of each other's religious beliefs and practices, and this ideological factor has tended to make conflict between Sunni and Alevi tribes quite bitter. In the Sunni Ottoman Empire the state and the Sunni tribes readily cooperated to impose political oppression on the Alevis. Understandably, their reaction to Mustafa Kemal's attempt at secularisation was generally positive. Several local Alevi tribes were to turn against Shaikh Said's rebellion and actively fight it, or rather, fight their traditional enemies, whose joining the rebellion provided a welcome pretext.

The nationalists

The rebellion which was actually led by Shaikh Said, was not originally his idea but rather that of the clandestine Kurdish nationalist organisation, Azadi (Freedom), which wanted to set up an independent state of Kurdistan. Although Azadi was not the first Kurdish nationalist organisation [cf. *Jwaideh, 1960; Silopi, 1969; Bruinessen, 1978*], it was better organized than its precursors. Its members were mostly military officers with tribal backgrounds, instead of urbanised aristocrats completely alienated from village life as had been their predecessors. Their nationalism had been awakened as a reaction to the Turkish nationalism that was rampant within the army, and by anxieties that the Kurds were in for a similar fate to that of the Armenians. The possibility of an independent Kurdish state, as well as an Armenian one, had been written into the Treaty of Sèvres of 1920, and it had led to some half-hearted British attempts to create a small Kurdish buffer state between Arab Iraq and Turkey. Despite their nationalist fervour, Azadi's members were well aware that they did not as yet have the support of the Kurdish masses, and that they lacked the power and appeal necessary to enlist mass support. They therefore approached influential traditional leaders in various parts of Kurdistan. Shaikh Said was invited by his in-law, Halid Bey, of the Cibran's ruling family, an army colonel who was one of Azadi's chief ideologues. The Shaikh responded enthusiastically and took a leading part in the planning, which got under way in 1924. May 1925 was originally set as the date for a major uprising which would encompass most or all of Turkey's Kurdish provinces. Operations were to be coordinated by Azadi officers, since they had military experience. Local leadership was to be provided by shaikhs and tribal chiefs. Yet the actual rebellion did not follow this pattern. Due to unforeseen circumstances, misunderstandings and a number of mistakes, the Turkish authorities' suspicion was aroused. By the end of 1924, most of Azadi's top leadership had been arrested and only a few succeeded in escaping to Iraq, where they were interrogated by British intelligence officers. Their grievances against the Turkish government show an acute awareness of discrimination, and a motivation that was nationalist, not religious in nature.[1]

The revolt (see map 4)

With Azadi's more important leaders now either in prison or exile, plans had to be revised. In December or January, a meeting took place between Azadi members and shaikhs and tribal chieftains, mainly from the Zaza district. It was decided to press on with the rebellion and the date was even brought forward to March. In January Shaikh Said started his annual tour of Zaza districts, doing his best to settle any conflicts that might disrupt the unity of the revolt, and discussing strategic questions with local chieftains. His inflammatory speeches inspired villagers with hatred against the Republican government [cf. *Cemal, 1955: 24; Toker, 1968: 38*]. On this tour the Shaikh was accompanied by an unusually large retinue which included many armed men. While he was staying in Piran, the village where his brother Abdurrahim lived, a minor incident prematurely triggered the revolt on February 13, 1925 [*ibid.*]. The Turkish gendarmerie at Piran village recognised from among the shaikh's retinue several fugitives from justice, some of whom were wanted for alleged murder. In an attempt to arrest these fugitives an exchange of fire occurred between the shaikh's men and the gendarmes, in which at least one policeman was killed. Since the preparations for the revolt were not yet completed the Shaikh did his utmost to hush up the whole affair, but in this attempt he was unsuccessful. The news spread rapidly, and in the nearby town of Hani the population expelled its governor and all Turkish officials. Near Lice a mail van was held up. Since the government had now been alerted, the general rising had to be brought forward. The Shaikh moved swiftly to Darahini, a small and rather inaccessible provincial capital, collecting on the way several hundred tribesmen. Darahini was easily taken and since most of its gendarmerie was Kurdish, they willingly joined the Shaikh. The town was turned into the rebels' provisional capital. Shaikh Said appointed his own governor, a *mufti* (expert of islamic law), and a gendarmerie commander. Lower officials simply continued their work under a new administration.

From Darahini Shaikh Said dispatched armed followers in all directions in order to take control of the region's administrative centres. Most of these irregular units were led by shaikhs. Capakcur was taken by the shaikhs of Can, who then marched on towards Kigi. Shaikh Abdullah, from the Solhan district, was dispatched to Varto and the area to the North of Mus. Shaikh Serif, the former militia commander, joined in the conquest of Capakcur, followed this up with the taking of Palu and then advanced to the important town of Elazig, receiving reinforcements at every village he passed. With a large body of followers Shaikh Said himself moved south from Darahini.

Meanwhile, an infantry and a cavalry regiment had been sent against the rebels from the region's major city, Diyarbakir. The Turkish infantry regiment was mauled by local peasants under Shaikh Mehmed Mehdi from the village of Serdi, near Hani, and a few days later routed by Shaikh Said's own forces. Its cannons were useful additions to the rebels' light and mostly old-fashioned arms. The Turkish cavalry force was ambushed and it surrendered to the Kurds on February 28, 1925. At that moment the entire Zaza area, from Ergani to Kulp was in open rebellion. The towns of Ergani, Hani and Lice had been taken by villagers from their local surroundings, although some urbanites had offered resistance. Self-confidently, Shaikh Said now concentrated his forces on the largest urban centre, Diyarbakir, whilst his brother. Abdurrahim, with a part of the Zaza forces, struck out to the west and took Maden, Cermik and Siverek. Shaikh Said toured the districts around Egil to solicit the support of the local chieftains. He sent messengers to major chieftains in other parts of Kurdistan such as to the strong Milan tribe around Viransehir and to the tribes around Bitlis, all of which had participated in Azadi's original plan. There was no response.

At the beginning of March, Diyarbakir was besieged by a large force of some 10,000 rebels, who were continually reinforced. Shaikh Said himself coordinated operations from a nearby village. With its numerous garrison, led by the able Mürsel Pasa, and with its solid walls, the city was virtually impregnable. Mürsel Pasa had taken care to disarm all civilians. During the siege he imposed a total curfew, reducing the risk of any civilian collaboration with the rebels. After a siege of several days with fruitless attempts by the rebels to storm the city, a small band did succeed in entering by night, apparently due to support from Zaza Kurdish inhabitants in the city. Their presence was discovered and in a bloody fight the garrison wiped them out, letting only a few escape (March 7–8). After this failure, Shaikh Said withdrew his men from the city walls and gave them a few days leave.

On the other fronts a number of successes were scored. Shaikh Serif took Elazig and scattered its garrison. In the northeast, Varto was captured and Hinis was raided several times. Although many Cibran and Hasanan joined the rebel forces, they were fiercely opposed by their traditional enemies, the Alevi Hormek and Lolan tribes. Plans to take Mus and Bitlis were wrecked by local tribes reluctant to join the rebels. The inhabitants of Farkin (Silvan) kept aloof until March 25, when the town was stormed by Zaza Kurds under the leadership of Shaikh Semsettin. It was lost to government troops within a few days. The original momentum of the revolt had been dissipated. Confident, open defiance now gave way to hasty preparations for defence against an imminent Turkish government counter-offensive.

The capture and loss of Elazig

Existing records say very little about motivation and behaviour of the rebel peasants who really made the uprising. Survivors embroidered the facts far too frequently, centring on their leaders too exclusively for any effective understanding of the rebellion as a whole. This makes the few eye-witness reports on the capture of the major regional town of Elazig by the rebels particularly important in showing how different sections of the population reacted [*PRO, FO 371, 1925: E 2359/362/65; Cemal, 1955: 32–4*]. Middle-class notables, such as officials, traders, lawyers, major craftsmen, and lower public servants, were mainly Turks, whereas menial jobs were mostly done by more recent immigrants from surrounding Kurdish villages.

Soon after the rebels had taken Darahini and Capakcur, rumours started reaching Elazig that several hundred Kurdish peasants were coming to reinforce the rebels in the city. A frantic band they were, wielding green flags and Korans, shouting unremittingly 'God bless the Prophet' and calling out to all in their way that they should surrender in the name of God. The town of Palu did surrender and with untiring fervour the rebel band went on to Elazig, asking everyone to join them. When the first three hundred Kurdish rebels appeared before the army lines outside Elazig, they presented a frightening spectacle. Soldiers rather took to flight than shoot at rebels who had tied Korans to their bayonets. The Kurds were welcomed by most of the city population, and they ransacked the gendarmerie station and court-house, storming the prison and burning the files. The released prisoners showed the Kurds the houses of the officers and the rich, 'so that the first could be made prisoner and the second looted'. The Kurdish porters and woodcutters of the city willingly joined in. Later that day, the rebel commander at this front, Shaikh Serif, entered the city and promised to re-establish order. He ordered the execution of looters, but the threat remained without effect. The next day looting was concentrated more purposefully upon the military depot and the tobacco monopoly. Many civilians did not resist the looting, for they regarded the rebels as an Islamic army. Hundreds of peasants from the surrounding countryside came to the city to congratulate the rebels, and some of them accompanied the main rebel army on its way towards Malatya. But Shaikh Serif did little to consolidate the rebel hold, merely assigning administrative responsibilities to the *mufti* (official expert of islamic law) and leaving a small garrison behind. When these continued looting, notables organised resistance groups to expel them. After Elazig, Shaikh Serif's rebels ran out of success [*Toker, 1968: 87*]. Apparently Malatya was never reached.

Suppression of the revolt

The government quietly prepared its counter-offensive, dispatching perhaps as many as 35,000 troops to the area. Kurdish chiefs from other areas were urged to show loyalty to the Republic by providing men to fight against their fellow Kurdish rebels. Some chiefs complied, although they do not seem to have fought Shaikh Said's men. Late in March the Turkish army started a three-pronged attack on the rebel area, receiving valuable assistance from the air force. Bombardments created great panic among the Kurds, most of whom had never seen aeroplanes before. In a matter of days the towns of Hani, Silvan, Palu, Piran and Lice were taken and the rebels were forced to flee to the less accessible, mountainous districts of Capakcut and Genc (Darahini). In spite of the late winter snow the army followed them here and in a few violent open battles destroyed the Kurdish forces. The remaining rebels split into small guerrilla units, continuing operations for years. Shaikh Said was arrested a few days later near Mus, apparently betrayed by a former ally who tried to save his own skin. After a short trial, Shaikh Said and forty-seven other leaders of the revolt, at least seven of whom were shaikhs, were condemned to death and executed on 4 September 1925. A law was then passed suppressing all dervish orders, their convents and shrines [*Albayrak, 1973: 186–206*].

Nationalist versus religious character of the rebellion

At the trial the Turkish authorities insisted that the rebellion was nationalist in inspiration, and that its leaders intended to establish an independent Kurdish state. The same claim was made by Kurdish nationalists of that time [e.g. *Chirguh, 1930*]. Shaikh Said's relations with Azadi as well as other, more conservative nationalists are beyond doubt. My chief oral informant, who was close to the Shaikh during the rebellion, claims that for the Shaikh himself, religious motivations were clearly secondary to nationalist ones. In fact, one of the Shaikh's closest aides, Fehmi Bilal Effendi, was a blaspheming atheist, tolerated only because of his courage and devoted nationalism. Neither the other leading shaikhs nor the common villagers seemed to have such clear and strong national feelings.

Shaikh Said used mainly religious arguments for village propaganda purposes – to the effect that 'Islam is under attack and has to be defended'. Rebel symbols were of a religious character – green flags and Korans, Islamic battle-cries, and holy war or *cihad*-terminology. There was a millenarian flavour to the rebellion, although no overt reference seems to have been made to messianic ideas. The rebels' behaviour strongly suggests that by merely marching on the cities they expected to bring about a restoration of Islam and establishment of a reign of justice. Among the long list of Kurdish nationalists' grievances only a few meant anything to the peasants – notably abolition of the Caliphate. The grievances mainly reflected the concerns of educated Kurds, and to some extent the interests of the traditional ruling stratum. Ideas of self-rule were very recent even among tribal chiefs. During the First World War, young Kurdish intellectuals making nationalist propaganda had still found the chiefs opposed to their appeals. Loyalty to the Ottoman sultan in his capacity of caliph was still paramount [*Silopi, 1969: 38–9*]. The victorious Allied powers seemed to be less opposed to the idea of a Kurdish state, which had alerted many chiefs to the possibilities of such a project. Yet Allied support never materialized, and Mustafa Kemal succeeded in gaining the loyalty of many of the bigger chiefs by offering them positions in the Turkish National Assembly. Real discontent showed itself especially among the smaller chiefs, who were left outside the political system. Many of these were receptive to Azadi propaganda. Since the peasants were more receptive to religious Islamic than to nationalist Kurdish agitation, Azadi sought to keep to the background as a planning and coordinating body, leaving the tasks of direct mobilization and field command to local chiefs and shaikhs. When Azadi broke up, only one supra-tribal organization remained that could possibly take over this coordinating role – the network of Naksibendi shaikhs. Moreover, among the influential leaders originally approached by Azadi, only Shaikh Said was determined to go on with the revolt. Shaikh Said in turn found no one except the smaller shaikhs and chiefs of his own local area ready to join him.

The political role traditionally played by these shaikhs assured them a prominent say in whether or not to join the rebellion. In the Mus district, where tribal chieftains were stronger than in the Zaza districts, the major shaikh was primarily a spiritual rather than political authority, who refused to join. So did the tribal chiefs of Mus as well as those of Dersim, several of whom had been in direct communication with Azadi. Toker [*1968: 83*] ascribes this to the fact that these chiefs were more nationalist-minded, and disliked the strongly religious character that the revolt acquired under the shaikhs' leadership. The Dersim tribes, being Alevi, had little reason indeed to join this staunchly Sunni movement that might easily be directed against themselves as well, despite Shaikh Said's letter of invitation to the Alevi Hormek tribe to join him in rebellion [*Firat, 1970: 200*]. These tribes were later to rebel on their own account.

Since the legitimation of the shaikhs' authority was primarily religious, the shaikhs' agitation naturally concentrated on the apparent threat to Islam and on the religious obligation to defend it. They had good reason to do so: even if the kemalist reforms did not endanger all of Islam, the threat to the shaikhs' positions was very real indeed. Kurdish villagers, who identified strongly with Islam and among whom the shaikhs' words carried enormous weight, were easily carried away, especially when the shaikhs used words associated with holy war (*cihad*). Thus, Shaikh Said styled himself *emir el-mücahidin* and declared that every rebel who was killed would be a martyr (*sehid*) and go straight to paradise.

Nevertheless, religious fervour was not the sole force that moved the rebel peasants. In Elazig and other towns courthouses were ransacked, gendarmerie posts raided, prisoners set free and the tobacco monopoly was looted. Rather than suggesting merely a desire for plunder, eye-witnesses claimed this indicated a strong, acutely felt discrepancy between traditional tribal and Islamic norms on the one hand, and the foreign, Europeanized judicial state system plus economic grievances among the tobacco growers on the other hand. The same discrepancy was evident in the endemic social banditry of the region. Several bandits joined Shaikh Said's retinue. In his march on Elazig, Shaikh Serif shared command with Yado, a renowned and admired bandit. After the defeat of the rebel army, small guerrilla units remained active, adopting the style of the traditional social bandits of the area. The chief factor lying at the root of this rebellion was the conflict between the Western, secularist ideas adopted and enforced by the new Turkish state and the traditional Kurdish value system with its popular forms of Islam. Abolition of the caliphate, which until recently had been a powerful rallying point uniting Kurdish tribes in a common struggle, was felt by the peasants to be a major symbolic attack on their own beliefs. Militant Kurdish shaikhs in the Zaza districts embodied these traditional values. They were the appropriate leaders to stem the tide of unbelief and foreign morality, and to re-establish traditional justice. At other occasions and in other parts of Kurdistan it was other leaders who took up this role, which lent those risings a less pronounced religious character. For the rank-and-file this may hardly have mattered: they fought to hold on to their traditional identity, irrespective of whether its religious or ethnic aspect was stressed.

Conclusion

The Naksibendi order played an important organisational role in the revolt. Kurdish grievances in the mid-1920s seem to show a remarkable similarity to those of Afghan islamic guerrilla forces in the 1980s. Even if we account for the obvious differences between both situations, it is clear that the Kurdish rebel actions showed more coordination and success initially than those of their Afghan counterparts. This difference may be due to the presence of the Naksibendi network in the Kurdish case. In three ways especially the Kurdish shaikhs' role was crucial. Firstly, their religious prestige, which included a belief in their supernatural powers made their agitation all the more effective and was responsible for the millenarian fervour of many followers. Secondly, shaikhs had authority in more than one tribe, which enabled them to arbitrate disputes and more readily unite the rebel rank and file. Thirdly, rebel shaikhs all belonged to the same section of the Naksibendi order, wherein they had previously cooperated, making coordination over a much larger area possible. The shaikhs' important function in preventing tribal disharmony from making the revolt impossible has its close parallel in the Sanusi movements of pre-independence Libya [*Evans-Pritchard, 1949*]. The Sanusiyah was also a popular mystical order. A network of the supreme shaikh's *halifes* (deputies) united Beduin tribes in a common anti-colonial struggle and laid the basis for Libyan independence. Where the Libyans succeeded the Kurds failed. External and environmental factors were more in favour of the Libyans. But there was a more important reason for the Kurdish failure. As usual with millenarian movements, Kurdish actions were of a highly symbolic nature and there was no strategic planning envisaging successive steps towards an ultimate goal. When the walls of Diyarbakir did not fall like those of biblical Jericho, many Kurdish peasants were demoralized. Turkish reinforcements then further undermined a belief in their own divine mission. For successful resistance against a modern state, a more 'modern' ideology and organization seemed indispensible. In subsequent Kurdish revolts these did indeed emerge.

Note

1. Public Records Office, London, FO 371, 1924: E 11093/11093/65. This is one of the very few contemporary sources on Kurdish complaints and demands. Most Kurdish sources on this period were written *after* the rebellion and are prejudiced by the Turkish reprisals following it. The Azadi members formulated the following grievances:
    i. A new law regarding minorities aroused suspicion. Was the government considering resettlement of Kurds in Western Turkey and replacing them with Turks?
    ii. With the abolition of the caliphate one of the last ties uniting Turks and Kurds had been cut.
    iii. The use of Kurdish in law court and school had been restricted. Due to the banning of Kurdish education, there were virtually no schools among the Kurds.
    iv. The name 'Kurdistan' had been deleted from all geography books.
    v. All senior government officials in the Kurdish provinces were Turks; minor officials were Kurds, but these were carefully selected.
    vi. No benefit was derived from the government in return for taxes paid.
    vii. The government interfered in the elections for the National Assembly in the Kurdish provinces.
    viii. The government followed a policy of setting one tribe continuously against the other.
    ix. There were frequent military raids on Kurdish villages, animals were commandeered and there was widespread corruption connected with receipts and payments for supplies requisitioned.
    x. The Kurdish rank-and-file in the army was abused and ill-treated; they were usually selected for the roughest and most unpleasant duties.
    xi. The Turkish government attempted to exploit Kurdish mineral wealth with the aid of German capital.

References

Albayrak, Sadik, 1973, *Türkiye'de Din Kavgasi* [The struggle for religion in Turkey], Istanbul.
Algar, Hamid, 1976, 'The Naqshbandi order: a preliminary survey of its history and significance', *Studia Islamica*, 44, pp. 123–152.
Arfa, Hassan, 1966, *The Kurds. An historical and political study*, London.
Bruinessen, M. M. van, 1978, 'Agha, Shaikh and State: On the social and political organization of Kurdistan', Ph.D. thesis, Utrecht University.
Cemal, Behçet, 1955, *Şeyh Sait isyani* [Shaikh Said's rebellion], Istanbul: Sel yayinlari.
Chirguh, Bletch, 1930, *La question kurde, ses origines et causes*, Cairo.
Dersimi, M. Nuri, 1952, *Kürdistan tarihinde Dersim* [Dersim in the history of Kurdistan], Aleppo.
Evans-Pritchard, E. E., 1949, *The Sanusi of Cyrenaica*, London.
Firat, M. Şerif, 1970 (1945), *Dogu illeri ve Varto tarihi* [History of the Eastern provinces and of Varto], Ankara.
Gologlu, Mahmut, 1972, *Devrimler ve tepkileri (1924–1930)* [Reforms and their reactions, 1924–1930], Ankara.
Hobsbawm, Eric, 1959, *Primitive rebels. Studies in archaic forms of social movement in the 19th and 20th centuries*, Manchester.
Hourani, A., 1972, 'Shaikh Khalid and the Naqshbandi order', in: *Islamic Philosophy and the Classical Tradition*, eds. S. M. Stern, A. Hourani and V. Brown, Oxford.
Jwaideh, Wadie, 1960, 'The Kurdish nationalist movement: its origins and development', Ph.D. thesis, Syracuse University.
Kisakürek, Necip Fazil, 1977, *Son devrin din mazlumlari* [People oppressed for religion's sake in the latest period], Istanbul, 5th impression.
Massacres kurdes en Turquie, Les, Publication de la Ligue nationale kurde Hoyboun, 1928, Cairo.
Olson, R. W. and W. F. Tucker, 1978, 'The Sheikh Sait rebellion in Turkey (1925)', *Die Welt des Islams*, N.S. XVIII: 195–211.
Silopi, Zinnar, 1969, *Doza Kürdüstan. Kürt milletinin 60 senedenberi esaretten kurtuluş savaşi hatirati* [The trail of Kurdistan. Memoirs on the 60 years' struggle to liberate the Kurdish nation from subjection], Beirut.
Toker, Metin, 1968, *Şeyh Sait ve isyani* [Shaikh Said and his rebellion], Ankara.
Wolf, Eric, 1969, *Peasant wars of the twentieth century*, New York.

Mahdism, Messianism and Marxism in the African setting

THOMAS HODGKIN

Reprinted with the friendly permission of author and publisher, from *The Sudan in Africa: Studies presented to the first international conference sponsored by the Sudan Research Unit, 7–12 Feb. 1968*, Y. Fadl Hasan, ed., Khartoum: Khartoum University Press, 1971, 109–127.

I wish in this paper to raise, very briefly and inadequately, some questions about the relationships between these three types of revolutionary ideology: Mahdist, Messianic and Marxist in the general context of African history. I do not propose to limit myself exclusively to *Bilad al-Sūdān*, since, while the Mahdist movements about which I shall have something to say arose mainly in that region, it seems useful to consider Messianic movements in a wider African setting. It is, I realise, presumptuous for one who has done no original work in this field to attempt to say anything about Mahdism in this historic focus of the most important Mahdist movement of modern times. But I hope the attempt can be justified by the fact that so much interesting work has recently been done, or is now in progress, on the contribution of Mahdist and Messianic ideologies to new political and social initiatives in nineteenth and twentieth century Africa. It may therefore be a good moment to look at some of the evidence in a comparative way. The references will give some idea of the people whose researches I have leaned upon most heavily and from whom I have learned most.

Although there has been a tendency for Mahdist and Messianic movements, because they have emerged in different types of cultural setting (Islamic and non-Islamic), to be studied from somewhat different standpoints, it seems generally recognised that they have certain common characteristics. These might provisionally be listed as follows:

(1) The central role of the Messianic leader, prophet, or Mahdī.
(2) The millenarian expectations, or hopes, of the movement.
(3) The rejection of established authority, both religious and secular, as oppressive and illegitimate.
(4) The appeal to 'the masses' and the effort to mobilise them in support of the Mahdist-Messianic idea.
(5) Associated with this, the attempt to use the universality of the Mahdist-

Messianic message as a means of overcoming traditional conflicts and antagonisms.
(6) The establishment of some form of continuing organisation, based upon adherence to this ideology.
(7) The use of certain external symbols to express the common purposes and beliefs and distinctive character of the movement.
(8) The assertion of puritan values in matters of personal conduct (abstinence, self-discipline, etc.); the rejection of 'the things of this world'.
(9) The situation of 'crisis' in which such movements tend to emerge.

Essentially both Mahdism and Messianism are ideologies which are, as [Lanternari, 1963] stresses, particularly appropriate for 'the oppressed' in situations in which they have not only become conscious of oppression but are willing to respond to a movement which seems to offer a revolutionary way out: 'If the present belongs to the oppressors, the future belongs to us, the revolutionary community and outside the community there is no salvation and no future'.

But, in spite of these basic resemblances, there are also some significant differences between movements that are generally described as 'Mahdist' and those described as 'Messianic'. In particular, Mahdist movements, emerging in societies which have been fairly effectively Islamized over a period of time, have had a well established body of Mahdist beliefs or, as *Holt* prefers to say, 'a deposit of ideas and hopes ... varying in their content and emphasis at different times and in different places' [*1958: 22*] on which to draw.

There is, of course, an extensive literature relating to the general theory of Mahdism.[1] Apart from the traditional corpus of beliefs regarding the Signs of the Hour and the distinctive characteristics of the Mahdī, the aspects of this theory which would seem to be of most importance in the present context are:

First, the concept of crisis, during the period preceding the end of time in which the Mahdī will appear. 'Upheavals and dissension (*fitan*) will divide the Muslim community (*umma*) and lead to political strife, social disorder and moral degeneration...' [*Al-Hajj, 1967: 100*].

Second, the idea that the Mahdī, as the divinely guided one, in direct communication with God or his Prophet, can exercise a special revolutionary initiative in his interpretation of the Quran and the Sunna, unrestricted by the established *madhhabs* [*Holt, 1958: 112*].

Third, the idea that the Mahdī, as Imam, or ultimate Caliph of the Prophet, has the responsibility for conducting *jihad*, particularly against nominal and backsliding Muslims who reject his mission, and ensuring the universal triumph of Islam.

Fourth, the association of the appearance of the Mahdī with the approaching end of the world and a brief intervening Golden Age, during which he will 'fill the earth with equity and justice, even as it has been filled with tyranny and oppression'.

The Messianic movements on the other hand which have emerged in non-Muslim Africa have generally drawn their basic ideas either from the Judaeo-Christian tradition, or from traditional African belief-systems, or, very often, from some combination of these (Mahdist movements have naturally tended to show a similar kind of syncretism, combining pre-Islamic with Islamic elements in their ideologies). But, while there is as ancient and important a 'deposit' of Messianic and millenarian ideas within the Christian as within the Muslim tradition, these have not in general been available to the membership of the various Christian churches and sects in Africa, in the modern period at least, in as well-defined and coherent a form as Mahdism. True, the ideologies of some African Messianic movements have been derived directly from a non-African prototype, as that of Kitawala in the Congo and adjacent territories, was derived from the *Watchtower*, though with important variations and modifications [*Kaufmann, 1964: IV–V; Shepperson, 1962: 148–56*]. But often, it would seem, the ideology has been worked out afresh by the movement through the application of certain basic concepts drawn from the Judaeo-Christian tradition of a Messiah, of an oppressed people, of salvation as an event in historic time (not essentially different from political liberation) to their own situation. The central idea is that the Kingdom of Heaven must be understood in a 'this-worldly', not in an 'other'worldly' sense as a perfected social order, to be achieved in the very near future and enjoyed collectively by the faithful [*Kaufmann, 1964: 25–6*].

Messianic movements in non-Muslim contexts would seem to differ from Mahdist movements also in that they are not committed to the same sort of attitude to institutions. It is an essential part of Mahdist theory to regard *jihad*, in the sense of an armed revolutionary struggle, as the method whereby a perfected social order must be brought into being. Messianic movements on the other hand, while they may accept the view that the expected transformation of society depends upon revolutionary action on their part, may also regard it as dependent upon some cataclysmic external event which it is their duty simply to await [*Shepperson, 1962: 44–5; Hobsbawm, 1959: 57–65*]. In other words Messianism seems compatible in some degree, with quietism as well as with activism. Similarly, at the level of objectives, Mahdist movements are committed to the idea of a Mahdist state, i.e. a perfected Islamic state, which they must seek to realise. Messianic movements are not necessarily concerned with state-building, though in practice this may become their objective. This, as Balandier points out in the case of Kimbanguism, follows logically from the interdependence of religious and political ends. The aspiration to establish a 'Congolese Church' cannot be separated from the aspiration to set up a 'Congolese State', detached from all forms of European control [*Balandier, 1955: 455*].

Through history clearly Messianic movements, expressing millenarian expectations, have provided the oppressed in societies dominated, or strongly influenced, by Christian or Islamic ideologies, with a particularly effective vehicle of protest. In such contexts a coherent, intelligible and relevant system of revolutionary beliefs has been, so to speak, ready to hand. But such movements have been important also in societies in which what may be loosely called 'traditional African systems of belief' have been dominant, and Islamic and Christian influences would seem to have been negligible. In this connection Terence Ranger's discussion of the part played by millenarian beliefs in the ideology of the Shona revolt of 1886–7 [*1967: 346–54*], and John Iliffe's study of comparable aspects of the Maji Maji rising of 1905–07 are of particular interest [*1966: 502–12; Gwassa & Iliffe n.d.: 17–20*].

From this point there are various questions which it would be interesting to discuss. How far back in African history, or in the history of particular African regions, can Messianic-Mahdist movements be traced? How far did particular movements, separated in time and space, influence one another? In what kind of crisis situation did such movements tend to emerge? From what social groups did they draw their leadership and support? How significant a part did they play in the development of 'primary resistance', or proto-nationalist opposition, to European colonial regimes? How far have they influenced the theory and practice of modern political movements? In this paper I can only touch on some aspects of such large questions in a very preliminary and inadquate way.

As regards this question of historical roots, in the Maghrib the Mahdist tradition is, of course, a very ancient one. Dr Holt has pointed out resemblances between the careers of Muhammad ibn Tumart, the founder of the Almohad movement, who assumed the Mahdiship in A.D. 1212, and Muhammad Ahmad, the Sudanese Mahdī, in the late 19th Century [*1958: 22–3*]. But I know of no evidence of the circulation of Mahdist ideas or prophecies in *Bilād al-Sūdān* at this early period. Indeed, it would follow from Ibn Khaldun's view, that within Sunni Islam Mahdism is essentially a *popular* belief, 'commonly accepted among the masses of the people of Islam', that Mahdist ideas could not be expected to emerge in any significant way until Islam had become fairly widely diffused among the Sudanese masses [*Ibn Khaldun, 1958: 156, 195–7*]. Hiskett has suggested that 'the first written record ... in Sudanese literature of the Messianic tradition, common throughout Islam', occurs in the following passage from the replies of Muhammad ibn 'Abd al-Karīm al-Maghīlī of Tlemcen to Muhammad Ture, the founder of the Askia dynasty in Songhai, (c.1500 A.D.):

> And accordingly it is related that at the beginning of every century God will send a learned man to the people to renew their faith, and the characteristics of this learned man in every century must be that he commands what is right and forbids what is

disapproved of, and reforms the affairs of the people and judges justly between them, and assists the truth against vanity, and the oppressed against the oppressor, in contrast to the characteristics of the [other] learned men of his age [*Hiskett, 1962: 583–4*].

But al-Maghīlī, as Hiskett points out, seems clearly to be referring here to the historic function of the *mujaddid*, the renewer and reformer of Islam, who, according to tradition, appears at the end of every century, and not specifically to the Mahdī (though admittedly there is a certain overlap between the two ideas) [*Al-Hajj, 1967: 107–8*].

At any rate by the turn of the eighteenth century Mahdist beliefs were sufficiently firmly implanted in the Central Sudan, and sufficiently widely accepted, for 'Uthman dan Fodio to devote several of his works to their discussion.[2] Muhammad al-Hajj has pointed out that the growth of interest in Mahdism at this particular time was probably connected with the fact that the twelfth century Hijra ended in A.D. 1785–6 and that, according to al-Suyūtī (whose writings were widely read and respected in the Sudan), A.H. 1200 or A.H. 1204 were alternative dates for the appearance of the Madhi [*Ibid. 109–13*]. He has also shown clearly the way in which what might be called 'latent Mahdism' persisted in the western and central Sudan throughout the nineteenth century. Hence it was natural that all the three major reforming leaders of the period: 'Uthman dan Fodio, Shehu Ahmadu and al-Hajj 'Umar Tal, should have been associated in the public mind with Mahdist hopes and prophecies [*Willis, 1967: 401–6*]. 'Uthman's own position (so far as I can understand it) seems to have been particularly interesting. He shared the widespread popular belief in the imminent appearance of the Mahdī and the approaching end of the world. At the same time he went to great pains to explain to the people that he was not himself the Mahdī, and precisely why he failed to meet the generally accepted requirements:

> Know, O my Brethren, that I am not *al-imam al-mahdī*, and I have never claimed the *mahdiyya* – even though that is heard from the tongues of other people. Indeed, I have striven beyond measure in warning them to desist from that, and declared its refutation in some of my writings, both in Arabic and 'Ajami . . . How can I claim the *mahdiyya* since I was born in *Bilad al-Sudan* in a place called Maratta and the Mahdi ought to be born in Medina? [*quoted by Al-Hajj, 1967: 111;* cf. *Last, 1967: ixxxi, 10*].

In his interesting Fulfulde poem, *Sifofin Shehu*, he takes the same general position, though mentioning thirty or more attributes of the Mahdī which he claims to possess [*Adeleye et al., 1966: 1–36*]. But, while denying his own claims to the Mahdiyya, 'in the early stages of the *jihad*', Al-Hajj argues, 'the Shehu consciously emphasised the prophecies about the End of Time in order to instil into his followers the love of martyrdom and the renunciation of this transitory world'. And at his important meeting with the eastern leaders at Birnin Gada in the dry season of 1805/6 Muhammad Bello delivered a message from the Shehu 'about the approaching appearance of the Mahdī, that the Shehu's followers are his vanguard, and that this *jihad* will not end, by God's permission, until the appearance of the Mahdī [*1967: 109*; cf. *Last, 1967: 36*]. By 1808, when the main phases of the *jihad* had been successfully completed, he had shifted his ground, and presented in his *Amer al-sa'a* an apology for the confusion caused by his previous books and a warning against indulgence in extravagant prophecies'. In his *Tanbih al-fahim*, written in the same year, he subjected his former views on the imminent appearance of the Mahdī to serve self-criticism:

> What we used to mention again and again during the gatherings for preaching, that the time for the appearance of the Mahdī had come, was based on the assumptions of al-Suyūtī. But, after investigation, we admit that we do not know the time with any degree of certainty.

And in 1814 his *Tahdhīr al-ikhwan* was written specifically to refute the claims of the Tuareg Hamma (whom the Sokoto government later defeated and crucified) to the *Mahdiyya* [*Al-Hajj, 1967: 110*].

This evidence would seem to fit with the fairly generally accepted view of 'Uthman dan Fodio as essentially a middle-of-the-road reformer, as much opposed to the leftist social-revolutionary ideas of Mahdism and Kharijism as to the rightist opportunist attitudes of the 'venal mallams' [*e.g. Hiskett, 1962: 591*]. At the same time it is natural that this reforming leadership should have been willing to promote and encourage Mahdist beliefs during the revolutionary phase of the *jihad*, when it was essential to mobilise the masses in its support, but should have found these expectations of a new world order an embarrassment, or even a positive threat to the regime, when it was attempting to consolidate the power of the Sokoto Caliphate on lines which offered relatively little prospect of fundamental social change. This dual attitude to Mahdism seems to have continued through the century. Since Mahdist beliefs remained current and officially approved it was necessary to keep the roads to the East, where the Mahdī was expected to appear, open. But active expressions of these beliefs, including attempts at mass migration to the East, were generally resisted on the ground that the time of exodus had not yet come, 'since there is still some good remaining among us' [*Biobaku & Al-Hajj, 1966: 429*].

Muhammad al-Hajj has shown very clearly how this two-way traffic in Mahdist ideas, between the Central and the Eastern Sudan, operated in the latter half of the nineteenth century and has indeed continued down to modern times. What perhaps one needs most to understand is what was the nature of the crisis that stimulated the transformation of latent Mahdism into active Mahdism during the period from 1880 on, above all in the Eastern Sudan, the only region in which an effective Mahdist state was able to establish and maintain itself for a substantial period, but also generally, in many parts of *Bilād al-Sūdān*. (It is odd that Holt, in his valuable study of the Mahdist state in the Eastern Sudan, should have described it as 'an apparently isolated and anachronistic phenomenon' [*1958: 23*]. In fact it was far from isolated and not in any intelligible sense anachronistic).

In a general way, no doubt, one can explain the activisation of latent Mahdist beliefs during this period by the increasing pressure of European imperialism upon the Muslim world and the economic, social and political disintegration arising out of these pressures and, later, out of actual European invasion and occupation and the defeat or capitulation of Muslim governments.[3] This, understandably, appeared to indicate the existence of the kind of crisis associated historically with the appearance of the Mahdī. (This identification had in fact already been made during earlier phases of European penetration into Muslim Africa: a Mahdist rising had occurred in Lower Egypt during Bonaparte's occupation [*Daniel, 1966: 98–9*]. 'Abd al-Qadir's revolt against French penetration into Algeria seems to have owed its popular support in part to Mahdist expectations) [*King, n.d.*]. More study of the literature of the period would enable one to grasp in more depth and detail how the crisis presented itself to Muslims in different parts of *Bilād al-Sūdān* at different phases of its development, and how far their reactions to it involved Mahdist ideas and symbols. We have poems of al-Hajj 'Umar ibn Abi Bakr al-Salghawi (of Ghana), for example, in which the European invasion of West Africa is associated with the conventional signs of the coming of the Mahdī.[4] At the level of practice Le Grip [*1952*] gives some rather fragmentary information, based mainly on Marty, relating to Mahdis who appeared during this period in various parts of the Western and Central Sudan and who led movements that provided, in one way or another, channels for 'primary resistance' to European imperialism. But the whole subject requires much more investigation.

One important theme which is beginning to be more seriously studied is the impact of the Mahdiyya in the Eastern Sudan on these various West-Sudanic Mahdist movements, particularly on the movements which emerged in the 1880's and 1890's in the Sokoto Caliphate [*Biobaku & Al Hajj, 1966*]. Here the situation involved at least four elements. First, there was the stimulus given to Mahdist beliefs by the successes of the Mahdī, Muhammad Ahmad, who in January 1883, after the capture of al-Obeid, opened correspondence with the rulers of Sokoto and Bornu, demanding recognition and support (which they refused) [*Holt, 1958a*]. Second, there was the special position of Hayatu ibn Sa'id, grandson of Muhammad Bello, with claims to the Caliphate, who identified himself with the Mahdist cause from the outset, and was appointed by the Mahdī (and confirmed after his death by the Khalīfa) as his agent (*'amil*), responsible for the affairs 'of all the people of Sokoto who were subjects of your great-grandfather, 'Uthman dan Fodio' [*Biobaku & Al Hajj, 1966: 433; Al Hajj, 128ff*].

Third, Mallam Jibril Gaini, a Fulani of Katagum, who described himself as *Amir al-jaysh* to Hayatu, established in about 1885 and maintained by military force an autonomous Mahdist state, based on Bormi in the Gombe region, on the Sokoto-Bornu frontier [*Lavers, 1967*]. Fourth, the situation was transformed by the conquest of Bornu by Rabih ibn Fadl Allah in 1893–4. Although Rabih's relationship with the Mahdiyya in the Eastern Sudan, and in particular with the Khalīfa, remained ambiguous, he clearly made use of Mahdist ideology and symbolism: 'His army wore the Mahdist uniform, read the *Ratib*, and fought under a Mahdist flag' [*Biobaku & Al Hajj, 1966: 434; cf. Tomlinson & Lethem, 1927*]. Initially Hayatu attempted to work in close association with Rābih, whose daughter, Hawwa', he married. Later he appears to have been kept virtually a prisoner at Dikwa, Rābih's capital, and was killed in 1898 by a force led by Fadl Allah ibn Rābih when attempting to escape with the help of an escort provided by Jibril Gaini [*Al Hajj: 135; Lavers, 1967, 27–30*]. But during the period 1894 to 1900 Bornu was ostensibly a Mahdist state.

Against this background one can understand how the idea of *hijra* became associated with, and reinforced by, Mahdist beliefs in the popular opposition to European-Christian rule which expressed itself in the final crisis of the Sokoto Caliphate. The choice of *hijra*, as opposed to collaboration with the unbelievers, had already been made by Ahmadu Shehu, son of al-Hajj 'Umar and ruler of Segu, who, after Bandiagara had fallen to the French, had moved east with a considerable following to Sokoto, where he died in 1898. His son, Bashir, together with a section of the ruling and scholarly classes from Sokoto and its dependent Amirates accompanied the legitimate (now officially deposed) Caliph, al-Tahiru Ahmad, when he opted for *hijra* after the fall of Sokoto in March, 1903. But what makes al-Tahiru's *hijra* particularly interesting historically is the scale of mass participation and support which it enjoyed, as Dr Adeleye shows from contemporary sources [*Adeleye et al. 1966: 294–5*]. Hence the strengthened appeal, in a situation in which the country was now in actual occupation by the Europeans, of Mahdist ideas reflected in the choice of the Mahdist town of Burmi as the place of refuge for al-Tahiru and his supporters and the base for their final stand against imperialism. At the battle of Burmi, on 27 July, 1903, al-Tahiru (who, it is claimed, first accepted Mahdism) was killed with some seven hundred of his supporters. But the *hijra*, involving many thousands of Westerners, to the Eastern Sudan continued, under the leadership of al-Tahiru's son, Muhammad Bello Mai Wurnu (after whom their eventual town of settlement was named) and others. And within the British-occupied territories of the Caliphate a succession of Mahdist, or post-Mahdist, movements emerged: 'the most celebrated ... (being) that which culminated in the Satiru rebellion of 1906' [*Ibid.*, and *Tamuno, 1965:291–3*].

If we turn from the Muslim to the non-Muslim world we can find a clear example of the use of messianic and millenarian ideas to provide ideological support for a movement of 'primary resistance' to European imperialism in Ranger's admirable study of the Shona rebellion. Like the later Maji Maji rising in Tanganyika, he argues, the rebellion involved:

> defiance of a power which enjoyed great technological superiority and began with a superiority of morale based upon it and upon confidence in its ability to shape the world. The [African] religious leaders were able to oppose to this a morale which for the moment was as confident, if not more so, based upon *their* supposed ability to shape the world; and they were able to oppose to modern weapons the one great advantage that the Africans possess, that of numbers [*Ranger, 1967:352*].

He goes on to stress the 'abiguity' of the attitude of these resistance movements to European ideas and technology. 'There is repudiation but also desire; a rejection of white mastery but a longing for African control of modern sources of wealth and power in an African environment ... Mkwati and Kagubi (religious leaders of the Shona rebellion) ... were not reactionary in the simple sense of looking to the restoration of the *status quo* of 1890; their programme was in some ways revolutionary in its vision of a new society'. In Mkwati's millenarian promises 'there was a strange mixture of return to the past and control of the new'.

> Lobengula was to return from the dead and to reign from Government House, Bulawayo. When Mkwati was trying to rally the north-eastern rebels in August 1896 it was reported that he promised them that they only 'had to wait until all the whites are dead or fled and then they will enjoy the good things of the town and live in palaces of corrugated iron'. 'Directly the white men are killed', a police inspector was told during the Inyanga scare of 1903–4, 'we will occupy your houses; all these nice things will be ours' [*Ibid. 354*].

There is, of course, ample evidence of the important part played by Messianic and Mahdist ideologies in the development of what may be loosely called 'proto-nationalist' movements during the main period of colonial domination.[5] Here again the use of these ideas as a basis for political action seems to have been associated with situations of crisis, or situations seen as such by substantial sections of the African masses, particularly the crisis of the years immediately following the First World War. Tomlinson and Lethem, in their interesting if lurid and occasionally fantastic report on the history of Islamic propaganda in Nigeria, mention as one factor contributing to the revival and spread of 'Mahdist propaganda' during the period 1918–1923:

The widespread belief (not, of course, confined to Nigeria) that the end of the world, which is to take place in A.H. 1400 (1979 A.D.), will be preceded by the supremacy of the false prophet ('Dajjal' or Anti-Christ), followed by the second coming of Nebi Isa (Jesus Christ), after which all the world will be converted to Islam. It has been the practice of agitators of late to identify the European conquerors of Muslim countries with Dajjal [*Tomlinson-Lethem, 1927: 10*].

The content of the 'Mahdist propaganda' is described as including:

The 'Vision of the Alfa Hashim', the Dajjal prophecies, encyclicals of the Mahdi, letters to Hayatu from the Mahdi and the Khalifa Abdallahi, garbled versions of Abderrahman's visit to England, ... old Fulani prophecies of the Fulani trek to the East, Muhammad Bello's prophecy as to his son Sa'id and his grandson Sa'id, and Hayatu's upon his son Sa'id ... Nonsense about 'the day' and the imminent appearance of Isa [*Ibid. 72*].

While the Eastern Sudan was regarded as the main source of Mahdist beliefs, with the Hijāz as a secondary focus and the *hajj* route providing the main communications network, in a more confused and shadowy way 'Mahdist propaganda was thought of at this time as associated with Bolshevism, the Third International, Egyptian nationalism, Pan-Islamism, and ideas of 'world revolution' in general [*Ibid., passim*].

The Messianic movement associated with Simon Kimbangu and his successor prophets among the Bakongo, which is one of the best documented among anti-colonial protest movements making use of an essentially Christian ideology, was at the same time one of the most highly developed from the standpoint of theory and most effective and stable in respect of its organisation, maintaining itself through a variety of institutional forms over a period of more than thirty years.[6] Balandier in his study of this movement emphasises the connection between its phases of greatest activity and situations of particular crisis in Bakongo society:

The moments of 'crisis' were coincident with the most violent protests on the part of the colonised society. In 1921–1922, after the decline in the trade in export crops, the messianic movement known as *Kimbanguism* established itself in the areas around Brazzaville. After the 1929 crisis violent incidents occurred in Bakongo country and in various parts of Upper Congo. In this connection it is significant that the preacher and inspirer of the Sanga revolts was concerned to announce, after the expulsion of the Whites, a true Golden Age – 'perpetual abundance of crops, game and fish'. Official reports, dating from 1931, refer to 'the actions of sorcerers who take advantage of the economic crisis to spread the rumour that the Whites are growing weaker and have no more money', stressing at the same time the 'troubles' which threaten the Belgian Congo for the same reasons [*Balandier, 1955: 55*].

However, one has not, I admit, made much progress towards answering some of the crucial questions: What during this phase of history, the period of the break-up of indigenous pre-colonial states and the imposition of European-dominated colonial systems, was the nature of the crises which led to the emergence of Messianic and Mahdist movements? Why have they played a particularly significant part in the history of some societies and not of others? At what point do the oppressed decide that oppression, or this particular form of oppression, is no longer endurable, and turn to a revolutionary millenarian ideology for a way out since clearly no Messianic leader can establish himself without a supporting popular movement? In this connection it is worth asking how important is the possession of a local tradition of popular protest. In the case of the Mahdist movements which emerged in the Sokoto Caliphate/Northern Nigeria during the late nineteenth and early twentieth century, we have seen that these drew upon a deposit of beliefs which had been in circulation in the region for at least a century. Among the Shona there was a tradition of resistance to Portuguese pressures going back to the early seventeenth century [*Ranger, 1967: 345*]. In the old kingdom of the Kongo there was a long-standing tradition of popular Christian heresies. At the beginning of the eighteenth century a Bakongo prophetess, Donna Beatrice, gave herself out to be St Antony, claimed to speak with God, prophesied that the Day of Judgment was at hand, and sent out her 'angels' as ambassadors through the country to summon the princes to San Salvador 'to restore the kingdom'. 'Almost the entire kingdom was disaffected and adhered to the Antonian sect'. Even after she had been condemned to death and burnt by the Portuguese, together with her principal 'angel', the movement remained a powerful force. Her supporters became 'more obstinate than ever' [*Andersson, 1958: 244–5*]. The existence of such traditions of protest within a particular society might seem to predispose its members to seek for a Messianic solution to the problems posed by modern forms of European domination.

It may help towards an understanding of the nature of the crises which have given rise to Messianic-Mahdist movements to note the distinction which Lanternari draws 'between movements generated by a conflict between societies or by the clash with an external force and those generated by dissensions within the pattern of one society', even though, as he says, 'we should view the distinction between external and internal motivation in a dialectical sense and not as a static condition' [*Lanternari, 1963: 309*]. In other words, during the phase of history with which I am particularly concerned, Messianic-Mahdist movements were always directed partly against the external forces of oppression (Western imperialism, or its associated sub-imperialisms, and the dislocations, tensions and problems to which it had given rise), partly against indigenous oppressive classes, interests and institutions. Sometimes one aspect is more in evidence, sometimes the other. In the case of the Mahdist movements in the Sokoto Caliphate it would seem that the increasing economic difficulties of the free peasants and small gentry during the latter part of the nineteenth century were a contributory factor. In the Eastern Sudan, Holt and others have stressed the importance of specific economic grievances associated with attempts to abolish the slave-trade supplementing and intensifying general popular opposition to the alien, oppressive and un-Islamic regime of the *Turkiyya* [*Holt, 1958: ch. 1*]. Naturally, where Messianic-Mahdist movements occur in an apparently firmly established colonial situation, as vehicles for some form of proto-nationalism, as in the case of Kimbanguism and its successor movements, the main emphasis tends to be upon opposition to external oppression and its local agents. As a sacred song from Musana (1930) has it:

> The Whites are about to be lost on account of the earning of money.
> Lord, pardon them that they may be saved.
> The chiefs are about to be lost on account of their money.
> Lord, pardon them that they may be saved.
> The police are about to be lost on account of the collecting of taxes.
> Lord, pardon them that they may be saved [*Andersson, 1958: 276*].

As Lanternari mildly puts it: 'Cultural conflict with the whites is by no means the only motivation behind the Messianic movements, but it is by far the most prevalent because of its disconcerting effects upon native society, culture and religion' [*1963: 310*].

Clearly one should not attempt to be too rigorous in considering whether a given movement was or was not Messianic or Mahdist in character. Even in the case of Mahdism, where one might think it sufficient to apply the simple criterion: Did this particular Muslim leader proclaim himself to be the Mahdi or not, things are not necessarily altogether clear-cut. One may be confronted with a popular protest movement in an Islamic frame of reference, such as the reformed Tijaniyya under the leadership of Shaykh Hama Allah (the so-called 'Hamalliyya') in the Mali region during the inter-war period, which seems to have had most of the characteristics of a Messianic movement, as I have attempted to define them. Yet Shaykh Hama Allah never (so far as I know) identified himself with the Mahdī, though he was certainly so regarded after his deportation by the French.[7] This kind of transformation of a given popular leader, after his exile, imprisonment or death, into a Mahdī or Messiah is a not uncommon phenomenon: e.g. the transformation of André Matswa of Congo (Brazzaville), founder of *Amicalisme* in the late 1920's, from a secular political leader into 'Père Matswa' or 'Jésus Matswa', third person of the Kimbanguist Trinity and focus of the Matswanist Church, after his trial and first imprisonment in 1930, and even more after his death in prison in 1942 [*Balandier, 1963: 397–416*]. It might therefore seem best to use the term 'Messianic movement' in a fairly general sense, recognising that movements of many different types (including modern secular national movements) may reveal

Messianic characteristics, reserving the term 'Mahdist' for movements whose leaders have claimed to be Mahdis (or representatives or agents of Mahdis) in the more strict and technical sense.

One needs to pay attention also to the later history of Messianic and Mahdist movements. There would seem to be a fairly general tendency for such movements, after their revolutionary phase has ended in defeat and repression and their millennial hopes have been disappointed, to adapt, or partially adapt, themselves, ideologically and structurally, to the new situation. The neo-Mahdist organisation of the Ansar, which during the period of the Condominium developed as a quasi-*tariqa*, is a case in point [cf. *Trimingham, 1949 : 157–163*]. Kimbanguism-Matswanism during its later phase, as the *Mission des Noirs*, is an interesting example of a somewhat comparable kind of development, with its hierarchical, semi-military form of church organisation (partly modelled on the Salvation Army), ethical and ritual prescriptions, calendar of holy days, sacred literature, esoteric interest in symbolic numbers, combined with its attitude of total rejection of the European missions and the colonial state:

> Thus the symbol 12 – a sacred number, which is expressed in the twelve 'persons' of Simon Kimbangu, the Council of twelve 'apostles', the obligation to observe the twelve 'days of grace' (the first twelve days of June), or in certain rules relating to personal hygiene (men had to cut their hair every twelve days) was associated not only with Biblical tradition ... but with a whole network of activities in which the faithful participate [*Balandier, 1963 : 450*].

But this attitude of rejection and withdrawal may, of course, relate to all forms of secular politics, not merely to European-dominated politics; and the conflict of a Messianic Church that is committed to this kind of attitude with the nationalist party, once it is in formal political control of the state, may be even more sharp than with the former colonial administration as in the case, particularly, of the Lumpa Church in Zambia [*Roberts, 1970*].

It is obviously difficult to try to answer large questions about 'historical significance' in relation to movements as complex and diverse as these, occurring in many different African territories, in very different kinds of historical context. None the less one can reasonably claim that these Messianic–Mahdist movements were important, both in themselves and as regards their influence on subsequent African history, in at least three ways.

First, through the universalism of their ideologies, and the forms of organisation which they attempted to construct, these movements tried, with varying degrees of success, to provide a new basis of solidarity, transcending the more restricted ties of kinship, locality, ethnic or linguistic group, or pre-colonial state. This is a point which is constantly stressed by those who have studied specific movements: for example, Ranger [*1967 : 352*], writing of the leaders of the Shona revolt:

They were very successful exponents of a type of leadership which appears to have been associated with most of the striking attempts to solve, on however impermanent a basis, the greatest political problem of pre-colonial Africa; the problem of scale.

Similarly Iliffe, on the organisation of the Maji Rebellion:

> Since the object was to organise anew, it was not sufficient merely to revitalize structures and beliefs which often reflected those divisions which had previously hindered effective action. Rather, it was necessary to enlarge the scale both of resistance and of religious allegiance. The central figure in such an enlargement was the prophet, proclaiming a new religious order to supersede the old, a new loyalty to transcend old loyalties of tribe and kinship. German observers saw in Maji Maji the signs of such a transformation. The *maji* – the water-medicine accepted by each rebel – united in common action peoples with no known prior unity [*1967:502*].

Compare also Balandier on the Kimbanguist movement among the Bakongo:

> The second remarkable fact (over and above its endurance through time) was its extension in space, which took less account of national than of ethnic frontiers. It expressed the profound reactions of a people who had rediscovered their sense of unity: the 'messages' circulated within the Congolese churches were described as 'bringing knowledge' to the faithful in the two Congos and in Angola. Unquestionably the movement for religious innovation lay at the root of a growth of 'national' consciousness. The new Church as the builder of social relationships, sought limits lying beyond the restricted framework of clan or tribe [*1963:427*].

The Mahdiyya in the Eastern Sudan asserted its own form of Islamic universalism:

> The fall of El Obeid opened to the Mahdi the prospect of a series of apocalyptic victories throughout the heartlands of Islam. The determination to undertake the conquest of the Sudan generally and then of the neighbouring lands was conveyed in the visionary form in which the Mahdi cloaked his decisions [*Holt, 1958:73*].

True, this new revolutionary form of *'asabiyya* was by its nature unstable and difficult to maintain over a long period. There was an understandable tendency, once the leadership had to confront the problem of constructing some kind of continuing system and preserving it against increasing internal and external pressures, to revert to reliance on those same traditional ties, loyalties, institutions, that the revolution had sought to abolish or transcend. Thus Holt describes how the Khalifa 'Abdallahi, during the later phases of the Mahdist state, found himself obliged to depend increasingly upon Ta'ishi political support, while attempting to 'restore the administrative system . . . by bringing back the men and methods of the old regime and thereby much of the corruption, dilatoriness and oppression which the Madhī had hoped to sweep away' [*Ibid. 246*]. (Modern analogies will readily suggest themselves.) In his account of the

Maji Maji rebellion Iliffe refers to 'a third phase, in which the failure of the *maji* obliged the rebels to return to customary methods of tribal warfare ... Thus the paradox of later nationalist movements, the need to use old loyalties in order to popularize an effort to transcend them, also characterized this earlier attempt to enlarge political scale' [*Iliffe, 1967: 511–2*]. None the less, the mere fact of asserting a universal idea, as the basis for a new and more comprehensive form of organisation, was itself of historical importance: 'God ... has sent us a Saviour of the Black race, Simon Kimbangu. He is the leader and Saviour of all Black people, in the same way as the Saviours of other races – Moses, Jesus Christ, Mohammed and Buddha' [*Balandier, 1963:431*].

Second, Messianic-Mahdist movements were in a basic sense forward-looking: they were 'movements of innovation', 'looking to the future and regeneration of the world' [*Lanternari, 1963:322*]. True, 'forward-looking' and 'backward-looking' are relative categories, and movements of popular protest and revolt normally contain elements of both. But what was significant about these particular movements was that they presented a view of a future social order which was essentially different from any kind of society that had existed in the known or remembered past. They might refer back to the early Caliphate or to the state of man before the Fall; the Mahdī-Messiah might see himself as re-enacting the life and experience of the Prophet or Christ; or they might make use of concepts and symbols derived from traditional religion. But they were essentially different from those forms of resistance or rebellion whose primary object was to retain or restore the pre-colonial political and social order. The revolution, as they conceived it, must involve the total transformation of society, and of man as a social being; the assertion of a new ethic and a new basis for human relationships; the ending of all forms of oppression, not merely those specific forms of oppression associated with external domination or the colonial state.

Third, Messianic and Mahdist movements have provided a structure of ideas and institutions through which 'the masses' have begun to play an active, formative and conscious part in modern history. Not much work (so far as I am aware) has yet been done on the social composition of these movements, on the lines of the studies of other revolutionary movements in other historical contexts. In particular one is not clear about the relative importance of rural and urban components, or the part played (in the Congo or Nyasaland, for example) by migrant workers [*Shepperson, 1962*]. But in broad terms these movements would generally seem to have involved some form of alliance between large sections of the peasantry (including semi-proletarianised elements) and, in the case of the Sudan, the nomad population, with a revolutionary leadership drawn largely (like the *prophetae* in mediaeval Europe) from what one might call the underprivileged intelligentsia: *sufi shaykhs*, small *ulama*, catechists, monitors, interpreters, clerks and NCOs who had worked in the administrative, commercial or military sectors of the colonial apparatus [*Andersson, 1958: ch. VII; Balandier, 1963: 401–3; Cohn, 1962: 314–8*]. It was essentially this literate leadership, with a grounding often in Islamic or Christian doctrine, which was able, as a member of the Khaki Movement (a successor to Kimbanguism) put it 'in various ways to "vana ngolo kwa bankwa brousse" (give power to the country people)' [*Anderson, 1958: 51*].

The points of resemblance between the theories of Messianic and Mahdist movements and certain aspects of Marxism are evident enough, and have been discussed from various standpoints (though more often, I think, in a European than an African or Third World context).[8] These include the idea of history as involving a continuing conflict between oppressors and oppressed, and leading, by a process conceived as historically necessary, to the ultimate victory of the oppressed; the 'apocalyptic' idea of the just, or classless, society, based on the principle of 'to each according to his needs', as in some sense the goal of history; the idea of the total corruption and degeneracy of the existing social order, and the consequent necessity for the total reconstruction of all institutions, all aspects of human life and relationships; the idea of social change in a progressive direction as depending not simply upon providential guidance, or some cataclysmic external event, but also (in part, at least) upon revolutionary activism and the intelligent and continuing participation of the masses in the effort to transform the actual world.[9] The list, obviously, could be extended.

Of course, the points of difference between the two types of theory are also substantial and important. In part these arise from the fact that Marxism involves a much more carefully constructed, and objectively better grounded, method of historical interpretation and sociological analysis than the methods employed by Mahdist and Messianic movements. The classless society of Communism is conceived, not as imminent, but as realisable after a complex and protracted period of effort, conflict and transition, involving many retrogressive as well as progressive phases, even though there have been moments in the history of the past hundred years when Marxists have in practice taken a somewhat millennial view of the prospects of world revolution. Moreover bourgeois society, and even the colonial systems which western bourgeois states have imposed upon the peoples of the non-western world, however distorted and oppressive, are conceived as containing within themselves possibilities for the kind of total transformation of society in a Socialist (and ultimately a Communist) direction which Marxists believe to be necessary and desirable. 'Millenarian movements', Hobsbawm argues, 'share a fundamental vagueness about the actual way in which the new society will be brought about' [*Hobsbawm, 1959: 58*]. But, while this contention is no doubt in general correct, I think he exaggerates the extent to which 'pure' millenarian movements have tended to adopt a passive, or 'waiting', attitude to revolutionary change: their 'followers are not makers of revolution. They expect it to make itself'. This is certainly not true of Mahdist movements, nor, I think, of most of the non-Muslim Messianic movements referred to here.[10] They are closer to the classic Marxist position that revolution is at the same time historically necessary and dependent upon the beliefs and actions of revolutionaries.[11] Their difficulty has been rather that of all Utopian movements: the lack of a clearly defined strategy of revolution, reliance upon a variety of methods: *jihad* or armed rebellion; magical-religious techniques (such as the *maji* water-medicine); *hijra* or withdrawal from the European-dominated political order; expectation of external support (e.g. from American Negroes) [cf. *Shepperson, 1962: 153–4; Andersson, 1958: 250–6*]; inadequate to achieve their revolutionary objectives.

Yet, when all this is said, it surely remains true that Utopianism, or 'impossiblism', is, as Hobsbawm suggests, in some degree a characteristic of all revolutionary movements, however 'primitive' or 'sophisticated' they may be in respect of their social theories or political strategies. 'Utopianism is probably a necessary social device for generating the superhuman efforts without which no major revolution is achieved. It is essential for revolutionaries to believe that the ultimate in human prosperity and liberty will appear after their victories' [*1959: 60–1*]. It seems doubtful even whether the fact that, for participants in Mahdist and Messianic movements, 'the future' normally includes the prospect of the enjoyment of bliss in some form of other-worldly existence, while for Marxists it is limited to future phases of human history, makes all that practical difference. In both cases suffering, death, martyrdom are endured for the sake of a future which is believed to be their entire and sufficient justification. Hence the efforts of 'venal mallams' among sociologists and political scientists to discredit revolutionary movements under Marxist (or partly Marxist) leadership on the ground that these are simply modern expressions of 'archaic' and 'primitive' millenarian ideas are otiose [*Cohn, 1962: 309*]. The resemblances, and the historical connections, between the two types of movement and ideology are a primary datum. But it is above all about this interesting question (which Hobsbawm has discussed in a European context) of the structural relations between millenarian and modern revolutionary movements that one needs to know a great deal more. How far, and by what kinds of historical process, has the one been transformed into the other, or provided necessary preconditions for the growth of the other? In the case of the Philippines the point has been made that the revolutionary Huk movement was able to stabilise itself most effectively in areas such as 'Laguna province, where the pre-war Sakdal movement (a messianic nationalist movement that staged an abortive revolt in 1935) had been strong' [*Pomeroy, 1968: 38*]. How far can comparable kinds of historical connection be traced in the African context?[12] Even where, as in the Sudan itself, there would seem to have been no significant structural relationship between the late nineteenth century Mahdist movement and the Sudanese Communist Party (which developed from quite different, and in some respects opposed, groups and interests), how far did the mere possession of a revolutionary millennial tradition contribute to the growth of modern forms of revolutionary organisation and consciousness?

Notes

1. See particularly Ibn Khaldun [*1958: II, 156–200*], and references under 'al-Mahdi', in the *Shorter Encyclopaedia of Islam* (Leiden, 1953) 310–13; further *al-Hajj, 1967:* 100–5.
2. For a list of 'Uthman dan Fodio's Arabic works dealing with Mahdism and the end of the world, see *al-Hajj, 1967:* 114.
3. See esp. *Smith, 1957: 52–3* and *ch. II*. For a discussion of the local situation in Sudan see *Adeleye, 1967 and 1968*.
4. Al-Hajj 'Umar also criticised a certain Musa who was active in northern Ghana at the turn of the century and who claimed to be the Mahdī (*Braimah-Goody, 1967: 191–2*].
5. In addition to the sources referred to below, see also *Balandier, 1953*; *Shepperson, 1962*; *Shepperson-Price, 1959*; *Banton, 1963*
6. See particularly *Balandier* [1963] and his bibliography; *Andersson, 1958* and references in *Banton, 1963*.
7. There is no satisfactory study of the Hamalliyya. The relevant chapter in *Goully, 1952* remains useful; *Hampate Ba-Cardaire*, 1957 contains interesting material, presented from a somewhat *engagé* standpoint. Jamil Abun-Nasr, *The Tijaniyya: a Sufi Order in the modern World* (Oxford, 1963) is disappointing in this topic.
8. See discussions from very different standpoints in *Cohn, 1962* and *Hobsbawm, 1959*; cf. also the writings of Engels in *Marx-Engels, 1955*: passim.
9. For texts illustrating Marx's approach to this thesis see *Bottomore-Rubel, 1955*.
10. But Hobsbawm would presumably regard the movements considered here as holding 'intermediate positions' between the 'two extremes of the "pure" millenarian and the "pure" political revolutionary' [*1959:59*].
11. Cf. *G. Plekhanov* [*n.d. 93*]: 'If I am inclined to take part in a movement whose triumph seems to me a historical necessity, this only means that I consider my own activity likewise to be an indispensable link in the chain of conditions whose aggregate will necessarily ensure the triumph of the movement which is dear to me'.
12. In addition to Ranger, John Saul's chapter 'Africa' in *Ionescu-Gellner, 1969: 122–50*, contains an interesting discussion of points which have some bearing on the question.

References

Adeleye, R. A. *et al.*, 1966, 'Sifofin Shehu: An autobiography and character study of 'Utman b. Fudi in verse', *Research Bulletin* (Centre of Arabic Documentation, Ibadan), 2:1, 1–36.
Adeleye, R. A., 1967, Overthrow of the Sokoto Caliphate 1879–1930. Ph.D. Ibadan.
Adeleye, R. A., 1968, 'The dilemma of the Wazir: the place of *risalat al-wazir 'ila ahl al-'ilm wa'ltadablu* in the history of the Sokoto Caliphate', *Journal of the Historical Society of Nigeria* 4:2.
Al-Hajj, Muhammad, 1967, 'The Thirteenth Century in Muslim Eschatology: Mahdist Expectations in the Sokoto Caliphate', *Research Bulletin* [as above] 3:2, 100ff.
Al-Hajj, Muhammad, 'Hayatu b. Said: A Mahdist revolutionary agent in the Western Sudan', *The Sudan in Africa, Studies &c.* 128–141.
Andersson, E., 1958, *Messianic Popular Movements in the Lower Congo* (Studia Ethnographica Upsaliensia 14), Uppsala.

Balandier, G., 1953, 'Messianismes et nationalismes en Afrique Noire', *Cahiers Internationales de Sociologie* 14.
Balandier, G., 1955, *Sociologie actuelle de l'Afrique Noire*. Paris.
Balandier, G., 1963, *Sociologie*... – [as above] 2d ed., Ibid.
Banton, M., 1963, 'African prophets', *Race* 5:2, 42–53.
Biobaku, S. and M. Al-Hajj, 1966, 'The Sudanese Mahdiyya and the Niger–Chad Region', *Islam in Tropical Africa*, I. M. Lewis, ed. Oxford.
Bottomore, T. B., and M. Rubel, 1955 (eds.], *Karl Marx: Selected Writings in Sociology and Social Philosophy*, London.
Braimah, J. A., and J. R. Goody, 1967, *Salaga: The Struggle for Power*, London.
Cohn, N., 1962, *The Pursuit of the Millennium*, London.
Daniel, N., 1966, *Islam, Europe and Empire*, Edinburgh.
Gouilly, A., 1952, *L'Islam dans l'Afrique Occidentale Française*, Paris.
Gwassa, G. C. K., and J. Iliffe, n.d., *Records of the Maji Maji Rising*, I (Hist. Ass. of Tanzania, Paper 4) Nairobi.
Hampate Ba, A., and M. Cardaire, 1957, *Tierno Bokar, le Sage de Bandiagara*, Paris.
Hiskett, M., 1962, 'An Islamic Tradition of Reform in the Western Sudan from the Sixteenth to the Eighteenth Century' *Bulletin SOAS* 25:3.
Hobsbawm, E. J., 1959, *Primitive Rebels*, Manchester.
Holt, P. M., 1958, *The Mahdist State in the Sudan*, Oxford.
Holt, P. M., 1958a, 'The Sudanese Mahdia and the Outside World', *Bulletin SOAS* 21: 276–90.
Iliffe, J., 1967, 'The Organisation of the Maji Maji Rebellion', *Journal of African History* 8, 3: 502–12.
Ionescu, Gh., and E. Gellner, 1969, *Populism: Its Meanings and National Characteristics*, London.
Ibn Khaldun, 1958, *The Muqaddimah*, Transl. F. Rosenthal, London.
Kaufmann, R., 1964, *Millénarisme et acculturation*, Brussels.
King, J. n.d., [Unpublished seminar paper. St Antony's College, Oxford].
Lanternari, V., 1963, *The Religions of the Oppressed*, London.
Last, M., 1967, *The Sokoto Caliphate*, London.
Lavers, J. E., 1967, 'Jibril Gaini: a preliminary account of the career of a Mahdist leader in North-Eastern Nigeria', *Research Bulletin* (Centre for Arab. Doc., Ibadan) 3,1: 16–38.
Le Grip, A., 1952, 'Le Mahdisme an Afrique Noire', *L'Afrique et l'Asie* 18: 3–16.
Marx, K., and F. Engels, 1955, *On Religion*, Moscow.
Plekhanov, G., n.d., *Fundamental Problems of Marxism*, Transl. E. and C. Paul, from the Russian ed. of 1928, London.
Pomeroy, W. J., 1968, 'Questions on the Debray thesis', *Monthly Review* 20, 3.
Ranger, T. O., 1967, *Revolt in Southern Rhodesia, 1896–7*, London.
Roberts, A., 1970, 'The Lumpa Church', in R. Rotberg and A. Mazrui, eds., *Protest and power in Black Africa*, Oxford.
Shepperson, G., 1962, 'Nyasaland and the Millennium', *Millennial Dreams in Action*, S. Thrupp, ed. (Comp. Studies in Soc. and Hist. Suppl. II) The Hague, 148–56.
Shepperson, G. and G. Price, 1959, *Independent African: John Chilembwe and the Nyasaland Rising of 1915*, Edinburgh.
Smith, W. C., 1957, *Islam in Modern History*, Princeton.
Tamuno, T. N., 1965, 'Some aspects of Nigerian reaction to British rule', *Journal of the Historical Society of Nigeria* 3, 2.
Tomlinson, G. J. F., and G. J. Lethem, 1927, *History of Islamic Propaganda in Nigeria*, London.
Trimingham, J. S., 1949, *Islam in the Sudan*, London.
Willis, J. R., 1967, '*Jihad fi sabil Allah* – its doctrinal basis in Islam and some aspects of its evolution in nineteenth century West Africa', *Journal of African History* 8,3: 401–6.

Religions and rural protests in Makoni District, Zimbabwe, 1900–80

TERENCE RANGER

Introduction: Types of Peasant

Makoni district lies some two thirds of the way between the capital city and the town of Umtali, on the border with Mozambique. Its colonial history has largely concerned the contestation between African and European agriculture; between black peasant production and white commercial farming. By 1900 most of the land in the district had been set aside for white farming, though it was not until after the second world war that white settlers took up all of 'their' area. However, although some Africans continued to live on 'unalienated' land or on land held by large investment companies, by far the greatest proportion of the African peasantry moved into the four Reserves set aside for African occupation. Most peasants in Makoni, therefore, did not pay rent for their land, nor a proportion of their crop, nor labour services. They were expropriated in other ways – through forced labour, through the low prices offered for crops by white traders, or through Governmental price fixing to the advantage of white producers.

Despite the fact that most peasants lived in the Reserves, holding their land by 'traditional' communal tenure, there were nevertheless considerable differences between types of peasants in Makoni. Peasants in the two small Reserves in the north of the district – Weya and Chikore – were too far away from the line of rail or from towns to be able to market their surplus; so also were peasants in the north-eastern portion of Makoni Reserve, who were cut off from markets by rugged granitic hills. For most of the colonial period peasant families in these areas were engaged in subsistence production, using the surplus of a fortunate year for beer brewing. Most of the adult men left these areas for work in the towns and mines.

In the rest of Makoni Reserve, however, and in the large Chiduku Reserve, peasant farmers were much closer to the halts on the railway lines or to traders' buying points. Peasant settlement in these Reserves clustered as close to such markets as possible. Until the mid 1920s hardly any male labour went out to work on European farms or mines, and virtually every family was engaged in small-scale production for the market. After the mid 1920s younger men began to leave the district to work but their fathers remained on their land. Peasants rapidly turned to the cultivation of maize, which had been little grown in the nineteenth century, but which became both the main cash crop and the staple of the district. In a good year such peasants might market up to ten bags of maize.

Within so-called 'traditional communal tenure', however, it was possible for entrepreneurial peasant farmers to emerge. In such a system land is allocated on the basis of capacity to work it. Some men were able to accumulate cattle and wives; or to invest savings from their salaries as teachers or policemen. Such men could make use of the labour of their own wives and of the wives of absent relatives; they could afford to keep their sons at home to work on their land rather than sending them out to wage labour; they could buy ploughs, carts and wagons. Men of this sort could obtain the usufruct of large tracts of land. By the 1920s several such men in Makoni were farming forty or fifty acres in the Reserves and marketing scores, or even hundreds of bags of maize. When the land they were using was exhausted, they could apply to the chief for land elsewhere in the Reserve. To be an entrepeneur in the Reserve, indeed, offered several advantages over acquisition of land in the Native Purchase Areas which the Rhodesian Government set up in the 1930s. Native Purchase Area farmers had to buy their land and they had to go on farming the same land in perpetuity.

Thus up until the 1930s when Government began to move against the Reserve entrepreneurs, peasant society in Makoni and Chiduku Reserves was divided into three groupings. There were the minority of relatively prosperous entrepreneurs; there was a much larger number of small peasant producers; and there were widows, the handicapped and those living behind the mountains or on the far side of unbridged rivers, who were engaged in subsistence agriculture. Chiefs and headmen stood rather apart from this pattern. None of the chiefs engaged in large-scale production for the market, though Chief Makoni at any rate possessed more land and controlled more women than even the most successful entrepreneur. In the earlier colonial period he continued to receive gifts of produce and tribute labour: he also received gifts of money from entrepreneurs to whom he allocated extensive land. All this enabled him to hold court and offer hospitality on something of the same lines, though on a much reduced scale, as his predecessors of the nineteenth century.

Varieties of Religion

As well as many types of peasant, there were also many types of religious profession in the Makoni district under colonialism. Pre-colonial religious observance was very much concerned with maintaining a proper relationship to the environment, with assuring fertility and an adequate supply of rain. The key figures were spirit mediums, men or women believed to be possessed by the spirits of founders of chiefly dynasties or by spirits of the land. Such mediums called upon the people, through the Chiefs, to make offerings for rain and fertility at the *rukoto* ceremony at the beginning of October and offerings in thanksgiving at the first fruits ceremony in February. The mediums and Chiefs controlled the agrarian cycle. They told people what crops could be grown and when planting could begin – and imposed penalties on anyone who planted a prohibited crop and who sowed seed too early. Before sowing, the people who lived near a major medium took their seed to a ceremony at his kraal; there the seeds were mixed with *divisi* medicine to ensure fertility. A mixture of seeds and *divisi* was sent by the medium to the Chief; people then brought their own seeds to the Chief to add to the mixture and a field at the Chief's kraal was cleared and planted before any other cultivation could commence. A special field was also maintained at every headman's kraal; the produce from which was sent to the Chief. Finally, the medium proclaimed, and the Chief enforced, rest days or *chisi* in honour of the spirit, on which no agricultural work has to be done.

In this way the mediums administered a set of rules of land management and conservation. They also gave spiritual sanction to the tributary demands of the Chiefs. As I was told by a senior medium of the Tandi chiefship in 1981: 'A Chief *must* have a spirit medium. The spirit medium *is* the chiefdom' [*Cf.* '*Gelfand, 1977: 134*]. Plainly these rules of land management and these tributary demands were not appropriate to entrepreneurial agriculture. An enterprising peasant farmer needed to take advantage of every local variation of soil and rainfall; to plant what he wanted when it was most profitable to plant it; to ignore the *chisi* rest days.

In the first decades of colonialism, then, certain correlations between economic position and religious observance were clear. Chiefs held aloof from mission Christianity – no Chief in Makoni was baptised as a Christian until the 1940s, though amongst their people there had been massive grass-roots movements towards Christianity from the 1910s. Chiefs had a traditional obligation to perform the rain ceremonies and their own economic interests lay in seeking to preserve the old systems of land management and tribute. Beyond that, oral evidence makes it plain that it was the peasantry in the zones of subsistence farming who most regularly observed 'traditional' ecological rituals. So long as there was not crippling land shortage, the old patterns suited them well enough. At the other extreme the Reserve entrepreneurs did *not* observe the old spiritual controls, particularly when the possession of ploughs allowed them to open up large areas of land.

The middle group of peasants producing small surpluses were in a more ambiguous position. There was nothing inherently hostile to the sale of agricultural surplus (in the attitudes of the mediums). So long as peasants were able to sell familiar grain crops, hoe-cultivated in the familiar way, and so long as they were prepared to offer beer to the spirits to keep the *chisi* days, the spirit mediums blessed their activities. Mediums – and small peasants for that matter – objected not to sale of the surplus, but to European enforcement of agricultural rules and levying of taxes and rates. So in their pronouncements the mediums often expressed the consciousness of the small surplus marketing peasant as well as the subsistence producer:

> The spirit disapproves of certain developments introduced in modern days (runs one such pronouncement). For instance it does not care for contour ridging because it causes too much work and has introduced features that were not in the landscape in former days. His spirit declares that there is no pleasure in walking the fields or bush as the contours make movement difficult. This innovation makes the tribal spirit angry and as a result people are short of food. The tribal spirit . . . dislikes the rising rates levelled by the rural councils . . . The spirit gave people soil on which to grow their crops . . . but nowadays they were being told to plough here and not there, only in particular places, unlike the instructions of the tribal spirit, which were merely to plant and water would be provided.

And if the mediums could express small peasant discontent with European interference, they could also express small peasant hostility towards the entrepreneur:

> Very rarely do Africans die of starvation. They have enough. They can get help from others . . . relatives and friends . . . If one brother needs help, another must come forward and help. . . . The sons of today expect something in return for what was given, but this is a European custom . . . Amongst the Shona there is no usury [*ibid. 140*].

From the time of the first world war onwards this level of peasant religion was overlaid by a movement of grass-roots 'conversion' to Christianity. All three missionary churches in Makoni – the Anglicans, the Catholics and the American Methodists – experienced the same rush of 'converts'; all three professed that this sudden success had little to do with their own activities and was either the work of the Holy Spirit or the consequence of the general desire for literacy. At this stage there was no correlation between the particular church to which peasants turned and their socio-economic position. There was a single movement on foot, powered by a very widespread desire to understand the new colonial order and also by the ambitions of young men returned from mines with a smattering of Christian literacy to set up their own villages of adherents grouped around a 'school'. But soon there *did* begin to develop a 'fit' between peasant type and particular Christian affiliation.

What happened was that core areas of Christian committment grew up in Makoni district – nuclei surrounded by a much more fluid and mobile religious pluralism. The Catholic core area came to be the mission farm at St Triashill and St Barbara's, on the eastern edge of Makoni district. Here the land was rocky as well as remote, cut off from markets. The peasantry were subsistence producers into the 1960s when the opening up of a good road through to Inyanga and the availability of fertilisers gave point and possibility to producing a marketable surplus. The peasants of this region remained faithful to the ecological rituals of the mediums. But they also took enthusiastically to a folk Catholicism. The successive Catholic orders which ran Triashill farm — Trappists, Mariannhill Fathers, Jesuits, Irish Carmelites — agreed at least on the ideal of maintaining an organic peasant community. The missionaries brought in the Ultramontanist peasant cults of nineteenth century Europe — the Lourdes Grotto, miracle-working statues of Our Lady of Fatima, pilgrimages to every hill on the mission farm designed to sacralise the land and to bring the migrant labouring men back home. Missionaries exorcised locusts, blessed seeds, prayed for rain. Their flock cheerfully held together this instrumental Catholicism with older eco-rituals. As one informant said in 1981, she had become a Catholic 'because they do not prohibit traditional practices such as brewing beer'; during her baptism she asked the Catholic Father whether it was a sin to brew beer for the spirits: 'It was replied that the dead do not partake in these ceremonies for none has ever been seen doing so. So there is no harm ... She was fully satisfied with these replies and has decided to remain a practising Roman Catholic and performs the necessary ceremonies for her ancestors'.[1] For their part, the spirit mediums showed a similar tolerance: around Triashill the mediums declared Fridays and Mondays as *chisi* days but the people complained that since they kept the Catholic sabbath this would leave 'four days only during which they could work in the fields and Monday was dropped out'.[2]

If Catholicism came to be the religion of subsistence peasants, Anglicanism came to be the faith of the small surplus-marketing peasants of Chiduku Reserve. A network of Anglican church and schools, maintained by teacher-catechists, sprang up in Chiduku in all the surplus producing zones. The teacher-catechist ruled his flock with great dignity and honour and in return gave them access to literacy and to basic 'modernising' skills — village hygiene, the growth of groves of gum-trees, and so on. Village life focussed round the church, with its carved animal clan totems; villagers marched on high days to the mother church of St Faiths, carrying their totemic banners. Edgar Lloyd, for some thirty years the dominant influence on Makoni Anglicanism, accepted joyfully this village ministry. On leave in England he took a course in Peasant Pottery at the Camberwell School of Arts and Crafts; his wife Elaine took a weaving course at the Peasants Art Guild. The Anglican mission, wrote Lloyd in 1930 was:

> that of preaching Christ in the village ... Africa is a country of villages; of cultivated patches, often hand-tilled, of herds of small cattle, of wood fires in huts ... To hold

the villages for Christ is to hold Africa that now is, and to influence for good the Africa to be.³

Everywhere that Lloyd went in his ceaseless itinerations of Chiduku he met peasants carrying their crops to market — the surplus of their 'cultivated patches, hand-tilled'. The Resident Commissioner, touring southern Chiduku in 1920, found a network of Anglican outstations:

> in charge of a native teacher. These men are married, are well educated, and of more than usual intelligence. At each station there is a well built church ... replicas of the large Mission Church at St Faith's. It was also evident that some attempt was being made to keep the native kraals ... clean and tidy. In one case the native teacher had planted an avenue of eucalyptus trees leading to the kraal. The men and women were better dressed than is usually the case in kraals so far removed from centres of European occupation.⁴

These mild 'modernisations', however, were far exceeded by the quintessential American Methodist converts — entrepreneurs to a man. American Methodist missionaries aimed at economic transformation:

> Poverty is the word that perhaps best describes the lives of these people. Poverty of material comforts; poverty of social ideals; poverty of religious conceptions. Richness must be poured into their lives ... to bring regeneration to the entire economic, social and spiritual life [*O'Farrell, 1926: 28*].

From the beginning the American Methodists stressed 'improved' agricultural methods — and they found their core areas in villages particularly close to market opportunity. The most prominent of these was Gandanzara in the east of Makoni Reserve, close to the Umtali market. Here the headman himself converted to Methodism and to entrepreneurial agriculture, enthusiastically seconded by many male household heads:

> The success of our native people in agriculture (wrote the Mission Agriculturalist in 1923) is really wonderful ... At present there are hundreds of plows owned by natives and the crops grown are really wonderful. Some of our best stations like Gandanzara where the new methods of agriculture have taken a firm grip are a wonderful demonstration. At this particular station every person who has any cattle has a plow and there are forty-three plows owned by the people there. These people who own the ploughs are no longer poverty stricken. They are the foundation of progress in the village [*Roberts, 1923: 67*].

In Gandanzara there was a complete Christian substitution for the old eco-religion. In place of the ritual field cultivated for Chief Makoni, 'the people cultivate some acres which they call "The Garden of God", sell the crop and bring the proceeds to the mission'. In 1922, during severe drought, 'the heathen came to Philip, son of Gandanzara, and said "Allow us to be given spirit that the rain come" '; the headman refused sacrifice to the spirits; there was constant prayer in the church so that 'it rained hard, and the gardens of the people have good crops'.[5] Thereafter, a sequence of charismatic African ministers made rain for Gandanzara.

The successive Gandanzara headmen broke away from spiritual dependence on the mediums and economic dependence on tribute: they opened up fields of new cash-crops, cultivated with the aid of the Government/Agricultural Demonstrators. The women of the American Methodist Rukwadzano association gave free labour in these 'progressive' fields. After Phillip Gandanzara's death a kinsman summed up his modernising achievement:

> The late headman was a Christian ... He refused the brewing of beer in his area ... His village became a centre of civilisation and attraction ... people of Makoni as a whole had refused the idea of contour ridges but ... he introduced the idea.[6]

In these core areas, then, a peasant folk Christianity developed – or rather a series of folk Christianities, appropriate to a series of peasantries. In the 1930s yet another variety of religious committment developed in Makoni. Prophetic, pentecostal movements sprang up under African leadership, the most important of which was founded by a young man from the Gandanzara area, Shoniwa Masedza Tandi Moyo, who became known as Johana Masowe, John of the Wilderness. Johana's church emphasised healing, exorcism, the eradication of witchcraft. It attracted particularly those groups who had least status in Makoni's peasant economy – women, young men without land of their own, those families in Gandanzara and elsewhere who did *not* own ploughs and who lived in the shadow of the successful American Methodist entrepreneurs. It also established itself particularly strongly in western Chiduku, on the far side of an unbridged river and hence in effect cut off from trade in agrarian products. Johana preached a radical criticism both of the mission churches and also of the religion of the spirit mediums. In *his* 'spirit-filled' universe only the Holy Spirit possessed benevolent power: all other spirits were defined as evil. Members of his church had to withdraw from all 'traditional' ecological rituals. Johana preached that fertility would be restored to the land only when the African people repented of their particular sin – witchcraft.

At the same time he preached an economic doctrine – a doctrine of withdrawal from dependence on the white trader or employer:

> Baba Johan had the conviction (says Amon Nengomasha) that one could not lead a proper and holy life unless he could fend for himself. This is the most important belief expressed by Baba Johan. If he satisfied his material needs, he would be able to satisfy his spiritual. It was very difficult at first because most of his converts lived in rural areas and knew only about agriculture. The first message to these people was, 'first of all, all you people must learn to work together. Have a common field; you might have

individual fields but at least you must have one field designed for the Church.[7]

Later Johana led many of his followers out of the rural areas altogether and they became self-employed artisans – shoe-makers, basket-makers, etc – on the outskirts of Southern Africa's towns.

Varieties of Protest

In this society of varied peasant experience and of varied religious commitment, there were many grounds for protest. There were tensions between one stratum of peasants and another – as land came to be less and less freely available within the Reserves, so there was hostility towards the entrepreneurial peasants who farmed such large acreages and who rapidly exhausted soil fertility with their ploughing. There were tensions between one generation and another – for example, between the generation of the first Christian converts, many of whom had become small or large surplus-marketing peasants, and their sons and daughters, many of whom had to go out of Makoni district to seek work or found themselves providing additional labour to cultivate land controlled by the Christian elders. Then there were a number of tensions between peasants and the whites – ranging from the bitterness of the peasant evicted from white farms and unable to get adequate land in the Reserves, through to the anger of small peasant producers at the low prices offered by traders, and on to the sense of betrayal felt by the Reserve entrepreneurs as white officials turned against them and sought to drive them out of the Reserves altogether.

These tensions formed a complex pattern. At one time one peasant stratum or one generation would find allies in the whites; at other times another stratum or generation. Thus, for example, from 1900 to 1920 white missionaries and administrators favoured the mission Christian 'youth revolution' and the entrepreneurial peasant farmer; in the 1920s and 1930s the administration increasingly came to opt instead for rural stability and backed chiefs, elders and small or subsistence peasants against entrepreneurs. In the earlier period the administration was deeply suspicious of spirit mediums, whom it believed both desirous and capable of fomenting armed insurrection. By the 1930s, however, Native Commissioners were requesting white farmers and even missionaries to allow 'traditional' ecological ceremonies to take place on their land.

From the 1940s onwards, by contrast, almost all peasant interests had reason to be hostile to the whites. All peasants who were living on white-owned or 'unalienated' land were evicted from it into the already over-crowded Reserves. There was official interference and coercion in farming methods, land allocation and conservation measures. Cattle were destocked. Government control of prices meant that black maize producers got much less than white. Government tried to destroy the Reserve entrepreneurs by insisting that each family be allocated the same amount of land. All this united the subsistence, small and entrepreneurial peasantries against white settlers and officials.

These complexities of tension mean that it is not possible to identify any one of the religious traditions of Makoni district as the tradition of peasant protest. At different times *all* of them were acquiescent; at others all of them – Anglican, Prophetic, American Methodist, Catholic and 'traditional' – were drawn on as ideologies of peasant protest. I propose to demonstrate this by taking four sequences of protest in chronological order. The first is protest by the Anglican spokesmen of small producing peasants against forced labour in 1911. Next is the protest of the Prophetic churches against the misery of the Depression of the 1930s. Then comes the protest of the American Methodist 'progressives' in the early 1970s against a projected settlement to the Rhodesian problem which would have denied them opportunity. Finally I shall describe the involvement particularly of spirit mediums and of Catholic priests in the guerilla war in Makoni from 1976 to 1980.

Anglican teacher-evangelists and the forced labour crisis of 1911

It is important to understand that the very process of becoming a surplus-marketing peasant in early colonial Makoni district was in itself a defiance of settler society and of the colonial state. After the repression of the 1896 uprisings and the execution of the 'rebel' chief Makoni, the district was defined as a zone of white commercial agriculture. The role of African males was to supply cheap labour – labour to build the railway between Salisbury and the Mozambique coast; labour to clear the land on white farms; labour for the mines. For a year or two after the risings, labour *did* flow out – African cultivation had been badly disrupted by the military repression and where men did not voluntarily seek work to provide for their families, armed police were sent in to the kraals to compel them. But once the railway was built through the district and once the British Government began to frown on forced labour, the possibility of becoming a peasant rather than a labour migrant arose. The railway ran more or less parallel with the eastern border of the Chiduku Reserve, and grain-traders took their wagons into Makoni Reserve. In both areas men and women began to open up extensive fields in order to produce for the market. Soon there was an acute labour shortage on white farms.

Prices for grain were good and people were readily able to meet their tax obligations and other cash needs in years of good harvest. It was more difficult to sustain the peasant strategy through years of drought and dearth. At such times white traders were eager to sell back grain at high prices, and happy to get peasants into their debt; the Native Commissioner was prepared to offer famine relief but only in return for men volunteering to go out for work. So peasants in

Chiduku and Makoni had somehow to manage to refuse to buy grain from traders and to refuse to accept official famine relief. They *did* manage — by trading their own grain for high famine prices and then travelling into remote areas to buy grain more cheaply, by offering their labour or their cattle to peasants in areas where there had been rain, and so on. And at the end of each such drought the peasants enlarged their lands in hopes of a good year and a good market. It was during these years that Anglicanism spread in Chiduku. Meanwhile the white farmers of Makoni could get hardly any local labour. Even the men of Weya and Chikore Reserves or from Triashill, who had to go out to work, refused to work on farms and went instead to the towns. So the white farmers began to import labour from Nyasaland and Northern Rhodesia. They detested the Anglican mission at St Faith's, which they regarded as sustaining the African peasant strategy:

> St Faith's mission was then very powerful (an old white farmer told me in 1981). The Africans used to think it was their head . . . St Faith's was a thorn in our side from the start. Their whole idea was educating the African to be as good as the white man . . . They had a little education and wanted to be as good as the master.[8]

The white farmers tried a series of attacks on Chiduku Reserve — the bastion of the peasant strategy. They suggested in early 1911 that a great belt of land in the north of the Reserve was too rich for African cultivation and that it should be taken out and made available for white settlement. This proposal was in the end defeated by protests to the High Commissioner by the Anglican missionaries at St Faith's, as was a later proposal by the 1915 Reserves Commission that the southern third of Chiduku should be excised from the Reserve. In September 1911 a more direct assault was attempted. Nyasa labour supplies fell away; white farmers went to Salisbury *en masse* and demanded that the administration help them to get local labour. As a result Native Commissioners were told to seek the cooperation of chiefs and headmen in getting labour for white farms.

The Native Commissioner in Makoni put these orders enthusiastically into effect. He told chiefs that if they didn't produce labour the Reserves would be taken away. He authorised his Native Messengers to go into the Reserves and take men — and this at a time when male labour was needed to open up and plant land for peasant production. Men were taken, and where they had run away their wives were taken so as to force husbands to give themselves up. Peasant production was seriously disrupted and labour was instead made available to the white farmers.

Who was to protest against this blatant transfer of labour from one agrarian sector to the other? Male peasants offered no overt resistance but fled into the hills. Spirit mediums had no message to give, though they later explained the drought of the 1911–12 season in terms of the anger of the spirits at the treacherous actions of the Native Messengers. The Catholic missionaries had only just arrived on the scene. The American Methodists were anxious that their converts should stand well with the administration and in any case there were few Methodist entrepreneurs in 1911. It was the Anglicans – and pre-eminently the teacher-evangelists – who offered effective protest.

The teacher-evangelists of Chiduku witnessed the labour raids and saw their schools empty as their pupils took to the hills. Then they wrote full accounts of the incidents and sent them to the white missionaries at St Faith's. Edgar Lloyd and his colleagues compiled a dossier which they sent to the Resident Commissioner and High Commissioner; an inquiry was ordered, which reluctantly found that illegalities had taken place. The Native Commissioner was officially censured and the Government made it clear that they would not again ask Native Commissioners to recruit labour. In this victory for the peasant strategy, the teacher-evangelists played a key role. Their oral evidence was crucial at the inquiry. These new men struck a new note. Matthew, teacher at Gushiri's kraal, where people had been very actively engaged in grain production and marketing as well as in the pursuit of literacy, spoke up in their interest and in the interest of Anglicanism:

> I consider it my duty should I hear of any irregularity by officials of the Native Department to report to the head of the mission. In my opinion the Native Commissioner exceeded his authority by giving the instructions to the Messengers... I should like to see those who seized people punished... If the Native Commissioner acted wrongly I should like to see him punished.[9]

Prophetic Apostolics and the Depression of the 1930s

The Anglican victories in Chiduku were followed by a period in which the peasant strategy came to maturity; in which Methodist entrepreneurs began to flourish and the folk Catholicism of Triashill grew up. Peasants faced plenty of difficulties in the 1920s but in retrospect this decade came to seem a golden age. Small peasants looked back on it as a time when one could market a surplus without abandoning 'traditional' methods of extensive farming and long fallows; the entrepreneurs came to look back on it as a period of steady grain prices, of missionary backing and of profitable collaboration with government Agricultural Demonstrators. The mission churches began to develop schemes of local financial self-support. The Depression which began at the end of the 1920s brought this heyday of Christian peasant agriculture to an end.

Markets for African grains and cattle collapsed and there were no jobs for the young men who left the district as labour migrants. The young men returned home full of resentment and with articulate political ideas encountered in the towns. Older people shared the resentment, if not the urban political ideas. None of the mission folk Christianities could adequately express this resentment because the mission churches were themselves soon under attack. The mission strategies of peasant production for the market and of education for employment now looked like mere deceit. Mission emphases on 'self-help', on church dues and taxes now seemed like oppression. All three of the major missions came under attack from their adherents. Around Triashill African Catholics protested bitterly against the Jesuits who had just taken over the mission and some of those who lived on the mission farm joined the millenarian Watch Tower church. Many of the old Anglican teacher-evangelists, bitter at the increasing emphasis on formal educational qualification and their consequent loss of status, shared the general bitterness and three of them broke away from the Church of England to found their own sects. Boys and girls left the Anglican schools. As for the American Methodists, the prominent entrepreneurs were able to weather the Depression but others came to criticise the acquistive ideology which marked Methodism in Makoni. American Methodist evangelists found that 'our Christian people are gradually withdrawing themselves from the Church and they regard it as an instrument of oppression'.[10]

If there was going to be a religious expression of protest, of repudiation of a failed system, it had to come from somewhere outside the mission churches. It might have seemed an opportunity for the spirit mediums, and there is indeed evidence of unusual activity amongst them at this time. Many mediums called upon the people to return to the old eco-rituals, neglect of which was being punished by immiseration. Chiefs and headmen pressed the Native Department to make it possible for ceremonies to be held at sacred places on 'white' land. Chiefs also made use of a new non-Christian prophetic movement, Mchape. Increasing mortality among children – the result of a combination of disease and malnutrition – led to an increased fear of witchcraft. Mchape claimed to be able to eradicate witchcraft, to protect the innocent and punish the guilty, to cleanse the land and to renew society by means of collective confession and a ritual meal. Mchape ritual was a dramatisation of the divisions which economic differentiation had brought to Makoni and a means of re-integrating the repentant Christian 'moderniser' back into the collectivity of the chiefdom: but for this very reason it took place only in the kraals of chiefs, who stood outside the Christian 'progressive' system, or in zones of subsistence peasant farming. Thus the folk Catholics of Triashill performed the Mchape rituals, but they did not take place in Gandanzara, where the Methodist entrepreneurs were still too influential to have to expose themselves to humiliating public repentance.

The major religious protest came, in fact, not from any revived or innovated 'traditionalism' but from Christian prophetic independency. The 1930s saw the rise of the *Vapostori* church of Johana Masowe. Johana came from a small kraal in the Gandanzara area, an island of Anglican relative poverty in a sea of American

Methodist enterprise. His preaching combined the enthusiastic dimensions of folk Methodism with a scathing critique of the entrepreneurial ethic. His message was profoundly inward-looking: the white system had reneged on its promises and Africans should turn their backs on it, contracting out of both peasant agriculture and labour migration. White missionaries had proved incapable of speaking to African needs or healing African sins. But Johana did not glorify African tradition either. Chiefs and headmen, in his view, still demanded tribute without any longer providing services in return for it; fathers and elders oppressed the young. A profound internal Christian revolution was required to bring about a just society.

So the thousands of *Vapostori* converts in Makoni in the 1930s offered a largely symbolic but infuriating challenge to chiefs and headmen as well as to Native Commissioners, to spirit mediums as well as to missionaries. Children ran away from mission schools and gathered on nearby hillocks to praise the Holy Spirit in tongues; young men and women married without bride price; *Vapostori* refused to perform corvee labour in the Reserves, and danced around Native Messengers and Native Commissioners in holy ecstasy; Johana and his preachers destroyed the regalia of spirit mediums. An Anglican African priest itinerating in the rural areas of Makoni found:

> Apostolics ... a mixed lot of lapsed Christians from the American Methodist, the Roman Catholic and our Church. ... They claim themselves to be the true followers of the Apostles, and the other Christians of other Churches are false, their priests are not true ministers of Christ. 'You are not true ministers of the word because you sell it for money. Our Lord did not do that nor His Apostles. But you do. Our Lord cast out devils and evil spirits, you cannot'.[11]

American Methodism and Protest against the Rhodesia Front

By the last years of the 1930s the mission churches – and their varieties of folk Christianity – had weathered the challenge of independency. As markets for agricultural produce began to recover, so the Christian peasant solution seemed pertinent once more. By the end of the 1930s Native Commissioners were talking once again about grass roots demands for baptism and for education. Confidence in the schools recovered and only the *Vapostori* stood aside from a scramble for educational qualifications which was as hectic in the zones of subsistence production as in those of peasant marketing.

Still, the 'golden age' of the 1920s did not return. During the 1940s there was a great boom for white commercial agriculture in Makoni: in the years of the war African labour was once more conscripted in the Reserves and delivered to white farmers for 'war production'; 'white' land long left vacant was now cut up into 'tobacco units' and settled with new white farmers; Africans were driven off this land into the Reserves. In order to create anything like room for them, Native Commissioners sequestered the large land holdings of the Reserve entrepreneurs and allocated them only six or seven acres per family. In the small Reserves in the north of Makoni there was crippling overcrowding by 1950 and even in Chiduku and Makoni Reserve there was profound opposition to Government coercion and interference. By the 1950s peasants in Makoni were ready to link up with anyone who would help them combat land alienation, the enforced construction of contour ridges and so on.

In this way there developed connections between Makoni peasants and the successive mass nationalist movements of the late 1950s and early 1960s. In northern Makoni especially these were years of violent peasant opposition; of collective refusals to pay tax or dip fees; of attacks on African Agricultural Demonstrators; of the breaking down of contour ridges. The connection between all this and religion was complicated. On the one hand there *was* – especially in the early 1960s – a cultural nationalist criticism of mission Christianity and a proclamation of the 'religion of our ancestors'. The spirit mediums' opposition to the enforcement of agrarian rules fitted neatly into such a development. But on the other hand, precisely because peasant nationalism *was* a mass movement it was bound to contain very many of the folk Christians of Makoni's various traditions. Thus, although some churches and schools were burnt down and life was difficult for African agents of the churches especially in 1964 – when the nationalist parties were finally banned by Government – it would not be possible to say that nationalism as a whole was anti-Christian.

As for the churches themselves, they all had an ambiguous relationship to nationalism. For a period the experiment in co-operative farming based at St Faith's and led by Guy Clutton Brock made it seem as if there might even be an alliance between Anglicanism and nationalism. But that possibility vanished when an alarmed hierarchy restored a narrow and authoritarian priestly control and wound up the co-operative. The age of Edgar Lloyd and the defiant teacher-evangelists seemed completely to have ended. The Irish Carmelites who now ran Triashill and St Barbaras began by being shocked at the local folk Catholicism. Faced by nationalism, however, they began to play up folk piety, to preach sermons about the virtues of traditional African religiosity and the contrasting horrors of Communism. The *Vapostori* shared the nationalist repudiation of official intervention in rural society, but they certainly did not share nationalist admiration for the ancestor spirits. *Vapostori* solutions were spiritual, not political and there were severe tensions between *Vapostori* leaders and nationalist militants. Even some of the spirit mediums were more inclined to work with the administration towards a revived tribal traditionalism than to collaborate with the nationalists.

As for the American Methodists, nothing would have seemed less likely in the

1960s than that they should take a lead in nationalist opposition. When the Methodist missionary, Norman Thomas, carried out doctoral research in the 1960s he found that of all the religious denominations in Makoni district the American Methodists and their adherents stood most apart from nationalism. He found that folk Catholics and folk Anglicans belonged to the nationalist parties in their thousands. But to be an American Methodist was still much more a matter of core commitment: Methodists were churchmen first and foremost, as well, of course, as being 'modernising' progressives.

And yet the unlikely came to pass. After the banning of the nationalist parties and the detention of most of their leaders in 1964, there were eight years without any open or formal organisation of African opposition. When one *did* emerge in 1972 it was improbably led by Abel Muzorewa, first African bishop of the American Methodist Church. In Makoni district, at any rate, Muzorewa's African National Council acquired much of its energy from the ardent participation of American Methodist clergy, teachers and laymen – and especially from the militancy of the church's women's organisation. How did this happen?

There were no doubt many reasons, among them being the gradual development within American Methodism generally of a social gospel which emphasised the need to attack societal poverty as well as to save individuals. But it is not too reductionist to see the long-established entrepreneurial nature of Makoni Methodism as also being at the root of things. The point was that under the revived segregationist ideology of the Rhodesia Front Government, Methodist rural entrepreneurs once again felt themselves being forced out of their deserved opportunities.

Muzorewa's family history illustrates perfectly the chequered career and constantly frustrated aspirations of the Makoni entrepreneurs. His father had been a pastor-teacher in the A.M.E.C.; in the early 1930s he decided to 'try his hand at farming'. Together with two other ex pastor-teachers he settled at Chinyadza village in Chiduku Reserve, where he 'discovered some forty to fifty acres of relatively rich soil' and opened up 'rich green fields of maize, groundnuts, rapoko and beans'. 'Released from pressures to conform with past ways', the three Methodist families prospered. Their waggons carried scores of sacks of maize to market in Rusape. Then in the 1940s these entrepreneurs were forced out; the 'cattle were sold ... farmlands surrendered'; Muzorewa's father had to accept 'almost desert-like' land in Mangwende Reserve and to go to South Africa to work as a waiter. Returning in 1948 he showed all the resilience of the Methodist moderniser by irrigating a half acre garden and producing carrots as a cash crop. At last, he managed to acquire a farm in the Native Purchase Area. For a time he did well enough, in common with other Purchase farmers who were on good terms with Government in the 1950s. But Rhodesia Front policy threatened once again to reduce the Native Purchase entrepreneurs to peripherality [*Muzorewa, 1978*].

Martin Meredith has described Abel Muzorewa as coming from 'a simple peasant family'. Plainly in Makoni terms, it was by no means so simple. Muzorewa was a quintessential product of the Methodist entrepreneurial tradition. He himself served his first pastorate in Chiduku North Circuit, at one of the long-established Methodist entrepreneurial villages, Muziti. There is no doubt – even when one takes into account his genuine concern for the poor – that Muzorewa's fundamental opposition to the Rhodesia Front's policy was that it left no room for the honest, industrious, entrepreneurial African farmer to reap his just reward. Thus in 1972 – when the African population of Southern Rhodesia were asked to express their opinion of the proposed terms of a constitutional settlement between Britain and Rhodesia – 'the overwhelming majority of (the) relatively privileged group' in the Native Purchase Areas 'unequivocally rejected the terms'. Muzorewa emerged as leader of the African National Council campaigning for rejection. The A.M.E.C. journal, *Umbowo*, began to carry the speeches of this 'Moses of his day', side by side with its articles on the importance of education and on the techniques of progressive farming. Muzorewa sketched the past of American Methodism: 'We want to be counted as good people by those in power. We want to feel secured, comfortable and enjoy a life of luxury.' He also suggested its future – to 'choose life, as Moses did in leaving the palace by simply disagreeing with the powers that be' [*Muzorewa, 1982*]. Gandanzara became a stronghold of opposition.

When Muzorewa turned the A.N.C. into a permanent organisation it was very strong for a period in Makoni district. It won the support of the radical peasant nationalists, even if many of these were using it as a cover for continued activity on behalf of the banned nationalist parties. But it added to this a dimension missing from the nationalism of the 1950s and 1960s – the wholehearted commitment of the Methodist machine and of Methodist modernisers.

Guerilla war and religious ideology: 1976 to 1980

Although Muzorewa claimed the loyalty of many of the guerillas as the war developed after 1972, the natural inclination of his movement and of its quintessential support was towards negotiation. When Muzorewa came to terms with Ian Smith in the 'Internal Settlement' and formed a Government after his victory in the 1979 elections, the nationalist front in Makoni was broken beyond repair. There was a split between those who worked with the guerillas from Mozambique – who had entered Makoni in 1976 – and those who retained faith in Muzorewa. It would be an over-simplification to analyse this split either in purely class or in purely confessional terms. Muzorewa recruited African

Auxiliaries who were largely drawn from the under-educated unemployed of Makoni. Many entrepreneurs in Makoni – especially store-keepers – worked with the guerillas. Nevertheless, there *was* an underlying division.

In the files of the Catholic Commission for Justice and Peace are two reports which illustrate the predicament of the rural entrepreneurs during the guerilla war. One was by 'A Middle Class Business Man in a War Zone', a store-keeper who complained that he had been victimised by all sides: as for the guerilla:

> his demand for money is quite above human dignity. He does not allow anybody to show that whatever one has worked for must be asked for, but just takes unconditionally... The number of shops that have been emptied by them without buying anything are not countable. How many people have been killed because they are said to be sell outs are not countable... You can see gentlemen that it is a middle class person who suffers from both sides for no cause of his.[12]

The other was from the Native Purchase Area Farmers' organisation which protested that since the Internal Settlement agreement the guerillas 'were not sure of the local attitude to the Agreement and so have hardened towards African farmers... Prominent African Farmers are being killed simply because they are better off than most of the people'.[13]

In Makoni district these patterns are also detectable. It was the zones of historically subsistence peasant agriculture – Triashill, St Barbaras, the northern Reserves – which supported the guerillas most strongly. On the other hand, Gandanzara was several times attacked by guerillas and its impressive buildings left in ruins. But what was the role of religion in this radical peasant guerilla war?

The evidence available while the war was going on, suggested that something very unusual and significant was happening, namely that for the first time peasant protest in Makoni had been separated from religious expression. It was reported that Catholic, Anglican and Methodist missionaries had been forced to withdraw from the Reserves; that abandoned mission stations had been looted and broken up; that one of the independent church leaders, Basil Nyabadza of the Church of St Francis, had been murdered by guerillas; even that the medium of the greatest of the Shona spirits, Chaminuka, had been killed by the guerillas. Government propaganda portrayed the guerillas as Communist enemies of religion; the mission churches feared that their converts, in supporting the guerillas, were moving irrevocably away from Christianity; guerilla support groups in Europe and America depicted the guerillas as educators, teaching the peasants a rational, secular doctrine of political action and leading them out of supernaturalist superstition.

Field inquiry shows that this picture is in many ways misleading. Basil Nyabadza was in fact killed not by guerillas but by Government police disguised as guerillas. If the Chaminuka medium was killed by the guerillas – as he undoubtedly was – many other mediums worked with them closely. If some mission stations were wrecked, others were left untouched and their resident missionaries came to be regarded as invaluable allies of the guerillas.

In particular, guerillas worked with spirit mediums and with spokesmen of folk Catholicism. This was partly because the key guerilla strong-holds lay in the old subsistence peasant areas where folk Catholicism and 'traditional' eco-religion were both deeply rooted. Thus Triashill and St Barbaras became almost no-go areas for Government forces. Guerillas interacted intensely with the people and came to recognise how profoundly their consciousness was shaped by their folk religion. For their part, the local people applied their composite religious rituals to the war situation. Old Bepas Manyoka Chiro, baptised a Catholic in 1914, married in Triashill church in the 1920s, subsistence farmer and migrant labourer, was worried about the safety of the Catholic secondary school for girls near Triashill. He met with the headmaster of the school: 'They then agreed to brew beer and make an offering to ancestors through the spirit mediums. Beer was brewed, an offering was made to the ancestors and the rest of it was drunk by the villagers. It so happened that none of the buildings were destroyed and Mr Chiro believes that the offering was heeded'. At the same time, meeting with the guerillas at a politicisation gathering, Bepas told them of a former white priest who had prophesied 'that there was going to be a war which was to come from the east which I interpret as this very one ... the first and last war in our country'.[14]

The Irish father in charge of St Barbaras remained there throughout the war; so too did the Irish father at St Killian's in the Makoni Reserve. They came to terms with each successive guerilla band; provided them with medical supplies and clothes; worked to release members of their flock who had been arrested as well as those who were tortured at Security Force camps. Although the Catholic church had given up its ownership of the mission farm and the peasant Catholic Association was disbanded so as not to clash with primary loyalties to the guerillas, the size of the St Barbaras and St Killians congregations grew.

But interactions between guerillas and peasant religion were not restricted to guerilla sensitivity to the folk religion of the old subsistence zones. It was not only in these zones but throughout the district that guerillas worked closely with spirit mediums. There were cultural nationalist reasons for this – guerillas had named two of their major war zones after the great spirits and a major spirit medium was based at a guerilla transit camp in Mozambique. But there were also strong local reasons. As a matter of guerilla policy, the young men fighting in Makoni district were overwhelmingly strangers to it. It was not easy for the peasant elders, who had headed the old nationalist movement in Makoni, to cede dominance to these strange young men. Moreover, the guerillas could not legitimate themselves by working with chiefs and headmen; these had come to be so closely connected with the Government that they mostly became the object of armed guerilla attack, though chief Makoni himself did manage to work with the comrades. Hence they needed to achieve the legitimation which the spirit mediums, as 'owners' of the land, could provide. For their part, the Makoni peasants — no matter how strongly they supported the guerillas — wanted some means of turning arbitrary guerilla action into a mutually agreed code of conduct. For them, the spirit mediums acted as 'Holy Men', giving the laws of internal peace.

Throughout Makoni district, therefore, spirit mediums mediated between the guerillas, the peasants and the land. According to Amon Shonge, founder of a cooperative farm in the northern Reserve:

> There are many spirit mediums in Weya . . . The main medium the comrades used was the chief medium of headman Mwendaziya, Mukuwamombe, the greatest spirit of them all. The comrades brought him into Weya. They wanted him here, because he was supposed to be the one who could make the land safe. This use of mediums was the same everywhere. The comrades had to contact the spirit medium first to introduce themselves. Then they would be told what to do. They were told which were the holy places and given some sort of by-laws to guide them. They were told that they must not kill innocent people. Nearly everyone then started to feel that the mediums were very important people. The mediums felt that they had been forgotten but now they were remembered.[15]

In this way, folk Catholicism and the spirit mediums interacted with guerilla war. Anglicanism was largely discredited by the break-up of the St Faith's cooperative and the condemnations of the guerillas by the Anglican episcopacy. American Methodism was discredited by its association with Muzorewa. Nevertheless, under certain circumstances local agents even of these churches could play the same role of peace-making Holy Man. One example of this was the Anglican headmaster and 'supplementary' priest, Stephen Matewa, at Toriro school in Chiduku. Matewa disliked guerilla recourse to spirit mediums — wars were won, he urged, by guns, not magic. But he himself took much the same role. He provided the guerillas with clothes and food, had his school declared by the authorities as an 'open zone' and then allowed the guerillas to use it for recuperation. In return, he wrote, 'the boys now have respect for the tribesmen and talk with them as with their parents. The killings in this area have ceased and people are a little happier than before'.[16]

Conclusion

It is clear, then, that politicisation during the guerilla war did not secularise Makoni. Still, it did undoubtedly produce very significant changes in most of the equations established in this paper. Most of the chiefs and headmen were killed or ran away during the war, and since the 1980 elections the executive and judicial role of the chiefs has been more or less brought to an end. Spirit mediums still enjoy prestige, and some are being paid a salary by the ruling party. But it remains to be seen how the prestige of the mediums works out in an era without chiefs. The Mugabe Government has called upon the mission churches to help with restoration and expansion of education. Anglicanism is now fully under African control. The Catholic priests who stayed on throughout the war are still there, much honoured. And yet the war *did* change the character of Makoni folk Christianity:

> Since the 4th April, 1966, when the first guns were fired at Sinoia (wrote an African Anglican priest in July 1980), Christians in Tribal Trust Lands became open to war propaganda. This propaganda has shaped the thinking and life of these Christians to such an extent that some of these Christians are now different Christians they were before the war. Their thinking has been very much coloured by the events of the war [*Mudzvovera, 1980*].

What the new colours are to be will depend on what patterns African agriculture in Makoni develops out of the present confusion made up from Government resettlement schemes, peasant squatters, revived Native Purchase farmer ambitions, and the purchase of farms in the commercial areas by black entrepreneurs on a new and grand scale. But it seems to me certain that the close interaction between peasant types and types of religious expression will continue for a good while yet.

Notes

1. Interview between P. M. Chakanyuka and Mapani Magadza Rinah Gertrude, Nedewedzo, Chiduku, 9 January 1981.
2. Interview between Sister Emilia Chiteka and Denis Tahusarira, Triashill, 11 January 1981.
3. Canon E. W. Lloyd, Report, 1930, SPG Reports, USPG Archives, Westminster.
4. High Commissioner to Administrator, 4 March 1920, A 3/18/39/10, National Archives. Archives.
5. Daniel Chipenderu, Report from Gandanzara, 7 January 1923, NUA 3/1/1, National Archives
6. T. Gwatidzo to District Commissioner, Makoni, 10 August 1975, file 'Makoni: Headman Gandanzara', District Commissioner's office, Rusape.
7. Interview with Amon Nengomasha, 17 February and 3 March 1977, AOH/4, National Archives Oral History project.
8. Interview with Leonard Ziehl, Rusape, 19 February 1981.
9. Evidence of Matthew, 13 November 1911, A 3/18/33/2, National Archives.
10. 'Christian Conference. Agenda and Minutes, July 3 1935', Green files, Old Umtali Archives.
11. Yakobo Mwela, 'The Mission of Renewal', 1934, USPG Archives.
12. Pasipanodya, 'A Middle Class Business Man in a War Zone', Catholic Commission for Justice and Peace Archives, 'Guerilla Reports'.

13. African Farmers' Union Report, 13 February 1979, CCJP Archives, file 'Political'.
14. Interview between Sister Emilia Chiteka and Bepas Manyoka Chiro, Chewa, Makoni, 4 January 1981.
15. Interview with Amon Shonge, Weya, 25 March 1981.
16. Stephen Matewa to Bishop of Mashonaland, 4 November 1978, Matewa letter-book, Toriro, Chiduku.

References

Gelfand, M., 1977, *The Spiritual Beliefs of the Shona*, Gwelo.
Muzorewa, A., 1978, *Rise up and Walk: An Autobiography*, London.
Muzorewa, A., 1982, 'Bishop's Corner', *Umbowo*, Febr.
Mudzvovera, N. P., 1980, 'Hopes and Aspirations of the Black Anglican Christians', *The Independent Zimbabwe*, 9 July.
Roberts, G. A., 1923, *Journal*.
O'Farrell, 1926, 'Report', *Journal of the Rhodesian Annual Conference*.

Additional bibliography

N. Bhebe, *Christianity and Traditional Religion in Western Zimbabwe 1859–1923*, London 1979.
P. Fry, *Spirits of the Protest: Spirit Mediums and the articulation of consensus among the Zezuru of Southern Rhodesia*, Cambridge 1976.
I. Linden, *The Catholic Church and the Struggle for Zimbabwe*, London 1980.
D. Martin and P. Johnson, *The Struggle for Zimbabwe*, London, 1981.
M. Meredith, *The Past is Another Country: Rhodesia 1890–1979*, London, 1979.
M. W. Murphee, *Christianity and the Shona*, London, 1969.
T. Ranger and I. Kimambo, eds. *The Historical Study of African Religion*, London, 1972.
T. Ranger and J. Weller, eds. *Themes in the Christian History of Central Africa*, London, 1975.
T. Ranger, 'Developments in the historical study of African religions: relations of production and religious change in Central Africa', R. Willis, and R. Ross, eds., *Religion and Change in African Societies*, Edinburgh, 1979.
T. Ranger, 'Religious studies and political economy; the Mwari cult and the peasant experience in Southern Rhodesia', W. Van Binsbergen, and M. Schoffeleers, eds. *The Social Science of African Religion*, London [forthc.].
T. Ranger, 'The death of Chaminuka: Spirit mediums, nationalism and the guerilla war in Zimbabwe', *African Affairs*, July 1982.
T. Ranger, 'Tradition and travesty: Chiefs of the administration in Makoni District, Zimbabwe, 1960–1980' *Journal of Southern African Studies* 9 (1982).
J. M. Schoffeleers, *Guardians of the Land: Essays on Central African Territorial Cults*, Gwelo 1978.
M. J. Van Binsbergen, *Religious Change in Zambia: Exploratory Studies*, London 1981.
R. P. Werbner, ed. *Regional Cults*, London, 1977.

Modern China

Preface

DANIEL L. OVERMYER

There is a long history of popular uprisings in China, beginning with the rebellions led by Ch'en She and Liu Pang at the end of the third century B.C. which led directly to the founding of the Western Han dynasty (206 B.C. − 8 A.D.). In the People's Republic 'peasant wars' are understood to be a driving force in Chinese history, and in Chinese museums that history is divided in part by the sequence of 'peasant rebellions'. There were many different types of uprisings, from local riots against corrupt officials to huge movements which led to civil war and the displacement of dynasties. They were motivated by a variety of factors: protest against unusual suffering and injustice, utopian hopes for a better society, desire for booty and power, competition to take over the empire. Participants in these rebellions came from different social and economic backgrounds. They were usually led by men from a middle level of literacy and influence; artisans, merchants, government clerks, military officers, or scholars who had passed the first set of civil service examinations but were still not eligible for employment. There were some uprisings dominated by miners, salt transport workers or canal boatmen, but most movements of any substantial size included large numbers of peasants, if only because peasants made up 85% of the population.

However, from an intentional point of view peasant participation does not necessarily mean that the movement was a 'peasant rebellion' or a 'rural revolt' as usually understood, particularly in the European context. Early modern Chinese society was more integrated than that of Europe. Though there were powerful local families which might have influence for generations, there was no hereditary aristocracy, and no entrenched church with vast land holdings. In China by the period in question power could be obtained and held only by continuous ability in civil service examinations, trade or military service. Gentry status had to be won and could easily be lost. In such a situation there was a fair amount of social mobility. Gentry and peasants lived together in the villages, with many gradations of land owning and tenancy between extremes. Local elites were expected to provide leadership in the community, and to mediate between the people and government officials.

Chinese villages were components of larger marketing networks through which goods and ideas circulated up and down the social scale. In addition, literacy was more widespread than in contemporary Europe (Cf. Evelyn Sakakida Rawski, *Education and Popular Literacy in Ch'ing China*, Ann Arbor, 1979), and through it values, beliefs and story cycles were shared. All this meant a degree of social integration that makes it difficult to specify class orientations in popular uprisings. There were disturbances led by farmers protesting unfair rents or taxes, but beyond such local incidents the terms 'peasant rebellions' or 'rural revolt' are of limited utility in the Chinese situation.

Violent uprisings in China had varying relationships with religion, ranging from none at all, through divination and prayer for victory in battle, to movements which were predominantly religious in structure and intent. There were many rebellions in which religion played an important role, almost all of which were led by popular religious sects with their own forms of organisation, leadership, worship centres, rituals, scripture texts and beliefs. Most of these groups lived and died in obscurity as pious voluntary associations promising aid in this life and salvation in the next. They tended to go unnoticed, and might exist for scores or even hundreds of years without drawing official attention. However, from their inception in the second century A.D. such sects were considered illegal by a state which tended to be suspicious of all voluntary associations, so that the arrival of a zealous local official or the implication of some members in a disturbance could result in attempts at suppression. As a result, some groups were eliminated but others resisted, by protest or force of arms. As was the case with European sects discussed in this volume, the basic concern in such uprisings was self-protection.

However, from the Yellow Turban rebellion in 184 A.D. on there was a millennial element present in the beliefs of some sects, at first Taoist, but later reinforced by ideas from Manichaeism and Buddhism. In particular, from the sixth century on the Buddhist idea of the coming of a future saviour, Maitreya, played a powerful role in popular thought. Maitreya's coming would herald a new age of faith, peace and prosperity, an age that was correlated with cycles of cosmic time. To some this new order could be hastened if present obstacles to it were removed, by force if necessary. So arose a Maitreya sect, beyond the bounds of monastic orthodoxy, which was known for its propensity for violence. By the fourteenth century the Maitreya belief became a part of the emerging White Lotus tradition, the characteristic form of early modern sectarianism. By the sixteenth century faith in the Buddha of the future was firmly embedded in sectarian scripture texts and tracts, some of which identified Maitreya incarnate with living sect leaders. In the name of such beliefs uprisings could be started to prepare for the saviour's coming by putting a pious ruler on the throne. In some cases it is clear that these uprisings were motivated by internal pressures and expectations and not by abnormal economic or political difficulties. Violence began at the conjunction of eschatological hope with particular forms of organisation and aggressive leadership. The result could be isolated attempts to take over county towns, or full-scale civil war that raged across provinces for years. The Yüan (Mongol) dynasty (1271–1368) collapsed in part because of attacks by White Lotus armies, and there were sporadic wars with similar groups into the nineteenth century. In such large scale movements motivations were mixed, and the majority of troops and followers might have only a nominal understanding of sectarian beliefs, but the core was formed of religious leaders and their disciples, gathered and trained over a period of years.

Thus, the articles in this section deal with the last phases of a long tradition of sectarian religion in China. The Taiping Heavenly Kingdom of the mid-nineteenth century, discussed by Elizabeth Perry and Rudolf Wagner, combined a variety of indigenous motifs with evangelical Protestant ideas from that West. Wagner's essay does much to clarify the exact nature of these imported beliefs, and thus helps us understand how they resonated with Chinese ideas. It was a case of the combination of lively popular religious concerns from two cultures. Perry's contribution demonstrates the ambiguity of such phenomena, and the ways in which beliefs were interpreted in different ways by those at varying distances from the centre of the movement. Robert Weller's paper reminds us that the Chinese sectarian tradition is still alive in Taiwan, with many new scripture texts believed to be direct revelations from the gods. He discussed the teachings of these texts in the larger context of religion in Taiwan. The conservatism of these teachings demonstrates afresh the cultural integration of Chinese society mentioned above.

It is no accident that the theme of religion and rural revolt is discussed in the Chinese context in relationship to popular religious sects. By the late traditional period monastic Buddhism and Taoism had long accommodated themselves to the political order, and non-sectarian popular religion was too diffused in family and community structures to become a focal point of resistance. On the whole, religiously oriented violence in China was most likely to arise from a confrontation between lay voluntary associations and an imperial state which claimed hegemony over all dimensions of existence, both religious and secular. In the long run religious sects in China were unable to prevail except at a limited local level, because unlike their European counterparts, they lacked educated leadership and the opportunity to gain the support of separate states.

Selected Bibliography

Susan Naquin, *Millenarian Rebellion in China: The Eight Trigrams Uprising of 1813* (New Haven and London, 1976).

Susan Naquin, *Shantung Rebellion: The Wang Lun Uprising of 1774*, (New Haven, 1981).

Daniel L. Overmyer, *Folk Buddhist Religion: Dissenting Sects in Late Traditional China* (Cambridge, MA, 1976).
Daniel L. Overmyer, 'Boatmen and Buddhas; The Lo chaiao in Ming Dynasty China', *History of Religions* 17.3–4 (1978) 284–302.
Daniel L. Overmyer, 'Alternatives: Popular Religious Sects in Chinese Society', *Modern China* 7.2 (April 1981) 153–190.
Shek, Richard Hon-chun, 'Religion and Society in Late Ming: Sectarianism and Popular Thought in Sixteenth and Seventeenth Century China', unpublished Ph.D. dissertation, University of California, 1980 (UMI// 8029585).

Taipings and Triads:
the rôle of religion in inter-rebel relations*

ELIZABETH J. PERRY

China's colorful two thousand year history of rural rebellion has long been linked, in Chinese government documents and Western scholarly works alike, to the strength of popular Chinese religious traditions. Whereas orthodox Confucianism prescribed subordination to existing sociopolitical authority, the heterodox religious beliefs of Daoism, Buddhism, and syncretic secret societies were said to be laden with rebellious potential. Because they acknowledged sources of supernatural power that transcended the dictates of the imperial Chinese state, religious organizations seemed a natural rallying point for opposition to the status quo. Thus Confucian bureaucrats anxious to maintain order instigated periodic crackdowns on religious sects, while scholars seeking the roots of China's turbulent rebellious tradition have also devoted special attention to the heterodox side of her social history [Muramatsu Yuji, 1960: 241–67; Yang, 1961: 218ff.].

There is certainly much justification for this identification of religion and revolt in the Chinese context. As early as the Yellow Turban uprising of 184 A.D., religious beliefs are known to have played an important role in inspiring insurrectionary activity. During the nineteenth century, the period with which this paper will be most concerned, religious persuasions were key ingredients in many of the massive revolts that sapped the strength of the Qing dynasty and led to the fall of the imperial system. The White Lotus Rebellion (1796–1805), Taiping Rebellion (1851–1864), Muslim Rebellion (1862–1878), and Boxer uprising (1899–1900) all showed clear signs of religious inspiration.

On the other hand, the very fact that government authorities viewed popular religion as dangerously conducive to revolt tended to perpetuate a self-

---

* The author gratefully acknowledges the Committee on Scholarly Communication with the People's Republic of China and the Graduate School Research Fund of the University of Washington for financial support that facilitated the research and writing of this paper. Professors Mao Jiaqi and Cai Shaoqing of the History Department of Nanjing University also deserve special thanks for providing generous research direction during the author's residence in China.

fulfilling prophecy. In case after case of Chinese rebellion, the heavy hand of government repression was a major precipitant of the outbreak. Indeed, the resulting conflagration often was due more to government interference than to any inherently rebellious urge on the part of the religious community itself.

The research of Daniel Overmyer has shown that even the allegedly most rebellious Chinese religious sect, the White Lotus Society, could be politically quiescent for centuries in many locations [*Overmyer, 1976; 1981*]. As with religious groups the world over, White Lotus sects were concerned primarily with ministering to the spiritual needs of their membership. Again like religious bodies elsewhere, Chinese sectarian groups typically strove to establish an institutional base to safeguard and expand their endeavors. When this institutional base, congregations, temples, or religious leadership, was threatened by government intrusion, the sect was prone to rebel in self-defense.

Just as religious groups were not always inclined to rebel, so rebel groups were not invariably motivated by religious concerns. Recent research suggests that both the massive Nien Rebellion of 1851–68 [*Perry, 1980*] and the White Wolf (Bai Lang) uprising of 1911–1914 [*Perry, 1981*] were secular movements, contrary to earlier scholarship which had argued for religious roots [*Chiang Siang-tseh, 1959; Teng Ssu-yu, 1961; Friedman, 1974*]. In both of these cases, rebellion occurred after government pressure was brought to bear upon bandit outfits whose original operations were fundamentally a peasant strategy for economic survival, rather than a religiously or politically motivated challenge to central authority.

To understand Chinese peasant rebellion, whether secular or religious in nature, thus demands attention to ways in which the state interacted with ongoing rural organizations to generate a rebellious situation. As we will see in examining relations between the Taipings and the Triads in mid-nineteenth century China, the role of religion was quite variable. Religious precepts could be a vehicle for popular mobilization, but they could also serve as a barrier to alliances between rebel groups. The impact of religion was in all cases mediated through the intervening factors of local environment, leadership personality, government activities, and the like.

The quasi-Christian Taiping Rebellion, estimated to have included several million followers at its height, was a major watershed in modern Chinese history whose effects will be studied and debated by scholars for years to come. The fighting that accompanied the rebellion brought death to some 25–30 million persons, rendering it the most costly civil war in human history. Much has been written about this uprising, its ideology, and its long-term sociopolitical impact [*Jen, 1974; Michael, 1966; Shi, 1967; Kuhn, 1970*]. We will focus here on but one aspect of the movement: the role of its religious system in facilitating or hindering the recruitment of new members.

Like many millenarian movements, the Taipings were led by a charismatic figure whose hallucinatory visions had convinced him of his divine mission. As is well-known, repeated failure in the official examinations, the route to bureaucratic position in imperial China, plunged Taiping leader-to-be, Hong Xiuquan, into nervous collapse. In this state of delirium, Hong dreamed he had ascended to a high place to meet with an old man and his son who commanded the frustrated scholar to return to earth to slay demons. After recovering his health, Hong examined a Christian tract that he had picked up without reading some years earlier. Now he felt he had an explanation for his peculiar visions. The old man was God the Father, his son was Jesus Christ. And, concluded Hong in a burst of heretical enthusiasm, he himself was none other than the younger brother of Jesus Christ, divinely appointed to deliver the Christian message to his countrymen. Armed with these convictions, Hong Xiuquan began to recruit followers, principally among his own ethnic group, the oppressed Hakka minority of Guangdong and Guangxi provinces.

Although he subsequently received religious instruction from a Western missionary in Canton, the Rev. Issachar T. Roberts, Hong persisted in his idiosyncratic interpretation of Christian doctrine. Misguided as many of his precepts seemed by orthodox Christian standards, they were the cornerstone of Hong's fast-growing Society of God Worshippers (*Bai shangdi hui*). While many of the new recruits were undoubtedly attracted to the Society less for its religious doctrine than for the material security it offered Hakkas in their struggles against other local inhabitants [*Hamberg, 1854: 49*], Society members were required to abide by a strict religious regimen. The discipline fostered by this rigorous routine of worship services, dietary restrictions, etc. engendered a certain community of spirit, binding the God Worshippers together in a sense of shared purpose. At the same time, the religious coloration of the group rendered it a target of government suspicion. When local militia and official troops were called in to rout the God Worshippers from their Guangxi base, the group was transformed from an organization whose political activities had been limited to local ethnic conflicts into a movement overtly aiming to topple the imperial state.

As the Taipings developed revolutionary designs, they began to reach out in search of allies in the anti-government cause. An especially promising source of such comrades-in-arms were Triad societies, secret associations which had been active since the late eighteenth century in promoting anti-Qing struggles. Although their precise origins are still somewhat obscure, by the mid-nineteenth century Triad groups were numerous in much of South China in market towns and rural villages alike. While Triad members engaged in a variety of ritualistic practices, some of which may be characterized as religious, theirs were a far cry from the strict regimen of the God-worshipping Taipings. Triad rites consisted of a blood-oath initiation ceremony followed by the memorization of various code phrases and gestures. Although some Triad groups established altars to the legendary Five Patriarchs who were believed to have founded the Society, in fact most of their worship rituals were a loose imitation of popular Buddhist and Daoist practices [Lu Baoqian, 1975: 71–76; Taiping Tianguo Qiyi Diaocha Baogao, 1956: 80–81; Hongjinjun Qiyi Zilioaji, 1959: I/2]. Differences between the Taipings and the Triads make a study of their relations an interesting starting point for examining the role of religion in inter-rebel relations.

In early 1851, pressed by government suppression efforts in the Guangxi area, two female Triad chiefs, Qiu Er and Su Sanniang, agreed to accept the rules of the God Worshippers. Each of the chiefs brought about 2,000 followers to augment Hong Ziuquan's army. Not long after, eight other Triad chiefs expressed interest in joining the Taipings. Again Hong was happy to welcome them, with the proviso that they, too, conform to the required religious regimen. To instruct them in the faith, Hong dispatched sixteen members of his congregation, two to each Triad chief. After completing their course of instruction, the chiefs paid their religious tutors a liberal sum of money for their efforts. Then the chiefs and their followers all duly enlisted in Hong's army. As required by the God Worshipper's code, fifteen of the sixteen religious tutors deposited the compensation they had received from the Triads into the God Worshippers' common treasury. However, one teacher, who had previously committed offenses of opium smoking and drinking for which he had been spared punishment only because of his eloquence in preaching, tried to pocket the money for himself. When this breach of discipline was detected, Hong Xiuquan and the man's own relatives agreed that the culprit should be beheaded as called for in their religious law. The Triad chiefs, despite their recently completed course of religious instruction, were shocked to see that a teacher was to be killed for so minor an infringement. Fearful that they too would be likely to incur a death penalty at some future point, seven of the chieftains deserted with their followers. Only Triad chief Luo Dagang, convinced of the benefits of Taiping discipline and doctrine, elected to remain [Hamberg, 1954: 54–55].

Luo Dagang became an important officer in the Taiping Army, whose loyalty was later rewarded by appointment to commander of the city of Zhenjiang, the eastern gateway to the Taiping capital in Nanjing. Along with Su Sanniang, whose commitment to the Taiping cause was also unswerving after her recruitment in early 1851, Luo is often cited as the exemplar Triad-turned-Taiping [Zhong Wendian, 1962: 166–167]. There is no doubt that his contribution to the rebellion was substantial, or that Luo endeavored to be a faithful steward of the Taiping enterprise. Charles Taylor, an American missionary who visited Zhenjiang for several days in the spring of 1853, reported favorably on the worship routine of Luo Dagang's army. The men were said to have chanted hymns and doxologies in a very solemn manner twice or thrice daily and to have recited grace before and after meals [*Meadows, 1856: 283–284*]. Even so, it seems that Luo Dagang's early experience as a Triad may not have been entirely erased by his conversion to the Taiping cause. While the Taipings were known for their ruthless destruction of other religious institutions, Buddhist temples, Confucian tablets and the like, there is evidence that Luo Dagang was less zealous in persecuting competing faiths. Thus Luo issued orders to spare Zhenjiang's famous Chan Buddhist temple, Jiaoshansi, from attack. As one Chinese historian has speculated, such leniency suggests that Luo Dagang's religious ideology may have been at odds with that of other Taiping leaders [*Huang Zheng, 1980: 143–144*]. Luo Dagang's view in this matter was possibly the result of imperfectly grasped Taiping doctrine. As Charles Taylor, his missionary visitor, reported, Luo Dagang's 'literary attainments were of the scantiest; and there were in consequence manifest signs of some confusion in the Chin keang (Zhenjiang), secretariat' [*Meadows, 1856: 277*]. However, since Luo had been with the Taiping Army on its temple-smashing march through south-central China, it is likely that his loose interpretation stemmed less from ignorance than from inclination.

If even the most loyal of ex-Triad leaders could diverge from the strict demands of the Taiping code, what of some of the less committed Triads-turned-Taipings? Information on the attitudes of rank and file followers is scant at best. Nevertheless, there is fragmentary evidence to suggest that at least some Triad members who joined the Taipings did so without a full conversion to the Taiping faith. Indeed, their cooperation seems to have been dependant on the misconception that the Taipings were just another branch of the Triad brotherhood.

Some fascinating hints of this phenomenon appear in a letter to the editor of the *China Mail* written on July 7, 1853 by a Western missionary in Canton who signed his initials A.P.H. He relates how a representative from the Taipings in Nanjing had come to his house a couple of months before with a letter addressed to the Canton Chapel of Rev. Issachar Roberts, the missionary with whom Taiping leader Hong Xiuquan had studied some years before. But Roberts was not in Canton and the letter remained undelivered. The Taiping emissary returned to the home of A.P.H. about a month later, after an inducement reward had been posted by the missionary. To prove he was an officer of the Taipings, the representative used the Triad code word 'hong' (which was, entirely coincidentally, also the surname of the Taiping leader) and demonstrated a secret sign made of the given name of the Taiping leader, Xiuquan. He then transcribed some lines of poetry from the *Book of Celestial Decrees*, a Taiping religious document.

A few days later the emissary again visited A.P.H. to explain more about his background. He informed his listener that he came from Dongguan district, twenty miles east of Canton. He had gone to Guangxi several years before as a government volunteer to fight against the Taiping rebels. However, when the rebels threw into the government camp evidence that they were Triads under another name, the many Triad volunteers in the government army like himself refused to continue to fight the Taipings. Instead, a number of them converted to the rebel side. He explained that the rebels had at first used the slogan, 'Overthrow the Qing dynasty and restore the Ming', a traditional Triad phrase. But after the battle at Quanzhou in north-eastern Guangxi where many of their members had been killed, their watchword was changed to a call for the complete liquidation of the Manchu race.

The informant was able to identify all the Triad literature that his missionary interrogator could produce. He informed his listener that the term *Shangdi hui* (God Society) was, like the traditional names of *Tiandi hui* (Heaven and Earth Society), *Sanhe hui* (Three Harmonies Society), and *Hong jia* (Hong family), simply a different designation for the Triad fraternity. The name *Shangdi hui*, he insisted, had been adopted to conceal the fact that the God Worshippers were really Triads. He understood Hong Xiuquan's *Shangdi* (the Protestant term for God) as possessed of a three-in-one nature, in keeping with the mystic significance which the Triads attributed to the number three. According to the emissary, Hong Xiuquan had been the acknowledged head of the Triad fraternity for years. Although after 1850 he had assumed the title of Taiping King, prior to that time Hong had been known simply as First Brother (*yige*), the usual designation for a Triad chieftain [*China Mail, July 7, 1853*].

In reality, we know that much of the emissary's account was factually incorrect. Hong Xiuquan's God Worshippers were a quasi-Christian sect entirely distinct from the Triad associations that had antedated them by a century. As Hong himself is said to have declared,

> Though I never entered the Triad Society, I have often heard it said that their object is to subvert the Tsing (Qing) and restore the Ming dynasty. Such an expression was very proper in the time of Khang-hsi (Kangxi), when this society was at first formed, but now after the lapse of two hundred years, we may still speak of subverting the Tsing, but we cannot properly speak of restoring the Ming ...
>
> There are several evil practices connected with the Triad Society, which I detest; if any new member enter the Society, he must worship the devil, and utter thirty-six oaths; a sword is placed upon his neck, and he is forced to contribute money for the use of the society. Their real object has now turned very mean and unworthy [*Hamberg, 1854: 55–56*].

From this it is clear that Hong Xiuquan was not the commander-in-chief of the Triad league that the emissary described him to be. But the interest of the informant's testimony lies not in its veracity as a characterization of the Taiping movement, but rather as a possible clue to the outlook of a Triad-turned-Taiping. Although sufficiently trusted by the Taipings to have been made an officer in their army and an emissary to contact the Western missionaries, the man's understanding of Taiping doctrine was in terms of his earlier Triad beliefs.

Further evidence of this same phenomenon is provided in the report of a government military officer who had interrogated a number of captured rebels during campaigns against the Taipings in Guangxi and Hunan, areas where recruitment of Triad allies had been most successful. From a rebel hideaway, the government seized two objects of worship common to Triad groups: a wooden doll, clothed in yellow silk dress, and a wooden plaque with the name of the sect leader. According to the officer's report, the captured rebels testified that the founder of their religion was known as the prince (*taizi*) because he revered *Tianzhu* (the Catholic term for God) as his father. Hong Xiuquan's name, these rebels claimed, was an assumed one. The surname of Hong had been adopted, in traditional Triad fashion, when he had founded his association. The given name 'Xiuquan' had been formed by an ingenious combination of four Chinese characters meaning, I am the king of men (*wo nai ren wang*) [*Taiping Tianguo Shiliao Congbian Jianji, I/6–7*]. Although the content of the rebel testimony was far from an accurate portrayal of Taiping reality, it is probably a useful guide to the mentality of Triads who joined the Rebellion. For these allies the Taiping religion seems to have held an attraction, but only as interpreted in terms of pre-existing Triad precepts.

It is unclear to what extent the Taipings themselves actually tried to blur their differences with the Triads in an effort to attract more followers. The testimony of the rebel envoy to the missionaries in Canton suggests that the Taipings may have posed as members of the Triad fraternity in order to win the allegiance of Triads among the government army. Another hint of Taiping accommodation to Triad traditions was the use of the reign year title of *Tian De* (Heavenly Virtue) in early Taiping documents. This had been a favorite title of southern sectarian groups, especially Triads, for years prior to the Taiping Rebellion. As early as 1707, the title appeared in the reign year of an anti-Qing uprising in Zhejiang Province that went by the name of Great Ming Heavenly Virtue (*Da Ming Tian De*) [*Cai Shaoqing, 1979: 56*].

During the early years of the Taiping movement, there were widespread rumors that the Taipings had found a descendant of the Ming imperial house and crowned him King of Heavenly Virtue (*Tian De Wang*) to attract followers from among the south China sectarians [*Brine, 1862: 136*]. The rumors came to a sensational head in 1852 when the Qing government publicized the confession of a captured rebel leader, one Hong Daquan, who claimed to have been designated King of Heavenly Virtue by the Taiping authorities.

The mystery surrounding the capture of Hong Daquan has been meticulously explored in a number of informative essays. [*Jen Yuwen, 1944: 274–277; Peng Zeyi, 1957: 50–54; Curwen, 1972: 70–75; Luo Ergang, 1979: 49–52; Cai Shaoqing, 1979: 53–56*] and need not concern us in detail here. For our purposes it will suffice to summarize the major conclusion of this research: Hong Daquan, whose original name was Jiao Liang, was a Triad leader from Xinning county in Hunan who had apparently joined up with the Taiping rebels in Guangxi before being captured by the government authorities. However, evidence does not support Hong Daquan's assertion that the title of Tian De Wang had been conferred upon him by the Taipings. The title seems to have been adopted as a continuation of age-old sectarian practice, rather than at the behest of the Taipings. In 1796, a White Lotus leader in Hong Daquan's home county of Xinning had also called himself Tian De. Claiming to be the incarnation of the Maitreya Buddha, this earlier King of Heavenly Virtue had raised a following of tens of thousands of devout believers, including a corps of rebel women who waved white fans and chanted charms to frighten off the government soldiers [*Fu Cheng, 1869: 5/3–6*]. Although Hong Daquan belonged to the Triad rather than the White Lotus persuasion, his use of the Tian De title perpetuated a rebel tradition of his native area.

It is plausible that the many reports of a Tian De leader in the Taiping Rebellion were references to a number of different Triad chieftains who cooperated with the rebel movement. The missionary A.P.H. wrote that his informant had heard that the Tian De Wang drowned after jumping into a well in Guangxi to escape being taken prisoner [*China Mail, July 7, 1853*]. A captured rebel in Guangxi in 1852 reported having seen the King of Heavenly Virtue in Daozhou. By his account the Tian De Wang was a heavy set youth of seventeen or eighteen years of age named Zhu (the surname of the Ming imperial family). He is described as attired in a black silk mandarin's hat and yellow dragon robe with large sleeves [*F.O., 682/112.4*]. Quite possibly these and many other similar reports circulating in the early years of the Taipings reflected the existence of several allied Triad chieftains who had independently assumed their traditional title of King of Heavenly Virtue.

In using the Tian De title as their own reign year designation, the Taipings were probably also following the common practice of rebel groups in their native locale rather than implementing a conscious design to attract Triad followers. Still, the identity of nomenclature in this early period must have made it easier for Triads to throw in their lot with the Taiping rebel enterprise. After the Taipings moved north to establish their Heavenly Capital at Nanjing, they dispensed with the earlier reign year title. Proclamations were thenceforth stamped with the seal of the Taiping Heavenly Kingdom, in place of the Tian De designation.

The Taipings' consolidation of power at Nanjing ushered in a period of less cordial relations with Triad groups. To some extent this was a result of the increased strength of the Taiping movement. Having accomplished the impressive feat of taking the ancient capital of Nanjing, the Taiping leaders felt more confident in asserting their own doctrines. Support from ideologically impure allies no longer seemed so necessary. Thus religion became a greater barrier to cooperation during the era of Taiping strength. In part, however, the lack of cooperation between the Taipings and Triad groups at this time was due to objective limitations imposed by the government's military blockade of Nanjing. Even if the Taipings had wished to provide aid to Triad uprisings, they would have been severely hampered by the government presence.

Relations between the Taipings and the Small Swords of Shanghai, a Triad rebellion that held the treaty port for some seventeen months, reflected these dual obstacles of doctrinal differences and state intervention. Although the endurance of the Small Swords was due in large measure to the buffer created by the presence of the Taipings in Nanjing, in fact the two groups were never able to forge a lasting alliance. Part of the difficulty lay with the reluctance of the Small Sword leaders to shed their Triad practices for the Christian faith. Shortly after the Small Swords occupied Shanghai in September 1853, the Reverend Issachar Roberts on his own initiative paid a visit to Small Sword commander Liu Lichuan in his headquarters at the Shanghai Confucian temple. There Roberts found the pale, emaciated young rebel chief in the act of smoking opium. Liu told Roberts that he had already sent two letters, one by land and the other by water, to the Taiping Heavenly King, requesting that an emissary be sent from Nanjing to arrange joint operations. Thereupon Roberts showed Liu a copy of the Ten Commandments and told him that the Taipings had adopted them as their sacred code. Roberts went on to explain that he had been the Heavenly King's religious teacher and that he now wished to instruct the eight or nine thousand Cantonese under Liu's personal command. At this suggestion, the rebel chief demurred, saying that all such arrangements should await the arrival of the deputy from Nanjing [*North China Herald*, October 1, 1853: 34].

It is possible that neither of Liu Lichuan's letters reached the Taipings at Nanjing. Nevertheless, emissaries from Nanjing were apparently sent to make contact with the Small Swords. The *North China Herald*, Shainghai's English language newspaper, in December 1853 reported the rumor that Taiping envoys had arrived on a special mission to the Small Swords and had immediately denounced the immoral habits and vicious propensities of the local rebels as an insuperable barrier to amalgamation with the Taiping Rebellion [*NCH, December 3, 1853: 70*]. British observer Thomas Meadows noted that two Taiping emissaries to Shanghai 'found the gods all standing in the temples and opium smoking' and reported back to Nanjing in such a way that the Taipings rejected all Small Sword overtures [*Meadows, 1856:452*].

The missionary William Medhurst provided further evidence of Taiping deputies. On December 14, 1853 Medhurst received permission to enter the walled city of Shanghai to preach to a large congregation at the London Missionary Society chapel. In the middle of Medhurst's sermon about the folly of idolatry and the necessity of worshipping one god, a man stood up and shouted, 'That is true, that is true, the idols must perish, and shall perish. I am a Kwang-si (Guangxi) man, a follower of Tai-ping-wang (the Taiping king); we all of us worship one God and believe in Jesus...' The man went on to inveigh against opium smoking and told the crowd to be swift in abandoning their evil ways, for the Heavenly King was coming and would permit no infringement of his rules. Medhurst, who was intimately familiar with Taiping doctrine, observed that this man was thoroughly trained in Taiping beliefs and must have been a Taiping follower [NCH, December 17, 1853: 78].

There is some evidence that these efforts at transforming Small Sword ideology eventually bore limited results. In April 1854, Liu Lichuan issued a remarkable proclamation in which he explained the origin of the universe as God's creation and called on the people of Shanghai to abandon Buddhist and Daoist idolatry, to accept the true God, to pray regularly, and to observe the Sabbath [NCH, May 20, 1854]. There is, however, no evidence to suggest that these injunctions were enforced in any way. And the next month Liu issued another proclamation in which his caution against idolatry drew more from Confucian than Christian inspiration:

> There is a class of ignorant people who repair to the temples, ignite incense sticks, burn paper-money, and contribute to the gilding of the Buddhist images; why do they not with this money purchase articles with which they may show their filial piety and respect towards their parents?... Now it behooves us who are brethren of the Hung family with faithful hearts to manifest our patriotism and he who is a son must show filial piety towards his two parents... I have no object in this than to act according to the ancient national laws and regulations of the Ming dynasty, in promoting the practice of loyalty and filial piety [NCH, May 20, 1854].

Thus the gap between Triad and Taiping beliefs and practices remained substantial.

But even had the Taipings been willing to overlook matters of doctrine, and there has been much recent debate among Chinese historians over whether they were in fact anxious to ally with the Small Swords, there were obvious military obstacles to such an alliance. East of Zhenjiang (where Triad-turned-to-Taiping Luo Dagang was in charge), Qing control of the Yangzi was secure enough to deter any Taiping effort at linking up with the rebels in Shanghai. Attempts by the Taipings to move east in November 1853 and August 1854 were blocked by overwhelming government opposition [Jiaoping Yuefei Fanglue: 67/101–102].

Taiping relations with Triads in Guangxi and Shanghai defy any simple formula for explaining the role of religion in peasant rebellion. Although the religious doctrine of the Taipings seems to have served as an attraction to some Triads, in such cases Taiping precepts were often misunderstood as a variant of Triad traditions. In other cases there is clear evidence that Taiping religion worked against alliance with Triad groups. This was certainly true for the eight Guangxi chieftains who deserted the rebellion once they had encountered a demonstration of its religious discipline. It was equally true for Taiping relations with the Small Swords of Shanghai, although in this case the difficulties seem to have stemmed as much from Taiping repugnance at Triad improprieties as from the Small Swords' own fear of religious restrictions.

Religious ideology was an important factor in many peasant rebellions, but seldom was it a determining one. Local socioeconomic conditions, rebel leadership and state actions frequently exerted a more compelling influence upon the outbreak and destiny of rural insurrection.

References

Brine, Lindesay, 1862, *The Taeping Rebellion in China*, London.
Cai Shaoqing, 1979, 'Guanyu Hong Daquan de shenfe' (Concerning the identity of Hong Daquan), *Lishi Yanjiu* (Historical Research), VI: 53–56.
Chiang Siang-tseh, 1959, *The Nien Rebellion*, Seattle.
Curwen, Charles A., 1972, 'Taiping Relations with Secret Societies and with Other Rebels', in *Popular Movements and Secret Societies in China, 1840–1950*, Jean Chesneaux (ed.), Stanford: 65–84.
Curwen, Charles A., 1979, *Taiping Rebel*, Cambridge.
F.O. (682 series in the Public Records Office, London).
Friedman, Edward, 1974, *Backward Toward Revolution*, Berkeley.
Hamberg, Theodore, 1854, *The Visions of Hung-siu-tshuen and origin of the Kwang-si Insurrection*, Hong Kong.
Hongjinjun Qiyi Ziliao Ji (Collection of Materials on the Red Turban Army Uprising), 1959, Guangdong.
Huang Zheng, 1980, 'Luo Dagang zai Zhenjiang shiji kaolue' (A brief study of the activities of Luo Dagang in Zhenjiang), *Taiping Tianguo Shi Luncong* (Collected essays on the history of the Taiping Heavenly Kingdom), Nanjing University, II: 136–148.
Jen Yuwen, 1974, *The Taiping Revolutionary Movement*, New Haven.
Jen Yuwen, 1944, *Taipingjun Guangxi Shou Qiyi* (The first uprising of the Taiping Army in Guangxi), Beijing.
Jiaoping Yuefei Fanglue (Annals of suppressing the Guangdong bandits).
Kuhn, Philip A., 1970, *Rebellion and its enemies in late Imperial China*, Cambridge, Mass.
Lu Baoqian, 1975, *Lun Wanqing Liangguang de Tiandihui Zhengquan* (On the Triad regime in Guangxi-Guangdong during the late Qing), Taibei.
Luo Ergang, 1979, 'Tiandewang Hong Daquan wenti de buchong zhengju' (Supplementary evidence on the question of King of Heavenly Virtue Hong Daquan), *Lishi Yanjiu*, VI: 49–52.
Meadows, Thomas Taylor, 1856, *The Chinese and their Rebellions*, London.
Michael, Franz, 1966, *The Taiping Rebellion*, Seattle.

Muramatsu Yuji, 'Some themes in Chinese rebel ideologies', in Wright, Arthur, ed., *The Confucian persuasion*, Stanford.
NCH, *North China Herald*, Shanghai.
Overmyer, Daniel L., 1981, 'Alternatives: Popular Religious Sects in Chinese Society', *Modern China*, VII, ii: 153–190.
Overmyer, Daniel L., 1976, *Folk Buddhist Religion*, Cambridge, Mass.
Peng Zeyi, 1957, 'Guanyu Hong Daquan de lishi wenti' (On the historical problem of Hong Daquan), *Lishi Yanjiu*, IX: 50–54.
Perry, Elizabeth J., 1980, *Rebels and Revolutionaries in North China, 1845–1945*, Stanford.
Perry, Elizabeth J., 1981, 'Social Banditry Revisited: The Case of Bai Lang, a Chinese Brigand', unpublished ms.
Shi, Vincent, 1967, *The Taiping Ideology*, Seattle.
Taiping Tianguo Qiyi Diaocha Baogao (Report on investigation of the Taiping Heavenly Kingdom uprising), 1956, Beijing.
Taiping Tianguo Shiliao Congbian Jianji (Collected excerpts from historical materials on the Taiping Heavenly Kingdom).
Teng Ssu-yu, 1961, *The Nien and their Guerrilla Warfare*, Paris.
Fu Cheng, ed., 1869, *Xinning Xianzhi* (Xinning County Gazetteer).
Yang, C. K., 1961, *Religion in Chinese society*, Berkeley.
Zhong Wendian, 1962, *Taipingjun Zai Yongan* (The Taiping Army in Yongan), Beijing.

*God's country in the family of nations:
the logic of modernism in
the Taiping doctrine of international relations**

RUDOLF G. WAGNER

The Problem

The Taiping rebellion shook the southern and central parts of the Chinese Empire between 1850 and 1864. It was seen by all, observers as well as participants and enemies, as an important international event, influencing both the future of the Empire and of the Western interests in the Far East. The Western governments were wary of recognizing the Taiping government in Nanjing regardless of its professed Christianity and friendly attitude towards the 'transoceanic brethren'. After initial hesitation the powers deemed it to be of greater advantage to them to deal with a weakened Manzhu government in Beijing (Peking) and eventually intervened indirectly against the Taiping. The attitude of the Western traders and merchants was more ambivalent. They were apprehensive about the rigorous Taiping ban on opium, wine and tobacco and the perspective of a prolonged civil war; but the Taiping's assurances of free access to the inner markets after their victory gave many of them hope. But when their governments secured ample economic privileges in the treaty of Tianjin (1858) they mostly sided with their governments against the rebels. The evangelical and mostly revivalist early missionaries like Issachar Jacox Roberts from the Mississippi valley or Theodore Hamberg, a Swede who served with the Basel Missionary Society, saw in the rebellion the outpouring of the Spirit preceding the imminently expected Millennium. Only when they learned that the Taiping insisted on their own reading of the Bible and their own authentic vision of God did they abandon them. The same rapid change took place with some European revolutionists like

---

* Research for this paper was conducted while I was a Fellow of the Cornell University Society for the Humanities in 1981/82; I am exceedingly grateful to the Society, its staff and my co-fellows for their support, help, and encouragement. The superb Wason collection at Cornell has provided me with a unique research opportunity, and my thanks go to Diane Perushek, James Cole, and Paul Cheng.

Marx. In 1850 when he heard the first rumours about the rebellion he saw it as the beginning of grave economic tribulations for England. These, he expected, would eventually lead to an economic crisis, which in turn would promote revolution. The despondent capitalists would find, when their flight from the enraged workers would finally bring them to the Great Wall of China, that the words *Liberté, Egalité, Fraternité* were already engraved there [*Marx, 1850: 445*]. When the British revolution had failed to materialize, Marx abandoned the rebels and affirmatively quoted the British consul Harvey's statement that 'their mission seems to be nothing else but to oppose the conservative marasmus with destruction in grotesquely abominable forms' [*Marx, 1862*].

Taiping international relations have been extensively documented by Teng Ssu-yu [*1971*], Gregory [*1959, 1963, 1969*], and others. The historians' perception of them, of Taiping motives in dealing with the Westerners and of the rationale in their attitude, imputing traditional categories of 'interest' and 'tactics' are quite at variance with both the self-perception of the Taiping themselves and with that of the evangelical missionaries. The assumption prevails among historians subscribing to quite diverging philosophies that ideas and religious elements are nothing but a 'cloak' for the crude and direct interests. Therefore, not much attention has been paid to the inner logic of the arguments and behaviour of the protagonists. In addition, the Taiping movement, subsumed under the category of rebellion or revolution is studied with a concomitant emphasis on internal political and military aspects. Thus the numerous works dealing with the genesis of 'modern' ideas and attitudes on international relations in nineteenth century China, like Immanuel Hsu's *China's Entrance into the Family of Nations* (1960), do not deal with the rebels as one of the 'modernizing' groups. It is the purpose of this paper to help in filling this gap. More specifically, I will try to prove the following hypotheses:

1. The Taiping perception of the world and China's place in the world is stringently and rationally deduced from the authenticated sources of their creed. They adhered to this perception even against clear evidence that it did not tally with their crucial experience.
2. The inherent modernism of the Taiping perception of the world was not a product of a cool and detached assessment of China's interests and possibilities, but was the product of a quite different set of categories, into which both traditional Chinese and new religious elements entered.
3. The Taiping idea of a family of nations under God only included Christian nations, e.g. the West and China. Each of these equal children of God would have his/her own colonial/tributary subsystem to hold the idolatrous nations at bay.
4. The Taiping idea of international relations is based on two authenticated precedents. The relations between the various Chinese states during the latter

part of the Zhou dynasty gave the model for the relations among Christian nations. The relationship of Israel with the other nations, be they their oppressors like Egypt, or be they inhabiting the land assigned to Israel by God, was the model for the Taiping behaviour towards the Manzhu government of the Qing Dynasty.
5. The Taiping attitude towards the Manzhu combined two elements; they were attacked as idolatrous adherents of Satan, that is, on religious grounds. But different from the Han-Chinese whom they had deluded, they could not be 'brought back'. Their very nature was devilish. This is a proto-nationalist perception of a fundamental ethnic rift between the Manzhu and the Han-Chinese.
6. Each of the key ingredients of the Taiping ideas on international relations was also present within the categorical arsenal of those Westerners who were in closest contact with the rebels, confirming it as a part of a Christian frame of reference.

The Taiping perception of the world and of China's place in it

It has been extensively documented that conditions 'were ripe for rebellion' in China in the middle of the last century. The government was in the hands of the Manzhu, who were seen as a 'barbarian' tribe by most Han-Chinese. The government had decayed into corruption and inefficiency, receiving the death blow to its prestige from British cannon during the Opium War. Regional famines were rampant and no or little relief was forthcoming. The ecology of coastal piracy and inland transport was greatly disrupted by the foreign presence and the shift of trade from Canton to Shanghai. Pirates driven on land and unemployed transport labourers swelled the already floating population. The government had permitted the establishment of local militia against the British and against robbers; thus arms, military skills and leadership experience were available in many areas of China.

Among the numerous rebellious groups which emerged as local rebels, some attempting to overthrow the Dynasty and restore the (Han-Chinese) Ming Dynasty, the Taiping finally became by far the most 'successful' organized and 'modern' force. Many of the other rebellions had religious motivations: a direct mandate had been conferred onto them by a deity through visions, omens, or dreams. But due to their closeness to popular beliefs which were mostly restricted to a limited area and local character of their social networks these movements remained parochial and were not able to become national forces with a strength to challenge the government [*Naquin, 1976, 1981; Overmyer, 1976*]. The Taiping were an exception.

The later Taiping leader Hong Xiuquan had several times tried and failed the entrance examinations on the provincial level for the government bureaucracy. On one such occasion, in 1837, he fell ill in his distress and had a vision: He was transported to Heaven where, after being properly cleaned and purified he met an old man and his son. Together with Hong the old man looked down to earth; with tears in his eyes he complained about man's ingratitude. Men had forgotten him, their creator, who also cared for their livelihood. They had fallen prey to the delusions of 'demons'. He instructed Hong – whom his son called his 'younger brother' from which Hong deduced that he himself was the old man's second son – in proper behaviour, and gave him ample evidence and proof of his heavenly mandate; he then ordered him to exterminate the demons. In the vision the expected attitude of the different sections of the populace is indicated in a symbolical manner. For example, Confucius sides with the 'demons' after being charged by the old man as the person responsible for China's desertion of the old man. He is caught and brought back by Hong, and finally permitted to stay in Heaven, but not allowed to teach. In the symbolical person of Confucius the reaction of the Confucian literati to Hong's actions is anticipated and the proper policy towards them is indicated. All relevant problems were dealt with in this symbolical manner.

In the vision the old man announced to Hong that he would find his name and new Heaven-conferred title written at the door, and that at some later time he would find a book which would explain this vision to him. Hong was then sent back to earth as the Heavenly King of the Kingdom of Great Peace. Being well aware of the possibility that this vision was just a delusion of his overexcited mind, he proceded with great care to verify the divine origin of his vision. The slip of paper with his name and title was instantly forthcoming. But the second proof failed to materialize until 1843. During this time Hong behaved in no unusual way; he tried the examinations again, and became a schoolteacher. But in 1843 his attention was drawn to the *Good words to Admonish the Age*, a compilation of Bible extracts and homilies put together by the most influential early evangelical convert, Liang Afa. This tract indeed explained everything Hong had seen in his vision: the old man was God himself (Shangdi), his son, who had been 'sent down' earlier, was Christ. Hong as God's second son would usher in the millennium of the Heavenly Kingdom which would come after a desperate battle with Satan and his demons. For the battle the Pentateuch offered a vivid picture of the relationship between God, his appointed leader (like Moses) and the mixed multitude of the host. It requires some effort to imagine what went on in the head of this obscure school teacher when he felt forced to recognize what God had in store for him [*Michael, 1971: 3ff, 51ff*]. Hong now proceeded with the great care and circumspection to obey – even though reluctantly – the mandate of his powerful and raging Father. With the *Good Words* his own vision was authenticated as orthodox, and from the Gospels Hong now developed a world view capable of challenging the imperial ideology on every level. The vision, had predicted to him in symbolic form the actors of the drama that was to come and their actions. As God's obedient son he could but reenact in the most meticulous manner what God had decreed to happen, hoping that his Father would then do his share. He, therefore, repeated each and every detail from the vision, from his own headgear and that of his staff, to the treatment of the Confucian literati, the people and the Manzhu. This interpretive mode was reinforced by the tremendous success of his army from the beginning; this success again increased the credibility of the visionary scenario with both adherents and enemies [*Wagner, 1983*].

Most Chinese rebel movements at the time did not develop a recognizeable view of international relations. The Taiping, however, were no rebels. While Shangdi had appeared earlier to and for the benefit of Chinese emperors, there was no rebel movement ever claiming a mandate from him. The visionary, as a rule, would deduce the geographical dimensions of his action from the power of the divine protector: so, for example, Bao Lisheng, an enemy of the Taiping in Zhejiang province, had a mandate from a local immortal, and as a consequence he never ventured beyond the confines of this godhead's power [*Cole, 1982*]. But Hong's heavenly interlocutor had been God, who controlled not only China, but the whole world. Hong was thus forced to see himself as having a mandate for all 'ten thousand nations' of the world. Therefore, he had to develop a concept about his and China's relationship with them. Hong had grown up in a world where it was commonly held that China stood at the center and zenith of the world. It was surrounded by peoples of lower cultural level who recognized China's superiority by paying tribute. With increasing distance from China the tribute missions would come at ever greater intervals. There were countries about which one had only heard, such as the Europeans; these were placed in the category of barbarians for whom no interval for tributary missions had been as yet fixed [*Hsu, 1960*]. This model did not go unchallenged. The British insisted on their recognition as a power equal to the Chinese Empire and proceded to impose their view with cannon, without, however, planning to transform China into a colony. Although the government had to make verbal concessions in the Treaty of Tiantsin in 1859, most of the high officials retained their old assumptions. John K. Fairbank [*1957, 1968*] has convincingly argued that this was not so much due to a particularly pronounced obstinacy of the Chinese officials, but to the fact that the 'Chinese world order' continued to remain viable in many respects into the 1880s. There was nothing surprising in the doing of the mighty western barbarians: as everyone knew, barbarians were both martial and greedy; this the officials felt was amply confirmed by the British. The time honoured antidote against barbarian menace was applied, namely, to gradually submit them to Chinese civilizing influence while making temporary concessions to their lust for profit.

Seeing the world from the high vantage point of God's seat, Hong Xiuquan beheld quite a different picture. All men were Godfather's children. They were one family under Him. 'Shangdi, the Heavenly Father, is shared by each human being. "All under Heaven is one family" this is transmitted since olden times; since Bangu [the Chinese Adam] down to the Three Dynasties both princes and people as one body worshipped August Heaven,' wrote Hong around 1844, when it dawned on him that he was to be the earthly master over this family [*Hong, 1861: 87; Michael, 1971: 25*].

> Under Heaven all are one family and in the world all are brothers. Why is this so? Speaking about the physical bodies of human beings, each has his father, mother, his family and given names. Seemingly there are the divisions of borders here and frontiers there but (in fact) the ten thousand families all spring from one and the same family, which again hails from one ancestor; thus their origin is nowhere dissimilar. Speaking about man's soul, from whence are they born, from whence do they spring? They are all born and they have all sprung from the breath of the one origin of August Shangdi.

This is how Hong was arguing for the common physical and spiritual origin of all human beings [*Taiping zhaoshu, 1852: 92f.; Michael, 1971: 37*]. His early poems express his exultation about his own rôle in the world. 'Holding the three-foot sword in hand, I consolidate the mountains and rivers. Within the four seas all are one family all in harmonious union. . . . The East, the West, the South and North venerate the sovereign supreme . . .' [*Hamberg, 1854: 25*].

This emphasis on 'one family' referred to the relationships both within China and between China and other countries. Against the narrow-mindedness and egotism of his countrymen Hong proclaimed two new virtues: broadmindedness (*liang*) and public-spiritedness (*gong*). He assailed his compatriots:

> Those of this country dislike those of that country, and vice versa. This is because their views are confined to one individual country and they are ignorant of everything beyond their own country. Hence they love those of their own country and dislike those of other countries. Those of this province, this prefecture or that district dislike those of that province, that prefecture and that district.

From his lofty vision of the various regions and nations and of their equality before God he apostrophies his countrymen as 'frogs at the bottom of a well' who see nothing but the small segment of the sky which is perceptible through the mouth of the well [*Taiping zhaoshu, 1852: 91f; Michael, 1971: 37*]. The ensuing recognition of the equality of nations before God and hence the possibility of borrowing liberally all that might be good and useful – such as God's earlier revelations in the Bible and practical mechanic devices – while rejecting what was repulsive, like opium, attracted the earlier generation of Chinese gentry reformers to the Taiping. All of them had some form of contact with the West and opted for a form of cooperation with the West which would keep China independent [*Wagner, 1983*]. The doctrine itself, however, did not appear to be a foreign message for the Taiping. Liang Afa's tract and Gützlaff's translation of the Bible which the Taiping adopted spoke of God as Shangdi. Shangdi was the highest God in the China before the Qin dynasty, which began in 255 B.C. In Hong's vision the 'old man' had complained that men in China had fallen away from him, which implied that they had originally honoured him. And indeed Shangdi had been honoured before the Qin; the manufacture of gods and their worship had started with the Han and had spread with Buddhism; the Manzhu again followed a form of Buddhism, e.g. Lamaism. 'The Chinese in the beginning were looked after by God. Together with the foreign nations they were on a common way,' said the Trimetrical Classic, an early official Taiping publication [*Sanzi jing, 1853: 226; Michael, 1971: 156*]. The time referred to as 'in the beginning' is the time before the Qin Dynasty. This time thus became the original good time to which China should return. The Taiping modelled their institutions on an idealized description of the 'golden age' conditions, as found in the *Rites of Zhou* [*Couvreur, 1950*]. The Taiping Utopia is taken from this text [*Hong, 1861: 92; Michael, 1971: 35f.; Couvreur, 1950: I, 497f.*]. At that time China was not unified, but consisted of different states. The intercourse between these Chinese states becomes the model for the envisaged intercourse of Taiping China and the Western nations. Hong wrote:

> Recall the times of Tang and Yu and of the Three Dynasties; in that world those who had and those who had not were mutually compassionate, and in calamity they aided one another ... Yao and Shun ... made no distinction between this land and that land ... Yu and Ji ... made no distinctions between this people and that people ... Tang and Wu made no distinction between this country and that country. Confucius and Mengzi ... made no distinction between this state and that state. It was because all these illustrous ones saw that the mortal earth, when spoken of in its parts, comprised the ten-thousand kingdoms, but when spoken of collectively, constituted one family. ... China, which is near to us, is governed and regulated by the Great God; in foreign nations, which are far away, it is also thus [*Hong, 1861: 91f; Michael, 1971: 35*].

The ancient Chinese sage emperors and heroes thus showed the proper attitude in international relations. Even the key slogan 'all under Heaven is one family' comes from the *Rites of Zhou*. It says:

> Therefore, that the Sage can unify all under Heaven as one family and treat all of China as one human being, is not due to his (simply) wanting it. He has to know their feelings, has to gather what is their duty, to elucidate what is of benefit for them and

to understand what is harmful for them; then only will he be able to achieve this [*Couvreur, 1950: I, 516*].

Thus it is an ideal that all under Heaven should be one family; it is to be achieved through the proper policies of the Sage.

Consistent with this basic view of international relations, developed from their authenticated sources, the Taiping, met the Westerners with the greatest friendliness, calling them 'transoceanic brothers' and repeated at every opportunity that they were all one family under God. On this basis they freely adapted the Bible and collected tracts on mathematics, mechanics and science translated by missionaries; they adopted foreign habits like shaking hands; the children of a number of Taiping leaders learned English. Hong Rengan, the cousin of Hong Xiuquan, proposed a wide-ranging reform of the country including modern technology in railways and mining, modern institutions such as those he had seen in Hongkong: social services, general education for boys and girls, hospitals, newspapers and examinations based on the authenticated texts [*Hong Rengan, 1859; Michael, 1971: 748ff.*]. Rev. Yates recalled what Captain Fishbourne of the HMS Hermes, that visited Nanjing in 1853, told him about his conversation with the rebels:

> He was most cordially received by the rebels, who welcomed him as a brother, and told him that in the future foreigners should have steamboats, railroads, telegraphs and all Western appliances without any restriction. They told him: 'We are going to be just as you are. We worship the same God and would live together like brethren' [*Yates, 1876: 7*].

It might be and has been argued that this attitude was dictated by tactical considerations. This argument is based on general assumptions about human nature, not on available sources. It is my contention that this attitude was not derived from any actual experience with the British nor from considerations about its potential power, but that it was derived in a rational and coherent manner from the authenticated sources of Taiping religion. This, is confirmed by a curious episode. In the Spring of 1861 Hong Xiuquan had received from God the unequivocal command to 'receive the British with friendliness' [*Lindley, 1866: 418*]. This was but a confirmation of the policy they had already followed. In 1860 the Taiping approached Shanghai with a small contingent; they justly expected substantial support from the population and had obviously been invited to take Shanghai by various Westerners. A 'correspondent of the *North China Herald*,' the major English language paper in Shanghai, wrote about the Taiping encounter with the British and French on the ramparts of Shanghai:

> When it was discovered that they were real rebels, orders were given to fire on them. They waved the hand, begged our officers not to fire, and stood there motionless,

wishing to open communication and explain their object. No notice was taken of this, but a heavy fire of rifles and grape was kept up on them for about two hours, when they retired with an estimated loss at two hundred.

On the next day the following went on:

> Now the firing and shelling commenced. The insurgents stood it for several hours like men of stone, immovable without returning a single shot. At length a well-directed shell from HMS Pioneer, bursting in the midst of one of the hamlets, and another from the Race Horse, which followed the former in about two seconds, bursting in the midst of the other hamlet, started them fairly [*Lindley, 1866: 297f.*].

From this scene it is evident that the Taiping had not developed their attitude towards the West from experience; as a consequence it could not be altered by contrary experience. They followed their authenticated sources, which, within the logic of the Heavenly scenario, would guarantee victory. The way to a modern program for the development of China and its interaction with the world was thus opened from a quite unexpected angle, namely Taiping theology.

The independent brother

These events may have given the impression that the Taiping, just as other first generations of Christianized elites in colonial countries have shown a most docile and submissive attitude towards the Westerners, especially towards the missionaries. The glorious phrase about 'all under Heaven' being 'one family' might be read as but a thin disguise of a *de facto* acceptance of Western superiority. Nothing, however, could be further from the truth. China had been spared the experience of Western colonization. It had been subdued, it is true, by the Manzhu, but especially in the South there had been a strong resistance which provided a historical legitimacy for defiant attitudes towards the Manzhu. As far as the Taiping behaviour towards Westerners was concerned, the latter, be they soldiers, diplomats or missionaries, were stunned by the unexpected combination of an unfailing friendliness towards them as the 'transoceanic brothers' and the most unequivocal independence of the Taiping in their thought and action.

The revivalist theology embraced by men like Gützlaff and Roberts emphasized direct relationships between the individual and God, and paid little attention to church organization. In addition it envisaged the conversion of the Chinese through 'native evangelists'; this implied a great independence of Chinese Christians. Hong Xiuquan had gone to Canton in 1847 to learn more about the Gospel. Roberts [*1847*] was exhilarated about Hong's vision, seeing it as a sign from the Spirit that China was being moved. There was thus nothing in Hong's experience with Roberts which would have instilled into him the catechete's submissiveness. Hong returned to his 'Association of God

Worshippers' which he had formed earlier on the basis of his confirmed vision, and from then on the Taiping operated in complete theological independence. Through his vision Hong had direct and independent access to God, who with many signs led his host from victory to victory, thus reinforcing this direct link. The evangelical missionaries were in a unique position. They were invited to Nanjing, the Taiping capital, to preach the Gospel. In their enthusiasm about the sudden conversion of the Chinese they printed well over a million Chinese bibles to be distributed after the Taiping victory. (After the failure of the rebellion it took them well into this century to dispose of this stock.) Roberts went to Nanjing and became the first Taiping Secretary of State. Although the missionaries were enthusiastic about the new Christian kingdom, they had fought for so many decades about theological questions that they could not accept that the Taiping be just 'Christians', they had to be Baptists like Roberts or follow some other established denomination. These differences split the evangelical community to the extent that in the revised Bible translation they decided to leave the words for 'baptism' blank, to allow each denomination to fill in the term for 'immersion' or for 'sprinkling with water'. When the missionaries arrived in Nanjing as theological inspectors, they found 'Socinian', 'puritan', 'unitarian', 'mormonite' and other heresies in Taiping writings, and demanded in no unclear terms that these flaws be expunged. But all their letters and remonstrances were refuted by Hong who referred to the Chinese Bible and his own experience in Heaven, while all the way retaining a friendly attitude, even though some of the foreigners wrote quite rude rebukes. Edkins sadly stated:

> The truth has been laid before [Hong], and all his cherished errors exposed and assailed. But he has not abated an inch of the contested claims. He has shown himself decided and unyielding, while maintaining a kindly manner. The self-styled prophet and iconoclast proceeds with his enterprise, unimpeded by the presence of those from whom, as he well remembers, and cheerfully acknowledges, he received the knowledge of Christianity [*1863: 299*].

This statement is fairly typical for the evangelical missionaries who sympathized with the rebels.

Hong Rengan, who became the Taiping Prime Minister, after having been for many years in the service of the London Missionary Society where he was held in high esteem, made it clear to Rev. Muirhead that this theological autonomy was a question of principle for the Taiping:

> He [Hong Rengan] then stated that the desire of his royal master was to evangelise the country; and when asked if that was their mutual intention, he at once replied, 'Most certainly it was; the thing had been contemplated from the first, and would be strenuously followed out. But it was necessary to observe,' he added, 'that the king intended to prosecute this object in his own way.' 'In what way?' [Muirhead] asked.

'By native means,' he said ... 'Well then,' it was asked, 'what position would foreign teachers have in the case? He stated that 'at first they would be useful in diffusing among the scholars and people a general knowledge of Christianity; but the fact was, that the king did not like the idea of depending on foreign aid in the matter. He thought that the thing could be done by the Chinese themselves, who were naturally proud, and not disposed to accept the Gospel at the hands of foreigners ...' [Brine, 1862: 286f.].

There was more to come. As Hong Xiuquan had been mandated by God as His second son this new revelation, not contained in the earlier Gospels, there was to be a Taiping 'New Testament'. Hong politely turned the tables on his teachers and asked them to accept the Taiping revelation. Roberts even suspected that Hong wanted to use him as its missionary to the West. Thus the missionaries encountered an unprecedented combination of friendliness and independence. It was based on Taiping sources, but at the same time quite explicitly corresponded to the doctrine of missions as enunciated by men like Gützlaff and Roberts. The verbatim enactment of their doctrine of the conversion of the heathen by native evangelists was more than they could swallow, and they turned against their Eastern brethren.

In economic and technical matters things were similar. The Taiping advocated free and equal trade with the Westerners; in fact, during their rule, silk and tea exports from rebel controlled areas to Shanghai increased. They explicitly stated that all of China and not just some coastal ports would be open for trade in the event of their victory. But there was no question that the foreigners would have to abide by the Taiping laws and they set up Roberts as the responsible person to deal with infractions committed by foreigners. Opium, wine and tobacco were banned in Taiping areas under threat of decapitation. The ban, of course, was not fully effective under the prevailing conditions, but there is no question that serious and quite successful efforts were made to enforce this law. Opium and tobacco, however, were very major articles of trade for a segment of the Western merchants, who as a consequence turned against the Taiping even more after the British government had succeeded in legalising its opium imports with the Treaty of Tiantsin in 1859. In Hong's vision God had made it quite clear that these obnoxious items of trade should be banned, although there was no indication that he held the foreigners responsible for it; the spread of these intoxicants was rather seen as a part of the Manzhu strategy to befuddle the heads of the Chinese. Hong referred to the Opium pipe as a 'gun to kill oneself,' but the Taiping even accepted the first Opium war in Canton as a legitimate British action against the Manzhu and their Chinese servants like Lin Zexu, who eventually was sent to suppress them, and died on the way [Hamberg, 1854: 47; Michael, 1966: 64]. This attitude of the Taiping found a strong support among many of their Western friends. Opium imports to China had been attacked in the British parliament for many years and the correspondences of missionaries and the English language papers appearing on China's fringes were replete with scathing attacks against drug imports. In military and diplomatic matters we discern the same pattern of behaviour. It seems to have been a quite conscious policy of the Taiping to evade conflict with the 'transoceanic brothers'. They did not march on Canton; when they went for Shanghai and Ningbo they tried everything to insure that contact was established with the 'brethren' beforehand and that their lives and property be protected. This attitude was well received by the powers and interpreted as due respect for British cannon. Brine, however, reports about the impression of Meadows who had accompanied Sir Bonham to Nanjing in 1853 as a translator:

> The most noticeable point in this conversation [with Meadows] as reported, is the supreme indifference with which the chiefs seemed to regard our proffered neutrality. Knowing the province from which they had sprung, and supposing that frequent mention must have been there made of the power of our forces in 1841–43, it is strange that more anxiety should not have been shown to obtain our approval of their acts; the similarity of their faith with ours was the only point in which they appear to have felt interested [*Brine, 1862: 169*].

Captain Fishbourne who joined the same trip, quotes affirmatively the conclusion of Rev. Medhurst:

> Another thought struck my mind; viz. this is a class of men that can with difficulty be controlled. They must for a time be allowed to go their own way. It may not be in every respect the way which we could approve, but it does not appear to run directly counter to our objects [*Fishbourne, 1855: 353*].

This independent and friendly attitude strongly contrasts with the treatment meted out to the Western barbarians by the Manzhu representatives. They used all traditional devices of their diplomacy from copious tears at the negotiating table to move the barbarians' hardened hearts, gifts of classical Chinese writings to let them exert their civilizing influence, to verbal concessions in the negotiations while later organizing opposition to their fulfillment.

The Taiping behaviour impressed many Western observers who linked Christianity with personal dignity, freedom and high moral standards, and felt that the behaviour of the average Chinese and Manzhu was a product of idolatrous morass and Tartar oppression. The Rev. Kloekers, indeed no friend of the Taiping, could not help approving the comportment of the Taiping. 'The male population looks strong and well-fed, while I have nowhere in China seen such respectable and thriving women;' the struggle against the oppression of women in non-Christian countries being one of the main motives for missionary work [*Ostertag, 1862: 74; Brumberg, 1981*]. Lindley, a British officer who together with a Greek who had fought against the Turks, and a Corsican eventually joined the Taiping host, showed the peculiar mixture of enthusiasm for the freedom fighter à la Lord Byron, with the firm belief in the instant civilizing influence of Christian religion, when he wrote his most glowing statement:

> One of the most remarkable contrasts between the Ti-pings [Taiping] and their enslaved countrymen, the Imperialists [e.g. the Manzhu and their Chinese followers], and the first to attract the observation of foreigners, is their complete difference of appearance and costume. The Chinese are known as a comparatively stupid-looking, badly-dressed race; the disfigurement of the shaved head not a little causing this. One presents a type of the whole – a dull, apathetic countenance, without expression or intelligence, except what resembles the half-cunning, half-fearful manner of slaves; their energies seem bound, their hopes and spirits crushed by wrong and oppression. The Ti-pings on the other hand, immediately impress an observer by their intelligence, continual inquisitiveness, and thirst for knowledge. It is indeed utterly impossible, judging from their different intellectual capacities, to come to the conclusion that they are both natives of the same country – a difference more marked cannot be conceived. The Ti-pings are a clever, candid, and martial people, rendered particularly attractive by the indescribable air of freedom which they possess. Where you would see the servile Tartar-subdued Chinamen continually cringing, the Ti-pings exhibit, even in the face of death, nothing but the erect, stately carriage of free men [Lindley, 1866: 67].

Where does this exceedingly 'modern' bearing have its logic?

It seems to be such a coherent pattern of Taiping behaviour that one has to wonder whether it is not mandated by the Taiping vision as a collective and collectively known scenario of action. This does not exclude the existence of strong traditional elements; but they would find their legitimate articulation and appropriate reinforcement from the new authenticated sources. Hong Xiuquan had been taken up to Heaven by way of 'the Great Eastern Road', or 'by that great road which is leading up from the East' [*Taiping tianri*, 1862: 632; Michael, 1971: 53; Hong Renfa, 1860: 510, cf. 513; Michael, 1971: 9, cf. 14] apparently an independent, direct, Eastern (i.e. Chinese) road. The vision does not portray any intermediary between God and Hong who could be interpreted as the foreign missionary, such as the Evangelist in Bunyan's *Pilgrim's Progress*. The West and the Westerners were patently absent in the heavenly battles with the 'demons'. Hong as God's second son, with a direct mandate to exterminate the demons on earth was assigned a palace in the 'Eastern Part' of Heaven, indicating the domain of his rule. Further events proved to Hong and his host that God and Christ had indeed 'personally taken charge' of his kingdom's fate. Hong did not import a foreign religion, but restored China's original creed which coincided with that of the foreigners. China was God's chosen country where He had sent down His second son to usher in a worldwide millennium. In His own secretive way God had indicated this choice already in China's ancient names. Was it not called *shenzhou*, 'Realm of the Spirit' or 'Realm of God?' It was also called *Zhong hua* ('Central Flowery'). God's Chinese name, the transscription of Jehova, was *Ye Huohua*; Hong read this as a Chinese family name. In good esoteric tradition God had referred to Hong with Hong Xiuquan's second personal name, *quan*; hence God's 'second personal name' was *hua*, enshrined in China's name *Zhong hua*. And indeed 'the Father has established the Kingdom of Heaven' which He announced in the Bible, 'in China' said Hong [*1861: 678; Michael, 1971: 940*]. The Taiping pattern of behaviour towards the Westerners in both of its main aspects had its logical foundation and explanation in the scenario which propelled their rebellion.

There is one point which remains slightly ambiguous. Religious and secular authority were not divided in the Taiping kingdom. Thus it was not quite clear what Hong's world-wide role would be. Did he demand the submission of the Western nations under his political rule, as some have suggested at the time? In actual Taiping documents nothing indicates this. True, on some rare occasions lower charges of the Taiping hierarchy employed the terminology of 'barbarians sending tribute to the Chinese emperor' in regard to visiting Westerners, but apologies were offered for this insult and Hong Rengan explicitly forbade its use. However, Hong clearly had a world-wide mandate. In homiletic language and missionary hymns Christ was often addressed as 'master' or 'lord' of the world. In religious terms Christ had a world-wide mission, but he never demanded political authority of the myriad states. Hong as the second son seems to have followed this pattern. He ushered in the Kingdom of Heaven and demanded recognition of his mandate as God's second son. There is no indication that he ever claimed a political mandate beyond the 'East'. But exactly on the religious level this led to a serious conflict. The evangelical missionaries had come from societies impregnated with a strong millennial expectation. American evangelical movements expected that the United States would be the promised land. From this belief they drew their motivation to rapidly convert the heathen prior to the Second Coming. And suddenly they were confronted with God's Second Son who had descended in China whence he proceded to establish the Kingdom of Heaven, demanding their acceptance of his claim. This could not but enrage them to the utmost, and so it did. Roberts left Nanjing and demanded that the Powers should exterminate the 'coolie king' and his ilk. Others said that the perversion of Christianity by the Taiping was even worse than the open idolatry practised by the 'imperialists'. The attitude of the Taiping in their dealing with the West had evolved into a pattern – and the West's reaction as well.

One cannot but consider a later parallel. Soon after their initiation to Leninist Marxism under Soviet guidance the Chinese Communists developed their own 'line', while retaining friendly relations with the Soviet Union. Eventually they maintained that Mao Zedong Thought had further developed Marxism-Leninism-Stalinism; as the new revelation Mao Zedong Thought claimed spiritual authority even over the original 'missionaries', who reacted with no surprising outrage. The Great Eastern Road to truth is also seen as an obstacle by foreign experts and businessmen, used to docile Third World cooperators. Many are shocked by the peculiar Chinese mixture of friendliness and 'supreme indifference' toward their judgement. It seems that a strong self-consciousness of China as a land of an old culture of its own was a crucial ingredient enabling the Chinese to create this form of autonomous adaption of foreign things [*Wagner, 1981*].

The members of God's family of nations

International relations in nineteenth century China meant not only relations with the West. The country was occupied by the Manzhu, who were 'foreign barbarians' in the eyes of many Chinese; and China was surrounded by tributary nations. The set of categories which regulated the relationship with the West was clearly inappropriate for the regulation of relationships with the 'demon' Manzhus and other barbarians. Thus we have to proceed to a second reading of the relevant Taiping writings and actions to understand more in detail what their terminology implies. When speaking about nations with direct relationships with God Taiping sources only mention the Christian Westerners and China before the Qin and under the Taiping. There was the Great Eastern Road, and there obviously was a Western Road as well, as Christ was descended there. The direct access from West and East was there independent of the actual moral state of the country; China was the 'Realm of the Spirit' and named after God although it had fallen away from the Creator and had been punished with foreign domination and famine. Israel was the elect nation even when the children of Israel cast the Golden Calf. There is no specific reason given why just China and the Western countries should be thus selected. Neither is there a reason given in the Pentateuch why God entered a covenant with Israel. The Pentateuch, the main precedent for the behaviour of the Taiping host, does not speak of converting the other nations to God. The nations which previously occupied the promised land were not converted, but slain, man, woman, child and cattle. They certainly were no children of God. This was a familiar thought in China. Traditional religious topography knew of 36 Caves Opening Towards Heaven (*dongtian*) and 72 Auspicious Places (*fudi*). All of these had good access to Heaven; temples would be built there and pilgrims would deposit their written prayers there with greater chances to speedy delivery to their heavenly address [*Fu, 1937: 110ff; Stein 1942: 43*]. When Nanjing had become the capital of the Taiping Kingdom many authors of commemorative essays written for this event referred to this New Jerusalem as a *fudi*, an Auspicious Place, from which 'a way led to Heaven', ensuring direct and rapid communication [*Wu Rongkuan,*

1853: 252; Huang Congshan, 1853: 257; Lin Yihuan, 1853: 258; Michael, 1971: 254–9]. The Chinese religious map was transferred by the Taiping to the globe with such 'Auspicious Places' only in the West and China. It was in no way surprising that the 'demons' as well as the tributary and other intermediate nations should have no direct access to Heaven. They could only – if at all – reach it through these elect places. This eliminated the multitude of 'barbarian' nations from being 'equal' members of God's family. Hong Rengan observed [*1859: 531f*] that countries like Persia and Turkey were backward because of their idolatrous religion [*Michael, 1971: 762ff.*].

It was known to the Taiping that the Christian British and French had colonies all over the world, but there is not a single word in Taiping sources expressing dismay over this fact. The 'transoceanic brothers' were accepted by the Taiping as heads of their own subsystems, or colonial empires of tributary nations. The Taiping did neither identify with the Chinese rebel tradition (which they unequivocally denounced) nor with the rebellions of the colonies like the Sepoy rebellion in India. Hong evidently saw it as a normal thing that the nations elect would each have such a colonial or tributary subsystem, encompassing those backward barbarian nations unhappy enough to lack God's direct protection. Taiping China was one of the nations elect. The traditional Chinese 'family of nations' under the Chinese emperor ruling over the adjacent barbarians was to be continued under the Taiping, although in the framework of new categories of legitimation. During the late stages of the rebellion we even see a mimicked enactment of the tribute paid by these nations to Hong [*Michael, 1971: 1028f.*]. The 'family of nations' under God the Father only consists of Christian nations with their own subsystems holding backward and idolatrous barbarians under control. While this idea was directly deduced from the authenticated sources of the Taiping, it again coincided with a Western pattern of thought.

It is not known whether the Taiping had access to the translations of manuals on international law which had been made in Hongkong, although this is quite probable. The implied assumption in international law was that its rules prevailed only among civilized, i.e. Christian, nations. Caleb Cushing, a senior American statesman to whom Rev. W. A. P. Martin addressed three open letters in 1856 to forestall an intervention of the Powers against the Taiping, is quoted by Martin as saying 'the law of nations is in fact only the international law of Christendom' [*Teng, 1971: 191*]. By referring to this statement Martin argued for the recognition of the Taiping kingdom as a Christian kingdom to which international law was accordingly applicable. And this indeed was the problem which also gave some of the purely theological judgements of missionaries on Taiping beliefs their very practical importance. The Taiping fully accepted Cushing's view quoted above, but included themselves into the category of Christendom with all its ensuing consequences, while the Powers tended to exclude Taiping China from 'civilized Christendom'.

The 'demonic' Manzhu

In his vision Hong had been mandated to exterminate the 'demons'. 'Demons' are a large class of noxious spectres believed to populate the universe. God had given to Hong the proper and familiar devices to deal with their menace, a magic seal, a *jian* sword and His personal support. In the beginning Hong interpreted the symbolical figure of the 'demons' in his vision as a reference to the idols which filled the temples and houses especially in South China. He and his followers proceded to publicly exterminate local gods and to smash ancestral tablets. Once, however, the Taiping came into conflict with the authorities, they were in a quandry; the vision did not indicate how they should react. God himself freed them from this predicament by personally descending in 1848 to identify the Manzhu as the demons, and ordering the Taiping to exterminate those who happened to run the government of China. This explosive help of exegesis (the Taiping commemorated the day by making it into a holiday) gave the rebellion a clear political orientation. The original religious meaning of 'demons' was retained however; the Taiping argued that the Manzhu, who followed the Lamaist version of Buddhism, prayed to the Black Dragon, Yanluo, who in the Taiping Bible was no other than Satan himself. The Manzhu were Satan's servants and underlings, pulling the Chinese away from God. Taiping documents do not use the term 'man' or 'human being', *ren*, indiscriminately. To 'become a human being' meant to convert, repent, and submit to the one God, Shangdi. God Himself declared on Jan. 23 1852: 'Now you know that you have a sovereign, and you may become human beings,' referring to the advent of Hong [*Tianming zhaozhi shu, 1852: 62; Michael, 1971: 102*]. The Taiping leaders complained that 'there are no human beings in China' [*Hong Rengan, 1861: 570; Michael, 1971: 806*]. Losing contact with the one God means to become a 'demon' in Taiping language. The class of 'demons' is again subdivided. There are the Chinese who have been deluded by the Manzhu demons and have themselves turned demonic. But they basically remain 'brothers and sisters' as they can be 'brought back' and can 'become human being' again. Their 'original nature' (*benxin*) is 'correct' as they are members of a nation elect. The Manzhu, on the other hand, are demons by their very nature. They cannot be converted, and there are no instances of Manzhu siding with the Taiping, although large bodies of imperialist troops went over to the Taiping. The Manzhu demons can be either exterminated or restricted to their 'hell' in the northern provinces so that they do not 'dare to commit further absurdities' as it was said in the vision. The struggle against the Manzhu thus contained a proto-nationalist ethnic element. The entire set of traditional beliefs and practices existing in China at the time was identified by the Taiping as demonic delusion; their vituperous attacks against the 'demons' also carried the message, that only through the most radical break with the 'narrow-mindedness', 'egotism', 'idolatry', 'worldy customs', would their compatriots be able to 'become human beings' again and return to a paradisiac state of affairs under God's direct protection and stern command.

References

Brine, L., 1862, *The Taiping Rebellion in China: A Narrative of Its Rise and Progress, Based upon Original Documents and Information Obtained in China*, London.
Brumberg, J. J., 1981, 'Zenanas and Girlless Villages: The Ethnology of American Evangelical Women, 1870–1910', paper read at the 1981 Berkshire Women's History Conference.
Cole, J. H., 1982, *The People versus the Taipings: Bai Lisheng's 'Righteous Army of Dongan'* (China Research Monograph 21, Institute of Asian Studies) Berkeley.
Couvreur, S., 1950, *Mémoires sur les Bienséances et les Cérémonies*, Leiden.
Edkins, J., 1863, 'Narrative of a Visit to Nanking', in: Edkins, J. R.: *Chinese Scenes and People*, London.
Fairbank, J. K., 1957, 'Synarchy under the Treatise', in: J. K. Fairbank (ed.), *Chinese Thought and Institutions*, Chicago.
Fairbank, J. K., 1968, 'The Early Treaty System in the Chinese World Order', in John K. Fairbank (ed.), *The Chinese World Order*, Cambridge.
Fishbourne, 1855, *Impressions of China and the Present Revolution: Its Progress and Prospects*, London.
Fu Qinjia, 1937, *Zhongguo daojiao shi* [A History of Daoist doctrines in China] Shanghai.
Gregory, J. S., 1959, 'British Intervention against the Taiping Rebellion', *Journal of Asian Studies* XIX.
Gregory, J. S., 1963, 'British Missionary Reaction to the Taiping Movement', in *Journal of Religious History*, II.
Gregory, J. S., 1969, *Great Britain and the Taipings*, London.
Hamberg, Th., 1854, *The Vision of Hung-Siu-Tshuen and Origin of the Kwang-si Insurrection*, Hongkong.
Hong, 1861, Tianwang zhaozhi [Decrees of the Heavenly King], 2, in: *Xiang, 1953*: I, 678–9.
Hong Renfa, 1860 (and Hong Renda, eds.), Wangzhancixiong qinmu qiner gongzheng fuyinshu [Gospel jointly: witnessed and heard by the Imperial Eldest and Second-eldest Brother], in: *Xiang, 1953*, II, 507–16.
Hong Rengan, 1859, Zizhen xianpan [A new work for aid and administration] in *Xiang, 1953*: II, 521–41.
Hong Rengan, 1861, Qinding yingjie guizhen [A hero's return to the truth] in *Xiang, 1953*: II, 563–94.
Hsu, I., 1960, *China's Entrance into the Family of Nations: The Diplomatic Phase 1858–1880* (Harvard East Asian Studies 5), Cambridge, Mass.
Huang Congshan, 1853, Jian Tianjing yu Jinling lun [On establishing the Heavenly Capitol in Junling], in *Xiang, 1953*: I, 256–7.
Lin Yihuan, 1853, Jian Tianjing yu Junling lun [as above], in *Xiang, 1953*: I, 258.
Lindley, A. E., 1866, *Ti-Ping Tian-Kwoh: The History of the Ti-Ping Revolution including a Narrative of the Author's Personal Adventures, by Lin-Li*, 2 vols, London.
Marx, K., 1850, Article in Neue Rheinische Revue, written Jan 31., 1850 in London, in: F. Mehring (ed.), *Aus dem literarischen Nachlaß von K. Marx, F. Engels und F. Lassalle*, Stuttgart, 1902, III, 445ff.

Marx, K., 1862, 'Chinesisches', in: Die Presse no. 185, July 7, 1862, *Marx Engels Werke* 15: 514ff.
Michael, F., 1966, *The Taiping Rebellion, History*, Seattle.
Michael, F., 1971, *The Taiping Rebellion, History and Documents*, vols II and III: Documents and Comments, Seattle.
Naquin, S., 1976, *Millenarian Rebellion in China: The Eight Trigram Uprising of 1813*, New Haven.
Naquin, S., 1981, *Shantung Rebellion, the Wang Lun Uprising of 1774*, New Haven.
Ostertag, A., 1861/2, Die Taipings in China, *Evangelisches Missionsmagazin*.
Overmyer, D. L., 1976, *Dissenting Sects in Late Traditional China*, Cambridge.
Roberts, I. J., 1847, For the Banner and Pioneer, in: Baptist Banner and Western Pioneer XIV. 30, July, 118. Reprod. in: Coughlin, M. M., Strangers in the House: J. Lewis Shuck and Issachar Roberts, First American Baptist Missionaries to China. Ph.D., University of Virginia, 1972.
Sanzi Jing, 1853, [The 'Three Character Classic'] in: *Xiang, 1953*, I. 223–228.
Stein, R., 1942, 'Jardins en miniature d'Extrême-Orient', *Bulletin de l'École Française d'Extrême-Orient* XVII.
Taiping tianri, 1862, [Heavenly chronicle of the Taiping] in: *Xiang, 1953*: II, 629–650.
Taiping zhaoshu, 1852 [Taiping proclamations] in: *Xiang, 1953*: I, 85–89.
Teng, S. Y., 1971, *The Taiping Rebellion and the Western Powers*, New York.
Tianming zhaozhi shu, 1852, [Heavenly decrees and proclamations] in: *Xiang, 1953*: I, 59–70.
Wagner, R. G., 1981, 'Staatliches Machtmonopol und alternative Optionen: Zur Rolle der 'Westlichen Barbaren' im China des 19. Jahrhunderts' in: J. G. Grevemeyer (ed.), *Traditionale Gesellschaften und europäischer Kolonialismus*, Frankfurt.
Wagner, R. G., 1983, Reenacting the Heavenly Vision: The Role of Religion in the Taiping Rebellion [forthc.].
Wu Rongkuan, 1853, Jian Tianjing yu Jinling lun [On establishing the Heavenly Capitol in Jinling], in *Xiang, 1953*: I, 251–2.
Xiang, Da, 1953, (et al., eds.) *Taiping tianguo* [The Taiping Heavenly Kingdom] 8 vols, Shenzhou.

The fate of the Heavenly Gates: rebellion, religion and repression in Republican China

RALPH THAXTON

Like autumn exploding into red and gold a spectacle of religiously colored peasant rebellions erupted in rural Asia on the eve of the World Depression. In the Philippines Florenico Natividad raised the banners of an anti-tax movement, and established a short-lived millennial empire of poor peasants, hired hands, and mill workers in the Central Visayas [*Sturtevant, 1976: 158–174*]. In Burma reduced rice prices and rigid taxes set the stage for Saya San, a member of the Buddhist clergy, to declare himself a Burmese messiah ready to deliver peasants from the all-encompassing British colonial tax order [*Cady, 1976: 124–131*]. In China peasant jacqueries sprang up nearly everywhere, so that in North China we discover a rock quarry worker by the name of Han Yuming drawing peasants, quarry workers, and coal miners into the Heavenly Gate Society, a millennial movement which promised to sweep away the military tax machine of the Kuomintang (KMT) warlords and to replace the Republic of China with a new Ming empire [*Cf. Thaxton, 1982: Chapter 3*].

Indeed, it seems that as international depression took its toll on the revenue making schemes of political orders, rulers centered in urban capitals set out to make up their fiscal deficits by increasing taxes on marginal village populations. The Heavenly Gate rebellion, which took place in China's Henan province from 1925–32, presented a formidable challenge to this type of political taking. The fate of the Heavenly Gate Society was decided ultimately by the oppressive army of the KMT warlord regime under Chiang Kai-shek. By sketching its origins, development, and goals we may begin to get some feeling for how military governments were able to demobilize and defeat one of the more broad based millennial movements in agrarian Asia during the interlude between the great wars.

The origins of the Heavenly Gate Uprising

The Heavenly Gate Society grew up in response to bad government, warlordism, and banditry in Henan province during the 1920s. Peasants in Lin county, the birthplace of the Heavenly Gates, had been suffering from a dual squeeze at the hands of landlord rent collectors and government tax collectors for nearly a decade before the massive uprising of 1926–27.

The Heavenly Gate uprising occurred in the context of unrestrained exploitation in rural class relations. To be sure, landlord exploitation of the peasantry was not the precipitant of the rebellion, and the Heavenly Gates did not rise up against landlordism *per se*. Whereas landlord actions, which were cruel enough, did not trigger the rebellion, landlordism was an important underlying cause.

By the 1920s there were few restraints on exploitation within the villages of Lin county and the surrounding region, and relations between peasants and landlords were infused with rancor. Already by 1919–20 a ruling clique had begun to overturn the older informal system of settling disputes and demands at the local level. An elite composed of *nouveau riche* landlords and gentry had begun to dominate village and county affairs exclusively in the name of their own illegal interests, which included water-use-fees, gambling dens, and grain monopolies. These *tuhao lieshen* or local bullies and evil gentry [Wei, 1978: 20–30] no longer honored the traditional intra-village procedures for resolving disputes involving peasant claims to land and water. When proven wrong by the respected villagers who presided over the local mediation process landlords used their relations with relatives in Lin county government to override popular will.

The same peasants who stood to lose from such an arbitrary system of law and order were producing income that was providing less security than before. Their relations with landlord often involved them in insecure economic arrangements which over time compelled them to give up village roots. As severe drought settled over Lin county in the early 1920s peasants who owned tiny plots and small family businesses turned to landlords to rent several *mu* of land in order to supplement the income derived from family based agriculture and trade. This in turn was necessitated in part because landlords had usurped water supplies and diverted the underground water table to feed their own fertile rental fields. These water-rich landlords required peasants who rented their fields to pay a fixed crop rent, and they collected this rent whether the harvest was good or bad. The land hungry peasants had taken up these fixed tenancies to steady household income, but when the crop failed – and it invariably did in the drought-prone 1920s – they found themselves still owing the fixed rent. Landlords also began utilizing the system of fixed rent to drive hundreds upon hundreds of peasant families into indebtedness, intensifying their exploitation by drawing the rent from family grain harvests and business income rather than by collecting it from crop yields actually produced on the fixed rent fields. The level of peasant family income was thus being reduced significantly in a milieu where the older village-based means of settling grievances over basic rights had collapsed under new landlord rules.

The hard-pressed smallholders turned to cash cropping, mining, and migration for survival. By 1917 they were cultivating the opium poppy for income. Many of them, however, lost this income to landlord-run gambling rings or to the local Opium Tax Bureau, today in the hands of one militarist, tomorrow in the hands of his competitor.

In the years following the first World War the international demand for coal fell off drastically, and the new wave of post-war taxes imposed on the coal mines by Hebei and Henan militarists further crippled the hand-powered coal mine industry. By 1923–24 the local gentry mine bosses were making tax payments to regional militarists by paring wages to mine workers. Many of the desperate peasants who had departed the villages to work in the coal mines were greatly disappointed by the wages and working conditions they encountered in the mines.

Many peasants turned to migration to escape drought, cruel landlordism and taxes. This strategy of survival took them to villages in neighboring districts and counties, where they worked as hired hands and herdsmen. At first, migration was a short-term affair, involving one or two members of the family work force, but as the 1920s wore on, whole families took to the migration trails, leading west into the Taihang Mountains. The Taihang, however, offered a slim prospect for survival, for its soils were extremely poor and its landlords were extremely ruthless in tightening the terms of work life. By 1926–27, many of the more desperate migrants were pouring back to their old home villages in Lin county, living in the abandoned temples near the villages that were to become Heavenly Gate strongholds.

Although the Heavenly Gates would strike against some of the worst features of landlord exploitation, what triggered the Great Rebellion of 1926–27 was the illegitimate extraction of the ruling political élite. Prior to the 1920s peasants in Lin county had petitioned local government to reduce grain taxes when drought made for a poor harvest, but after the death of warlord Yuan Shih-kai the Lin county officials were less willing to honor this practice. Beginning in 1919, the year of the Big Drought in folk memory, and continuing through the North China Famine of 1920–21, the Lin County officials refused to postpone or cancel taxes when drought settled over the fields. The rigidity of government taxation, coupled with official refusals to negotiate a 'just harvest tax', prompted peasants from various parts of the county to turn to begging and banditry. These uprooted peasants organized themselves into popular bandit leagues of 100 and 1,000 people. The leagues embraced as many as seventeen villages within one district, as was the case in central Lin county in 1921.

In 1922 the Lin county officials decided to eliminate the popular bandit leagues. But the head of the Lin county militia, turned over his stock of government weapons to the popular bandit leagues in exchange for money and a position of leadership in the popular bandit countermovement. From this time on, roughly October 1922, the Lin county government had no way of controlling its own territory. If they were to maintain their version of law and order then they had to enlist new force from outside the county: they invited bandits from neighbouring Anyang county to quell the tax avoidance protests. The Anyang bandits arrived in Lin county in late October 1922 and stayed on until 1927 – the high tide of the Heavenly Gates. In the day time the Anyang bandits served as soldiers of the Lin County Tax Bureau, but at nightfall they donned masks and robbed the village people from their headquarters. The Tian Men Hui uprising of 1926–27 grew out of a series of failed peasant attempts to fight off these predatory bandits, including the anti-bandit revolt of 7,000 peasants in He Shun in late 1922.

From 1922 to 1924 the soldier bandits added kidnapping and ransom to their tax collection activities. The peasants who did not cooperate with this pillage had their homes burned to the ground. The market roads were unsafe day and night. Lin county became so much a bandit world that many people fled their home villages in the rain and snow. Only the richer landlord families with a relative in county government were safe. Government complicity in this predatory banditry helped to create the conditions which triggered the Heavenly Gate Uprising.

There were two significant triggers to the uprising. In 1925 the Anyang soldier-bandits struck the village of You *cun* in one of their raids, and burned the homes of villagers. The future leader of the Heavenly Gate Society, Han Yuming, was the son-in-law of one of the families who lost everything in this bandit raid. When he heard about the raid he confronted the raiders with a small group of locals, but they were no match for the bandit-soldiers. The raiders tracked Han Yuming into a nearby field where he was nearly beaten to death.

In the following months Han Yuming, once recovered from the beating, began to go from village to village in an effort to organize poor peasants, quarry workers, and coal miners to resist the Lin county government and its bandit lackeys. In late 1925 Han Yuming and Li Youyu assembled with some forty peasants in You village where they turned their faces to Heaven and proclaimed a rebellion that would open the gates to a just world for the next thousand years.

Membership in the Heavenly Gates swelled to ten, twenty, and one-hundred thousand in the next year. The explosion in Society membership, however, was triggered by unwarranted and harmful government extraction, and not by the religious ideology of the emergent rebel leadership. To supplement county level finances and strengthen local security forces, the governments in Lin county and Ci county had imposed a new surtax in addition to the regular land tax (*di ding*). The *di ding* itself already was ten times greater than the customary land tax, which itself was not to exceed 30 per cent of the harvest yield. Therefore, the new surtax far surpassed the tax bearing capacity of both smallholders and small merchants, all of whom became desperate to avoid government taxes on land and harvests. The origins of the Heavenly Gate Society lay in peasant attempts to avoid these new unbearable surtaxes on the autumn harvest. In 1926, just prior to the harvest, the Lin county government announced its intentions of sending surtax collectors into the villages. Han Yuming and Li Youyu responded by raising the banners of an anti-surtax movement in You village, and then invited peasants from surrounding villages and counties to form the Heavenly Gate Society to resist taxes. The peasants who flocked to the Heavenly Gates did so in response to a promise that members of the Society would not have to pay any illegal taxes, especially the new surtax and troop support tax. Within a very short time, the Heavenly Gates sprang up like wildflowers in twenty other counties of the Shanxi-Hebei-Shandong-Henan border area.

Religious Rebellion

As the Tian Men Hui grew, it took on a religious character of a distinctively heterodox nature. Han Yuming declared that he had discovered a Book of Heaven in the Taihang Mountains, and that this set of commandments called for the replacement of the Lin county government by the Heavenly Gates, who were to usher in an eternal peace. Thus behind the specific sociopolitical demands of the Society there existed a set of millennial aspirations rooted in a nostalgia for past order, security, and peace [*Zhou Ran, 1935: 118–120*].

The messianic promise of the Heavenly Gates was evident in its earliest pronouncements. In 1926 Han Yuming declared his intention to establish a dynasty in place of the Republic of China. By August of that year Han Yuming was rumored to be a new Ming Emperor, and Han and his lieutenants were receiving thousands of peasants seeking salvation from warlord and bandit taxes within the 'Empire of the Heavenly Gates'. From 1926 on, the revivalist politics of the Heavenly Gates was clear, and shortly thereafter Han proclaimed himself the leader of a movement that was going to bring back the Ming dynasty, the pure Han Chinese dynasty that had been the victim of the Manchu conquest in 1644.

The recruitment and training, actions, and accomplishments of the Heavenly Gates reflected the millennial tone of the movement. The Heavenly Gate Society was a movement of the poorest rural people. Massive numbers of poor land-hungry peasants, small bandits, journeymen, stonemasons, and miners flocked to its banners. These people were part of a floating population whose membership was experienced in working outside of the villages – a semi-proletariat whose lot was threatened collectively and simultaneously by drought and tax disaster.

Most interestingly, the Heavenly Gates were notoriously illiterate as well as poor. The leadership of the Society initially established a special rule that only poor people without any education could join the Society. Once the rebellion snowballed this rule was relaxed, but it was unmistakably a measure designed to prevent literate secular persons with aspirations to become rebel officials from joining the Society and diluting the anti-Republican religious content of Han Yuming's message to the country people [*ibid., 138–142*].

The Heavenly Gates also sought to check foreign missionary influence in Lin County and Northern Henan. Their membership was drawn largely from local religious families that were not in the thrall of the Roman Catholic missions and the leadership remained in the hands of Han Yuming and native priest-advisors. In an important sense, the Heavenly Gates followed in the footsteps of the anti-Western missionary struggles begun in the Zhangde, Anyang, Hua County area from 1901 to 1904, when French priests who meted out punishment for interference in official missionary work came under popular attack [*Zhang Kaiyuan and Lin Zeng Ping, 1980: 265*].

By 1926 Han Yuming was conducting a military training course for Heavenly Gate members. The training generally took place around temples which were assembly grounds for peasants and semi-peasants coming to district level market fairs from different villages. The individual warriors were known to swallow yellow strips of paper which symbolized the talisman, and this assured them of invulnerability in battle. The Heavenly Gate Society had its own official stamp for these yellow strips, and its warriors lined up to have the stamp issued in the name of the True Son of Heaven, Han Yuming.

The Heavenly Gates drew on the myth of 'the just emperor' to create an earthly paradise in which faithful followers would receive salvation, and follow the one who would revive the protective duties of the Ming dynasty. In one sense, Han Yuming was but one of many rustic pretenders who wanted to raise a rebellion against the Republic of China. In Anyang, around April 1925, Wang Liuzai had proclaimed himself to be the True Son of Heaven, gathered 300 bandits to his cause, and then attempted to steal weapons from the militia. A similar effort to start a new Empire was undertaken by Zhu Hongdeng in Lin *xian* about this same time. Han Yuming's Heavenly Gates built their power in part by uniting many of the remnant disciples of these earlier aborted rebel attempts to lead isolated crusades against the Republic.

What enhanced the potential for Heavenly Gate success was Han Yuming's insistence on putting force behind these earlier rebellions of the poor. The Heavenly Gates gained momentum as they began to attract leaders from surrounding counties who were committed to the idea of inaugurating the millennium by the sword.

The riotous eruptions of the Heavenly Gates were directed at Republican local government in Lin county and elsewhere in the region. The first attack, and the unexpected victory that followed it, was hardly a rebel conspiracy. It proved a real inspiration to rebellion on a greater scale, however. On August 14, 1926

Han Yuming and ten of his followers had gone to Lin county town to buy shoes, but when they were denied admission to the town they grew angry and began a small guerrilla action inside the capital. The Lin county government thereafter dispatched a security force unit to You village, the Heavenly Gate headquarters. But the Heavenly Gates ambushed the security force and killed twenty of its members. This little victory threw the Lin *xian* government into a panic, and raised the prestige of the Heavenly Gates in peasant villages of Lin *xian*, Ci *xian*, and several other counties [*Takeshi, 1975: 75–81*]. Shortly thereafter, Li Youyu, a native of Ci county, called on peasants and miners in Ci county to follow the Heavenly Gate example in resisting the imposition of taxes by the Fengtien Warlords, and then came to Lin county to ask Han Yuming for assistance and advice. On January 25, 1927 after returning from a meeting with Han Yuming, Li led a force of ten thousand people to burn the Ci county Military Garrison and Police Station, whose officers were enforcing the tax directives of the Fengtien warlords in the county. Several police officers were killed and the Police chief was taken into custody by the Heavenly Gates. Then the joint Lin-Ci Heavenly Gate forces even beat back two Fengtien units sent to reinforce the Ci county garrison. This was a crucial turning point. Now the Heavenly Gates were able to capture small firearms and some rifles before thousands of additional Fengtien cavalry arrived to drive them toward the wild back county of the Zhang River. Several months later, in the spring of 1927, Han Yuming forged a federation of Heavenly Gates in the counties of Anyang, Lin, Ci, and Linzhang to stage a combined attack against the Fengtien Warlords. The Heavenly Gates struck in March. They annihilated a unit of the Fengtien cavalry, and then drove the Fengtien Warlords back to the major points of the Beijing-Hankow Railway [*Ibid., 75–81*].

Political Accomplishments

Having established their military superiority the Heavenly Gates moved to create an alternative system of power in place of the lawless Republic. The changes they carried out were aimed at recapturing the security of the traditional world. Although the movement's emphasis was on the perfection of age-old village society and culture, this backward thrust did not prevent its leadership from creating a multifaceted network for political mobilization and economic revitalization.

In April 1927 the Heavenly Gates took a giant step toward resurrecting a sound agricultural base: they delivered peasants from the burden of the Republican tax structure. The Society refused to collect the inflated land tax (*di ding*) for the Henan provincial government, and it put an end to the endless surtaxes taken by the Lin county government-bandit tax authority. This drive to simplify and sweep away the emergent Republican tax machine was followed by a Heavenly Gate campaign to combat predatory banditry. Within one year peasants and merchants were able to travel once again throughout the county on safe market roads. Suddenly, it seemed as if Heaven had hurled the tax-soldiers back over the Anyang county line.

Though we are often told that peasant movements are prone to fanatical religious outbursts which inhibit mobilization for power goals, the Heavenly Gate movement was both a religious and a political mobilization, and it clearly was aimed at overthrowing Lin county government. It was, to be sure, a movement to remedy the worst abuses of power, but its leadership was nonetheless committed to providing a transformationist framework in which such abuses would be corrected once and for all, and the supernatural world be harnessed to the everlasting service of village society. The disciples of Han Yuming paid homage to a supreme deity, who symbolized China's first emperor, and the flag of the Heavenly Gates was said to be the same as used by Zhu Yuanzhang, the leader of the rebellion that ushered in the Ming dynasty.

From its earliest development the Heavenly Gate Society was determined to do away with the new, illegitimate powerholders who were furthering government intervention into village life. In 1926 the Heavenly Gates killed ten members of the He Jian militia and captured its leader Li Peiying. This action struck terror into the hearts of Lin county officials, and paralyzed their capacity to make decisions on how to handle 'popular disturbance'. Then, in June of the same year, the Heavenly Gates defeated a small pro-government bandit force and took several hostages. This bold action, which went unanswered by the Lin county officials, prompted hundreds of peasants with primitive guns to come to You village to join the Society. The Heavenly Gates also began to confront the gentry and landlords who were cooperating with the Lin county bandit government in its efforts to 'institutionalize the villages', that is, integrate them into its schemes of extraction and regimentation. The Society created a popular system of counter-espionage in order to root out gentry spies and informants at the village level, and dispatched units to disarm the evil gentry. According to Han Yuming and his lieutenants, the Heavenly Gates were going to reverse the roles of oppressed and oppressors.

Religion served as a bridge to political rebellion for the Heavenly Gates. Han Yuming was both military commander and spiritual head of the movement. His dual role seems to have given the Society ever greater drawing power when it came to the issue of recruiting peasant followers. To the rural people, Heavenly Gate rejection of the Republic was all the more attractive because it was rooted in the notion of reviving a world without the armed tax state.

As the Heavenly Gates captured the Lin county capital, they called on peasants to organize self-defense units to keep out warlords and the gentry who had corrupted the peace of the villages. The peasants and merchants supported the Heavenly Gates by financing the purchase of weapons and by giving food and travel money to members going off to do battle. It was the lower nobility, however, who paid the price of village protection. As part of a system of Heavenly Gate fines and punishments, the hated gentry were made to contribute their own guns to the movement or to contribute the cash needed to purchase weapons. A 'weapons contribution deadline' was established, and when no guns were forthcoming the gentry were sentenced to be shot to death. Understandably, a number of the gentry fled the county, and the larger mansions stood empty.

A third goal of the Heavenly Gates was to make the county more modern. The development projects started up by this religiously colored mass political movement after 1927 make us think harder about the Western image of peasant based rebellions being inherently reactionary throwbacks to pre-modern forms of life. To be sure, the Heavenly Gates wanted to go back to some older parochial forms of rule, but on the other hand, the Lin county Heavenly Gates equipped the capital with street lights, drew up plans to improve the highways, and declared war on drug-related spiritual demoralization. None of these rebel development projects was at odds with Heavenly Gate attempts to reunite peasants with the valued products of their labor or to reestablish the recently threatened sense of traditional community.

Repression: The Kuomintang Strategy of Counter-Rebellion and Political Demobilization

From the standpoint of the Chiang Kai-shek Kuomintang [*henceforth KMT*] whose goal was to take over and tax the countryside, a strategy of anarchy prevailed in the rebellious North China interior after 1927. The April 12–13, 1927 KMT *coup d'etat* against the Chinese Communist Party did little to tame the rural Heavenly Gates, Red Spears, Yellow Sands and other peasant-membered societies in China. Chiang Kai-shek's armed forces were still based in South China, and the Heavenly Gates were able to thrive in the interstices of the incessant wars between the Northern Warlords. From 1924 until 1927 the peasant movement was gaining momentum within the power gaps fostered by the growing splits in the ruling warlord army – which had begun to fall apart after the death of Yuan Shikai. The situation was so serious that Chiang Kai-shek's emergent *junta* could not get its provincial level tax officials into the places where they were scheduled to go.

There were several reasons why the Heavenly Gates under Han Yuming were taken as a threat to the KMT. On the one hand, the Society was experienced as yet another 'criminal mob' contributing to the collapse of state power, and inimical to the Kuomintang policy of integration. Hence the name illegal bandits was bestowed upon the Heavenly Gates by the new Nationalist government under Chiang Kai-shek. On the other hand, Chiang and his men saw the folk millenarian ideas of the Heavenly Gates as a backward peasant rejection of Republican authority, and a heterodox peasant movement which was impossible to integrate into the secular KMT order – an order which elevated its goals to a level above and separate from the survival goals of illiterate, insecure villagers. The Heavenly Gates were demanding freedom to escape the military tax machines of the Republic of China. The KMT, however, was attempting to organize these machines into its own more rational, and more efficient tax order. The two were incompatible from the beginning, and the Heavenly Gate outcry for a return to a 'Just Empire' drove home this incompatibility to the Nationalist officials who were secretly sent to investigate the movement in late 1927 [*Zhou Ran, 1935: 118–120*].

In this situation, Chiang Kai-shek chose to deal with the Heavenly Gates by a two pronged strategy. Chiang first attempted to defeat the Heavenly Gates by armed force. When this policy led to stalemate, Chiang turned to peace-offerings and patronage. Then, when the Heavenly Gate leadership let its guard down, the Kuomintang followed with a *volte-face*. From 1928 until 1932 a big three stage battle was fought between the Kuomintang Army and the Heavenly Gates in the rebel strongholds of Lin county, but by 1932 the tide had turned and the soil of northern Henan was stained crimson by the blood of Heavenly Gate members who fell victim to the Chiang Kai-shek takeover.

But how, exactly, did the Kuomintang succeed in defeating a peasant movement which by 1928 outnumbered Kuomintang forces 20 to 1; believed in the righteousness of its own Little Tradition religious world view; enjoyed an alliance with a major warlord foe of Chiang Kai-shek, the Manchurian Warlord Zhang Xueliang, and basked in territorial security from any direct foreign military presence? The question is all the more intriguing when we recall that by 1930–32 the Kuomintang was concentrating its crack army divisions *en masse* on the Chinese Communist Party bases in South China (Kiangsi and Fujen), so that Chiang Kai-shek had a less than iron-grip on North China. To answer this, we must delve into the wider political background.

The essence of the problem was that Chiang Kai-shek had not yet consolidated his power over the countryside, and that both North and South China were being set afire by an anti-tax peasant movement of which the Chinese Communist Party was becoming a part. Rebel movements like the Heavenly Gates taken together, outnumbered those of any one provincial warlord contender for national level power. By late 1927, for example, the Heavenly Gates had grown to 100,000, and one scholar had put them at 300,000 [*Slawinski, 1972: 206*]. In Lin county, Anyang and elsewhere they established themselves as the county level

Hunger Prevention Forces, and they expected the National Revolutionary Army to recognize them as a popular militia that would put an end to warlord tax plunder – a point which Chiang Kai-shek, who was taking control of the National Revolutionary Army during its 1927–28 drive into North China, undoubtedly understood.

Following the Shanghai coup, the KMT occupied Peking [*Beijing*], and from there began to absorb many of the militarists. By early 1928 Chiang Kai-shek was in a position to strike against the peasant movement throughout China. In North China, Chiang Kai-shek decided to destroy the Heavenly Gates, who stood strategically between the Kuomintang and its warlord allies in Shaanxi, Shanxi, and Henan, and who posed a threat to the big landlords and big warlords who comprised Chiang's KMT.

At first the KMT encouraged the Heavenly Gates to fight the Fengtien warlords, who were enemies of Chiang Kai-shek. As the newly victorious Heavenly Gates proclaimed their Empire, however, the KMT Army began occupying the Hebei-Henan area, and prepared to wipe out the religious zealots who were challenging the Republic of China. In March of 1928 Chiang's troops, converged on Lin county from the rail depots in Xinxiang, Anyang, and Zhengzhou. The KMT scattered the poorly armed rebels, and put the Heavenly Gate leadership to flight. After 1928, Lin county was under KMT occupation, but this initial advance soon received a serious attack at the hands of the Heavenly Gates.

Han Yuming understood that the basic reason for KMT success was that poorly armed locals were no match for well-armed nationals. In 1928, therefore, Han Yuming went underground, reemerging in Northeast China in order to cooperate with warlord Zhang Xueliang, the enemy of Chiang Kai-shek. Han Yuming was able to secure a promise from Zhang Xueliang to help him organize a popular army against the occupying KMT. Military advisors and weapons followed Han Yuming's return to his stronghold in Henan, and the Heavenly Gates thereupon staged a successful comeback against KMT general Pang Bingxun.

Once it became clear to Chiang Kai-shek that the KMT Army was not going to be able to subdue the rebellion, the method of dealing with the Heavenly Gates was changed. The KMT offered to hold a discussion with Han Yuming about a peace settlement, and to provide Han with military advisors and weapons. A military post in the Official Kuomintang Army was presented to Han Yuming. The total package was taken seriously, and by 1929 KMT officials were inspecting the training of Heavenly Gate militias near the City God temple in Lin county.

To Han Yuming and the Heavenly Gates, the KMT offer only confirmed the recently established right to determine the amount of outside government meddling in local politics and society. The negotiated settlement with the KMT, in other words, was taken by the rebels as a product of their strength, and it in no way implied a willingness to give up rights won through rebellion. If the KMT interpreted this new relationship as the first step toward a subordinated peasant entry into the Republic of China, the Heavenly Gate leadership continued to run county level affairs from its rural headquarters in You village and the peasant members continued to associate the Heavenly Gate order with a 'People's Republic'. However, this situation did not last for long.

In 1930 the KMT reversed its policy of negotiation with the Heavenly Gates. This *volte-face* was in line with the growing repression fostered by the North China KMT after 1927, but it caught Han Yuming and his lieutenants off-guard and dealt the Heavenly Gates a blow from which they never fully recovered.

Early in 1930 Han Yuming was expecting Liu Xuixin, a KMT commander from the Shaanxi-Henan-Shanxi Military Area, to come to Lin county to help train Heavenly Gate troops. The former Lin county magistrate, now serving as a consultant to the Heavenly Gate cause, collaborated with the KMT to arrange a big banquet in celebration of the meeting between Han Yuming and Liu Xuixin. The banquet was held in the reading garden of a schoolyard dating back to the Qing dynasty. Kuomintang soldiers surrounded this banquet and seized Han Yuming with his lieutenants as the toast was being given. Yuming was duly executed by the KMT warlords Liu Chenhua and Liu Maowen in Xinxiang county.

This betrayal was accompanied by a KMT strike against six of Han Yuming's personal lieutenants. Most were killed in Lin county shortly after Han Yuming's execution. Kuomintang hostility during 1930 precipitated a second Heavenly Gate uprising in the form of uncoordinated assasinations of KMT agents in the villages of northern Lin county. Confusion over the new leadership meant that by late 1930 the Heavenly Gate Society retreated into the Taihang Mountain wilderness, disbanding its village associations.

But in 1932 there was yet another Heavenly Gate uprising against the KMT. About ten thousand members of the Society rallied in Dong Gang and Yao districts. They held their own within these districts until the KMT magistrate assembled an armed force of 3,000 under Ma Jongyue, who dispersed them at Yi Jiajia village in today's Yao district, and then proceeded to garrison the entire county. This Heavenly Gate failure marked the end of organized peasant rebellion in Lin county until the revolutionary army of Mao Zedong and Zhu De entered the country in 1938.

From 1928 until 1938 the KMT instituted a reign of terror in former Heavenly Gate strongholds, though, significantly, its power remained far stronger in southern districts where the Heavenly Gates had not taken hold. During this decade the KMT Lin county government, which also took over other

Henan counties where the Heavenly Gates had prospered, became the tax arm of the Chiang Kai-shek Nationalist government. In Lin county, KMT commander Pang Bingxun extended the tax machine into districts where the Heavenly Gates had made headway, and a new tax order, enforced with the help of the returning predatory bandits from Anyang, was imposed on the county.

At the national level, the Kuomintang government was able to sustain itself in the antistatist countryside because it could unite with provincial Bonapartists, and because the Soviet Union and the United States were coming to aid Chiang Kai-shek's apparent success in reunifying China. The aid, in either case, was awarded to the same KMT that was standing in the way of peasant movements for survival and social justice. The fate of the Heavenly Gates bears testimony to this deadly convergence of Russia and America on the side of the arch enemy of China's peasant masses, Chiang Kai-shek.

Reflections on the Failure of the Heavenly Gates

In establishing the categories for debate around the Cold War, Western scholars have generally failed to explain why so many rural people were attracted to a movement such as the Heavenly Gates: that is, to a popular rebellion which would later style itself native Communist. With few exceptions, the notable one being John King Fairbank [1979], Western intellectuals explained the origins of the Chinese revolution in terms which did not challenge superficial and supercilious notions of why the West 'lost' China. Foremost among these was the idea that peasant rebellions were only contributing insurgency and anarchy, thereby complicating the task of the chosen instrument of political order in China, the Kuomintang. Despite absurdity of this received wisdom, the study of peasant rebellion in pre-Liberation China became so unsafe that it was hardly undertaken. To do so was to reopen the question of whether something other than deceitful Chinese Communists or defeatist American Democrats got the Chiang Kai-shek KMT into trouble with China's rural people. The case was closed: so closed in fact, that for thirty long years Western scholars by and large wrote about the rise of revolutionary China as if there were no peasant rebellions in places where the KMT prevailed. The view was that the KMT only put out the fire started by the Communists, and so the issue always came back to the insufficient support for, and relative strength of, the Kuomintang.

This image of the Republic of China, championed by a Chiang Kai-shek out to restore law and order, obscured the political dynamics of peasant rebellion in the countryside. The fact is that rebellion was there, and even KMT writings on crime and banditry tell us this much. But rebellion did not grow out of Communist-inspired assaults on legitimate KMT authority. Rather, the painful burden of newly illegitimate taxes, imposed on the villages and the mines by the

Beiyang warlords and by subsequent KMT warlords, compelled the Heavenly Gates to rise up in defense of a long established right to deal with local authority on the matter of a 'just tax'. The Heavenly Gates were, in one sense, merely a peasant movement for simple traditional tax justice which used religious heterodoxies to aid the fight for material survival. Here were humble folk who had grown indignant over the growing warlord-bandit enroachment on local harvests and households, and they expressed their indignation partly through religious protest.

Long before the West was supposed to have 'lost' Chiang Kai-shek's China, rural rebel movements such as the Heavenly Gates were taking up arms to free themselves from the dearth-bearing tax grip of incoming KMT warlord order. With the coming of this order, there was less allowance for tax reduction or tax rebate, and there was more of the kind of suffering that had moved peasants to rebel in the first place. What had changed was the penalty for rebellion which, as the fate of the Heavenly Gates illustrates, grew year by year under the white hand of KMT betrayal and terror. The real tragedy of the Chinese revolution, therefore, was that the West backed the very force which made it necessary, and then stood in the way of its natural course of development.

Which brings us to another major question of interpretation: why were the Heavenly Gates labeled 'Communist', and why was it that this alleged Communism, more than the actual religious motivations of the rebels, should be registered in the writings of Western historians and diplomats to explain what was going on in rural China during the 1920s? The Heavenly Gates were called 'Communist' because they decided to share in the struggles of the poor. The poor, for their part, were rebelling only in reaction to the arm of institutionalized oppression. This arm was creating a situation far from acceptable to the marginal poor country people who had no choice but to join the Heavenly Gates. Kuomintang investigators, who feared the apocalyptic visions of the Heavenly Gates, Red Spears, and Black Flags in North China, found it necessary to ascribe modern political motivations to these dissenting peasant secret societies only after it became clear that the KMT itself could not control the spread of rebellion in 1927–28. Other observers, who rightfully doubted that the KMT could ever win the hearts and minds of China's peasants, nonetheless reported the issue in the terminology preferred by the KMT – 'Communism'. For this was the magic word which brought in the money and guns to smash the Heavenly Gates, and hence reinforced those very KMT government actions that were responsible for the conflict in the first place. Ironically, it was this conflict that gave the Chinese Communists the peasant audience they needed if they were to pick up where the Heavenly Gates left off.

The primitive religious doctrines of the Heavenly Gates were an outright rejection of the major political orthodoxy of the Kuomintang, namely its presumed legitimacy to penetrate the village world as the national Chinese authority. Naturally, the KMT officials branded the Heavenly Gates as religious fanatics. The rebel order which the Heavenly Gates attempted to realize, however, proved far more peaceful and workable for the illiterate peasants, miners, and bandits who joined the Society than did the intruding KMT tax authority. The latter seemed to be the real source of fanaticism to the rural people. That the Heavenly Gates were aiming to develop an alternative order based on reduced taxation and increased marketing of practical significance to the countryside was not missed by the Chinese Communist Party, whose cadres would expand this aspect of the movement when they opened yet another Gate of Heavenly Peace for Lin county and the regional peasantry a decade later.

Yet it is doubtful that the Chinese Communists won because they, as some scholars imply, abandoned the traditional millenarian platform of the Heavenly Gates for a modern, antireligious order. Like the Heavenly Gates the Communists would preach that life was sacred; like the Heavenly Gates, the Communists would win a place in the hearts of inarticulate folk because they too would sacrifice their lives to prevent the Kuomintang tax system, and its Japanese successor, from violating this sacred gift. In a rural society where actions weighed more than words leftist party cadres who opposed the oppressive 'taking-arm' of the KMT were inevitably regarded to be advanced millenarians by peasants who had borne witness to the Heavenly Gates. In this sense, the Chinese communists did not have to go to any great effort to 'fit' the goals of the Heavenly Gate peasantry into their allegedly more complex ideological cause.

It is tempting to explain the Heavenly Gate failure as the product of its 'primitive' millenarian outlook. Perhaps, as Hobsbawm [1959] would suggest, the Heavenly Gates failed because they lacked the Marxist intellectual tools to prepare them for sustained class struggle, and the Leninist organization weapon with which to seize political power. True, the Heavenly Gates did not have these modern things. But they were no less committed to a practical defense of peasant rights and no less determined to overthrow the hated Republic. Moreover, the Chinese Communist Party, which was working alongside other peasant secret societies in the Great Rebellion of 1925–27 and which had all the advantages of leftist ideology and organization, proved no more or less successful in forging an independent political alternative to the emergent warlord Republic. Does this mean that the very Communist Party, which was to win eventually, was also 'primitive'?

In China in 1927, national and international conditions were not yet favorable for a successful peasant revolutionary mobilization. The leaders of the Heavenly Gates did not fully comprehend the ruthless double-face of the KMT, with its capacity to pragmatically utilize internal and international power rivalries to reinforce its own hand: neither did the Communist Party. Time and again its cadres were also caught off guard in this first Civil War with the Kuomintang, and they were too frightened and scattered to impart effectively their own cruel lesson to hinterland rebel movements like the Heavenly Gates. The lesson would be left for Mao Zedong to formulate as a future party canon: never trust, and never underestimate the power of your enemy. The Heavenly Gates did, and they were defeated.

Finally, there is uncertainty as to whether the secret brotherhood of Han Yuming failed because of certain religious misgivings about the necessity of seizing power. The Heavenly Gates were not apolitical simply because they were rural/backward/religious, as Hobsbawm's model of peasant millenarianism would have it [*1959:98*]. The problem was not how to seize power, but how to hold on to it and build it after the spontaneous seizure. Here we find the Heavenly Gates pursued a policy that played into the hands of counter-mobilization. One cannot help but wonder if the fact that Han Yuming and his lieutenants were about to receive favors and posts from the KMT warlords somehow caused them to lose sight of the necessity to create their own alternative instrument of power if they were to hold and protect any local territory. Perhaps, in this sense of comparison, Hobsbawm does begin to capture the fate of the Heavenly Gates when he writes of the destiny of Andalusian peasant anarchism: 'it is likely to go down in the books with the Anabaptists and the rest of the prophets who, though not unarmed, did not know what to do with their arms, and were defeated forever' [*ibid., 92*].

Yet China was not Spain. The millenarian peasant movement would come back once Mao Zedong's Red Army and the Japanese Imperial Army challenged KMT oppression. The Communists, for their part, would not win by changing the millenarian content of the peasant movement, but rather by arming it to the teeth and by building into it a people's army as effective protection against the warlord Republic. The Communists, no less than the Heavenly Gates, first had to learn that, without an independent army, rebels of any stripe would be crushed.

References

Adas, Michael, 1980, 'The Avoidance to Confrontation: Peasant Protest in Pre-Colonial and Colonial Southeast Asia', *Johns Hopkins Symposium on Peasant Rebellions*, Baltimore.
Butterfield, Herbert, 1981, *The Origins of History*, New York.
Cady, John F., 1976, *The United States and Burma*, Cambridge, MA.
Critchfield, Richard, 1981, Villages, Garden City, NY.
Dai Xuanzhi, 1973, *Hong Qianghui* [The Red Spear Society], Taibei.
Hobsbawm, E. J., 1959, *Primitive Rebels*, New York.
Fairbank, John King, 1979, *The United States and China*, Cambridge, MA, (fourth edition).
Slawinski, Roman, 1972, 'The Red Spears in the Late 1920s', in Jean Chesneaux, ed., *Popular Movements and Secret Societies in China 1840–1950*, Stanford.
Sturtevant, David R., 1976, *Popular Uprisings in the Philippines 1840–1940*, Ithaca, NY.

Takeshi, Baba, 1975, 'The Red Spear Society', *Studies in Society and Economy*, 41.
Thaxton, Ralph, 1982, 'Land Rent, Peasant Migration, and Political Power in Yao cun, 1911–1937', *Modern Asian Studies*, (Cambridge), 16, part 1.
Wei, William, 1978, 'Law and Order: The Role of the KMT Security Forces in the Suppression of the Communist Bases during the Soviet Period', *ACLS Workshop on Chinese Communist Rural Base Areas*, Cambridge, MA.
Zhang Kaiyuan, Lin Zeng Ping, eds., 1980, *Xinhai Geming Shi* [History of the 1911 Revolution], Beijing.
Zhuo Ran, 1935, 'Ji-Lu Huifeizhi', [The Record of the Criminal Societies in Hebei and Henan], *Zhengfeng* [Rectification] No. 13–16.

Ideology, organisation and rebellion in Chinese sectarian religion

ROBERT WELLER

Political violence in China often took a religious form, and Chinese officials thus often repressed 'heterodox' (*xie*) sects. Many of these sects, however, never took part in any political violence: the government repressed them because it considered the ideology itself dangerous. To what extent were sectarian ideologies really 'heterodox', that is, to what extent did they offer genuine ideologies to orthodox authority?

Chinese scholars in the 1950s and 1960s often maintained that religion was the most likely garment to clothe revolutionary ideas in the feudal period. For example:

> Chinese peasant revolutions used religion not simply because their thinking was relatively backward, nor simply because they wanted to use an organizational form that was already familiar, but more importantly, because they wanted to combine the battle against feudal political power with the battle against feudal spiritual power. Moreover, the original teachings of some religions were easily borrowed to realize peasant revolutionary ideology, and may thus have become powerful weapons for the propagation and organization of peasant revolution [*Yang, 1960: 332*].

In the West, Overmyer [*1981: 188*] has written similarly that 'the sects seem to point to a basic aspect of Chinese consciousness and modes of social organization, an aspect at odds with the demands of a centralized state'. Unlike the Chinese, however, Overmyer stresses that this 'basic aspect of Chinese consciousness' did not necessarily lead to political action.

Since the death of Mao, many Chinese scholars have criticized the earlier work, and argue that neither peasant violence nor sectarian religion was truly revolutionary – peasant wars could not transcend the feudal system [*Liu, 1981*]. Several cite the case of Zhu Yuanzhang, a sectarian rebel who turned increasingly to Confucianism as his power increased. Having taken the throne, he completed his ideological reversal by declaring many of the sects illegal [*Dardess, 1972; Liu, 1981: 300; Taylor, 1963*].

The general outlines of this debate are familiar outside China. On the one hand, for example, James Scott [*1977: 224*] writes that peasant culture and religion 'contain almost always the seeds of an alternative symbolic universe... This symbolic opposition represents the closest thing to class consciousness in pre-industrial agrarian societies'.

On the other hand, however, Godelier (writing about tribal societies) holds that:

> Religion legitimates the domination of the chiefs of the dominant lineages. But one also perceives that this domination is shared by both the dominated and the dominating. There inheres in religion, therefore, the source of a violence without violence, the ideal cement for exploitative social relations [*1975: 84*].

This paper examines 'heterodox' religious sects that exist in Taiwan now, and discusses the relation between the particular beliefs of the sects and their traditional reputation for political violence. My findings do not resolve the arguments about the revolutionary nature of sectarian beliefs. By examining sectarian beliefs as they have been used in specific contexts in Taiwan, I show instead that, while the beliefs may be open to alternative, even rebellious interpretations, people also sometimes interpret them in politically conservative ways. Religious beliefs in general, and Chinese sectarian beliefs in particular, are inherently flexible. Out of context, we can only say that they have a *potential* for political action.

I demonstrate this by examining some of the most striking aspects of 'heterodox' sects that currently exist in Taiwan – the influence of the Buddhist cosmology, the presence of a very maternal goddess, the general use of spirit mediums, the important position of the deity Guan Gong, the worship of a consciously syncretic pantheon, and the creation of new forms of organization.[1] I compare each of these aspects to the other major religious traditions in China: sectarians share many symbols with the other traditions, but they often give those symbols new interpretations. Each of the sets of beliefs I discuss can take on new meanings in new religious contexts. Even within the sectarian tradition, people can use beliefs flexibly to promote either alternative or conservative political interpretations.

The special aspects of the sects that I examine thus help distinguish them from Buddhism and Daoism, which have established priesthoods and long textual traditions recognized by both Western scholars and the Chinese government. I also differentiate between these sects and 'popular worship' – the set of beliefs and rituals that the great majority of Taiwanese share (see, for example, the essays in Wolf [*1974*]. Many Taiwanese do not consider this 'religion' at all. When I asked informants who I knew worshipped every day what religion (Hokkien: *cong-kau*) they adhered to, they often replied, 'I do not have any religion at all, I just offer incense'.[2] Religion, to most Taiwanese, involves an established institution which must be officially joined. Buddhism, Daoism, and the heterodox sects qualify as religion, by this definition, but ordinary popular workship does not.

I divide heterodox sects in Taiwan into three broad (but overlapping) categories, based primarily on how closely they resemble Buddhism:

(1) Vegetarian halls (Hokkien: *chai-tng*) are superficially very similar to Buddhist temples (also called *chai-tng* by most Taiwanese). The most commonly mentioned sects in Taiwan are the Xiantian (Former Heaven) and Longhua (Dragon Flower); both are vegetarian, both sponsor sutra-singing groups, and both have lay followers who sometimes live in their temples. In the popular view, they are simply sects of Buddhism, and sectarians living in the vegetarian halls often reinforce that view by remaining celibate and (for the men) shaving their heads. A Japanese anthropologist working in the 1920s described the 'Vegetarian Religion' as a sect of Buddhism divided into three subsects: Xiantian, Longhua, and Jinchuang [*Suzuki, 1978 (1934): 38–40*]. De Groot mentions the same three sects in Amoy (a point of origin for many Taiwanese) at the end of the nineteenth century, and discusses their official persecution [*De Groot, 1903: 170*].

(2) Another group of sects is also apparently Buddhist in origin [*Overmyer, 1977*], but is currently less easily confused with orthodox Buddhism than the vegetarian sects. They worship the Eternal Venerable Mother (a non-Buddhist deity typical of these sects; she is discussed below), they place great emphasis on spirit writing, and they are very active in propagating their religion. The largest and most active of these 'Venerable Mother' sects in Taiwan is the Cehui Tang (Religion of Compassion), and the most notorious is the illegal Iguan Dao (Religion of Unity).

(3) The final group of sects also stresses spirit writing, but worships the deities of the popular tradition instead of the Eternal Venerable Mother. They are extremely active in publicizing their message; many of them publish regular journals to disseminate the results of their spirit writing sessions. The most active of these groups is the Shengxian Tang, which publishes both a journal and large numbers of tracts urging people to be upright citizens.

The following section discusses two major non-sectarian religious traditions in Taiwan – the popular worship and Buddhism.[3] I concentrate on the political implications of these traditions in order to create a base of comparison for the discussion of sectarian ideology that makes up the latter part of this paper.

Non-sectarian religion

Popular Worship

The popular pantheon in Taiwan consists of three primary types of beings – gods, ghosts, and ancestors – who closely reflect the social world [*Jordan, 1972; Wolf, 1974*]. Wolf, for example, writes:

> The conception of the supernatural found in Sanhsia is thus a detailed reflection of the social landscape of traditional China as viewed from a small village. Prominent in this landscape were first the mandarins, representing the emperor and the empire; second the family and the lineage; and third, the more heterogeneous category of the stranger and the outsider, the bandit and the beggar. The mandarins became the gods; the senior members of the line and the lineage, the ancestors; while the stranger was preserved in the form of the dangerous and despised ghosts [*1974: 175*].

The analogy between gods and bureaucrats is important for understanding the contrast between the popular and Buddhist (or sectarian) cosmologies. Evidence for the bureaucratic nature of the popular deities comes from many areas. Temple architecture provides one of the clearest examples. Temples are explicitly modeled on yamens, the traditional residence of government officials. Traditional sumptuary laws, for example, limited use of the colorfully decorated and sharply curved roofs typical of temples to the houses of official degree-holders. Temple architecture also distinguishes the relative rank of various gods, for example by the amount of roof decoration, or the type of door gods.

Many informants make an explicit analogy between the gods and the government. The Jade Emperor, they say, is like President Jiang, lower gods are like governors or magistrates, the Earth God is like a policeman, and so on. The detailed parallel between the religious and secular bureaucracies meant that the popular pantheon was not used to question the general system of bureaucratic authority.[4]

Popular worship in Taiwan includes more than metaphorical bureaucrats, fathers and strangers: there is also a female undercurrent which stresses compassion and birth [*Sangren, 1979: 371–375*]. Popular worship borrowed one of its most important goddesses from Buddhism: Guanyin, the goddess of mercy, is one of the most popular deities among Taiwanese, and she is also a primary deity in the vegetarian sects [*Suzuki, 1978 (1934): 39*]. Guanyin is known for her deep compassion for humanity, and for her boundless abilities to save people. Popular temples sometimes depict Guanyin holding a small child, in which form people beg her for help in bearing sons. Guanyin thus combines features of the two remaining important goddesses in Taiwan – Zhusheng Niangniang (who helps women conceive and give birth safely) and Mazu (who is best known for saving seafarers in distress). Many people in Taiwan in fact claim that Guanyin and Mazu are the same goddess. As I will show below, this female undercurrent is adopted and magnified by the sectarian traditions.

The popular deities and their temples relate closely to local social organization, as well as to the political hierarchy that I have been discussing.

The individuality of a village is inseparable from the particular configuration of gods who guide its policy, and its conflicts with other villages necessarily entail conflicts between the divinities that each side is able to muster. Accordingly, alliances between men and gods are a common idiom in which historical events are recounted [*Jordan, 1972: 42*].

Earth God (Tudi Gong) temples, for example, govern mutually exclusive territories, whose boundaries closely follow neighborhood divisions. Higher ranking gods may be associated with entire marketing areas. Major temples unite communities both through their major festivals, and through their managers, who are often tied to the local political elite.

Buddhism

Buddhas and Bodhisattvas do not have the same links to local communities that gods of the popular religion have. Buddhist temples, similarly, do not have close community ties, and the monks or nuns who run them often come from other areas. They do not organize local residents in the same way as a major community temple would, and they do not perform rituals for the benefit of the community as a whole.

Orthodox Buddhist cosmology also differs markedly from the popular tradition. In contrast to the popular division into gods, ghosts and ancestors, orthodox Buddhists in Taiwan conceive of ten types of beings which fall into two main categories: those who have transcended the wheel of reincarnation (the Four Saintly Planes), and those who are still subject to the agonies of rebirth (the Six Ordinary Planes). The unenlightened beings consist of gods, humans, demons, ghosts, denizens of hell, and animals. Gods, according to Buddhists, include the entire popular pantheon. Gods live in a more pleasant world than humans, but even the Jade Emperor is unenlightened and will eventually suffer the pains of rebirth.

The most important implication of this is that for Buddhists every being in the popular world view is in exactly the same position: none have transcended the most basic feature of life, the bitter cycle of birth, sickness, old age, and death. Not only have the Buddhists ignored the precise appreciation of secular hierarchy found in the popular tradition, but they have made the more radical assertion that everyone, whether god or man, magistrate of peasant, is fundamentally equal.

More detailed analysis shows the thoroughness of the difference between the popular and Buddhist cosmologies. First, although Buddhas constitute the top of the spiritual hierarchy, they are totally unlike the rulers of the secular hierarchy or their heavenly counterpart, the Jade Emperor. There are many Buddhas, they do not take an active part in the affairs of the world, and they have no bureaucratic authority. Thus, while the Buddhist deities form a hierarchy, it is in no way bureaucratic. Position in the Buddhist hierarchy depends not on political ability to deal with the world, nor on authority to wield power, but rather on faith and a personal commitment to transcend the affairs of the secular world.

Second, rank is determined only by the personal merit and personal commitment of the deities of the Four Saintly Planes; the bureaucratic principle of appointment to official position is never evoked. Bodhisattvas are not at the highest level (Buddhahood) only because they have made a personal choice to remain in this world. This contrasts with the deities of the popular tradition, whose only orthodox path to power is enfeoffment by the Emperor.

Finally, the beings of the Four Saintly Planes differ fundamentally from the popular gods and from men in having transcended the physical and emotional limits of humanity. Buddhist deities have unlimited vision, knowledge, and abilities to transform their outward appearance; they have also given up all secular passions. Gods, on the other hand, do most things better than men, but there is no real qualitative difference. The Emperor, like the gods, is far more powerful than most people, but even he is not omnipotent. Thus people's relationships with popular gods are based on their relationships with other humans. Buddhism requires people to abandon these secular principles. Faith is not an important concept in the popular religion, just as it is not an important feature of political bargaining. In Buddhism, however, faith becomes one of the keystones. The most impressive acts of worship done without faith accomplish nothing, but a simple prayer said with true faith can accomplish anything.

The Buddhist cosmology thus offers people an alternative interpretation of the political world. Bureaucratic hierarchy gives way to spiritual equality, political manipulation gives way to personal freedom, and secular desire gives way to faith. The Buddhist alternative to the secular world did not usually lead its adherents to rebellion. Instead, the alternative was realized through a monkish withdrawal from secular desire. Sectarians, on the other hand, reinterpreted the Buddhist alternative, making it more amenable to political action.

Sectarian religion

In this section I show how a number of special features of sectarian ideology compare to the traditions I just discussed, I discuss how those features may (or may not) have led the sects to oppose the government, and I emphasize how they have been used flexibly to achieve different purposes at different times. I begin with the influence of Buddhism on the sects.

The sects and Buddhism

Buddhist influence on sectarian religion is very strong. Many sects share not only a part of the Buddhist cosmology, but also many sutras (including the Heart Sutra and the Diamond Sutra), the hope of rebirth in a paradise (see Overmyer

[*1976: 85–89*] on the relation between Pure Land Buddhism and the White Lotus), and a belief in the eventual arrival of a new Buddha, Maitreya. The sects, like Buddhism, reject the popular pantheon and its concommitant approval of the secular political hierarchy. They emphasize instead faith, equality, and compassion. The Xiantian and Longhua vegetarians in Taiwan have borrowed so much from Buddhism that most Taiwanese do not distinguish their temples from orthodox Buddhist temples. For example, a Xiantian vegetarian hall near my fieldsite was famous for the 'Buddhist monk' who told fortunes; only near the end of my stay did I discover that he was a layman and that the temple was not orthodox.

The sects, however, reinterpreted many Buddhist concepts to fit their own needs. Sectarian use of Maitreya is the best example of reinterpretation of a Buddhist symbol. Both orthodox Buddhism and the sects speak of history as a series of kalpas – long periods of time whose beginning is marked by the arrival of a Buddha, whose development is marked by a steady deterioration in human values, and whose end is marked by devastation preceding the beginning of the next kalpa. In orthodox Buddhism kalpas are extraordinarily long; one illustration says that if a soft cloth is passed over a solid rock 40 *li* in size once every hundred years, a kalpa still will not have passed by the time the rock is entirely worn away [*Soothill and Hodous, 1937: 242*]. In the sects, however, the period is shortened to the point where the end of the kalpa is imminent. Sect leaders sometimes proclaimed themselves to be Maitreya, the Buddha who marks the beginning of the new kalpa and the end of the old. The orthodox Buddhist interpretation was appropriate to a pacific life of moral cultivation, while the sectarian interpretation of Maitreya could be used instead to justify violent political action.

The symbol of the Future Buddha was thus made potentially useful for rebels. The idea of successive kalpas resonated with the traditional Chinese concept of changes in the Mandate of Heaven, which justified revolt against an emperor who no longer held divine approval. At the same time, a claim to be the incarnation of Maitreya could also give supernatural sanction to the actions of a sectarian leader. Let me stress again, however, that this heterodox reinterpretation of Maitreya was only a potential, and that this potential was only sometimes realized. Orthodox Buddhists shared the idea of Maitreya, and of kalpas, but neither they nor all of the sects used these beliefs to support millenial revolt. Even within the sects, the Maitreya saw very different uses. To be sure, the White Lotus and other sectarian rebels often used the Maitreya to support their political violence [e.g. *Naquin, 1976: 92*]. On the other hand, however, the self-proclaimed incarnation of Maitreya of the Iguan Dao (Religion of Unity) cooperated with the Chinese puppet government during the Japanese occupation of China [*Deliusin, 1972*]. Sectarian reworking of the Buddhist alternative thus helped to create the *potential* for a revolutionary ideology, but the sects did not realize this potential in all conditions.

Eternal Venerable Mother

The Eternal Venerable Mother (*wusheng laomu*), goddess of infinite compassion and mother of the world, was the primary deity for the White Lotus and most of its offshoots [Overmyer, 1976; Naquin, 1976]. She is worshipped in Taiwan by the Religion of Compassion, the Religion of Unity, and others.[5]

The Eternal Venerable Mother's creation of the world, and her position at the top of the sectarian cosmology seem to suggest a comparison with the Jade Emperor, the highest deity in the popular cosmology. The Venerable Mother is sometimes called Golden Mother of the Jasper Pool (Yaochi Jinmu), whom many people in Taiwan identify as the wife of the Jade Emperor. In fact, however, the Venerable Mother figure is in every way closer to the Buddhist than to the popular deities. Like a Bodhisattva, her powers transcend the abilities of any of the popular gods, and her wisdom exceeds that of all others. Most importantly, she embodies the Bodhisattva ideal of infinite compassion for the beings of the Six Ordinary Planes. Her primary concern is to save as many people as possible from the sea of evil.

The Venerable Mother's compassion and her creative abilities also relate her to the important female deities worshipped in the popular tradition (discussed above). The key position that the Eternal Venerable Mother occupies in the sects nurtures the female undercurrent of popular worship at the expense of the more standard god-bureaucrats. Fittingly, the most active members of both sectarian and orthodox Buddhist groups in Taiwan are women, and women are able to achieve positions of relative authority in many of the sects.

The Eternal Venerable Mother is another case of sectarian adaptation of a borrowed symbol. In this case, the sects have reworked a secondary theme of popular worship into a major theme. Putting a Boddhisattva-like female figure at the head of the pantheon again helps the Eternal Venerable Mother sects deny the secular bureaucratic hierarchy, and it may also increase sectarian support by appealing to women.

Spirit possession

All the sects in Taiwan except the Xiantian and Longhua vegetarians feature active spirit possession cults. Spirit writing and spirit mediumship are also important features of the popular religion, and I will discuss them first as one of several methods for communicating with the non-sectarian gods.

Important popular communication with gods involves drawing from a set of (usually sixty) lots. Each lot has a number on it; these numbers encode a set of slips of paper with verses printed on them. The entire set is posted somewhere in the temple, and the patron can find the verse that goes with the lot he or she has chosen. These verses are generally metaphoric to the point of incomprehensibility, and very few people feel competent to interpret them. As an aid to these people, the slip of paper on which each verse is printed usually includes a list of possible questions and very brief indications of how the poem answers them. The slips supply a very limited range of questions; there is no way to ask, for example, about whether a rebellion will succeed or whether to join a heterodox sect [Ahern, 1982]. Many people turn to the temple management for interpretations of the verses, and unusual questions can only be answered by the management. The temple management, however, especially in the more important community temples, are usually members of the local elite. They are unlikely to provide interpretations which challenge their own positions of authority. In general, therefore, drawing lots allows only for very orthodox, politically safe answers to questions. It is taking gradual steps to outlaw them. They were equally discouraged in late traditional times.[6] Spirit possession may not often have led to politically dangerous claims, but the potential was always there, and this was recognized by the government.

Spirit possession also characterizes many of the sects. Sectarian mediums generally write divine commentaries which are often in verse, and occasionally include hidden acrostics that spell out further messages.

The sectarian attitude toward these texts differs from the popular attitude. In the popular tradition, divine replies are simply answers to questions, while in the sectarian version, the texts are objects for study. Many sects, for example, begin each session with mutual discussion and interpretation of the texts written during the last session. These discussions could reinforce any tendency to create new (and thus potentially politically challenging) interpretations. Influential members of the sects can give concrete political meaning to ambiguous texts. These regularly scheduled sessions for ideological development may help institutionalize the potential for political improvization that exists in the popular tradition of spirit possession.

Although spirit writing provides a greater potential for divine approval of political alternatives than does temple worship, it is not inherently rebellious. Indeed, much of the sectarian spirit writing in Taiwan appears politically conservative. Many spirit texts are published in Taiwan, some in regular magazines, others in 'morality books' (*shanshu*) which are distributed free. Wealthy patrons often underwrite these publications, and they stress the importance of traditional moral values. Some of the publications rewrite their divine texts as ordinary prose; this is part of a conscious attempt to appeal to intellectuals, as well as to the very religious.[7] The Shengxian Tang is one of the most active publishers of the results of its spirit writing sessions. A typical text is the 'Compass for the Cultivation of the Dao' (*Xiudao Zhinan*) a panel discussion by the 'Founders of the Five Religions' (Confucius, Sakyamuni, the Primordial Heavenly Worthy [central deity of the Daoist Trinity], Jehovah, and Mohammed) moderated by Guan Gong (whom I discuss below). The Primordial Heavenly Worthy summarizes the panel discussion as follows:

(1) Those who cultivate the Dao should respect the Constitution, be faithful to the nation, be faithful to human plans, not abandon the laws, and behave as good citizens.

(2) Those who cultivate the Dao should be filial to their parents, carefully attend to their funeral rites and make sacrifices to them [*Shengxian Tang, 1978: 10*].

This very prolific spirit writing cult thus promotes a conservative ideology that explicitly supports the government. Earlier cults have also been used to support the authorities: I mentioned in the section on Buddhist influences that the Religion of Unity (Iguan Dao) cooperated with the Chinese puppet government.

Many of the scriptures of the *rebellious* sects were also revealed by spirit writing [*Overmyer, 1976: 185*]. Spirit writing in both the sectarian and popular traditions thus had the potential for both conservative and critical uses. The sectarian emphasis on spirit writing did not necessarily lead to an oppositional ideology, but it did give greater opportunities for flexibility than ordinary worship in popular temples.

Guan Gong

Red-faced and black-bearded, Guan Gong is one of the most respected figures in the popular religious tradition. Guan Gong was a hero from the Three Kingdoms period. He is reknowned for his prowess in battle, for his loyalty to his friends, and above all for the oath of blood brotherhood he swore with two comrades. This oath has provided a model for sworn brotherhoods ever since including the initiation ceremonies of secret societies like the Triads. Guan Gong is also one of the most frequently seen images in popular temples and on domestic altars.

Guan Gong's popularity is apparently increasing in Taiwan. A peddler turned coal mine owner, for example, who credits Guan Gong with his rise to wealth, built three large and popular temples in northern Taiwan to honor the deity under the name of Enzu Gong, Lord Patriarch of Kindness. The cult has a large following which wears robes similar to the robes favored by members of sectarian spirit writing cults. Indeed, Guan Gong is a favorite of spirit writing cults, especially those with less Buddhist influence [*Seaman, 1978: 22-24*].

There is a rumor now in Taiwan, especially popular among members of sectarian spirit writing cults, that Guan Gong has replaced the old incumbent and is now the Jade Emperor. Some of the cults have gone farther than simply whispering rumors. I saw one temple in Gaoxiong in which Guan Gong was dressed and posed according to the conventions which normally indicate the Jade

Emperor. A publication put out by another spirit writing cult claims that, 'In 1864, on the first day of the first lunar month of the *jiazi* year [that is, at the beginning of a new sixty-year cycle], the founders of the Five Religions [Confucius, Taoism, Buddhism, Christianity, and Islam] elected the Sage Emperor Guan to the position of Jade Emperor' [*Shengxian Tang, 1977: 5*].

Why is Guan Gong so popular among sectarians? The most important reason is probably his association with sworn brotherhood. Although few of these religious sects involve swearing blood brotherhood, Guan Gong is nevertheless an appropriate symbol for an organization which cuts across ordinary local and elite ties, and which is united by bonds of shared loyalty.

Guan Gong's increasing popularity in Taiwan may be the result of yet another role which he plays – he is considered a patron of businessmen. It was in this role that the coal magnate I mentioned above worshipped him, and in this role that he appears on many domestic altars. As patron of the bourgeoisie, Guan Gong helped provide a base for opposition to the Japanese government in Taiwan, which generally discouraged the development of the Taiwanese bourgeoisie. Seaman translates a portion of a Japanese police report which describes some of the problems caused by a cult that worshipped Guan Gong during the early period of the Japanese occupation of Taiwan:

> During this time many wild stories and pathetic rumors went around, stiring up the people. This not only disturbed the public order, moreover it damaged not a little the relationship between the Japanese and the Taiwanese natives. Let us give some examples of these disruptive beliefs:
> 1. The gods of the spirit writing cult hate the Japanese and detest their gods. Thus if a person use Japanese goods or make friends with a Japanese, he will find the punishment of the gods unavoidable.
> 2. The only source of income for the Japanese government of Taiwan is the opium monopoly. If Taiwanese give up the smoking of opium [and the cult attempted to cure opium addiction], then the Japanese government will be pressed for funds and will raise the price of opium to get more out of the people [in *Seaman, 1978: 26–27*].

In present-day Taiwan, on the other hand, a god of business should mesh well with the political goals of the government. The portion of the panel discussion moderated by Guan Gong that I translated above is a good example of this kind of political orthodoxy. The heavenly participants all espouse a very traditional Chinese morality of filial piety and loyalty to the government. Guan Gong as an abstract symbol is thus open to varying political interpretations. In twentieth-century Taiwan, he has been used to express both rebellious and politically conservative messages.

Syncretism

A number of the sects are insistently syncretic. Many teach that the three religions are one (*sanjiao wei i*), and some (e.g. the Gelao Hui [Chesneaux, *1971: 47*]) worshipped the Founders of the Three Religions (Confucius, Sakyamuni, and Laozi). Current sects have increased the count to five by adding Christianity and Islam. Indeed, DeGroot [*1903: 192*] praises some of the sects for their openness to Christian doctrine.

The Compass for the Cultivation of the Dao, from which I quoted briefly earlier, is a good example of the sectarian doctrine of syncretism. The Founders of the Five Religions discuss the major concepts of their respective belief systems, and each shows how his own concepts are identical with the basic Confucian virtues. For example:

> Sakyamuni: Buddhist disciples who cultivate the Heavenly Dao also do not depart from 'loyalty, filial piety, benevolence, and justice' [the virtues which Confucius has recommended in the previous speech] ... Thus, those who cultivate the Dao should respect the laws of their country ...
> Jehovah: The goal of those who cultivate the Dao is to rise to Heaven after their death. Yet they do not know where to begin their cultivation. The disciples of this religion, for example, although they take brotherly love as their basis, yet they must embrace brotherly love toward everyone. Brotherly love is the same as Confucian benevolence. If brotherly love is combined with loyalty and filial piety, then the Dao can be achieved, and one can rise to Heaven [*Shengxian Tang, 1978: 8–9*].

Syncretism thus meshes with the other main features of sectarian ideology – it claims access to a greater truth than any other tradition, and it challenges some of the principles of the more orthodox traditions. Both the Buddhist and non-Buddhist influences on the sectarians deny the secular political hierarchy, claim a higher legitimacy, and offer a greater flexibility of message than popular religion. Yet there is nothing inherently rebellious about any of these ideas. Their flexibility and independence gave them a greater *potential* for use in opposition to the government than any of the other traditions, but the ideology in itself was not necessarily rebellious. Sectarian ideologies sometimes supported and sometimes opposed both the native Chinese and occupying Japanese governments.

Sectarian Organization

Chinese popular worship is a very individualized procedure. Unlike Western churches, whose members worship in unison as a congregation, Chinese popular temples host a constant flow of individual worshippers, each acting in isolation from the others. Even on festival days, there are rarely set times for worship, and people come to burn incense for the gods at their convenience.

Sectarian religion offers a sharp contrast to the popular pattern. While people may continue to worship as individuals, there are also carefully orchestrated communal ceremonies that feature group singing (sometimes accompanied by electric organ in Taiwan) and simultaneous bowing. Sects that stress spirit writing also often have classes on the supernatural texts before each session; there is no equivalent propagation of a group ideology in the popular religion. Members of the sects also often wear identical robes while they worship, further emphasizing their shared membership in a single congregation.

Sectarian deities are universal; they are not tied to local communities in the same ways popular dieties are. In contrast to the popular tradition, loyalty to the sectarian deities thus does not necessarily mean loyalty to traditional community structure. Sects, like Buddhist temples, also differ from popular temples in performing no community functions. Many of the Taiwanese sects are instead involved with their congregations as individuals. In the vegetarian sects, for example, family members must join as individuals, not as members of a kin group or community. If the child of a member wants to be admitted, he or she must apply separately [*Suzuki, 1978 (1934): 39*].

Sects typically consist of a number of semi-independent branches. Master-pupil ties often connected branch leaders, and these ties could be used to unite the various sect branches. On the other hand, there was rarely a tightly organized central administration during non-violent times. Naquin [*1976*] describes the organization of the Eight Trigrams, which rebelled in 1813, and shows how its leaders pulled the various branches together before the rebellion. Overmyer [*1977*] discusses the relatively loose organization of the Religion of Compassion in modern Taiwan. The Red Spears [*Perry, 1980: 155–156*] were community based, but they existed within a broader framework provided by the sect. The sects thus offered the potential for an organization that cross-cut local community ties, and that demanded loyalties transcending clan and neighborhood.

Conclusions

Religious symbols are inherently flexible. The Buddha, for example, may have different meanings in the sects, in the popular tradition, and in Buddhism. Much of the sectarian ideology is a reworking of borrowed symbols to deny the secular political hierarchy, to claim a higher legitimacy, and to offer a greater flexibility of message than any other Chinese religious tradition. Sectarian organization also had the potential to challenge the more regular ties of lineage, neighborhood, or political faction.

These ideas offer people an alternative to the secular political world, but they are not inherently rebellious because they are themselves open to differing uses. The flexibility and independence of sectarian beliefs and organization gave them a greater *potential* for use in opposition to the government than any of the other traditions, but the sects were also open to conservative uses. Sectarian ideologies sometimes supported and sometimes opposed both the native Chinese and occupying Japanese governments. This potential sufficed to arouse the fear of the central government, even in cases where there was no rebellious activity.

I began this essay by reasking an old question: is Chinese sectarian religion really a radical political alternative to the established system? I have tried to make clear in my analysis, however, that the question is essentially misleading. Abstracted from the social conditions in which they are used, the sects are indeed a genuine alternative. Yet every feature of this abstract alternative was open to reinterpretations and new uses. Religions often claim eternal and unchanging truths, but in practice they can be very flexible. The Chinese sects illustrate this clearly: they realized their potential for radical political violence only occasionally; most of the sects, most of the time, provided people with apolitical social support, and some even engaged in active support of the political status quo.

In what contexts was the rebellious potential of the sects actually realized? There is still very little known about the actual day-to-day uses of religion by rebels, but let me nevertheless offer some speculative suggestions.

In a few cases, sectarian ideology itself seems to have been the prime inspiration for some short-lived rebellions. The Wang Lun uprising of 1774, for example, was rooted in a sect that was strongly influenced by Buddhist millennialism [*Naquin, 1980*]. Naquin finds no increased exploitation, no threat to subsistence, and no violations of traditional norms leading to the uprising [*1980: 17*]. Instead, she explains the revolt as one of the sect's major techniques for strengthening its interests and asserting its structure [*1980: 18*]. The Wang Lun uprising never attracted a large popular following, largely because the ideology-based rebellion held no appeal for the unconverted masses. Rebellions based solely on sectarian ideology thus did exist, but they apparently never spread beyond the ranks of the true believers in the absence of political, economic, or social causes of unrest. Indeed, many sects with Buddhist-based ideologies were never violent at all; violence was only one of their many options [*Overmyer, 1981*].

The Eight Trigrams rebellion of 1813 also originated in the ideology of the true believers. The decision to rebel

> came as a logical outgrowth of tendencies inherent in the ideas and structure of White Lotus sects. Certain leaders motivated both by conviction and ambition had encouraged these tendencies by stimulating the sometimes dormant anxieties of their followers about the long-predicted arrival of the apocalypse [*Naquin, 1976: 90*].

As the rebellious branches of the sect gained momentum, they began to attract non-sectarian followers, including both opportunistic looters and entire villages faced with the threat of violence [*Ibid.: 203–204*]. Most of these people had at best a cursory knowledge of sectarian ideology; they joined partly out of fear, partly out of greed, and partly out of desperation following several years of floods. The Eight Trigrams thus began ideologically, but it spread to non-sectarians who rallied around sectarian banners for more mundane reasons.

Still other sectarian violence was rooted in the political struggles of local elites. These struggles often grew far beyond the scale of purely ideological rebellions like Wang Lun's. Taiwan's Dai Wansheng rebellion (1863–1864), for example, was based in communal rivalries between settlers from Zhangzhou and Quanzhou Prefectures on the mainland. As the battle lines were drawn, the Quanzhou people allied with the government, and the Zhangzhou people organized a branch of the secret Heaven and Earth Society [*Meskill, 1979: Ch. 8*]. Both sides were led by local powerholders, and much of the activity (both for the government and for the rebels) consisted of one strongman trying to take over the turf of another.

Perry also gives several examples of sects that protected the established interests of local communities. She sees them as

> one of many organizations through which villagers mounted collective solutions to mundane problems. The visionary – even millenial – ideology of many secret societies did not necessarily put them on the side of the poor. To the contrary, in the case of both the Old Cows and the Red Spear Society, we have seen sects directed by members of the privileged rural elite, striving to defend their property against assault [*Perry, 1980: 254–255*].

Here, sectarian organization and ideology helped to mobilize people against bandits or against the excesses of the government. The scale of these uprisings could be huge, even by Chinese standards – Dai Wansheng threatened all of Taiwan, and the Red Spears fielded armies of several hundred thousand.

The sects existed most of the time as independent entities that housed special ideologies and opened up new lines of organization. These groups occasionally rebelled as a way of fulfilling and concretizing their ideas. More effective rebellions, however, took place when people with underlying political economic problems – from subsistence crisis, to struggles between local powerholders, to suddenly increased demands of the state – were able to take advantage of the mobilizational potential of sectarian beliefs and organization, either by joining an ideological uprising (as in the Eight Trigrams) or by inviting sect teachers into an area to help mobilize the population (as in the Red Spears).

Notes

1. I conducted field research on religion in Sanxia Township, Taiwan from August 1977 to February 1979. I would like to thank Arif Dirlik, Elizabeth Perry and Steven Harrell for their comments on various drafts of this paper. A revised form of this paper appeared in *Modern China*. I thank the publishers of *Modern China* for permission to reprint parts of that paper here.

2. Hokkien terms are romanized following Bodman [1955]. Terms not specifically noted as Hokkien are Mandarin, and are romanized in the pinyin system.
3. I ignore Daoism due to limitations of space. Including Daoism would not alter the basic lines of my argument.
4. The system did permit, however, criticism of specific gods or specific magistrates for misbehaviour.
5. Topley [1963] writes that she is also the primary deity for the Xiantian sect in Singapore, although DeGroot gives a deity called 'the very highest Wu-kih, our Old Patriarch' (Taishang Wuji Laozu) this role for the Xiantian in Amoy [1903: 179–180], and Suzuki [1978 (1934)] mentions only orthodox Buddhist deities and a few popular deities for the 'vegetarian sects' of Taiwan.
6. Overmyer [1976: 24], for example, translates a Ming Dynasty prohibition against planchette writing and other forms of spirit possession.
7. This is based on research into these publications conducted by John McCreery. I am also grateful to him for an introduction to some sects in Taiwan.

References

Ahern, Emily Martin, 1982, *Chinese Ritual and Politics*, Cambridge.
Bodman, N. C., 1955, *Spoken Amoy Hokkien*, Kuala Lampur.
Chesneaux, Jean, 1971, *Secret Societies in China in the Nineteenth and Twentieth Centuries*, translated by Gillian Nettle, Ann Arbor.
Dardess, John W., 1972, 'The Late Ming Rebellions: Peasants and Problems of Interpretation', *Journal of Interdisciplinary History* 3: 103–117.
Deliusin, Lev, 1972, 'The I'kuan Tao Society', in Chesneaux, Jean (ed), *Popular Movements and Secret Societies in China, 1840–1950*, Stanford.
DeGroot, J. J. M., 1903, *Sectarianism and Religious Persecution in China*, Amsterdam.
Godelier, Maurice, 1975, 'Toward a Marxist Anthropology of Religion', *Dialectical Anthropology* 1: 81–85.
Jordan, David K., 1972, *Gods, Ghosts, and Ancestors: The Folk Religion of a Taiwanese Village*, Berkeley.
Liu Kwang-Ching, 1981, 'World View and Peasant Rebellion: Reflections on Post-Mao Historiography', *Journal of Asian Studies* 40: 295–326.
Meskill, Johanna Menzel, 1979, *A Chinese Pioneer Family: The Lins of Wu-feng, Taiwan, 1729–1895*, Princeton.
Naquin, Susan, 1976, *Millenarian Rebellion in China: The Eight Trigrams Uprising of 1813*, New Haven.
Naquin, Susan, 1980, 'Millenarian Rebellion in Late Imperial China: The Uprising of Wang Lun in 1774', Paper presented at the Symposium on Peasant Rebellions, The Johns Hopkins University, January 24–25, 1980.
Overmyer, Daniel L., 1976, *Folk Buddhist Religion: Dissenting Sects in Late Traditional China*, Cambridge.
Overmyer, Daniel L., 1977, 'A Preliminary Study of the Tz'u-hui t'ang', *Bulletin of the Society for the Study of Chinese Religions* 4: 19–40.
Overmyer, Daniel L., 1981, 'Alternatives: Popular Religious Sects in Chinese Society', *Modern China* 7: 153–190.
Perry, E. J., 1980, *Rebels and Revolutionaries in North China*, Stanford.
Sangren, Paul Steven, 1979, 'A Chinese Marketing Community: An Historical Ethnography of Ta-Ch'i, Taiwan', Ph.D. dissertation.
Scott, James, 1977, 'Protest and Profanation: Agrarian Revolt and the Little Tradition', *Theory and Society* 4: 1–38, 211–246.
Seaman, Gary, 1978, *Temple Organization in a Chinese Village*, Taipei.

Shengxian Tang, 1977, 'Yuhuang Pudu Shengjing, Taishang Wuji Hunyuan Zhenjing Zhushi' (Notes and Explanations to the Jade Emperor's Holy Sutra of the Ferrying Across and the True Sutra of the Infinite Chaos Origin of the Great Above), Taichung.
Shengxian Tang, 1978, 'Xiudao Zhinan' [Compass for the Cultivation of the Dao], Taichung.
Soothill, William E., and Hodous, Lewis, 1937, *A Dictionary of Chinese Buddhist Terms*, London.
Suzuki, Seichiro, 1978 (1934), *Taiwan Tiuguan Xisu Xinyang* [Old Customs and Traditional Beliefs of Taiwan], edited and translated into Chinese by Gao Jianzhi and Feng Zuomin, Taipei.
Taylor, Romeyn, 1963, 'Social Origins of the Ming Dynasty, 1351–1360', *Monumenta Serica* 22: 1–78.
Topley, Marjorie, 1963, 'The Great Way of Former Heaven: A Group of Chinese Secret Religious Sects', *Bulletin of the School of Oriental and African Studies* 26: 362–392.
Wolf, Arthur (ed.), 1974, *Religion and Ritual in Chinese Society*, Stanford.
Yang Kuan, 1960, 'Lun Zhongguo Nongmin Zhanzhengzhong Geming Sixiang de Zuoyong ji qi yu Zongjiao de Guanxi' [On the Functions of Revolutionary Thought in Chinese Peasant Wars and their Relation to Religion], Shi Shaobin (ed.), *Zhongguo Fengjian Shehui Nongmin Zhanzheng Wenti Taolunji* [Collection of Discussions on Problems of Peasant Wars in Feudal Chinese Society], Beijing.

Latin America

Preface

CATHERINE LeGRAND

When Latin Americanists think of religion and rural revolt, several specific incidents come to mind. We think of the Caste War of the Yucatan – a revitalization movement of Mayan peasants who in the 1840s rose to expel the whites from their land and to create a new religion blending elements of the Mayan past with the Spanish present [*Reed, 1964*]. We also think of the various messianic movements centered in Brazil in the late nineteenth and early twentieth centuries which have evoked some of the most moving literature on popular protest to come out of Latin American [*da Cunha, 1944; Pereira de Queiroz, 1972; Della Cava, 1970; Vargas Llosa, 1981*]. Yet another revolt relevant to our subject is the Cristero Rebellion which pitted hundreds of rural communities against the Mexican government during the later 1920s. Finally, the theme of religion and rural revolt calls to mind the profound influence of Liberation Theology in galvanizing the struggle for justice in the Latin American countryside today. The murder of nuns and priests by right-wing death squads in Central America bears tragic witness to the importance of the new Catholic Church which emerged in the 1960s in mobilizing peasants for social change [*Gutiérrez, 1973; Lernoux, 1980*].

Of the four Latin American papers included in this volume, only one – Jean Meyer's article on the Mexican Cristeros – deals directly with these well-known movements. The other three papers focus on less familiar developments in the Andean countries of Ecuador, Peru, and Bolivia. Their contributions, nevertheless, are basic to understanding the varied and sometimes contradictory functions of religion in the multi-ethnic societies of Latin America. Taken together, these essays illuminate the complex interaction between religious institutions, popular consciousness, and rebellion among rural populations of Indian extraction.

To understand the religion of the rural peoples of Latin America, the experience of colonial rule must be taken into account. In pre-Columbian times, Mexico and the Andean countries were the sites of the great Aztec and Incan civilizations, each of which was composed of a mosaic of diverse Indian groups. These were civilizations with a religious world view in which political and religious authority were vested in the same individuals. The dense Indian populations of these regions, estimated to have reached as high as 50 million (?)

people, were peasants, in the main, for whom religious rituals associated with agricultural production formed an essential aspect of everyday life.

The Spanish conquest of the Americas in the sixteenth century was not just a military conquest, but a spiritual conquest as well. The spread of Catholicism – the 'One True Religion' – both fuelled and justified the imposition of Spanish colonial rule. A strange undercurrent of mutual comprehension marked this epic confrontation of two worlds which had been separated for millenia – the Amer-Indian world and the European world. For the Spaniards, as for the Indians, political power and religious power went together: Church and State were mutually reinforcing.

Supported by fervent missionaries and a strong institutional Church with direct links to the Crown, the Spanish evangelization effort appeared remarkably successful. Just as the Spanish incorporated the Indians into colonial society as peasant laborers and miners, so they also brought the Indians into the Catholic Church. Today almost everyone in Latin America officially adheres to Catholicism: indeed there are more baptised Catholics in Latin America than in all of the rest of the world combined.

For many years most urban Latin American and foreign scholars took it for granted that the devastating experience of conquest followed by centuries of colonial domination had swept away the indigenous systems of belief. No one who visits Latin America can help but notice the many folk aspects of Catholic ceremony there, but these elements were thought to be relatively superficial and unintegrated remnants of the past. It was assumed, then, that the peasant population had become fundamentally Catholic in outlook and belief.

Isolated revolts like the Caste War of Yucatan should have indicated to us that this was not so. But it has been the work of anthropologists in the last twenty years that has brought dramatically to our attention the extraordinary resilience and continuing vitality of pre-Columbian religious traditions in the peasant and mining communities of Mexico, Guatemala, and the Andean highlands [*Vogt, 1969; Isbell, 1978; Nash, 1979*]. Such traditions provide the rural peoples with a shared set of beliefs from which they draw a sense of history and cultural identity at variance with that of their mixed blood and Spanish compatriots.

So what we find in Latin America is that just as Catholicism and its institutions and clergy are deeply rooted in the peasant communities, indigenous beliefs and practices persist as well. This interpenetration of two religious traditions renders particularly complex and interesting the study of religion in Latin America and its role in rural revolt. In this context, popular religion mirrors that ambivalence basic to peasant society which tends toward cultural autonomy, but is at the same time imbedded within national society, that is, within larger structures of belief and control. The major questions that rise out of this situation are: What is the content of popular religion in any given time and place? What elements of popular belief do specific groups call on to fuel protest movements? And what specific historical circumstances either facilitate or inhibit the expression of such movements and the use of religion within them?

The papers presented here address these issues in different settings and from different points of view. The essays by Muratorio and Stein both stress the role of religion as an instrument of domination, while, in contrast, Nash and Meyer show the potential of religion to foster revolt. Blanca Muratorio focuses on the religious dimension of the process of colonization in northwestern Ecuador. Although the people with whom she is concerned are forest Indians, the missionary strategies she describes were common throughout Latin America. Evangelization of the Indian people implied not only conversion, but also profound changes in native structures of authority and social and economic organization in accordance with Spanish conceptions and needs. As the Indian leaders took cognizance of the challenge to their authority and, beyond this, to a whole way of life, they rebelled: the Great Revolt of 1578 represented at once a clash of competing authorities and a bid for economic and cultural autonomy in which both sides used religious ideologies. Muratorio suggests that such rebellion was possible only in the early stages of missionary activity before the Church had fully undermined native leadership and disrupted native social organization. Thereafter Indian resistance to mission authority was expressed only in self-destructive ways and through individual acts of defiance.

William Stein's article on a nineteenth century Peruvian uprising reiterates the theme that the Catholic Church was an obstacle to successful peasant revolt. Stein argues that the peasants who took part in the Atusparia rebellion were defeated by an unscrupulous priest who understood and manipulated them and by their own religious world view which led them, in the midst of battle, to waste precious time on religious rituals. Of particular interest in this case is the figure of Pedro Pablo Atusparia, the leader of the revolt, who was an Indian with a foot in two worlds and ambitions to match. Drawing his peasant following in part from his position as an Indian religious leader, once the revolt began, Atusparia sought to win power and recognition from the provincial gentry as well by identifying himself with the Catholic establishment in town. Ironically, it was Atusparia himself who approved the activities of the priest who eventually undermined the movement. Here the overt conflict between Indian and white religious authorities described by Muratorio for the early colonial period is no longer manifest. In nineteenth century Peru the relation between popular religion and formal Church institutions had become both closer and more complex. Stein presents a clear picture of religion binding people together across class lines in such a way as to subordinate the peasants to a larger structure of domination.

While admitting the social control function often exercised by religion, the papers by June Nash and Jean Meyer take a different perspective. They focus on the positive relation between religion and rural revolt. Both Nash and Meyer argue that under specific structural conditions, the religiosity of rural peoples may contribute in profoundly important ways to protest movements.

An anthropologist who has done field work among Bolivian tin miners of Indian extraction, June Nash elaborates in convincing detail the amazingly rich belief system of the miners today. The belief system incorporates elements of Catholic dogma and radical labor ideologies, but fundamentally it is rooted in pre-Columbian agricultural values and observances. The constantly evolving popular religious tradition provides the tin miners with a sense of community, history and distinctiveness which, Nash maintains, constitutes a form of cultural resistance in and of itself. This independent vision holds the potential for active resistance as well, but whether it is realized depends on other factors, beyond the miners' control. At certain times in Bolivian history, the mine owners have successfully played upon popular religious practices to pit the miners against each other and reinforce identification with management, while at other times popular religion has served to unite the miners against their immediate employers and the government as well. Perhaps the most interesting conclusion of this article is that the maintenance of traditional religious beliefs and modern labor organization are not incompatible. Indeed, the tin miners are the best organized and most revolutionary sector of the Bolivian labor force. Nash argues that both the strength the miners draw from their pre-Columbian heritage and their outrage at management violations of religious obligations have reinforced the miners' combativity in seeking concrete improvements in working conditions.

Like Nash's work, Jean Meyer's paper on the Cristero Revolt deals with religion as a force for mobilization. But, unlike the preceding authors, Meyer's is not concerned with the distinct ethnic or cultural dimensions of popular religiosity. Rather, Meyer's paper serves as a reminder of the importance of Catholicism to the peasant communities of Latin America.

In the great Cristero rebellion which enflamed all of central Mexico in the late 1920s, religion functioned both as means and ends. The Catholic Church and the State were locked in a struggle for power and when the Church went on strike, the peasants rose against the government demanding that the sacraments be restored. Not only was this a revolt predicated on religious grounds, but it is a rare example of a rural revolt that was successful in its own terms. In 1919 the Church and State came to an accord, the village priests returned to their pulpits, and the rebellion died away as quickly as it had come.

Like Nash, Meyer argues that religious-based peasant revolts are not necessarily reactionary. He clearly shows how the Cristeros revolted against the 'modernizing' State that emerged out of the Mexican revolution because the religious and agrarian reform policies of the new government directly threatened vital economic resources and social relationships within the rural communities.

Thus, objective socioeconomic concerns were inextricably bound up with and came to be expressed through the religious issue. Meyer's work serves to point out that the interests of the peasant are not necessarily those of the State. Together with Sutherland and LeGoff's article on the French Revolution, Meyer challenges us to reexamine our assumptions of what reaction and progress mean, not in terms of any abstract theory of modernization, but rather in terms of concrete peasant interests and concerns.

This observation leads to the question of what peasants understand their interests to be. For the peasant, as for the social scientist, economics plays an important part, but the papers presented in this section emphasize that economic concerns are imbeded within a social universe. Peasants seek to create multiple, overlapping social ties, both horizontal and vertical, that provide security, protection and a sense of moral order. In Latin America, religious ceremonies play a central role in sanctioning social relationships between peasants and their superiors whether through indigenous rituals involving reciprocal obligations, as Nash describes for Bolivia, or through Catholic practices such as the godparent system (*compadrazgo*). Given the uncertainty of rural life, such relations make economic as well as political sense. They are not necessarily evidence of upper class manipulation, but rather are actively sought by peasants themselves and viewed by them to be in their interests. To a Marxist historian like Stein, the vertical bonding function of religion is a negative factor that inhibits class conflict and therefore authentic peasant revolt. Meyer and Nash, however, point out that the loss of such ties through the prohibition of essential religious activities may actually prove to be the catalytic factor that sets off revolt. Such revolt does not always mean a return to the past, but depending on structural conditions, may lead in various directions.

If the papers presented in this section underline the role of religion in creating larger social solidarities, they also shed light on the ways in which religion may reinforce group consciousness and organizational bonds among the rural poor themselves. Of particular interest is the evidence that popular religion can keep alive a collective memory of the past. As Nash and Muratorio show, the Indian peasants and miners of the Andes reenact each year the long social and economic oppression of their peoples through their religious processions. These processions etch into the popular consciousness a sense of history at variance with the official texts. Religion as history and myth provides these people with an analytical reference point through which to interpret their reality, a reference point which, by stressing social antagonisms, also may help to set the stage for rural revolt.

References

Da Cunha, Euclides, 1944, *Rebellion in the Backlands (Os Sertoes)*, Trans. Samuel Putnam, Chicago.
Della Cava, Ralph, 1970, *Miracle at Joaseiro*, New York.
Gutiérrez, Gustavo, 1973, *A Theology of Liberation*, Maryknoll, New York.
Isbell, Billie Jean, 1978, *To Defend Ourselves: Ecology and Ritual in an Andean Village*, Austin, Texas.
Lernoux, Penny, 1980, *Cry of the People*, Garden City, N.Y.
Nash, June, 1979, *We Eat the Mines and the Mines Eat Us: Dependency and Exploitation in Bolivian Tin Mines*, New York.
Pereira de Queiroz, Maria Isaura, 1972, *Images Messianiques du Brésil*, Cuernavaca, Mexico.
Reed, Nelson, 1964, *The Caste War of Yucutan*, Stanford, Cal.
Vargas, Llosa, Mario, 1981, *La Guerra del Fin del Mundo*, Barcelona.
Vogt, Evon, S., 1969, *Zinacantan: A Mayan Community in the Highlands of Chiapas*, Cambridge, Mass.

Evangelisation, protest and ethnic identity: sixteenth century missionaries and Indians in Northern Amazonian Ecuador*

BLANCA MURATORIO

Introduction

The native people of the Ecuadorian tropical forest have had almost 450 years of contact with different representatives of white colonial and post-colonial societies. Through these years, the presence of missionaries among the native groups has been the most pervasive. Missions have been consistently organized as institutions whose main objective was, at least until very recently, to radically change the natives' world view and way of life.

Until the State became interested in the economic resources and the potential for colonization of its Amazon region in the 1940's, the missionaries practically maintained the monopoly of the task of 'civilizing' the different native groups and integrating them into the larger society. The control the missionaries had over the Indians greatly conditioned the impact of other 'civilizing' agents and, in a sense, still does.

The Indians' responses to evangelization have varied greatly during these 450 years, from acceptance of a new religion, to passive resistance, to active rebellion, and very recently to open criticism and attempts to control the action of the missionaries. This recent reaction by the natives has been also influenced by a critical change of direction experienced by some missions after Vatican Council II, when their previous evangelization strategies among native cultures were seriously questioned, and their future objectives radically redefined.

The general problem discussed in this paper is the interrelation between different missionary strategies of evangelization and the varied responses elaborated by the native population. The paper focuses on the ideological aspects of the contact underlying the interaction between missionaries and Indians as a confrontation between two conceptual representations of the world. In order to

---

* I gratefully acknowledge an SSHRCC grant and the support of the University of British Columbia. In Ecuador, my research is sponsored by Facultad Latinoamericana de Ciencias Sociales and the Instituto Nacional de Patrimonio Cultural del Ecuador.

understand the real meaning of this symbolic exchange, however, it is necessary to analyze the relation between the economic and social structure of the larger society, where the missionaries belong, and that of the different native groups.

As Ribeiro has argued in his book on the Brazilian Amazon, the Indians, when evangelized, are not confronted with several rational alternatives among which they can choose one, after a thoughtful critique of their own belief system [*1973: 263*]. The ideological confrontation between Indians and missionaries is not a free intellectual exchange, but an important element in a situation of colonialism. The main goal of the missionaries was always to convert the Indians, by implanting the 'seeds of civilization' and new forms of social relations. Consequently, the ideological practices of the missionaries always meant a denial of the Indians' own system of values and beliefs, the very basis of their ethnic identity. This is why the reactions of the Indians to evangelization have often been inspired, in different forms, by a reevaluation of their own cultural identity.

More specifically, the problem will be examined in an area of the Napo province in the Northern Ecuadorian Amazon. During colonial times, and mainly for missionary purposes, this area was known as the Governorship of Quijos. Several different native groups inhabit the region now: Quichuas, Cofanes, Sionas, Secoyas, Teetetes, and Huaoranis. Many more lived there in colonial times, but have since become extinguished. This paper will focus on the Napo Quichuas who live around Tena, the capital of the province, in the region near Archidona, Sumaco, Avila, Loreto, and in the upper tributaries of the Napo river. When the Spaniards entered this area, the native people they contacted were known as Quijos. Their language was not Quichua and, despite the careful ethnohistorical work done by Oberem [*1980*], it is still difficult to understand the process by which they became present day Napo Quichuas.

These Indians share with all the other Amazonian groups a tropical forest culture, living by shifting cultivation, hunting, and fishing. However, for a long time, this area has been opened to white colonists who compete with the Indians for land and resources. This colonization, coupled with the 'modernizing' influence of the Josephine missionaries since the 1920's onwards, have contributed to the process by which the Napo Quichuas are transforming themselves into peasants. A majority of these Indians are presently engaged in cattle raising, and in producing commercial crops, such as coffee and cocoa, for a national market. As a result, they now confront the same structural problems which seem to affect small peasant producers all over the world.

The missionary strategies analyzed here only cover the attempts at converting the Quijos by the secular clergy during the sixteenth century. Consequently, the Indians' responses were still expressed in the ideological practices which correspond to their earlier form of economic, social, and political organization.

Early attempts at evangelization and first rebellions

In pre-colonial times, the Incas Tupac-Yupanqui, Huayna-Capac, and Atahualpa had attempted to conquer the Quijos region but were not able, or willing, to subjugate them [*Rumazo Gonzalez, 1946: 11–14*]. The fact that the Quijos were never incorporated into the socio-economic and political organization of the Inca Empire explains, in part, the difficulties the Spanish *encomenderos* and missionaries had in their attempts to transform these Indians into a disciplined labour force and to settle them into *reducciones* for the purpose of catechization. Although the Quijos were able to keep their independence from the Incas, they maintained regular commercial relations with the highland groups, interchanging cinnamon and gold for arms, tools, cloth, and other highland products [*Ibid: 15*].

Probably through their traders, the Quijos learned of the consequences of Spanish domination over the highland Indian population, and this accounts for their fierce armed resistance against the first Spanish expeditions into their territory. However, the coveted cinnamon and gold which the Quijos used to bring into the highlands, constituted a strong allurement for the Spaniards who, immediately after the conquest of Quito, started organizing expeditions in search of the Land of Cinnamon and El Dorado. The first attempt was that of Gonzalo Díaz de Pineda in 1538. The difficulties of the jungle terrain and its rivers, and the number of men lost in the battles with the Quijos, forced Pineda to return to Quito [*Ibid: 37–38*]. He learned, however, that the land was populated by a large number of Indians led by powerful caciques, but that they were dispersed over an immense territory [*González Suárez, 1970: 3, 69*]. In 1541, Gonzalo Pizarro was able to capture some Quijos and, after horrible tortures, forced them to guide him to the famous Land of Cinnamon. This turned out to be a great disappointment because the cinnamon trees were dispersed over a vast and rough terrain, and very difficult to exploit [*Oberem, 1980: 67*]. However, gold and cotton still continued to be an attraction for other Spanish adventurers, but subsequent expeditions were repelled by the Quijos. This contributed to the Quijos' reputation as 'rebellious and unruly Indians' [*Porras, 1974: 72*].

For the next sixteen years, the Quijos were left alone, until 1558 when they were again contacted by Spaniards, but this time peacefully, through a highland chief who was not only an ally of the Spaniards but also the brother in law of an important Quijo chief [*Rumazo Gonzales, 1946: 95–96*]. After long negotiations and an exchange of gifts, several Quijo chiefs invited the Spaniards into their territory. Gil Ramirez Dávalos was put in charge of contacting the Quijos. He took with him a Franciscan friar to evangelize the Indians. As an eyewitness of the negotiations, the friar reports that one of the caciques asked Gil Ramirez Dávalos for religious images and crosses 'because his father had died as a Christian, and his mother was a Christian from the time Gonzalo Díaz de Pineda entered the Land of Cinnamon and they were baptized by Father Carvajal, provincial of the Dominicans [*Vargas, 1977: 139–140*].

Given the short time Pineda and other Spaniards remained among the Quijos, and the character of the other Spaniard expeditions, it is doubtful that the Quijos as a whole were even superficially Christian by 1559. However, they could have known about the 'whites' religion' through their traders or through their relatives in the highlands.

To receive the Spaniards, the Quijos built houses all along the roads putting crosses inside [*González Suárez, 1970: 3, 64*]. They also honored them with music and dances, and women and children carried crosses knowing that this was the symbol of the whites [*Rumazo Gonzalez, 1946: 95*]. Probably, they did this to please the Spaniards and to entice them into their area, because the Quijos thought that they could probably increase their commercial exchanges if the Spaniards established their towns among them [*Ibid: 86–87*].

In May 1559, Dávalos founded Baeza, the first important town in the Quijos area. This event marked the beginning of the economic and political domination of the Quijos by the Spaniards through the establishment of *encomiendas* and *repartimientos*, as well as the more systematic attempts to convert them to Christianity. In the document written for the oath ceremony, the day Baeza was founded, it is already said that the Spaniards should make a list of the peaceful native chiefs, so that along with their people they could be assigned the work of building the church, the houses, and preparing the fields. They should also put their people at the service of the Spanish inhabitants. It is also ordered in this document that a mass should be celebrated 'with all devotion and solemnity to impress the natives and to move their hearts' [*Porras, 1974: 66–70*].

As first governor of the region, Gil Ramirez Dávalos gained a reputation among the Indians of being magnanimous and respectful of their land rights. When he was forced to leave the office to Rodrigo Nuñez Bonilla, the Indians complained to higher authorities [*Rumazo Gonzalez, 1946: 88*]. As a consequence, the Spaniards started to worry about the possibility of an Indian rebellion [*Porras, 1974: 72*]. According to the chronicles, Nuñez Bonilla actually created all the conditions which provoked the first general rebellion of the Quijos in 1562. He changed the location of Baeza, probably invading Indian communal lands [*Rumazo Gonzalez, 1946: 102*]. Unlike Dávalos, he did not order the cultivation of maize in the fields around the city and, consequently, the Spanish soldiers started stealing food and also gold ornaments from the Indians. Furthermore, the Indians were forced to make regular trips to Quito bringing heavy loads of food. Finally, Nuñez Bonilla started distributing the Indians to the Spaniards in *encomiendas*. Important caciques, with between 300 and 1,000 Indians under them, became dependent on the *encomenderos*. The Quijos, who knew already about the *encomienda* in the highlands, regarded it as practical 'slavery' [*Porras, 1974: 76–77*], because it meant a considerable restriction of their freedom and the exploitation of their labor through force.

Not long after becoming governor, Nuñez Bonilla died in Quito and Captain Bastidas was put in charge as provisional governor. He tried to avoid some of Nuñez Bonilla's mistakes and, for the first time, introduced cattle and new crops into this area. In order to pacify the Indians, he granted privileges to the caciques and presented them with gifts of meat, shoes, gunpowder, wicks and lead [*Rumazo González, 1946: 103–105*]. However, all his efforts did not succeed in preventing the general rebellion which took place in July 1562. The Quijos caciques joined forces to expel the whites from their territory, destroyed the bridges and barricaded the roads to prevent Spanish reinforcements coming from Quito. They attempted to kill Spaniards as well as highland Indian carriers, they burnt *tambos* (inns) and all the crosses located on the roads, *tambos* and towns [*Porras, 1974: 85*]. They attacked Baeza and burnt some houses but were repelled by Bastidas with silver bullets. Finally, Bastidas was able to calm the insurrection by the usual method of pacifying the most important chiefs with gifts and privileges. Other caciques, specifically the famous Jumandi, cacique of the Sumaco Province, preferred to warn the Spaniards against entering his territory. Jumandi threatened the Spaniards with an army of 15,000 warriors and went with his people to live deeper in the jungle [*Rumazo González, 1946: 127*], until he reappeared as the main leader of the second and most interesting of the Quijos general rebellions in 1578.

In 1563, Captain Bastidas was informed that Melchor Vásquez de Avila had been appointed governor of Quijos and granted several *encomiendas*. As he lived in Cuzco, Vásquez de Avila governed Quijos for fifteen years through his lieutenant governors [*Ibid.: 112*]. Under no direct official control, the *encomenderos* and their soldiers felt free to exploit the Indians' labor and to treat them with extreme cruelty. Many Quijos died as a result of these abuses which included hunting them with dogs, confiscating their food, letting them die of hunger, and mutilating Indian women who resisted the sexual advances of the Spaniards [*Ibid.: 131*]. Confronted with this extreme genocidal situation, and out of frustration and despair, the reaction of some of the Quijos was self-destructive. There were cases of suicide, and it is reported that women killed their babies so that 'they would not live through such miserable times' [*González Suárez, 1970: 3, 77–78*]. Other Indians fled into the highlands, because they preferred to live as slaves of the caciques in Quito than to suffer under the Spaniards [*Rumazo González, 1946: 203*].

During 1563, the lieutenant governor founded other towns in the area, such as Avila, in the land of Jumandi, Alcalá del Río in the Aguarico River, a tributary of the Napo, and Archidona in a densely populated area called *Los Algodonales*, rich in cotton and specially in gold [*Ibid.: 119, 126–127*]. Weaving and panning gold became the two main forms of labor through which the Spaniards exploited the Indians. In that same year, the Quijos living close to the rivers Misahuallí, Tena, and Hollín – all areas near Archidona – fought against the Spaniards, but were finally forced to submit [*Ibid.: 126*].

The oppression of the Quijos was denounced by several officials [*Ibid.: 203–204*]. The situation was so serious that in 1576 the King ordered a Visit of the Governorship of Quijos by the *Oidor de la Audiencia de Quito* Diego de Ortegón. From Ortegón's report it is clear that by 1576, the conversion of the Quijos to Christianity was still superficial. Two Dominican friars accompanied the *Visitador* to establish two religious communities of this Order in the region to attend the evangelization of the Indians which, according to Ortegón's report, has been 'considerably neglected' [*Porras, 1974: 96*].

While Ortegón was conducting the visit, the vicar of Quijos 'christened a great number of creatures' and Ortegón helped him with gifts for the Indians [*Ibid.: 97*]. They found a similar situation of neglect in Baeza and in Avila, where the Indians received religious instruction for the first time through the preaching of the vicar. In a report to the King about the 'sad situation of the Indians' another friar remarked that 'the *encomenderos* force the Indians to spin and weave continuously and they have them so occupied in these tasks that it seems that in this land they have forgotten about God ... there are no churches, no ornaments, no images, except old and smoked paper ones ... and in order to live the *Doctrineros* (priests) must collaborate with the *encomenderos*. We can clearly see the bad treatment and oppression of these Indians because a large number of them had died, and others are dying everyday' [*Rumazo Gonzalez, 1946: 242–243*].

It is quite clear that at this time, the missionaries who worked among the Quijos were an integral part of the socio-economic system which exploited the Indians. The *encomiendas* in this area were not very productive for the *encomenderos*, due to the small and decreasing number of Indian tributaries. Consequently, the Spaniards did not pay the diezmos and other dues to the priests, who received a salary of 300 golden pesos from the Bishop, and the accustomed food and other offerings (*camaricos*) from the Indians [*Ibid.: 186, 228*]. According to Porras [*1974: 100*] the priests had no alternative but to adapt themselves to the whims of the *encomenderos*, or to die of hunger.

Not many priests were willing to go to these forgotten regions. We get an idea of the type of priests who went to the area from information given by González Suárez about the priests working in another Amazonian Governorship further South: 'Some of the priests who entered in the Governorship of Salinas were fugitive monks from the Convents in Quito, and two of them had been excommunicated. It was not easy for them to learn the language of the barbarians, and evangelisation was done through interpreters. People were merely compelled to attend religious worship or to suffer the *Doctrinero*'s punishments [*1970: 3,*

91–92].

Given this picture of evangelization around 1576, it is obvious that when chronicles report that at this time 'more or less half of the 16,509 Quijos dependent on the Spaniards were Christians' [*Oberem, 1980: 85*] it probably only meant that they had been superficially baptized in large groups or that the Spaniards counted as Christians those 6,803 Indians who were already tributaries in Spanish *encomiendas*.

Ortegón's 'solution' to evangelisation was to create *doctrinas* some of which were assigned to the Dominican friars and others to secular priests [*Rumazo González, 1946: 225–226*]. The Dominicans did not last very long in the area [*González Suárez, 1970: 3, 91*]. In order to evangelize the Indians in the *doctrinas*, Ortegón had to introduce another Spanish institution, the *reducción*, by which Indians from small communities or from isolated dwellings were forced to congregate in one town. Unlike the highland Indians, who were settled agriculturalists long before the Spanish conquest, the Quijos were hunters and shifting cultivators. They resisted the Spanish attempts to settle them in *reducciones*, because this new form of social organization constituted a serious threat to their own reproduction as a group. It is important to underline the fact that the *reducción* also challenged the established power of the shamans, some of whom were important caciques having groups of extended families organized around them [*Oberem, 1980: 274*]. The attempt to settle the Indians in *reducciones* necessarily contributed to the breakdown of this form of social organization, and to weakening the social and political power of the shamans.

Discouraged by the fact that their *encomiendas* were not renewed for more than one life term and by the scarcity of Indian tributaries, many *encomenderos* began to leave the area. Those who remained became impoverished and indebted [*Rumazo González, 1946: 185–86*]. Ortegón's visit contributed only to aggravate the situation of the *encomenderos*, both because of the expenses they incurred in entertaining him and his large retinue, and because of the fines Ortegón imposed on them for the abuses committed against the Indians. However, the worst consequences of this visit were for the Quijos who ultimately paid for all those expenses. The *encomenderos* forced them to spin and weave great quantities of cloth through forced labor [*Ibid.: 185*].

The increased exploitation resulting from this visit, plus the fact that Ortegón destroyed the dreaded dogs trained to hunt rebellious Indians, are mentioned by several writers as the most immediate causes which encouraged the Indians to engage in the general insurrection against the Spaniards in 1578 [*González Suárez, 1970: 3, 76; Rumazo González, 1946: 185*].

The Quijos rebellion of 1578: the rebellion of the shamans

While most of the previous uprisings of the Quijos had been organized locally by one group of cacique in protest against specific abuses by the Spaniards, the rebellion of 1578 was a carefully planned general uprising of all the Quijos to exterminate the Spaniards and to do away with white domination forever. It was coordinated in conjunction with highland caciques and was planned to include the participation of the Omaguas, another large and powerful tropical forest group, well known for their reputation as warriors. Like many other Indian uprisings, it failed militarily due to the superiority of Spanish arms and strategy. However, the rebellion is interesting for what it reveals both about the dynamics of the Quijos social and political organization in a period of acculturation and about the ideological factors of evangelisation.

The rebellion was started by two famous shamans or *Pendes* (sorcerers or high priests) called Beto and Guami, respectively from the regions of Archidona and Avila [*see Rumazo Gonzalez, 1946: 198*]. They were already dependent on *encomenderos* [*Ibid.: 187*]. According to Diego de Ortiguera's chronicle [*Rumazo Gonzalez, 1946: 187–222*] on which all reports about this rebellion are based, Beto and Guami called all the caciques and their people to arms against the Spaniards. They succeeded in getting a large number to join the rebellion, not only because all the Indians hated the Spaniards, but also because the powerful shamans threatened them with 'turning their fields into poisonous toads and snakes' if they disobeyed [*Ibid.: 198*]. People in this area still believe today that shamans have the power to kill them. After a ritual fast, Beto proclaimed that the devil had appeared to him in the form of a cow claiming to be the Christian god who was very angry with the Spaniards living in the region. This devil ordered Beto to kill all Spaniards, including women and children. For his part, Guami claimed to have gone for five days into another world (probably under the effects of *ayahuashca*, a hallucinogenic still used today by shamans in this area as part of their ritual) where the Christians god had equally ordered him to kill all Spaniards, burn their houses, and destroy their fields. The god had also chosen him to be Supreme *Pende* [*Ibid.: 187, 198*]. This last statement is important, since the chronicler states that a power struggle had developed between Beto and Guami, joined later by Imbate, an older shaman from another area. They met to decide who was the most powerful shaman worthy of leading the rebellion. The dispute seemed to have been solved by an alliance between Imbate and Guami and, later on, by appointing Jumandi, one of the most powerful caciques in the Quijos area, as commander in chief of the rebels. Before he joined, the shamans were successful in destroying and burning both Avila and Archidona, killing all whites and the highland Indians who were servants of the Spaniards. The hatred of the Indians was not stopped by the pleas for mercy from priests or churches. In

Archidona, for instance, they tried to burn the priest inside his church. When he tried to escape, he was speared [*González Suárez, 1970: 3, 81*].

After their initial victory, the shamans retired to Jumandi's land to prepare the assault on Baeza following five days of ritual fast. This assault failed because, by this time, Baeza had received reinforcements from Quito and from a cacique from the highlands. The attack of more than 5,000 Quijos was repelled [*Rumazo González, 1946: 203*]. The Omaguas arrived after the rebellion had been crushed. Many Quijos escaped into the jungle, including Jumandi's son who reappeared in 1590 in connection with another attempted rebellion [*Ibid.: 203, 214*]. Responding to the Spaniard's promise of peace, the Indians started to surrender, except for Jumandi and the shamans who were able to escape for four months. Finally they were arrested and taken to Quito to be given an exemplary punishment. Standing in carts they were paraded through the streets, tortured with hot irons and quartered, after which their heads and limbs were exhibited in the city streets. The highland caciques who had participated in the rebellion were exiled to the coast [*Ibid.: 209–210*]. Although it took the Spaniards ten months to pacify the Quijos region, the punishments seemed to have cowed the Indians because they did not engage in any other rebellion. However, the Spaniards regarded this rebellion as a threat, important enough that they found it necessary to remind the Indians of the punishments in a fiesta celebrated in Quito in 1631, where the Spaniards exhibited prisoners in carts representing Jumandi and the shamans [*Oberem, 1980: 89*]. This was a form of Baroque symbolism which, along with the religious ritual, the Spanish authorities often used in an attempt to impress the Indians and win their submission.

An examination of this rebellion shows that, despite the early attempts by the Church to Christianize them, the Indians expressed a total rejection of the new faith and a re-affirmation of their traditional religious beliefs. Those beliefs were incarnated in the persons of the shamans who, among tropical forest groups, have the ultimate power to interpret and make sense of ordinary experience. Rather than a direct ideological challenge to the shamans, Christian evangelization meant a threat to their power, mainly because the *reducciones*, as we have already explained, concentrated Indians in circumscribed areas, away from their traditional authorities and under the strict control of the Spaniards and the missionaries. The symbolic behavior and the discourse of the shamans during the rebellion represented the display of a very common shamanistic practice by which power is diverted from a powerful source, in this case the whites, by invoking their gods [*Lanternari, 1974: 274–275; Taylor, 1981*]. The shamans tried to appropriate the power of the whites through the image of the Christian 'devil' in the form of a cow, which was a new source of wealth introduced by the Spaniards. Besides, still today in their magical songs, shamans include names of saints, of powerful mountains, and of objects of the white world, all in an effort to reinforce their own power.

In 1578, Christianity seemed to have been regarded by the shamans as an additional source of power which was re-interpreted within the traditional framework of their own magical vision of the world. Furthermore, it is clear from the chroniclers' accounts, that the shamans were not only fighting against the Spaniards, but also among themselves. The changes in the traditional social structure had unleashed an internal struggle for power, and an attempt to reorganize society along traditional lines. Consequently, the rebellion can be interpreted as a process of reassertion of native religious and cultural values and as a defense of the Quijos ethnic identity.

In 1578, evangelization among the Quijos was quite superficial, and the role of the priests too entangled with the worst aspects of Spanish domination for the missionaries to become effective competitors of traditional shamans. It was to take years of painful work by the Jesuits, Josephines, and Evangelical Protestant missionaries for this ideological competition to become a reality. But even today shamans are always respected, often feared, and regularly consulted by most Napo Quichuas, both Catholics and Protestants.

References

(Translations of quoted sources in Spanish have been made by the author.)

González Suárez, Federico, 1970, *Historia General de la República del Ecuador*, Vol. 3, Quito.
Lanternari, Vittorio, 1974, *Occidente y Tercer Mundo*, Buenos Aires.
Oberem, Udo, 1980, *Los Quijos. Historia de la transculturación de un grupo indígena en el Oriente Ecuatoriano*, Otavalo, Instituto Otavaleño de Antropología.
Porras, G., Pedro, I., 1974, *Historia y Arqueología de la Ciudad Española de Baeza de los Quijos*, Quito: Centro de Publicaciones de la Pontificia Universidad Católica del Ecuador.
Ribeiro, Darcy, 1973, *Fronteras Indígenas de la Civilización*, segunda edición, Méjico.
Rumazo Gonzalez, José, 1946, *La Región Amazónica del Ecuador en el Siglo XVI*, Sevilla: Escuela de Altos Estudios Hispano-Americanos de Sevilla.
Taylor, Anne-Christine, 1981, 'God-Wealth: The Achuar and the Missions' in Norman E. Whitten, Jr. (ed.), *Cultural Transformations and Ethnicity in Modern Ecuador*, Urbana.
Vargas, S. I., José María, 1977, *Historia del Ecuador, Siglo XVI*, Quito.

Religion and clergy in the Atusparia uprising, Peru, 1885*

WILLIAM W. STEIN

A social movement, in order to develop its own identity and to exert control over its environment, requires association and organization: that is, people in relation to one another based on common interests, with consciousness of their purposes and the means for achieving the latter. Peasant movements may constitute a special case, in view of what Graus [*1976: 8*] calls 'great objective and subjective obstacles in the rural environment' to the realization of organized action by peasants because they are 'bound throughout the year to their fields and villages' and because the enemy is 'often perceived only in a vague and frequently incorrect way' in terms of the conception of the misuse of lordship rather than a challenge to the existence of lordship and a 'belief in the good ruler'. Although this statement was intended to characterize social conditions of late medieval peasant wars of Europe, it would seem to have wider applicability. This essay will attempt to apply this perspective, as well as add to it the dimension of religious ritual and ideology, in the case of the Atusparia Uprising, a peasant movement which took place in Perú's central highland region in 1885, beginning in the town of Huaraz, capital of the Department of Ancash and situated centrally, at around 10,000 feet above sea level, in a large and densely populated valley running north and south between two mountain ranges.

Just as peasants tend to cease social struggle to plant, cultivate and harvest their crops, they are also likely to interrupt action for purposes of religious ritual, to forge or renew the bonds between people and the animating forces of their environment [*Custred, 1979: 288–289*]. This spontaneous and direct

---

* The research on which this essay is based was made possible by several grants from the State University of New York at Buffalo. I wish to express special gratitude to Señorita Graciela Sánchez Cerro and the staff of the Oficina de Investigaciones Bibliográficas of the Biblioteca Nacional, and Señor Alejandro Lostaunau of the Library of the Instituto Riva Agüero, in Lima, for their assistance in locating sources. The Huaraz office of SINAMOS graciously made available a transcript of its 1974 symposium on the Atusparia Uprising. I thank the following for their help: Señor José Sotelo, Señorita Elia Lazarte Ch., Dr. Luis Millones, Carmen Salazar, Enrique Sánchez, Pilar Suárez, Maria Julia Woillús, Dr. Thomas M. Davies, Jr., and by no means least, Florence E. Babb.

connection between getting a living and worship appears to be as old as cultivation in the central Andean area, and after four and a half centuries of forced hispanicization and Christianization, it is still possible to discern the native Andean concept which is relatively unconcerned with the *más allá* – the 'beyond', i.e. afterlife, because it is orientated to the *más acá* – the 'nearer', i.e. here and now [*Marzal, 1977: 34*]. Andean peasants appear to ascribe more importance to the celebration of a ritual than to personal faith; ritual seems to have the purpose of obtaining something specific, rather than for worship; peasants resort to priests as clients of professional religious services more than as members of a community of believers; and it appears that religion is more useful for the resolution of life's material problems than it is to assure ethical behavior or to question personal conduct [*ibid, 231–3*]. In opposition to the notion of 'magicization' of peasant religion, Custred [*1973: 79–80*] says that this 'ritual is an analogue of the things peasants must do to survive', in order to carry on subsistence activity and social life. Peasants do not need a complete understanding of the symbolism to make the ritual work, 'any more than it is necessary for the operator of a machine to understand the working of the machinery he deals with'. Like the machine, the ritual 'had an origin somewhere and at some point in time and is an artifact of human invention'; its component symbols, therefore, would have had an explicit meaning which, at least in part, constituted a rationale to continue its performance. However, the 'really effective rationale for the ritual efficacy' rests upon 'the associative value of the symbolism with basic peasant experience' in subsistence activities: 'this symbolism, although not explicitly explained by the peasants, is nevertheless implicitly understood by them'.

It should come as no surprise that rural producers, engaged in the transformation of nature into the many different kinds of use-values and commodities [*Fonseca Martel, 1973: 120*], in control of the means of production as well as their own labor, should possess a non-alienated, and thus non-mystified, conception of the universe and their place in it, a world in which spiritual needs and satisfactions more directly reflect [*Hahn, 1978: 61*] material activities. Peasants as direct producers, are not concerned with the existential justifications needed by the indirect producers and social parasites who are supported by their rent; nor must peasants endure the existential agony of expropriated laborers doomed to superannuation and superfluity. Peasant religion has a base which is different from that of the town, as different as the promotion of fertility and rainfall is from the promotion of commodity exchange. In order to keep the flow of rent and commodities coming from the rural sector, the urban sector exercises dominance over a dependent countryside; its religion reflects that condition.

In the Andean part of Perú, peasants have been called 'Indians' since early colonial times, as distinguished from townspeople who have been known as *mestizos*, 'creoles', or 'whites', terms which over the centuries have become much more associated with landed-property ownership, regional control, and position in the chain of commercial intermediaries which reached from the smallest hamlet to the great metropolitan center of Lima. the terms which were originally linked with Native American, in contrast with European biological roots, have in reality had little to do with race since those early times of the Spanish invasion and occupation; rather, they have reflected much more accurately the position of Peruvian people in the tax rolls. This is not to say that one does not observe in modern Perú that a European physical appearance is associated with a higher class position; however, such a correlation is far from perfect; moreover, physically the urban masses are indistinguishable from the rural masses. Townspeople, of course, are bilingual in both Spanish and Quechua, while peasants tend to be Quechua-speakers only, a condition which was more extreme in the last century.

Town and country were not two homogeneous categories but were themselves segmented by diverse socio-economic conditions [*Stein, 1974*]. The peasants consisted of small farmers and herders, in large part micro-holders, living in *estancias*, freeholding communities; *colonos*, peasants who paid labor-rent to the proprietors of *haciendas*, large landholdings, in return for an allotment of land; micro-holding clients of town patrons in a variety of servile relations on smaller rural properties or in town activities; wage-workers; petty commodity-producers; and petty buyers of agricultural produce on the lowest commercial levels. These peasants supported and otherwise served the interests and needs of townspeople, both as individuals and as a class; they supplied the town with labor-power, in the form of rent or as wage-labor for produce or cash, for the production of commodities for sale in the national market, as well as with a variety of goods and services for consumption. Peasants worked as agricultural laborers, burden-bearers, message-carriers, street-cleaners, house servants, providers of draft animals, mounts, and fertilizer, provisioners from their own small food and handicraft production, and even as cattle rustlers and squatters in townspeople's property struggles, and irregular troops in town feuds and factional quarrels. As a whole, the rural sector rendered tribute to the town in two ways: in the form of a number of different taxes paid in cash and produce and in the form of corvée labor on town projects such as public buildings, the construction and repair of streets and highways, the maintenance of the district's water supply and drainage, the cultivation of flower beds in the public squares, and so on. Townspeople, at the top of this servile social order, were segmented into the owners of large, medium, and small properties, often combined with a position at one level or another in the commercial intermediary network and/or with the practice of a profession. Townspeople were literate, voted in national elections, controlled the courts and the police force, and were easily distinguished by their clothing from peasants. While townspeople understood the peasant language, and often spoke it at home rather than Spanish, and participated to a degree in peasant culture, especially its pleasures, lore, and ritual, they considered themselves far superior to 'brutal', and 'savage' people of the countryside who did hard work for a living. The need to reproduce in this social environment was also reflected in peasant religious ritual and ideology.

In the discussion of the Atusparia movement it will be useful to bear in mind that peasants formed part of the population of towns, that many of them lived in close association with townspeople, and that the structure of patronage pervaded the social system. This in itself constituted an obstacle to peasant movement: it made doubly difficult the definition of the enemy and caused interruptions in peasant action.

The Atusparia Uprising takes its name from its leader, Pedro Pablo Atusparia, a small-scale operator of lands in an *estancia* who worked as an artisan in a small dye-plant owned by a mestizo in Huaraz. In 1885, Atusparia happened to be the incumbent of the office of *alcalde pedáneo*, the leading position of some forty peasant officials in one of two ceremonial divisions into which the District of Huaraz was and is divided. An alcalde, newly appointed each New Year's Day, is responsible for directing, together with his group of lesser officials and the personnel of different Roman Catholic saints' cults, the yearly round of festivals and other ritual occasions. The alcalde and his officials, *varáyoq* (from Spanish *vara*, 'staff of office', together with a Quechua suffix indicating possession) as they are called,[1] are also charged with supervising communal public works in their territorial division, and the maintenance of ceremonial structures, such as chapels, shrines, and crosses, but also including the construction and repair of roads and bridges. The *varáyoq* also supervised corvée labor for townspeople and collected the taxes which, traditionally, were divided between the regional administration and the central government in Lima. In the middle of the nineteenth century, the poll tax alone provided between one-third and one-half of the national budget [*Pásara, 1970: 53*].

The peasant movement began when Atusparia presented a petition, signed by himself and the other varáyoq with 'X's' — for none of them could read or write — to the recently appointed Prefect of the Department of Ancash, whose main task was to generate funds for the national treasury. They requested the reduction of the poll tax, and the amount of corvée labor so that the peasants might have more time to attend to their crops. The Prefect, alert for subversion as well as funds and suspecting that the assistance provided to the varáyoq in preparing their petition by some literate person or persons was founded in opposition to the government, ordered Atusparia's arrest, imprisonment, whipping, and the cutting off of his braids, in order to force a confession from him. When the other varáyoq came to protest this treatment, they too were seized, jailed, and their braids cut off. This last event seems to have occurred on March 1, a Sunday and market-day in Huaraz when a peasant mass was given, and when the varáyoq appeared at the municipal office to receive their corvée orders for the week and to deliver the tax monies they had collected. On the following day, there were skirmishes between hundreds of peasants, who came down from the heights to protest and see what could be done to free their officials, and the Huaraz garrison of police and soldiers, in which casualties were suffered on both sides after the nervous troops fired on the peasants. On March 3, the peasant attack was renewed, this time by thousands of insurgents who succeeded in driving the remnants of the government forces out of the city in the middle of the afternoon.[2]

In order to appreciate the forces which were at work in this situation, it will be useful to elucidate the crisis which Perú was suffering at the time. The country had just experienced disaster of the greatest proportions in losing the War of the Pacific, 1879–1883, to Chile, in which revenue was cut off, coastal sugar and cotton plantations were wrecked, Perú's southern provinces in which valuable nitrate deposits were located were removed, and Lima was occupied by Chilean troops for three years. Although resistance continued in the interior, Perú's plantation owners and exporters realized that the only way they could carry on their business was to settle the War. Eventually, in 1883 a government acceptable to the Chileans was formed by President Miguel Iglesias who signed the peace treaty in October of that year. The hero of the resistance was General Andrés Cáceres, a nationalist and populist figure who harassed the Chileans with troops which contained large numbers of peasant irregular forces. He was opposed to the peace treaty and, after the Chilean forces left Lima in January 1884, he continued to harass the Iglesias government. However, he did not appeal to the country's financial and commercial rulers, the large coastal landlords, until he cut himself loose from the peasants. When he finally obtained landlord assistance, he was able to put together the force needed to take Lima and the presidency from Iglesias in December 1885. Iglesias, whose reputation was tinged with illegitimacy because he signed the treaty with Chile, was disposable once a more effective substitute was found; Cáceres, who proved to be anything but a patriot in his settlement of foreign bondholders' claims, managed to maintain this popular image, at least long enough to become Perú's President [Basadre, 1969, vols. VIII–IX; Pike, 1967].

In 1885, many of Perú's highland towns contained large numbers of the supporters of General Cáceres. Huaraz was no exception, and it is possible that the Prefect was correct in his assessment of Atusparia's petition. Here there appear parallels with the process which Spalding [1980: 95] describes for the southern Peruvian highlands. There small landlords and petty commercial intermediaries of the towns were squeezed by land concentration and the decline of local markets, which led to a number of uprisings, triggered by some 'new and onerous exaction, such as a labor levy or the imposition of a head tax'. However, there is no evidence of the participation of townspeople in planning the revolt, beyond the diplomatically worded petition.

Because our knowledge of the movement consists of fragments and images which the official bulletins and newspapers of the time wished to present and were willing to reveal [cf. *Stein, 1980a; 1980d*], and which the gatherers of oral history saw fit to write in later years, there is little agreement among its students. Certainly, the characterization of it as an 'Indian revolt' was a journalistic device of 1885 to satisfy the literate population of Perú as well as government determination to seek peace with the Huaraz dissidents, but it encompassed social sectors far beyond the peasantry. Quijano [*1979: 57, note*] defines it as a 'racist movement', pre-political in nature, that is, one with 'goals that are diffusely discernable or concrete and linked with the real situation only in a completely segmentary, tangential, or indirect way' [*ibid.: 52–53*]. The 'racist' character may be projected into the movement because of its goal of eliminating the 'white' population [*ibid.: 121*]. However, Valladres and Piel [*1977: 169*] remind us that 'whites' in fact meant 'landlords and authorities and represented the dominant minority of the region' as well as those 'big merchants who sold articles that peasants could not purchase ... [unless] they got indebted for an indefinite period'. Kapsoli [*1979: 247*] classifies the rebellion as one of a number of nineteenth century 'anti-fiscal movements with marked passivity of consciousness and without a greater questioning of society'. Espinoza Soriano [*1973: 145*] refers to it as a 'reappearance' of 'the entirely nativistic movements' of early colonial times; and, indeed, some aspects of the movement, particularly the call for the reestablishment of the Inca Empire sent out by townspeople, could very well have elicited a more serious peasant response in the context of peasant myth. My own feeling is that probably all of these interpretations are, at least in part, correct, for a peasant movement, being composed of the diverse socio-economic sectors which constitute a peasantry, need not set monolithic goals for itself: some peasants joined it to avoid taxation, some in the service of their town patrons, some for loot, while some may well have been impelled by myth.

The day after the peasants took Huaraz, on March 4, Atusparia appointed a mestizo townsman, named Manuel (or Nicolás) Mosquera, to the office of Prefect, since the government appointee was by that time in full flight. Atusparia, who remained alcalde of his division, retained the title of *Delegado*, ('delegate'). One of Mosquera's first actions was to force numbers of townspeople to sign a document in support of General Cáceres. While Atusparia was the only leader of the uprising at the time of its outbreak, and for the peasants remained the real supreme leader, once Mosquera entered the scene he was the one who actually directed the movement. After an interruption, which included a mass of thanksgiving in the main church of Huaraz, followed by a banquet for the insurgents, the rebellion moved down the valley from Huaraz to the provincial capitals of Carhuaz on March 16, Yungay on April 4, and Caraz on April 14. Carhuaz offered no resistance and was sacked. Yungay organized a civil guard and held out until ammunition was gone on April 2, when the city was partially evacuated. A priest from Huaraz, whose actions will be elaborated in the next section of this essay, appeared in Yungay to conduct a religious procession in the midst of its sacking by a peasant mob, and managed to quiet the situation, but not in time to save much damage to the city. The same priest led a procession from Caraz to meet the peasant forces at the approaches to the city, this time with success, for the peasants were held back while their leaders attended a banquet of welcome in the city.

While these events were taking place in the valley, Lima finally decided to take action. On April 8 a new Prefect was appointed to lead government forces in their putting down of the rebellion. The Ancash peasantry – equipped with slings, clubs, pikes, and a few rifles captured from the Chileans or carried in by deserters – was no match for two infantry batallions, a regiment of cavalry, and two brigades of artillery [*Piel 1973: 312*] armed with canister shot, and the rebellion was rapidly extinguished [*Stein, 1980c*]. The government troops entered Yungay on April 24 and retook Huarz on May 3, with little resistance, for the populace was in the midst of celebrating an important regional ceremony, the feast day of Nuestro Señor de Soledad (Our Lord of Solitude). Except for guerrilla action in the mountains west of the valley, which lasted until the end of September, led by another peasant, Pedro Cochachin, who, when captured, had on his person a commission from General Cáceres, the movement was over.

The processes of the Atusparia Uprising appear to have been slowed, interrupted, and even halted on various ceremonial and ritual occasions. These were not only matters of peasant requirements but in them the regional clergy played a strategic part. It must be understood that this clergy was and is rooted in the region, as is the case throughout Andean Perú: priests not only speak the peasant language formally but understand peasant needs, customs, and beliefs, in short, they function in peasant culture, as do townspeople as a whole, although priests are somewhat more removed from it in consequence of their training and the offices they occupy. Marzal [*1971: 297–298*], a priest himself, points out that a priest who is from elsewhere is from 'another cultural world', and even those with rural backgrounds undergo a process of cultural uprooting in their seminary training: in addition to their religious experience, they take on urban values. Moreover, some local clergy ignore or have less concern with peasant culture. Furthermore, the 'official posture of the Church', as Marzal (*ibid.: 516*) notes, changed from an original hostility to a 'non-aggression part', in which 'priests ignore or appear to ignore everything related to' peasant non-official rites and beliefs.

Of several priests who played some role during the revolt, one, a certain Fidel Olivas Escudero, seems to have been busily engaged in open counter-insurrectionary activity and to have understood the Ancash peasantry well enough to know which actions on his part, at which times, would do the most good for his cause. Klaiber [*1977: 64*] describes him as having come from 'a middle-class family in the district of Huari', which is located on the other side of the mountain range east of Huaraz; thus, he would have spoken a variety of Quechua very close to that of Huaraz and he would have possessed intimate knowledge of regional peasant culture. Olivas Escudero, ordained in 1874 and assigned to the diocese of Huaraz between 1878 and 1900 was 'tall, thin, and white-complexioned ... somewhat taciturn and even austere', 'highly respected' by both townspeople and peasants [*ibid., 65*]. Ponte González [*1945: 93–94*], a Huaraz priest who interviewed eyewitnesses of the revolt describes his actions on March 4, the day after the taking of Huaraz by the peasant forces:

> It was the first day for Huaraz in the power of the revolutionaries ... The Indians were drinking, breaking the necks of their bottles in the absence of other ways of opening them, and, when they were empty, they were thrown into the streets along with salmon tins and other refuse. Everyone feared a massacre. Saint Bartholomew's night was coming; the danger was imminent. Then was the time to think about priests.
>
> In truth, the figure of Olivas Escudero appeared like a ray of hope at the moment of greatest chill, when the irreparable was approaching. He hurried straight to the Prefecture, wrapped in his woolen cape, nervous and pale. He came to see Atusparia. The interview was brief and respectful on the leader's part. Olivas Escudero came out smiling, filled with optimism. The avalanche could be contained, transformed for the moment into an eddy, even later when new breaches appeared ... It was midnight, with a revel of drunken people and disorderly voices in the streets ... From a distance there quickly came the soft sounds of hand-bells. In surprise, people asked: 'Are they bringing the Viaticum for the dying?' In fact it was a small group of young men passing with a priest who carried the holy sacrament. It was Olivas Escudero, a man of nerve and idealism, who had had his interview with Atusparia a few hours earlier. He had been commissioned to attend to the wounded and was covering all the streets without entering any of the houses. He had devised that means to ward off the danger which hovered above Huaraz, and he managed to bring to the revolutionaries' notice the idea of a Supreme Being and to drive out of their minds the fatal thought of extermination. So it was: the hours of dawn passed and the plan of the drunken masses was not carried out. There were only isolated sackings and outrages during the days of the revolution, but not the slaughter desired and planned by the Indians' inflamed and vengeful spirit. The outbreaks and acts of savagery took place in towns in the valley where Atusparia's influence did not immediately come to bear ... Olivas Escudero's strategy had its success in Huaraz.

At the end of the first week of the rebel occupation of Huaraz, Atusparia proclaimed that on Sunday, March 8, a mass of thanksgiving would be heard, given by the parish priest, a man named Figueroa. Reyna [*1932: 35–36*] describes this event in his novelistic treatment of the revolt based on oral history, as follows:

> On Sunday, in the great church, the announced solemn mass was sung. Atusparia attended it in a black cape with a scarlet band. The priests seated him in the place of honor and, so he could rest his feet clad in rustic leather sandals, they set down for him a beautiful cushion bordered with gold thread. In the sermon, the priest Figueroa, with those rustic metaphors which highlanders employ to preach to the faithful, he told them that God was like a young lamb mounted in a bread oven. When He voided himself, His small pieces of dung rolled all over. Today the dung had fallen on the Indian side. What were the estancias without this fertilizer? Would it fertilize the young crops, and would there be a pleasant fire in the household hearth? When God saw them show mercy, He would make the grainfields produce and there would be no lack of maize in the pot! Further, if the dung was used in the forges where the implements of war were made, He would take his eyes away from the fields and there would be no rain, but plagues and hunger. God made men so that some would rule and others would obey; He asked recently born souls: Do you want to rule the land and be condemned to hell forever, or will you suffer on earth and enjoy heaven eternally? All the little Indian souls had chosen heaven; and obedience, submission, servitude, and poverty were pleasing to God. Christ had died, crucified like a criminal, without defending himself from his executioners, in order to give us the example of humility. If we were given a blow on one cheek, we must turn the other, and if we were kicked in the stomach, we must humbly turn our behinds. For those who want to go to Heaven, it is necessary to obey the authorities ...

Holy Week in Perú constitutes a significant interruption of routine; in Ancash, masses of peasants descend from their hamlets to the valley towns, bearing their patron saints on litters, to attend a series of rituals. Here is how Ponte González [*1945: 95–96*] describes Holy Thursday and Good Friday, which in 1885 came on April 2 and 3, in Huaraz:

> Atusparia was content with his successes and his power ... Many of the directors [*i.e. mestizo dissidents*] advised him and explained things to him. Illusions paraded through his imagination, dreams in the millenarian unconsciousness of his race ... Stimulated and embraced by those illusions and unconscious reactions, he wanted the days of Holy Week to be solemn and he wanted to preside as the whites were accustomed to do.
> In actuality, the church bells rang out on Holy Thursday in 'proud' Huaraz, capital of the Indian domination. Orders were given for official attendance. The urban parish performed the duties of bishopric and ministered to the authorities, inviting them to the traditional gathering. The Prefecture, on its part, circulated invitations indicating

that the 'Delegate', Señor Pedro Pablo Atusparia, would attend the religious ceremonies on Holy Thursday and Good Friday.

The main church was filled from end to end. Clearly, there was less elegance in the dress of most people ... More ponchos stood out, new ones with lively colors. The Indian aristocracy [*sic*] was at high tide. Curious people squeezed into the square and the streets. The official committee was going to pass by, and so they searched out the best places to catch sight of Atusparia. The cornet blew; people listened; the troops in correct formation presented arms. The martial chords of the band swelled. It was the committee coming with dignitaries in front, officials, governors, and magistrates with pikes and uniforms, and then the varáyoq in sandals, ponchos, and homespun trousers and shirts. They carried black staves with silver veneers and shining crosses on their handles. Last came the Prefect with the 'Delegate' on his right. The latter was the same: he had not changed his clothing, but for a new poncho with a fringed border in natural color, and his homespun trousers and shirt ended in tassels. When the leader passed there was emotion; the multitude greeted him. He answered courteously and cordially. Inside those scorned garments was a man who inspired respect and fear. The priests offered him hyssop. He made the sign of the cross and then entered the church. People stood up to watch him pass, severe, calm, and dominating. He took the seat of honor and the ceremony began. At the right moment the sign of peace was brought to him for the ritual kiss; he stood up and gave it. In the afternoon he attended the Lavation. He made his offering and kissed the feet of the 'apostles'. On Good Friday he performed his act of adoration and also offered his obolus.

Holy Week was invested with particular solemnity. The predominance of the Indian element and its official participation gave the event a unique and memorable color. The processions were rivers of human masses. Never had Huaraz felt such religiosity ...

It will be recalled that although Yungay was evacuated on April 2, rebel forces did not enter the place until April 4, Holy Saturday, after the rituals which have been described. It was undoubtedly the peasants' 'Good Friday orientation' that held up consolidation of the insurgent victory. The siege of Yungay seems to have begun on or before Palm Sunday but was interrupted by ritual observances. Then, having solemnly celebrated Good Friday, the revolt continued. As soon as the Indians were in Yungay, they began to sack it. Olivas Escudero arrived too late to stop them, even though he tried to restrain the rebels [*ibid.: 95*].

In Caraz, the story was different: Olivas Escudero arrived in time to save the city. According to Klaiber [*1977: 66*], he 'and other priests of the area stood on the outskirts of the town in full liturgical regalia with the monstrance and the Blessed Sacrament held aloft' as the rebel forces were approaching, an event which stopped and spiritually disarmed the latter. According to a collective account by a group of local historians [*Associación de Maestros 1945–1946: 39*], Olivas Escudero and the parish priest, a man named García, led a procession of town dignitaries out to meet the insurgents. The confrontation was described by

Don Fortunato Guardia García in unpublished oral-history materials[3] as follows:

> The Caraz authorities got together in an open council in the square. There were different opinions, as is the case in town when people are unsure what course of action to take. The priest played the main part. He was a strange person, a tall, fat, white man. He elected to receive the Indians in a Christian manner, a religious manner. They agreed to take the Host out in procession. They appointed some lookouts to watch the Indians' march on Caraz. Then the town was brought together, the priest dressed in sacred trappings, families attending with their flowers, and they took out the Host with everybody to meet the invaders. It turned out that when the crowd, with Pedro Cochachin Atusparia, and all, was entering the town, the Caracinos were also coming out in the procession. They were fearful and thought they were lost, but they did not think at all about the attitude of the invaders. When the Host arrived, it was Atusparia who was the first to hold the people back and wait for its arrival. He kneeled, and so did Pedro and all the rest. They all kneeled and worshipped the Host. The priest gave them his blessing and invited all the town authorities to move to the front of the procession with Atusparia; however, they preferred to remain behind. When the procession arrived at the church, he gave them his most holy blessing.

After the ritual, the rebel leaders were invited to a banquet, described by the local historians [*ibid.*] in the following way:

> In Don Francisco Almandoz's house a great banquet was offered to Atusparia and the other leaders of the revolution, attended by many ladies of the locality who offered them bouquets of flowers ... Atusparia occupied the seat of honor ... After the Caracinos conferred with Atusparia, they offered to furnish supplies to the revolutionary troops. On their part, the Indians agreed to respect lives and properties.

The last ceremonial event which interfered with the pursuit of rebel goals was the great festival of the Lord of Solitude on May 3. It centers on an image which is venerated not only in Huaraz and its surrounding hamlets but in the whole valley; its devotees come to Huaraz from the urban and rural sectors of all parts to celebrate the feast day. This date also marks the transition from the rainy season to the dry season, the harvest of the former crop and the preparation for planting the latter, and, thus, an occasion for making and carrying out pilgrimage vows. In 1885, it was the time when the insurrection paused, its masses in confused retreat after its efforts to retake Yungay from the government forces in bloody battles on April 25, 26, 27, and 28 [*Stein, 1980a; 1980d*] had failed. The masses were becoming segmented and disorderly and the mestizos were withdrawing from the movement, Mosquera himself in secret negotiation with the Prefect. What better time for what was left of the movement to hope for supernatural intervention in its favor? What better time for the commander of the government forces to choose for his entry into Huaraz? Antúnez de Mayolo [*1957: 10–11*] tells the story as follows:

(On May 3) the Fiesta of the Lord of Solitude was celebrated in the 'Very Generous City of Huaraz'. It has more *devotos* among the Huaraz Indians than the Lord of Miracles has in Lima. Like the latter, the Lord of Solitude has a history: among the people of the region there is a story about how it holds back a gigantic washout [a constant danger in the valley from the glaciers and lakes in the mountains to the east], and they say that it has a miraculous origin . . .

The procession, a solemn one as is the custom, began at eleven in the morning, accompanied by *Pallas* (women in festive regalia who dance and sing] and *Huanquillas* [male dancers with peacock-feather headdresses, boots with bells attached to them, and vests to which pounds of silver ornaments and mirrors are attached], and the din of musician instruments. It had hardly begun when the aureole [an elaborately decorated halo in the form of a frame to which flowers and other ornaments are attached] of the figure fell to earth with a crash [an exceedingly bad omen]. People had to stop for a moment to put it back in place, with the result that it fell again two or three more times. Just as the procession was ending, the light artillery was heard . . .

So ended the Atusparia Uprising. The government forces easily retook Huaraz from the rebels who offered almost no resistance. Atusparia was wounded in the skirmishing and sought refuge among the townspeople he had protected; he was later granted amnesty by the new Prefect. Pedro Cochachin regrouped part of the rebel force in the mountains west of the city. Fidel Olivas Escudero led an unsuccessful mission to seek peace with him; then, after several bloody and useless attacks on the city, Cochachin retired to the mountains to harass government forces until September when he was captured and executed.

It is appropriate to begin analysis of the ritual and ideological impediments to peasant revolt in rural Perú (and no doubt elsewhere) by emphasizing the central role of the religious festival in peasant life. It is a mode of worshipping and claiming the favorable attention of the forces of the universe and an assertion of social identity. The social elements which make up the fiesta consist of positions in a system of offices which include the varáyoq, members of saints' cults, dancers, banner-carriers, and other persons who assume the róle of sponsorship with some kind of contribution to the celebration. Each position is conceived of as a *cargo*, an obligation affirmed by a contribution or pledge to contribute. The reasons for accepting *cargos* are varied. For example, Marzal [*1971: 173–176*] found, in his study of the District of Urcos in the Cuzco region, that more urban people said they accepted them 'out of devotion', while rural people said it was 'so that people would not speak ill' of them or 'because it is customary'. Some did it because of a dream, or in order to keep in good health or recover it, or to get a good harvest, while others said simply that they were 'pressured' into it. The reward and punishment aspect of *cargos* is general in the central Andean region, and what Casaverde Rojas [*1970: 192*] says of the community of Kuyo Grande, near Cuzco, also applies to Ancash:

> The Saints are the direct representatives of God on earth and men should fulfil cargos as a way of paying for the usufruct of the lands they work. The people believe that the only form of living well is with God's blessing, which is obtained by remembering Him, praying to Him, and serving the Saints. If it is not done that way, frosts are strong, rain is scarce, hail ruins the crops, and the harvests are generally bad. For this reason, no person may refuse to fulfil cargos for fear of these and other punishments which the Saints may send... In contrast, those who fulfil cargos are rewarded...

Arguedas [*1964: 268–269*] notes the 'direct relationship between the prestige' of a person in the peasant community 'and the fulfilment of official religious obligations'. In reference to the Andean varáyoq system, Earls [*1973: 401*] calls these *cargos* 'age-grades' in which 'temporal and spiritual power... increases with each ascending position'. Fonseca Martel [*1977: 72–73*] observes that while the cargo system is 'a form of validating the power and prestige of wealthy peasants', and as such may be used 'to extract greater economic surpluses from the poorest peasants', it is 'a way of serving the community' which 'functions as a mode... of redistribution of supluses...'. Thus, the festival serves not only spiritual needs but also those for personal and family wellbeing, and for social reproduction. Finally, and highly significant in terms of the constant threat of land encroachment by both more powerful peasants and townspeople over the last century and a half of Republican history, as Custred [*1980: 203–204*] points out, community festivals have a vital function 'external to community organization':

> De facto recognition of communities by other peasants and by local elites is an important factor in maintaining claims on land and water resources made by those individual households comprising communities... Community feasts parallel and support in the ritual sphere what community organization does in the social and political realms... By organizing and celebrating the recognized feast of a community saint (a saint accepted with reverence throughout society), the community is asserting its identity to all concerned through ritual action, while at the same time supporting its own internal organization and its territorial claims.

In the same article, Custred [*ibid.: 201*] makes reference to fictive or ritual kinship both within and outside the peasantry and concludes that 'Church ritual... acts to seal these important social contracts both through the authority of the Church and through the solemnity of sacred ritual, and thus plays an important role in establishing and maintaining different kinds of social alliances'. This could be easily extended to the joint participation of peasants and townspeople in great regional festivals, in view of the existing socio-economic complementation of these two social categories. It is well to remember with Custred [*ibid.: 206*] that Catholic saints are 'polysemous' symbols, having different values for different groups: thus, 'the illusion of agreement is created, ... masking the different currents of belief and social and economic functions which underlie both the symbol and its corresponding ritual'.

While peasants and townspeople were allied in revolt, in terms of patronage and clientage, and in ceremony, this alliance was really an illusion covering up their real divergence and opposition, socially and culturally. For townspeople, the fiesta was and is disorder verging on the pagan; for peasants it is the best mode of worship they know in a world where spirit and substance are not separated. For townspeople, with their intrigue and grasping for advantage, the insurrection was a political thing; for peasants, it was a way of reorganizing the world. In its tendency to break away from the servile social order it was a danger easily perceived by townspeople who, by the end of the revolt, saw the government forces more as liberators and less as political antagonists.

The polysemous nature of the events which have been described here is clear in the mestizo manipulation of symbols to achieve a desired effect in the peasant mob on ritual occasions, and also in the conversion of secular scenes into sacred ones. Moreover, it constitutes pathetic evidence of peasant incapacity to organize its own liberation. Because the peasantry is not a class it is not capable of enforcing its class interests in its own name: peasants 'cannot represent themselves, they must be represented' [*Marx, 1963: 124*]. In 1885, the Ancash peasantry was its own obstacle to organized action. Its halts for ritual performance were as material as its arms; and its arms were as spiritual as its worship. Fidel Olivas Escudero, and the other mestizo priests – representing their own mestizo class and possibly with full awareness of the 'tricks'[4] they were performing in their management of ritual so as to gain a certain control in the insurrectionary process in order to protect the interests of that class – 'knew' full well what peasants could never know: that the material and the spiritual are eternally separate. Their intervention helped to seal the doom of the movement. However, it was not religious ideology and ritual, either in the form of the official Roman Catholicism or in the form of peasant versions of it, that hurt the peasant cause but, rather, the peasant inability to use religious ideology and ritual for peasant purposes.

Notes

1. There is as yet no published study of the varáyoq system in the District of Huaraz. The varáyoq of the Hacienda Vicos have been discussed in a short monograph by Vázquez [*1964*] and those of Hualcán, an estancia in the Province of Carhuaz, are presented in my ethnography [*Stein, 1961: 184–193, 195–197*].

2. Atusparia Uprising sources include Antúnez de Mayolo [*1957*], Meza [*1928*], Ponte González [*1945: 83–101*], and the novel by Reyna [*1932*], all of which include oral history. More fragmentary accounts by the Asociación Provincial de Maestros Primarios de la Provincia de Huylas [*1945–46; 39, 156, 247, 268, 276*], and Carrasco, Ramírez, and León [*1962: 37–45*] are also based on original work. Secondary accounts include research into the 1885 newspapers, such as Alvarez-Brun [*1970: 199–208*], Basadre [*1947: 244–248*], and Villanueva [*1973: 116–119*]. Maguiña Chauca [*1974*] is a synthesis. Reina Loli [*1969*] and Valladares and Piel [*1977*] are valuable for their critical examination of sources and their contribution of new perspectives on the 1885 event. For an English account of the revolt, see Klaiber [*1977: 58–67*] and Stein [*1978, 1980a, 1980b, 1980c, 1980d, and 1981*].
3. Based on interviews with Don Fortunato, May 17 and 22, 1977, in Carhuaz, and on a transcript of his talk to a conference held in Huaraz in 1974 by SINAMOS, and made available to me by that office for which I should like to express my gratitude.
4. In his study of religiosity in Qollana in southern Perú Michaud [*1970: 15*], points out that in local mythology the priest plays the part of a 'trickster': in relation to peasants: 'a rule similar to the one the fox plays in relation to the other animals: he is more cunning than the others but in the end he is defeated by them'. In the Atusparia Uprising, the mestizo priest defeated the peasants in a series of ritual encounters. It is well to recall what Ponte González [*1945: 93*] said of Olivas Escudero: 'The Indians knew him but they did not trust him. They had often heard him preach in their *estancias*. A severe man, and slave to discipline, he was a question to the Indians. 'Who knows?' But justice was with everyone, they thought.'

References

Albó Xavier, 1973, 'Santa Vera Cruz Tatita', *Allpanchis Phuturinqa, Revista del Instituto de Pastoral Andina* (Cuzco, Perú) 7: 163–215.

Alvarez-Brun, Félix, 1970, *Ancash, una Historia Regional Peruana*, Lima.

Antúnez de Mayolo, Santiago, 1957, *La Sublevación de los Indios del Callejón de Huaylas*, Lima.

Arguedas, José María, 1964, 'Puquio, una cultura en proceso de cambio'. *Estudios Sobre la Cultura Actual del Perú*, Luis E. Valcárcel, et al. Lima.

Asociación Provincial de Maestros Primarios de la Provincia de Huaylas, 1945–46, *Monografía de la Provincia de Huaylas*, Caraz, Perú.

Basadre, Jorge, 1947, *La Multitud, la Ciudad y el Campo en la Historia del Perú*, (2d ed.) Lima.

Basadre, J., 1969, *Historia de la República del Perú, 1822–1933*, (6th ed.) 17 vols, Lima.

Cadorette, Raimundo, 1977, 'Perspectivas mitológicas del mundo aymara', *Allpanchis Phuturinqa, Revista del Instituto de Pastoral Andina* (Cuzco, Perú) 10: 115–136.

Casaverde Rojas, Juvenal, 1970, 'El mundo sobrenatural en una comunidad', *Allpanchis Phuturinqa, Revista del Instituto de Pastoral Andina* (Cuzco, Perú) 2: 121–243.

Carrasco, Juan N., Joel Ramíez, and Delina León, 1962, 'Historia de Yungay', *Libro de Oro de Yungay*, Alberto Carrión Vergara, ed. Lima.

Custred, H. Glynn, Jr., 1973, Symbols and Control in a High Altitude Andean Community. Ph.D., Indiana University.

Custred, H. G., 1979, 'Inca concepts of soul and spirit', *Essays in Humanistic Anthropology: A Festschrift in Honor of David Bidney*, Bruce T. Grindal and Dennis M. Warren, eds. Washington D.C.

Custred, H. G., 1980, 'The place of ritual in Andean rural society'. *Land and Power in Latin America, Agrarian Economies and Social Processes in the Andes*, Benjamin S. Orlove and Glynn Custred, eds. New York and London.

Earls, John, 1973, 'La organización del poder en la mitología quechua', *Ideología Mesiánica del Mundo Andino*, Juan M. Ossio A., ed. Lima.

Ennew, Judith, Paul Hirst, and Keith Tribe, 1977, 'Peasantry as an economic category', *Journal of Peasant Studies* 4: 295–322.
Espinoza Soriano, Waldemar, 1973, 'Un movimiento religioso de libertad y salvación nativista. Yanahuara – 1596', *Ideología Mesiánica del Mundo Andino*, Juan M. Ossio A., ed. Lima.
Fonseca Martel, César, 1973, *Sistemas Económicos Andinos*, Lima.
Fonseca Martel, C., 1977, 'Diferenciación campesina en los Andes peruanos', *Vicus Cuadernos* (Amsterdam) 1: 61–86.
Graus, František, 1976, 'From resistance to revolt: the late medieval peasant wars in the context of social crisis', *The German Peasant War of 1525*, Janos Bak, ed. London.
Hahn, Erich, 1978, 'Ideology and reflection', *Revolutionary World* 27: 61–68.
Kapsoli, Wilfredo, 1979, 'En torno a los movimientos campesinos en el Perú contemporáneo', *La Investigación en Ciencias Sociales en el Perú*, Oscar Jara H., ed. Lima.
Klaiber, Jeffrey L. S. J., 1977, *Religion and Revolution in Peru, 1824–1976*, Notre Dame, IND.
Maguiña Chauca, J. Santiago, 1974, *La Revolución Indígena de 1885 en Huaraz y Ancash*, Huaraz.
Mallon, Florencia, 1980, Race, Class and the 'National Question' in the War of the Pacific, Electrostatic copy, Department of History, Marquette University, Milwaukee, Wisconsin.
Manrique, Nelson, 1978, 'Los movimientos campesinos en la Guerra del Pacífico', *Allpanchis Phuturinqa, Revista del Instituto de Pastoral Andina* (Cuzco, Perú) 11/12: 71–101.
Manrique, N., 1979, 'La ocupación y la resistencia', *Reflexiones en Torno a la Guerra de 1879*, Jorge Basadre, ed. Lima.
Marx, Karl, 1963, *The Eighteenth Brumaire of Louis Bonaparte* [1852] New York.
Marx, Karl, 1967, *Capital, A Critique of Political Economy*, Volume 1, [1867] New York.
Marzal, Manuel M., S. J., 1971, *El Mundo Religioso de Urcos, un Estudio de Antropología Religiosa y de Pastoral Campesina de los Andes*, Cuzco.
Marzal, M., 1977, *Estudios sobre Religión Campesina*, Lima.
Meza, Ladislao F., 1928, *Dictadura Atusparia*, Huaraz.
Michaud, Andrée, 1970, 'La religiosidad en Qollana', *Allpanchis Phuturinqa, Revista del Instituto de Pastoral Andina* 2: 7–17.
Ossio, A., Juan M., ed., 1973, *Ideología Mesiánica del Mundo Andina*, Lima.
Pásara, Luis, 1970, 'Situación tributaria del "indígena" entre 1821 y 1871', *Revista Campesina* 3: 53–51.
Piel, Jean, 1973, 'Rebeliones agrarias y supervivencias coloniales en el Perú del siglo XIX', *Revista del Museo Nacional* (Lima) 39: 301–314.
Pike, Frederick, 1967, *The Modern History of Peru*, New York and Washington.
Ponte Gonzáles, Alfonso, 1945, *Por la senda, breve ensayo historico-biografico*, Lima.
Quijano, Aníbal, 1979, *Problema Agrario y Movimientos Campesinos*, Lima.
Reina Loli, Manuel S., 1969, 'Causes del movimiento camiesino de 1885', *Revista Campesina* 2: 31–47.
Reyna, Ernesto, 1932, *El Amauta Atusparia*, Lima. [Originally published in *Amauta* (Lima), Volumes 26, 27, and 28, 1929–30. Republished in a facsimile edition by Ediciones Limitadas, Universidad Nacional Mayor de San Marcos, Lima, 1977.]
Sallnow, Michael J., 1974, 'La peregrinación andina', *Allpanchis Phuturinqa, Revista del Instituto de Pastoral Andina* (Cuzco, Perú) 7: 101–142.
Spalding, Karen, 1980, 'Class structures in the southern Peruvian highlands, 1750–1920', *Land and Power in Latin America, Agrarian Economies and Social Processes in the Andes*, Bejamin S. Orlove and Glynn Custred, eds. New York and London.
Stein, William W., 1961, *Hualcan: Life in the Highlands of Peru*, Ithaca, NY.
Stein, William W., 1974, *Countrymen and Townsmen in the Callejón de Huaylas, Perú: Two Views of Andean Social Structure. Special Studies Series Number 51*, Council on International Studies, State University of New York at Buffalo, Buffalo, New York.
Stein, William W., 1978, 'Town and country in revolt: fragments from the Province of Carhuaz

on the Atusparia Uprising of 1885 (Callejón de Huaylas, Perú)', *Actes du XLIIe Congrès International des Américanistes* 3: 171–187, Paris.

Stein, William W., 1980a, 'Rebellion in Huaraz: the newspaper account of an "obscure" revolt in Peru', *Dialectical Anthropology* 5: 127–154.

Stein, William W., 1980b, The Limits of Peasant Movement: Leaders, Followers, and Allies in the Atusparia Uprising of 1885, Perú. Paper presented in a conference on Peasant Production and the Evolution of Social Systems, University of Iowa, Iowa City. Typescript. Department of Anthropology, State University of New York at Buffalo, Amherst, New York.

Stein, William W., 1980c, The Military Apparatus Reports: The Peruvian Forces of Order Confront the Pesantry in the Atusparia Uprising of 1885. Typescript. Department of Anthropology, State University of New York at Buffalo, Amherst, New York.

Stein, William W., 1980d, Newspapers as a Data Base for Ethnohistory: Studying an Andean Peasant Movement of 1885. Typescript. Department of Anthropology, State University of New York at Buffalo, Amherst, New York.

Stein, William W., 1981, The Role of Non-Peasants in a Peasant Revolt: Mestizos and Indians in Nineteenth Century Perú. Paper presented at the Annual Meeting of the American Anthropological Association, Los Angeles. Mimeographed. Department of Anthropology, State University of New York at Buffalo, Amherst, New York.

Valladares, Manuel, and Jean Piel 1977, 'Sublevación de Atusparia', *Los Movimientos Campesinos en el Perú: 1879–1965*, Wilfredo Kapsoli, ed. Lima.

Vázquez, Mario C., 1964, The Varayoc System in Vicos. Comparative Studies of Cultural Change, Cornell-Perú Project, Department of Anthropology, Cornell University, Ithaca, New York.

Villanueva, Víctor, 1973, *Ejército Peruano: Del Caudillaje Anárquico al Militarismo Reformista*, Lima.

Wolf, Eric R., 1966, *Peasants*, Englewood Cliffs, NJ.

The Cristiada: *peasant war and religious war in revolutionary Mexico, 1926–9*

JEAN A. MEYER

Writing about the *Cristiada* in this volume, I am somewhat in a quandary. While this great war of Catholic peasants in Mexico certainly qualifies for inclusion in a collection on rural revolt, it was at the same time wider than a 'peasant' war as it was an expression of many concurring conflicts. Above all it was a struggle between church and state. It was national and international at the same time. It involved the Mexican Revolution, the agrarian reform, the oil companies, the army and the politically active Catholics of the urban middle classes as well as hundreds of thousands of peasants. It was also part of a diplomatic and political history in which Mexico, Washington and Rome played major rôles. Even though the fighters in arms were essentially the rural guerrilla (*cristeros*), it would be a mistake to separate them from all these many different connections and social groups, especially from the militant Catholics of the cities and the moral as well as material support they had received from almost the entire female population of Mexico, regardless of class.

I therefore beg the reader to bear these connections in mind, even if in the following pages I shall necessarily concentrate on the rural revolt proper.

Religion and history

In his book about the German Peasant War Ernst Bloch wrote:

> Although the economic desire is the most sober and constant, it is not the only one, nor the most persistently powerful, or the most privileged motive of the human soul, above all not in times of religious upheaval... In this way a purely economic analysis is insufficient... to solve the deeper meanings of human history, which flares up at this point, ... to bring it down to earth, to relieve it of its specific character, to reflect upon it and to deprive it of its reality by pushing it into the realm of the purely ideological [Bloch, 1966: 61f.].

It is in the light of my reading of Bloch that I understand religious phenomena and consider them in three dimensions: cosmological, institutional, and personal. Suffice it now to note the close relationships between certain social strata and certain religious attitudes. In our case, this is between early twentieth century Mexican rural society and a specific form of Roman Catholicism. It would be wrong to single out the religious elements without asking, why did they play such a crucial rôle in the *Cristiada*, integrating, as they did, the social, economic and political aspects into a totality that expressed itself in sudden armed rebellion. It may not be human consciousness that determines reality, but reality that determines consciousness; however, it is also true, in reverse dialectics, that consciousness determines social existence.

In the analysis of the peasant masses that fought the great war of 1926–29 in Mexico, I do not mean to dismiss statistics, economic models and sociological systems, but to understand this history it is also necessary to probe into the lost or forgotten mental world of the common people who leave so few records of their thoughts. Yet, sociology and ideology will not suffice here. The former tells us how mentality forms itself whereas for the latter, mentality is the matrix. However, 'mentality' itself does not offer any more an easy solution of explaining events by intention. It will only pose the question of responsibility in new ways, by raising doubts about explanations that assume that a social group such as the priests who roused the Christian peasants actually manipulates an ideology to its profit.

The rural masses were not devoid of their own ideas and traditions. They were the only ones who started the uprising in 1926 and they alone sustained it for three years. Religion was a fundamental element of their mentality, their manners, their thought and their actions. More cultural than ideological, more emotional than rational, it supplied them with a particular coding guiding their reactions to challenges. Rooted in the past and sensitive to the present they were much less concerned about the future, letting it take shape at the moment of great events, such as the revolution of 1926.

The Cristiada

It may be useful to recite briefly the historical frame of reference to the thesis which follows. To start with, the conflict between state and church was typical of all western countries in the nineteenth and twentieth century, as for example the *Kulturkampf* in Germany, and the fights about separation of church and state in the French Third Republic. It was a similar conflict that re-emerged in Mexico during the revolution (1910–1940), and reached its first apogee in 1926. In the course of a long tug-of-war, aggravated by national and international political crises, the state put the church up against the wall, and the latter, rather than surrender, retaliated with redoubled effort. Maintaining that under the new legislation its functioning was impossible, the Church decided to suspend all religious services. It was a brutal measure, similar to the one taken three hundred years before by a Mexican prelate against a viceroy. The whole country was placed under interdict, with silenced bells, suspended liturgy, and secretly administered sacraments, because the government in response to this 'strike' of religion had outlawed private religious service. Children were not baptized, marriages not consecrated, confession not heard. People 'died like dogs in the streets. It was almost better to die in battle' [Meyer, *1980a: 95–7; 1980b: 232–85*].

In this way it may be seen that state and church provoked the uprising of the *cristeros*. Once the services were suspended and once religious persecution had been introduced, an autonomous process of peasant mobilization took place which resulted in the uprising. Religious services were suspended on 31 July 1926 and the first riots took place on 2 and 3 August. Between then and All Saints there were some thirty outbursts all over the country, which were easily crushed by the army. However, in November and December tensions rose and in the first days of 1927 all of the west-central area was up in arms. Every village witnessed the same dramatic scenes. It is not very important who gave the orders. Even the *Liga Nacional de Defensa de las Libertades Religiosas*, a Catholic lay political organization, which actually did, would not have thought of acting before the many sporadic riots of 1926. Now it wanted only to exploit the movement, using it to rise to political power on the shoulders of the masses. The League gave the uprising no leaders, no material aid, and no money [*Meyer, 1980a: 50–95*].

The slowness and inefficiency of politicking shamed the traditionally quietistic villagers, their nerves already on edge because of the suspension of church services, into open warfare. Little did they realize what they were letting themselves in for. At the beginning of the mass uprising in January 1927 unarmed men and women of all ages gathered as though for a pilgrimage and deposed, amidst general rejoicing, the old authorities, and elected new leaders. Once the movement had spread to the villages of a large area, the government began to react swiftly. It concentrated armed forces systematically to pacify one village after the other. For forty-five days 'it was not a war but a hunting party', as one general remarked [*Meyer, 1980a: 126–35, 169–79*].

With these atrocities, the war inexorably escalated, fuelled by government oppression and by deadlock in the ecclesiastical dispute. In the summer of 1927 observers counted twenty thousand *guerillos* fighting in spontaneous and unorganised detachments of between twenty-five to five hundred in their own location where they could rely on native backing whilst working in the fields and fighting against the government. In a three year war the situation gradually deteriorated for the government. By June 1929 church and state had been forced to come to agreement, religious services were resumed, and within weeks the war was over. By this time, the *cristeros* counted some fifty thousand men and it seemed that they were invincible. No tactics of scorched earth, no punitive expeditions, and no deportation of civilians with widespread terror could succeed in cutting them off from their popular support. Although everyone, whether armed or unarmed, suffered incredibly, they faced their fate as a Biblical trial. The cristeros were the new Maccabees and the villagers the Israelites suffering flight, exile and persecution.

When church services began, the war ended as spontaneously as it had started. The fighters returned home, still poor, and even poorer than if they had never left. This ending to the uprising surprised as many observers as had its beginning. They foresaw a painful and gradual return to the normal and a growth of banditry, which was to be only a logical consequence of the three years spent as vagabond guerillas, and also the usual transition in Mexican revolutions. Nothing like it happened. By September 1929 there was not a single *cristero* in arms and not one bandit in the mountains. This was all the more surprising since many of the fighters had returned home very embittered. They felt that the government had got away too lightly, and they resented that the *cristeros* were never consulted during the negotiations, much as if they had never forced the government to give way [Meyer, 1980a: 199–353].

To complete the story, let us add a few sociological details. Mexico was a country of some 15 million inhabitants two thirds of whom were concentrated on the central plateau. The 50,000 *cristeros* came from this most densely inhabited plateau. The *Cristiada* was a peasant movement and the most important of the guerila wars during the whole thirty years of the Mexican Revolution. It was *Zapatismo* on a massive scale, encompassing the whole of old Mexico [Womack, 1969] from the West to a line connecting Mazatlan and Tehuantepec (see map no. 5). This rural Mexico rose in a *zapatista* tradition of guerilla war, mobilizing as many men as had guns and relying on the civilian population for supplies, military intelligence and communications. The Zapata rebellion had been limited to the state of Morelos and environs. At its height it counted ten thousand men. By contrast, at the end of the war there were five times as many *cristeros*.

There was no other peasant insurrection of such size in the course of the Mexican revolution. For a parallel, one has to go back over a hundred years to the September 1810 uprising led by the priest Hidalgo. January 1927 and September 1810 were as alike as were the guerilla war of 1811–14 and the *Cristiada*. In neither case can rural uprising be separated from national history, nor can the peasants in arms be split off from other classes of society.

The peasantry is of course not a social class, even if at times it seems to display its autonomy in motivations, organizations and action. It is perhaps altogether inappropriate to talk about classes in the context of the Cristiada, since all rural strata were represented in it, with the signal exception of two. The great landowners (*hacendados*) were of course not, neither were the *agraristas*, the

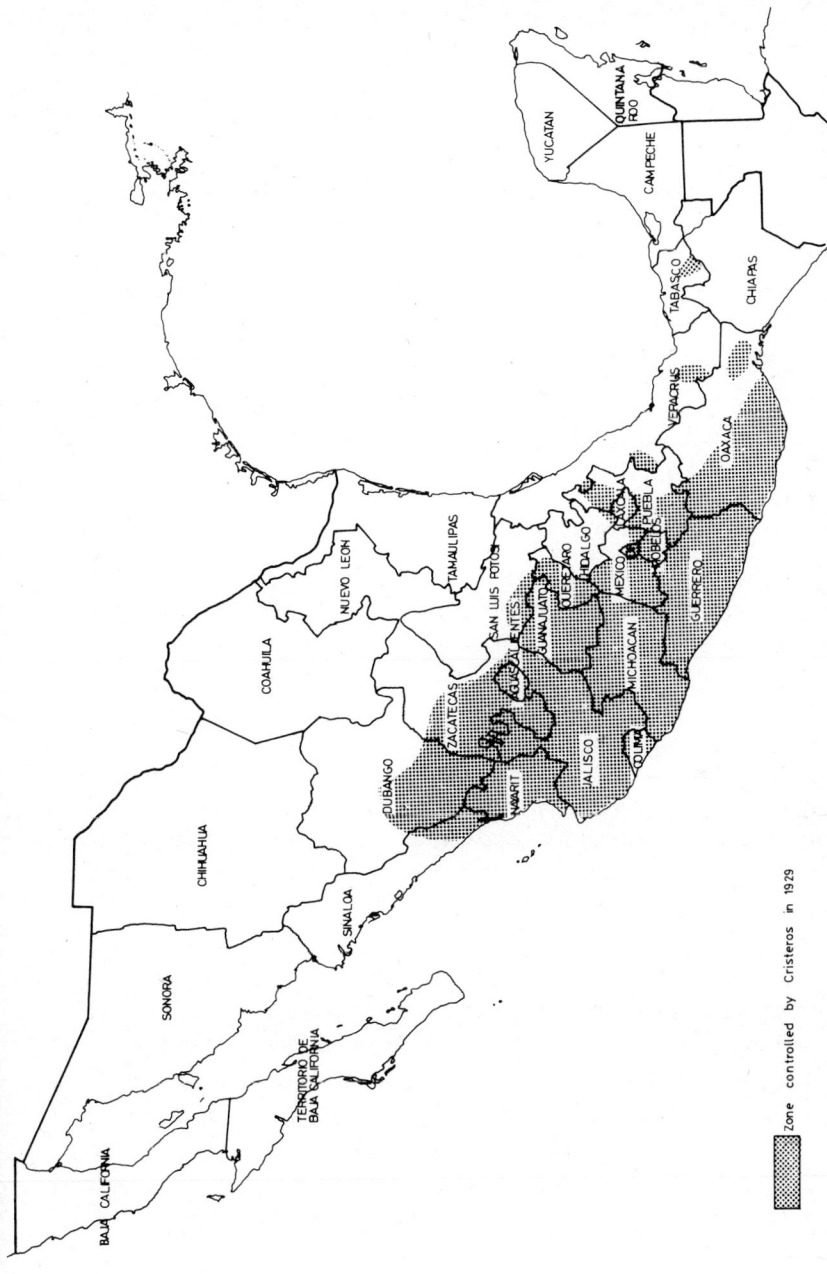

Map 5. The Cristiada in Mexico

beneficiaries of the agrarian form. We shall return to them.

The uprising cut deep into the fabric of society. Groups which in peacetime are usually noted by non-participation in national history and which display only local and particular interests, were pushed to the forefront of the events, as though a flood swept up the deep waters. The seriousness of the crisis was demonstrated by a unique harmony between the Indian communities and modern settler peasantries. In this segmented rural society each part was guided by different variables and had divergent interests marked by race, mix of blood, degree of urbanization, popular density and modernization. What if any were the common variables? Contrasts help to define them. The north of the country, with its peculiar white-urban American colonial frontier society was as conspicuously absent from the uprising as was the southwest, Yucatan and Chiapoas, the world of the Maya Indians. The *Cristiada* was fought on the Mexican high plateau, the cradle of Mexican nationality that had always been the spiritual and cultural focus for the Catholic Hispano-American *mestizo* [MacLachlan, 1980].

Rural class struggle and the 'clerical conspiracy'

Before examining the religious culture and its rôle in the dynamics of rural society, we have to ask ourselves, why the *Cristiada* cannot be explained by the agrarian reform and even less by the thesis of peasants manipulated by an institutional church.

The agrarian reform and class struggle

Because of the violent antagonism between *agraristas* and *cristeros*, I had been tempted to regard the uprising as a protest of peasants frustrated by ineffectual agrarian reform, or manipulated by great landowners (and their clergy). When I gave up this model of explanation, I did not intend to replace it by an exclusively religious motivation. I am, however, convinced that economic aspects of the collective mentality were embedded in a world of intermediate relations which cannot be forced into a simple determinist causality. The person of the *agrarista* and his rejection by the rural society is the proof of that.

The Mexican agrarian reform, which began in 1915 and has continued to our day, concerned in 1930 less than 500,000 peasants. This small minority – some 10% of all peasants – was, however, much more important than the mere numbers would imply, because it was concentrated in a few regions. Among these 500,000 *agraristas* were 30,000 men who served as political activists of 'Agrarianism', organized in self-defense militias at the disposal of the government. Never had a Mexican government had such an instrument of control in their hands: peasants, who in the heart of the rural community worked for the government against the old ideal of village solidarity and independence. Hostages of a government that held the strings to their land, the *agraristas* became for ten to twenty years the masters of community life. They were beneficiaries and at the same time victims of a situation in which they were wedged between the state and the rest of the peasants who considered them traitors and henchmen [*Friedrich, 1970*].

As a client of the state the *agrarista* was regarded a Judas at the very moment when religious conflict flared up between the peasants and the government. The *agrarista* could not change sides because he would lose his land. This actually happened to about three thousand *agraristas* who joined the *cristeros*. The *agrarista* was considered to be an agent who came from afar to ruin the already fragile and precarious unity of the rural community. Conflict between the *agraristas* and other villagers was universal and especially violent in close-knit Indian village communities.

Agrarian reform can be regarded best as a modernizing enterprise conceived by urban folk. Peasants wanted complete and total ownership which the land-reform never intended to give them. Therefore they saw it as a mere change of masters, and they preferred an individual and well-known local patron to an abstract and all-powerful state as their landlord. 'Do you know the mother of this government?' a peasant once asked *Juan Rulfo* [*1953: 102*]. That is why the old *Zapatistas* of Morelos refused to accept the land offered to them by the government as grants (*dotaciones*), insisting instead on having the land that belonged to them returned by way of *restitucion*. Faced with such refusals, the government had to give the land to people who were not peasants, but rather craftsmen, small merchants or settlers from elsewhere. In a village where everybody knew each other, no one accepted the validity of such property transactions whereby land was simply taken away from someone by the state and given to another who was often a stranger and an outsider. It was theft, and it carried a high political price. Thus the *agrarista* tended to be an alien from another world, and that only increased the local peasant hatred against him.

The *Cristiada* has been an occasion to settle old scores between the *agrarista* minority and the peasant majority. This does not make it into a reactionary movement manipulated by the great landowners.

The Church and the Cristiada

The church, which is to be understood as the official ecclesiastical authorities from the Vatican down to the bishops, has not spoken about the *cristeros* since 1929 for political reasons of its own. By contrast, the lay Catholic right wing has for a long time monopolized historical publications on this topic, whilst the non-Catholic Left has for obvious reasons always provided its own interpretation favorable to itself. In fact this version [*Jus, 1950–65*] amounts to an ideological reconquest of the *Cristiada* by the Right, just as the Vendée became in nineteenth century France the domain of the Catholic and royalist right wing. According to this consensus the *Cristiada* was the most spectacular manifestation of Catholic lay organisations linked closely to the bishops (and hence to Rome) and the clergy. Let us test this image on three levels: the Vatican, the bishops and the parish clergy.

The Vatican wanted peace and resented the anti-clerical offensive of 1925–26 since it threatened its own policy of political conciliation. Rome worked all the time towards another accommodation, such as the one finally agreed to in 1929. The bishops followed the Roman line with the exception of a small minority that enthusiastically hailed the war. The Vatican chose not to fight since its approach was political. It did not consider President Cales an Antichrist, as many Catholics did, but rather as a Philip the Fair or a Charles III of Spain with whom one had to keep negotiating. So churchmen at the top and the government kept negotiating throughout the war years, until they arrived at the *modus vivendi* of 1929.

If the war was not the Pope's it was neither the bishops', of whom only one openly defended and encouraged the armed uprising. Twelve were against it, and twenty-three remained neutral [Meyer, *1980a: 13–30, 1980b*]. Equally, the war was not supported by the overwhelming majority of the urban clergy who tended to ignore the crisis in the countryside. Village priests experienced the conflict in a different manner, and it was they who had to take sides [Meyer, *1980a: 30–50; 1980c: 291*]. They identified with the people of the countryside and their support for the rebellious peasants came as a major surprise to the social and ecclesiastical élites: both to the state and to their bishops. Rome explicitly prohibited the priests from supporting the uprising in any way, materially or morally by issuing a nuncial brief on 12 December 1927 [Meyer, *1980a: 18*]. Five village priests took an active part in the armed struggle, and about a hundred supported the *cristeros*. Another hundred opposed them and the rest of the 3,500 priests who stayed in Mexico, while another thousand had fled abroad, spent the war in the cities, as deportees of the government. Thus the villages were deprived of their clergy [Meyer, *1980a: 40, 49*]. This fact helps us to understand the relative autonomy of the movement, both in its widespread organisation and its internal dynamics and functions.

Religious culture in rural society

It is important now to examine the integral connections between a certain 'cosmic' Catholicism and the mentality of the peasantry in west central Mexico [Meyer, *1980c: 272–310*]. Natural conditions, the economy of property, labour and land use, and the social and political organization of the village community provided religion with an essential rôle, both as a world view and as the local church. Vicars and their curates played a vital, primary and irreplaceable role in the countryside. Whatever touched this church, was hotly debated in the community, and provoked a mass response. Peasants thought that without religion they could have no social life since the rites of passage within family and clan, regarded as basic to them, could not be carried out. The agrarian order was seen to rest upon family and the smallholding, which was supposed to transcend the opposition of classes. Class struggle existed, but rarely was it perceived of in terms of horizontal division of social groups. What really seemed to count with the peasants was a feeling for continuity of groups founded in the seventeenth century on an interdependence of interests in lineages, family ties, clientèles and loyalties. Groups of families were constituted according to different fortune and rank in such a way as to maintain a seeming unity by mutual relations in protection and other local services that inspire a sense of solidarity. The farm, the hamlet, the village, the canton, the clientèle of an oligarchic family were united by complex networks of blood relations, marriages, godfatherships, confraternities and the parish [*Meyer, 1980c: 8–43; Espin, 1978*].

In this context the so called 'ideological control' exercised by the church is a wrong formulation. Certainly, the influence of the parish priest was often decisive, and the role of religion primordial. However, the vicar was as much embedded in this society as he was controlling it. Most peasant clans made sure that they had at least a priest or a nun among their members. Priests were numerous, and they played many rôles especially as brokers and as social and economic innovators. But they were bound by family ties just as they were by local ones. Where property was held communally by the family, there labor, discipline, daily life and also religion were likewise shared rather than individualized.

A decade or so before the *Cristiada*, local conflicts had began to confront priests with the new men of the revolutionary state: the merchants, the civil servants, the *agrarista* chiefs. Their local squabbles were doubtless more profound than those at the national level where bishops opposed government, because they were more embedded in social reality.

Since religion seeks to bind together family, farm, work and village, when it is threatened, it seems that everything is. Communities mobilized in 1926 as soon as their church was closed and civil servants began to inventorize its contents. Peasants massed for a fight according to the same paternalistic rules of discipline that reigned in family and work. It mattered little, whether their priest was present or absent, hostile or favorable to the uprising. Defensive reflexes were at work without him. Hence it is unnecessary to propose a theory of conspiracy or manipulation: a whole social order defended itself in a global way. The extended family found themselves at the crossroads of small property, local patriotism and rural Catholicism on the one side and *agrarismo*, state intervention and anti-clericalism on the other. All the manifestations of central authority boiled down to one: the army. Thus the uprising could be seen as a total war because it was fought by a social totality that felt itself globally attacked.

Religion in the peasant war

The soldiers of the government christened their adversaries *cristeros* after their battle-cry '*Viva Cristo Rey!*' Then the whole war was called *Cristiada*. Considering that it began a few days after religious services had been suspended, and ended on the day they were resumed, the central rôle in this revolt of religion, which provided the language and the vehicle of its concepts and ideologies, cannot be denied.

The Kingdom (of Christ) was the focal point of these ideologies, mentalities and beliefs, centered in the specifically Mexican cult of the Virgin Mary, as the Virgin of Guadalupe, which is part and parcel of the popular national mind. Mexico is traditionally poor in civic historic consciousness, which belongs to the élite, and virtually all education has been Christian [Ricard, 1966; Kobayashi, 1974]. There are no other famous monuments in Mexico but churches, convents and episcopal palaces, so much so that governments have had to confiscate many of these for barracks, offices and gubernatorial palaces. Place-names are rural and religious, so that it is well founded to say: 'Mexico is the son of the priests' (*Mexico fue hijo de cura*). As Mircea Eliade has shown, in a world of suffering and labor the cross seems to be a reasonable mystery to believe in, whereby the kingdom of Christ is manifest in a crown of thorns.

The hope for the Kingdom and the heavenly Jerusalem, the faith in the Virgin of Guadalupe who appeared to the Indian Juan Diego to express her love for the people of Mexico were functional and highly effective. Politicians are unable to understand it, but the ecclesiastical establishment knows and distrusts that formidable energy which the *cristeros* were able to receive from it.

The motivation of the *cristeros*, uniting all their concerns, was a religious one, just as the crisis itself that marked the moment of revenge for centuries of history of bad government generally and of decades of revolutionary disorder especially. Between 1913 and 1920 peasants had been subjected to violence, famine and epidemics. Although one must appreciate the positive side of the Mexican revolution, one can not overlook the enormous human price that was paid for it, particularly by the rural masses.

The *cristero* movement caused an enormous social upheaval. Indians of the mountains, young men who had never before fired a gun, family fathers who had always been docile now rose in self-defense and in the defense of their religion, their icons and the church, which they and their forebears had built. For the first time they were united in a real common purpose: a desired social concord of peasants. Paradoxically, they fulfilled this dream by fighting against the so-called revolutionary government and dying for religion whilst chanting death to evil government – *Muera el Mal Gobierno!*.

Their attitude towards the state is not ours. That is why we tend to believe that peasant movements are backward-looking, that the Vendée was reactionary and the Afghan guerillas of 1980–81 are counter-revolutionaries. Our critique of bad government is different from theirs. For them, government was and is a necessary evil that has always existed and is called Ceasar. One has to render its due to it, but at the same time absolutely distrust it. In the countryside rebellion is rare but so is loyalty. Loyal are townspeople and *agraristas*.

These peasants, who did not rise against the *ancient régime* in 1910, found themselves in 1926 suddenly in full rebellion. This fact has often amazed Left intellectuals. How could these masses be mobilized? What was the secret of leadership? Well, exactly, there is no secret and the events cannot be repeated at will. The movement had its own peasant motivation, ideology and distinct aims, however disconcerting this fact may be to us, later observers and scholars.

From the outset, the insurgents expressed their intention to set up an independent government. These aspirations to village democracy and self-government were fostered by military necessity. Wherever liberated territories were secured against the federal army, civilian and military administration was established. Nevertheless the *Cristeros* did not plan to take over political power for good. Their aims were fulfilled by the resumption of religious services, even though they controlled an enormous military force after three years of ferocious war and devastating repression. In fact the war made Mexico similar to those former colonies where wars of national liberation have been fought, such as Algeria, Indochina or Afghanistan.

The semi-autonomous existence of these movements and their religious dimensions are essentially irritating elements, because the paradox that the popular masses are 'counter-revolutionaries' is clearly untenable. That is why many of us tend to employ all too readily reductionist explanations of manipulation and conspiracy. Or else, such ridiculous images are called upon as the fanaticism, the mental retardation, the illiteracy or the religious alienation of the masses which is supposed to have made them an easy prey to reactionary and ecclesiastical manipulation.

Although the *cristeros* were able to serve the cause of the institutional church, thereby offering hope to the Catholic right wing, they in fact kept their autonomy, their own logic and their own particular aims. One hears much about the passivity of peasants, their being subject to manipulation and acceptance of paternalism. The *Cristiada* offers an example to refute all that. These Mexican peasants were neither passive nor submissive. Their armed struggle was an expression of the long term consistence of their ideology founded on religion. It was an uprising of oppressed and exasperated people who had no other vision of the world but a religious one, which was neither alienated nor totally inefficient. As such the *cristeros* also saw history as a prelude to the Second Coming. They believed in the mystery of original sin whereby Satan was active in history. Saints and martyrs were thus needed to counteract him and bring history to its fulfillment. Is this concept so very different from the laicized versions of contemporary revolutionaries? [*Meyer, 1980c: 296f, 301f*].

References

Bailey, David, 1974, *Viva Cristo Rey! The Cristero Rebellion and the Church-State Conflict in Mexico*, Austin, Texas.
Bloch, Ernst, 1966, *Thomas Münzer als Theologe der Revolution*, Frankfurt.
Espin, Jaime – Patricia de Leonardo, 1979, *Economia y societad en los Altos de Jalisco*, Mexico.
Friedrich, Paul, 1970, *Agrarian Revolt in a Mexican Village*, ed. 1, Chicago.
Jus, publishers; some 30 publications related to the subject.
Kobayashi, Joseph, 1974, *La education como conquista*, Mexico.
MacLachlan, Colin – Jaime Rodriquez, 1980, *The Forging of the Cosmic Race: A Reinterpretation of Colonial Mexico*, Berkeley.
Meyer, Jean, 1974, *Apocalypse et révolution au Méxique 1926–1929*, Paris.
Meyer, Jean, 1980, *La Cristiada*, ed. 7, Mexico:-
    1980a: Vol. I La guerra de los Cristeros
    1980b: Vol. II El conflicto entra la Iglesia y el Estado
    1980c: Vol. III Los Cristeros.
Ricard, Robert, 1966, *The Spiritual Conquest of Mexico*, Berkeley.
Rulfo, Juan, 1953, *El llano en llamas*, ed. 1., Mexico.
Womack, John Jr., 1969, *Zapata and the Mexican Revolution*, New York.

Religion, rebellion, and working class consciousness in Bolivian tin mining communities

JUNE NASH

In the competition for the souls of indigenous people of the Americas, missionaries, spiritual leaders of the pre-conquest society, viceroys, governors, and populist leaders have tried for over four hundred years to create a sense of dissonance between the views they propose and other contending world views. This has been a means of promoting and maintaining exclusive authority and leadership. The people of the mining communities in highland Bolivia have resisted these attempts to wipe out their own beliefs [cf. *Nash, 1979*]. Mining families relate to a superhuman world of saints, devils, deities, and enchanted beings with which they live in the mine, the encampment, and the region. They tend to encapsulate the widely disparate, apparently contradictory ideologies to which they have been exposed in a unitary world view. They accomplish this not by syncretising indigenous and colonial beliefs with modern ideologies, but by separating out and assigning a separate place, time, and context in which each is appropriate. Tuesday, Fridays, the week of Carnival, and the month of August are the appropriate times for giving special recognition to the Pachamama, the ancient space-time concept immanent in the earth, and for the enchanted demons and spirits. Sundays and saints' days are devoted to the Catholic God and saints. May first and national holidays are set aside for remembering events in labor history. The settings for these celebrations are also distinct. While the entry level of the mines may contain a saint's niche and mass may be celebrated by the priest for the patron saint of the mine, no miner will mention the name of the Lord, the Virgin Mary, or of saints below level zero for fear of angering Supay, the Lord of the Hills, in his domain.

The technique of syncretizing elements as developed by the Spaniards in the early years of conquest is alien to the indigenous way of thinking. It relates to a mode of thinking that accepts only a single, hicrarchically defined system of ideas. Indigenous thought is capable of entertaining coexistent and apparently contradictory world views. The identification made between figures and concepts in the two systems, such as the transmogrification of Supay as the Devil, and Pachamama as the Virgin Mary, is only superficial, and as one becomes familiar with the culture, people deny the fit. In periods of stress, the calendar of

The belief system

The ritual cycle in Oruro is structured on two axes, one dealing with agriculture, the earth, and the Pachamama, the other with mining, the underground, and Supay. The overlay is Spanish colonial and post-Independence Catholicism, but the deeper structuring is pre-conquest agricultural rites, concerned with preserving the fertility of the land and maintaining harmony with the supernatural. The miners fit their industry into the old structure, maintaining equilibrium by sacrificial offerings to Supay for the mineral they extract.

Ritual time relates to the preindustrial agricultural cycles. The warming of the earth ceremonies in June with the onset of the cold dry season, the preparation of the soil in August for the planting in September, and even Carnival, the season for harvests and joy, relate to an agricultural culture. It is not as clear, however, that space is structured in terms of any significant social groupings in the four quarters of the compass. The shrines devoted to the monsters of the myth related above stand like sentinels at these compass points. But movement and activities in other ceremonial occasions relate to the location of work and residence.

Although miners defer to Supay in their productive base within the mines, the cycle of Pachamama is still the most pervasive. The *ch'alla* is performed as an offering to the Pachamama at all life-crisis ceremonies, inaugurations of new houses, work sites, and public buildings, and almost every social gathering. Alliance to the Pachamama relates the individual to life, while a contract with Supay brings luck and the chance windfall that might change one's circumstances but inevitably causes death in a short time. The Awicha tempers the anger of Supay. When a thundering blast of dynamite shakes the underground and threatens a cave-in, miners call on the Awicha, who figures as a companion of Supay and who is their intermediary with Supay.

This complementarity of the two forces is found along other dimensions of contrast. The Pachamama is a female force of continuity in subsistence production. Offering to her ensures continuity in the returns from crops and flocks. The offering of chicha, or in some more elaborate ceremonies, the fetus of a llama, guarantees equilibrium in the productive and reproductive forces. Supay is clearly a masculine force. Offerings to him are in the form of propitiation to gain his good will. They are not for maintenance of a *status quo* but for enrichment from the hidden treasures of the hills. A live, white llama is sacrificed and its heart interred in the mines to gain his good will twice yearly, during Carnival and on July 21, the eve of the month of Supay. It is both an offering to satisfy his voracious appetite so that he will not eat the men who work the mine, and a request that he yield to the workers some of the riches of the mine. Ceremonials to him are characterized by abandoned, passionate dancing, drinking, and chewing coca. Considering the peasant's awareness of the need to limit their flocks in order to maintain the life of the herd, it is perhaps justifiable to see in the offering of the aborted fetus to the Pachamama a recognition of human intervention to assure an equilibrium between the food resources and the animals that graze on her pastures. In contrast, the offering of a mature animal is a direct substitute for the human lives that Supay might otherwise claim.

Paralleling the opposition of the earth and the underworld is the cosmic equilibrium of the moon, as the force that generates cold, and the sun that warms the earth and the people. The conflict of the two cosmic forces comes to a climax at the time of the winter solstice, June 21, and of the summer solstice, December 21. Human ritual intervention is necessary at these times to ensure balance.

The celebration of the winter solstice is in conjunction with the fiesta of San Juan, June 24. As happens so often in Latin America, the Christian calendar provides a framework within which indigenous people accomodate their own ceremonies. Some miners have heard the story of how San Juan entered into competition with Jesus Christ to split a rock by blowing a wind so cold it could cause frost. Campesinos celebrate the day by burning the stubble grass over their fields, and in this way they help the Pachamama maintain the balance of heat and cold. Miners to this day celebrate the eve of San Juan by lighting fires around which they gather to drink and dance. For the campesinos, lighting the fires signifies the maintenance of fertility for their land and their flocks, and each faggot that they burn stands for the life of one animal for the year. The miners have generalized the theme of maintaining an equilibrium such that life itself can continue on earth.

For the miners, June 24 has a particular significance, since it was on the eve of San Juan in 1967 that General Barrientos sent in the troops to massacre the inhabitants. Barrientos, who had seized the presidency in November 1964, lowered wages and ordered the troops into the mines. In an attempt to recoup their position, miners called a meeting of the Federation of Mine Workers' Unions June 24 at the Siglo XX Catavi encampment at a time when Che Guevara was still engaged in guerrilla warfare in Santa Cruz.

On the eve of San Juan, June 23, delegates began to arrive in Llallagua, the town adjacent to Siglo XX mine. Band music greeted the visitors, who joined the workers of Siglo XX in the traditional fiesta of San Juan. Simon Reyes, one of the union leaders of Siglo XX (1967) described the evening's festivities:

> The enthusiasm for the night of San Juan was linked with the welcome to the delegates, demonstrating in everything a spirit serene and confident for the outcome of the meeting. The enthusiasm was prolonged until 4:30 a.m. when the people returned to their homes while some workers prepared to go to work.

It was at that moment that the military force, along with the national guard, armed with machine guns, mortars, and hand grenades, entered the encampment and attacked people who were still dancing in the streets. They fired machine guns and threw grenades into houses with sleeping occupants. In the streets everything that moved was fired on, even dogs. As one miner told me – 'And what kind of politics does a dog have?'

News of the atrocity seeped out slowly. *La Patria*, the daily newspaper of Oruro, reported on the following day that there were sixteen dead and 171 wounded, and that the operation had been carried out by the mining police, the Department of Criminal Investigation (DIC) and Rangers with airplanes circulating overhead. Colonel Prudencia, in charge of the operation, announced that the army had occupied the mine centers of Siglo XX and Huanuni with the object of capturing the pro-guerrillas in the encampment who were stirring up the union leaders. Later the papers revealed that at least 87 were killed, including men, women, and children, and there were many wounded. An eyewitness at the funeral assured me there were many more; he told me that the number of caskets he saw going by looked like a stream of ants, and that there were burials in common ditches of bodies so destroyed by bazookas that they were no longer intact. The ovens that were used formerly to dispose of the dead after such massacres were no longer in operation thanks to the new technology of the sink-and-float plant, and so there was no longer an efficient way of disposing of the evidence left by the atrocity.

The massacre of San Juan was more destructive than any previous terror let loose in the mines. The tactic seemed to be to inspire fear in the mining community, where the buildup of resentment against Barrientos was the greatest, at a time when Che Guevara was still operating in Santa Cruz. It was in no way a selective operation to eliminate guerrilla sympathizers, as the colonel in charge of the opposition claimed, nor an attempt to rid the community of labor agitators, but rather a totally indiscriminate attack on a whole class in order to break their resistance to the military.

December 21, 1942, was chosen as the day to stage a demonstration for higher wages in the mining encampment of Siglo XX-Catavi. The Federation of Mine Workers' Unions had just been organized the year before. With rising food prices coinciding with the inflated price of tin during World War II, the miners were determined to improve their lot by united action. Ceferino, who started work as a child during the Chaco War in the Siglo XX-Catavi mines, told me about this event.

> Then came the strike of 1942. We had fifteen to twenty days of strike. The company announced, 'The Miners who do not want to work will be killed'. They paid every man who went to work a bonus of two hundred pesos. With this tip, almost all of the

workers came in. Then the massacre came on December 21. Five hundred to eight hundred of the seven thousand workers were thrown out of work or killed for failure to conform. On the morning of the massacre, the workers of Cancañiri, Socavón, and Miraflores united at ten o'clock. There were six thousand of us. We were going down to the administration, calmly, without any weapons. We were a mixed lot, women, children, men. Maria Barzola was a delegate for the pallires. When she approached the soldiers, seizing the Bolivian flag when the men fell back fearing an attack, they shot her. We were about four hundred meters from the office, and they were firing on all of us. We couldn't advance, and so we escaped. We were surprised by the attack on us.

The choice of these seasonal transition dates for demonstrations is not coincidental. In 1970, the spring equinox on September 21, a time to celebrate youth and love in Bolivian tradition, became the chosen date for students and workers to enter into the streets in a major protest demonstrating against the government of General Ovando for his treatment of the guerrilleros of Teoponte. In the preceeding month, leaders of the National Army of Liberation (ELN) of Che Guevara had gone to Teoponte in a desperate attempt to off-set the turn to the right that Ovando's government had taken in the preceeding weeks. Failing to capture the ambassador of the United States, whom they had planned to hold hostage in order to strengthen the bargaining position of the Left in the government, their members, whilst sleeping, were captured by the armed forces. In captivity, a dozen of their leaders were blown up by hand grenades and bazookas. Fearing to reveal the cowardice with which the army overcame the rebels, Ovando resisted the pleas of parents and priests to surrender the bodies, at least until pressure had mounted to fever pitch in the early weeks of September. Finally he yielded, and the mutilated corpses were delivered to students in the Universidad Mayor de San Adrés. Bolivian popular outrage grew, and a procession of students and workers made a public demonstration on September 21. Shortly after, the government was ousted by a right-wing junta led by General Rogelio Miranda, who proved so unpopular even with the armed forces that the way was paved for the presidency of Juan José Torres, for Miranda had been the very General in charge of the San Juan Massacre.

Carnival

Carnival draws together myths and rituals of Christian and indigenous belief in ceremonies involving all the workers' unions and fraternal groups in the locality. Coordination depends on a municipal organizing committee but the real impulse comes from dance groups from the town as well as from occupational groups.

Each act of Carnival follows historical precedents relating to pre-conquest or early conquest days. The traditions of indigenous and Spanish populations are inter-woven as distinctive strands, whose elements are not as homogenised. Each appear in dances and dramas to interpret past and present. There are two main dramas. The first is the triumph over the monsters sent by Huari, which took place sometime before the conquest. Over the centuries it has assimilated post-conquest spirits and powers. The second is the conquest of the Indians by the Spaniards, with subjugation as labourers in mines and vine-yards. The first drama is played out in the Devil dance and in the propitiation of all the mythical monsters. The second is enacted on the plaza during Carnival Sunday by the Children of the Sun, as well as by dancing the *Diablada* and the *Morenada*.

Carnival dancing is both a propitiation of supernatural forces by temporarily assuming the powers that they represent. The magic of identification is contained in the mask. As long as dancers wear the mask, they are the figure impersonated. On Sunday the dancers remove their masks and dance under arches constructed on the plaza in front of the church of the mineshaft. Laden with silver, they enter the church to pray. Although the magical element is not always assumed by dancers today, a sense of transformation remains in the dance as they perform impossible feats, leaping and cavorting like devils; weaving to and fro whilst bearing the heavy suit of the Morenada; pole-vaulting as Tobas in long procession for several miles from the north of the town to the plaza of the church of the mineshaft, where the Virgin is ensconced. Dancers practice ardously from the first Saturday of November, and continue each Saturday until the Carnival in February or March.

The dances of the *Diablada* and the *Morenada* are especially important to the consciousness of labourers in relation to their work. Both dances show whereby dancers move from representing themselves as miners or slaves, accompanied by a single devil in each group, towards a configuration of prohibited but desired incarnation of evil. The devil mask worn by *Diablada* dancers combines the horns of Christian figures with three serpents which sprout from the forehead. The red-coverall worn by the dancers is decked with a tunic emblazoned with cut glass jewells and an apron of linked coins. Through the streets and up to the plaza leap the devil dancers with their temptresses, men dressed as women in satin and jewells, who lure men to work for the devil.

The *Morenadas* represent black slaves who once worked in the mines but were later transferred to the vineyards at low altitudes where, it is said, they could better endure the climate. The mask they wear caricatures negroid features, with flaring nostrils, protruding lips, and bulging eyes. The lead dancer, representing the *cabecilla* (foreman) is the most elaborately dressed. He carries a pipe and cracks the whip as he leads the other dancers. They carry jewelled flasks from which they drink the wine they were forced to produce. Their costume is like a wine cask, a synecdoche for the transformation they undergo in the dance from enslavement to the embodiment of joy made possible by the liberating effects of liquor.

The devil dance captures the essence of Carnival in Oruro. According to legend, the dance began when a miner fell asleep after the *ch'alla* to the devil in the mine. As he woke up, he saw the devil himself dancing and he followed him, dancing out of the mine. After that, the miners continued to dance in the streets following the *ch'alla* on the Friday of Carnival. The dance evolved from being a group of miners with a devil or two among their ranks towards one in which devils predominate. At first, miners were dancing in homage to the devil, according to one of the miners who has kept the mask he wore as a dancer ten years ago. In the dance the miners released their hopes, ambitions, fears, and joys. As the dance progressed, drawn to the devil, or Supay, who danced among them, they transformed themselves into the attractive, alluring figure to whom they paid homage. The dance is an act of devotion to the Virgin of the church of the mineshaft, in which dancers complain to her of their troubles, and finally give themselves up to joy as they receive her blessing.

The *Morenadas* reveal the deep impression made upon the indigenous population of slave labor in the mines. The choreography of the many *Morenada* dance groups tells the legend of a rebellion against a caporal in the vineyard called Maria Antoinette. A young black woman who was the delight of the old despot attracted the attention of the slaves. Burning with desire for her, they got the caporal drunk and then overthrew him in a rebellion. They forced the caporal to stamp on the grapes and move the winch, while they ridiculed him in satiric verses [*Alesandri 1968: 10*]. It is an incomplete rebellion, one in which the agent of oppression, not the forces of repression, is attacked and forced to take their position in the productive process.

Organization of dance groups provides institutional basis for important friendships and contacts. In Oruro there are four major groups among eighteen dance societies, each representing a major occupational confederation. The railroad workers and the miners form the largest contingents. The dance groups reinforce the solidarity of the work groups and link them to the community.

Two separate acts, divided by time and place but linked by the common elements involved, are the *ch'alla* to the Pachamama and to Supay performed during Carnival. The first takes place in most of the houses and yards of the townspeople at midday on the Tuesday of Carnival week. The second is performed inside the mines on Friday evening beginning about sundown and lasting until midnight. The first brings together the members of a household and assures their health and welfare, and the productivity of whatever subsistence crops they grow in their gardens. The second reinforces the solidarity of the work group and ensures the safety of men against accidents as well as their yield of minerals. In both cases offerings are made to gain the good will of spirits of earth and hills, through participation of all those involved in each setting.

In the inner recesses of the mine, just the work group of a section share their drink and coca with the Tío (the miners' name for Supay). When I was in Oruro, the *ch'alla* to the Tío had just been resumed after a five years' ban by Barrientos. Reenstatement of the *ch'alla* was taken to be a sign of greater freedom accorded to the miners by the regime of his successor, General Ovando, who had seized power in September 1969. The ingredients used in both *ch'allas* are liquor, coca, and cigarettes with dancing to the tune of a *chiranga*, similar to a mandolin, and of guitars.

During Carnival, and on 31 July, the offering to Supay should include the sacrifice of a llama or sheep. When tin barons Patiño, Hochschild, and Aramayo owned the mines before the Revolution of 1952 and nationalization, the sacrificial animal was purchased by the owner, who often attended. After nationalization the rituals continued. In fact, some of the miners complained that these rituals were performed in excess of the Tío's needs. Juan, whose autobiography I transcribed [*Rojas and Nash, 1976*] told me that going into the mine shortly after the revolution was like walking into a saloon. Such secular abuse of the ritual was curtailed in the latter part of the decade and, following military control in 1965, the rituals were entirely halted. It intensified the hatred miners felt for the regime of Barrientos. Although Ovando reinstated the rituals, his administration did not subsidize the cost of the llama. The ritual that I observed during Carnival was limited to hot beef stew brought into the mines by workers' wives. Not until the mine accidents of July did a complete *k'araku* take place (see below).

The Friday before Carnival is devoted to a *ch'alla* of the serpent at the southern end of town, and on the following Wednesday and Friday respectively, people on the north side of town attend to the toad and to the image of the condor. The condor is not one of the four monsters of the myth, but he is accorded the same treatment during his celebration. The special day for the serpent is on the Day of the Cross, May 3, and for the hoard of ants July 15. Each celebration combines a request for material goods, a house, a truck, good health or good fortune, with an offering of liquor, incense and a 'table'. In these active cults, people reveal the intensity of their desire for material improvement in their lives and their sense of the reciprocal balances in the universe. Most people I questioned said that they were successful in gaining the objects they requested of the enchanted images.

In contrast with celebrations in other places, Oruro Carnival processions were ordered with precise dance steps and lavish costumes. It is not a wild excess of sex and drink, but a precise channeling of some very deep passions and sentiments. It is both an expression of, and solace for, discontent.

In the main street on Carnival Sunday, a drama group of miners, friends and families from the encampment, who call themselves Sons of the Sun, present a play depicting the Conquest. Protagonists include Pizarro, Diego Almagro and his cohort, the priest Vicario Hernando Luque, the king of Spain, Atahualpa, king of the Incas, Hualla Huisa as chief diviner, and fifteen Nustas, or Inca maidens. The conquistadores are heavily bearded. The Spanish king and his priest wear pink gauze masks with brightly rouged cheeks and widely staring blue eyes. This contrasts with the unmasked faces of actors playing their Inca forebears without the need for falsification.

In the enactment of the death of Atahualpa, players reenacted their own conquest and subjugation. The drama reveals their rejection of this unjust act, and keeps alive the spirit of rebellion by repeating Pizarro's outrageous betrayal of his promise to release Atahualpa after he had received the royal treasure. The dialogue in Quechua language is an assertion of their own cultural survival in the face of Spanish domination. The effect of the drama is to reinforce resistance by enacting a moral triumph over unjust domination.

These are some of the events of Carnival, reenacted along the same pattern but always incorporating special features. In recognition of the flight to the moon in 1970 an astronaut danced with an American flag emblazoned on his space suit, and a machine gun in his hand. Carnival is always a time for cultivating one's luck, and overcoming the destiny to which one is assigned. It is a time for pursuit of the ordinarily unattainable. Good fortune is available to the lowliest. The only investment is faith plus a certain amount of ritual expenditure to secure the *aini* or reciprocal gift, due to the devout. The past is assessed and credits for the future are chalked up.

Carnival is often regarded as the drama of good over evil. After witnessing eight days of ceremonial offerings, processions, displays of faith in the Pachamama, the Virgin, the devil, and the enchanted images, my own view was that good and evil became totally blended. Fortune, power, riches, sex, strength, were available by appealing to the devil. But access to the values behind these desires required intermediacy of the Virgin, who now acquired her own court of devils as well as guardian angels. She, too, combined good and evil. Her very existence in the church of the mineshaft was due to a thief, Nena Nena, who by his veneration was able to transubstantiate her. Somewhat like Robin Hood, Nena Nena, the unemployed miner, who was forced to steal for a living, robbed the rich. Unlike Robin Hood, his First World prototype, he sold his goods to the poor, albeit only for a modest return. When one of his would-be victims turned upon him and stabbed him, he returned to his cave hollowed out of the mine hill, and there prayed to the Virgin. As he lay dying, she came to him in the form in which she is to be seen with the life-sized wooden painting which is housed at the altar of the church over the very opening of the mineshaft.

Why has Carnival not merely survived but also grown more elaborate over the years? Whenever people spoke about political repression and revolution, they concluded by asking me, 'But have you ever been here during Carnival?', and proceeded to describe past processions and their role in them. I sensed that it was not a shift in the dialogue but an extension of it. Carnival is an expression of a people's view of their history and an account of how they have transmuted their defeat into a triumphant statement of the value of survival and self-determination. Josermo Murillo Vacareza [*1969: 9*] says:

> The *Diblada* is a splendid transformation of the disenchantment that permeates the spirit of the pueblo, releasing the frustration from those forces that falsify its inner vitality. The daring and impetuous dance is the hidden impulse, equal to that of their ancestors, to demolish, fight, and subvert that which they oppose themselves to, whether to subjugation or inferiority; the epochal music is a stimulus to an insurgent movement, as a trumpet of continuity; its rich and beautiful clothing derives from a system of impoverishment, as if to say in the hyperbole of fired imagination, that we dare to believe that there is an end to it.

It would be simplistic to say that Carnival is a substitute for revolution. It is more accurate to say that it is a reminder to the people of the necessity for revolt when the historical conditions are appropriate, just as it is a denial of the misery and drabness of their everyday lives, and an expression of what they aspire to.

The month of Supay

The month of August is the time for the preparation of the land for planting in September. It is a time to propitiate the power of the hills, which is identified with both Supay and Huari, sometimes called Supay's father. Among the miners, the two beings are treated as one. It is simultaneously a time to recognize the Pachamama, since one must avoid the destructive potential of Huari at the same time that one wins the benefits of the earth's fertility. It is a time to ask for both fertility of the fields and mineral wealth from the mines.

The moratorium on the *k'araku* during the military occupation of the mines from 1965 was revoked in the year of 1970 when I lived in the encampment. In the first week of July, three young miners were killed at work. The workers asserted that the deaths were due to the failure in keeping up the ritual offering of the sacrificed llama to Supay. A delegation of workers urged the superintendent of the San José mine to permit them to carry out the ritual on the customary night of July 31, which was that very month. The superintendent agreed to this and offered to pay for the llamas when he saw that the men were reluctant to return to work. I arrived at 10:00 p.m. on the appointed evening. Many workers were gathered in level zero at the elevator shaft. One man offered me a drink from a plastic fish he wore suspended from a string around his neck. 'The k'araku is held in order that there be some development in the mine, or so that we might discover a vein that would benefit the company', he told me. 'If they [the managers] had come, we workers would want to work with greater enthusiasm and will. Here we are waiting for some improvement to take place so that all can benefit. But what benefit would it have? Only so that the administrators could take trips out of the country'. He went on to explain the sense of reciprocity played out in the rituals: 'We eat the mines and the mines eat us. For that reason, we have to give these rituals to the spirit of the hills so that he will continue to reveal the veins of metal to us so that we can live.' The miners blamed the deaths of the miners on the failure of management to permit them to carry out the regular rituals of sacrifice that fed the spirit of the hills and satisfied his appetite so that he would not eat the workers.

In the course of the sacrifice, the men call out to the Tío, the *awichas*, *machulas*, *tiyulas*, and throw the blood of the llama in all the danger points in the mine, the elevator, the winch, the machines, asking for safety and that there be no accidents in any of the work sites. The heart of the llama is buried near the image of Supay in a remote gallery of the mine where he could eat it in peace. The llama used in the sacrifice I attended was pregnant and the miners discovered the fetus when they butchered her. This was thrown on the pile of bones stripped clean in the banquet of baked flesh held on the following day. As the bones burned on the pile of faggots, surmounted by the fetus, a miner said to me:

> This is the luck of the working class. It is our thing because of our faith in the Tío Lucas. He is the owner of the mine. We walk with him. He takes care of us, and we arrive with him. He is still owner of the mine. Before, we worked with greater strength and without accidents. It is the fault of the security engineers that we had this accident. They are in collusion with the administration. We make claims without any effect.

Ritual and ideology

What is the meaning of these rituals and how do they relate to the new ideologies that express the class consciousness of the miners? These questions have to be answered on at least three different levels: (1) What happens with the people relating to each other in the scene? (2) How does the ritual relate these participants to other significant reference groups? (3) How has the significance of the ritual changed over time?

A simple Malinowskian functionalism helps us to answer the first question. The *ch'alla* integrates men within the work site and thus promotes the solidarity of the primary group. This is best expressed in the words of Manuel, a carpenter in the mine:

> This tradition inside the mine must be continued because there is no communication more intimate, more sincere, or more beautiful than the moment of the *ch'alla*, the moment when the workers chew coca together and it is offered to the Tío. There we give voice to our problems, we talk about our work problems, and there is born a generation so revolutionary that the workers begin thinking of making structural change. This is our university. The experience we have in the *ch'alla* is the best experience we have.

Manuel, who was one of the top leaders in the union before the Barrientos coup, was perhaps unusual in equating primary group solidarity with the basis for revolutionary action. Although it is a basic Marxist proposition about the beginning of class consciousness, many union leaders seem to negate it and often criticise traditional rituals. This may stem from the fear of deep-rooted levels of consciousness and self-determination that are not controlled through the bureaucracy of union management.

The second issue of how the ritual relates workers to other significant reference groups requires a historical perspective. In the days of the tin baron before the nationalization of the mines in 1952, the owners, especially Patiño, would come to the celebration of the *k'araku* and dance with the *palliris* and the men as they celebrated the feast. His administrators gave each miner a personal gift of a skirt or jacket, in return for which they gave him a lump of the richest metal they had uncovered in their work. This exchange of the *t'inka* (the management's gift to the worker) and the *achura* (the workers' gift of ore to the owners) symbolized the basic reciprocity in the labor relationship. It reinforced a set of paternalistic ties that gave the workers greater spirit to work and sacrifice themselves. In those days, the workers within each work group were paid according to a contract figured on the basis of the mineral content of the ores they produced. There was a great deal of competition between each work group to secure the richest vein, and the hostility engendered was worked out in witchcraft. An old miner who had worked in most of the mines of Bolivia and a copper mine in Chile, described these customs:

> The men in the mines who got high returns on their contracts were most often the targets of witchcraft. The miners used to go seek the shamans from among the campesinos who know more about this. These shamans have animal spirits. Here, and especially in Colquecharka, many miners use witchcraft to make their more fortunate companions lose the vein. They went into the mine with the shaman and they threw water with salt on the vein where their enemy was working and this made it disappear. Sometimes the miners knew they were being bewitched and they called on the Pachamama.

Other miners reported pouring the milk of a black burro mixed with garlic on the veins of their enemies to make them disappear. The miners also had to protect the veins against the 'evil eye' (*bankañowi*) of any workers entering their sector. When they struck a good vein, they sometimes slept in the mine to protect it. The miners never brought garlic into the mine, because this could make their own vein disappear since the Tío did not like it.

In short, hostile competition was intense, and the solidarity built up in the *ch'alla* was limited to the immediate group of men working on the same contract. Following the nationalization of the mines, the base pay was raised and equalized for all the mines, and the negotiation for the contract was carried out by the union agents in open bargaining procedures. Workers felt that one of the most important gains they made was to have the contracts figured openly with the superintendent of the mine, the mayordomo of the level, and the head of the work group witnessing the contract statement. After the revolution the contract was paid to work teams of two men rather than to a work gang, and it was based on total output measured in cubic feet regardless of mineral content. Thus the solidarity of the work group was weakened at the primary group level, but a larger unity was maintained in the work force as a whole as the union welded together not only the work units within a mine, but through the Federation of Mine Workers Unions of Bolivia (FSTMB) created a massive political force of all miners and, through the Workers Central of Bolivia (COB) linked miners to other industrialized workers.

During the period of nationalist solidarity within the populist revolutionary government, the *ch'alla* in the mines served as a recreation more than a point for mobilizing rebellion and focusing on dissatisfactions. This brief period of amicable labor-management relations came to an end with the Triangular Plan reorganization of the mines after 1960 and deteriorated still further after the military occupation of the mines by Barrientos in 1965. The miners say that Barrientos suppressed the *ch'alla* because he was afraid of the solidarity promoted in these drinking sessions. The suppression of the *ch'alla* added to the resentment of the workers against both management and the government.

Along with the suppression of the *ch'alla* came a sharp drop in the production of high quality ores. This was coincident with a falling off in exploration. Furthermore, the nationalized mining administration has never succeeded in developing work incentives. The wages of the workers were frozen at the level to which Barrientos had reduced them in 1965. This fact, coupled with rising salaries of administrators and army officers, has resulted in both alienation of the workers and stagnation in production. A brief respite came with the Torres regime in 1970 when wages were reinstated to the pre-1965 levels, but his presidency came to an end after ten months with the military coup of Colonel Hugo Banzer. The alienation of the worker expressed during the *ch'alla* reveals the complete transformation of the ritual from one in which worker-management solidarity was reinforced to one in which the ritual becomes the basis for communication of rebelliousness.

We have answered our third question, how the ritual has evolved over time, in the course of analyzing the changing structure of relations. This has not been a one-way street from paternalism to revolution. When the conditions were ripe for revolt in the past, especially in the early labor struggles of 1918 and during the Chaco War, the *ch'alla* became a point for mobilizing discontent. It did not come as a surprise when I learned that in 1918, when the management of the private mine of San José rejected the workers' petition for higher wages and union recognition, the workers chose the night of July 31 to declare the first strike recorded for the mine. Again, when there was extreme discontent over the Chaco War, the shrine of the Sapo was chosen as an assembly point. Recognizing this, the general ordered that it be destroyed.

The cycle of which I observed the latter stages in 1970 was one in which there was a shift from sponsorship of the rituals by the former owners and their foreign administrators, reinforcing an exploitative labor system, to a rejection of the belief and repression of the rituals of the *ch'alla* by the indigenous bureaucrats and technicians brought in after nationalization. These men may have opposed the rituals because of their fear of being identified with the Indian and chola classes from which they came. When the ritual was outlawed, the Tío was transformed into an ally of the workers. As one worker said, on the occasion of the *k'araku*, 'The Tío is the real owner here. The administrators just sit in their offices and don't help us in our work.' When Ovando permitted a limited *ch'alla* to take place in the 1970 Carnival, the men expressed some hope that their lot would improve, but the failure of the administration to make the traditional exchange and the impoverished nature of the celebration, because of insufficient funds, minimized the impact of the celebration. 'The Tío is still hungry', the miners said, 'and so are we'.

Assumptions about traditional and modern systems of belief often fail to capture the complexity of selective changes in symbol systems. The Tío is more important now in reference to accidents than as a generator of mineral wealth. This is tied to a contract system in which, after nationalization, the payoff depends on the total tonnage output rather than the mineral content of the ore. Its significance is directly related to this changing reality. The Tío is an explanation for the inexplicable, a rationale for the irrational destiny which is forced on the miner. Their faith in him enriches a barren existence of unremitting toil. In the colonial period, when he appeared before the workers, he had the face and figure of the enemy of their enemy, the devil, red-faced, horned, and dressed in the royal robes of a medieval underworld denizen. In the period of imperialist exploitation, he appeared as a gringo, wearing a cowboy hat, boots, red-faced, and larger than life. When one makes a contract with him, one is assured of riches even at the price of one's life, but he pays off with a greater certitude than government bureaucrats or officials. Supay transcends the medieval conception of the devil imported by the Spaniards; he is the source of wealth and desired power as well as the agent of evil. He is not only a projection of the fetishism of commodity production in capitalism, as one very imaginative ethnographer conjectures [*Taussig, 1980*], but a means to satisfy communal goals. The difference lies in whether the individual or the group as a collectivity enters into a contract with him. When a lone miner works with the devil in solitude, he will die within ninety days and his heirs will never enjoy the wealth he accumulates. In contrast, when the devil is given an offering by the miners as a group in the *k'araku*, he reveals to them the veins which all can work to make it possible for the mine to remain productive and sustain the people who live on it.

Supay is a multifaceted power neither all good nor all bad. As the central figure in Carnival, Supay is both an expression of the frustrations and anxieties in the lives of these people as well as a projection of their desire to overcome them.

Religious belief and political behavior

Pre-conquest beliefs provide deep roots for the people's sense of their identity and a baseline for their resistance to oppression by alien forces. Although this may lie at a nearly subconscious level, it nonetheless has a pervasive influence in determining the choice of timing for political acts of protest and consequently the reaction of the ruling group. The first strike in Oruro in modern times took place on July 31, 1918. Although there are no records to indicate how it started, I can imagine scenes such as I have witnessed on the occasion of much later *ch'allas* in the mines, when the workers were determined to take their destiny into their own hands after offering the *ch'alla* to the Tío. Perhaps it was an obdurate administrator, who refused to let the men close the mines for three days after making their offering, to enable the Tío to eat in peace, so the workers decided to act in response to the dictates of their own beliefs and to go out on strike. The massacre of December 21, 1942, occurred on the day the *malku* interred himself in his own blood, when the miners of Siglo XX and Catavi marched, ten thousand unarmed men and women, to the administrative offices of Patiño Mines Company to demand higher wages and a share in the war-inflated prices for tin. The massacre of San Juan took place when a congress was called to reinstate the wages Barrientos took from the workers when the revolution was over. Dedicated as the Day of Miners, during the MNR period, December 21 was again chosen by the women of Siglo XX to demonstrate against the Banzer government's military suppression of the mining community in 1978 with the resulting surge of democratic activities that unsettled the regime in the following year. Finally, the students and workers called a demonstration against the government on the Day of Spring, September 21, when the white condor was born and spirits were high.

It is during these rituals that the spirit of rebellion has come to the surface. Resistance may take many forms, but it is always strengthened by the self-determination of a people who have not yet lost their self-identity. Rituals and belief combine to reinforce the myths which encompass their history, and the celebrations of Carnival, the *ch'alla* and the earth-warming ceremonials, prepare the people for a time when they can shape their own destiny. Sectarian political leaders usually reject ritual protest as deviance. However, if one thinks of it as a rehearsal that keeps alive the sentiment of rebellion until a historically appropriate moment, it may reinforce political movements.

References

Alessandri, Arturo Z., 1968, 'Facetas de "la morenada", un ensayo', *Ensayo de interpretación del Carnaval Orurenco: Leyendas, tradiciones, costumbres*, Oruro.
Beltrán Herédia, B. Augusto, 1962, *Carnaval de Oruro y proceso ideologica e historia de los grupos folkloricos*, Oruro.
Murillo Vacareza, Josermo, 1969, 'El diablo de Oruro y la supervivencia de un anhelo', *Fraternidad Revista Cultural*, pp. 7–9, Oruro.
Nash, June, 1979, *We Eat the Mines and the Mines Eat Us; Dependency and Exploitation in Bolivian Tin Mines*, New York.
Reyes, Simón, 1967, *La masacre de San Juan*, Oruro.
Rojas, Juan and June Nash, 1976, *He agotado mi vida en la mina*, Argentina.
Taussig, Michael, 1980, *The Devil and Commodity Fetishism in South America*, Chapel Hill, N.C.

Epilogue

The politicisation of the transcendent: a quasi-sociological postscript

IVAN VARGA

It is not a matter of pure chance that no formal consensus emerges from these articles, and it was certainly no omission on the part of the organizers that there was no 'wrap-up' session at the workshop. The topic, *Religion and rural revolt* simply does not lend itself to a formal summary. The reasons for this stubborn resistance to formalization are manifold.

The first problem arises from the presentation of religion. At the workshop and in the articles two extremes could be observed. On the one hand, religion has been presented as a deeply personal, lived – and in any case, individual – belief; as, in Rebel's formulation, an 'internal factor'. On the other hand, religion has often been referred to as an 'external factor', namely, a social force with a community-building and -sustaining capacity, as having a dual character: a supporter of the status quo or, conversely, a set of ideas that creates justification for revolting against it.

In my view, this disagreement stems from the identification of religion and belief. Religion in itself is an abstraction even if it is, as Marx would say, a 'rational abstraction'. Religion is a doubly mediated symbolic expression of human existence: apart from the anthropological quality of human activity, that is, a necessary objectivation and symbolic expression of this activity, there is a second mediation as well, namely, a reference to the transcendence as the ultimate source and goal of human existence and activity. In this respect it is immaterial whether the reference is being made to a personified or impersonal transcendental force. When speaking of religion, we obviously cannot discard the element of belief, although, save from an extreme functionalist standpoint, not all beliefs are necessarily religious. The understanding of this doubly mediated nature of religion may help to understand better the autonomy *viz.* dependence of religion *vis-à-vis* society.

Without even attempting to give a definition of religion, I wish to point out that when we speak of religion, we have to assume intersubjectively shared meanings as well. The concept of religion as individual belief is typical of modern society[1] while in pre-modern societies, which occupy the centre of this volume, religion, precisely due to its nature of intersubjectively shared system of meanings, is communal, societal. Hence the propensity of religion to be social, i.e. to create religious communities or endow communities with religious content. Therefore, religion always tends to become institutionalized. Consequently, in speaking of religion, we have to take into account the institutional, organizational forms, the churches or other religious organizations as well, even though we cannot identify the two [*Le Goff-Sutherland*, above].

This dual nature of religion has some salient consequences. In traditional society religion is defined by an authority, namely, the church or 'religious experts', as Max Weber would say, and transmitted by religious communities – or communities *tout court*. From where does, say, a peasant, most probably illiterate, in sixteenth – seventeenth century Europe obtain his ideas? Are those theologies? Or else, are they defined by the social and cultural environment into which he is born? For this peasant the only source of meaning of his world and the universe, of ideas of good and evil, of 'ought' and 'is'; briefly, all ideas constituting a world view (including the meaning of his personal existence) come from religion and the church. The Bible constitutes the only source of knowledge about the origin and nature of the universe and to a large extent, his personal world. (I exclude here the empirically acquired everyday knowledge and rather focus on the interpretive aspects.) God and Satan, saints and witches, miracles and bewitching constituted the main – though not exclusive – concepts of this world view. Under these conditions the 'religious terms of discourse', 'vocabulary' or 'lexicon' provide the overarching frameworks of culture and meaning. True, religion was not the only supplier of culture, symbols and meaning – folk tales, for example, powerfully convey the peasants' longing for social justice – but this was their only institutionalized purveyor.

But not only this. While folk tales, for example, can give an idea about some aspects of reality, such as justice and injustice, they do not provide an ordering meaning system. Moreover, religion is the only possible provider of a universal, unifying principle for large groups of people that extends beyond their small, limited communities. In this sense religion is the only catholic world view.[2]

For, as has been strongly emphasised by the participants of the workshop, religion possesses a community-forming power. A sociologist, naturally, is interested in the social causes of this capacity. One of the most obvious reasons is the aforementioned rôle of religion in the provision of culture and meaning. But beyond this, peasants – be they food producers or small commodity producers – are tied to land thus, as R. DeKoninck pointed out, territoriality plays an intrinsic and vital rôle in peasant life. Community, however, is but a 'rational abstraction'. A community is formed and sustained by a multitude of factors: economic, political, kinship, cultural and symbolic ones. Moreover, we are talking of rural communities that are mainly characterised by agricultural productive activity. This, as anthropology demonstrates, was closely interrelated with religious ideals and rituals. I do not think it would be too far-fetched to assume that this intertwined (productive-religious) character survived over millennia. If so, however, communities in pre-modern societies are also religious communities. Rites of passage are performed in religious garb, kinship ties receive religious affirmation (e.g. in this institution of godparentship). The ritual aspect of religion thus acquires a paramount importance in the life of the community (cf. *Le Goff–Sutherland above*]. To belong to the community and to a religion meant the same. The church steeple towering over the village symbolises the role of the church – or religion – in sustaining community. This dual character of religion: system of meanings and ideas on the one hand and institution on the other, could explain certain contradictory features of religion's role in rural revolt.

The first question that arises in this context is that religion in its concreteness is understood, assimilated, lived and recreated differently by different social strata.

> Religion [became] intertwined with other elements of society in a complicated way. Religious ideas and religious values are in part influenced by the social groups among whom they originate; they express the needs, the thought-ways, the perspectives upon the world of social strata. But once they become established as elements of the culture and are taught as the belief system of a religion, they have a formative influence upon the values and motivations of men. Thus religion is both affected by, and affects, social conditions. It can be either cause or effect [*O'Dea, 1966:79*].

From different theoretical premises Buganov [*above*] expressed the same idea, namely that religion can have different meanings for, say, those whose interests are linked to the maintenance of the existing social order and for those who want to change society. As already Max Weber pointed out, the demands of different social groups towards the same religion are different. Thus religion, in particular in pre-modern societies, is a cultural system as well. Religious discourse cannot take place outside the totality of culture. The meaning-giving function of religion can be seen only in the broader cultural context, and religion is at the same time creating this context and building upon it. However, as is so well known in cultural studies, culture is stratified. The same symbols, ideas, etc. do not mean the same to people who have different interests.

In the case of rural revolts we do not deal only with meanings and perceived interests, much as they are important in looking at motivations of people. Rural revolts are social actions of large social groups who either question the legitimacy of the political order (or the system of rule) or want to establish their rights within the system that they hold by and large for legitimate. It is, however, a somewhat abstract statement that religion means different things for different groups in different societies. In order to attempt an analysis of the rôle of religion in rural revolts, one has to ask the question, why did peasantry have to recur to religion as motivation for revolt or rebellion.

There are several reasons for this, and one cannot explain the whole complex phenomenon by simply referring to the overwhelming cultural impact of religion. Other factors have played an important – and I venture to say, often more important – rôle. First of all, pre-capitalist societies did not develop clear-cut class relations. Customary, traditional, legal overlays, the very personal character of dependency in feudal societies complicated social relations to the extent that the underlying class relations remained quasi imperceptible for the actors of social life. Many sociological traditions, notably the Weberian, would certainly deny the existence of social classes in feudalism. This, among other factors, would point out the tremendous importance of distinguishing between rural revolts that have occurred under pre-capitalist conditions and the more recent ones that, even though they took place in societies at least not fully capitalist, have been influenced by capitalism [*Nash, above*]. Furthermore, peasantry has not produced an ideology of its own, one that would reflect the peasants' own interests, aspirations, separate position in society. Peasants have always accepted – and eventually assimilated – ideologies that have been developed by other social strata. This, quite clearly, expresses the historically constant 'underdog' situation of peasants and might explain, why peasants in rural revolts have so often appealed to the 'good king' against the excesses of their immediate lords. One possible explanation for that blatant lack of consciousness of the social structure is that the ruler (king or emperor) derived the most important aspect of legitimation precisely from religion.

Peasants have rarely embarked upon ventures profoundly to transform society. Our image of a peasant revolt or rebellion is very often that of violence: armed hordes ('mobs') of peasants, indiscriminately killing, setting fire to the lord's home, and so on. But exactly these elements show the lack or limitation of goals of peasant revolts. As Jerome Blum succinctly puts it:

> Their rising, with only rare exceptions, did not embrace revolutionary goals, nor did the rebels ever offer a worked-out program of social and political reform. Whatever their reasons – whether it was the lowly status of the peasants, their self-deprecation, their ignorance, the weight of tradition, the conservative influence of religion (Otto Hintze called Lutheranism a 'useful instrument for the domestication of the [German] peasant') – peasant movements lacked ideological content [*1978: 335*].

Of course, this deficiency, which proved to be fatal for so long a time, can be explained among others by the lack of leadership from within peasantry. It reflects the 'underdog' situation of peasantry, as T. Shanin [*1971: 15*] so aptly put it. Blum expands on the same problem:

> The leadership in peasant disturbances came often, and not surprisingly, from the upper ranks of social hierarchy of the village. [...] Generally, they were the wealthier people of the community. Village officials, too, or schoolmasters, or parish priests

emerged as the commanding figures. Sometimes townsmen acted as instigators and directors. And there were instances, as in places in Hungary, when lesser nobles, burdened with many of the obligations demanded from their peasant neighbours, took over the leadership in rural protest [*1978:335–6*].

If one doesn't think of religion as abstraction but rather considers religion's concrete manifestation as particular denominations (a feature that in our context acquires special importance after the Reformation), then one has to appreciate that belonging to a particular church, or denomination, carried an allegiance to that particular church, denomination or sect. Since various Christian churches or sects as well as Islam generally show strong proselytising tendencies, any attachment strengthens particularistic ideas and feelings. If one adds to this that religious attachments often signified attachment to a nation or ethnicity, it is not too difficult to understand that particularistic tendencies frequently override common class or social interests. A good example would be the bloody revolts of Ukranian peasants in the eighteenth century against their predominantly Polish landlords. In these cases it is outright impossible to separate the particular components: revolt of peasants against their landlords (class aspect); Ukranians against Poles (national aspect); Orthodox against Catholic (religious aspect). Blum illustrates this point with the 1747 Horia-Closca rising in Transsylvania where the leaders of the revolt

> issued a list of demands that defined the dimensions of the social revolution they had in mind. They called for the abolition of the nobility, the distribution by the emperor of the land of the nobles among the peasants, equal taxation for all, and the *conversion of the nobility*, who were predominantly Hungarian Calvinists, to the Greek Orthodox faith. The demand for conversion alienated the Hungarian peasants, who had joined their Rumanian brethren in the revolt, and brought on ethnic and religious clashes among the rebels themselves [*1978: 349*, italics added].

Klibanov's argument about the lack of expressed religious character in the 'multinational' peasant revolts in Russia demonstrates this in the reverse.

Territoriality implies the allegiance not only to a territory but also to a lord or ruler, and makes peasants prone to this particularism at the expense of their class interests.[3] The lack of a marked awareness of peasants' vested interests, that would distinguish those from the idea (eventually illusion) of common interests, results also in the acceptance of the superiority of nobility and in the illusion of the good and just ruler who can, and would, correct the excesses of their lord.

This leads us to the problem of legitimation of a social order. Generally speaking, the legitimate character of a social order or system becomes problematic when the difference – non-identity – of society and state becomes recognized, in particular when it is so perceived that society enamantes from the state and not the other way around, that is, when the state is not viewed as an institution of society. In our example the king or emperor is considered as the supreme embodiment of a higher principle and accepted as a legitimate ruler on the basis of divine ordination. Under the concrete socio-cultural conditions the claim of a social order (together with its institutions) to correspond to a transcendentally or divinely determined natural order of things, remains unchallenged. As Weber emphasized, a social order is considered legitimate if at least part of the population acknowledges it as binding and exemplary, whereas the other part does not confront the existing social order with the image of an alternative, held equally binding.

But how can an alternative be found when the order of society is considered transcendentally legitimised? On what idea would the alternative order of society rest, when the prevailing or even all-embracing culture is still permeated by religious ideas, when religion is the culture of the society? When it represents 'the other world of this world'? Religion is the 'other world' of society (and this is not meant in the rather one-dimensional Durkheimian sense) insofar as it recreates societal relationships, conflicts and processes at the ideological level, elevates them to the other world and provides them with a supernatural aura. Thus, it is capable of presenting this-worldly phenomena as a preordained, supernaturally sanctified state of affairs, albeit with a sharp distinction between this and the other world, between the 'city of God' and the 'city of man'. Even in a largely secularized society religion still performs an important, although no longer exclusive, meaning-giving function. A great number of people still assess their world in terms and meanings provided by religion. In this sense religion, taken in its *abstract* sense, is basically neutral as far as the legitimation of the social order is concerned, it has no intrinsic legitimising propensity. In its *concrete* form, however, i.e. as organised religion, as church, it does perform the legitimising function mainly because of its cultural preponderance. It, therefore, lends itself to a hegemonical use by those whose interests are linked to the maintenance of the existing social order.

In its concrete form, embodied in a church, religion thus assumes the function of an ideological apparatus. In Gramsci's analysis, well summarised by Portelli [*1974: 39–50*], this links the church closely to the existing state. It would however, be a very one-sided view to hold the church merely for the servant of the state. The church constitutes also an autonomous intellectual caste, that of 'religious experts', and as such – and only as such – is it linked to the state, in particular through its legitimising function. The importance of Gramsci's considerations lie in their re-formulation of what defines the state. To him, the state is the totality of civil and political society. Its repressive apparatus unifies the function of domination with that of hegemony as expressed through the corresponding ideological apparatuses. These latter retain a certain independence from the state organizations, an autonomy in relation to the state, a 'private' character of some sort. In Gramsci's view, this was the case with the medieval church. Gramsci also remarks that 'Since cultural differentiations are numerous and profound, society embraces an extraordinary variation of trends that, according to the historical tradition, display a religious or political colour' [Portelli, 1974: 43].

Thus, the afore-mentioned factors, in particular religion's relative autonomy and ambiguous relation to legitimation of a political system, combined with its capacity to express different, and conflicting, life-situations and life-worlds in religious terms, makes it understandable that diametrically opposed social forces can claim religious legitimation. This is why from the Albigensian crusade through the peasant wars in fifteenth–sixteenth century Europe, to the *comuneros* rebellion in eighteenth century South America, to the Taiping and Mahdist and Babist movements outside Europe, all could equally be religiously motivated revolts against the status quo; even contemporary movements resort to religious ideas or are inspired by them. In this context one cannot neglect the impact of the Reformation because it signified the destruction of a quasi-monolithic religious culture of Europe. It both allowed and necessitated the reinterpretation of the doctrines of the old church, not the least its social doctrines. Reformation opened up the possibility to legitimise a radically different social order with reference to divine will, based on an alternative interpretation of God's will as expressed by the scriptures.

Owing to these characteristics, religion can be, and indeed has been, used for legitimising the maintenance of, as well as for revolting against, an established social order. Still, the religious motivation of social protest or rural revolt, requires also a brief evaluation of the role of utopia in social thinking and action. In one way, the existence of utopias is embedded in the nature of human activity. They are expressions of the self-transcending character of human activity insofar as by setting goals and attempting to achieve them, human activity transcends the given state from which it departs. In this sense human activity is always future-oriented. Utopias, however, as Ernst Bloch [*1969: 177–82*] pointed out, cannot be equated simply with this future-oriented nature of human activity since they are not 'concrete anticipation'. Utopia therefore represents, again in Bloch's words, 'the dream of mankind'. But precisely because of this lack of 'concrete anticipation', utopias can be powerful moving forces of creativity and search for the absolute, as millenarian or messianistic movements show. They can also be linked with, and inspire, social protest.

At least since the emergence of societies where domination prevails, utopian thinking permeates the desires of mankind. In this respect, considerations about folk tales hit a historically valid point. Folk tales or fairy tales invariably include reference to social justice but also often express wishes to improve the lot of the people. Motifs like mountains transformed into cheese, rivers flowing with wine, and, of course, the land of Cockaigne are to be found in nearly all peasant cultures. The mutual relationship between folklore and religious 'high culture' is worth more study. Folk tales, however, are not utopias *per se*, even though they include some elements of utopian thinking. Utopias differ from myth, too, for they do not express relations of human beings to nature, the cosmos or time. On the contrary, social utopias, even in their abstract forms, emphasise the conditions for achievement of human happiness and construct reasoned images of a society that would provide conditions for human dignity. In this sense, they represent the accomplishment of ideas of humanism and raise hope for a better future of man.

Thus, utopias are part of the broader process of symbolic reproduction of society. Even though utopias still exist as ideas, their mobilizing and community-forming force was more powerful in the past than nowadays. Since the emergence of industrial capitalism, class relations, as mentioned before, are manifested in an unmediated form, thus the possibility to fight out this-worldly contradictions in secular terms is incomparably greater than in pre-capitalist societies. There, utopias provided no specific directions for the realization of the state of society they depicted. Karl Mannheim's remark on modern revolutions sheds light on the difference between utopias and revolutions: 'One of the features of modern revolution [...] is that it is no ordinary uprising against a certain oppressor but a striving for an upheaval against the whole existing social order in a thorough-going and systematic way' [*1954: 195*].

The basically a-historical character of utopias prevents them from performing this function. In this context 'a-historical' does not mean to be outside of history but rather that utopias do not grasp the real possibilities of historical action and therefore remain abstract expressions of a hope for liberation or a better future in general. 'The responsibility for world renovation usually lies with saviours, mythical heroes or miracle workers who somehow transform the imperfect present into a perfect "not-yet"' [*Gross, 1973: 97*]. But this abstract character, the postulation of perfection, the introduction of the idea of 'not-yet' (*Noch-Nicht*, in Ernst Bloch's expression) is the feature that brings utopia and religion so close together. Religiously formulated utopias emphasise collective salvation, the perfect world eventually created right away, or else they are formulated in a millenarian projection. 'In this, utopia is distinguished from all elitist manifestations of religion that culminate in a purely individual salvation or in ascetic and mystical currents' [*Houtart, 1980: 21; 17–23*].

The emphasis in utopias on this 'not yet' is expressed in the biblical tradition by the distinction between 'this' and the 'other' world. In Ernst Bloch's interpretation this also includes the distinction between present and future. It is, however, not an absolute distinction; there is a dialectical relationship between 'here' and 'there': 'The "other world" was the utopian earth with a utopian heaven above... The goal was not a beyond after death, ... it was the terrestrial as well as supraterrestrial kingdom of love, with its first enclave already constituted by the original community' [*1971: 123*]. Bloch also remarks the lack of social utopia in the Bible. 'No social utopia was worked out in the Bible ... But even though the Bible contains no social utopia, it does most strongly, in negation as well as in affirmation, point to this sort of exodus and to this sort of kingdom' [*Ibid; 125*]. 'In negation as well as in affirmation' – perhaps this is the key to the understanding of the rôle of religion in the utopistically formulated social protest and its unavoidable failure.

The negation of this – imperfect – world, this 'valley of sorrows', implies a negation and rejection of the existing social conditions, or at least a critical attitude toward them. But it is at the same time the affirmation of the future: the other-worldly kingdom. There is a tension between the two realms and the two attitudes. The negation of the present involves the affirmation of the future – the 'not yet'. This tension is creating a forceful drive for social action, for protest movements, offering, as it does, an idea and an image that is superior to the powers-that-be in this world, a legitimation for revolt. Justice is divine, thus the attempts to achieve this justice must correspond to the superior will. Rebellion is just; the present (i.e. social conditions) can be rejected, since the future, the 'above', overrides this world. Utopias in this sense are not reactionary or retrograde because they do not want to achieve a state of affairs which would continue with inequality, deprivation, misery.

Yet, actions based on these abstract utopias are doomed. They are doomed for two reasons: first, their goal is not only the 'not-yet' but a future which is not solely in this world. In the second place, one ought to pose the question, who are the social carriers of religiously motivated utopias; in other words: to whom are these utopias plausible. As to the former, the abstract-utopian orientation, in spite of its activistic impact, does not foster the mapping of a realistic action based on the analysis of social power relations. It tends to veil the fundamental community of interests between ruler and landed nobility, between the church and the feudal system as it existed, at least, in the European context. The social basis of religiously motivated utopias is largely the peasantry which, as argued above, depends on other layers of society for its ideology. Therefore its interests are usually not fully represented or poignantly expressed. Religious social utopias and ideologies of rural revolt often appear as heresies. Thus the ground is shifted from the social to the religious field or, more precisely, the fights, differences, controversies, feuds, accusations and counter-accusations in the religious field often divert the attention from social issues and act divisively. Hence one can conclude that, in spite of their activising rôle, utopias develop only rudiments of critical consciousness, and this fatefully influences the character and outcome of collective social action.

So far the analysis centered around the late medieval and early modern

Europe, although, as papers dealing with non-European peasant revolts or later developments [*Kippenberg, Greussing, Grevemeyer, Weller, Meyer, Nash*, etc. above] show, at the level of abstraction there are some basic similarities to other movements. The concrete rôle of religion ought to be assessed from case to case. Obviously, this is an important methodological imperative not only for the historian but also for the sociologist. The dynamics of religion – rural revolt relationships underwent thorough changes from the nineteenth century onwards. Especially important is the sociopolitical and geographical shift in the field of peasant revolts. It raises such questions as: how does the character of peasant revolts change under the conditions of developed capitalism, colonialism, neo-colonialism? What new elements emerge in the interaction between religion, political activity and social change? Are religious ideas still fostering social revolts or rather reacting to them? What is the relationship between religion and nationalism?

It would be impossible to give here even a partial answer to those questions, and of course, many more questions could be raised. Only as a matter of illustration, I shall mention some cases indicating the extreme difficulty of generalizations. These illustrations also show the importance of the distinctions underlined in the Introduction, namely not only between different historical situations in which revolts occur but also between the religions that provide their ideology.

Twentieth century peasant revolts tend to be purely political when, for example, their goal is the achievement of national independence. In these cases religion – depending on the circumstances – may have no significant rôle, if at all. It is, for example, highly questionable whether religion played any rôle in the Mau Mau revolt in Kenya. True, members of the movement were admitted by ceremonies and oath-taking that stem from the Kikuyu culture and were reminiscent to rituals of secret societies. One certainly can say that in this particular culture this was a religious element. Accounts of participants, however, do not make any particular reference to influence by religion – not even in traditional African terms – but instead emphasise political and economic goals: independence and land. By contrast, during the struggle for independence in North Africa, Islam served as a rallying point, combining religious and national identity. Nevertheless, the struggle was primarily political, and as soon as independence was achieved, sharp differences emerged concerning the rôle of religion in the newly formed states, or, rather, societies. Not only is the rôle of religion different in different states – neighbouring Tunisia and Algeria are good examples – but the islamic tradition of *umma* (community of believers) has been so far largely ignored. The focus in those societies has now shifted toward economic and social development.

In connection with contemporary peasant movements, two recent developments cannot be by-passed: Islamic fundamentalism in the Middle East and liberation theology in Latin America. Since both problems are complex and involve contentious issues, I make just a few remarks. Islamic fundamentalism, unlike fundamentalist movements in developed capitalist societies, expresses a vehement and often violent reaction to enforced modernisation and destruction of traditional cultures. Their excesses (Iran, Egypt) frequently evoke emotional reactions from the outside observer which, however, disguises the fact that the aim of Islamic fundamentalism is not a full restoration of pre-modern socio-economic conditions and that social and political as well as economic development might occur in forms other than the West European and North American model. For example, certain social institutions, such as the family, may persist in their traditional form even under significant technological and economic advance. One certainly cannot engage in predictions as to the future course of events. A more nuanced approach is necessary. Liberation theology in Latin America advocates Catholic social activism, raising the conscience of the mainly peasant masses with a fight for the abolition of exploitation and social injustice. Here again, as is the case with Islamic fundamentalism, it is not the peasants who produce these ideas. Priests and religious laymen disseminate them among peasants and attempt to mobilise the oppressed. However, it would be erroneous to conclude from this fact that there is no difference from the past. First of all, liberation theologians couple their references to the Bible with critical, often Marxist, analysis of the social and economic conditions as the basis for action, from peaceful protest to violent resistance. Second, the type of action has been shifted from the spontaneous, often anarchistic rebellions of the past to organized movements, and, finally, alliances are built with other elements of progressive movements.

So, even contemporary peasant or rural movements are in one way or another connected with religion. The reason seems to be that they are peasant movements and everything that has been said about the relative weaknesses of peasantry and its movements still holds true to a large degree. These movements emerge in societies that are far from developed capitalism and, therefore, display many fundamental features of pre-capitalist societies, in particular in terms of culture and polity. No wonder that religion still largely retained its previous rôle in formulating goals of social and political protests.

In conclusion, temporary and incomplete though it may be, one could remark that religion plays an ambiguous rôle in rural revolt – traditional and contemporary alike. What ought to be emphasised, however, is that religiously motivated rural revolts cannot be called reactionary or conservative without first analysing the political and economic situation of the societies in which they take place, their goals and the consequences of the revolts. Religiously motivated rural revolts can play a progressive rôle, even if they are crushed. In many societies, due to historical traditions, specific conditions, weak political organizations and the precarious situation of peasantry, the 'transcendentalization' of political protest is the only way toward politicization of the transcendent.

Notes

1. I am using the terms 'modern' and 'pre-modern' rather reluctantly, and only in the meaning of modernity as 'institutional concomitants of technologically induced economic growth' [Cf. Berger, Berger, Kellner, 1973: 9] and, in particular, as pluralistic ideological and political arrangements.
2. In the European development at least, the emergence of Protestantism signified a tremendously important change in this respect as well: the possibility of choice. True, initially this choice did not extend beyond religious ideas and communities, however, the very fact that options were available, opened up the way toward a secular world view.
3. This is quite understandable. Even in capitalism, where territoriality plays a much lesser role, internationalism does not extend to the worker. As human beings, they have a language, family and kinship ties, a particular culture, etc., and their perceived interests are primarily linked to the well-being of their country.

References

Berger, P., B. Berger, H. Kellner, 1973, *The Homeless Mind*, New York.
Bloch, E., 1969, *Freiheit und Ordnung*, Reinbek bei Hamburg.
Bloch, E., 1971, *Man on His Own*, New York.
Blum, J., 1978, *The End of the Old Order in Rural Europe*, Princeton.
Gross, D., 1973, 'Marxism and Utopia', in: B. Grahl-P. Piccone (eds.), *Towards a New Marxism*, St Louis.
Houtart, F., 1980, *Religion et modes de production précapitalistes*, Brussels.
Mannheim, K., 1954, *Ideology and Utopia*, London.
O'Dea, T. F., 1966, *The Sociology of Religion*, Englewood Cliffs.
Portelli, H., 1974, *Gramsci et la question réligieuse*, Paris.
Shanin, T., (ed.) 1971, *Peasants and Peasant Societies*, Harmondsworth.

Authors

Bak, János M., Dept. of History, University of British Columbia, Vancouver B.C., V6T 1W5, Canada [UBC].
Benecke, Gerhard, Faculty of Humanities, Darwin College, University of Kent, Canterbury, Kent CT2 7NY, U.K.
Broadhead, Philip, Dept. of Hist., University of London, Goldsmiths' College, Lewisham Way, London S.E.14, U.K.
Bruinessen, Martin van, Haverstraat 15 bis, 3511 NA Utrecht, Netherlands.
Buganov, Viktor I., Inst. Istorii SSSR, Akad. Nauk SSSR, ul. Dm. Ulyanova 19, 117036 Moskva W-36, USSR.
Burke, Peter, Emmanuel College, Cambridge CB2 3AP, U.K.
Frey, Herbert, Eden 10/204, Las Aguilas, Mexico 20 D.F., Mexico.
Friedrichs, Christopher R., Dept., of Hist., UBC.
Greussing, Kurt, Weizeneggerstr. 5, A 6850 Dornbirn, Austria.
Grevemeyer, Jan-Heeren, Nollendorfstr. 28, D 1000 Berlin 30 Berlin-West.
Hill, Christopher, Woodway House, Sibford Ferris, Banbury, OX15 5RA, U.K.
Hodgkin, Thomas, Crab Mill, Ilmington, Shipston-on-Stour, U.K.
Kippenberg, Hans G., State University of Groningen, Nieuwe Kijk in't Jatstraat 104, Groningen, Netherlands.
Klibanov, Aleksandr I., Institut istorii SSSR, Akad. Nauk SSSR, ul. Dm. Ulyanova 19, 117036 Moskva W-36, USSR.
LeGoff, T. J. A., Dept. of Hist., York University, 4700 Keele str., Downsview, Ont. M3J 1P3, Canada.
LeGrand, Catherine, Dept. of Hist., UBC.
Ludwig, Karl-Heinz, Universität Bremen, Schwerpunkt Geschichte, Bibliotheksstrasse, D 2800 Bremen, Federal Republic of Germany.
Meyer, Jean A., Colegio de Michoacán Madero 310 Sur, Zamora, Mich. Mexico.
Mitchell, Harvey, Dept. of Hist., UBC.
Muratorio, Blanca, Dept. of Anthropology and Sociology, UBC.
Nash, June, Dept. of Anthropology, City College CUNY, New York, N.Y. 10012, U.S.A.
Nicholls, David, 27 Harehills Ave., Leeds LS8 4EX, U.K.
Overmyer, Daniel L., Dept. of Asian Studies, UBC.

Perry, Elizabeth J., School of International Studies, University of Washington, Seattle, WA 98195, U.S.A.
Ranger, Terence O., School of History, University of Manchester, Manchester M13 9PL, U.K.
Rebel, Hermann, Dept. of Hist., University of Arizona, Tucson AZ 85721, U.S.A.
Rothkrug, Lionel, Concordia University, 1455 De Maisonneuve blvd. West, Ste N-205, Montréal, Que. H3G 1M8, Canada.
Stein, William W., Dept. of Anthropology, SUNY at Buffalo, Spaulding Quadrangle, Buffalo, N.Y. 14261, U.S.A.
Sutherland, Donald M. G., Dept. of Hist., Brock University, Region Niagara, St Catherine's, Ont. L2S 3A1, Canada.
Thaxton, Ralph, Dept. of Politics, Brandeis University, Waltham, MA 02254, U.S.A.
Varga, Ivan, Dept. of Sociology, Queen's University, Kingston, Ont. K7L 3L6, Canada.
Vogler, Günter, Humboldt-Universität, Sektion Geschichte, DDR 110 Berlin, Unter den Linden 6, German Democratic Republic.
Wagner, Rudolf G., Martin-Luther-Str. 78, D 1000 Berlin 62, Berlin-West.
Weller, Robert, Dept. of Anthropology, Duke University, Durham NC 27706-2590, U.S.A.
Wirtz, Rainer, Universität Konstanz, Phil. Fak., Fachgr. Geschichte, Pf. 5560, D 7750 Konstanz, Federal Republic of Germany.

Index

compiled by KATHLEEN D. SCARDELLATO
University of British Columbia

The intention of this index is to facilitate a comparative approach to the events and processes, spanning several centuries and continents, which are discussed in the volume. Only revolts analysed in some depth are listed by name (*see:* uprisings); other topics have been subsumed under collective subject headings. A few geographical and personal names were included for orientation, but the regional and chronological organisation of the volume made their systematic listing redundant. Modern authors (set in **bold**) are listed only when their views are quoted extensively.

Afghan Communist [Kalkh-Parchan] Party, 270–71
Afghanistan, 9, 270–80 *passim*
Africa, *see:* Sokoto, Sudan, Zimbabwe
agrarian reform, 271, 446–7
anti-clericalism, 42, 90, 154–5, *see also:* clergy; mission
anti-colonialism, *see:* colonialism, opposition to
atheism, 99, 114, 291
Austria (Inner & Upper, Salzburg, Tyrol), 6, 10, 154–60 *passim*, 188–205 *passim*

Baha'i, 265–6
Bahrain, 251–2
banditry, 76, 81, 113–14, 293, 375–6, 444
Bible, 98–9, 228–31, 235, 356, 444, 471, 478 (*see also:* legitimation, scriptural)
Bloch, Ernst, on religious upheaval 441, on utopia 476–8
Blum, Jerome, on rural revolts 473–4
Bois, Paul, on counter-revolution 67
Bolivia, 6, 11, 408, 411, 453–68 *passim*
Buddhism, 339–40, 342, 346, 391, 394–6, 399–401 *passim*
 Lamaism, 211, 215, 360, 370
 Maitreya, 339, 349, 396
 sects related to, 395–7 *passim*
Büchner, Georg, *see: Hessischer Landbote*

capitalism, merchant, 257, 259
Chartism, 101
Chiang Kai-Shek, *see:* Kuomintang
China, 338–406 *passim*
Chinese Communist Party, 387–8 (*see also:* Mao Zedong)
Christianity, 20–21, 22–8, 212–13, 474
 and shamans, 423
 as 'civilising agent', 206
 as 'religion of the oppressed' 22, 176, 178–9, 206
 disciplinary function of, 184
 in China, 344, 350–51, 354, 363–5 *passim*, 369–70
 in Taiwanese sects, 400–401
 (*see also:* church, Christian; feudalism; Protestantism; religion; Roman Catholicism; Russian Orthodoxy)
Church, Christian:
 as central to village, 7, 175, 231, 448
 as landowner, 33, 36, 78–9, 161–4, 175
 its concepts and practices: (God) 358–9, 360, 370, 421; (Blood of Jesus) 31–2, 35–6, 42, 51; (Sacred Heart) 125; (Corpus Christi) 191, (Mary, the Virgin) 8, 48–9, 79, 82–3, 319, 450, 453, 461; (saints, martyrs) 49, 51–4 *passim*, 436, 451–2; (relics) 33–5 *passim*, 567; (Devil, Satan) 219, 420–22, 452,

453, 458–9; (Antichrist) 225, 447; (demons) 370; (Host) 434; (Holy Week) 432–3; (Cross) 417–18, 450; (Kingdom) 83, 450; (Second Coming) 452; (penitence, practices) 36–7, 39–40, 52–3, 119, 232; (indulgence, plenary) 7, 34–5, 39, 45, 47–9 *passim*, 51–2; (Jubilee) 35, 39, 46, 49, 52; (interdict) 443; (Inquisition) 80 (*see also*: Crusade, festivals, pilgrimage)
  (*see also*: clergy; Protestantism; religion; Roman Catholicism; Russian Orthodoxy)
class, 16–18, 270, 279, 473
  antagonism, 94, 270–71
  consciousness, 464–5
  struggle, 449
clergy, 17, 38, 67, 72, 78, 87–8, 95, 100, 225
  Catholic (priests, parish priests), 68, 120, 128, 410, 419, 421–2, 430, 442, 445, 448–9; frustrating an uprising, 431–5 *passim*
    Civil Constitution of, 125–6, 129, 131, 133; recusant, 129, 133; constitutional, 131–2, 135
  Muslim (molla, ulama), 241, 260–61, 276–7
  Protestant (ministers) 191, 328–30, 344, 346, 350, 354, 362–3
  Russian Orthodox (priests, monks), 208–9, 216–18 *passim*
  (*see also*: anti-clericalism; élites: religious; mission; movements: leaders)
colonialism, 257–8, 266–7, 311, 315–16, 358, 458, 460
  opposition to, 322–3
'common man' (14th–16th C.), 37–8, 41, 43–5, 52
communism, anticipation of, 266, 268, 270
confessionalism, 180–83, 474
Confucius, Confucianism, 342, 357, 400–401
Counter-Reformation (Catholic), 150, 155–6, 180–82, 189–90, 199
counter-revolution, popular, 10, 82, 123–42, 452
Crusade, 2, 3, 48–52 (*see also*: Holy War)

Dahrendorf, Ralf, on bureaucratisation, 198–9
Daoism, 391, 399–401 *passim*

'dechristianisation', 123, 125, 128, 133–4
Diggers, 87–8, 91, 94, 100

Ecuador, 414–23, *passim*
élites:
  gentry (Chinese), 338, 380–81
  nobility, 51–3, 248–9
  religious, 271, 276, 285–7, 291–4
  urban, communal, 427–8
  tribal, 273, 276, 278, 283, 317, 416–20 *passim*
equality, 394
  in dress, 53
  in ritual terms 232–3
  (*see also*: legitimation, of equality)

family, peasant, 188–9, 200, 204, 449
famine, 225–7, 356
Febvre, Lucien, on laicisation 65–6
festivals, religious (fiesta etc.), 232, 422, 435–6, 454–6
  and revolt, 422, 432–5
  Carnival, 457–62
  (*see also*: church, Christian; ritual)
feudalism, feudal system, 22–5, 266, 279
  abolition of, 124, 130, 136
folktale, 7, 471, 477
France, 6, 46–59 *passim*, 67–72 *passim*, 75–7 *passim*, 81–5 *passim*, 104–45
French Revolution, 9, 68–71 *passim*, 83, 123–45 *passim*

Germany, 32–46 *passim*, 173–87, 223–37
Godelier, Maurice, on pre-class society, 16; on religion, 391
'godly law', *see*: legitimation
Gramsci, Antonio, on church and state, 475–6
Graus, Frantisek, on peasant revolts, 425
Guevara, Ernesto 'Che', 456–7

Habermas, Jürgen, on religion, 65
Heaven:
  access to, 368–9
  denial of, 98
  vision of, 344, 357–8
heresy, 3, 28, 87, 214–15, 218, 285
  persecution of, 156–8
  Bogomilism, 216
  Khorramdinites, 245–7
  (*see also*: Protestantism, radical sects)
Hessischer Landbote, 228–34 *passim*
Hobsbawm, Eric, on millenarianism 311–12, 387–8

Holy War [*jihad, cihad*], 2, 20, 82, 278, 291, 293–4, 297, 298–301 (*see also*: Crusades)

Ibn Khaldun, 243, 250, 299
imperialism, 257–60, 272 (*see also*: colonialism)
Inca (Empire and ruler), 408, 416, 460
  idea of return to, 429
Indian, as social category, 425–6
Indians:
  Amazonian, 11, 414–23 *passim*; conquest and genocide of, 416–18
  Highland, 416, 421–2
  Maya, 446
  Mexican, 446, 450
industry, rural, 83–4, 88, 89, 91, 92, 130, 139, 249, 259
Iran, 241–69 *passim*, 480
'irreligiosity', 12, 183, 214–22 *passim* (*see also*: atheism; religious tolerance)
Islam, Muslims, 79–81, 211, 215, 240–314 *passim*, 399–401, 474, 480
  opposition to, 246, 249, 252, 257, 261–2
  relations to state, 282–3
  sects and orders, 241, 276–7, 282, 285–6, 293
  Shi'ites [Twelver'], 244–5, 253, 257
  Sunnites, 283, 287, 292
  (*see also*: Holy War; Mahdi; pilgrimage)
Italy, 75–9 *passim*, 82–5 *passim*

Japanese, occupation, 400–401
Jews, 227, 232 (*see also*: Judaism)
Joan of Arc, 47, 53–4
Judaism, 21–2
  Ten Commandments, 21, 27

Khomayni, Ruholla, ayatollah, 241
Koran [Quran, Q'oran], 262, 290
Kosselleck, Reinhard, on *politiques*, 203–4
Kuomintang [KMT], 373, 381–8 *passim*
Kurds, Kurdistan, 281–95 *passim*

Lamennais, Félicité R., de, 230–1
Lefebvre, George, on autonomous peasant revolts, 68–9, 123–4, 126, 134
legalisation of social conflicts, 105, 183, 232, 235
legitimation, 475
  of equality (freedom, etc.): natural law, 32, 183; penitential practices, 52–3; scriptural, 90, 94

  of resistance, revolt: religious (incl. millenarian, Mahdist), 243–4, 251, 296–314 *passim*, 332–3, 399; scriptural (incl. 'godly law'), 7, 11, 31–2, 78, 176–7, 179, 208, 219, 227–34 *passim*, 240–41, 476; traditional: dynastic, 210, 212, 277, 348–9, 356, 377–8, 380; 'old law', 11, 33, 39–40, 84, 232
  of status quo (inequality, expropriation etc): religious, 15, 317; scriptural, 7–9, 23, 225, 253
Le Roy Ladurie, Emmanuel, on social conflict, 115, 119
Levellers, 86–7, 94–5, 100–101
Liberation Theology, 408, 480
Lollards, 67, 88–9, 91–100 *passim*
Luther, Martin, 3–4, 36, 41, 87, 94, 176–8 *passim* (*see also*: Protestantism; reformation, Protestant)

Mahdi, Mahdism, 3, 241, 243–51 *passim*, 261, 296–314 *passim*
  as 'ideology of the oppressed', 297
  vs messianism, 297–8, 304–5
  vs Marxism, 311–12
  (*see also*: millenarianism; uprisings, Babi, Mazyar, Moqanna')
Mannheim, Karl, on utopia and revolution, 477
Manzhu [Manchu], 356, 362–71 *passim*
Mao Zedong, 367–8, 388, 390
Marx, Karl (and F. Engels), 7, 16–17, 174, 179, 355
Marxism, 25, 66, 270–71, 311–12, 367
messianism, 298, 305–10 *passim*
  vs Mahdism, 297–8, 304–5
  vs Marxism, 311–12
Mexico, 9, 11, 411–12, 441–52 *passim*
migration (emigration, flight, *hijra*), 75, 82, 88, 191–2, 200, 165, 178, 283, 303, 324–5, 375, 418
millenarianism, 3, 12, 42, 48, 81, 83, 95–6, 101, 263, 291, 294, 296–9, 304, 308–13 *passim*, 339
  (*see also*: Buddhism, Maitreya; Islam: Mahdi; messianism)
Milton, John 87, 94, 98, 99
miners, 6, 150, 154–60 *passim*, 318, 375, 411, 453–68 *passim*
  associations and unions, 157, 455–7 *passim*, 465
  mine-owners and, 157, 159, 460, 464
mission, missionary:

opposition to, 216–17, 325–7, 378, 420–23
Catholic, 67, 409–10, 414–20 *passim*, 423
Protestant, 319–21 *passim*, 324–5, 362–4 *passim*, 367; Anglican, defending peasants, 323–5
(*see also:* Christianity; clergy)
modernisation, 11, 69–70, 124, 130, 211, 219, 261–2, 272, 319–21 *passim*, 355, 365–6, 381, 411–12
theory of, 11, 68–9, 130, 139
Mohammad Ali Barforushi, 3, 262–3
monarchism, peasant, 48, 54, 197, 207–8, 212, 227, 232, 473–4
(*see also:* legitimation, dynastic)
moral economy, 68, 77
Mousnier, Roland, on peasant revolts, 76–7
movements, popular [in the widest sense, from religious dissent to peasant war and armed uprising]:
causes and catalysts: changes in tenancy, 104–5, 161, 189, 259–60, 275, 374; conscription, 129, 134, 137–8, 141; forced labour, 323–5, 416–17, 420–22; heavy taxation, 76–7, 89–90, 108–10, 131, 140, 274–5, 373, 375–7, 386, 427; increased exactions (billeting etc.), 77, 107–8, 132–3, 275, 417–18; insufficient reforms, 71, 126, 131, 446–7; other economic and demographic, 46, 89, 104–5, 109, 266–7; religious persecution, 79–82 *passim*, 189–90, 201–2, 208–12 *passim*, 221; restriction of peasant (village, family) autonomy, 71, 151, 189, 200–201, 246–9 *passim*, 427–8, 443; secularisation, 82–3, 211, 274–5, 281–2, 293
defeat, factors of, 267, 291, 294, 425, 431–7 *passim*
leaders: artisan, rural 'bourgeois', 31–2, 83, 209, 192–6 *passim*, 209, 410, 427–35 *passim*; clergy, 3, 38, 45, 78, 95, 107, 112, 115, 177, 208–9, 262–3, 281–93 *passim*, 241; 'intelligentsia', 12, 310–11, 344–5, 347–8, 356–71 *passim*; prophetic, 42–3, 307, 246–8, 421; soldiers, warriors (incl. Cossack), 281–93 *passim*, 208–11 *passim*, 345–6; traditional élite, 275–7, 418, 421–2; uprooted peasants, 45–6, 376–9, 383–4; women, 263, 306, 345
leadership, problems of, 109, 152, 192, 197–8, 267, 287, 473–4
problems of assessment, 10, 76–7, 83–4, 115, 124–5, 148, 196, 338–9, 411, 441, 447, 451
programme, ideology, 32, 38–9, 151, 178, 196, 199–202 *passim*; 'backward'/'forward' looking, 11, 119, 310, 381, 447, 477; millenarian, 42–3, 48, 210, 240–50 *passim*, 304, 306, 308–9, 373, 403; its limitations, 12, 267, 294
rôle of settlement and land-holding patterns in, 67, 69, 75–6, 78, 87–8, 118–19, 126–7, 130–33, 138–42 *passim*, 246, 271, 283–5, 317, 374, 444, 446
sources [quoted in extenso]: contemporary (near-contemporary) assessments, 87, 109–10, 116–17, 133, 140, 172, 178, 245–8 *passim*, 256–7, 305, 334, 347, 361–6 *passim*; contemporary reports, 109–10, 180, 247, 263–5 *passim*, 277, 290–91, 304, 331–2, 431–5 *passim*, 455–7 *passim*, 463–4; texts advocating opposition/resistance, 32, 91, 111, 128, 181, 227–30 *passim*, 300–301, 351, 359–61 *passim*, 401
symbols, 125, 177, 212, 291
(*see also:* Islam: Mahdi; messianism; millenarianism; uprisings)
Münzer, Thomas, 3, 98, 177
Muslim, *see:* Islam
Muzarewa, Abel, bishop, 329–30
myth, 14–15, 18, 457, 459

Napoleon, Bonaparte, reaction to, 225, 227–8, 230, 302
nationalism, 282–3, 287–8, 291–2, 328–9, 332, 479
proto-nationalism, 116, 307, 356
Normandy, 9, 81, 84, 104–21 *passim*

'old law', *see:* legitimation, traditional

patron–client relations, 271, 275, 427, 436–7, 448
peasant war, *see:* movements, popular; uprisings
peasantry [rural populations in general]:
differentiation, conflict within, 132, 134–5, 151, 196, 316, 322, 426, 444, 447

ideology, 120, 290, 292–3, 473, 478
outsiders' images of, 38, 41, 118, 184, 224–6, 451
relationship: to other classes (groups), 64–6, 76, 78, 107–8, 112–13, 148, 163–4, 208–12 *passim*, 276–9, 426, 428, 437; to the state, 9, 11, 164–5, 181–2, 198–9, 201, 211, 219, 246–7, 249, 272, 451
religiosity, 5, 6, 8, 212–13, 321, 331
territoriality, 471, 474
Permian Komi (people), 410, 424–40 *passim*
pilgrimage, 33–4, 38–44 *passim*, 49, 52, 223–4, 443
sites and geography of conflict, 33, 38–9
Pillorget, René, on revolts and communities, 76
popular religiosity, 8, 64, 174, 217, 282, 285, 291, 326–8, 391–4 *passim*, 401
Porshnev, Boris, on revolts, 76–7, 118
pre-class society, 15–16
property:
common, 94–5, 263–7 *passim*; private, 26; opposition to, 219, 262
Protestantism, 5, 81–2, 104–17 *passim*, 136–41 *passim*, 340
Anabaptism, 3, 86, 89, 96, 166, 169
Anglicanism, 319–20
radical sects (Anti-Trinitarians, Familiarist etc.) 87–102 *passim*
revivalist, prophetic churches, 298, 321–2, 328, 426–8
(*see also:* Christianity; clergy; radicalism, religious)

Qoran, Q'uran, *see* Koran
Quakers, 89, 91–2, 94, 97, 100–101

radicalism, religious, English:
continuity by regions, 87–92
continuity of ideas, 94–100; in America, 101–2
reformation, religious:
and social reform, 3–4, 159, 169–70
Babist, 256–7, 261–4 *passim*
Protestant, 6, 33–4, 182–3
religion [mostly Christianity]:
as belief, devotion, solace, 4–5, 8, 12, 15, 72–3, 78, 175–6, 470–72
as 'internal' and 'external' fact, 213, 471–2
its ideological functions, 7, 14–29 *passim*, 72, 132, 156, 207, 225–6, 279, 380, 402, 410, 412, 471–2, 475–6, 477

its social functions, 5, 66, 149, 178, 223, 244, 319, 402–3, 470; as a community-building force, 83, 119, 149, 175, 234, 244, 279, 404, 412, 448–9
scholarly analyses of, 8, 65, 71, 152
(*see also:* legitimation; Christianity; the different religions)
religion royale, 47–59 *passim*
religions:
monotheist, 19–24, 360, 370
natural ('pagan'), Eurasian, 211, 215–17, 219
pre-Colonial, African, 316–17, 326
pre-Columbian, 11, 17, 23, 409, 411, 452–4, 458–9, 461–7 *passim*
sectarian, 339, 342, 391–2, 401–3
(*see also:* Baha'i' Buddhism; Christianity; Judaism; Islam; Protestantism; Roman Catholicism; Russian Orthodoxy; Zoroastrianism)
religiosity, popular [rural], 4–6, 10, 71, 128, 151–2, 225, 231, 321, 340, 342, 392–5, 409, 425
its synchrestism, 4, 308, 318–19, 400–401, 409, 421–2, 453–4, 455, 459, 461
religious tolerance, 184, 211–12, 215, 220–221
revolution, *see:* French Revolution; uprising
Ribeiro, Darcy, on Indian mission, 415
Ricoeur, Paul, on mimesis, 72
ritual, 317, 425, 437, 454–65 *passim*
and revolt, 454–7, 465–6, 468
and social relations, 460, 464
Roman Catholicism:
conversion to, 78–81 *passim*, 189, 191, 201–4 *passim*
relations to the state, 224, 235, 409, 411, 442–3, 448, 452
rural society and, 107, 116–17, 319, 332, 430–31, 442
(*see also:* religiosity, popular; Christianity, church, Christian; clergy)
Russia, 206–222 *passim*, 257–8, 272
Russian Orthodoxy, 207–210 and 215–20 *passim*
dissenters: Old Believers, 5, 10, 208–21 *passim*; Spiritual Christians, 219–20; Dukhobors, Molokans, 220
popular ('everyday'), 217–18
(*see also:* clergy)

St Ambrose, on servitude, 27

St Augustine, bishop of Hippo, 22, 26–7
St Bernard, abbot of Clairvaux, 49
Scott, James, on traditions, 234; on peasant revolts, 390–91
secret societies and comparable networks, 12, 137, 214, 244, 246–9, 287, 339–40, 343–52 *passim*, 373–89 *passim*, 396, 402–4 *passim* (*see also*: religions, sectarian)
shamans, 420–23 *passim*
slaves, 18, 459
Smith, Adam, on religion, 64–5
Sokoto, Caliphate, 302–3, 306
Spain, Spaniards, 75–7 *passim*, 79–81, 84–5, 416–17, 421–3 (*see also*: colonialism)
spirit mediums, spirit writing, 317–18, 322, 331–3, 397–9
Sudan, 296, 299, 300, 301–3 *passim*
suicide, 418
Swiss Confederation, 41–2, 161–72

Taiwan, 9, 340, 391–404 *passim*
Taoism, *see*: Daoism
taxation, 259–60, 274–5 (*see also*: movements, causes)
Taylor, Charles, on epistemology, 73
theology, rational, 224–6 (*see also*: Liberation Theology)
town and country, 76, 78, 249, 259, 284–5, 289, 290, 425 (*see also*: peasantry, relations to other classes)
trade unions, *see*: miners, associations and unions
tradition, 'little' and 'great', 149, 152, 226, 382
transformation, social (incl. 'bourgeois', 'socialist'), 224, 230–33, 311, 320, 323–4, 415
Turkey, 281–95 *passim*

uprisings [incl. revolts, riots, peasant wars; discussed in some length]:
  Alpujarra Mountains (Granada, 1568), 79–81
  Astrakhan (Russia, 1705–6), 210–11
  Ariège (France, 1799), 137–8
  Atusparia's (Peru, 1885), 427–35
  Babi (Iran, 1848–52), 12, 256–69
  Bohemia (1775), 181
  Brittany (1590–95), 116–17
  Calabria (1799), 82–3
  Camisards (Languedoc, 1702–4), 10, 81–2
  Catalonia (1640, 1688), 76–7, 84
  Chouannerie (Brittany, 1793–1832), 130
  Cristiada (Mexico, 1926–9) 9, 11, 83, 408, 411–12, 441–52
  Don [Cossacks] (1688–9), 209–10
  Eshaq Khan's (Afghan-Turkestan 1888), 9, 11, 241, 270–80
  Essex riots (1629, 1638–42), 89–90
  Gautiers (Normandy, 1589), 112–15
  German Peasant War (1525–6), vii, 3, 11, 32–3, 79, 165, 176–9, 200, 229, 232
  Heavenly Gates (Henan, China, 1925–32), 373–89
  Hidalgo's (Mexico, 1810), 445
  Jacquerie (1358), 48, 50, 53
  Jalès, camps de (1791–2), 136–7, 139–40
  Kett's rebellion (1549), 31–2, 89
  Languedoc (France, 1792), 135–6
  Maji Maji (Zimbabwe, 1905–7), 299, 304, 310
  Marchland (Austria, 1632–6), 181
  Mazyar's (Iran, ninth century), 240
  Moqanna's (Transoxania, 775–83), 240–50 *passim*
  Moscow ['raskolnik'] (1682), 209
  Niklashausen 'commotion' (1476), 41–3 *passim*, 176
  Nîmes, election riots (1790), 136
  Nu-pieds (Normandy, 1639), 76, 78, 114–15
  Quijos [Indians] (Ecuador, 1562), 418; (1578) 410, 421–3
  Russian Peasant Wars, First [I. Bolotnikov's] (1606–7), 214; Second [S. Razin's] (1667–71), 208–9, 215–16; Third [K. Bulavin's] (1707–10), 211; Fourth [E. Pugachev's] (1773–5), 211–12, 214–15
  St Gallen (Switzerland, 1490), 162; (1529), 150, 161–71
  Salzburg & Tyrol [miners] (Austria, 1525), 154–60, 173
  Saxony, Hesse, Baden (1848), 227
  Shaik Said's (Turkey, 1925), 288–94
  Shona (Zimbabwe, 1886–7), 299, 304, 306
  Small Swords (Shanghai, 1853), 350–52
  Solovetsky (Russia, 1668–76), 208, 221
  Taiping (China, 1850–64), 11, 12, 340, 342–72 *passim*
  Upper Austria (1626), 150–51, 173, 180,

192–202
Vendée (1793), 125, 129–32
White Lotus (China, 1796–1805), 340, 343
Zapata (Mexico, 1910–19), 444, 446
Zambabwe, guerilla war (1976–80), 330–33
(for regional surveys, consult: geographical headings)
(*see also*: counter-revolution, popular; millenarianism; movements, popular)
Urban II, pope, 47–9 *passim*
USA, 385
USSR, 279, 395
utopia, 24, 218, 476–8 *passim*

Vatican, 447
   Vatican II, council, 414
visions, 177, 344, 357–8, 359, 421, 460

Weber, Max, on holy war, 20; on Judaism and Near Eastern religions, 21
Weidig, Friedrich, *see: Hessischer Landbote*
Weitling, Wilhelm, 223–4
'When Adam delved . . .', 45, 94
White Lotus, *see:* secret societies; uprisings
witch, witchcraft, 43, 89, 463
Wolf, Arthur, on sects, 393
women, 88, 95, 99, 128, 156, 209, 248, 263–5 *passim*, 321, 329, 365, 397, 418, 441, 457 (*see also:* movements, leaders)
Wyclif, John, 87, 95, 98, 100

Zimbabwe, 315–35
Zoroastrianism, 249
Zwingli, Ulrich, 162–71 *passim*